General Principles of Constitutional and Administrative Law

CW01066943

Palgrave Macmillan Law Masters

Series Editor **Marise Cremona**

Stephen Judge
BUSINESS LAW (2nd edn)

Janet Dine
COMPANY LAW (4th edn)

John Alder
GENERAL PRINCIPLES OF CONSTITUTIONAL AND ADMINISTRATIVE
LAW (4th edn)

Ewan McKendrick
CONTRACT LAW (4th edn)

Priscilla Sarton
CONVEYANCING (3rd edn)

Jonathan Herring
CRIMINAL LAW (3rd edn)

Debbie J. Lockton
EMPLOYMENT LAW (4th edn)

Raymond Emson
EVIDENCE

Kate Standley
FAMILY LAW (3rd edn)

David Cowan
HOUSING LAW AND POLICY

Tina Hart and Linda Fazzani
INTELLECTUAL PROPERTY LAW (2nd edn)

Kate Green and Joe Cursley
LAND LAW (4th edn)

Margaret Wilkie and Godfrey Cole
LANDLORD AND TENANT LAW (4th edn)

Jo Shaw
LAW OF THE EUROPEAN UNION (3rd edn)

Catherine Rendell
LAW OF SUCCESSION

Ian McLeod
LEGAL METHOD (4th edn)

Ian McLeod
LEGAL THEORY

Robert East
SOCIAL SECURITY LAW

Alastair Mullis and Ken Oliphant
TORTS (3rd edn)

General Principles of Constitutional and Administrative Law

Fourth Edition

John Alder
Professor of Law, University of Newcastle upon Tyne

With contributions from
Michael Haley, Barry Hough, Richard Mullender

Law series editor:
Marise Cremona
Professor of European Commercial Law,
Centre for Commercial Law Studies, Queen Mary, University of London

First published 2002 by
PALGRAVE MACMILLAN
Houndmills, Basingstoke, Hampshire RG21 6XS and
175 Fifth Avenue, New York, N.Y. 10010
Companies and representatives throughout the world

PALGRAVE MACMILLAN is the global academic imprint of the Palgrave Macmillan division of St. Martin's Press, LLC and of Palgrave Macmillan Ltd. Macmillan® is a registered trademark in the United States, United Kingdom and other countries. Palgrave is a registered trademark in the European Union and other countries.

ISBN 0–333–97164–7

This book is printed on paper suitable for recycling and made from fully managed and sustained forest sources.

A catalogue record for this book is available from the British Library.

10   9   8   7   6   5   4   3   2   1
11   10   09   08   07   06   05   04   03   02

Typeset by Aarontype Limited
Easton, Bristol, England

Printed and bound in Great Britain by
Creative Print & Design (Wales), Ebbw Vale

Contents

Preface

The aims of this edition remain the same as those of previous editions: namely, to explain and discuss critically the general principles of the constitutional law and administrative law of the UK and to identify their historical and political foundations. This edition has been recast and substantially rewritten and expanded in order to take account of major changes in the law, notably the burgeoning case law generated by the Human Rights Act 1998, and to consider recent scholarship and political developments. I have tried to make the book clearer and easier to use both as an introductory text for law degree students and as a self-contained text for more basic courses. I have also tried to emphasise difficult and controversial issues.

The law and its political foundations are constantly changing. Since the last edition in late 1999, litigants have begun to exploit the Human Rights Act 1998 in a variety of contexts. These include, for example, immigration, asylum, and prisoners' rights, the eviction of tenants, pawnbrokers' rights, access to adoption records, victims' rights, press freedom and euthanasia. The *Alconbury* case in particular involved the relationship between political decisions taken by a minister and the rule of law. It is too early to suggest any general tendencies towards a distinctively British human rights jurisprudence. On the one hand, the Strasburg case law seems to have been systematically applied and a moderate approach adopted. On the other hand, significant differences of approach are emerging between individual judges.

Other developments have been influenced by the 'Nolan Principles of Public Life' which have pervaded several areas of law, including bringing political parties within a legal regime. There have also been changes in electoral law and developments in the law of judicial review, notably in relation to the doctrines of 'unreasonableness' and legitimate expectations and the bias rule. There has also been important new literature including extra-judicial writings from senior judges and dealing with the influence of the common law on the constitution.

Other developments have been disappointing. The long-awaited reform of the House of Lords is unfinished business and the Wakeham Report raises concerns about the dangers to democracy of a legislative chamber which includes persons hand-picked by those already in positions of power. There have been limited reforms in local government law which have to some extent strengthened local democracy although, characteristically the centre retains comprehensive powers. There have been a desultory Freedom of Information Act 1999, and increased state powers in relation to official surveillance, police investigations and public order. Some of these were a response to the terrorist attack on the World Trade Centre on 11 September 2001 but go well beyond terrorism.

The main standpoint of the book is that constitutional law pre-eminently concerns the management of disagreement about the exercise of power. As Holmes J remarked, 'the Constitution is made for people of fundamentally different views' (*Lochner* v. *New York* (1905), 19 US 45 at 767). Hence, in a democracy, the task of constitutional law is to provide mechanisms that prevent one set of values from being permanently dominant while at the same time trying to keep order and to adjudicate fairly between competing pretenders to power.

Part I has been substantially rearranged and discusses fundamental principles and concepts, including revised treatment of the rule of law to reflect developments in scholarship. In particular the introductory chapters have been recast. I have also attempted to provide an overview of the history, structure and main concepts of the UK constitution in the hope that this will signpost later chapters. Part II is new, in which I have brought together topics relating to the geographical separation of powers, namely, devolution, local government and the European Union. Part III discusses the main institutions of government, namely Parliament, the Crown, ministers, the civil service, the armed forces and police. Part IV concerns the citizen and the state, and includes an expanded treatment of judicial review of administrative action and human rights together with a more detailed discussion of freedom of expression, police powers and state secrecy. However the increasing legislation relating to public order, terrorism, immigration and state surveillance have made detailed treatment of particular civil liberties unrealistic as part of a general constitutional law course. For this reason I have concentrated in this edition upon general constitutional principles The case law is, as far as possible up to date to 10 April 2002.

I am grateful to many people who directly and indirectly helped me to produce this edition. These include, pre-eminently, Michael Haley of Keele University who prepared Chapter 21, Barry Hough of Southampton Institute who made substantial contributions to Chapters 3, 13 and 14 and Richard Mullender of Newcastle Law School who prepared Chapter 20. I am also indebted to Rui Verde of the Universidade Independente Lisbon who critiqued several chapters and made invaluable suggestions and to Ann Sinclair of Newcastle Law School who revised the bibliography. I am of course wholly responsible for the mistakes that remain.

JOHN ALDER

Newcastle, April 2002

Table of Cases

Table of Statutes

Part I

Fundamental Principles

1   The Nature of Constitutional Law

1.1   Introduction: What is a Constitution?

In this introductory chapter, in order to provide a perspective for the rest of the book, I shall discuss some concepts, themes and issues relating to constitutions generally. In democratic countries, constitutional structures concern the competition between the collective goals of the community and ideas of individual equality and freedom. Constitutional law makes it possible for us to act collectively by co-ordinating the interests of many individuals, for example by voting mechanisms or judicial decisions. It also protects individuals against abuses by those to whom we entrust power it being a sad feature of human nature that those who seek power may be unfit to exercise it. The political system of which the constitution is a skeleton can of course be anything that the dominant groups in the community manage to impose on the people by appeals to morality or self-interest or by means of violence, charismatic leadership, or reliance upon apathy. A constitution provides safeguards which at the very least facilitate peaceful change (or in some versions of democracy provides a means of legitimating forcible change according to majority opinion).

There are debates concerning what should be the role of the state in respect for example of providing public services or regulating the economy. These debates do not always involve constitutional matters. On the other hand it is arguable that democracy entails certain basic rights of the individual, broadly encompassed within the concept of the 'rule of law', for example freedom of expression and a right to a fair trial. It is arguable that, except in a situation of extreme emergency, no government should trespass upon these even for a good social purpose. Moreover economic decisions impact on constitutional concerns in as much as the economically powerful have a lever in that they may be able to manipulate those with political power to ensure that the constitution works in their interest. At these points particular political issues interact with constitutional concerns.

Constitutional law therefore concerns the struggle between rival contenders for power, the constantly changing relationships between the different governmental institutions and the limits imposed on the government. Sir John Laws (1996) described a constitution as 'that set

3

of legal rules which governs the relationship in a state between the ruler and the ruled'. This can be compared with the following broader description. 'A constitution is the set of the most important rules that regulate the relations among the different parts of the government of a given country and also the relations between the different parts of the government and the people of the country' (King, 2000). Constitutional questions therefore concern the rules which identify the ruler, which define the nature and extent of the rulers' power and which set the conditions for its exercise.

Sir John Laws's approach is that of a lawyer whereas Professor King writes as a political scientist. Although law is a manifestation of politics, law can be distinguished from other aspects of politics in at least the following respects: its reliance on formal sources of authority, usually in the form of written texts; its emphasis upon dispute resolution; and its authorisation of violence against individuals. The legal perspective is therefore particularly concerned with the relationship between the citizen and the state. It is also worth remarking, as King points out (above), that a constitution deals only with the most important aspects of government. We might reasonably disagree about what is important and what is peripheral so that any attempt to explain the constitution is inevitably subjective although there is likely to be a core of common ground. A study of constitutional law must therefore be selective but should at least include the broad purposes of the political arrangements of the country in question and the main rights of the individual which are protected by the law. We shall not therefore take up Sir Stephen Sedley's dauntingly all-encompassing definition of a constitution as 'the totality of arrangements that we make for ourselves as a society' (Nolan, 1997: 49).

In his Hamlyn Lectures (2000), King makes a useful distinction between three kinds of constitution. Before examining them it must be noted that, as with most attempts to squeeze human institutions into general concepts, these are abstract models which are unlikely to exist in a pure form in any single country but which serve as reference points. Most systems will show signs of all three and, at any one time, one of them is likely to be dominant.

First, there are what King calls 'power-sharing' constitutions. These disperse the powers of government between different institutions in a co-ordinated manner. They try to minimise conflict by seeking consensus perhaps at the expense of efficiency and decisive government. An example of a power-sharing constitution given by King is the Netherlands. This kind of constitution may require elaborate legal mechanisms such as federal structures in which power is divided between different geographical units, each being protected against interference by the others, or a formal separation of powers between the executive, the legislature and the judiciary (see Chapter 5). It is also likely to involve elaborate arrangements for consultation between different official bodies and to result in a relatively inactive and non-interventionist form of government. Accountability might also be difficult where power is shared.

Secondly, there are what King calls 'power-hoarding' constitutions. These concentrate power in a strong central authority. Plato, for example, thought that government was a skill like any other and should be concentrated in the hands of a specially trained elite. Power-hoarding constitutions have the opposite advantages and disadvantages to those of the power-sharing variety and, in democracies, emphasise strong and accountable government with clear lines of responsibility. Thus, while we may accept that in the interests of efficiency powers should be concentrated at the centre, we expect to be able to dismiss a government easily if it does not perform to our liking. Power-hoarding constitutions might be divided into those where the central power is elected directly by the people, those where it is hereditary and those where it is appointed. In the case of power-sharing constitutions the different government bodies might also be selected by any permutation of these means.

Thirdly, King (2001) identifies 'power-fractionated' constitutions, where power is broken up into fragments. Unlike the power-sharing variety there is little formal machinery to resolve disagreement between the competing power centres resulting in a permanent state of political conflict and instability. A power-fractionated constitution is therefore little more than an assemblage of competing bodies perhaps representing the nature of our culture better than the other more authoritarian models. The US constitution might be regarded as power-fractionated although the competition between its many power centres is to some extent mediated by the courts. For example, the failure of the presidential electoral process in November 2000 to produce a clear winner was resolved by the Supreme Court in accordance arguably with the political preferences of its own members.

Which of these models represents the contemporary constitution best is for you, the reader, to decide. The UK constitution has usually been regarded as a power-hoarding constitution. Lord Hailsham in his 1976 Dimbleby lecture, famously, if unoriginally, described the UK's constitution as an 'elective dictatorship'. If we take the UK constitution to be a power-hoarding constitution we would locate the centre of legal power in Parliament. The centre of political power is concentrated in whatever group manages to control both Parliament and the executive, since as a deliberative assembly Parliament could not run the country by itself. In law the executive is the Crown, which since 1688 conceded power to Parliament and is effectively appointed by Parliament. The history of the UK constitution tells a story of conflict between different interest groups to control Parliament and the executive, in particular the monarch, the land-owning families, organised labour, and latterly political parties supported by business interests.

On the other hand the fact that we can argue about where power lies suggests that the position may not be so straightforward. The UK constitution has been described in terms more akin to the power-sharing variety, as a 'mixed' or 'balanced' constitution, where power is shared between different interest groups not necessarily in different institutions. This relates to Aristotle's famous division of constitutions. Aristotle regarded participation in the life of the community as essential to human well-being. 'Justice' consisted of each person playing his allotted part in the community whether as slave or king, an idea that throughout history has been used to protect established interests. Aristotle postulated three basic forms of constitution: monarchy which provides authority; aristocracy (literally government by the 'best' people) which provides wisdom; and democracy which provides power. Aristotle himself favoured a constitution that mixed these elements within a legal framework thereby promoting the values of equality and balance beaten competing forces. The nineteenth-century commentator de Toqueville (1945, p. 285), writing about the USA, saw courts and lawyers as a kind of aristocracy who are a check against the mob. 'Men who have made a special study of the laws derive certain habits of order, a taste for formalities and a kind of instinctive regard for the regular connection of ideas which render them very hostile to the revolutionary spirit and to the unreflecting passions of the multitude. A leading contemporary judge, Lord Hoffmann (1999), referring to political parties, described the UK constitution as 'aristocratic.'

During the eighteenth century in particular the British constitution was often portrayed as a mixed constitution with the King, the House of Lords and the House of Commons supposedly working together in harmony each representing different 'estates' or interests in the country (see Chapter 5). However, until the beginning of the twentieth century the aristocracy in the House of Lords was dominant, although its influence had been steadily declining. Lord Salisbury was the last prime minister to sit in the House of Lords (1895–1902). The majority, who owned no land and had no vote were said to enjoy 'virtual' representation through the landowners who were regarded as having a natural stake in the country. Until the extension of the franchise to most of the population, which evolved by stages from 1832 to 1928, elections to the Commons were largely controlled by aristocratic land-owning families with a power base both in the Lords and in local affairs. Suspicion of democracy and the privileging of aristocrats have been powerful themes in English constitutional thought in competition with the liberalism of Locke, Paine and later Mill (see Chapter 2). For example Edmund Burke (1729–1797), concerned at the violence unleashed by the French revolution, thought that the notion of individual rights was nonsense and favoured a society based on custom and tradition which evolved pragmatically guided by paternalistic aristocrats. The relatively peaceful development of the UK governmental system during the eighteenth and nineteenth centuries is often attributed to the openness and flexibility of the ruling classes in absorbing others into their ranks, particularly the new industrial wealth.

Today, the institutions of the mixed constitution remain but their importance is debatable. The monarch does not in practice exercise a veto and the House of Lords has lost most of its legal power to veto the Commons. On other hand the House of Lords retains genuine power and the reforms that are currently in progress may reinforce its political influence although they are unlikely to enlarge its formal powers. The common law in the hands of the courts and lawyers is also an important source of power. Indeed, in *R. v. Secretary of State for the Home Department ex parte Fire Brigades Union* (1995), Lord Mustill spoke of the courts occupying the 'dead ground', where other means of protecting the citizen have failed.

King himself suggests that recent uncoordinated developments in the UK constitution may be producing the power-fractionated model. These developments include devolution of substantial lawmaking and executive power to elected bodies in Scotland and Northern Ireland, devolution of a smaller amount of lawmaking and executive power to an elected assembly in Wales, the introduction of referendums in respect of some political issues, what King calls the 'disembowelling' of local government by dispersing its functions to many different private and private bodies, membership of the European Union, House of Lords reform without a clear purpose, the delegation to the Bank of England of the power to influence the economy by setting interest rates and the increased volatility of the electorate. Perhaps of most importance from the legal perspective the courts have become more prominent. This has been generated by several factors, notably the alleged supremacy of EC law, the enactment of the Human Rights Act 1998, an increasingly active and wide-ranging approach to reviewing government action and a new willingness on the part of the higher judiciary to enter into public debate about constitutional matters.

1.2 Civic Republicanism

Power-sharing constitutions have close links with the classical 'civic republican' tradition. This tradition inspired by Aristotle and developed in Ancient Rome, challenged the idea of Plato that government should take the form of an elite of experts. It was revived in the Renaissance, together with the development, promoted by Machiavelli (1469–1527), that disagreement rather than harmony was the natural state of political communities. Republicanism influenced the English civil war in the mid-seventeenth century, was developed by eighteenth-century advocates of limited government such as Montesquieu (1689–1755) and influenced the French and American revolutions in the late eighteenth century.

Republicanism explains many traditional constitutional concepts and values. Its central idea is that no single interest group, not even a majority, should be dominant in society so as 'to be able to interfere on an arbitrary basis – at their pleasure – with the choices of a free person' (Pettit, 1997, p. 271). Republicanism is often used as a contrast with an inherited monarchy. In this sense many European states, including France and Germany are republics. However, republicanism does not require any particular form of government but requires that no single group should be in a position of dominance.

Crucially, republicanism distinguishes between non-interference and non-domination, the latter meaning the existence of objective limits on the power to interfere (see Pettit, 1997). Domination means the power to interfere. A person in a dominant position may in fact be liberal minded and not interfere but it is nevertheless offensive that such a relationship of domination should exist. A kind master is still a master so that a person subject to domination is not free. Republicanism therefore insists that powers to interfere should be defined by law and that those exercising such powers should be forced to justify any interference with others. Thus republicanism embodies the traditional virtues of the rule of law such as that no one should be punished or restricted without legal authority, that laws should be justified on the basis of the public interest, and that judges should be impartial (see Chapter 5). Republicanism also entails the belief that governmental institutions be representative of different sections of the community and that everything the government does should be justified by reason and open to challenge by the people. Republicanism also requires that there should be protection against vested interests, not only within government but also, for example, those of business and professional organisations.

Perhaps the hallmarks of the republican tradition are firstly its emphasis on equality and secondly its reliance on traditional mechanisms in the form of checks and balances between the different branches of government so as to ensure that no one group can be dominant. These include the following which are represented in imperfect form in the UK constitution.

- 'federalism' which divides up government responsibilities between central and local units;
- bills of rights preventing governments from interfering with defined individual rights or, less common, requiring governments to positively protect stipulated interests such as health or education;
- 'checks and balances' between branches of government such as judicial review of the executive;
- provisions requiring 'super-majorities' of the legislature such as a 75% vote on particular matters. These devices are used in connection with the Council of Ministers of the EC and also in relation to certain powers of the Scottish Parliament and the Welsh Assembly. Such requirements of course amount to minority control and are unlikely if they are frequently used to withstand the inexorable force of the majority.
- provisions for referendums on particular issues. These are increasing in the UK.

Above all republicanism rejects the traditional English attitude to constitutional affairs which relies heavily upon networks of officials linked by personal relationships and upon informal and voluntary custom and practices generated within government itself. For example it is often asserted that the anomalies and lack of formal controls in our constitution do not matter. This is because we can rely on the general benevolence of our rulers whom we can trust to honour voluntary codes whether written or unwritten, what Peter Hennessey has called the 'good chaps' theory of the constitution (below Chapter 3). As against this for example, the Commissioner for Standards, appointed as an independent regulator to counter corruption in Parliament, recently published a letter claiming that her work had been undermined by campaigns against her by MPs, civil servants, ministers, and even the Speaker (see *Times*, 5 December 2001).

However, the UK constitution is arguably moving in a republican direction influenced in particular by the Human Rights Act 1998, the legalistic culture of the European Union and the legalistic nature of the devolved regimes in Scotland, Wales and Northern Ireland against a background of wide spread distrust in the integrity of politicians. This might be a counter-trend to that towards fragmentation which I mentioned earlier.

1.3   Representative Democracy

Democracy cannot easily be justified as the most efficient form of government but rests on ideas of human equality and dignity. As with many general political and legal ideas there is no consensus about what democracy means and what it requires in practice. The basic meaning of democracy is that of government by the people as a whole. However, in any but the smallest community, direct democracy is impracticable and the notion of democracy has been narrowed to mean government with the consent of the people. This is a more slippery idea since an authoritative decision maker is needed to interpret the people's consent. The UK constitution is democratic in the sense that the government's authority derives from the consent of the people (or at least those whom Parliament permits to vote). This is given every four or five years in a general election in which the electorate choose representatives who form the main part of the legislature, the House of Commons. The House of Commons in turn chooses the leader of the executive who appoints the rest of the executive.

Democracy also requires that nothing should be immune from change and that the state must not permanently commit itself to any particular set of social, economic or political values Thus no one should be able to make irreversible decisions which tie the hands of future generations. James Madison for example, one of the founders of the US constitution, thought that all laws should be 'sunset laws' which automatically lapse after a given period of time. UK law does not go this far but the possibility of changing any law, including the constitution itself, is secured in the UK by the doctrine of parliamentary supremacy according to which no Parliament can bind its successors or indeed itself.

Democracy is also said to mean that laws should be made by a body that represents the wishes of the majority from time to time. Parliament votes by means of a simple majority, and elections are fought on the basis of a 'relative majority' in the sense that the candidate with more votes than any other candidate is the winner. (If we combine these rules we can see that it is not unlikely for a measure to be passed that enjoys the support of only a small minority of the people.) The nineteenth-century commentator de Toqueville, in his famous attack on the 'tyranny of the majority' (de Toqueville, 1945, pp. 269–71), made the point that there is no particular reason to suppose that a majority is right about anything any more than is the case with an individual. Majorities merely represent force and magnify the vices of individuals. We use majority voting only because it gives a clear outcome and because it is the fairest system of participatory decision making that we can think of in that it gives each participant equal value.

Another aspect of democracy emphasises that every member of the community is of equal value. One interpretation of this requires that individuals be protected against majority decisions that threaten equality since majoritarian democracy would entitle the majority to oppress minorities. If we wish to put limits on the majority we might therefore have to use non-democratic mechanisms such as the courts. In *R. (Alconbury)* v. *Secretary of State* [2001] 2 All ER 929 at 980, Lord Hoffmann endorsed this general view of democracy by saying that although decisions as to what the general interest requires are made by democratically elected lawmakers, 'respect for human rights requires that certain basic rights of individuals should not be capable in any circumstances of being overridden by the majority.'

Perhaps the most well-known version of this approach is that of Dworkin (1996), who from an American liberal perspective, offers what he calls a 'constitutional conception of democracy. This regards democracy as what Dworkin calls 'government subject to conditions', these being the equal status of all citizens. Dworkin argues that equality depends on individual liberty and that there is no logical or moral reason why these conditions should be under the control of the majority or indeed any other group. Dworkin favours a compromise between courts and politicians with the courts having the power to override the majority in defence of fundamental freedoms. He suggests that the courts may be better guardians of democracy than politicians. They are under less political pressure and are required to consider both sides of the case in public and to justify their decision by reasoning (see also Allan, 2001, 1993; cf. Steyn, 1997).

Other liberals, for example Waldron (1998), preferred the majority on the ground that, despite the risks involved, it is better that the majority should have the last word in the interests of fairness, accountability and the desire that those affected by a law should be able to participate in its making. On the other hand it could be argued that our practice of making decisions through elected representatives is an unfortunate second best because it would be impracticable for all to participate directly in decision making in an ideal democracy. This being the case it seems reasonable to put curbs on our representatives enforced by a trusted external body such as a court.

1.3.1   The nature of representation

Our system of democracy involves government by elected representatives. The term representative is ambiguous. In one sense a representative is the agent of whoever he represents reflecting their wishes. In another sense a representative substitutes for those he represents exercising his own judgement in the same way that a trustee represents his beneficiaries. This creates several problems. In particular is a representative elected as a member of a political party bound or entitled blindly to follow the party line? Is a representative bound to those who voted for him to obey the 'mandate' embodied in his party election manifesto? There is also the question of how far MPs are entitled to assist private interests for whom they may act as consultants or advisers.

There is a strong tradition that the House of Commons does not directly represent those who elected it in the sense of being required to follow their wishes. Moreover Parliament is self-governing and immune from interference by the courts (see Chapter 10). In the eighteenth century the idea that the people should be directly represented was widely regarded as unconstitutional. Therefore in order to protect their independence, legislators, like judges, could claim to be insulated from populist pressures. In his famous speech to his Bristol electors in 1774 Burke said: 'if government was a matter of will upon any side, yours without question ought to be superior. But government and legislation are matters of reason and judgement and not of inclination' and 'mandates issued which the member is blindly and implicitly to obey ... these are things utterly unknown to the law of this land and, and which arise from a fundamental mistake of the whole order and tenor of our constitution.' Similarly, in 1784 Lord North said of members of Parliament that: 'to surrender their own judgments, to abandon their own opinions, and to act as their constituents thought proper to instruct them, right or wrong, is to act unconstitutionally ... they were sent there as trustees to act for the benefit and advantage of the whole kingdom' (see Briggs, 1959, p. 98). Writing in 1867, Walter Bagehot thought that an elite made up of reasonably independent men (*sic*) of property to whom the populace defers should get on with the practical business of running the government without outside inter-ference. Bagehot, along with many of his propertied contemporaries, feared popular democracy because in his view it was likely to lead to the government being captured by powerful vested interests who could manipulate the mob. The independence of Parliament has also been endorsed in modern times. Erskine May, the authoritative guide to parliamentary law and practice, asserts that an MP's vote is to be cast neither for locality nor for party but for the good of the nation and according to conscience (Nolan, 1997, p. 82). However, there is no method of policing this other than through Parliament itself which is controlled by political parties.

The principle that our democracy is channelled through Parliament has significantly influenced the development of the constitution. For example the notion that government is accountable to Parliament has been used to deny the existence of a public right to access to government information (see *British Steel* v. *Granada TV* (1981); *Bushell* v. *Secretary of State for the Environment* (1981)). The Bill of Rights 1688 conferred a right to freedom of speech on members of Parliament (Art. 9), but the only public political right it conferred was to petition the Crown. The ordinary courts have no jurisdiction over the internal proceedings of Parliament which polices itself, assisted since 1997 by the office of Parliamentary Commissioner for Standards and by the Committee on Standards and Privileges. At local government level, however, the courts have attempted to compromise between traditional values and the reality of party discipline by holding that while it is lawful for a councillor to vote according to the party whip, the councillor must still consider at each vote whether there are reasons of conscience for not doing so (*R.* v. *Waltham Forest DC ex parte Baxter* (1988)).

The courts defer to representative democracy at central government level but less so at local level. Usually the view has been taken that, because of its subordinate nature, the democratic nature of a local decision-making body does not entitle it to any special consideration (see *R.* v. *Somerset CC ex parte Fewings* (1995) per Laws J; compare the different views expressed in *Roberts* v. *Hopwood* (1925) both in the House of Lords and the Court of Appeal). The rule of law requires that a democratic mandate cannot bind an authority to decide in a particular way to the exclusion of other concerns required by the governing legislation, but this of course begs the question, as to what assumptions the court should make about democracy when interpreting the legislation (see *Bromley LBC* v. *GLC* (1983)).

In the case of central government the courts have been influenced by the existence of parliamentary scrutiny. They have not withheld from review altogether. Indeed they have emphasised that legal review by the courts is independent of political accountability (*Hoffman-La Roche Ltd.* v. *Trade and Industry Secretary of State* (1974)) but have deferred to executive discretion particularly in cases involving sensitive political or financial issues (*Hammersmith and Fulham LBC* v. *Secretary of State for the Environment* (1990); or where Parliament itself is involved (compare the majority with Lord Mustill in *R.* v. *Secretary of State for the Home Department ex parte Fire Brigades Union* (1995)). Under the Human Rights Act 1998, the question of deference to political discretion arises in acute form. In many cases the right in question can be overridden by various categories of the public interest subject to the test that interference with the right 'is necessary in a democratic society'. The courts will defer to 'an area of judgement' within an elected body in cases which involve matters of social or economic policy (Chapter 18). Thus in his famous dissent in *Lochner* v. *New York* (1905), Holmes, J emphasised that the social or economic policies adopted by governments were not appropriate matters for constitutional review. However, this must be a question of degree in that, according to the broader view of democracy, there may be cases where government policies of any kind place at risk basic values of equality and freedom.

Recent cases suggest an increasing concern for direct public involvement in governmental decision making. Decision-making processes relating to transport, planning and the environment provide for public inquiries, and the courts have recognised that public opinion, even if 'irrational' should be taken into account in relation to sensitive development proposals even if the decision is already adequately informed (see *Berkeley* v. *Secretary of State for the Environment* (2000)). At a political level a convention may be emerging that the government is morally bound by the promises in the election manifesto on which it was elected. Referendums have been held in relation to EC membership (1976) and devolution proposals and arrangements for referendums have been placed on a legal footing (Political Parties, Elections and Referendums Act 2000). The government has undertaken to hold a referendum in relation to the proposal to enter the European single currency.

Summary

1.1   This chapter discussed some general themes which influence the different ways in which constitutions develop and which will be drawn on throughout the book. We first discussed the function of a constitution emphasising that a constitution deals with the most basic principles and values as to how the community should be governed. We then looked at broad types of constitution using King's typology, namely 'power-sharing', 'power-hoarding' and 'power-fractionated' constitutions each of which has advantages and disadvantages. We characterise the UK constitution as power-hoarding with a tendency to become fractionated. It may be that recent constitutional reforms, particularly devolution, have begun to disperse political away from the central executive.

1.2   We distinguished between descriptions of the constitution and evaluations of it and between the constitution in its normative sense of rules and the actual political relationship between the different parts of government. We pointed out that, while the rules of the constitution may facilitate or exclude particular political outcomes, at any given time the two do not necessarily correspond. The principles of the UK constitution are sufficiently open-ended to permit a wide range of political outcomes. We contrasted the political relationship between the executive and the legislature with that between the courts and the other two branches.

1.3   We used the notion of constitutionalism to refer to values which are intended to limit the powers of government and to make government accountable. We mentioned the traditional doctrine of the separation of powers between the legislature, judiciary and executive, pointing out that it has some influence on the UK constitution but that, because of the pragmatic and evolutionary nature of the UK constitution, it has not been systematically adopted.

1.4   We emphasised the wider principle of civic republicanism. This links many of the constitutional concepts and values offered by different perspectives. Civic republicanism does not substantively limited the power of government but attempts to ensure that no particular interest group, not even a majority, can dominate the government. It relies on mechanisms which disperse power in order to achieve this. In relation to this we introduced examples such as that of the separation of powers, judicial review, fundamental rights, and the mixed constitution representative of different interest groups. The notion of dispersal of powers includes but is wider than the doctrine of the separation of powers and influences for example, devolution and the debate on the future of the House of Lords. According to the republican perspective, informal conventional restraints whereby those in power follow a benevolent practice of not interfering are inadequate since human dignity requires formal constraints on power.

1.5   We discussed the principles of representative democracy drawing attention to the problems of majoritarianism and the ambiguity in the notion of representation in relation to the independence of a representative, in particular from party political control. We also briefly considered the courts' attitude to democracy. This raises the question whether there are certain basic principles which are essential to democracy such as equality and freedom of expression which should be outside the reach of democratic decision making. There is no consensus on these matters. The courts have not deferred to local democracy but have been more cautious in interfering with central government powers.

Further Reading

Allan, *Law, Liberty and Justice*, chapter 1.
Ewing, K. (2000) 'The politics of the British constitution', *Public Law* 405.
Finer, Bogdanor, Rudden, *Comparing Constitutions*, chapter 1.

Harlow, C. (2000) 'Disposing of Dicey: from legal autonomy to constitutional discourse', 48 *Political Studies*, 356.
Held, *Models of Democracy*, chapter 10.
King, *Does the United Kingdom Still have a Constitution?*
Laws, (1995) 'Law and democracy' *Public Law* 72.
Laws, (1996) 'The constitution, morals and rights' *Public Law* 622.
Pettit, *Republicanism*.
Seidentop, *Democracy in Europe*, Chapter 5.

Exercises

1.1 To what extent does the UK constitution conform to Professor King's system of classifying constitutions?

1.2 'A constitution is not the act of a government but of a people constituting a government and a government without a constitution is power without right' (Paine). Discuss in relation to the UK constitution.

1.3 To what extent should the courts defer to elected bodies?

1.4 'That every Member is equally a Representative of the *whole* (within which by our particular constitution, is included a Representative not only of those who are electors, but of all the other subjects of the Crown of Great Britain at home and in every part of the British Empire, except the Peers of Great Britain) has, as I understand, been the constant notion and language of Parliament' (Speaker Onslow (1728–61). Comment. To what extent do these remarks apply today?

1.5 There is a proposal in your town to build a secure hospital for sex offenders. Your MP is a member of the government the election manifesto of which included a promise to ensure that 'sex offenders are kept off the streets'. A public inquiry into the scheme is to be held and you ask your MP to appear at the inquiry to represent local public opinion which is against the proposal because of fears of escapes and the likely fall in property values. The MP refuses to appear on the ground that the government is committed to the scheme. The inquiry inspector decides that because expert evidence is that the risk of an escape is negligible the views of the local people are irrelevant. Discuss any constitutional implications.

1..6 To what extent should a constitution provide for direct public participation in governmental decision making? Outline the advantages and disadvantages of a referendum as a means of making government decisions.

2 Constitutional Values

2.1 The Nation State, the Enlightenment and the Social Contract

A convenient starting point is the emergence of the independent nation state. This is based on the concept of a republic developed in ancient Rome. It re-emerged throughout Europe in the sixteenth century for military purposes. Following the collapse of the unifying authority of the Catholic church, the nation state displaced the medieval diffusion of power between king, church, corporations and feudal barons as the ultimate source of political authority. In England, however, the common law, claiming to be rooted in community custom and values, opposed the development of the idea of an all-powerful state.

The rise of the state corresponded to the beginning of the Enlightenment, which reached a high point in the late eighteenth century and which still provides the dominant intellectual force in European societies. Enlightenment or 'modernist' thinking places the individual at the centre of the political process and regards reason as the key to human happiness. One task of the Enlightenment was to justify state power by reason. As an impersonal and neutral form of organisation the state, in its ideal form, treats all persons equally and releases the individual from dependence upon customary, religious and traditional ties.

Broadly speaking the state means the government of a country. The term is also used in international law to describe an independent country and as such a full member of the international community. The term 'state' derives from 'status' or 'estate' and originally meant a position in the overall scheme of things. Thus the legislatures of the Channel Islands are called the 'states'. The state could be regarded as merely an organised body of people issuing orders, its function being to provide services for the public. What is special about the state is the notion that the state must be accepted by the community as having a monopoly of physical force either directly or indirectly as when it permits the use of force by others in self-defence.

We can go further by recognising special features associated with the state. For example the state represents the whole community rather than any particular section of it and therefore carries special authority. Moreover the state should be subject to higher standards of conduct than other persons with regard in particular to its duty to treat people

17

equally, to act altruistically and to be accountable (see *R*. v. *IRC ex parte Unilever* [1996] STC 681 at 695; *R*. v. *Somerset CC ex parte Fewings* [1995] 1 All ER 513 at 524; *Reynolds* v. *Times Newspapers* [1998] 3 All ER 961 at 1004). Conversely, in order to perform its duties, the state might have privileges not available to other bodies such as immunity from legal enforcement.

The terms 'state' and 'nation' could overlap. The state is a legal and political concept. A nation is a cultural, political and historical idea signifying a relatively homogenous community featuring possibly but not necessarily a common language, a common territory, and shared religious, or cultural traditions. Legally speaking there is no necessary link between a state and a nation. For example, most of the African states are artificial constructs devised in the interests of colonial rulers and relatively unstable as political units. Within the United Kingdom which is a state but not a nation there are the nations of England, Scotland and Wales and some argue Cornwall. The problems of Northern Ireland are connected with the fact that the Irish nation was partitioned in 1921 between two states, the UK and the Republic of Ireland. Until the Union with Ireland in 1801, Britain was a state, as was England before the Union with Scotland in 1707.

The English nation has no legal or political institutions as such whereas the other nations of the UK have a certain degree of autonomy. (The term 'country' has no legal significance and is used loosely to refer either to a nation or to a state in their geographical senses.) A community that considers itself to be a nation has a moral claim to the legal powers that go with statehood. Indeed it is arguable that association with a place – England – is a stronger source of political legitimacy than the institutions that embody the state as such. The French Declaration of the Rights of Man (1789) announced that the source of all sovereignty lies in the nation, although some communitarian beliefs would devolve power to smaller groups linked by ethnic ties.

The period from 1770 to 1820 is widely regarded as marking the birth of the modern political age. Influenced by the writings of the previous century, the French and American revolutions generated written republican constitutions which were copied later on, when aristocratic regimes were overthrown throughout Europe and colonial rulers expelled. The English revolution and the subsequent union with Scotland had taken place a century earlier. Even though the British system of government was widely admired, no other state adopted the loose unwritten British model but preferred the rationality of a written blueprint in accordance with Enlightenment philosophy.

The experience of the twentieth century in which states use technology as a means of mass extermination and set up regimes designed to subjugate communities by terror may have damaged the credibility of the 'Enlightenment project' and in recent decades there has been a reaction against the supremacy of reason and indeed against the validity of the state. This has taken the form of self-consciously 'post-modern' and 'critical' approaches to law which have emphasised law as a propaganda instrument of powerful vested interests rather than as one of reason and justice and which have drawn attention to what are presented as irresolvable contradictions in the law (see Ward, 1997; Dworkin, 1986, p. 275). Solutions have usually centred upon participatory mechanisms that devolve decision making to lower levels so as to allow those most affected to exercise control. The obvious danger here is the sacrifice of the neutrality and equality associated with the idea of the state in favour of self-appointed vigilante and vested interest groups.

A method of justifying the state which was popular with Enlightenment thinkers and is still used today is the idea of the 'social contract'. This is a hypothetical agreement made by the community under which individuals voluntarily give up some of their freedom in return for the benefits of the law. The social contract therefore regards government as based on the consent of the people and treats each member of the community as equal. It does not matter that there was no actual contract. According to Kant for example an arrangement is unjust if free individuals would not have agreed to it. Rawls, an important modern contractarian, seems to take a similar approach by having a system of justice on what we might agree to if we were unaware of the social and economic disparities between us. According to Hart (Rosen, 71) the obligation is one of mutuality in the sense that, because I enjoy the benefits of law and order, I must accept its burdens. However, it is not easy to understand why any individual should be morally bound by a social contract on Hart's basis since we cannot choose to opt out of the 'benefits' of the law. Nor is there any reason why future generations should respect contracts made by their forebears. Moreover the idea of contract makes sense only if there is some already existing reason why agreements should be binding.

2.2 Incommensurables and Uncombinables

A constitution must either impose a particular value system by force or must reach a voluntary accommodation between incommensurable values and interests. Incommensurable values reflect the fact that human nature comprises contradictory elements. For example, we are at the same time, individuals who want to be left alone to pursue our own versions of happiness and social animals who could not survive without the help of others. Each of us possesses these contradictory features in different proportions. This leads to competing goals in the law. Each goal may be desirable in itself but one cannot be achieved without sacrificing the other. Incommensurables cannot be brought within a principle that everyone can unite behind other than one so general as to be meaningless such as 'the public interest' or 'human dignity'. Nor can incommensurables be weighed according to any rational measure. For example how is it possible to compare the risks of an obscene publication corrupting people with the good of any artistic merit such a publication may have (see Obscene Publications Act 1959, s. 4).

For the purposes of constitutional law the most fundamental incommensurables are the two freedoms identified by Sir Isaiah Berlin (1968). On the one hand there is the 'negative freedom' of the absence of restraint, reflecting our wish not to be interfered with. Negative freedom includes, for example, personal liberty, freedom of expression, freedom of association, freedom of religion, privacy etc. On the other hand there is positive freedom which, reflecting the social side of our nature, is the freedom of the community to take collective action to advance the general welfare. Positive freedom includes the democratic right to choose and control the government and, through the government, to make collective decisions about taxation, public services and the regulation of private activities.

The two freedoms cannot be reconciled although they may overlap. For example liberals would support some exercises of positive freedom on the ground that, without minimum standards of welfare, public order and education, it is difficult to exercise the negative freedoms, (some of which such as freedom of expression and privacy may conflict with each other) to which we are entitled. The reason to insist on this distinction is to emphasise that different freedoms may conflict, so that any constitution has to make what has been called 'tragic choices' in the sense that one cannot further a given interest without injuring others. For example Sedley (2001) describes a case where the French Conseil d'Etat upheld a ban on local funfairs where revellers had been permitted to shoot a dwarf from a cannon. The decision was made in the name of public morals and human dignity even though the dwarfs made their living from the spectacle and were among the chief opponents of the ban (Sedley, 2001a, p. 11) In other words the conflicting ideals of law as a bulwark of liberty and law as 'social solidarity' cannot be harmonised. At best we can seek a provisional accommodation that is widely accepted and can be used as a reference point for settling disputes.

Incommensurability must be distinguished from 'uncombinabilty' (see Raz, 1986). Interests are combinable when both happen to be achievable at the same time. This is a matter of fact in the particular context and there is no logical connection between incommensurability and uncombinability. For example in *R.* v. *Brown* (1993), the House of Lords held that a group which voluntarily indulged in homosexual sado-masochism were guilty of an offence. The majority started from the communitarian stance that the deliberate infliction of pain was an affront in a civilised society unless it could exceptionally be justified as being for the public good for example in the cases of surgical operations and sport. The two dissenting judges took the individualistic stance that people should be free to do what they like unless it is clearly harmful. They held that the accused were not guilty since their behaviour even if immoral happened to carry no danger to the public. Had their behaviour happened to be a public danger then, by a happy chance, the two approaches, though incommensurable, would have been combinable in a unanimous decision.

There are two opposite attempts to combine incommensurables. One often favoured by academics attempts to impose some assumed grand harmonising principle usually based on the writer's personal preferences. One such principle is utilitarianism (below) which looks to the 'greatest good of the greatest number'. Dworkin (1983) uses concepts of equality and integrity as harmonising principles. However, *Airedale NHS Trust* v. *Bland* (1993) shows that the search for a harmonising principle may be illusory. The House of Lords had to decide whether doctors should withdraw medical support from a man who had been so severely injured in the Hillsborough stadium disaster that he would never recover consciousness. Lord Hoffmann identified the issue as that of Berlin's tragic choice, in this case between the sanctity of life and 'the principle that the individual should be free to choose what should happen to him and, if he is unable to choose, we should try our honest best to choose as we think he would have chosen'. His Lordship thought that there was no single formula which can help us choose between incommensurables, and rejected the Attorney General's argument that they could be harmonised, as rhetoric, 'intended to dull the pain of having to choose'. The House of

Lords unanimously held that the patient should be allowed to die. Their basis for so doing seems to derive from no more than their intuitions as to a solution that many people would find morally acceptable.

Similarly in *A (Re), children: conjoined twins: surgical separation* (2000), the Court of Appeal chose what it regarded as the lesser of two evils in allowing the weaker of the twins to die in order to save the stronger. Brooke LJ applying a doctrine of necessity against the views of many moralists recognised that there was no combinable solution (see pp. 1042, 1051.)

The other approach is to recognise and encourage disagreement between competing views as a sign of a healthy society and to concentrate on methods by which disagreements can be resolved on a temporary and provisional basis without precluding change. The law can assist the process of managing disagreement by identifying incommensurables and trying to combine them, ensuring that value judgements are exposed and that decision makers take into account all relevant interests. In this context lawyers often use metaphors such as 'balancing' interests to give an illusion of objectivity, for example, between the claims of freedom of expression of the media and personal privacy. Such metaphors are sometimes useful, for example where the competing interests can be expressed as money. In the case of incommensurables they are misleading because there is no common measure and no way of avoiding the hard choice between competing interests.

Fairness is not enough in itself. For example we would probably object to what Dworkin calls a 'checkerboard statute' (1986, p. 179) under which abortion is permitted on odd days but not on even days with a view to compromising between pro- and anti-abortionists holding sincere but incommensurable views. Different judges may have irreconcilable points of view but we accept the decision of the judge or of a majority, not because they are necessarily right but in the interests of keeping the peace. We could equally fairly decide such disputes by tossing a coin but we prefer some reasoned justification and we require our decision makers to be personally accountable.

The clash between the incommensurable values of individualism and communitarianism comes into the open in the context of the Human Rights Act 1998 (see Chapter 18). Few of the rights protected under that Act are absolute. In most cases the court must decide whether they are overridden by various social concerns, which among other things must be justified as 'necessary in a democratic society'. This requires firstly value judgements to be made about what democracy means. For example do we consider like Rousseau that democracy requires all to be roughly equal in terms of economic wealth so that we participate on a level playing field? Secondly, the Act requires the decision maker to make a choice between the right in question and the social goal. In relation to this choice the point at which one must give way to the other cannot be justified by reason alone (at least short of the extreme case where protection of the right would destroy the society altogether). The decision maker may get some help from widespread social consensus or from the principle of 'proportionality', which requires that protected interests be interfered with no more than is necessary to achieve the social goal in question but in the end the choice is a subjective one.

This leads to another problem. The techniques we use to choose between incommensurables may themselves be controversial and incommensurable. For example should the courts decide whether there is a right to abortion, which is the solution chosen in the USA, or should it be left to the democratic process? It is arguable that incommensurable issues should be the province of elected bodies since the irrational element that determines both the starting point and the accommodation between conflicting interests requires the support of public opinion. Elected bodies have the merit that the decision is the outcome of deliberation by the interests concerned being a voluntary rather than an imposed outcome. The contrary argument is that there are certain basic values such as freedom of expression that are so important that they should be put beyond the reach of volatile public sentiment by being guarded by expert judges. This reveals a contempt for democracy.

Furthermore, the democratic process may itself raise incommensurables. For example some voting systems, notably the 'winner takes all' system used in elections to the UK Parliament, favour strong accountable government. Under this system the government is rarely supported by a majority of the popular vote and minority parties tend to be under-represented (see Chapter 11). By contrast, systems of proportional representation such as apply in the case of elections to the EU Parliament, the Scottish Parliament and the Welsh Assembly favour fairness in the form of an outcome which reflects the spread of votes cast. The price for this may be uncertain and weak government, although some may think this is a virtue.

A democratic constitution attempts to provide a non-violent battleground between incommensurables. Some constitutions, notably that of the USA, are carefully crafted so as to prevent a particular point of view from permanently triumphing. This is the driving force of the civic republican tradition (chapter 1). There may be an illogical and unstable compromise with a different compromise being struck at different times. Tribe (1988, pp. 1–7) sees the US Constitution, as 'a historically discontinuous composition; it is the product, over time, of a series of not altogether coherent compromises; it mirrors no single vision or philosophy but reflects instead a set of sometimes reinforcing and sometimes conflicting ideals and values'. The same can be said of the UK constitution which has been formed out of 'collaboration, negotiation and consent' although it contains no formal mechanism which prevents any one group from permanently holding power (Van Caenegen, 1995, p. 173).

In the following sections I shall outline four influential models which I suggest embody the fundamental incommensurables which dominate constitutional law. These are firstly the individualistic model proposed by Thomas Hobbes; secondly the liberal, quasi-democratic model of John Locke, which represents a notion of limited and accountable government; thirdly the democratic communitarian model of Jean Jacques Rousseau, which takes the idea of the state to an extreme by privileging the collective over the individual; and fourthly the conventionalist pragmatic version of David Hume. It is important to remember, however, that these thinkers responded both to the political agenda of their times and to their personal circumstances.

2.3   Hobbes: Constrained Individualism

Thomas Hobbes (1588–1679) explained the nature of the modern state from an individualistic perspective. Hobbes is pivotal to modern democratic thought in that he broke away from the mythology grounded in Plato that good government is a matter of expert knowledge in the hands of an elite. He recognised that human affairs are based on irreducible disagreement and therefore that a constitution has solid foundations only in the minimum on which it is possible to agree. According to Hobbes this is an independent mechanism to resolve disputes. Although one of the earliest of the modern political theorists, Hobbes's insights may well provide the most universally valid approach to the foundations of the modern state exposing as they do the frailty of human values and the contradiction between the individualist and the social aspects of human nature.

Hobbes wrote his most influential work, *Leviathan* (1651) during a time of widespread political unrest throughout Europe when England was in the grip of civil war between the King and Parliament. He was a materialist sceptic who doubted whether it was possible to discover objective truth about the world. He thought that moral and political values were no more than subjective human attitudes and that the natural state of humanity is mutual conflict – a war of 'all against all' – so that, without government, we would destroy each other. He regarded individuals, on the analogy of the particles envisaged by the physics of his day, as moving indefinitely and colliding with each other unless restrained by a superior force.

Hobbes did not believe that humans are inherently wicked but thought that our different ideas of good inevitably set us in conflict with each other unless we accepted the need for a supreme authority. According to Hobbes we are motivated by three impulses: competition, fear and the desire for power over others. We constantly strive to fulfil new desires in a never-ending and ultimately doomed search for what Hobbes called 'felicity'. Hobbes therefore argued that the purpose of government is to keep order and that any government is better than none. The one thing we could all agree upon would be that we want to survive so that we would each submit to a ruler as the lesser of evils.

Hobbes's most famous passage encapsulates the beauty of his language:

> Hereby it is manifest, that during the time men live without a common Power to keep them all in awe, they are in that condition which is called Warre; and such a warre, as is of every man against every man ... In such condition, there is no place for Industry: because the fruit thereof is uncertain; and consequently no Culture of the Earth, no Navigation, nor use of the commodities that may be imported by Sea; no commodious Building; no Instruments of moving and removing such things as require much force; no knowledge of the face of the Earth; no account of Time; no Arts; no Letters; no Society; and which is worst of all, continuall feare, and danger of violent death; And the life of man, solitary, poore, nasty, brutish and short (Hobbes, 1973, p. 65).

Hobbes's government has three crucial features. Firstly the sovereign – 'Leviathan' – must have unlimited powers to issue commands These are automatically binding because of the subject's prior agreement. Otherwise the very conflicts that the sovereign was created to resolve would inevitably arise. Hobbes's sovereign is not itself a party to the social contract which is hypothetically assumed to be made by the people with each other. The people are then assumed collectively to have made a covenant, a one-sided promise, to obey the sovereign, in effect making a free gift of power to the sovereign. The sovereign, who has promised nothing, cannot be subject to legal controls. Indeed Hobbes thought that by definition the sovereign can never act unjustly to a subject because the subject has agreed to accept every decision of the sovereign. Similarly Bentham famously observed that the notion of rights except in the sense of rights created by positive laws was 'nonsense on stilts'.

Second, in order to minimise disagreement, the sovereign must be a single unitary body, an 'artificial man'. This could be either a monarch or an assembly, although Hobbes preferred monarchy as being less prone to disagreement. Hobbes's sovereign has no special claim to rule nor indeed any particular qualifications for ruling. It is a representative of the community and is not necessarily better or worse than anyone else. Hobbes therefore rejected the classical notion that government is a matter of enlightened expertise. He also rejected the claims of the common lawyers that the common law is the embodiment of reason. However, in his later work, *The Dialogues*, Hobbes conceded that the sovereign should secure the assent of Parliament before enacting laws (Postema 1986, p. 46).

Third, Hobbes's sovereign exists for one purpose only, that of preserving life and has no authority to use the law for any other purpose. The moral obligation of the sovereign, according to Hobbes derives from its gratitude to the people for the free gift of power. Thus the sovereign is required to act 'so that the giver shall have no just occasion to repent him of his gift' and 'all the duties of the rulers are contained in this one sentence, the safety of the people is the supreme law.' Therefore the individual life comes first and we have an inalienable right of defence even against the sovereign. Hobbesian thinking therefore supports the importance that the law gives to public order and national security, sometimes justifying the infringement of basic freedoms. Thus, in *Entick* v. *Carrington* (1765) 19 St. Tr. 1029 at 1074 Lord Camden reflected on the Hobbesian view that people need government no matter how tyrannical and that the price to be paid is the risk that those in power would be vindictive towards the people.

The Hobbesian approach has an important influence on the development of the constitution. Firstly it promotes the notion of equality between citizens. In a state subject to a single omnipotent ruler all are equal, both subject to and protected by the law and no one has powers or privileges or is subject to special rights or obligations based solely on custom or tradition, such as feudalism or on membership of religious, family or other cultural groups. Secondly there is the notion of freedom as the natural state of affairs as opposed to a gift bestowed by authority. It is true that the sovereign can make any law but unless it positively does so the individual is free to do what he or she likes – 'freedom lies in the silence of the laws' (*Entick* v. *Carrington* (1765)).

Thirdly Hobbes generates the distinction between the public and the private sphere. In relation to areas of life not controlled by the state, namely those where public order and safety are not at risk, what I do is not the law's business. Fourthly, Hobbes encourages change and frees the individual from commitments to the past. Nothing is immune from change and arguments based upon custom or tradition do not in themselves have legitimacy. This runs counter to the strong tradition in English constitutional thought that custom is an indication of success and should not be lightly changed.

Hobbes's ideas influenced what many believe to be the central doctrine of the UK constitution, that of parliamentary sovereignty. A line of thought can be traced from Hobbes that a state requires a single ultimate source of authority with unlimited lawmaking power and with no superior authority. However, there is arguably a dual sovereignty between parliament and the courts in the sense that the courts have the last word both as to what counts as an Act of Parliament and what an Act of Parliament means. Because the common law does not derive its authority from Parliament this tension between a court-centred notion of the constitution and a political notion centred on Parliament remains unresolved.

The notion of sovereignty is controversial but few modern thinkers support the view that there is a need for some kind of indivisible omnicompetent supreme ruler (see MacCormick, 1993). A republican form of constitution such as that of the USA, limits the powers of all branches of government. Even Dicey (1823–1921), the jurist who is sometimes credited with creating the doctrine of parliamentary sovereignty, did not regard the doctrine as a necessary one but merely as an empirical fact about the UK constitution. Legal power can be divided in many ways dependent on the particular interests who manage to control it. For example a modified Hobbesian version of the sovereign, strictly limited to the primary goal of protection, expounded by the twentieth-century authoritarian political theorist Karl Schmidt (1888–1985) is the person who can decide the 'exception', that is the person who can intervene as a last resort where the normal machinery of government breaks down.

2.4 Locke: Liberalism and Majoritarianism

It is arguable that, even from a Hobbesian perspective, the stability of the state depends upon the sovereign conforming to widely shared moral values and cultural practices within the community. These matters were taken forward by John Locke (1632–1704), whose writings were aimed at justifying the 1688 revolution against the claims of absolute monarchy. Locke's approach was grounded in the Protestant religion. He argued that the community had a duty to ensure that people were treated as equals. Locke proposed a social contract, sharply different from that of Hobbes, one in which governmental power is limited in favour of individual rights. For this reason Locke is usually regarded as a proto-liberal. In his *Second Treatise of Government* (1690), Locke took a more optimistic view of human nature than did Hobbes. He regarded most humans as essentially sociable and anxious to help each other. He also believed that individuals had certain natural rights, most notably property rights, that, according to him, existed independently of the law.

According to Locke sovereignty lies collectively with the people, an idea which Hegel (1770–1831) ridiculed on the ground that the people comprise an amorphous mass and that, in any sense possible in a constitution, the state comes first and creates 'the people'. According to Locke, however, the people first hypothetically contract with each other unanimously to establish a government and then choose an actual government by majority vote. The form the government takes is less important. The government as such does not enter into a contract but takes on a trust, a one-sided promise, whereby it undertakes to perform its functions of protecting natural rights, respecting individual freedom and advancing well-being. This is not a contract so that the government has duties but no rights of its own (see Laws J in *R* v. *Somerset CC ex parte Fewings* (1995)).

Locke called for restraints upon the powers of government in the form of a separation of powers between the different branches of government to make it difficult for any one group to gain absolute power. He emphasised the rule of law in the sense that the government should be bound by the same law as everyone else and there should be a judiciary independent of the legislature. However, unlike modern theorists, he was less concerned with the executive and combined it with the judiciary. His writings have influenced the common law in respect of its emphasis upon private property rights (see *Entick* v. *Carrington* (1765); *Burmah Oil Corp.* v. *Lord Advocate* (1965)).

Locke also influenced the American revolution by virtue of his belief in the importance of individual rights and the limited role of the state. Indeed a modified passage from Locke, famously prefaced the United States Declaration of Independence (1776). Locke wrote in the second edition of his *Essay on Human Understanding*: 'Civil interests I call life, liberty health and indolency of the body (substituted in the Declaration by 'the pursuit of happiness'). It is the duty of the Civil Magistrate, by the impartial execution of equal laws, to secure unto all the people ... the just possession of these things belonging to this life.'

Locke did not, however, favour legal constraints on the lawmaker itself. He regarded the contribution of lawyers as 'artificial ignorance and learned gibberish' (*Two Treatises on Government,* para. 12, p. 275) and preferred to restrain the lawmaker by political means. Locke can claim to have introduced the notion of representative democracy. According to Locke, government should be appointed and dismissable by a majority vote representing those with a stake in the community. He justified this on the basis that the majority commands most force. He also upheld a right to rebel against a government that broke its trust. The ideas of rights protected by the courts and majority rule by equal citizens were developed by later eighteenth-century writers such as Thomas Paine and Jean Jacques Rousseau and implemented in the French Revolution.

2.5 Rousseau: Communitarianism

Hobbes and Locke in their different ways were concerned to justify particular forms of government for the purpose of protecting individual liberty. However, neither dealt in detail with the problem of how to reconcile the interests of the community with those of individuals. Jean Jacques Rousseau (1712–1778), in his personal life a pathological loner, attempted to do this by claiming that social co-operation was the highest form of individual happiness. Like Locke, Rousseau believed that man was by nature good, but thought that people had been corrupted by a society dominated by vested interests ('man is born free but everywhere he is in chains'). Rousseau believed that individuals had natural rights but argued that, because we are social animals, there is no conflict between the needs of the individual properly understood and the interests of the community provided that we participate in government on equal terms. Thus Rousseau attempted to square the circle by claiming that 'true' freedom lies in obeying a democratic state. Rousseau was therefore a founder of the communitarian thought that underlies modern collectivist visions of the good society. His thinking particularly influenced the French Revolution with its slogan of 'liberty, equality and fraternity' but had only limited influence in Britain. It is important to remember however that political and philosophical ideals such as those proposed by Hobbes, Locke and Rousseau had resonances and implications for their times which may be lost to us. For example, in pre-revolutionary France, unlike England, the monarchy and the rights-bearing landowners were in alliance. Lockeian thinking was therefore unhelpful to the French revolutionaries who needed a philosophy that gave power to people without property rights. In the American revolution by contrast Lockean property rights were asserted as a philosophical justification.

Rousseau presented a social contract under which the people give up their selfish, irrational, individual wills in favour of contributing to what he called the general will. The general will is our 'higher' altruistic or more rational will. It is what an assembly of equals *ought* to decide. This must be distinguished from what Rousseau called the 'will of all', namely the views of a numerical majority of people each voting for his or her own self-interest. The general will should ideally be expressed by a vote of the whole community but in practice the lawmaker is likely to consist of elected representatives. However, contrary to the traditional approach taken in English law, Rousseau's representatives are bound by the views of those who have elected them.

When we vote for the general will we are voting unselfishly for what we now call the 'public interest'. Rousseau asserted that when we conform to the general will we are 'free' in a higher sense, in that our thinking is not distorted by selfishness nor slave to our animal instincts nor dominated by the vested interests of others. Rousseau spoke of being 'forced to be free' just as bossy persons talk about what is in our own 'best interests' did we but know ourselves. Rousseau said that the general will could never be wrong but was apparently thinking of the general will as an ideal rather than of any application of it in the real world. Some modern lawyers such as Lord Devlin have put forward similar views to those of Rousseau when they argue that the community is held together by a shared morality which the law is entitled to enforce.

Even if the people can make laws collectively they cannot enforce them directly by mob rule but must devolve power to some form of executive government. Rousseau therefore vested day-to-day government in a body of experts preferably chosen by the people. The job of government was to propose laws to the people and to make decisions in individual cases within the laws given to it by the people. In modern conditions, however, the distinction between lawmaking and executive government is less clear-cut. The executive has to make general rules in order to carry out the complex tasks required of it, and the lawmaker, which is usually an elected assembly, has neither the time nor the knowledge to make all the laws required.

Rousseau therefore introduced the modern notion of the collective state. Rousseau's constitution favours the collective good of the majority against individual liberty and minority groups. The issues that he raises are fundamental, in particular whether there is such thing as the 'public interest' as opposed to an irreconcilable mixture of gains and losses to individuals. Rousseau is important to modern constitutional law partly because he shows how difficult it is to produce democratic government in which all participate without large sacrifices of individual liberty. For example he favoured state censorship and rejected 'mini-general wills' such as trade unions within the state and would restrict the freedom of expression and association in order to promote the 'right' way of thinking on which the general will depends. He also favoured compulsory state education and a state religion. He thought that people must be roughly equal in terms of wealth in order for the general will to operate effectively.

Rousseau assumes that the public are united by strongly held shared values and will vote altruistically whereas decisions made by an elite or by 'experts' are more likely to be corrupt and self-seeking. The German philosopher Hegel (1770–1831) also supported a collectivist view of the state but did not favour democracy. According to Hegel the state is the highest creation of reason through which we can reconcile our selfish impulses as individuals with the influences that necessarily constrain us as members of communities such as families, ethnic and social groups etc. The value of a person can therefore be realised only by immersion in the state. Hegel favoured the Hobbesian idea of an independent ruler such as the militaristic monarchy of his native Prussia who, having in Hegel's view no axe to grind, can be relied upon to rule rationally. However, Hegel did not favour the kind of totalitarian regime such as fascism that is the logical extension of the collectivist tradition but recommended safeguards against abuse of power such as independent courts and human rights.

Some variants of communitarianism (multi-layered communitarianism) do not support the notion of a single general will embodied in the state but favour decentralised government with power dispersed between different ethnic, economic, social and geographical groups. They emphasise the desirability of the constitution providing for the active participation of citizens, both individuals and groups, in the governmental process and reject liberalism as merely tolerating rather than embracing diversity (see Gray, 1993; MacIntyre, 1968; Morison, 1995). This variant of the communitarian idea recognises the inherent conflict between incommensurables and seeks a practical *modus vivendi*. However, multi-layered communitarianism does not explain how, in a complex society, disagreements can be resolved. Rousseau's general will would brook no rival to the state and would therefore suppress smaller groups that might create mini-general wills at odds with the community as a whole. In Hobbesian terms these rival groups would be analogous to individuals at war with each other in a state of nature.

2.6   Hume: A Common Law Approach

David Hume (1711–1776) provides a more flexible and open-ended communitarian approach for which the common law provides a vehicle. He thought that government is a matter of practical compromise driven by our psychological need to co-operate with each other and built on custom and greed for material possessions. Law is a tool of government, and ideas such as justice and appeals to 'the ancient constitution' are imaginative myths useful for persuading people to obey the law, just as are the courtroom panoplies of robes and honorific titles, a theme which was later taken up by Walter Bagehot in the particular context of the British Constitution. Hume said 'since 'tis impossible to change or correct anything material in our nature, the utmost we can do is to change our circumstances and situation and render the observation of the laws of justice our nearest interest' (*Treatise of Human Nature*, p. 537).

Hume therefore advocated a pragmatic society based on co-ordinating individual interests with those of the community but without the mystical overtones of Rousseau or the authoritarian aspects of Hobbes. Hume's approach therefore favoured the common law which he described as a happy combination of circumstances, according to which the law is developed pragmatically by the courts in the light of changing social practices and values. He relies on the common law as harnessing the common sense reasoning and attitudes of the community in order to achieve the same objective as Hobbes, that of resolving disagreement. Like Hobbes, Hume did not believe there are objectively valid moral and political principles but thought that long term self-interest and our natural imaginative concern for others would lead us towards developing principles of co-operation such as justice and fulfilling expectations.

2.7   Liberalism and Utilitarianism

Liberalism, is based on the idea that human beings are valuable as equal beings and are responsible for deciding our own goals in life. According to Lord Steyn, the basic premise of UK law is a liberal one.

'Parliament does not legislate in a vacuum. Parliament legislates for a European liberal democracy founded on the principles and traditions of the common law. And the courts approach legislation on this initial assumption' (*R*. v. *Secretary of State ex parte Pierson* [1997] 3 All ER 577 at 603). However, his Lordship immediately went on to recognise that this can be displaced by a 'clear and specific provision to the contrary', thus recognising the supremacy of the 'general will' of the majority expressed through Parliament. The starting point is all important since it determines where the burden of proof lies. Do our constitutional arrangements start with individual liberty and require the government to justify its interference or do we assume the right of the majority and have to make a special case for individual rights?

2.7.1 Liberal individualism

Lord Steyn seems to conflate two kinds of liberalism. In one, 'liberal individualism', the individual is valued for his or her own sake and is free to pursue a personal understanding of the good life provided that this does not harm others (there are of course large questions here as to what counts as harm which are outside the scope of the present book). Thus Kant (1724–1804) argued that an individual must be treated as an end in itself and not as a means to an end such as the public welfare. The role of the law is to provide a framework of procedures for resolving disputes but it is not for the state to impose its vision of the good life on individuals. The state has a right and duty to protect its members, and citizens arguably have a duty by virtue of our dependence on others to co-operate with society's reasonable demands. Subject to those limits, liberalism would limit the freedom of the individual as little as possible, and, as Allan (1999) argues, only to achieve goods which are common to all.

Nozick (1974) goes further arguing that the fact that I am born into a community does not give me any moral obligation to obey its requirements since I have no choice but to accept its power and also that doing good to others because I am forced to do so is morally worthless. Nozick supports the idea of a minimal 'night-watchman' state which does only those things for which compulsion is essential such as keeping order and enforcing contracts. According to Nozick no one should be sacrificed for the benefit of others without their consent. Any attempt by the state to force people to help each other, for example by raising taxes for welfare services is, according to Nozick, a violation of their rights and essentially slavery and theft.

Similarly taxation for the purpose of redistribution or providing public services is a form of theft. Nozick concedes that the state can legitimately tax for the purpose of its basic function of protection, using the money so raised to pay for the protection of those who could not afford to pay for themselves. He argues that taxation for this limited purpose is not redistribution but a form of compensation, whereby I am paying the state not only to protect me but as my agent in order to compensate other people who have to give up some of their freedom in the interests of my safety.

2.7.2   Liberal utilitarianism

The other version of liberalism, liberal utilitarianism, is a subjective view of the good life no different in this respect from, say, Islam or communism. Liberal utilitarianism is one of a group of utilitarian theories. Utilitarianism claims that the goal of government is to achieve 'utility'. This means the greatest amount of general well-being or 'the greatest happiness of the greatest number'. Thus utilitarianism attempts resolve all problems in terms of measurable units of human welfare. There are several versions of utilitarianism which differ from each other in respect of how to maximise welfare. They all seem to share the assumption that the individual is valued not for his or her own sake but as a vehicle for happiness.

One version of utilitarianism propounded by the great law reformer, Jeremy Bentham (1748–1832), measures utility by people's actual demands and interests. It is egalitarian in that each interest counts equally in the calculation and the preferences of the decision maker are irrelevant (a view that is problematic when it comes to voting). This permits an unlimited degree of state interference provided that there was a net gain in well-being. For example utilitarianism is consistent with slavery in that the standard of living of an elite majority might be held to outweigh the loss of freedom of a servile underclass. Moreover a utilitarian could reasonably think that wrongly convicted people should be kept in jail in order to preserve public confidence in the police.

This kind of utilitarianism, in its modern guise of economic cost, benefit analysis, has a substantial effect on policy making. However, another version of utilitarianism, liberal utilitarianism, has probably had greater influence upon our legal values. Propounded most influentially by John Stuart Mill (1806–1873), liberal utilitarianism argues that maximising individual freedom is the best way to achieve the overriding goal of advancing overall well-being. Its recommendations are often therefore similar to those of liberal individualism (above) in the sense that they prefer freedom provided that others are not harmed. There is, however, the crucial difference that liberal utilitarianism regards individual freedom as no more than a means to a specified end directed by the state, whereas for liberal individualists, individual freedom is an end in itself because the community has no inherent right to impose itself on its members.

2.7.3 Liberal constitutional mechanisms

From the legal perspective liberalism might take two competing forms. One is to rely on community customs and values generated by the voluntary relationships of individuals in making contracts and forming associations. The law steps in only to settle disputes and to facilitate private dealings. Public officials and private citizens alike are subject to the ordinary general law of private rights and freedoms. Hayek (1973) favoured this approach. He regards human affairs as being too complex to be regulated by any single body. He believes that no government can have sufficient skill, foresight, objectivity and knowledge to do more than provide a mechanism for doing justice and keeping order, and that attempts to redistribute wealth are likely to be corrupt. He drew attention to what is now called 'public choice theory' namely that the self-interest of officials in expanding and protecting their own territories is an important aspect of the political process. According to Hayek, the market is the only effective instrument for co-ordinating the individual plans of a host of different agents. He thought that legal institutions and principles of justice should evolve out of the community rather than be imposed from the top and that legal certainty was vital as a hedge against tyranny. Hayek therefore envisaged a common law framework which, as we shall see in Chapter 4, is similar to Dicey's influential version of the rule of law.

Within the utilitarian tradition neither Bentham nor Mill placed faith in the courts as guardians of constitutional values. Bentham thought that the notion of individual rights except in a technical legal sense was 'nonsense on stilts' while Mill placed faith in engineered forms of representative democracy which favoured the educated and property owners. Bentham supported central control as being, on the whole, more likely than not to maximise the happiness (utility) of its members but thought the notion of the interests of the community as such was a fiction masking the competing interests of individuals. The aim of the law was to achieve the greatest happiness of the greatest number on a scientific basis. Happiness was to be measured on a democratic basis which gave equal weight to the interests claimed by every individual. According to Bentham the only acceptable form of government was democracy through representatives who would engineer utility.

Mill's version of utilitarianism places stress on the active participation of citizens in public affairs particularly at local level (see Chapter 8), not merely as a means of identifying interests but as a means of self-improvement. Mill advocated the Aristotelian notions of citizenship according to which a purpose of government was to develop the higher faculties of human beings, namely their capacity to make reasoned choices. The protection of individual freedom, dispersed institutions and public participation in them are therefore ingredients of a good constitution valuable for their own sake.

> The first element of good government, therefore, being the virtue and intelligence of the human beings composing the community, the most important point of excellence which any form of government can possess is to promote the virtue and intelligence of the people themselves. The first question in respect to any political institutions is, how far they tend to foster in members of the community the various desirable qualities moral and intellectual.

However, Aristotle and his contemporaries had a limited idea of participation, restricting it to an elite of well-educated males who knew each other personally. Nevertheless citizen participation has been advocated by many modern writers, notably Jürgen Habermas (1996), as an appropriate goal of a constitution the ideal being a debate between equal citizens until a mutually acceptable compromise is reached. Given human nature this seems to be wholly impracticable and indeed incoherent in that there is no particular reason why any interest should be willing to compromise. The 'iron law of oligarchy' suggests that any form of participation will be stage-managed by an elite who take it upon themselves to select the 'participants', decide the terms of the debate and interpret its outcome. Habermas's notions of 'deliberative participation' and 'non-dominant discourse' have been unkindly described as 'the appeal of the intellectual salon with a dozen or so erudite and witty discussants' (Hardin, 1995; cf. Prosser, 1982). What is arguably more important is that all governmental decisions should be challengeable by the people, that officials should have to justify their actions and that all laws can be changed.

The other kind of liberal mechanism which appeals particularly to the individualistic end of the spectrum concentrates on the republican devices for limiting power which we outlined in Chapter 1.

Summary

2.1   We briefly introduced the development of enlightenment thought and the state as the foundations of modern constitutionalism.

2.2   We introduced the notions of incommensurability and uncombinability as tools of analysis. These notions suggest that democratic constitutions cannot create consistent or harmonious principles without sacrificing other valuable goods, so that a constitution is likely to be an untidy mixture of different ideals. Example of incommensurables include the distinction between positive and negative freedom and the apparent clash between majoritarian democracy and equality. Incommensurables are sometimes combinable in the sense that the objects of all happen to be achievable at the same time. A good working constitution would aim at this common ground. Where this is not possible, the constitution would provide procedures whereby a temporary accommodation between different viewpoints could be reached. In some cases, notably human rights cases, it seems to be impossible to avoid making a choice between incommensurables that cannot be wholly justified by reason. In such a case there is disagreement, not only as to the proper choice that should be made but also as to the most appropriate mechanism for making the decision, in particular whether it should be a court or an elected body.

2.3   We set out the different approaches of Hobbes, Locke, Rousseau and Hume to the question of the foundation of a constitution against the broad distinction between liberal and communitarian values. These writers express foundational approaches to the problem of government and the relationship between the citizen and the state. Hobbes favours government with unlimited powers as a necessary evil for the purpose protecting individuals. This has important implications both for individualistic aspects of a constitution leading to notions of equality and freedom and also for the collective aspect in the idea that the state cannot act unjustly. Locke's version uses government to protect natural rights, would limit the powers of government and make government accountable to the people. Rousseau believed that humans were only fully free if acting within the community for the general good and regarded individual freedom as exercisable only through collective action and the state as superior to other forms of organisation. Hume favoured a pragmatic form of community driven by accommodating competing interests in the context of custom and practice. This supports a common law view of the constitution.

2.4   We discussed different kinds of liberal values, including individualism, and utilitarianism through the writings of Bentham and Mill, with a view to suggesting that there are irreconcilably different versions of the proper basis of a constitution and suggested constitutional mechanisms which appealed to the different values.

Further Reading

Dworkin, *Freedom's Law*, chapter 1.
Hampshire-Monk, *A History of Modern Political Thought*.
Held, *Political Theory Today*, chapters 1, 6.
Loughlin, *Public Law and Political Theory*, chapters 3, 4.

Postema, *Bentham and the Common Law Tradition*, chapters 1–4.
Van Caenegem, *An Historical Introduction to Western Constitutional Law*, chapters 1, 5, 7, 8.
Waldron, *Law and Disagreement*, Introduction, chapters 7, 8, 9.
Wolf, *An Introduction to Political Philosophy*, chapters 1, 2, 3, 4.

Exercises

2.1   Explain and illustrate the nature of incommensurable constitutional values in relation to the UK constitution.

2.2   To what extent could Hobbes be regarded as the founder of modern constitutional ideas?

2.3   What are the practical implications for a modern constitution of following the ideas of Hobbes, or Locke or Rousseau and what differences would their ideas produce?

2.4   Bentham regarded natural rights as 'nonsense on stilts'. What did he mean and do you agree?

2.5   Distinguish between the ideas of Bentham and Mill in terms of constitutional mechanisms.

2.6   John Major, a former prime minister, said that democracy is a threat to liberty. Discuss.

3 The Sources of the Constitution

3.1 Written and Unwritten Constitutions

The term constitution is ambiguous. In one sense dating from the late eighteenth century, it has come to mean a special written document or a series of documents. In a second and older sense, which was used by Aristotle (384–322 BC), it means the arrangements, however they may be recorded, that function as a constitution. It is sometimes said that, because the UK has no written constitution, it has no constitution at all. This is a *non sequitur* and historically short-sighted. The term 'constitution' and the ideas of limited government associated with it were prominent features of the disputes between Crown and Parliament that dominated much of the seventeenth century. It may indeed be true that we have no constitution but the argument does not turn on the absence of a written document but whether our law includes basic principles that structure and limit the government. Thomas Paine, the eighteenth-century radical whose writings influenced both the French and the American revolutions and who denied that we have a constitution, said that 'a constitution is not the act of a government but of a people constituting a government and a government without a constitution is power without right', and that 'a constitution is the property of the nation and not of those who exercise the government ... a constitution is a thing antecedent to the government and always distinct therefrom' (1987, p. 291). There may be practical differences between the written and the unwritten kinds of constitution but there seems to be no difference in principle between them. Indeed in *R.* v. *Secretary of State for the Home Department ex parte Simms* [1999] 3 All ER 400 at 412, Lord Hoffman remarked that 'the courts of the United Kingdom ... apply principles of constitutionality little different from those which exist in countries where the power of the legislature is expressly limited by a constitutional document.'

The notion of a written constitution was the product of a period of revolutionary change throughout Europe and America that began in the late eighteenth century. New regimes liked to enshrine their practices and aspirations in grandiose written declarations. The UK is unique among the major nations in not having a written constitution in this sense. Our constitution has developed pragmatically usually out of accommodations struck between different sectional interests and we value the appearance of continuity and tradition as a means of social cohesion (or social control). For example our most recent revolution in 1688 was presented to the public as a return to ancient values which the Stuart monarchs were supposed to have subverted rather than the establishment of a new regime. During the following century the ruling elite continued to promote the constitution as resting upon widely accepted traditions. For example, Lord Chesterfield remarked that 'England is now the only monarchy in the world that can properly be said to have a constitution' (King, 2000, p. 79 quoting OED). During the eighteenth century Britain's unwritten constitution was widely admired as a source of stability and justice (although historians disagree as to how impartial that justice was in practice; see Thompson, 1975). Latterly our constitution has become less admired and is sometimes regarded as the least democratic constitution in western Europe in its concentration of power in the hands of the executive.

Our unwritten constitution must therefore be imagined partly out of the general sources of law, namely Acts of Parliament which are effectively made by the government of the day, common law in the form of decisions of the higher courts, and the 'laws and customs of Parliament' made by each House in order to control its affairs. In particular the common law as a source of general principles and values is sometimes regarded as the most basic source of our constitution. Statutes enacted to deal with specific matters are depicted as isolated islands in a sea of common law (see Nolan, 1997, ch. 2). The common law develops incrementally case by case focused on private rights and duties. Radical institutional changes therefore require statute such as for example the Act of Settlement 1701 that established the modern monarchy, the Parliament Acts 1911 and 1949 that reduced the powers of the House of Lords and the European Communities Act 1972 which subjected UK law to European law.

The UK constitution also relies heavily upon unwritten rules known as constitutional conventions. These are not strictly speaking law at all because they are not directly enforceable thorough the courts and have no authoritative sources other than recognition and obedience by those affected by them. However, conventions are closely related to law and are used by the courts at least as background to help them interpret the law. Most conventions concern the relationship between the different branches of government, both defining their powers and providing accountability. Examples include the rules that the Queen must appoint as prime minister the person who commands a majority in the House of Commons, and must act on the advice of ministers, and the rule that the government must resign if it loses the confidence of the House. The combination of these conventions creates what are perhaps the central political tensions in our constitution namely the concentration of power in the executive and the responsibility of Parliament both to sustain the executive, in the sense of providing the resources to keep the government functioning, and to hold the executive to account. As we shall see below, conventions are politically binding even if they are not legally enforceable.

There are also 'practices' which are of constitutional significance even though they are not in any sense binding. The most obvious of these is of course political parties through which contenders for power organise themselves. There is no legal or conventional requirement that there be political parties and strictly speaking a political party is a private voluntary organisation. However, in a large and complex society containing many different points of view the existence of parties as means of co-ordinating and organising competing claims is inevitable and no one would doubt that political parties are in fact a central feature of the constitution. Because the majority party in Parliament also forms the executive, party leaders can control both the legislature and the executive. Indeed it has been said that 'parties have substituted for a constitution in Britain. They have filled all the vast empty spaces in the political system where a constitution should be and made the system in their own image' (Wright, quoted in Nolan, 1997, p. 83). The importance of parties has been recently recognised by legislation which attempts to ensure that the funding of political parties is fair and transparent (Political Parties, Elections and Referendums Act 2000).

Some modern writers argue that the dependence of the UK constitution upon conventions and practices makes it no more than the wishes of those in power: hence Griffiths's much quoted aphorism 'the constitution is no more and no less than what happens' (1979, p. 19). Similarly Hennessy (1995, ch. 1) describes the UK constitution as an 'insiders' constitution' which is under the control of the government of the day and in particular the unelected officials who secure the continuity of the system at times of political crisis or change. He recounts the Victorian conceit that conventions embody 'the general agreement of public men about "the rules of the game"' (ibid. 37), a proposition that remains significant today. Thus Bogdanor describes the UK constitution as 'a very peculiar constitution which no one intended whereby the government of the day decides what the constitution is' (ibid., p. 165).

Conventions and practices are not peculiar to the UK constitution although we probably rely upon them more than most. Human beings survive by copying each other and in any political system custom and practice inevitably play large parts. Moreover every important matter is unlikely to be included in a written constitution. For example the US constitution contains considerable detail on matters which were thought important at the time it was framed (1788), such as the age composition of the legislature, and the quartering of soldiers, but makes no express provision for the judicial review of legislation, a gap that was later filled by the Supreme Court in accordance with its own idea of the purpose of the constitution (*Marbury* v. *Madison* 5 US 137 (1803)). Moreover a written constitution which is drafted in vague terms, as are parts of the US constitution, is capable of being interpreted in many different ways and is as much a vehicle for the opinions of those in power as is the case with the unwritten constitution of the UK.

Our constitution, in common with written constitutions, also depends on diffuse sources in the sense of uses of language, practices and attitudes which express the evolving political culture of the dominant sections of the community. It is often remarked in this connection that constitutions are organic, developing in response to cultural and political changes and also influencing those changes. There may be an underlying pattern forming a constitutional culture which shows itself particularly in changing relationships between institutions and in the way individual rights are conceived. In the case of a written constitution this pattern may be revealed by changing ways in which the courts interpret the constitution. For example the US Supreme Court has at different times interpreted the same constitutional language as both supporting and outlawing racial segregation (see *Plessey* v. *Ferguson* (1896); *Brown* v. *Board of Education* (1955)). In the UK there has been an evolutionary change in legal culture over the last 40 years in the courts' willingness to review governmental decisions and to apply international treaties concerning the protection of human rights. In all countries the language and imagery by which constitutional matters are expressed, not only in official documents but also in literature and the media, generates legal, ethical and political assumptions that are brought to bear on problems (see Ward, 2000). We have already met examples of this in the form of vague but evocative phrases such as 'the rule of law', 'balanced constitution', 'harmonious constitution', or 'ancient constitution'. These tend to change their meaning over time being put to different uses by different generations for their own political purposes.

The influence of customary values is not necessarily benevolent and custom may become dead wood but still inhibit legal change. For example during the extension of the franchise that took place during the late nineteenth century the cause of female suffrage was hampered by the courts refusing to interpret the word 'person' in legislation as including a woman on the ground that this violated the tradition that women did not hold public office or vote so that very clear parliamentary language was needed to change the status quo (*Nairn* v. *University of St Andrews* (1909)).

Moreover, the mind-set that has produced our heavy reliance on conventions has also caused us often to rely upon informal non-legally binding mechanisms on the grounds that they can be implemented quickly and co-operation may be secured more easily where there is no legal threat. This blurring of the distinction between law proper and conventions may be one factor contributing towards the deference to officials that is a prominent cultural phenonomen in the UK. For example, under the auspices of the Committee on Standards in Public Life various non-statutory codes of conduct have been made in respect for example of ministers and civil servants. In the case of the Ministerial Code it is not clear who is responsible for enforcement although, according to the Committee (6th Report cm. 4557-1), it should be the prime minister. In this respect a written constitution has the advantage that it is a public commitment to at least some of the basic principles of the community to which officials can be held. It can establish clear lines of political and legal accountability.

A written constitution can also be given a special status requiring changes to be made according to a special process, independent of the government of the day and which reflects the importance of the constitution, a device known as entrenchment. The special procedure might involve for example a referendum of the people, or, as in the USA, a weighted legislative procedure which takes into account the views of each state within the federation. In the UK any constitutional provision can be changed in the same way as any other law. This makes changes, for example electoral reform, against the interests of the government in office difficult to achieve.

On the other hand, if a written constitution is difficult to change it can be accused of inflexibility. Indeed, it is often maintained that a constitution changes organically as society changes so that a written document merely freezes the whims of whoever happens to make it at the time. Hence, in the USA there is a continuing debate as to whether the 300-year-old constitution should be interpreted in the light of the intentions of its framers or in accordance with changing circumstances and values (see Dworkin, 1986, ch. 10). An analogous debate applies in the UK to any legislation as to whether the actual or presumed intention of the lawmaker should be decisive or whether the words should be reinterpreted according to the opinions of successive generations of interpreter (see *Fitzpatrick* v. *Sterling Housing Association* (1999)).

A way of dealing with this kind of issue is to distinguish between 'general' intention and 'particular' intention.' The framers of the constitution might express a general intention, for example that everyone should have a fair trial, or be equal before the law while recognising that the particular ingredients of fairness or equality might change in different circumstances and over time. Hence, in 1791 when the Bill of Rights was added the framers of the US constitution saw no contradiction between their belief in equality and the inferior positions of slaves, women and native Americans.

Another advantage of a written constitution is that it can act as a convenient source of information and propaganda in order to give the governing arrangements a particular legitimacy. For example the UK constitution does not give clear answers to several fundamental questions. These include the extent to which the monarch has personal powers, and the reconciliation of disputes between the common law and Parliament. Moreover many constitutions set out a list of basic rights of the citizen, and a federal constitution which divides power between a central government and geographical units within it may focus the sense of identity of the citizen. Similarly an explicit separation of powers enshrined in a formal document announces that government is limited.

The differences between a written and unwritten constitution may therefore be differences of degree and of practical convenience rather than differences of fundamental principle. Nevertheless by constraining and structuring change a written constitution may provide stronger safeguards against the short-term concerns of the government in power than is the case in the UK. The status of the constitution is, however, primarily a matter of political and cultural attitudes. For example in the USA there is an attitude of reverence towards the written constitution that in the UK has been attached at various times to institutions such as the monarchy.

3.2   The Common Law Constitution

There are two fundamental and potentially rival sources of legal constitutional power. First there are Acts of Parliament. and secondly there is the common law applied by the judges in theory on the basis of community values mediated by reason and precedent. The judges also have the power conclusively to interpret Acts of Parliament. A written constitution in the form of 'articles of government' was introduced in England by the revolutionary regime of Oliver Cromwell in 1653 but after a year was superseded by a military dictatorship. No written constitution was adopted by the 1688 revolutionaries perhaps because the revolution was presented as a return to older tried and trusted customary arrangements. The absence of a written constitution means, however, that the ultimate source of legal power or sovereignty is open to debate. Is it the Crown, or Parliament or the common law? Suffice to say here that the 1688 revolution determined that the Crown is subordinate to Parliament but the relationship between Parliament and the common law has not been authoritatively settled. We shall discuss Parliament's claim to supremacy in Chapter 6. In this chapter we shall consider the common law as a source of constitutional principles.

There is a tension between the classical common law view of the constitution advocated with varying degrees of emphasis in the seventeenth and eighteenth centuries by writers such as Matthew Hale and Edmund Burke and the modern political notion of the constitution initiated, as we have seen, by Hobbes as the application of sovereign power, in our case vested in Parliament, able to make whatever laws it wishes. Laws made by Parliament can be arbitrary; the exercise of will as opposed to reason. The classical view envisages the common law constitution as the product of organic development, binding even the Crown, deriving its authority from the community, as interpreted and rationalised by independent judges, adapting the law an evolutionary fashion to meet changing circumstances. Hale's famous metaphor of the Argonauts' ship has often been used with the 'same ship returning that had set sail but having been so often mended, no piece of the original remains' (Hale, 'A History of the Common Law', p. 43). Thus the common law embodies a communitarian theory although its actual output happens to have put great stress on individual rights and duties.

There is also the rather obscure claim of Coke, the seventeenth-century Chief Justice, that the common law is a matter of reason, but 'the artificial perfection of reason ... gotten by long study and experience .... No man (out of his private reason) ought to be wiser than the law, which is the perfection of reason' (1 Institutes, 21, 138, see Postema, 1986, p. 61)). Coke used this notion of artificial reason to support the independence of the judiciary against the king (*Prohibitions Del Roy* (1607)). Artificial reason is apparently the collective wisdom of the judges refined over long periods of time and organised through precedents. Coke referred to the judges as '*lex loquens*' the mouthpiece of a law which transcends the judiciary (Postema, 1986, p. 9).

From our contemporary perspective we might be cynical about the notion that the common law represents community values. We might be more predisposed to view the common law as the creation of a professional elite of lawyers, concerned to protect the traditional status quo, and therefore filtering experience through their own self-interest even if unintentionally. Hobbes roundly condemned Coke's claims. He denied that there is anything special about lawyers' reasoning and refused to accept that custom and tradition in themselves carry any legal authority. According to Hobbes the rule of law derives from authority, subject to natural reason which is the prerogative of everyone. He objected to the common law on the ground that disagreement between judges picking over conflicting precedents creates the very uncertainty that the law exists to prevent. Nevertheless, Hobbes was not an absolutist. He believed for example that the sovereign, whose own reason was no better or worse than that of anyone else, should secure the assent of Parliament representing the people before enacting law (Postema, 1986, p. 46). Jeremy Bentham also objected to the common law on the ground that relying on precedent was contrary to reason and also likely to create uncertainty since each case is different.

This debate remains important surfacing in particular in relation to the question whether there should be legal limits on the power of Parliament. The same debate can take the form of asking whether the constitution is a majoritarian one in the sense of a vehicle for the changing wishes of the representatives of the electorate or whether there are overriding principles, such as freedom of expression, a fair trial etc. which, although political in a broad sense, are overriding conditions of democracy and as such protected, perhaps by the courts, against changing politics (Ewing, 2000; Allan, 2001). Some modern judges have attempted to resolve the debate by postulating a 'twin' or 'bi-polar' sovereignty between Parliament and the courts according to which Parliament makes legislation and the courts interpret it in the light of basic values of justice and respect for individual rights, each respecting the autonomy of the other in its own sphere (*X* v. *Morgan Grampian Publishers Ltd* [1991] 1 AC1 at 48; Nolan, 1997, p. 26). However, this does not fully accommodate the notion of the common law as an independent source of law historically and perhaps logically prior to Parliament. It is therefore possible to go further and argue that Parliamentary supremacy is itself a gift of the common law and therefore dependent on acceptance by the courts (see Nolan, 1997, ch. 2 and below ch. 6). Both sides of course regard values such as freedom of expression as important. However, the first view would treat them as values which in common with others must be fought for in a political forum such as Parliament and a practicable accommodation struck whereas the second view would treat them as special and, to an extent, non-negotiable.

3.3 Conventions

In this section we shall look at conventions in a little more depth. Conventions express the contemporary political morality of the constitution, and one argument for their existence is their achievement in continually modernising the constitution. Conventions are binding principles or rules, often derived from the practices of politicians, which confer obligations on those to whom they apply. For example, convention (and not law) requires that the Queen must grant her assent to a Bill passed by both Houses of Parliament, and that Parliament must meet annually.

However, the existence of conventions generates controversy. The most fundamental problem is that conventions do not meet one of the most basic requirements of constitutionalism, namely that there is no authoritative means of settling disputes either about whether a convention exists or whether it has been broken. If the purpose of a constitution is to impose external limits on government, then conventions which are generated *within* government are highly suspect. Horwitz, has argued, for instance, that conventions were developed as undemocratic devices to reassure the ruling class that constitutional fundamentals would continue to be developed within government largely beyond the influence of the rising middle classes following the rapid extension of the franchise after the Reform Act 1867 (1997 *OJLS* 551). Further, the absence of formal parliamentary debate in the evolution of conventions exposes an important concern about their democratic legitimacy. Who determines the timing, nature and shape of the reforms which conventions introduce? Why should not fundamentals of the constitution such as responsible government be protected as law? If conventions exist as a matter of politics and not law does it mean that the constitution is merely what the government of the day claims it to be?

3.3.1 Conventions and practices

It is important to distinguish conventions from other forms of constitutional behaviour, such as practices, traditions and legal principles. However, commentators disagree as to the tests used to identify conventions. Most fundamentally, this signals doubt about the very nature of conventions and, indeed, the nature of law. At a practical level, there is inevitable uncertainty as to whether some practices really are conventions (and so become obligatory). For example doubt surrounds the codes of public morality that have recently been promulgated by bodies such as the Nolan Committee (see Marshall, 1984, p. 3). The crucial evidence in establishing the existence of a convention is the belief of the politicians to whom it applies that there is an obligation to act in a particular manner. A convention exists if, as a matter of fact, the belief is present. But it is possible to argue that a conventions ought to engage what politicians *should* consider themselves bound to do and not merely what they actually consider their obligations to be.

A further issue concerns the extent to which a practice must be accepted as binding before it is recognised as a convention. It is arguable that *any* disagreement about the status of the practice prevents the practice from being a convention. This seems unsatisfactory because, unanimity suggests that a person whose actions ought to be governed by an existing conventional obligation can destroy that obligation by disputing its existence. An alternative approach might be to identify a convention where there was a *consensus* as to the binding nature of a constitutional practice. A consensus may be said to arise without unanimity provided there is overwhelming support for the proposed convention. Nevertheless, establishing the point at which a consensus can be said to have been reached may be difficult to determine. Evidence might be found through the collective memory of senior officials or constitutional 'experts' thereby privileging non-elected persons who represent the continuity of power, such as Hennessy's 'golden triangle' of cabinet secretary, the Queen's advisers and the prime minister's principle private secretary (Hennessey, 1995).

Dicey famously defined conventions negatively. He stated that apart from laws, '(t)he other set of rules consist of conventions, understandings, habits, or practices which, though they may regulate the conduct of several members of the sovereign power, of the Ministry, or of other officials, are not in reality laws at all since they are not enforced by the courts' (Dicey, 1959, p. 24). Thus, for Dicey, it is the absence of judicial enforcement which fundamentally characterises conventions. Dicey's approach ventures a clear distinction between law and politics; but it does not clearly explain the nature of conventions. This is so because Dicey seemed to have envisaged an inferior class of usages and customs which are not binding on those to whom they applied and so are not conventions. Since neither conventions nor non-binding practices are enforced by the courts, Dicey's test does not identify that which is a convention as opposed to non-binding practice (cf. Munro,

1999, p. 81 arguing that non-legal rules are best viewed as of one type provided we accept that conventions vary in stringency).

Jennings offered three tests to identify a convention (Jennings, 1959, p. 136). First, are there any precedents? Secondly, do those operating the constitution believe that they are bound by a rule? Thirdly, is there a constitutional reason for the convention? This has been accepted by the Canadian courts (*Reference re Amendment of the Constitution of Canada (Nos. 1, 2 and 3)* (1982) 105 DLR (3d) 1), but it has been subjected to a variety of criticisms (Jaconelli, 1999). Jennings's definition emphasises the importance of precedent in interpreting conventions. Hennessy (1995, ch. 1) describes how private secretaries, the sovereign's advisers at Buckingham Palace and officials of the cabinet office monitor and record practice in a 'Precedent Book', which, characteristically of the UK constitution, is not open to public inspection. Officials and politicians refer to the records contained within this collection to guide future behaviour, and this may eventually lead to a consensus that the practice is obligatory.

There are plainly difficulties in this because there may be many occasions on which politicians disagree about the precedents they are supposed to follow. This uncertainty clouds even established conventional rules, making fundamentally important conventions difficult to apply. An example is the preference expressed by the King and Chamberlain that Chamberlain should be succeeded as prime minister by Lord Halifax (and not Churchill) at a crucial moment for the nation in the conduct of the Second World War. This was so notwithstanding the established convention that a prime minister should have a seat in the Commons.

Sometimes precedent is unnecessary because a convention can be created by agreement, for example by the cabinet, or even laid down unilaterally by the prime minister. The important principles contained in the *Ministerial Code* (Cabinet Office, July 2001) may well furnish an example of conventions laid down by prime ministerial edict (Hennessy, 1995, pp. 36–7). However, Lord Nolan thought that the Code's predecessor, known as *Questions of Procedure for Ministers*, lacked constitutional status (see *First Report of the Committee on Standards in Public Life*, Cm. 2850, 1995).

Jennings also suggested that those operating the constitution should regard themselves as bound. Practices are merely regular habits of behaviour and are not binding at all. However, whilst conventions are obligatory they do not all have the same degree of binding force. Some are vague (e.g. ministerial responsibility), some may have exceptions (e.g. the personal powers of the monarch), some may not be regarded as important (see Jaconelli, 1999; Munro, 1999, pp. 81–7). Nevertheless it is still necessary to distinguish between conventions and practices because practices, however important, are not binding at all. The party system provides an example of a practice which is fundamental to the workings of the constitution but which has no binding force. Furthermore a practice ceases to exist if it is broken. If a convention is broken it ceases to exist only if no criticism follows. However, the line between convention and practices is blurred in that well-established practices carry at least a presumption that they ought to be continued. This seems to be a basic psychological fact about human motivation.

3.3.2   The purposes of conventions

Conventions concern in the main the distribution of power and political accountability. They deal mainly with the relationship between the different branches of central government, the Crown, the executive and Parliament, ministers and the civil service, the prime minister and the cabinet. Dicey made it clear (p. 429) that this group of powers is intended to ensure that power is exercised according to the wishes of the majority of the electors. Allan (1993, p. 253) concluded that conventions 'give effect to the principle of governmental accountability that constitutes the structure of responsible government'.

Many conventions relate to the exercise of prerogative powers which survive as vestiges of the legal powers of the Crown. For example conventions relating to the monarch ensure that vestigial prerogative powers are normally exercised only in accordance with advice received from ministers who are themselves accountable to Parliament. These powers, if exercised, could have profound political consequences, determining who, for example, should form the government. There would be no legal impediment if the Queen chose to dismiss all her ministers and appoint her friends in their place. These powers are, however, required to be exercised according to the convention that only a prime minister (who himself has the support of Parliament) can appoint and dismiss ministers. Thus a fundamental shift of power, which has largely been achieved by conventions, has significantly reduced the role of the sovereign since the eighteenth century without the controversy which might have been associated with a series of statutory reforms.

However, the supposed chain of accountability is weak. Dicey had not anticipated the dominance of the executive in Parliament nor the dispersal of executive power to miscellaneous bodies, including private companies outside the central government structure. If ministerial accountability is to be effective it assumes that members of Parliament will act as parliamentarians and not through party loyalty. Accountability to Parliament is often accountability to the minister's own party against the background of the adversarial nature of party politics and the government's desire to avoid political embarrassment (see Chapter 14).

3.3.3 Conventions, constitutional change and power

An unwritten constitution such as the UK constitution assumes that change and flux are permanent. This insists that constitutional fundamentals can be modified or abandoned according to their contemporary context. As we have seen, conventions have discreetly achieved such major changes as the transfer of power from monarch to Parliament.

New conventions are developed, and others abandoned. In the former category may well be the possible right of the Prince of Wales to communicate and meet with ministers, to obtain information from them, to comment on their policies, and to argue for alternative policies (Brazier, 1995). The former parliamentary convention governing the rules under which the Table Office of the House of Commons refused to allow a written parliamentary question to a minister to be tabled if the minister had earlier refused to answer it has also disappeared, although ministerial conventions on this matter still operate (*Second Report of the Public Service Select Committee*, HC 313).

Conventions change their meaning incrementally as they are applied, that being one of their alleged advantages. For example, since the late 1970s it has become apparent that a government need not resign merely because it suffers a major defeat. A formal Commons vote of no confidence is needed. This makes it very difficult to remove a government. There is considerable debate about the extent to which the monarch can exercise personal powers, and if so on whose advice. There is doubt, also, as to whether there is a convention embodying the 'mandate' doctrine, that is the idea that governments are bound to attempt to honour election promises. If this doctrine exists it would complete the 'democratic chain' between monarch and people. On the other hand it seems artificial to suppose that when people vote for particular governments they are endorsing every proposal made by the aspiring government.

However, the need to evolve the constitution is not in itself a conclusive case for the existence of conventions because parliamentary sovereignty ensures that any anachronistic laws can simply be repealed.

However, there would have been political risks in incrementally curtailing the powers of the Crown by repeated legislative means which might have risked constitutional confrontation. Conventions can also offer advantages in a society in which constitutional reform often finds a low place in the public's (and thus the government's) view of political priorities.

Thus the ability of conventions to generate change raises questions about the location of power within the constitution. Conventions help to ensure that power remains within a self-selected elite. A breach of convention which is not met with objection can effect constitutional change because the convention in question simply disappears. This places the constitution largely within the trust of the governing party since they can alter it without reference to Parliament. For example it is arguable that the cabinet has ceased to play a significant constitutional role, power having accumulated in the hands of the prime minister. Hennessy (1995, p. 37) raises this important issue in his discussion of *Questions of Conduct and Procedure for Ministers* (now the *Ministerial Code*, Cabinet Office, July 2001). For him this important document satisfies Dicey's definition of a convention and so should be binding. But both Lord Nolan and a former cabinet secretary have riposted that it lacks conventional status because, according to the former cabinet secretary, it would be possible for the prime minister to annul the *Code* and substitute another (laying down different obligations of ministerial accountability). Whether or not the *Ministerial Code* is a convention is, in one sense, beside the point. The essential issue is whether it can be altered by the prime minister. This perhaps illustrates how issues of such fundamental importance as ministerial accountability are prisoners of prevailing political power.

3.3.4   Why are conventions obeyed?

There are many reasons why conventions are normally obeyed, not least because of the adverse political consequences which might result from their breach. This is unsurprising since conventions are traditionally regarded as a matter of political ethics. As we have seen, Dicey distinguished conventions from laws by the absence of judicial enforcement. However, this did not mean that Dicey was content with exclusively political redress for breach of convention, and his argument somewhat undermines his distinction between law and politics. He stated (p. 439 *et seq.*) that conventions are not laws and so not enforced by the courts, but he argued that even the 'boldest political adventurer' would be restrained from breaching conventions because it would eventually lead to the offender coming into conflict with the courts and the law of the land (pp. 445–6). He gave as an example the consequences which might follow if Parliament did not meet at least once a year, or if a government did not resign after losing a vote of confidence. Dicey argued that the government would not have the statutory authority for raising (some) taxes, or for spending money.

This explanation is, however, incomplete, for not all conventions can be similarly treated. For example, if the Speaker showed party political bias the consequences are more likely to be in the political arena. Moreover, the adversarial nature of politics means that even political sanctions are far from inevitable. The pressure of political opponents, party and the strength of prime ministerial support as well as the reaction of the public, play a large part in determining the fate of a minister whose department's performance has been found wanting. The absence of adverse political repercussions may fortify ministers who give parliamentary answers that are incomplete. This failure is also unlikely to lead to a breach of the law.

Most conventions are respected because they are part of a shared system of values. This is evident in the commonly accepted definitions of conventions which emphasise the consent upon which they depend for their existence (e.g. Wheare's definition above). Whilst the values which underpin conventional obligations are shared by those to whom they apply a breach is unlikely. However, the disregard of a widely shared political ethic might threaten the career of the offender, about which there might also be adverse publicity. Social disgrace should not be ignored.

If some conventions are breached Parliament might be compelled to intervene to prevent a recurrence. Most famously, this occurred after the Lords refused to pass the Finance Bill 1909 thereby disregarding the conventional principle that the Lords should ultimately defer to the wishes of the elected Commons. The Parliament Act 1911 removed the veto power of the Lords in respect of most Public Bills. If the sovereign (without ministerial advice) were to refuse to grant the royal assent to a Bill passed by both Houses, the prerogative power to refuse would soon be removed by legislation.

Conventions may be breached or qualified (depending on one's view-point) where there is a conflict between what is normally constitutionally expected and current political consensus or expediency. In 1975 the prime minister 'suspended' the principle of collective cabinet unanimity to allow ministers to express their views openly in a referendum campaign concerning membership of the EEC. Any referendum on the future of sterling as British currency might result in a similar temporary modification to collective ministerial responsibility. Political opponents argued after 1975 that this first so-called 'suspension' was a clear breach of a convention but, according to a counter-argument, conventions are sufficiently flexible to admit of exceptions where prevailing political consensus demands it.

3.4   Law and Convention

For Dicey, the distinction between legal and political rules depended on the absence of direct coercive legal power to enforce conventions. Jennings, by contrast, argued that law and convention share common characteristics, each resting ultimately on public acquiescence. But as Munro (1999, ch. 3) argues the fact that law and convention have some features in common does not make them the same. In particular Jennings does not explain the different attitude of the courts to conventions when compared with laws.

At one level it is possible to understand how laws and conventions differ. A law does not fall into desuetude, yet a convention can disappear if it is not followed for a significant period, or if it is broken without objection. Another difference is that laws emanate from definite sources the courts and Parliament. In the case of conventions there is a lack of an authoritative source which might declare or establish the existence of conventions and provide for their interpretation and application and change. Moreover a breach of the law does not call into question its existence or validity, but this is not so with conventions. Nor do individual laws rest upon consent – an unpopular law or a widely disregarded law is nevertheless a valid law. But a convention is only valid if it is accepted as binding.

Nevertheless, Dicey's distinction between law and convention has been criticised as misleading. For example, the variability of the force of different conventions does not distinguish conventions from law. Some laws are less binding than others. For example, procedural requirements stipulated by statute are sometimes 'directory only'. This means that such requirements need not always be obeyed (see Chapter 16). Sometimes a statute specifically requires that it is not enforceable. The immigration rules made under s. 53 (2) of the Immigration Act 1971 comprise a mixture of binding rules, general guidance and advice. Which of these are 'law' is debatable (see *Singh* v. *Immigration Appeal Tribunal* (1986)). However, in all these cases a positive law determines the extent of enforceability rather than, as with conventions, the nature of the rule itself.

It is sometimes said that conventions differ from laws because they lack certainty. Uncertainty is, however, irrelevant. Many laws are uncertain whereas many non-legal rules, for example the rules of chess, are relatively certain. Generalisations about the relative importance of laws and conventions are also unhelpful. Many conventions function in a close relationship with laws since they direct how discretionary legal power will be exercised or prevent the exercise of anachronistic prerogative powers. Conventions provide the principles and values which form the context of the strict law. Thus conventions can be as important as laws; and some conventions may be more important than some laws.

The courts do not apply conventions directly. This means first, that there is no remedy in the courts for breach of a convention as such and, second, that the views of a court as to whether a particular convention exists and what it means are not binding. The existence and meaning of a convention are matters of fact that must be proved by evidence and not matters of law for the court. On the other hand the courts do not ignore conventions. A convention may form the political background against which a law has to be interpreted. For example, the convention of ministerial responsibility had enabled the courts to permit the powers of ministers to be exercised through civil servants in their departments, a principle that does not apply in other areas of government where statutory authority is required before powers can be delegated.

Two cases may help to illustrate the difference between law and convention in the courts. First, in *Reference Re Amendment to the Constitution of Canada* (1982) the Canadian Supreme Court, relying partly on British authority, recognized but refused to apply a convention. Under Canadian law, any amendment to the Canadian Constitution required an Act of the UK Parliament, following a request from the Federal Government of Canada. The Canadian government wished to amend the constitution so as to free itself from this legal link with Britain. The UK Parliament would automatically pass any legislation requested by Canada,

However, there were important conventions which required that the governments of the Canadian provinces be consulted about, and give their consent to, any proposed changes in the constitution that affected federal/provincial relations. Some claimed that this had not been done. The Supreme Court was divided as to whether the convention in question existed. A majority held that it did, and indeed went on to explain in some detail what the convention meant. Some of the judges doubted whether the court should have gone even this far, but as long as we remember that the court's view about the meaning of a convention is not in itself binding it seems acceptable. In any event a larger majority held that, whatever the convention meant, it could not affect the *legal* rule that empowered the Federal Government to resolve to seek an alteration to the constitution. Thus the convention could not be enforced by legal remedies. The judges also denied that a convention can ever crystallize into law, for example by becoming established over a period of years. This seems to be equally true of English law (see Monroe, 1999, p. 72 *et seq.*).

Our second case is *A-G* v. *Jonathan Cape* (1975). The government sought to prevent publication of the diaries of Richard Corpsman, a former Labor cabinet minister. It relied upon the legal doctrine of breach of confidence. This involves balancing the confidential nature of any material against any public interest in favour of its disclosure. The government based its case upon the convention of collective cabinet responsibility, arguing that this necessarily required that cabinet business remain confidential to cabinet ministers. The Lord Chief Justice, Lord Widgery, refused to apply the convention as such. However, the convention was relevant to the problem of deciding where the balance between confidentiality and the public interest lay. His Lordship held that the diaries could be published because they dealt only with matters of historical interest. Thus the convention was a crucial strand in the argument, but not the law itself.

It is possible that the courts will develop the common law so as to enforce at least some conventional obligations by allowing the law to endorse the values currently expressed in important conventions, or by developing judicial review. In relation to the first possibility, the constitutional ideas underpinning some conventions might be better protected if conventions can develop into laws. Moreover, the law/ politics dichotomy disintegrates where courts develop law by evolving a legal rule which underpins a convention. For example in *Carltona Ltd* v. *Commissioner for Works* (1943) the courts accepted the legitimacy of civil servants taking decisions which are in law the responsibility of the minister without reference to the minister personally. A counter-argument to this kind of incorporation is that, if courts enforce conventions, their existence becomes 'fixed' as a matter of law, thus taking judges into the political arena and losing the flexibility which is supposed to be a reason for conventions.

There are arguments that the demands of political morality ought to be a matter of collective decision reached through the medium of politics and so fall outside the proper scope of the judicial function. The abandonment of the law/convention dichotomy might not therefore lead to judicial enforcement of many of these rules because most would either be regarded as inherently non-justiciable or non-justiciable in the circumstances. To take the example of ministerial responsibility, we may conclude that apportioning blame is a political matter not a legal one. This means that the question of whether a minister's conduct in office is such that he or she should resign would seem to be a non-justiciable question, depending as it does on party support, the timing of the discovery, the support of the prime minister and cabinet and the public repercussions. But the issue is not so clear if a minister denied an obligation to answer *any* questions in the House of Commons. What would prevent the court granting a declaration that such behaviour was unconstitutional? Would the arguments be equally as strong if a minister deliberately misled Parliament where resignation should be automatic? (See *Ministerial Code*, Section 1, para. iii; and the 2nd Report of the Public Service Select Committee, 19956, HC 313, para. 26.)

3.5   Codification of Conventions

The argument surrounding codification of conventions is similar to the arguments for a written constitution. However, the case for codification involves two distinct positions. The first asserts that conventions should both be codified *and* given legal force; the second asserts that conventions could be codified in an authoritative text but without legal force. Even under this version, however, which has been adopted in Australia in relation to 34 constitutional practices, it is likely that the courts may cite those conventions which the process codified (Sampford, 1987). Such an approach would address the lack of precision in the scope of some conventions, and would enable us to say with certainty which usages are, and which are not, conventional. For example, the present lack of agreement about the conventional powers of the monarch to dissolve Parliament could damage the monarchy by accusations of political partiality. Establishing the certainty of conventions could safeguard the neutrality of those who apply them.

The more adventurous position involving codification *and* enactment arouses a number of concerns. The first is that such a model of codification would damage the flexibility of the constitution and inhibit its evolutionary role in maintaining the relationship between the constitution and contemporary political values. One of the purposes of conventions has been to annul anachronistic law. It would be undesirable if conventions were to become fossilised and so impede further constitutional change. This might even prevent the development of qualifications limiting the scope of some conventions (as in the case of the 'suspension' of collective cabinet unanimity in 1975).

Moreover, as conventions are enforced as a matter of political dynamic, some argue that political flexibility might also be curbed if the courts were invited to pronounce on the breach of a conventional obligation. As we have seen, there are concerns about embroiling the courts in the political process, and it is by no means certain that the courts would exercise a jurisdiction over issues which traditionally have not been seen as justiciable. Ultimately there might be practical difficulties in systematic codification. It would be impossible to identify all usages which are currently conventional, and immediately after the code was established, there would be nothing to prevent the evolution of new conventions.

The case for a systematic codification of conventions is not self-evidently of merit. One possible approach (which would not overcome all the difficulties mentioned above) might be to enact some of the most important conventions. This would place those selected outside the scope of the executive and locate more extensive power in Parliament. Constitutional development would then be a matter of statutory reform which would follow from more open debate and discussion.

In fact some of the main conventions have been enacted as law in the Scotland Act 1998, and the Government of Wales Act 1998 (below, Chapter 7). A limited and 'soft' version of codification currently operates where the conventions are expressed in instruments such as the *Ministerial Code*. This has the advantage of greater clarity, but it allows for future change since the *Code* can be amended at the discretion of the prime minister.

3.6   The Dignified and Efficient Constitution

Related to the nature of conventions, it is often said that the glue which holds our unwritten constitution together is trust in and deference to the discretion of officials (Hennessy, 1995). Bagehot, writing in the mid-nineteenth century, regarded social class deference and superstition as the magic ingredients. He distinguished between what he called the 'dignified' and the 'efficient' parts of the constitution. Bagehot took a jaundiced view of the political sophistication of ordinary people and thought that government could only work effectively if its authority was buttressed by dramatic and personalised institutions, preferably of a traditional kind, which command people's emotional allegiance and make them deferential to the rulers. These comprise the dignified part of the constitution. Since the First World War, however, this deferential glue may have ceased to work. Cynicism about the competence and honesty of government, and realisation of the impotence of governments against economic forces created a climate of opinion which demanded greater accountability of public officials. However, the distinction between the dignified and efficient still performs a useful function by separating authority from power. For example the monarch has authority but no power while the government has power without authority thus making it easier for us to remove governments that are not to our liking.

According to Bagehot, the monarchy and Parliament constitute the main dignified elements of the constitution. The 'efficient' part of the constitution, which Bagehot located in the cabinet and which depends on the political balance of forces at any given time, harnesses the dignified element in order to carry out the business of government. The eighteenth-century Hanoverian kings lost public respect by becoming virtually party politicians, but in the mid-nineteenth century Queen Victoria re-dignified the monarchy by distancing herself from political partisanship and introducing the kind of pomp and ceremony which characterises the UK monarchy today. Bagehot thought that it would be dangerous to shed the light of reality upon the constitution.

The 'noble-lie' postulated by Plato (*Republic*, pp. 414–15, 459–60), re-enforces the dignified constitution. The noble lie was designed to keep people happy with their designated roles. It was that when humans were formed in the earth, the rulers had gold mixed with them, the military silver and the workers lead. Even Plato's pupils found this hard to swallow but, they thought that it is sometimes right to lie in the interests of the state. There is an element of the same thinking in the contemporary constitution. For example in *McIlkenny* v. *Chief Constable of the West Midlands* [1980] 2 All ER 227 at 239–240 Lord Denning MR took the view that it was better for the 'Birmingham Six' to remain wrongly convicted than to face the 'appalling vista' of the police being found to be guilty of perjury, violence and threats. The Scott Report (1996) revealed that ministers and civil servants regarded it as being in the public interest to mislead Parliament, if not actually to lie, over government involvement in arms sales to overseas regimes.

Summary

3.1 We discussed how constitutional law is identified in terms of the distinction between written and unwritten constitutions, pointing out that the constitution is found not only in legal sources but also in the practices, attitudes and culture of the dominant sections of the community. From this perspective the difference between a written and an unwritten constitution may be of limited importance. However, a written constitution has the advantage that it can be made relatively difficult to alter and so provide enhanced protection against the abuse of power. A written constitution may also provide a focus for important values and for regional and local identities.

3.2   The UK constitution is unwritten and based upon a mixture of ordinary laws, customs and practices, the most important of which are called conventions, which are intertwined with law but are not directly enforceable in the courts. There is therefore no authoritative mechanism for interpreting or identifying conventions. The reasons for this are largely historical since the UK constitution has never been the subject of a grand plan or a fundamental political change. The difference between written and unwritten constitutions as such is not fundamental, and a written constitution is unlikely to be comprehensive and is subject to interpretation against unwritten principles and practices.

3.3   Conventions are of fundamental importance in the UK constitution. Those relating to the monarch, for example, limit anachronistic prerogative powers, ensuring that these legal powers are only exercised in accordance with advice given by ministers. The modern UK constitution would be unrecognisable without conventions.

3.4   There is disagreement about the definition of conventions. Accordingly, it is not always clear which forms of constitutional behaviour are conventions and which are mere practices. Conventions are binding rules of constitutional behaviour, whilst mere practices are not.

3.5   Conventions have played an important and continuing role in the evolution of the constitution. New conventions continue to emerge, whilst others are abandoned. There is, however, a concern that the creation and development of conventions lack democratic legitimacy. Conventions can be introduced, altered or abolished by the government of the day without reference to Parliament. The enforcement of conventions is also a political matter. Can we be content that core constitutional principles of accountability and responsible government depend on political choice and the ebb and flow of party political power?

3.6   Conventions are distinct from law firstly in that there are no authoritative formal tests for the validity of conventions and secondly because conventions are not directly enforced by the courts. However, there is no inherent difference in the content of laws and conventions and the courts use conventions, as they do moral principles to help interpret, develop and apply the law.

3.7   Some commentators have argued that conventions could be incorporated into the law, but even if this is achieved, how many such laws would be justiciable? Codification might offer certainty in respect of those conventions included in the code, but new conventions would be evolved after the code was introduced, and some flexibility in adapting existing conventions might be lost. There may be scope for extending 'soft' forms of codification, such as the *Ministerial Code*.

3.8   There is a distinction between the dignified and the efficient elements of the constitution. The dignified element relies on the deference of the people reinforced by pomp and ceremonial to give the law its continuity and authority. The efficient element is the working machinery of government and changes with events.

Further Reading

Allott, P., 'The theory of the British constitution', in Gross and Harrison (eds), *Jurisprudence: Cambridge Essays*.
Bagehot, *The English Constitution*, chapter 1.
Barendt, *An Introduction to Constitutional Law*, chapter 2.
Economides, etc (eds), *Fundamental Values*, chapter 12
Laws, J. (1989) 'The ghost in the machine: principles of public law', *Public Law* 27.
Munro, C. (1999) *Studies in Constitutional Law*, 2nd ed, chapters 1, 3.
Nolan and Sedley (eds), *The Making and Remaking of the British Constitution*, chapters. 2, 4, 6, 7.
Postema (1986) *Bentham and the Common Law Tradition*, chapters 1, 2.
Ward, I. *A State of Mind?: The English Constitution and the Public Imagination*.

Exercises

3.1   An American enters into an argument with you about constitutional law. He says that the British do not have a constitution worthy of the name. How would you respond?

3.2   'It is both a strength and a potential weakness of the British constitution, that almost uniquely for an advanced democracy it is not all set down in writing', Wakeham Report, 2000. Discuss

3.3   'The British constitution presumes, more boldly than any other, the good faith of those who work it' (Gladstone). 'The constitution is "... what happens"' (Griffith). Explain and compare these two statements.

3.4   Explain, illustrate and criticise Bagehot's distinction between the 'dignified' and the 'efficient' parts of the constitution. Is this a useful way to analyse the constitution?

3.5   'Parties have substituted for a constitution in Britain. They have filled all the vast empty spaces in the political system where a constitution should be and made the system in their own image' (Wright). Explain and criticise this statement.

3.6   'A constitution is not the act of a government but of a people constituting a government and a government without a constitution is power without right' (Paine). Discuss in relation to the UK constitution.

3.7   To what extent is the UK constitution a common law constitution and how important is this in contemporary conditions?

3.8   What is the relationship between law and convention? Does it serve a useful purpose to distinguish between law and conventions?

3.9   Consider the advantages and disadvantages of the UK's reliance on conventions. Should conventions be enacted into law?

4 The Structure of the UK Government: An Overview

In this chapter I shall attempt to highlight the main features of UK government that have constitutional implications. I shall emphasise in particular the checks and balances within the constitution hoping that this can serve both as a self-contained overview and also a guide to the more detailed topics that follow.

4.1 The Informal Constitution

The constitution is society's provisional accommodation between competing claims to power. The most striking feature of the UK constitution is perhaps its informal nature in the sense that its most basic principles depend upon voluntary restraint and consensus among those holding positions of power without strong lines of political accountability and outside the supervision of the courts. Thus the constitution is held together essentially by an assumption that established practices will be followed.

Traditionalists claim that the UK constitution is the happy and pragmatic outcome of an evolution towards democracy and the rule of law. According to this view, symbolised by Magna Carta (1215), the Crown gradually gave way to Parliament as an assembly representing those who were deemed worthy to have a stake in the community. Parliament steadily broadened its membership until eventually the people as a whole controlled the government. Abuse of governmental power is checked by a combination of Parliament and the courts. Parliament chooses and dismisses the government, provides it with the power to raise and spend money and scrutinises its activities. The courts protect the rights of individuals and groups treating all equally and ensure that the government keeps to the laws that it enacts. According to traditionalists pragmatic reforms such as strengthening the powers of the courts, reforming parliamentary procedures to give backbenchers greater independence, creating regulatory bodies, and publishing wish-lists of desirable behaviour such as those promulgated by the Committee on Standards in Public Life can preserve constitutional equilibrium.

Another view is that the constitution is driven by chance circumstances and personalities. For example a pivotal event of the English revolution was arguably 'Pride's Purge' in 1648 which was precipitated by the fortuitous (and temporary) escape from custody of Charles I. In Pride's Purge most of Parliament was ejected leaving the 'Rump Parliament' of army supporters to arrange the execution of Charles I. Had this event not occurred, an accommodation with the King would have been likely and the subsequent course of the constitution might have been different, leading perhaps to a later and more radical revolution.

More radical commentators suggest that the UK constitution is fundamentally flawed, democracy having ineffectively been grafted onto an authoritarian form of government concentrated in the Crown (see Morison and Livingstone, 1995). A fatalistic perspective is that such is inevitable, a sad truth of the human condition being that those who seek power over others tend to be unfit to exercise it, hence the importance of constitutional checks and balances. From this perspective all government boils down to a king and his favourites who surround him as courtiers and ultimately bring him down. In our case the 'king' is the prime minister and his courtiers are individuals whom he has appointed to high office or relies upon as advisers – 'the caterpillars of the commonwealth, which I have sworn to weed and pluck away' (Bolingbroke, Shakespeare, *Richard II*, Act 2, Scene 3). There are no legal constraints over senior public appointments. This allows prime ministers to appoint ministers and they in turn to appoint influential advisors from among their family, friends and personal networks. Lord Irvine the current Lord Chancellor is a paradigm case (see *The Independent*, 22.11.01).

A riposte commonly made by the courtiers themselves is that abuses will not happen, because, apart from the odd maverick, we can trust our rulers who are persons of high ability and integrity and are subject to legal, political and social pressures to conform. But:

> Why should we, in the compass of a pale,
> Keep law and form and due proportion,
> Showing as in a model our firm estate,
> When our sea-walled garden, the whole land,
> Is full of weeds, her fairest flowers choked up,
> Her fruit trees all unpruned, her hedges ruined,
> Her knots disordered, and her wholesome herbs
> Swarming with caterpillars. (ibid. Act 3, Scene 4).

Whether or not this is convincing, (see 4.7), our informal constitution fails to meet the republican requirement of non-domination which emphasises that it is offensive to human dignity to rely on the good will even of a kind master.

4.2   Crown v. Parliament: Historical Outline

During the sixteenth and seventeenth centuries medieval ideas of limited monarchy within the common law clashed with newer ideas of absolute monarchy and the nation state. Such a clash had been foreshadowed by the late medieval notion of the Crown's 'two persons', the one a symbolic and semi-divine personification of the state, the other an official whose day-to-day duties were subject to the law (see *Duchy of Lancaster Case* (1567) 1 Plow 325 at 327).

The seventeenth century was dominated by religious and financial conflicts between the Crown and Parliament. The Stuart monarchs seemed to respect the supremacy of the common law and to subject their powers to scrutiny by the courts (bearing in mind that judges, 'lions under the throne', were dismissable by the king (see e.g. *Case of Proclamations* (1611); *R.* v. *Hampden* (1637)). Coke CJ's stand against royal interference in the *Case of Prohibitions* (1607) was followed by his dismissal for taking a similar stand in 1616 in the *Commendum* case.

From 1629, Charles I attempted to rule without Parliament on the basis of taxes extorted from the rising middle classes. However, when he attempted in 1639 to impose the Anglican prayer book on the Scots the resulting uprising forced him to summon Parliament in 1640 (the 'Long Parliament' which technically survived until 1660), in order to raise funds. A short-lived compromise was reached in 1641 after Parliament's 'Grand Remonstrance' which detailed acts of royal misrule. In particular the Star Chamber and other special prerogative courts introduced by the Tudors to support an administrative state were abolished. Civil war broke out in 1642 resulting in victory for Parliament in 1646.

The civil war was followed by a wide-ranging debate at Putney between the ruling establishment of landowners led by Oliver Cromwell and the army rank and file represented by the 'Levellers', about the fundamentals of government. The Levellers proposed a new constitutional settlement – the 'Agreement of the People' – based on religious freedom, equality before the law and universal suffrage. This remains an important source of democratic ideas (see the writings of Richard Overton (1631–64)). However, Cromwell invoked custom and tradition in favour of more limited reforms. The Levellers were defeated by force in 1649.

In 1648 Parliament attempted to disband the army but most members were ejected in 'Pride's Purge' leaving only the 'Rump Parliament' of army supporters. In 1649 Charles I was executed on the authority of the Rump Parliament, the House of Lords abolished and a republic declared. In 1653 Parliament was dismissed and a military dictatorship led by Oliver Cromwell as 'Lord Protector' introduced. After Cromwell's death in 1658 it seemed that chaos could best be avoided by restoring the traditional constitution. The House of Lords had been restored in 1657 and the Long Parliament met in 1659 only to dissolve itself in favour of a self-appointed 'Convention Parliament'. This restored the Crown in 1660 in the form of Charles II, the lawful heir of Charles I.

4.2.1 The 1688 revolution

Charles II and James II ruled on the basis that there had been no republic and the republican legislation was expunged from the statute book. A limited religious toleration was declared and a relatively liberal regime introduced. The uneasy stalemate was broken when James II began to assert the interests of Catholics and to attempt to override Parliament. Catholicism was associated in the public mind with absolution, an association that still scars the constitution (below p. 292). The foundations of the modern constitution were laid by the 1688 revolution when James dissolved Parliament and fled the country. He was replaced by the Protestants William of Orange and his wife Mary (James's daughter) backed up by the Dutch navy. Neither had a lawful claim to the Crown.

1688 therefore marks a break in the constitution although in political terms the revolution was relatively conservative being a compromise designed to satisfy all influential interests. It was justified in two inconsistent ways. On a Hobbesian premise James II had abdicated leaving a power vacuum that the common law doctrine of necessity said must be filled in order to avoid chaos. On the other premise, based on Locke, James had broken his trust. This entitled the people to rebel.

The settlement formalities were entirely unlawful according to the previous constitution, unless we can say they were underpinned by the common law. A group of leading politicians summoned a 'Convention Parliament' which met early in 1688. This appointed William and Mary jointly to the Crown and enacted the Bill of Rights 1688 which limited the powers of the Crown against Parliament enshrining the principles that had been fought over earlier in the century. These prohibit the Crown from exercising key powers without the consent of

Parliament, such as the power to make laws to tax, to keep a standing army in peacetime, and to override legislation. William and Mary then summoned a Parliament which ratified the Acts of the Convention (Crown and Parliament Recognition Act 1689). The Act of Settlement 1701 provided for the succession to the Crown and gave superior court judges security of tenure and therefore independence from the Crown. Church and state were also linked by requiring the monarch to be a Protestant and not to marry a Catholic. In the case of Scotland and Ireland, force was needed to crush support for the Stuart monarchs.

The medieval institutions remained in place but it was made clear that the monarchy was subordinate to Parliament. The common law courts backed Parliament and it is plausible that in 1688 the judges accepted parliamentary supremacy in return for security of tenure. At any rate modern judges have assumed that the doctrine of parliamentary supremacy is grounded in the 1688 revolution (see *Pickin* v. *British Railways Board* [1974] 1 All ER 609 at 614). However, there is no clear historical evidence for this and it was not until the nineteenth-century disputes over the construction of railways that the courts unequivocally accepted parliamentary supremacy. (Compare e.g. *City of London* v. *Wood* (1710) 10 Mod 669 at 686–8; *Lee* v. *Bude & Torrington Railway Co. Ltd* (1871) LR 6 CP 577.)

The 1688 settlement was not therefore based on full-blooded ideas of the sovereignty of the people and the fundamental rights of the individual such as a century later would influence the French and American revolutions. If anything it confirmed the principle of aristocratic rule. The House of Lords was a powerful body and the House of Commons was largely made up of landowners and traders dependent on the patronage of the Lords. Thomas Paine, who fled the country in 1792 having been charged with sedition for denying that Britain had a constitution, said 'What is [the Bill of Rights 1688] but a bargain which the parts of the government made with each other to decide powers. You shall have so much and I will have the rest; and with respect to the nation, it said, for your share, you shall have the right of petitioning. This being the case the Bill of Rights is more properly a bill of wrongs and of insult' (Paine, 1989, p. 181).

4.2.2   The development of democracy

Early legislation ensured that the monarch could not keep Parliament in abeyance and that there should be regular elections (see Septennial Act 1715 as amended by Parliament Act 1911). During the early eighteenth century the monarch still claimed to run the government personally and to choose the ministers although a convention existed from the outset that the Commons could dismiss a ministry of which it disapproved. However, as late as 1812 it was argued that it would be unconstitutional for the king not to appoint the government personally (see Williams, 1960, ch. 2). During the eighteenth and nineteenth centuries the skeleton of the present system evolved. This replaced the personal power of the monarch with that of the cabinet, a core of ministers chosen by the prime minister and supported by Parliament. Bagehot regarded this as the central principle of the constitution. The Crown's influence in choosing a prime minister and dissolving Parliament was replaced by the conventions that the Crown must appoint the leader of the majority party, that the executive is collectively and individually responsible to Parliament and that Parliament must be dissolved if the government loses the confidence of the House of Commons. By the end of the eighteenth century the official status of the opposition was recognised.

During the eighteenth century the notion of the 'mixed constitution' was predominant in which monarch, Lords and Commons acted as checks on each other. For example Blackstone (1765, vol. 1, p. 153) announced that the royal veto on legislation meant that the king could not propose evil but could prevent it and went on to eulogise the mutual checks between nobility, king and people which Parliament embodied. However, of the three elements, until the end of the nineteenth century the aristocracy in the House of Lords remained a powerful force. Until the extension of the franchise to most of the population which evolved by stages between 1832 and 1928, elections were largely controlled by aristocratic land-owning families with a power base both in the Lords and in local affairs. There was also a tension, which is still significant between the notion of a constitutionalism based upon custom and tradition as interpreted by an elite, represented for example by Edmund Burke (1729–1797), and the republican ideals of individual rights and the rule of law represented in the eighteenth century by Thomas Paine (above). The relatively peaceful development of the UK governmental system during the eighteenth and nineteenth centuries is often attributed to the openness and flexibility of the British ruling classes in absorbing others into their ranks, particularly the new industrial wealth creators.

In the eighteenth century when most mainland European states were absolute monarchies, the British constitution was widely regarded by overseas observers such as Montesquieu as a stable and liberal regime embodying the values of the rule of law and separation of powers. From inside Britain the picture was more blurred. The courts protected rights in the formal sense that whatever rights a person had were impartially adjudicated. However, the content of those rights was affected by draconian legislation passed in the interests of aristocratic landowners, such as anti-poaching laws and a tax system that put the overwhelming burden upon consumption as opposed to property, thus penalising the poor (see Thompson, 1975).

On the other hand it would be wrong to get a one-dimensional picture. As usual there was a continuing accommodation between competing interests (see Thompson, 1975; Langbein, 1983). For example the poor were able to call on the protection of the courts as well as the rich and judges and juries were on the whole reluctant to impose draconian penalties. Moreover, during this period, the common law, albeit reluctantly, rejected slavery (*Somersett's Case* (1772)), and personal liberty and freedom of expression were upheld (e.g. *Leach* v. *Money* (1765); *Entick* v. *Carrington* (1765); *Wolfe Tone's Case* (1798); Libel Act 1792 – verdicts to be left to the jury).

Britain did not escape the social dislocations that were a prominent feature of the late eighteenth and early nineteenth centuries but, for reasons that are not fully understood, managed to escape the revolutions that brought down many European regimes. A possible reason lay in the flexibility of our constitutional arrangements and the willingness of the aristocratic elite to give way gradually in the face of pressures for reform. Thus it took nearly a century to complete the process towards popular democracy. Other reasons lay in the relative flexibility of the social class structure in Britain and with the deference of the English character (see Bagehot, in Crossman (ed), 1963).

From the mid-nineteenth century Parliament gradually and reluctantly extended the right to vote as utilitarianism and economics replaced law as the intellectual fashion of the day. This extension of the franchise culminated in 1928 when women were given the franchise. The extension of democracy led to a debate about the common law. Traditionalists such as Dicey regarded the common law as a hedge against tyranny while reformers such as Bentham despised the common law as an enemy of democracy and efficient management. '(E)ighteenth century veneration for the law was giving way to pungent criticism of it' (Briggs, 1959, p. 92).

Power became increasingly concentrated in the House of Commons and the executive. Lord Salisbury whose final administration ended in 1892 was the last prime minister to sit in the House of Lords and the Labour Party was founded in 1900. It was during this period when Parliament began to be genuinely representative that the courts explicitly recognised the principle of parliamentary supremacy. In relation to the common law it is arguable that the broad justice-based system that predominated during the eighteenth century was challenged by more formalistic rule-based conceptions of law that suited the development of capitalism and free markets in the nineteenth century.

During Queen Victoria's reign (1837–1901) the monarchy reshaped itself as a symbolic representative of the nation standing outside party politics. The increasingly important legislative role of Parliament awakened conflict between the two Houses of Parliament. The House of Lords, representing traditional landowners and the House of Commons, representing mainly commercial interests, struggled for dominance over issues such as Irish home rule and the introduction of social reforms. The Parliament Act 1911 resolved the matter in favour of the Commons although the House of Lords retains significant influence.

4.3 The Growth of the Executive

During the late nineteenth century, impelled by the demands of a larger electorate, the executive branch of government began to increase in size and range of discretionary powers. Governmental functions which had previously been exercised by local bodies were increasingly concentrated in central departments under the control of ministers answerable to Parliament. An important landmark was the Northcote–Trevelyan Report of 1854 which led to the creation of a permanent, professional and impartial civil service, appointed on merit (replacing a system of patronage and sinecures). In the USA for example the top ranks of the civil service change with each new president. In recent years, however, tensions have been created as ministers have increasingly relied on 'special advisors' appointed personally who, although paid from public funds, are more closely associated with party politics than are regular civil servants.

The eighteenth-century statute book had been dominated by laws protecting property policed by the courts. During the nineteenth century the wider franchise led to social welfare legislation which required a large and powerful executive. Nineteenth-century local government, public health and safety legislation was followed, in the early twentieth century, by substantial housing, education and urban development legislation. Immediately after the Second World War a wide-ranging welfare system was introduced. It was widely accepted that the economy should be driven by the state. Subordinate legislation and non-statutory rules were made by the executive on a large scale with limited parliamentary scrutiny. Thousands of administrative tribunals staffed by government appointees were created to deal with the disputes generated by this expansion of state activity. Other bodies outside the traditional umbrella of parliamentary accountability were created to run particular services or to give advice.

The constitution made only marginal responses to these fundamental changes. The traditional ideal of the rule of law as embodied in the common law and of accountability to Parliament were not seriously challenged even though the executive seemed to have outgrown both these constraints. The Donoughmore Committee on Ministers' Powers (1932, Cmd. 4060) and the Franks Committee on Tribunals and Inquiries (1958, Cmnd. 218) recommended marginal reforms which strengthened the powers of the courts and supplemented parliamentary scrutiny of the executive. These included a parliamentary committee to scrutinise such subordinate legislation as statute required to be laid before Parliament (Statutory Instruments Act 1946), increased rights of appeal and the creation of a Council on Tribunals with powers to approve procedural rules for most administrative tribunals and statutory inquiries (Tribunals and Inquiries Acts 1958–92). From the 1960s various 'ombudsmen' were set up to investigate complaints by citizens against government but without enforceable powers.

Recognising the inevitability of executive discretion and reluctant to appear to be challenging the majority, the courts began to defer to political decisions, an attitude which was particularly strong after the Second World War compared with the more robust attitudes expressed earlier in the century (below Chapter 16)). Dicey (1915) began to question his earlier belief in the rule of law. In the inter-war period, both ends of the political spectrum were worried. Some believed that the executive had taken over, others that an individualistically minded judiciary would frustrate popular programmes (see Stephens, 1993). More recently, dating from the mid-1960s, the courts have developed a more interventionist approach in relation to the executive which continues today (see Sedley in Nolan, 1997).

4.4   The Concept of the State

There is no coherent concept of the state in English law which regards government as comprising separate legal entities, Parliament, the Crown, local authorities, the police etc. each of which is linked to the others by pragmatic rules and practices. We use the terms 'Queen', 'Crown' 'state' and 'nation' with little discrimination. For example we refer to secretaries and ministers of state but also to ministers of the Crown and the Crown Prosecution Service. We refer to state schools, state papers and state secrets but to National Insurance and the National Health Service. The courts are the Queen's courts, laws are made by the Queen in Parliament but civil servants are servants of the Crown. Central government property is Crown property unless it is owned by an incorporated government department such as the Ministry of Defence.

By contrast, in 'statist' constitutions such as those of France and Germany, the various departments of government, and indeed the law itself, emanate from a single monolithic state created by law and whose powers are defined and limited by the law (*rechtstaat*). In statist theory a constitution arises from the act of a 'constituent power' which might for example be a revolution or a referendum of the people. The constituent power creates the constitution which in turn creates the state and authorises the enactment of laws in a logical self-contained hierarchy. The courts interpret the laws of the state. They do not, as in the common law system, provide their own independent source of law.

The term 'state' is sometimes used in legislation where its meaning depends on the particular context. Sometimes the state means the executive arm of government, sometimes the government as a whole, and sometimes the 'sovereign power' (see e.g. *General Medical Council* v. *BBC* (1998); *D.* v. *NSPCC* (1978)). In *Chandler* v. *DPP* (1964), which concerned the Official Secrets Act 1911, Lord Devlin described the state as 'the organs of government of a national community'. Lord Reid on the other hand thought that 'the organised community' was as close to a definition as one can get (see also *D.* v. *NSPCC* (1978)). There is a crucial ambiguity as to whether 'the interests of the state' are taken to be the interests of the government as such or include the broader interests of the people, usually expressed by the term 'public interest'. Sometimes the terms 'nation' and 'state' are used loosely and interchangeably, for example where the law refers to 'the national interest' or 'national security' (see *Council of Civil Service Unions (CCSU)* v. *Minister for the Civil Service* (1985)).

The non-statist nature of English law has at least the following important consequences:

- There is a distinction in statist constitutions between 'public law' which regulates the state itself and its relationship with citizens through its powers of compulsion (*imperium*) and 'private law' which the state uses to regulate the relationship between its citizens and that between itself and citizens in connection with contracts or other voluntary transactions. The UK does not have a concept of functions that are peculiar to the state although in some contexts, such as human rights and judicial review such a concept may be developing. In some constitutions the notion of the 'police power' encapsulates powers inherent in the nature of government. Not surprisingly the limits of the police power are controversial. Traditionally the police power relates to 'peace, order and good government' and includes the protection of 'public safety, health and morals' (see *Berman* v. *Parker* 348 US 26 (1954) at 32; Commonwealth Constitution (Australia) s. 51).

- In a non-statist framework, officials are on the face of it the same as ordinary persons so that, unless a particular law provides otherwise, public servants have no special powers or status and are individually responsible for any legal wrongs they commit. This depends on ensuring that public bodies keep within powers given to them by particular statutes (e.g. *R.* v. *Somerset County Council ex parte Fewings* (1995)). In *M* v. *Home Office* (1993) the House of Lords insisted that a court order was enforceable against a government minister as such even if the Crown itself was immune. Lord Templeman remarked (at 541) that to hold otherwise would reverse the result of the civil war.

- Our non-statist tradition means that government powers can be distributed haphazardly between government bodies proper, and private bodies. Contemporary privatisation policies are an example. There are some advantages in this. Particular decision-making bodies must be openly identified and cannot hide under the general state umbrella. There are also disadvantages in that there seems to be no constitutional principle to prevent public powers being farmed out to bodies that are not democratically accountable. There is no clear notion of what is a public body or a public function. The matter depends on the particular context. For example the Freedom of Information Act 2000 and the Regulation of Investigatory Powers Act 2000 provides a list of public bodies which can be altered by ministers. The Government Reserves and Accounts Act 2000 refers to a 'government department or a body exercising public functions' (s. 7 (3)). The Human Rights Act 1998 s. 6 contemplates that some bodies exercise a mixture of public and private functions but otherwise does not provide a definition. For example the exercise of statutory powers to regulate businesses is clearly a public function, but voluntary bodies such as the Jockey Club also influence important areas of public life.

- In a statist system the state is both a creation of the law and the producer of law. The judges are the authoritative interpreters of the law but not its creators. Judicial opinions are regarded as making more concrete the laws emanating from the state but do not traditionally have an independent law-making role. Judgements are often short with little detailed reasoning and dissenting opinions are not normally published. By contrast the historical basis of the common law gives the courts an independent basis of legitimacy. The authority of the common law lies in community values and does not depend on a theory of the state. In the common law system, the judges are regarded as individuals charged with doing justice. Judicial decisions are normally fully reasoned and dissents are published.

The traditional state has been attacked both from without and within. The 'global economy' is a fashionable idea. It will be recalled from Chapter 2 that the origins of the state were military as a method of defending a community against foreign aggression. Until the Second World War the international community was regarded as a Hobbesian state of nature while the rule of law operated within state boundaries. However, the Second World War persuaded the international community to develop common principles for defence and for regulating the economy, the environment and human rights through bodies such as NATO, the World Trade Organisation, and the Council of Europe.

Technology has speeded up communications and flows of resources to such an extent that states have become economically and militarily interdependent to a much greater extent than before. Some large international firms are wealthier than many states and it is often suggested that private bodies, and small local communities, can provide welfare services more efficiently than can governments in that governments cannot obtain sufficient information for the task. Moreover the balance of power that concentrated military efforts on perceived threats from identifiable states was destroyed in the 1980s by the collapse of the Soviet Union. This released pressures based on ethnic, religious and racial conflicts and led to an increased concern with terrorism, with large-scale population movements and with human rights all of which transcend state boundaries.

These developments do not, however, make the nation state redundant. The core Hobbesian task of keeping order cannot be carried out without a central authority. Indeed sentiments about globalisation and the obsolescence of the nation state, similar to those expressed today, were widely expressed in the nineteenth and early twentieth centuries until the dream was interrupted by the First World War. Moreover territorial units seem to cater for an essential human need. The state therefore remains vital as a guarantor of order, a major contributor to economic well-being and a last resort for the vulnerable.

4.5   The Legislature

The legislature is composed of the Queen in Parliament and is commonly believed to have unlimited legal power, although in recent years this has been subject to considerable questioning. By convention the Queen is bound to assent to any bill presented to her by Parliament. By convention Parliament must meet annually and by law expires automatically after five years unless it is dissolved earlier. The prime minister by convention can require the Queen to dissolve Parliament and must do so if the government loses the confidence of the Commons. Upon dissolution there must by law be a general election.

Parliament is bi-cameral. The House of Commons is elected. Its role is to make legislation to sustain the government by providing it with funds, to hold the government to account, to debate matters of public concern and to redress individual grievances, The House of Commons is superior to the House of Lords. The House of Lords comprising nearly 700 members is one of the largest legislative bodies in the world, is wholly non-elected and most of its members are entitled to sit for life. The House of Lords is normally confined to revising the details of legislation proposed by the Commons, holding general debates and reporting on matters of public concern through its committees. It acts as a limited check on the Commons in that it can delay legislation to give time for second thoughts. Subject to certain exceptions the Lords cannot veto legislation. The most important of these exceptions is a bill to extend the life of a Parliament which would enable the government to avoid facing an election. The government proposes to reform the House of Lords but there is no consensus as to whether or not it should become an elected chamber.

4.5.1   Referendums

Referendums have traditionally been regarded as constitutional anomalies in that they seem to conflict with the principle of representative democracy. On the few occasions on which they have been used referendums have been governed by particular statutes and have been advisory only, leaving Parliament with the last word. In recent years referendums have been used more frequently, in connection with general constitutional matters notably devolution to Scotland, Wales and Northern Ireland. The Local Government Act 2000 also contains provisions for referendums which can veto proposals to introduce new executive arrangements (see Chapter 8).

The Political Parties, Elections and Referendums Act 2000 has given referendums a general legal framework. Under the Act a referendum is defined as where 'one or more questions specified by or under an Act of Parliament' are put to the voters (s. 101 (2)). First the Act has imposed controls over campaign expenditure in relation to referendums similar to those applicable to parliamentary elections. The Act also introduced measures designed to enhance the fairness of a referendum campaign. First, after the relevant bill authorising a referendum has been introduced, the Electoral Commission can publish views as to the intelligibility of the wording of the question (s. 104). However, this would not allow the Commission to comment on whether the question is biased in favour of the answer the government hopes for. Secondly the Act designates 'permitted participants'. These include the following: registered parties, resident individuals or those on the electoral register, firms, voluntary bodies etc. based in the UK. Thirdly the Act empowers the Commission to give grants of up to £1,000,000 to one designated applicant representing each outcome in the campaign. This is intended to encourage bodies such as pressure groups to join forces so as to focus the issues. The designated applicants can also have free facilities including a referendum address, room for a public meeting and a campaign broadcast.

4.6   The Central Executive

In legal theory the Crown is the executive but by convention can act only on the advice of ministers. For most practical purposes, the Crown is represented by the government of the day. The executive enforces the law and makes and implements government policy. Historically, all executive powers were vested in the Crown subject to rights established by the common law or by particular charters and customs (cf. Magna Carta, 1215). The distinction between the functions of lawmaker and executive is blurred in that in practice the executive is the primary generator of law the legislature being confined to the more passive role of approving or amending laws proposed by the executive. In strict law the legislature may be the most important part of the constitution but in practice the executive is the dominant force.

Executive bodies have no legal powers other than those conferred by statute. There are two exceptions to this. First the Crown has a residue of inherent power as head of state (the royal prerogative). Since the seventeenth century most royal prerogative powers have been abolished and it has become clear that new prerogatives cannot be created except by statute. Nevertheless prerogative powers still pose problems in that they can be exercised by ministers without the need for parliamentary approval and might therefore escape democratic scrutiny. Secondly a constable (and possibly any citizen) has a common law power to take reasonable steps to prevent a breach of the peace. This might involve for example entering private premises or preventing public access to land (see Chapter 19).

Most powers are conferred by statute on specific ministers and there are no particular constitutional principles relating to the form and structure of the executive. Indeed it is widely accepted that the executive should have the freedom to determine its own internal organisation. In a general sense the executive comprises the Crown together with all bodies exercising power to enforce or implement the law. There are a wide variety of such bodies ranging from elected multi-function local authorities to specialised tribunals and advisory bodies.

The prime minister is in practice the chief executive although he has few legal powers. By convention the prime minister is the leader of the majority party in the Commons. He has two fundamental powers, namely to appoint and dismiss other ministers and to dissolve Parliament. The prime minister has other important powers, mainly based on convention which give the holder of the office unique political influence. Senior ministers under the chair of the prime minister form the cabinet which is responsible for overall government policy. The prime minister is also the minister for the civil service.

In the nineteenth century Bagehot claimed that the cabinet was the essential link between Parliament and the executive this arrangement giving the constitution its motive power and balance. It is often argued, however, that the cabinet is losing political power because a group of this kind cannot deal with the size and complexity of modern government and may be merely a rubber stamp for decisions taken elsewhere.

The Crown acts through its servants. These comprise ministers and permanent civil servants. Civil servants have no constitutional or legal status as such. They act only under powers flowing to them through ministers. Indeed the law has treated civil servants and ministers as a single body for the purpose of excluding any duty to disclose communications within a government department at a public inquiry (see *Bushell* v. *Secretary of State for the Environment* [1981] 1 AC 75 95; *Alconbury Holdings* v. *Secretary of State* [2001] 2 All ER 929, 995). Senior civil servants (of whom there are about 30,000) have the competing functions of offering impartial advice to ministers and carrying out ministerial instructions. In a system designed to allow political power to change hands abruptly, a permanent civil service is an essential source of continuity and a repository of knowledge. In recent years the independence of the civil service may have been diluted by the appointment of about 81 special advisers who, although civil servants also have political duties including liaison with the media. Special advisers are appointed by ministers to whom they have direct access. They are not required to be politically neutral. The delicate relationship between the civil service and political advisers has been put into question by empowering some special advisers to give orders to civil servants (Civil Service (Amendment) Order in Council 1999). On the other hand special advisers might also protect civil servants from political involvement. There is no systematic body of civil service law, the civil service being subject to an untidy mixture of royal prerogative, convention contract and practice with little statutory element. The Committee on Standards in Public Life in its 6th Report (Neill, 2000a), recommended that the civil service be placed on a statutory basis so as to protect its objectivity, and that the role and number of special advisers be clarified.

The distinction between Crown servants and others is of limited significance since many of the traditional immunities enjoyed by the Crown have been abolished. Most importantly the Crown is not bound by statute in the absence of express language or necessary implication. However, where powers are conferred by Parliament directly on a minister the courts are not prepared to let the minister shelter behind Crown immunity. In *M.* v. *Home Office* (1993), Lord Templeman remarked (at 541) 'that the argument that there is no power to enforce the law ... against a minister in his official capacity would, if upheld, establish the proposition that the executive obey the law as a matter of grace and not as a matter of necessity, a proposition which would reverse the result of the Civil War'.

4.7 Parliamentary Government and Ministerial Responsibility

The core of the constitution is that the Crown rules on the basis of powers given or allowed to it by Parliament and by convention the executive powers of the Crown are exercised by or on the advice of ministers who must be members of Parliament. The Queen must usually dissolve Parliament if requested to do so by the prime minister who must request her to dissolve Parliament if defeated on a vote of confidence in the Commons thereby precipitating an election. In many other systems, the legislature runs for a fixed term, in some cases subject to the government being defeated on a vote of confidence. If this were to be adopted here, Parliament would be strengthened. In exceptional cases where the normal processes have broken down, the Queen might have a residue of personal power. Thus the monarchy acts as a last resort to safeguard the constitution.

The conventions relating to ministerial responsibility are intended to make the executive responsible to Parliament and so indirectly to the people. Ministerial responsibility has two limbs. The cabinet is collectively responsible to Parliament for the conduct of the government as a whole while individual ministers are responsible to Parliament for the conduct of their departments. Thus there is a chain of accountability.

When ministerial responsibility was developed in the eighteenth century government departments were small enough for ministers to be personally in control. The position is different today since many government departments are multi-million pound businesses staffed by hundreds, sometimes thousands of civil servants. It is therefore impossible to expect a minister to be personally in control of the many detailed decisions that are made on a day-to-day basis. The meaning of the convention is therefore unclear. In an extreme case the minister should resign but in practice this is likely to happen only where the minister is personally at fault or where the problem is the result of a policy for which the minister is directly responsible.

Collective responsibility can be used to justify government secrecy on the basis that the unity of the cabinet would be threatened if its inner discussions were exposed. This attitude is embodied, for example, in the Freedom of Information Act 2000, which exempts matters affecting collective responsibility and other internal policy documents from disclosure. Ministerial responsibility also shields civil servants who are protected by anonymity, appear before Parliament only with the permission of the minister and owe duties only to the minister. This might be regarded as unreal. On the other hand their protection is said to secure their impartiality and ability to serve every kind of government. There is nevertheless a gap in the chain of accountability. However, various devices including investigatory bodies such as the Ombudsman, who investigates maladministration, and the National Audit Office, which investigates government spending, can probe behind the facade of ministerial responsibility and question civil servants directly.

Ministerial responsibility also affects the courts. The conventional wisdom is that accountability is split. Government is accountable to the courts for the legality of its conduct and to Parliament for the merits of its conduct i.e. whether its conduct is good or bad. Therefore the fact that a decision has been approved by Parliament does not normally restrict judicial review (*Hoffman – La Roche Ltd* v. *Trade and Industry Secretary of State* (1974)). Nevertheless, as we shall see, the line between legality and merits is blurred and judges disagree (Chapter 16). A court, aware of the weakness of Parliament, might be tempted to stretch the notion of legality in order to do justice (e.g. *R.* v. *Foreign Secretary ex parte World Development Movement* (1995)). On the other hand the existence of parliamentary accountability may work the other way and persuade a court not to interfere in a politically sensitive area (e.g. *Nottinghamshire County Council* v. *Secretary of State* (1986); see also *R.* v. *Secretary of State ex parte Fire Brigades Union* (1995)).

Another recent development has further distanced ministers from the operational work of executive departments and put a strain on the credibility of ministerial responsibility. During the 1990s executive power was reorganised and redistributed and the methods of governmental decision making changed. Traditional bureaucratic hierarchies have in many cases been replaced by looser quasi-autonomous structures copied from the private sector. The central civil service has been split into two kinds. The day-to-day work of delivering services has been delegated to 'executive agencies', sometimes known as 'Next-Steps' agencies (see Jenkins *et al.*, 1988). Each agency, although having a parent department with a minister retaining overall responsibility, has significant management autonomy and is organised more along private sector lines than according to traditional civil service practices. Executive agencies now comprise about three-quarters of all civil servants. They range from the Inland Revenue which is a self-contained government department, through bodies such as the Prison Service, the Benefits Agency and the Court Service to the Vehicle Inspectorate and the Public Records Office. The core civil service remains responsible for policy making, research, advising ministers and supervising the agencies, thus forming an elite corps. In theory ministers remain fully accountable to Parliament for executive agencies. However, given the amount of operational independence exercised by the agencies, in practice this is blurred and unrealistic.

4.8 'Hollowed-Out' Government

Apart from executive agencies the provision of public services has in recent years been dispersed among many different bodies. The election of the Conservative government in 1979 led to a return to individual-istic ideology perhaps generated by the belief that the welfare state cost more than the UK's declining economy could support. The driving force behind these changes was the desire to cut public costs and so lower taxes. The rationale is that of 'public choice' which assumes that self-interest is the driving motivation of public officials. This was thought to require self-contained units subject to competition with those providing the service, being personally accountable. Rather than the traditional hierarchical bureaucracies, each unit has relative freedom to manage its own affairs. The public interest is served by various regulatory devices. These include competition with the private sector for the provision of services, and published performance stan-dards and indicators of achievement. Regulation is carried out in some cases by the central government directly, in others by special regulators created by statute, such as the various utilities regulators. These are subject to varying degrees of central government control by means of ministerial powers to give directions, or guidance.

Miscellaneous devices have been used to achieve this fragmented form of government (see Jenkins *et al.*, 1996). Most of the nationalised industries including gas, electricity, rail, telecommunications, and steel and water supply were privatised by creating commercial companies each having one or more statutory regulators. In some cases, notably social housing, non-profit-making bodies partly funded by govern-ment have been the preferred vehicle. Some public services remain but their day-to-day running has been partly contracted out to private bodies. This includes education and the prison service. In certain cases, notably trunk roads and hospital building, 'public/private' partner-ships have been created whereby private funding is put into a public service in return for a share in the assets thereby generated (Govern-ment Reserves and Accounts Act 2000). The National Health Ser-vice, although operated as a conglomerate of separate 'trusts' entity, remains part of the Crown and the Post Office is a statutory body with certain market freedoms. British Waterways remains a wholly public body. Parasitic on this structure are numerous statutory authorities, some acting as regulators, some directly providing finance or services, and some giving 'advice'. Some, such as the Housing Corporation, combine all these functions in a farrago of conflicts of interest (see Housing Act 1996).

In addition the central government increased its powers over bodies which had previously enjoyed relative autonomy. It strengthened its control over local authorities so as to prevent them retaining the traditional communitarian public service orthodoxy and in particular encouraged them to transfer their housing stock to non-profit-making housing associations, these being hybrid bodies with both public and private characteristics. State schools have been given increased independence from local control. The central government also tightened its control over universities by exercising detailed powers of direction over the Higher Education Funding Council, and through its patronage over research funding bodies.

It has been argued that this dispersal of public functions is likely to weaken government overall. This is because, although it retains formal control through its lawmaking powers and its powers of patronage, the central government has neither the resources nor the will to co-ordinate its increasingly dispersed progeny (see Rhodes, 1996). On the other hand it is arguable that the arrangements are held together by the established tradition of deference to ministers and tribal loyalties that ensure that positions of power are kept within overlapping networks of personal and family relationships.

4.9 Ethics in Government

There are three broad methods of ensuring governmental accountability. First there is the accountability of ministers to Parliament (above). Second there is accountability to individuals through the courts (Chapters 16, 17). Third, and increasingly common, there is accountability through non-legally binding codes of conduct either self-regulated, as for example the House of Lords prefers for itself, or policed by a range of commissions, advisory bodies etc. appointed from the insider networks and working with varying degrees of informality. These do not usually have enforcement powers nor does a citizen have a right to an investigation. However, their reports are usually published and can be implemented through internal enforcement mechanisms within government. We shall meet many examples throughout the book.

As we have seen, the informal nature of much of the UK constitution, particularly at the higher levels, makes our arrangements heavily dependent on trusting those in power, a trust which history suggests is often misplaced. A series of scandals from the 1980s exposed significant corruption, ambivalence and incompetence within central government and Parliament. These included the following: the 'arms to Iraq' affair which involved allegations that ministers had tried to cover up breaches of UN sanctions against Iran and which resulted in the Scott Report (1996, HC 115); the clumsy prosecutions or censorship of civil service whistleblowers such as Kathie Massister, Clive Ponting and Peter Wright who made allegations of misconduct against ministers and officials; the Westlands affair in 1987 where civil servants appeared to disregard the traditional principle of impartiality and ministers to conspire against each other; cases where MPs and ministers were found by courts and parliamentary committees to have received bribes from business interests; claims that favours are performed in return for donations to party funds; conflicts between governmental media-management and civil service objectivity.

The result was an attempt to lay down standards to be expected from persons in public life. The Committee on Standards in Public Life was appointed by the prime minister in 1994, but without a statutory basis as a standing (permanent) committee. Its wide terms of reference included the UK and European Parliaments, central and local gov-ernment and other publicly funded bodies such as universities and local voluntary bodies. In its first report (Nolan, 1995) the Committee promulgated seven 'Principles of Public Life' that subsequently became widely regarded as representing the core values applicable in public life and public service of all kinds. These principles are as follows: 'selflessness, integrity, objectivity, accountability, openness, honesty, and leadership'. The principles are supported by what Nolan called 'common threads', these being mechanisms used to imbed the prin-ciples into governmental institutions. These are codes of conduct, independent scrutiny and guidance and education. The Committee, currently chaired by Sir Brian Wicks, reports to the prime minister in relation to standards of conduct of all holders of public office but does not investigate complaints against individuals. It quickly became very influential and generated other regulatory bodies. A Parliamentary Commissioner for Standards was created in 1996 to adjudicate upon questions arising out of MPs' interests and to report to the Standards and Privileges Committee of the House of Commons thus creating enforceable adjudicative machinery. However, being appointed by the Commons, serving only for a fixed renewable term and depending on the Commons for resources the PCS has limited independence. Furthermore the Commissioner cannot publish its own reports. There is also a Commissioner for Public Appointments created under the royal prerogative, a civil service commission (which long pre-dated Nolan), and a House of Lords Appointments Commission. Codes of conduct have been produced for MPs, non-departmental public bodies and existing ministerial, civil service and local government codes have been revised (see 1st Report 1995 cm. 2850). The most recent report (Neill, 2000b) suggested that the House of Lords should be subject to a formal code relating to conflicts of interest. The Committee is currently examining standards in the Commons and the relationships between ministers, political advisors and civil servants.

The Nolan principles have also been incorporated into the law both directly by statute and indirectly by the courts (e.g. Northern Ireland Act 1998 s. 16(4); see Bridge in Economides *et al.*, 2000). After its Fifth Report (1998) on the funding of political parties a statutory Electoral Commission was created to ensure openness and accountability in the conduct of elections and campaign funding (Political Parties, Elections and Referendums Act 2000). There is also a commission to enforce standards in local government (Local Government Act 2000). It has been suggested that the standards of public life translated into legal principles such as fairness, rationality, proportionality and respect for rights might form the basis of general public law reform (see Oliver in Taggart, 1997; Harlow, 1997).

4.10 The Judiciary

The third branch of government is the judiciary. The judges act in the Queen's name since their powers historically derive from the royal functions of keeping order and doing justice. However, since the seventeenth century, the judicial function has been separate from the executive functions of the Crown and it is settled that the Crown cannot establish new courts or interfere with judicial decision making. Moreover the common law is generated by the judges themselves and derives from the values of the community rather than from the will of the government. On the other hand the appointment powers, procedures and administration of the judiciary is regulated by statute and is subject to considerable executive influence. It is particularly important for the judges to be independent and we shall deal with this in the next chapter in relation to the separation of powers. In this section we shall outline the law governing the status of the judiciary.

Judges of the Court of Appeal and the House of Lords are appointed by the Queen on the advice of the prime minister. Other judges including magistrates are appointed on the advice of the Lord Chancellor. Tribunal members are appointed by ministers under particular statutes but sometimes from a panel nominated by the Lord Chancellor. Tribunals are supervised by an independent Council on Tribunals which is concerned to protect their independence from the executive (see Tribunals and Inquiries Act 1992).

Superior court judges, that is judges of the High Court and above, cannot be dismissed by the Crown except following a resolution of both Houses of Parliament (another constitutional safeguard in the hands of the House of Lords), and then only for misconduct (Supreme Court Act 1981, s. 11 (3); Appellate Jurisdiction Act 1876 s. 6). An alternative interpretation of these provisions is that the Crown can dismiss a judge for misbehaviour without an address from Parliament, but on an address a judge can be dismissed by Parliament irrespective of misbehaviour. In exceptional circumstances judges can be removed by the Lord Chancellor on medical grounds (Supreme Court Act 1981 s. 11 (8)). Superior court judges must retire at 70 (Judicial Pensions and Retirement Act 1993). The salaries of superior court judges are also safeguarded by statute.

The bulk of the judiciary (about 97%) are inferior court judges, magistrates or tribunal members. These comprise (i) circuit judges who hear criminal cases in the Crown court and civil cases in the county court; (ii) district judges who hear minor civil matters in the county court; (iii) magistrates both lay and stipendiary (full-time professionals); and (iv) part-time assistant recorders and recorders who hear certain criminal cases. Inferior court judges are appointed on the advice of the Lord Chancellor. They do not have full security of tenure but are appointed under various statutes which make different provisions for dismissal. Part-time judges are appointed for fixed periods, and whether they are renewed is in the hands of the Lord Chancellor (see Courts Act 1971 s. 21 (5)). Full-time judges, that is circuit judges and stipendiary magistrates, hold office until the retirement age of 70. They can be dismissed by the Lord Chancellor for incapacity or misbehaviour (Courts Act 1971 s. 17, s. 20). Lay magistrates hold office until retirement but may be removed by the Lord Chancellor without any particular grounds being specified (see Justices of the Peace Act 1997 ss. 5, 11, 16). Tribunal members are usually appointed for fixed terms and within that can in most cases be dismissed only with the consent of the Lord Chancellor (Tribunals And Inquiries Act 1992 s. 7).

4.11   The Privy Council

The Privy Council is the descendant of the medieval 'inner council' of trusted advisers to the King. Members of the Privy Council are appointed by the Queen on the advice of the prime minister. There are currently over 400 privy councillors including cabinet ministers, senior judges and miscellaneous worthies who have attracted the approval of the prime minister. The cabinet is sometimes said to be a committee of the Privy Council although there is no legal basis for this assumption. Apart from its judicial function, the role of the Privy Council is largely formal, or, in Bagehot's terms, dignified. Its approval is needed for certain important exercises of the royal prerogative known as prerogative orders in council, including for example the dissolution of Parliament and the regulation of the civil service, and also for 'statutory orders in council' where Parliament gives power to the executive to make laws in this form. Approval is usually given by a small deputation of councillors attending the Queen. The Privy Council also confers state recognition and legal personality by granting charters to bodies such as universities and professional, scientific and cultural organisations. It can exercise some degree of supervision over such bodies.

Committees of the Privy Council have certain important functions. In particular the judicial committee is the final court of appeal from those commonwealth countries who choose to retain its services, in which capacity it is familiar with broad constitutional reasoning. The judicial committee is made up from the Law Lords together with judges of the country under whose laws the appeal is heard. Importantly the Privy Council has jurisdiction over devolution issues including human rights matters under the Scotland Act 1998, the Northern Ireland Act 1998 and the Government of Wales Act 1998. It also has jurisdiction in respect of ecclesiastical courts, medical professional bodies, peerage claims, election petitions and appeals from the Channel Islands and the Isle of Man. Not being strictly a court, the judicial committee can give advisory opinions to the government (Judicial Committee Act 1833 s. 4). It has been suggested that recent constitutional reforms, notably devolution and the Human Rights Act 1998, call for the introduction of a constitutional Supreme Court. This might replace, both the Privy Council and the House of Lords the status of which as part of the executive and legislature respectively is explicable only historically and seems to serve no useful purpose.

4.12 Citizenship

Citizenship in the sense of a participating member of a political community is an idea originating in ancient Greece and revived in eighteenth-century Europe. This is, however, a sense unknown to English law, the objects of which are in theory 'subjects' of the Crown with rights and duties flowing from that relationship. Subjection to the Crown arises out of either presence in the territory or a claim of allegiance (below). Citizenship is one way of creating allegiance and also confers certain specific rights.

Entitlement to British citizenship is governed mainly by the British Nationality Act 1981. The subject of citizenship is complex due to the collapse of the British Empire after the second World War and to the many changes that have been made subsequently in order to control immigration. Citizenship can be acquired by birth in the UK or the Falkland Islands (British Nationality (Falkland Islands) Act 1983). At least one parent must also be either a citizen or settled in the UK. Citizenship can also be acquired by descent from a British citizen, adoption, registration or naturalisation. Registration is a right available to persons born in the UK or who fulfil certain requirements of residence or parentage. Naturalisation is a matter for the discretion of the Secretary of State and is available to anyone, subject to conditions of residence, language and good character. In certain cases such as conviction of a serious offence naturalised citizens may be deprived of citizenship.

Citizenship as such is legally important in the following respects:

1. Citizenship confers a right of abode in the UK under immigration law (Immigration Act 1971 s. 1). Certain commonwealth citizens who can trace historic connections with the UK also have a right of abode (which cannot be exercised by polygamous wives (Immigration Act 1988 s. 2). European Union nationals also have certain rights of residence in relation to working in the UK. Citizens of the Republic of Ireland are exempt from immigration control but can be expelled (Immigration Act 1971 s. 1 (3)).

2. British, Irish and commonwealth citizens, lawfully resident in the UK may vote in parliamentary and local elections (Representation of the People Act 2000). Non-citizens (other than Irish citizens) cannot be members of either House of Parliament.

3. Honours and titles cannot be conferred upon non-citizens.

4. British citizens have a right to call upon the protection of the Crown when abroad, although this is not enforceable in the courts. The main consequence of the Crown's duty to protect British citizens abroad is that the Crown cannot require payment for such protection unless the person concerned voluntarily exposes him or herself to some special risk (see *China Navigation Co. Ltd* v. *A-G* (1932); *Mustasa* v. *A-G* (1980)).

5. British citizens abroad are subject to special taxation laws.

   British citizens cannot generally be removed (deportation) or excluded from the UK, but there are two exceptions. Firstly a citizen can be extradited to stand trial or serve a sentence in another country with which the UK has an extradition treaty. This requires a court recommendation and a decision by the Home Secretary. The offence concerned must also be an offence of substantially the same kind in the UK (Extradition Act 1989 s. 2). In the case of commonwealth countries no treaty is required (Fugitive Offenders Act 1967), and there are special arrangements with Ireland. Secondly, under emergency legislation relating to Northern Ireland, the Home Secretary can exclude or remove even a citizen from Great Britain who has not been 'ordinarily resident' for at least three years (see Chapter 19).

6. Non citizens, whom the Secretary of State suspects to be involved in terrorism can in certain circumstances be detained without charge (Anti-Terrorism, Crime and Disorder Act 2000).

There are other categories of British dependent territories' citizenship, but these do not confer substantial rights. Under the British Nationality (Hong Kong) Act 1997 the Secretary of State was empowered to confer citizenship on certain residents of Hong Kong. This was to enable the UK government to select persons it deemed suitable to live in the UK after the return of Hong Kong to China in 1997. The government has announced an intention to confer British citizenship upon the citizens of the remaining dependent territories of the UK.

4.12.1 Allegiance

The legal basis of the relationships between the Crown and the individual is that of monarch and subject. The linking concept is the feudal bond of allegiance. This has two main practical consequences. Firstly, the Crown probably cannot plead the defence of 'Act of State' against a person who owes allegiance (see Chapter 12). Second, the offence of treason is committed against the duty of allegiance.

All British citizens owe allegiance wherever they are in the world (see *R.* v. *Casement* (1917)). Aliens resident in the UK also owe allegiance (*de Jager* v. *A-G* (1907)). A person who holds a valid British passport apparently owes allegiance even if he has never visited the UK and even if the passport has been fraudulently obtained (see Joyce v. *DPP* (1946)). Allegiance cannot be voluntarily surrendered (*R.* v. *Lynch* (1903)), nor probably can the Crown remove the status since it binds the Crown as well as the subject. Thus allegiance could be regarded as an assertion of individualism compared with the communitarian concept of citizenship, conferring as it does rights against the Crown.

4.13   Constitutional Reform

The Labour government, which was elected in 1997 and re-elected in 2001, embarked on a wide-ranging programme of miscellaneous constitutional reforms. This programme remains incomplete but was claimed to disperse power, to enhance individual rights and create greater openness. However, the desire for reform may conflict with the self-interest of the government in protecting its own power. We shall discuss the individual reforms in their context but for convenience will list the highlights here.

1. Political and legal power has been devolved to some extent away from the centre towards regional bodies in Scotland, Wales and Northern Ireland each of which now has an elected government, albeit subordinate to the Westminster Parliament. It is an 'asymetrical' devolution in that each region has a different extent and structure of devolved government. For example Wales has no power to make legislation but depends on power being delegated by Parliament. England alone has no elected government of its own.
2. The European Convention on Human Rights has been incorporated into UK law by the Human Rights Act 1998 thereby allowing the courts to pronounce upon the compatibility of UK law with broader international ideas of human rights, although not to override Acts of Parliament.
3. The House of Lords, is currently undergoing reform to remove the hereditary element although the details of this remain uncertain.
4. The question of electoral reform remains somewhat precariously on the political agenda due to a widespread belief that the current simple majority voting system produces governments that do not represent a sufficiently wide range of political opinion. The electoral system for the devolved governments, for the London Mayor and for the European Parliament all depart from the simple majority system so that UK voters now experience a variety of electoral methods.
5. There have been reforms in relation to the financial affairs of political parties in order to ensure accountability and openness (Political Parties, Elections and Referendums Act 2000).
6. The Freedom of Information Act 2000 gives the public access to official documents but is widely regarded as weak, with the government retaining control over several categories of information. It is unlikely to be implemented before 2005.

7. Local government has been reformed by requiring local authorities to put in place structures which separate the executive from the elected council with a view to increasing accountability. In the case of London there is now an elected mayor with a wide range of policy-making functions but limited executive powers.
8. It is proposed to strengthen the independence of the civil service by statute.

Summary

4.1 Dicey regarded the primary characteristics of the UK constitution as (i) the rule of law; (ii) parliamentary supremacy; (iii) the ultimate political sovereignty of the electorate. According to the traditional model of the constitution there is a democratic chain of accountability that makes the Crown subject to elected ministers, and ministers subject to the people through Parliament. In practice, however, the executive is usually able to dominate Parliament and ministerial responsibility may obscure rather than focus responsibility. There is considerable reliance on extra-parliamentary sources of influence in particular by means of the prime minister's power of patronage.

4.2 The historical development of the constitution has been evolutionary in the sense that the same basic institutions of Crown, Parliament and courts have remained and adjusted to changing circumstances. However, there has been continuous struggles for control of Crown and Parliament. Parliament triumphed over the Crown in the 1688 revolution. During the following three centuries, the monarchy lost personal power, Parliament gradually became democratic, the House of Commons became superior to the House of Lords and the executive increasingly dominated Parliament. During the eighteenth century the UK constitution was widely admired as a stable balance between the forces of monarchy, aristocracy and democracy but until the extension of the franchise in the late nineteenth century was actually dominated by aristocratic interests. From then on, political parties came to dominate Parliament, in effect controlling the Crown as well.

4.3 The traditional constitution is often attacked. On one view, the executive has become all-powerful. On another view, power has been dispersed upwards into international bodies and downwards into unelected specialist bodies, in both cases beyond the reach of Parliament and only spasmodically controlled by the elected government.

4.4 The Crown is the central executive with inherent royal prerogative powers. However, Parliament can give executive powers to anyone, and in recent years executive powers have been distributed across a wide variety of public and private bodies using mechanisms copied from the practices of commercial companies. This raises fundamental questions of accountability.

4.5 According to the doctrine of ministerial responsibility ministers are responsible to Parliament for the conduct of their departments and for executive agencies sponsored by their departments. The civil service is responsible to ministers but not directly to Parliament. This protection aims to provide a continuity and stability enabling the civil service to carry out the policies of successive governments with equal commitment. However, ministerial responsibility may be regarded as an unrealistic burden in the context of the size and complexity of modern government departments and it is not clear how far a minister should be regarded as personally culpable for the wrongs of his or her department. Nevertheless, apart from the courts there is no alternative accountability mechanism.

4.6 Perceived weaknesses in the traditional methods of accountability have led to attempts to formulate standards of behaviour for persons holding public office. Except in the case of Northern Ireland these are without direct legal force.

4.7 Superior court judges comprise the High Court, Court of Appeal and House of Lords together with certain specialised courts and tribunals. These have almost complete security of tenure. Their salaries and pensions are safeguarded by statute and they can be dismissed only by both Houses of Parliament.

4.8 Inferior court judges comprise circuit judges, who hear criminal cases in the Crown court and civil cases in the county court; recorders, who hear criminal cases; and also various kinds of magistrate including lay part-time justices of the peace. Their security of tenure varies with the legislation relating to the particular post. Lay justices have no legal security of tenure.

4.9 Judges are protected against legal actions, and can punish for contempt of court those who hamper the legal process.

4.10 The Privy Council while being a legacy of the medieval and Tudor constitutions has important functions as an appeal court in commonwealth cases, devolution cases and in connection with professional discipline and the regulation of chartered bodies. It is sometimes argued that the Privy Council should take on the role of a supreme or constitutional court.

4.11 Citizenship entitles a person to reside in the UK and has certain other miscellaneous consequences. However, the basic legal relationship between the state and the individual is one of Crown and subject, involving the concept of allegiance. The Crown has (unenforceable) duties to protect the individual while the individual has a duty of loyalty. Allegiance carries few specific legal consequences.

Further Reading

Bridge, 'Standards, principles and values in the public law of the United Kingdom', in Economides *et al.* (eds), *Fundamental Values*.

Committee on Standards in Public Life, 6th Report, 1999, cm. 4557.

Finer, Bogdanor, Rudden, *Comparing Constitutions*, Chapter 2.

Hennessey, *The Hidden Wiring*, Chapter 1.

Himsworth C. (1996) 'In a state no longer: the end of constitutionalism', *Public Law* 639.

Holiday, I. (2000) 'Is the British State Hollowing out?' 71 *Political Quarterly* 167.

Irvine, Lord D. 'Government's Programme of Constitutional Reform' http://www. open.gov.uk/lcd/speeches/1998/lc-const.htm

Jenkins, K., Caines, K. and Jackson, A. (1988) *Prime Minister's Efficiency Unit: Improving Management in Government. The Next Steps*, London: HMSO.

Jenkins, S. (1996) *Accountable to None*.

Marr, A. (1996) *Ruling Britannia*.

Morison and Livingstone, *Reshaping Public Power: Northern Ireland and the British Constitutional Crisis*, Chapters 1, 2, 6.

Nolan and Sedley (1997) *The Making and Remaking of the British Constitution*, Chapters 1, 3, 5.

Oliver, D. (1994) 'Law, politics and public accountability: the search for a new equilibrium', *Public Law* 238.

Oliver, D. (1995), 'Standards of conduct in public life: what standards?', *Public Law* 497.

Rhodes, R. (1994) 'The hollowing out of the state: the changing nature of the public service in Britain' 65 *Political Quarterly*, 138.

Rhodes, 'The new governance: governing without government' (1996), 44 *Political Studies* 652.

University of Cambridge Centre for Public Law (1998), *Constitutional Reform in the United Kingdom*, Cambridge: CUP.

Willet (ed.) *Public Sector Reform and the Citizen's Charter*.

Exercises

4.1   To what extent is the historical development of the UK constitution an example of the triumph of democracy?

4.2   You are a civil servant asked to draft a written constitution for Britain. Unfortunately you only have the information available in this chapter and the preceding chapters. Produce a draft.

4.3   Explain the significance of the distinction between a parliamentary constitution and a presidential constitution.

4.4   Argue the case for and against an independent civil service with particular reference to 'special advisers'.

4.5   To what extent is the traditional doctrine of ministerial responsibility to Parliament an adequate basis for government accountability?

4.6   To what extent is it possible to classify executive bodies in a legally significant way?

4.7   What constitutional problems are raised by a), 'the new public management' and b) non-departmental public bodies?

4.8   What problems of constitutional accountability are raised by public/private partnerships?

4.9   Bill, a High Court judge, is alleged to have been sexually harassing the junior staff of the High Court Registry. Parliament is not sitting and the Lord Chancellor advises the Queen to make an example of Bill by dismissing him forthwith. Advise Bill.

4.10   Compare the position of superior court judges with judges of the lower courts as regards judicial independence.

5 Constitutionalism: The Rule of Law and the Separation of Powers

5.1 Introduction: The Nature and Purpose of the Rule of Law

The concept of the 'rule of law' is paradoxical. In a literal sense it requires us to be prisoners of an impersonal authority and subject to unpleasant consequences if we transgress. In *The Pilgrim's Progress* Bunyan asks, '(h)e to whom thou was sent for ease, being by name legality, is the son of the Bond-woman ... how canst thou expect by them to be made free?'. On the other hand the rule of law is often regarded as a liberal, and indeed as liberating idea. This is because, as Hobbes perceived, 'freedom lies in the silence of the laws'. Law is therefore two faced. It confines us but outside its limits we are free and equal, authority having no place. Thus the emphasis of the rule of law is upon ensuring that those who enforce the law keep within its limits.

There is, however, disagreement as to what we mean by asserting that law has limits. The Hobbesian view is that the lawmaker has unlimited power so that the limits of the law are purely formal in the sense that that they lie in the structure and processes of the law irrespective of its content. Nevertheless, it is an important safeguard that those in power must justify their decisions by reference to an existing law. A broader view, rooted in Locke, is that the rule of law requires the law to have a certain substantive content which reflects the fundamental values of 'constitutionalism' in a democratic society, in particular respect for equal individuals. These approaches were combined by Lord Griffiths in *R* v. *Horseferry Rd Magistrates Court ex parte Bennett* [1993] 3 WLR 90, 104, when he said 'the judiciary accept a responsibility for the maintenance of the rule of law that embraces a willingness to oversee executive action and to refuse to countenance behaviour that threatens either basic human rights or the rule of law.'

The term constitutionalism expresses this idea. Hunt (1997, p. 22), supporting the broad view of the rule of law, describes the notion of constitutionalism thus: 'in any democratic system there are certain transcendental values that which enjoy a "constitutional" status, in the sense that they embody fundamental ideas or aspirations which democracy itself presupposes and which therefore cut across the political programmes of particular governments ... the bare minimum that is required of a commitment to constitutionalism is a rejection of the instrumentalist conception of law which sees it as a mere tool to be used by governments in order to achieve their political goals'. Allan (2001, p. 2) expresses a similar sentiment: 'the equal dignity of citizens, with its implications for fair treatment and respect for individual autonomy is the basic premise of liberal constitutionalism, and accordingly the ultimate meaning of the rule of law'.

The idea of the rule of law is deeply embedded in European political culture. In its different aspects it plays a dominant role in literature such as the *Antigone* of Sophocles and Shakespeare's *Merchant of Venice*. Aristotle (384–322 BC) pronounced that it is better for the law to rule than for any of the citizens to rule (*Politics* III.16, 1087a 19). The rule of law was described by the thirteenth-century jurist Bracton in terms that 'the King should be under no man but under God and the Law because the Law makes him King'. Magna Carta (1215) expresses the core concept (and its ambivalence): 'no freeman shall be taken or imprisoned or be disseissed of his freehold, or liberties or free customs or be outlawed or exiled or in any wise destroyed ... but by ... the law of the land'. In *X Ltd* v. *Morgan Grampian Publishers Ltd* [1990] 2 All ER 1 at 13, Lord Bridge said 'the maintenance of the rule of law is in every way as important in a free society as the democratic franchise' (see also *Pierson* v. *Secretary of State* (below)). Both the public order and the democratic aspects of the rule of law are central to the European Convention on Human Rights (see *Klass* v. *Federal Republic of Germany* (1978)).

The ideal of the rule of law goes back to the Anglo-Saxon notion of a compact between ruler and ruled under which obedience to the king was conditional upon the king respecting the law. Magna Carta (1215) symbolises this, notably in the principle of due-process in independent courts and, in the subject's right to refuse financial support to a king who violates the law. The eighteenth-century constitution was particularly influenced by the rhetoric of the rule of law. The constitution was regarded as a delicately balanced machine held in place by the rule of law; as George III put it, 'the most beautiful balance ever framed' (Briggs, 1959, p. 88). The rule of law protected individual rights imagined as being grounded in ancient common law tradition. Unlike the case in France, there was no doctrine that state necessity could override the ordinary law (*Entick* v. *Carrington* (1765)).

During the early nineteenth century too, there was a widespread belief that the relative stability and economic prosperity enjoyed by Britain was connected with a commitment to the rule of law. By contrast France with its 'demagoguary, revolt, beheadings and ... unruly mobs stood in English "common sense" as a dreadful warning of all that can go wrong, a sort of conceptual opposite to England's altogether more sensible ways' (Pugh, 1997, p. 168). However, with the expansion of democracy that took place from the mid-nineteenth century, common law ideas became increasingly confronted by the demand for greater state provision of services which could only be delivered through Parliament by radical reform which changed the balance of the constitution in favour of the executive.

5.2   The Core Meaning of the Rule of Law

There is a basic meaning of the rule of law in the sense of government through general rules laid down in advance by an accepted authority. We shall call this the core meaning of the rule of law. The rule of law in this sense is concerned with law as a means of guiding the behaviour of its subjects. The notion of a general rule entails the basic principle of equal treatment under it and this is perhaps the most important idea captured by the rule of law. If they are genuinely to guide behaviour, laws require good qualities such as non-retrospectivity, stability, accessibility, advance publicity, and open access to a means of settling disputes impartially and consistently perhaps even a right to legal advice (see Raz, 1977). There should also be safeguards against the abuse of official power, otherwise the enterprise of government by rules loses public credibility.

Even Hobbes acknowledged the rule of law in this sense. It will be recalled from Chapter 2 that Hobbes regarded law as the absolute command of a sovereign who, although not having any special powers of goodness or reason, is authorised by the people in the interests of resolving conflict to act on their behalf. Nevertheless Hobbes emphasised that the sovereign's commands must be recognised by formal public signs, must be general and must be clear and determinate. Moreover there must be institutions such as courts empowered to adjudicate conclusively upon disputes thus bringing qualities of fairness and independence into play. Moreover, where the law is unclear, the judge must 'mimic the sovereign' by bringing to bear his or her 'natural reason' on the matter. Where Hobbes and the common lawyers parted company is that Hobbes denied that the judges and the common law have any special claim to 'right reason'. He regarded the pretensions of professional lawyers as merely claims to power (see Postema, 1986, p. 46 *et seq.*).

The core version of the rule of law can be described as a formal con-cept since it seems to allow any infringement of liberty provided that it is carried out through legal processes. To its detractors, formalism is a term of abuse carrying the implications of sterile hair-splitting and pedantic legalism at the expense of the achievement of the preferred goals of the detractors. This point of view is usually associated with a utilitarian perspective and regards law as a delivery mechanism for state policy (see Harlow and Rawlings, 1997, ch. 2).

To its liberal supporters on the other hand, formalism is a valuable achievement of the human mind as a defence not only against tyrants but also against well-meaning busybodies who seek to impose them-selves on us. Formalism also ensures that the judges have to justify their decisions rationally and by reference to existing principles thereby limiting their power.

On the other hand it could be maintained that the core rule of law comprises no more than administrative regularity that enables des-potic government to rule efficiently since people are more likely to fall into line where rules are enforced in accordance with a predictable procedure. If government merely took the form of the whim of a tyrant, people would be more likely to risk disobedience and the tyrant would lack the means to ensure that his wishes were given effect. Furthermore, the protection of law can most effectively be taken advantage of by the wealthy and privileged classes, that is, those who benefit from the governing regime (Horwitz, 1977). On the other hand, as Thompson points out (1975, p. 264) 'it was inherent in the nature of the medium which they had selected for their own self-defence that it could not be reserved for the exclusive use only of their own class. In order to retain credibility a tyrant must conform to his own rules. The law in its forms and traditions, entailed principles of equity and universality which perforce had to be extended to all sorts and degrees of men.' The core idea of rule of law is therefore morally ambiguous.

5.3 The Extended Rule of Law

Some writers, notably Fuller (1969) and Allan (2001), have promoted the notion of the rule of law in an expanded sense as supporting the substantive values of a liberal democracy. This means a commitment to government by consent which respects equality and human dignity and which through obedience to the law honours its obligations to the people. This meaning of the rule of law reflects the social contract of

Locke. For example, according to Allan (2001, p. 62), '(t)he principle that laws will be faithfully applied, according to the tenor in which they would reasonably be understood by those affected, is the most basic tenet of the rule of law: it constitutes that minimal sense of reciprocity between citizen and state that inheres in any form of decent government, where law is a genuine barrier to arbitrary power.'

In this extended sense the rule of law has three main aspects. Firstly it means that no one is above the law in the sense that officials must justify any interference with individual liberty by reference to a power given to them by the law; secondly, there is arguably a right to disobey a law that violates the basic values of liberal democracy. Thirdly there are certain values of fairness and justice particularly associated with law. For example Fuller (1969) includes stability, openness, clarity, coherence and fair procedures such as a right to be heard before an unbiased judge that he calls the 'inner morality of law.' This is similar to Raz's list (above) although the latter justifies the list on efficiency rather than moral grounds. A similar approach was endorsed by Lord Hoffmann in *Alconbury Developments* v. *Secretary of State* [2001] 2 All ER 929, 981) when he emphasised that in a democratic society the rule of law means that the legality of government action must be subject to review by independent and impartial tribunals.

Allan (2001) goes further by adding substantive values such as freedom of expression, a right to information and non-discrimination. He also emphasises the importance of the adversarial method of deciding disputes which treats the parties as equals, each having a right to present their case to an impartial judge. According to this version of the rule of law, the state has no power to override these basic rights except for justifiable reasons of the public welfare (see also Lord Hoffmann in *Alconbury* (above) at 980). The rule of law can therefore be regarded as a set of moral and political values intrinsic to the legal process that supports a democratic society.

It is often suggested that the rule of law in this sense is so vague as to be no more than flag-waving rhetoric amounting merely to asserting what the protagonist would do if he or she ruled the country. The expanded rule of law is indeed a political preference and whether any particular preference is part of our constitution is purely a question of historical fact. In other constitutions the rule of law may be based on different premises. For example the constitution of Iran is based upon the rule of a supreme jurist as interpreter of divine law. It is plausible as a matter of historical fact that liberal individualism has a powerful influence on the political arrangements of the UK and there is no reason to think that any alternative is more influential.

A range of consequences follow including the need for a separation of powers between the lawmaker, the executive and the courts and the giving of special weight to individual rights. Moreover there must be political machinery to ensure that the actions of public officials serve the common good. This includes open government, a right to reasons for decisions and frequent elections. There must also be legal mechanisms to ensure legality. In this connection the extended rule of law has concrete recommendations about what should be done in order to ensure that all relevant points of view are treated with equal respect. These include judicial review (Chapter 16), the Human Rights Act 1998 (Chapter 18), and the freedom of the media to criticise government (Chapter 19).

5.4 Dicey's Version of the Rule of Law

There is a particular English version of the rule of law famously promoted by A.V. Dicey (1885) which still influences the way lawyers conceive the constitution. Dicey's version of the rule of law emphasises the ideas of generality, certainty and equality but goes further in stressing the common law basis of the constitution with its emphasis on the individual and its independence of government (see *R. v. Secretary of State ex parte Pierson* [1997] 3 All ER 577 at 606 per Lord Steyn).

Dicey formulated a threefold version of the rule of law.

(i) *The absolute supremacy or predominance of 'regular' law as opposed to arbitrary power and the absence of discretionary authority on the part of government. 'No man is punishable or can be lawfully made to suffer in body or goods except for a distinct breach of law established in the ordinary legal manner before the ordinary courts.'*

This means firstly that no official can interfere with individual rights without the backing of a specific law. For example in *R v. Somerset CC ex parte Fewings* [1995] 1 All ER 513 Laws J said (at 524) that the principles that govern the application of the rule of law to public bodies and private persons are 'wholly different' in the sense that 'the freedoms of the private citizen are not conditional upon some distinct and affirmative justification for which he must burrow in the law books' ... But for public bodies the rule is opposite and so of another character altogether. It is that any action to be taken must be justified by positive law.' Laws J described this as one of the sinews of the rule of law and, as Hobbes put it, 'Freedom lies in the silence of the laws.' However, this only applies to acts that interfere with legal rights as such. For example in *R* v. *Secretary of State for Social Services ex parte C* (2000), it was held that a government department was entitled to place a man's name on a child abuse black-list without giving him a prior right to be heard. Although entry on the register harmed the individual by destroying his job prospects, his legal rights were not infringed.

Secondly Dicey believed that officials should not have wide discretionary powers. For example in *Rantzen* v. *Mirror Group Newspapers* (1994) the Court of Appeal condemned the wide discretion given to juries to fix the amount of damages in libel cases as violating the rule of law. However, governmental discretion is inevitable. Rules cannot be devised to deal with every possible case, and modern government with its concern for child welfare, public health and education could hardly operate without discretionary powers in order to tailor decisions to individual circumstances. Resources also run out and choices have to be made between competing goals (see e.g. *R* v. *Cambridge Health Authority ex parte B* (1995); experimental medical treatment). Discretion is also essential to lighten the burden of the strict law. The police do not have to prosecute everyone. The Revenue may release a taxpayer from a tax burden.

It is often asserted, particularly by those in power, that discretion is good because it enables power to be exercised benevolently. For example the Anti-Terrorism, Crime and Security Act 2001 gives wide powers to official bodies to exchange information both with each other and with overseas police which they hold about individuals. This has been defended on the basis that the officials concerned have a discretion which they will use reasonably (see *Observer*, 25.11.2001, www.observer.co.uk/libertywatch). Dicey emphasises the republican belief namely that it is degrading to rely on the notion of a kind master. Moreover, Dicey did not rule out all discretionary power but only 'wide arbitrary or discretionary power of constraint' (1915, p. 184). He insisted on limits to and controls over the exercise of discretion. These include guidelines based on the purposes for which the power is given and standards of reasonableness and fairness. In other words, the rule of law is a broad guide to the values which should underpin the law (see Endicott, 1999).

(ii) *Equality before the law; everyone whether high official or ordinary citizen is subject to the same law administered by ordinary courts.*
Dicey believed that everyone is subject to the same law administered by the ordinary courts. He did not mean that there are identical rules for everyone and that no one has special privileges. This would have been obviously untrue. The law singles out many groups, for example,

the Crown, MPs, foreign governments, judges, diplomats and police officers all of whom have special duties and privileges. The rule of law, however, requires that any special treatment must be justified on the ground of public welfare and also in accordance with current ideas of human rights (see *R.* v. *Port Talbot BC ex parte Jones* (1988)). By contrast for example the Hampshire police force once announced that it gave special treatment to 'high-profile' people accused of offences (see *Guardian*, 19 November 1998).

Most importantly Dicey meant that officials enjoy no special protection as such. This has two aspects. Firstly, if an official exceeds or abuses his power, he is personally liable just as if he were a private citizen. For example, a policeman who unlawfully enters property is a trespasser whom I can sue for compensation. Nevertheless this is not adequate to remedy abuses of the wide-ranging powers of modern government. Many official powers, for example the improper refusal of a welfare payment or of a council home, have no parallel in the world of private citizens, thus making Dicey's principle irrelevant (see *Cocks* v. *Thanet DC* (1983)). Secondly disputes between government and citizen are settled in the ordinary courts according to the ordinary law rather than in some special governmental court such as the notorious prerogative courts, including the Star Chamber, which were abolished in the seventeenth century. In this respect Dicey (1915, p. 333) compared English law favourably with the law of France where there is a special system of law and courts dealing with the powers of government (*droit administratif* enforced by the administrative *Conseil D'Etat*). Dicey thought that special administrative courts would give the government special privileges and shield the individual wrongdoer behind the cloak of the state. Jennings (1959), however, argued that Dicey had misunderstood the system of *droit adminstratif* which in fact provided effective remedies for abuse of power. Moreover the *Conseil D'Etat* can be defended on separation of powers grounds providing a good example of how the rule of law can be understood differently in different political cultures.

This aspect of Dicey's teaching has had great influence upon the UK constitution. Until as recently as the 1970s there was resistance to the idea of special courts and judges to deal with disputes involving governmental powers. Since 1977, however, a version of public law has been introduced, albeit within the ordinary court system. This centres upon a special procedure in the Administrative Court designed for the purpose of challenging government decisions. In partial vindication of Dicey, however, attempts to distinguish between public law and private law have floundered (see below, Chapter 17). There are also numerous 'special' systems of law, such as social security law and immigration law, which deal with disputes between the individual and the state. These are administered by specialist tribunals outside the ordinary courts which often include lay people. Such tribunals are speedier, cheaper, more informal, and even sometimes more expert than the 'regular courts'. However, they are usually subject to the supervision of the ordinary courts.

(iii) *The constitution is the 'result' of the ordinary law.*
Dicey's third meaning of the rule of law derives from the common law tradition and relates to the extended notion of the rule of law. He believed that the UK constitution, not being imposed from above in the form of a written constitution, was the result of decisions by the courts in particular cases, and was therefore embedded in the very fabric of the law and backed by practical remedies. This promotes equality between citizen and state by treating private law with its concentration on individual rights as the basic ideological perspective of the constitution and encouraging the courts, not to construe a statute as violating basic rights. For example in *R.* v. *Lord Chancellor ex parte Witham* (1997) it was held that regulations made by the Lord Chancellor which provided for a minimum fee of £100 to issue a writ were invalid because that they discriminated against low-income people. Laws J put the matter in constitutional terms. 'In the unwritten legal order of the British State, at a time when the common law continues to accord a legislative supremacy to Parliament, the notion of a constitutional right can in my judgement inhere only in this proposition that the right in question cannot be abrogated by the state save by specific provision in an Act of Parliament ... General words will not suffice. And any such rights will be creatures of the common law, since their existence would not be the consequence of the democratic process but would be logically prior to it'. (See also *R.* v. *Secretary of State for the Home Department ex parte Simms* [1999] 3 All ER 400 at 411.)

The seminal case of *Entick* v. *Carrington* (1765) brings together all three aspects of Dicey's rule of law. The Secretary of State ordered two King's Messengers to search for Entick, accused of sedition, and to bring him with his books and papers before the Secretary of State. Entick sued the Messengers. The court held that the plea of 'state necessity' is unknown to the common law because there was no precedent from which it could be derived, that the practice of issuing general warrants giving a wide discretion is unlawful and open to challenge in any court, there being no special rights available to officials as such, and that the Messengers had no specific statutory authority regarding the particular papers that they seized. On the other hand, the more recent case of *R.* v. *IRC ex parte Rossminister Ltd* (1980) where Parliament had given a general power to tax officials to enter and search private premises illustrates the tension between the common law and parliamentary supremacy. Dicey tried to reconcile his rule of law with parliamentary supremacy but not entirely successfully. We shall discuss this in Chapter 6. Perhaps Dicey's version of the rule of law shows only that he trusted judges as a hedge against the popular democracy which he feared.

5.5 The International Rule of Law

Since the Second World War there have been several attempts to draw up internationally binding codes of basic human rights and to adjudicate in international courts promoting international rule of law standards. Modern international instruments include the United Nations Universal Declaration of Human Rights (1948), and the Declaration of Delhi (1959), an unofficial pronouncement of lawyers from 53 countries concerned primarily with the rule of law in the sense of fair procedures. There is also the Genocide Convention 1951 and the Torture Convention 1984. War Crimes Tribunals have been established by the UN Security Council to try those accused of atrocities in the former Yugoslavia and in Rwanda. These fail to meet the rule of law insistence on generality by being limited to particular countries. It is proposed to create a general international criminal court to deal with offences of this kind but the USA has not accepted this jurisdiction. Under the International Criminal Court Act 2001 there are powers to arrest persons suspected of genocide, crimes against humanity and war crimes, question them and deliver them to the International Criminal Court. The Act also creates offences of genocide, crimes against humanity and war crimes, wherever committed.

Of most immediate concern to UK law is the European Convention on Human Rights (ECHR). The European Convention on Human Rights, which drew heavily on the UN declaration (above), came into effect in 1952 under the auspices of the Council of Europe as a response to the fascist and communist atrocities that had disfigured much of the twentieth century. Individuals have a right to petition the European Court of Human Rights in respect of violations by states. Under the Human Rights Act 1998, most provisions of the Convention have belatedly been made binding in UK law although they do not override

Acts of Parliament (Chapter 18). The rule of law is central to the workings of the ECHR. For example, exceptions to the rights protected by the convention must be 'prescribed by law'. In this context 'a norm cannot be regarded as a law unless it is formulated with sufficient precision to enable a citizen to regulate his conduct: he must be able if need be with appropriate advice – to foresee, to a degree that is reasonable in the circumstances, the consequences which a given action may entail' (*Sunday Times* v. *UK* (1979); see also *Observer and Guardian Newspapers* v. *UK* (1992)).

The idea of the rule of law comes under particular stress when we realise that there is more than one kind of legal order and that clashes between the requirements of different legal orders, in particular between international law and domestic law may raise incommensurable values. International law as such is not automatically part of UK law, which has adopted a 'dualist' approach. This means that an international treaty, if it is to alter domestic law, must first be incorporated by statute into UK law. However, customary international law is recognised by the common law (*Chung Chi Cheung* v. *R.* [1939] AC 160 at 168; *R.* v. *Bow Street Magistrate ex parte Pinochet* (No. 3) [1999] 2 All ER 97 at 177). Therefore a treaty which embodies customary law may be part of UK law whether or not it is enacted.

The rule of law also comes under stress where its requirements clash with important political concerns, thus raising the question of immunity from the normal operation of the law. As we have seen, immunity is compatible with the rule of law provided that it is conferred by the law itself, for acceptable and proportionate reasons and its limits are clearly defined. *R.* v. *Bow Street Magistrate ex parte Pinochet Ugarte* (No. 3) (1999) revealed two broad approaches to immunity, one being concerned to harmonise domestic law with international values, the other being formalist, concerned with traditional notions of legal certainty.

The Spanish government had requested that Pinochet be extradited to Spain to stand trial in respect of murders and torture which he was alleged to have organised in Chile during his term of office. Traditionally the attitude of international law has been not to intervene in the internal affairs of a state except with its consent. In recent years, however, international concerns have begun to erode this principle and the Torture Convention 1984 requires a state either to prosecute or extradite an alleged offender. The Torture Convention had been translated into English law by the Criminal Justice Act 1988. Pinochet, however, relied on the widely accepted doctrine of state immunity, according to which a head of state cannot be tried in a domestic court. Complete immunity applies to serving heads of state. Immunity also applies to former heads of state but only in relation to official acts committed while they were in office. The traditional attitude of international law has been that the express consent of a state is required in order to override the immunity. The Torture Convention does not mention immunity at all.

The House of Lords, unusually comprising seven judges, eventually held that Pinochet was not entitled to immunity. However, their Lordships took different routes to their conclusions some applying the international rule of law directly while others looked for a peg in UK law.

Lords Browne-Wilkinson, Hutton, Saville and Phillips held that the matter depended on the 1988 Act but, because it was intended to implement a treaty, the Act must be construed in the light of that treaty rather than in accordance with English legal values. They held that state-sponsored torture violated fundamental principles of international law which Chile had accepted by signing the convention and was therefore not to be regarded as part of the official functions of a head of state which the immunity protected. They held, however, that Pinochet could only be extradited for offences which were alleged to have taken place after 29 September 1988 which was the date on which the Criminal Justice Act 1988 came into force. This reflects the rule-of-law value of non-retrospectivity.

Lord Millett, supported partly by Lord Hope and Lord Hutton, took a more radical approach. He argued that, irrespective of the Torture Convention, official torture was an international offence under a developing customary international law and was therefore unlawful at common law. For him there was no immunity even in respect of crimes committed before the 1988 Act. Similarly Lord Hutton said that 'certain crimes are so grave and so inhuman that they constitute crimes against international law and that the international community is under a duty to bring to justice a person who commits such crimes' (at 163).

Lord Goff, dissenting, took the 'core' rule of law perspective. He read the texts more strictly than the others, holding that the State Immunity Act 1978 s. 20 gives immunity to a former head of state in respect of official acts wherever committed subject to the established international principle that immunity must be expressly waived. He emphasised the value of legal certainty, pointing out the difficulty of drawing lines between overriding international offences as perceived by the majority and ordinary offences for which immunity can be claimed, and the problems that would be faced by former heads of state (such as Margaret Thatcher) who ventures abroad.

Pinochet therefore illustrates the conflict between the core and the expanded conceptions of the rule of law. The outcome seems to reinforce a cautiously expanded concept of the rule of law, namely that the courts will try to integrate domestic law with substantive values in the international order, at least where there is a statutory link between the two legal orders. However no single rationale commanded unanimous support.

5.6.   Dissent and the Rule of Law

Allan (2001, ch. 4) claims that the rule of law requires the individual to have the last word. He argues that, 'at the heart of the rule of law is the role of the individual moral conscience: any rule's entitlement to obedience, even when issued in apparent exercise of the state's authority, is ultimately a matter of personal moral judgement. This general principle governs the identification of relevant legal obligations as well as (other) moral obligations'. This seems to go beyond the commonplace observation that a person may sometimes have a moral right to break the law. Allan seems to suggest that an individual may have a *legal* right to disobey a law that violates his or her fundamental values, such a law being no law at all. This argument depends on the premise, derived from the social contract, that the rule of law depends on the consent of equal individuals. However, the consent normally envisaged is to the legal system as a whole rather than to particular rules within it. An invalid law or executive act is a nullity because it is not part of the system so that the citizen is entitled to ignore it although in practice the endorsement of a court is usually needed (see e.g. *Entick* v. *Carrington* (1765); *Boddington* v. *British Transport Police* (1998)). Allan's reasoning apparently means that a law could be a nullity against one person and not another.

However, in order to exercise his right to dissent the individual has to act rationally so as to consider the virtues of obeying the law in terms of co-operation with others and the fact that a given law has been enacted by democratic means. In other words the communitarian values proposed by Rousseau (Chapter 2) come into play in the sense that the citizen should subordinate his or her rationality to that of the 'general will'. The right to dissent therefore entails important supporting constitutional rights. These include a right of freedom of expression which extends to advocating disobedience to the law and also a right to information from the government so that the individual can make a proper informed decision.

Allan is not explicit as to how the right to dissent is to be protected. He accepts that the state, representing the community, has a right to enforce its laws but at the same time seems to regard the final decision as lying with the individual. Presumably the opinion of a court can be no more decisive on this matter than that of any other state agency. On the other hand, as Hobbes emphasised, the point of law is as an external and artificial *public* decision-making process intended to resolve disagreement, even if arbitrarily, since reason alone cannot resolve disagreement between incommensurable values, of which the right to dissent is an example. On this basis a legal right to disobey the law is contradictory. On the other hand even Hobbes accepted that a ruler who violates its basic duty to preserve life forfeits its authority. Therefore there is wide agreement that obedience to the law is conditional and the argument is really about what the conditions are.

5.7 The Separation of Powers

The doctrine of the separation of powers divides government between groups with different interests or purposes so that no power centre can act without the co-operation of others and each 'checks and balances' the others. Thus the separation of powers is a way of protecting the rule of law. Article 16 of the Declaration of the Rights of Man (1789) states that 'a society where rights are not secured or the separation of powers established has no constitution'. The separation of powers is associated with the civic republican tradition the aim of which is to prevent domination by any single group (Chapter 1). For example the notion of law would be meaningless if the lawmaker could interpret its own laws. In the words of James Madison 'The accumulation of all powers, legislative, executive and judiciary, in the same hands, whether of one, a few or many, and whether hereditary, self appointed, or elective, may justly be pronounced the very definition of tyranny' (*The Federalist* 4, 1987, p. 303). Thus in England the competition between two branches of government, parliament and the king, was settled by war in the seventeenth century while the third branch, the courts, stood on the sidelines.

In his most famous work *The Republic,* written in the third century BC, Plato's solution to the problem of ensuring just government was to train a specialist corps of philosopher kings with no other purpose but to rule. This classical ideal is reflected in the development in the late nineteenth century of the British higher civil service as an impartial elite of well-educated generalists. Today, however, there are pressures for civil servants to specialise and to be closer to politics and to the commercial world. Another way of supporting government by an elite is through a text claimed to be divine revelation authoritatively interpreted by a priesthood. This solution was rejected in Britain as result of the sixteenth-century reformation, producing a state church which over time ceased to have a significant role in government and which came to support religious freedom.

The opposite perception of government, endorsed by Hobbes, is that, disagreement is the condition of politics. Rulers are not necessarily wiser or better than anyone else. Indeed it can be argued that those who seek power over others are the very people least trustworthy to exercise it. Although Hobbes himself did not address the issue of controlling power, this perception leads to elaborate separation of powers structures designed to ensure that decisions are supported with as broad a consensus as possible between competing groups. The US constitution provides an extreme example.

5.7.1   The mixed constitution

There are several ways in which the powers of government can be divided. For example the idea of the 'mixed constitution' involves, not necessarily a distinction between the functions of the different bodies but ensures that the main interest groups have equal status with no single body able to act alone so as to check each other and to encourage co-operation and compromise. An early version of the mixed constitution featured in the Roman republic where power was divided between an aristocratic Senate and elected Tribunes. There is also the notion of the 'harmonious constitution'. This goes beyond the mixed constitution in emphasising what is in effect a safety mechanism, which requires intervention by one or other of the power-sharing groups in order to restore the balance where harmony is breaking down. For example when power is concentrated in an overactive executive with a frail parliamentary opposition and weak local government it may be important for the courts to be more active in exercising their powers (Verde, 2000; see *R.* v. *Secretary of State ex parte Fire Brigades Union* (1995), per Lord Mustill).

The mixed constitution relates to Aristotle's famous division of constitutions. Aristotle regarded participation in the life of the community as essential to human well-being. 'Justice' consisted of each person playing his allotted part in the community whether as slave or king, an idea that throughout history has been used to protect established interests. He postulated three basic forms of constitution, these being monarchy which provides authority, aristocracy (literally government by the 'best' people) which provides wisdom, and democracy which provides power. Aristotle thought that each was capable of corruption: monarchy into tyranny, aristocracy into oligarchy (the rule of a selfish minority) and factionalism, and democracy into chaos.

During the eighteenth century in particular the British constitution was often portrayed as a mixed constitution with the King, the House of Lords and the House of Commons each representing different 'estates' or interests. Blackstone (1723–80) praised this arrangement although he possibly underestimated the dominant influence held by the aristocracy of his day.

> Herein indeed consists the true excellence of the English government that all the parts of it form a mutual check upon each other. In the legislature the people are a check on the nobility and the nobility a check upon the people ... while the king is a check upon both which preserves the executive power from encroachments. And this very executive power is again checked and kept within due bounds by the two Houses ... For the two Houses naturally drawing in two directions of opposite interest, and the prerogative in another still different from them both, they mutually keep each other from exceeding their proper limits ... like three distinct powers in mechanics, they jointly compel the machine of government in a direction different from what either acting by itself would have done ... a direction which constitutes the true line of the liberty and happiness of the country.

Today, the mixed constitution remains in structure but has little practical reality. The monarch does not by convention exercise a veto and the House of Lords has lost most of its power over the Commons. Political parties have replaced the aristocracy leaving the courts as, arguably, the only effective independent element in the constitution. On the other hand the doctrine retains some resonance, most recently in the form of the Report of the Wakeham Commission on Reform of the House of Lords (2000). A central theme of the report was the desire, to ensure that the second chamber comprised a mixture of persons, mainly appointed but with a minority elected, who would make an engineered balance of interest groups deemed worthy by the ruling elite to participate. Wakeham rejected the idea of a wholly elected second chamber, on the ground that this might unacceptably restrict the elected House of Commons and therefore the government.

5.7.2   Montesquieu's version of the separation of powers

The mixed constitution must be distinguished from what is usually called the doctrine of the separation of powers. This divides government according to its functions. The doctrine has surfaced in various forms over the centuries. Locke, for example, distinguished between legislative, executive and what he called federative functions, these being concerned with the conduct of foreign affairs. He treated the judicial function as a particular aspect of the executive. The most influential version was formulated by Montesquieu in *The Spirit of the Laws* (1748). Modifying Locke, Montesquieu distinguished between legislative, executive and judicial functions arguing that if any two of these fall into the same hands there is a risk of tyranny. Montesquieu believed that the British constitution of his time embodied the separation of powers but possibly did not take into account the extent to which conventions were beginning to blur the distinction between the legislature and the executive.

There are three aspects to Montesquieu's version of the separation of powers. Firstly separation of function, secondly separation of personnel and thirdly checks and balances. When the courts refer to the separation of powers they may therefore use the concept in different senses. For example in *W.H. Smith Do It All Ltd* v. *Peterborough* [1991] 4 All ER 193 at 196, Mustill LJ remarked, apparently from a functional point of view that 'according to the doctrine of the separation of powers as understood in the United Kingdom, the legislative acts of the Queen in Parliament are impregnable'. On the other hand, in *X Ltd* v. *Morgan Grampian Publishers Ltd* [1990] 2 All ER 1 at 13 Lord Bridge seemed to have had the notion of checks and balances in mind when he referred to the 'twin foundations' of the rule of law namely 'the sovereignty of the Queen in Parliament in making the law and the sovereignty of the Queen's courts in interpreting and applying the law.' Sir Stephen Sedley referred to the 'discrete though interdependent' dual sovereignty between Parliament and the courts, each respecting the functions of the other (Nolan, 1997, p. 26).

R v. *Secretary of State for the Home Department ex parte Fire Brigade's Union* (1995) illustrated judicial disagreement between different versions of the separation of powers. The Criminal Justice Act 1988 provided a compensation scheme for the victims of crime. However, the Act was only to come into force on a day appointed by the Home Secretary. Claiming to act under the royal prerogative the Home Secretary introduced his own cheaper non-statutory scheme and did not arrange to bring the 1988 Act into force. A majority of the House of Lords, applying the checks and balances approach, held the minister had acted unlawfully by disabling himself from keeping under review, as required by Parliament, the decision to bring the Act into force.

However Lords Keith and Mustill (dissenting) took the view that the matter was a political one for which the minister should be held responsible to Parliament rather than the courts. The dissenters were apparently upholding the separation of powers in its functional sense. This was a question of lawmaking in respect of the minister's duty was only to Parliament. In *R* v. *H.M. Treasury ex parte Smedley* (1995), the 'checks and balances' separation between the executive and the judiciary was regarded as a matter of constitutional convention. The court deferred to Parliament, not by refusing to intervene where a government draft order giving effect to an EC treaty was alleged to be invalid, but by not making an enforceable order. (See also *R* v. *Secretary of State for Health ex parte Imperial Tobacco Ltd* (2000); – interim injunctions refused against an allegedly invalid EC ban on tobacco advertising because of deference to EC policy (Laws LJ dissenting).

These cases suggest that, while the separation of powers does not provide a grand constitutional framework, the doctrine has influence on a pragmatic level in particular contexts.

Some modern commentators have concluded that the separation of powers as such has little significance today. This is partly because the legislature is dominated by the executive and partly because it is claimed that the concept has little meaning, being used as an umbrella for different and conflicting ideas (see Marshall, 1971). Others have identified important separation of powers aspects in the UK constitution (see Allan, 2001; Munro, 1999, ch. 9; Barendt, 1998).

As often is the case the truth may lie in the middle. In the UK we do have three bodies with broadly different functions and our arrangements are certainly influenced by the separation of powers. Parliament is the legislature with the roles of making law and controlling the executive. The executive is the Crown which manages the resources of the state, implements and enforces the law, develops policy, conducts foreign affairs and is the last resort in an emergency. The judiciary is independent of both Parliament and the executive in relation to particular disputes before it.

On the other hand the UK constitution has no conscious design based on the separation of powers. Historically all three branches of government originated with the monarch, and this remains the case in strict theory today. There is substantial overlap of personnel and function between the three branches and our checks and balances are unsystematic. For this reason the Wakeman Commission (2000) was content to leave the status quo in place of the highest appellate tribunal being part of the legislature apparently thinking it unnecessary to examine the merits of the matter. In the following sections I shall sketch the main examples.

5.7.3   Separation of function

It is possible broadly to identify the separate functions of lawmaking, administering and judging and to ensure that each is carried out only by the proper body according to an appropriate procedure. For example, according to the assumptions of a liberal democracy, judging requires that the parties before the court are treated equally, and have an adequate right to present their cases before an impartial tribunal. The judiciary resolves particular disputes brought to them by others but cannot initiate policy nor, strictly speaking give general advice un-related to a case before them. Lawmaking requires that the lawmaker be chosen and removed by the people and should deliberate in public. The executive function requires subordination to general rules made by the legislature.

It is widely accepted that a rigid distinction of function between the three branches is not practicable in contemporary society. This is by virtue of the amount and complexity of business that governments are expected to handle. For example, the executive branch contains the expertise of government. It is commonplace for modern legislatures to delegate power to the executive both to exercise wide discretion in individual cases and to make detailed laws such as land use planning, traffic and public health regulations of the kind necessary in a complex society. These are known as delegated or subordinate legislation. If we wish the legislature to represent the community in the determination of the most important matters it would be impossible for it to produce all the laws required to run the country efficiently or to react flexibly to unforeseen events. Moreover even primary legislation is usually pre-pared and proposed by the executive the legislature being essentially a reactive and scrutiny body.

Moreover the common law system requires judges to make law in contexts where Parliament has not done so. It is also sometimes con-venient and relatively cheap for the executive to exercise the judicial function of resolving disputes, concerning for example the allocation of resources which closely affect government policy. Here the matter is more doubtful in that confidence in the judicial process depends upon the decision maker being seen to be impartial. Nevertheless the House of Lords has recently upheld the practice of ministers determining planning appeals as not violating the right to a fair trial under the ECHR (*R. (Alconbury)* v. *Secretary of State* (2001)).

Normally Parliament and the courts avoid interfering in each other's business. Cases in progress should not be discussed in Parliament except in relation to matters of a national importance or the conduct of ministers (see HC 214–I (1998–99)). Ministers do not answer questions on legal matters. No reflection must be cast on a judge's personal character, competence or motives except on a substantive motion for his dismissal, although backbenchers, but not ministers, may criticise individual judgements. In relation to its own composition and internal affairs the House of Commons has exclusive power to decide disputes and punish offenders and cannot be interfered with by the ordinary courts.

Traditionally judges have not participated in public debate. However, in 1983 the Lord Chancellor relaxed the notorious 'Kilmuir' rules which restricted such participation and the matter is now left to the discretion of the individual judge (see Brazier, 1994, pp. 283–4). Judges are sometimes appointed to hold inquiries into matters of public concern which may involve politically sensitive issues (such as Lord Scarman's Report into the Brixton Riots (1981 Cmnd. 8427) and the Scott Report into Arms Sales (HC 115 (1995–6). It could be argued that this places the judge in the political spotlight and so threatens judicial independence (see Drewry, 1996).

There are other overlaps between judiciary and executive. Firstly appellate judges are appointed on the advice of the prime minister and other judges and magistrates by the Lord Chancellor, a member of the executive. There is no mechanism for independent scrutiny of judicial appointments such as exists in many countries. There appears to be a process of private informal consultation involving mainly the sounding out of opinion within the legal profession (*Judicial Appointments*, HMSO, 1990). Lay magistrates are appointed on the advice of local advisory committees. Again the process is a secret one.

Secondly the Home Secretary has various powers to intervene in the sentencing process of the criminal law. Sentencing itself is a classic judicial function but originally the Home Secretary could order early release on parole, and fix the 'tariff' (a period of punishment) of a person serving a life sentence or, in the case of a child, detained 'at her majesty's pleasure'. As a result of challenges made under the ECHR, based on the right to a fair trial, most of these powers must now be exercised by judges, and in relation to parole by the Home Secretary must act on the recommendation of an independent parole board (see *Thynne* v. *UK* (1991), *Wynne* v. *UK* (1995), *T* v. *UK* (2000), Crime Sentences Act 1997 ss. 29 (1), 35 (2)). However, in the case of a mandatory life sentence it appears that executive discretion remain lawful presumably because administrative discretion alleviates a punishment already fixed rather than imposing a punishment (*see R. (Anderson)* v. *Secretary of State for the Home Dept* (2001)). Again this topic reveals the pragmatic nature of the separation of powers in English law.

5.7.4   Separation of personnel

The second aspect of the separation of powers is that of separation of personnel. For example the US constitution has been particularly influenced by Montesquieu. The president who forms the executive, and Congress the legislature, are elected separately and the same persons cannot be members of both (except that the vice-president is chair of the Senate). The US constitution is designed to encourage conflict between the two branches and regards weak government as desirable, whereas the UK system is more interested in ensuring that the will of the executive is carried out. The UK constitution does not embody a separation of personnel except on a pragmatic and ad hoc basis, arising, characteristically out of particular historical circumstances.

The UK constitution is less strict. The distinguishing element of the parliamentary system in the UK is that by convention ministers must also be members of Parliament, with a majority in the elected House of Commons. Parliament indirectly chooses the executive in that by convention it appoints the prime minister who appoints the other ministers. Bagehot saw this as a fusion between executive and legislature which he regarded as the driving force of the constitution enabling a strong government to get its way but allowed the people to get rid of a bad government readily in that both depend on the same electorate. Thus the checks and balances perspective may call for the violation of the separation of personnel. There is, however, some separation between executive and legislature. No more than 95 ministers can be members of the Commons (House of Commons (Disqualification) Act 1975 s. 2 (1)), thus preventing the government from packing the Commons with sycophants. Moreover, certain kinds of official (civil servants, police, regulators, members of the armed forces, etc.) cannot be members of the Commons (ibid., s. 1).

The judiciary has a stronger but still incomplete separation of personnel. The Appellate Committee of the House of Lords is a committee of Parliament, thus violating the separation of powers. Under the Judicature Act 1873, Gladstone's Liberal administration abolished the judicial functions of the Lords in favour of a final court of appeal. However, Disraeli's Conservative government quickly restored the Law Lords, apparently as a political ploy to counterbalance the influence of the bishops in the Lords (Appellate Jurisdiction Act 1873). There are up to 11 Lords of Appeal in Ordinary appointed on the advice of the prime minister. By convention only these and other peers who hold or who have held high judicial office are eligible to sit on the Appellate Committee. The Law Lords can, however, participate in the legislative business and debates in the House. It is arguable that the dual role of the Law Lords as judges and legislators violates Art. 6 of the European Convention on Human Rights which confers a right to a fair and public hearing by an independent and impartial tribunal established by law.

The Lord Chancellor is often described as a walking contradiction of the separation of powers. The Lord Chancellor is appointed by the prime minister and has no security of tenure. He is a member of the cabinet and heads the executive department dealing with the court system, thus being responsible for judicial appointments and promotions. The Lord Chancellor also presides over the House of Lords but unlike the Speaker of the Commons has no disciplinary powers. The Lord Chancellor is also a member of the Appellate Committee of the House of Lords.

The Lord Chancellor therefore has to balance executive and judicial interests. There is a threat to judicial independence in certain of the Lord Chancellor's functions. These include his control over the administrative and financial aspects of the courts, his power to dismiss magistrates and other lower court judges and his powers to regulate legal education and rights of audience in the courts (see Courts and Legal Services Act 1990; Access to Justice Act 1999). It could be argued that, where the Lord Chancellor sits as a judge the right to a fair trial under the Human Rights Act 1998 is compromised (see *McGonnell* v. *UK* (2000): Bailiff of Guernsey). However, it might be counter- argued that a fair trial is threatened only if the influence relates to the particular case. It has also been suggested that judicial independence could be compromised by a narrow 'executive-centred' model of the separation of powers whereby judicial independence is limited to the trial with other aspects of the court process including staffing, administration and distribution of business for the executive (see Purchas, 1993; Browne-Wilkinson, 1988). In a 'judicial-centred' model such as that in the USA, the judges themselves are given a budget within which they control the administration of the courts.

The Attorney-General also has conflicting roles, being a member of the government and its chief legal advisor, but also having powers to bring legal proceedings against public authorities on behalf of the public interest and to consent to many kinds of prosecution including political offences under official secrets and public order legislation. The Attorney can also intervene by means of a *nolle prosequi* to prevent criminal proceedings. The Attorney's powers to take legal action are apparently not subject to judicial review (see *Gouriet* v. *UPOW* (1978); *R.* v. *Comptroller of Patents* (1899)). The Scott Report (1996) revealed an official culture in which the advice of the Attorney-General was treated as if it had legal force, a practice condemned by the court in *R* v. *Brown* (1993).

Successive Lord Chancellors and Attorneys have relied on the characteristically English argument that eminent public figures can by definition be trusted so that a formal separation of powers is not required. It has also been argued that the office of Lord Chancellor, straddling all three branches of government, actually safeguards the separation of powers by providing a voice in the executive and legislature which can defend judicial independence (e.g. Irvine, speech to the Third Worldwide Common law Judiciary Conference, University of Edinburgh, 5 July 1999).

Allan has suggested that while an independent judiciary is essential, provided that the legislative function and its special procedures are clearly distinguished, it does not violate the rule of law for the same persons to exercise both legislative and executive functions (2001, p. 31). This can be supported on the basis that the executive exists to do the legislature's bidding. In the case of the judges by contrast the rule of law requires them not to be subject to any potential conflict of interest. Nevertheless, as we have seen, contemporary party politics has shifted the balance of power away from Parliament to the executive so that Parliament no longer enjoys public confidence as representing the electorate. Nor does Parliament reflect Allan's idea of a 'deliberative process, sufficiently detached from everyday pressures and immediate political ambitions to ensure, as far as possible, that pertinent requirements of justice are identified and affirmed' (Allan, 2001, p. 47). It may be that Parliament's role as a scrutiny body and public confidence in its integrity would be strengthened by excluding members of the executive.

5.7.5   Checks and balances

The third aspect of the separation of powers is that of 'checks and balances'. This lies at the heart of the republican version of constitutionalism and the rule of law. It involves each branch having some control over the others but also requires each branch to be protected against undue interference by the others thus entailing the need for pragmatic compromise. There are examples of checks and balances throughout the book but some highlights can briefly be mentioned here.

- The House of Lords can veto any bill to extend the life of Parliament, thus preserving the democratic right to an election.
- The Queen in an emergency could invoke her royal prerogative powers to dismiss the prime minister or government, dissolve Parliament or refuse to dissolve parliament.
- Parliament can dismiss the government.
- The higher judiciary has security of tenure against the executive but Parliament exercises a check over the judiciary in that as a last resort it can dismiss superior court judges (Chapter 4).
- The courts provide a check over the executive by means of judicial review, where they try to draw a line between the legality of government action which they are entitled to police and the merits of government action which is a matter for Parliament. As Nolan LJ put it in *M* v. *Home Office* [1992] QB 270, 314, 'The proper constitutional relationship between the executive and the court is that the courts will respect all acts of the executive within its lawful province, and that the executive will respect all decisions of the court as to what its lawful province is.' However, this line is sometimes difficult to draw. As Lord Mustill pointed out in *R.* v. *Secretary of State ex parte Fire Brigades Union* (1995) (above, p. 109), there is a tendency for judicial intervention to expand to fill the 'dead ground' where other safeguards fall short.
- The courts have the exclusive power to interpret statutes hence the claim that there is a balance of power in the sense of 'twin sovereignty' between courts and Parliament (*X Ltd* v. *Morgan Grampian Publishers Ltd* [1991] 1 AC1 at 48). Thus in *Hamilton* v. *Al Fayed* [1999] 3 All ER 317 at 320, Lord Woolf MR referred to 'the wider constitutional principle of mutuality of respect between two constitutional sovereignties'.
- The courts seek an objective independent approach to the interpretation of legislation. In *Duport Steels Ltd* v. *Sirs* [1980] 1 All ER 529 at 551, Lord Scarman said that 'the constitution's separation of powers, or more accurately functions, must be observed if judicial independence is not to be put at risk'. He meant that that the judges must observe the law by sticking to the language of legislation even at the expense of their own views of justice, otherwise, as his Lordship went on to say, 'confidence in the judicial system will be replaced by fear of it becoming uncertain and arbitrary in its application.

Society will then be ready for Parliament to cut the power of the judges'.

It is sometimes said in this connection that a statute should be interpreted according to the intention of the lawmaker. Leaving aside the practical problem of how several hundred members of Parliament can form a single intention and how a court can discover it, this threatens the rule of law and the separation of powers since it would enable the lawmaker by explaining what it meant, even after a law has been enacted, to give a law any meaning it liked. Against this background, the case of *Pepper* v. *Hart* (1993) can be criticised. The House of Lords held (with a dissent from the Lord Chancellor on the ground of cost), that where the language of an Act is ambiguous the court can look at reports in *Hansard*, and perhaps in other official documents, of statements made by the sponsors of the Act in Parliament (usually government ministers) in order to see what they intended. This threatens the independence of the judges and puts the executive in a privileged position. A statute is the *collective* enterprise of Parliament over which the executive should not have special control. However, later cases have emphasised that a cautious approach should be taken to this kind of material which should be taken into account only if the legislation is obscure, ambiguous or would lead to absurd results and then only if the effect of the material is clear (*R* v. *Secretary of State ex parte Spath Homes* (2001)). Moreover the court should not perhaps take into account extra parliamentary remarks made by ministers, in for example speeches or articles since these tell us only what the executive is thinking rather than what Parliament takes note of. On the other hand, under the Human Rights Act 1998, a court may have to decide whether Parliament's purpose justifies overriding a human right. In this kind of case the court can examine in depth evidence of government intentions, apparently from any source.

A position that reflects the rule of law is that the judge should be in the position of the user of the law rather than that of the lawmaker and reflect the moral values and understandings of the community, albeit filtered through those of legal professionals. Subjective judgement can never be eliminated and indeed is necessary for Hobbesian reasons in that objective reasoning may pull in different directions.

- Judicial independence requires that judges should be protected against attacks on their conduct in court. Judges are immune from personal actions for damages in respect of their official actions done in good faith (below p. xxx.). Anything said in court by judges, advocates and witnesses is absolutely privileged against an action in libel and slander. Another vital safeguard is that juries should not be vetted (*R.* v. *Crown Court at Sheffield ex parte Brownlow* (1980)) and cannot be required to give reasons for their verdicts or punished for giving or failing to give a verdict (*Bushell's Case* (1670)). It is an offence for anyone to publish information as to what was said in a jury room (Contempt of Court Act 1981 s. 8 (1); see *A-G* v. *Associated Newspapers Ltd* (1994)).

5.7.6 Treaties and the separation of powers

Treaties raise important separation of power issues between judiciary and executive. A treaty is an agreement made between the executive and another state which should not affect the law unless the democratic lawmaker has either approved the treaty or has at least authorised the executive to create legally binding obligations, for example in the case of the EC. The position differs in different countries. In the UK a treaty in itself can neither create nor take away legal rights because of the principle that the executive cannot change the law (see *Maclaine Watson* v. *DTI* (1988); *The Parliament Belge* (1879)). Thus Parliament must pass specific legislation implementing the treaty. This must not be confused with *ratification* of a treaty which merely makes the treaty binding in international law on the government.

Treaties are also non-justiciable in the sense that a court cannot review the validity of a treaty as such, although if there are statutory requirements before a treaty takes effect, the courts can of course ensure that these are obeyed (see *R.* v. *Secretary of State for Foreign and Commonwealth Affairs ex parte Rees-Mogg* (1994)).

However, the courts take treaties into account when interpreting legislation, in applying the common law, and in exercising discretionary powers (see *Derbyshire County Council* v. *Times Newspapers Ltd* [1993] 3 All ER 65 at 77–79; *R.* v. *Khan* (1996)). The courts will certainly take a treaty into account where a statue is ambiguous (see *Buchanan* v. *Babco* (1977); *Brind* v. *Secretary of State for the Home Department* (1991)). There is also a broad view, supported by ambivalent dicta that the courts will interpret all legislation enacted after the relevant treaty in the light of the treaty on the assumption that Parliament would not have intended to contradict treaty obligations (see *Garland* v. *BREL* [1983] AC 251 at 277; *Pan American World Airlines Inc* v. *DoT* [1976] 1 Lloyds Rep 257 at 261; *A-G* v. *BBC* [1981] AC 303 at 354; *A-G* v. *Guardian Newspapers Ltd* [1987] 1 WLR 1048 at 1096; cf. *Blackburn* v. *A-G* [1971] 1 WLR 1037 at 1039. Both views rest on the premise that

Parliament has recognised the treaty, thus giving the court the key to enter. It seems, however, that a minister exercising a statutory discretion is not required to take a treaty into account unless required to do so by statute (*Brind* (above)).

Summary

5.1   Constitutionalism means limited government and includes the ideas of the rule of law and the separation of powers as means of restricting and controlling government. The rule of law in its core sense emphasises the importance of formal rules, agreed methods of interpreting them and fair procedures, as binding on government and citizen alike. The core sense of the rule of law is morally ambivalent since it can be regarded as an efficient tool of tyranny.

5.2   In an extended sense, appropriate to a liberal democracy the rule of law requires the law reflects certain basic values derived from the notion of equal respect for individuals. These are translated into rights closely associated with legal processes such as non-discrimination, freedom of expression, and access to government information.

5.3   The rule of law as expounded by Dicey has significantly influenced the UK constitution. Dicey advocated that government discretion should be limited by definite rules of law, that the same law could in general apply to government and citizen alike, and that Britain does not need a written constitution because, in his view the common law made by independent courts with practical remedies provides a firmer foundation for individual rights. This has greatly influenced the thinking of the legal profession, but may be unsuited to the control of modern government. It is also difficult to reconcile the rule of law in this sense with the principle that Parliament has unlimited power that can be harnessed by a strong executive.

5.4   Other modern ideas of the rule of law include the increasing importance of international treaties which attempt to establish codes of fundamental rights and freedoms that governments should respect.

5.5   The doctrine of the separation of powers means that government power should be divided up into legislative, executive and judicial functions each with its own distinctive personnel and processes and that each branch of government should be checked so that no one body can dominate the others. A strict separation of functions is probably impracticable. A separation of personnel is essential in respect of judicial functions but arguably less so in other cases. In all cases the notion of checks and balances is essential in order to maintain the rule of law.

5.6   The separation of powers in its several senses plays an important part in the UK constitution, but there is no coherent theory. The eighteenth-century constitution which provides the framework of our modern system was proclaimed as a 'mixed' or 'balanced' constitution. The three 'estates' of Crown, Lords, and Commons shared power, so that each countered the excesses of the others. This version of the constitution was displaced by the growth of the executive and its dominance of the House of Commons through the party system. We now have an 'unbalanced' constitution kept in place by an untidy and imperfect set of checks and separations, which to a large extent preserve the independence of Parliament and the judiciary but where there are certain tensions. Particular aspects of the separation of powers should be noted throughout the book.

5.7 The separation of powers is most important in relation to the judiciary, where it requires judges to be protected against interference from the executive, to interpret the law according to principles that do not depend on the wishes of the executive but also to restrain themselves from interfering with the executive too far. The courts have a large degree of independence from the executive although there are important links with the executive, notably through the office of Lord Chancellor, particularly in relation to the administration and financing of the courts and the regulation of the legal profession. Superior court judges have security of tenure and protection against legal actions but the protection of inferior court judges varies. Judges are appointed and promoted by politicians, in particular by the Lord Chancellor. Convention requires that party political factors are not taken into account when making judicial appointments.

5.8 Treaties made by the executive do not in themselves change the law thus preserving a separation of powers but the law must, at least where it is ambiguous or uncertain, be interpreted in line with them.

5.9 The rule of law may also include a right to disobey the law on moral grounds. This includes a right to advocate disobedience and a right to information so as to make a properly informed decision which take into account communitarian reasons for obedience. It is unclear what this means and how the law should protect this right.

Further Reading

Allan, *Constitutional Justice*, chapters 1, 2, 3, 4.

Allan, 'The rule of law as the rule of reason: consent and constitutionalism' 115 *Law Quarterly Review* 221.

Allan, *Law, Liberty and Justice*, chapters 2, 3, 5.

Barendt, *An Introduction to Constitutional Law*, chapter 7.

Barendt, 'Separation of powers and constitutional government', *Public Law* 599.

Craig, P. 'Formal and substantive concepts of the rule of law: an analytical framework', *Public Law* 467.

Dicey, *The Law of the Constitution*, Part 2.

Jowell and Oliver, *The Changing Constitution*, chapter 3.

Lester, A. (2001) 'Developing constitutional principles of public law', *Public Law* 684.

Marshall, *Constitutional Theory*, chapters V, VI, VII, IX.

Steyn, 'The weakest and least dangerous department of government', *Public Law* 84.

Sugerman 'The legal boundaries of liberty: Dicey, liberalism and legal science', *Modern Law Review* 102.

Tivey (1999), 'Constitutionalism and the political arena', 70 *Political Quarterly* 175.

Waldron, *The Law*.

Woodhouse, D. 'The office of Lord Chancellor', *Public Law* 617.

Exercises

5.1 Do you agree with Thompson that the rule of law is an unqualified human good?

5.2 To what extent is Dicey's version of the rule of law of value today?

5.3   Is the rule of law any more than an appeal to a particular political ideology?

5.4   To what extent can disobedience to law be justified under the rule of law?

5.5   Does the rule of law have a substantive content in terms of individual rights?

5.6   'The principle that laws will be faithfully applied, according to the tenor in which they would reasonably be understood by those affected is the most basic tenet of the rule of law' (Allan). Discuss critically.

5.7   Does the idea of the mixed constitution have contemporary value?

5.8   Distinguish and illustrate the possible different meanings of the separation of powers. To what extent does the UK constitution embody a separation of powers?

5.9   It is sometimes said that the UK constitution embodies a 'fusion' between the legislature and the executive. Do you agree? Is it desirable that the composition of the executive and legislature be separate?

5.10   Is there an adequate separation between the judiciary and the executive in the UK constitution?

5.11   The Ruritanian government requests the UK to surrender to it, a former British prime minister now living in retirement in Devon, on the ground that, during his tenure of office, the UK's treatment of asylum seekers from a previous Ruritanian regime amounted to torture contrary to an international treaty. Advise the United Kingdom government.

6 Parliamentary Supremacy

The conventional basis of the UK constitution is parliamentary supremacy or sovereignty. This maintains that Parliament has unlimited *legal* power to enact any law whatsoever, without of course denying that there are many political and practical reasons why a particular Parliament may in fact be restricted. In the absence of a written constitution the foundations of the doctrine, lying as they do in no more than general acceptance, look frail. Indeed there are three possible contenders for sovereignty, namely Parliament, the courts and the Crown, although the latter conceded defeat in the 1688 revolution.

There is no logical reason why there should be a single sovereign with unlimited powers, although, as we have seen, Hobbes believed that such an authority was desirable in order to resolve disagreement. For example in the USA power is carefully divided so that no single entity has unlimited legal power. The doctrine of parliamentary supremacy and indeed the concept of sovereignty itself has in recent years been subject to attack from several perspectives as being unreal and unjust in a modern community which depends on international consensus and accommodations between competing interests and values rather than the crude solution of Hobbes (see e.g. McCormick, 1993; Hunt, 1996; Allan, 2001; Barber, 2000). Defenders of the doctrine of parliamentary supremacy claim that the doctrine is consistent with democracy in that it allows the people through their elected representatives to have the last word. To this the opponents would rejoin that, as we saw in Chapter 1, democracy involves wider values concerning the protection of individual rights which the majoritarian principle does not necessarily respect and which can be policed by the courts. There is also a middle view which postulates a 'dual sovereignty' between Parliament and the courts according to which the courts when interpreting statutes will assume that Parliament intends to respect basic values. This view is unclear as to how far 'interpretation' can extend; a problem that arises particularly in the context of the Human Rights Act.

The foundation of parliamentary supremacy is normally said to be the 1688 revolution which was a decisive political act establishing the parliamentary basis of our constitution (Wade, 1955). An alternative view is that parliamentary supremacy is the creation of the common law whereby in the interests of democracy the courts have conceded power to Parliament. This view leaves open the possibility that some common law principles are so fundamental that the courts would resist any attempt to override them. Indeed, on one view, parliamentary supremacy presupposes a law which identifies Parliament and states how its will is to be expressed. Because we have no written constitution, the nature of this law is contested. On another view, parliamentary supremacy may amount to no more than a political practice of obeying Parliament.

6.1   The Meaning of Parliamentary Supremacy

According to Dicey (1915, pp. 37–8), 'The principle of parliamentary sovereignty means neither more nor less than this, namely that Parliament has, under the English constitution, the right to make or unmake any law whatever; and further that no person or body is recognised by the law of England as having a right to override or set aside the legislation of Parliament.'

This has three aspects. Firstly Parliament has unlimited lawmaking power in the sense that it can make any kind of law. Secondly, the *legal* validity of laws made by Parliament cannot be questioned by any other body. Thirdly, a Parliament cannot bind a future Parliament. Dicey tried to split sovereignty into separate legal and political elements, arguing that Parliament was legally sovereign in the sense that the courts must obey it, but not politically sovereign. Dicey (1915, p. 70) described legal sovereignty as 'the power of law making unrestricted by any legal limit' and contrasted this with political sovereignty, as in the sense of the body 'the will of which is ultimately obeyed by the citizens of the state' (ibid.). He recognised both 'internal' and 'external' political limits on the lawmaker. Internal limits are limits inherent in the culture of the people who make up Parliament. The political and moral pressures imposed by constitutional conventions, patronage and party discipline are internal limits. The external limits consist in what those subject to the law are prepared to accept. Parliament cannot in practice pass any law it wishes, and its laws might be condemned as morally or politically bad or even as unconstitutional in a broad sense. Dicey thought that political sovereignty lay in the electorate.

Dicey's distinction between legal and political sovereignty may be too sharp. Firstly, law derives from politics so that there must be a political reason why Parliament rather than some other body should be obeyed by the courts. Secondly, legal rules are powerful political weapons since they authorise violence against persons and property. Thus whoever is able to control the legal sovereign is likely also to be the political sovereign. Thirdly, parliamentary sovereignty is bound up with the political issue of national sovereignty. The legal doctrine is sometimes raised as a reason for not surrendering national sovereignty in the international arena.

On the face of it, parliamentary supremacy is in the Hobbesian tradition of an absolute ruler. However, Dicey's version of parliamentary supremacy differs crucially from Hobbesian thinking. Firstly, the Hobbesian sovereign exists to protect life, so that, although the sovereign has unlimited powers, if it fails to protect life there is no longer a duty of obedience. Secondly, Hobbes did not separate legal and political sovereignty. Thirdly, Hobbes's sovereign must be a single unitary body, either a monarch or an assembly. Dicey's legal sovereign is divided comprising three bodies, namely Queen, Lords and Commons. Only in combination can they exercise the power of Parliament. Thus, Blackstone who defended parliamentary supremacy in the eighteenth century, linked the doctrine with that of the separation of powers. Indeed at the time Dicey first wrote (1885), the House of Lords had substantial power to block legislation. Dicey's doctrine does not therefore depend on the doubtful assumption that there must be a single ultimate source of power. Indeed Dicey denied that there was a logical need for an ultimate sovereign (1915, p. 143) merely pointing out that the evidence suggested that we have in fact adopted the doctrine of parliamentary supremacy.

6.2 Historical Development

Despite eschewing historical methods, Dicey (1915, p. 67) said that England had always been governed by an absolute legislator in the form of the Crown, originally alone and later in partnership with Parliament. However, a widely recognised feature of English constitutional history was that absolute notions of monarchy never took hold as they did in other European states during the sixteenth century. The medieval idea of the monarch being subject to the common law remained influential, and until the sixteenth century Parliament was primarily regarded as a body which declared existing law rather than making new law.

As early as the fourteenth century it became clear that the king could not exact taxes without the permission of Parliament, and from this power base Parliament could control the making of laws. A statute of Edward III (14 Edw. III, stat.ii.c.1) declared that the nation 'should be no more charged or grieved to make any common aid or sustain charge except by the common assent of the prelates, earls, barons, and other magnates and commons of the realm and that in Parliament'. 'Nor does the king by himself or by his ministers impose tollages, subsidies or any other burdens whatsoever on his subjects, nor change the laws nor make new ones without the concession or assent of his whole realm expressed in Parliament' (Sir John Fortescue, *De Laudibus Legum Angliae* (1468–70)). On the other hand, Parliament could not act without the king's consent, hence the notion of the English constitution as a 'harmonious' constitution driven by the co-operation of the powerful groups within the realm.

By the sixteenth century it had become clear that Parliament could change the common law. Even the Tudor monarchs who developed a strong central executive recognised that the full power of the Crown could be exercised only in combination with Parliament. In 1543, Henry VIII declared 'We be informed by our judges that we at no time stand so highly in our estate Royal as in the time of Parliament wherein we as head and you as members are conjoined and bound together into one body politic'. The most dramatic example of this was the Reformation Parliament (1529 to 1536) which destroyed the medieval social order by making the Church part of the English state.

Throughout the seventeenth century the political struggle between the king and Parliament was punctuated by a series of inconclusive lawsuits which raised the question whether the king could make law without parliamentary consent. The Stuart kings challenged traditional doctrine by drawing on new ideas of the state personified by the crown. The cases seem to assume the ultimate supremacy of the common law as mediating between Crown and Parliament. It was established in 1611 that the monarch cannot legislate without Parliament (*Case of Proclamations*) but other cases upheld wide prerogative powers. For example in *R* v. *Hampden* (1637) it was held, albeit by a divided court, that the king has emergency tax raising powers (see also *Godden* v. *Hales* (1686); *Thomas* v. *Sorrell* (1674)).

Parliamentary supremacy might be said to derive from the 1688 revolution (see *Picken* v. *BRB* (1974)). However, the revolution established only that Parliament was superior to the king and did not deal explicitly with the relationship between Parliament and the common law. Indeed, the revolutionaries claimed that their arrangements could be justified under the common law doctrine of necessity in that by abdicating King James had created a power vacuum. The revolution was also rationalised on the basis suggested by Locke that a lawmaker holds power on trust to protect the 'rights' of the people. A realistic assessment might be that the courts were responding to a political change begun in 1688 by accepting the doctrine of parliamentary supremacy in return for security of tenure which they were given by the Act of Settlement 1701.

However seventeenth-century dicta, notably Coke CJ in *Dr Bonham's Case* (1610), and *Day* v. *Savidge* (1615), and even post-revolutionary dicta (*City of London* v. *Wood* (1710); *Forbes* v. *Cochrane* (1824)), could be read as asserting that an unreasonable Act of Parliament is void. By the middle of the eighteenth century this had been 'revised' in favour of the modern compromise that the courts *interpret* statutes so as to avoid an unreasonable or unjust meaning (see Blackstone, 1776, Comm. 91, 160; cf. Jennings, 1959; Wade, 1955). Blackstone also emphasised the importance of the legislature being 'less corrupt' than the executive. Thus Blackstone anticipated the modern position that Parliament might be too corrupt to use its sovereignty against the executive.

By Dicey's time, parliamentary supremacy met the political needs of the day. It conformed to the extension of democracy and the increasing need for drastic governmental powers of intervention in a changeable industrial society. Case law emerged in support of parliamentary supremacy during the middle of the nineteenth century (e.g. *Lee* v. *Bude and Torrington Railway Co.* (1872); *Edinburgh and Dalkeith Railway Co.* v. *Wauchope* (1841)) which has been consistently confirmed throughout this century (see *Manuel* v. *A-G* (1983); *Pickin* v. *British Railways Board* (1974)).

6.3 The Application of Parliamentary Supremacy

The legal doctrine of parliamentary supremacy is concerned only with an Act of Parliament (a statute). An Act of Parliament, as the preamble to every Act reminds us, is an Act of the monarch with the consent of the House of Lords and the House of Commons, the Queen in Parliament. In certain circumstances, however, the consent of the House of Lords can be omitted under the Parliament Acts 1911–1949 (see below 12.3.4). Even if we believe that the House of Commons is the political sovereign, a resolution of the House of Commons has in itself no legal force, except in relation to the internal proceedings of the House (*Bowles* v. *Bank of England* (1913); *Stockdale* v. *Hansard* (1839)).

6.3.1   Freedom to make any kind of law

It will be recalled that Dicey identified two facets of parliamentary supremacy. The first is that Parliament can make any laws it likes irrespective of fairness, justice and practicality; hence Sir Ivor Jennings's famous example that Parliament can make it an offence for Frenchmen to smoke in the streets of Paris (1959, p. 170). The UK courts are bound to obey a statute applying anywhere and whether or not the relevant overseas courts would recognise it is immaterial (e.g. *Manuel* v. *A-G* (1983)). It has been said that Parliament cannot make a man a woman, or a woman a man, but this is misleading. The so-called laws of nature are not rules at all. They are simply facts which occur in a predictable pattern. A statute which enacted that all men must be regarded as women and vice versa would no doubt be impractical, but would be legally valid.

Dicey relied on examples of valid statutory provisions that in countries that do not recognise a principle of legislative supremacy would arguably be unlawful. However, these examples do not prove that the courts will not refuse to apply a statute that they consider even more unjust. All Dicey was saying is that the evidence to date was consistent with parliamentary supremacy. Modern cases continue to support Dicey. They include retrospective legislation (*Burmah Oil Co. Ltd* v. *Lord Advocate* (1965); War Damage Act 1965); statutes conflicting with international law (*Mortensen* v. *Peters* (1906), *Cheney* v. *Conn* (1968)), or with fundamental civil liberties (*R.* v. *Jordan* (1967)). *Picken* v. *British Railways Board* (1974) goes further since the House of Lords expressly affirmed that the courts must obey any law made by Parliament and could not even examine whether the legislation had been made in good faith in accordance with the proper parliamentary procedures.

6.3.2   Parliament cannot be overridden: implied repeal

Turning to the second limb of Dicey's formulation, that no other body can override Parliament, this has two aspects. Firstly, neither the UK courts nor international courts such as the European Court of Human Rights have the power to declare an Act of Parliament invalid (*MacCormick* v. *Lord Advocate* (1953)). Secondly, in the event of a conflict between a statute and some other kind of law, the statute must always prevail. As regards Dicey's third limb, a statute cannot be restricted even by another statute. However, this presents two opposite possibilities. It could be argued either that an earlier statute cannot be repealed by a later statute or that a later statute should always repeal an earlier one. The solution chosen by the law is that a later statute can indeed repeal an earlier one, in other words Parliament cannot bind its successors. This principle can be justified as democratic since it would be wrong for any group of people to tie the hands of the future. For example, Edmund Burke argued that the 1688 revolution had permanently enshrined a constitution which included the House of Lords. Thomas Paine answered this as follows: 'Every age and generation must be as free to act for itself, *in all cases* as the ages and generations which preceded it. The vanity and presumption of governing beyond the grave is the most ridiculous and insolent of all tyrannies' (1987, p. 204). However, Parliament could bind its successors by abolishing itself, having first created a body with more limited powers.

The approach taken by the English courts makes it relatively easy to override earlier statutes. This is the 'implied repeal' doctrine according to which a later statute which on an ordinary reading is inconsistent with an earlier statute impliedly repeals the earlier statute to the extent of the inconsistency. The court is not required to attempt to reconcile the two, and it is irrelevant that the earlier Act states that it cannot be repealed: *Vauxhall Estates Ltd* v. *Liverpool Corporation* (1932); *Ellen Street Estates Ltd* v. *Minister of Health* (1934). However, the implied repeal doctrine, although consistent with parliamentary sovereignty, is not essential to it. It is merely a particular approach to interpretation and there is nothing to prevent a statute from requiring the courts to interpret legislation as overriding another statute only if express or very clear language is used, thus putting a partial brake on the majority. For example s. 3 of the Human Rights Act 1998 requires all other statutes to be interpreted in accordance with the rights protected by the Act 'if it is possible to do so' (see Chapter 18). As regards a statute passed before the Human Rights Act the implied repeal doctrine therefore does not apply. The court must try to reconcile the two and, if this fails, the earlier statute must prevail.

6.4 The Ingredients of an Act of Parliament

The courts obey, not Parliament as an institution but a law which counts as a valid 'Act of Parliament'. Two questions arise from this. First, what rules create an Act of Parliament? Secondly, to what extent can the courts investigate whether these rules have been obeyed? There are complex procedural rules for producing statutes but not all of them affect the validity of a statute. Three kinds or levels of rule can be distinguished.

1. There is the basic definition of a statute as a document that received the assent of the three institutions that comprise the Queen in Parliament. The basic procedural requirements for passing an Act are currently the separate consents of the three elements, i.e. Queen, Lords and Commons . The preamble to a statute invariably recites that the required assents have been given. A court is not bound by a document that does not appear on its face to have received the necessary assents but conversely must accept the validity of a document that does so appear (*Prince's Case* (1606); *Hall* v. *Hall* (1944)). This is called the 'enrolled Act rule' and precludes the courts from investigating whether the proper procedures have been complied with (*Edinburgh and Dalkeith Railway* v. *Wauchope* (1842); *Manuel* v. *A-G* (1983)). The official version of a statute was traditionally enrolled upon the Parliament Roll. Today there is no Parliament Roll as such, but two official copies of the Act are in the House of Lords' Library and the Public Record Office.

2. A second layer of rules regulates the relationship between the three institutions. Some are conventions with which the courts are not concerned, for example the rule that the monarch cannot refuse the Royal Assent. Others are statutory. For example the Parliament Acts of 1911 and 1949 restrict the power of the House of Lords to refuse its consent to a bill passed by the Commons. In principle the court should be able to decide whether these rules have been obeyed. However, the Parliament Act 1911 foresaw this possibility, and excluded it by providing that a certificate given by the Speaker under the Act to the effect that the requirements of the Act have been complied with, is 'conclusive for all purposes and shall not be questioned in any court of law' (Parliament Act 1911 s. 3). Similarly, the Regency Act 1937 provides that the Royal Assent can be given by a regent if the monarch is under 18, or ill, or in certain other events. The court may be able to investigate whether the Act has been properly applied.

3. Thirdly, there is a complex network of rules concerning the composition and procedure of each House. These include the various stages of passage of a bill, voting procedures, and the law governing qualifications for membership of either House. They comprise a mixture of statute, convention and the 'law and custom of Parliament' enforced by the House itself. It is settled that ordinary

courts have no jurisdiction to enquire into any matters related to the internal affairs of the House. Quite apart from the enrolled Act rule (above), these are matters of parliamentary privilege and are exclusively within the jurisdiction of the House itself. This is true even if it is alleged that the House has violated a statute, or that a bill has been introduced fraudulently (see *Pickin* v. *British Railways Board* (1974)).

6.5 Dividing Parliamentary Supremacy?

There are arguments that Parliament can, in particular contexts be limited by the law either by transferring its power to others or because Parliament is the product of a previous transfer of power the terms of which limit Parliament. In other words sovereignty is divisible. However, if this is so, then it seems pointless to use the concept of sovereignty at all. The point of the concept is to express the Hobbesian assertion that we are prepared to trust a particular body with unlimited lawmaking power. If sovereignty can indeed be divided, all we are saying is the truism that each power holder has freedom within its allocated sphere whatever that might be.

Cases where sovereignty may have been divided are as follows:

- Parliament may not legislate for former British territories which have been granted independence (politically but not legally true).
- Parliament may not alter certain provisions of the Acts of Union with Scotland and Ireland because these created Parliament (unlikely).
- Parliament may be able to alter the 'manner and form' of legislation and so effectively restrain itself (plausible).
- Parliament has surrendered some of its sovereignty by joining the European Community (misleading).

6.5.1 Grants of independence

For example the Canada Act 1982 s. 2 provides that 'no Act of the United Kingdom Parliament passed after the Constitution Act 1982 comes into force shall extend to Canada as part of its law'. Could Parliament repeal that statute thus taking jurisdiction over Canada again? The answer is yes as far as the UK courts are concerned (*British Coal Corporation* v. *R.* (1935), *Manuel* v. *A-G* (1983)). However, only those who recognise Parliament's power, that is, UK courts, are legally obliged to obey such a statute and a UK court would even be required to hold that Canadian courts should obey the statute. Whether Canada falls into line is entirely a matter for its own legal and political institutions.

Such a statute is of course likely to be politically impracticable. There is a dictum by Lord Denning in *Blackburn* v. *A-G* (1971), that legal theory must give way to practical politics. All his Lordship seems to be saying is that it would be, in a practical sense, impossible for Parliament to reverse a grant of independence. On the other hand, Blackstone (1776, p. 160) said that an 'impossible' statute would be invalid and a legal principle that is so out of line with common sense might well be worth reconsidering.

6.5.2   Acts of Union: was Parliament born unfree?

The modern UK Parliament is the result of two treaties. First the Treaty of Union with Scotland, 1706, created the Parliament of Great Britain out of the former Scottish and English Parliaments. The treaty required, among other things, that no laws which concern private rights in Scotland shall be altered 'except for the evident utility of the subjects within Scotland'. There were also powers securing the separate Scottish Courts and Presbyterian Church 'for all time coming'. The new Parliament was created by separate Acts of the then Scottish and English Parliaments, giving effect to the treaty (see Act of Union with Scotland 1706). Some Scottish lawyers therefore argue that Parliament was 'born unfree', meaning that the modern Parliament cannot go beyond the terms of the Acts that created it. They suggest that the protected provisions of the Act of Union, cannot be altered by Act of Parliament. In effect, the union created a new Parliament which, in relation to the protected Scottish provisions, does not necessarily have the quality of supremacy inherent in the former English Parliament (see, generally, Munro, 1999, p. 137, Upton, 1989, p. 105; LQR, p. 75).

In the case of Northern Ireland there was a Treaty of Union in 1798, which preserved certain basic rights in Ireland including the con-tinuance of the Protestant religion and the permanence of the union itself. The Treaty was confirmed by the Act of Union with Ireland, 1800, which created the UK Parliament. The Act covered the whole of Ireland but, what is now the Republic of Ireland later left the Union. It might be argued that the Northern Ireland Act 1998 s. 1 which provides for the Union to be dissolved if a referendum so votes, would be invalid as contrary to the Act of Union. The 1998 Act makes no express reference to the Act of Union with Ireland, s. 2 merely providing that the Act overrides 'previous enactments'. This lets in the argument that even if the Act of Union is not sacrosanct, the implied repeal doctrine is not strong enough to repeal it by means of general language (see Hadfield, 1998). Political circumstances in Northern Ireland make this ambiguity understandable.

The crucial provisions of the Scottish Union have not been altered, but s. 37 of the Scotland Act 1998 expressly states that the provisions of the Act are to take priority over the Act of Union. This rules out the implied repeal argument but begs the question whether an Act can do this at all. The issue has surfaced in a few cases in all of which an Act of Parliament was obeyed. In *ex parte Canon Selwyn* (1872) (Ireland), the court denied that it possessed the power to override a statute. In two Scottish cases, *MacCormick* v. *Lord Advocate* (1953) and *Gibson* v. *Lord Advocate* (1975), the Scottish courts were able to avoid the issue by holding that no conflict with the Acts of Union arose. However, in both cases the argument in favour of the Acts of Union was regarded as tenable, particularly by Lord Cooper in *MacCormick*. However in *MacCormick* his Lordship, with the apparent agreement of Lords Keith and Gibson, suggested that the issue might be 'non-justiciable', that is, outside the jurisdiction of the courts and resolvable only by political means. On this view a statute that flouts the Acts of Union may be unconstitutional but not unlawful. In both cases the courts left open the question whether they could interfere if an Act purported to make drastic inroads into the Act of Union, for example by abolishing the whole of Scottish private law (see also *Sillers* v. *Smith* (1982)). The better view is probably that parliamentary supremacy is an evolving doctrine which developed after the Acts of Union, the latter being no different in law than any other statute.

6.5.3 The redefinition theory

This is an attempt to circumvent the rule that Parliament cannot bind its successors. The argument has various labels, sometimes being called the 'new view', sometimes the 'entrenchment' argument, sometimes the 'manner and form' theory and sometimes the distinction between continuing and self-embracing sovereignty. It has attracted considerable academic discussion and can draw support from certain overseas cases (see below). Apart from a brief discussion by Slade LJ in *Manuel* v. *A-G* (see above) it has not yet surfaced in the English courts (see Munro, 1999; Jennings, 1959; Winterton, 1976).

The redefinition argument is essentially that, if Parliament can do anything, it can prescribe what counts as a solid Act of Parliament and in so doing make it difficult to change an Act that it 'entrenches'. It can be supported as follows:

1. There must be rules of law that tell us what counts as an Act of Parliament. The redefinition theory relies on the proposition that in making law it must comply with the procedures for making a valid law that are in force from time to time. A document which purports to be a statute but which has not been passed according to these basic rules is not a statute and has no legal force.
2. The courts are obliged to apply only a law that has a valid pedigree in this sense. The crucial question therefore is whether an Act of Parliament can modify the procedural rules which prescribe what counts as an Act of Parliament. If Parliament can indeed do anything then we must concede that it can redefine what counts as a valid law. If this is so then Parliament can after all bind its successors by creating a procedure that makes it difficult to change the law. Suppose for example a statute enacts a bill of rights and goes on to say that 'no law shall be passed that is inconsistent with the bill of rights without a referendum of the people nor shall this statute be repealed without a referendum of the people'. This is known as double entrenchment. Another version of entrenchment might be a 'notwithstanding' clause, stating that the bill of rights shall be repealed only by an Act which expressly states that it is to apply 'notwithstanding' the bill of rights (Oliver, 1991, p. 158).
3. An entrenched statute can still be repealed but not without the special procedure. Those who reject the theory argue that if Parliament ignores the special procedure the courts will simply obey the most recent Act of Parliament and thus treat the special procedure as impliedly repealed. However, this misses the point since, according to the argument, a document which has not been produced under the special procedure is not a valid statute and so must be ignored, just as an ordinary law, however, strongly promoted by Parliament itself would be ignored if it did not have the Royal Assent. Parliament would remain supreme but would, for the purpose of the statute which it is intended to protect, now mean for example Queen, Lords, Commons and the referendum.
4. Some would go further and argue that the special 'entrenching' procedure could consist of a procedure within the traditional Parliament, for example a two-thirds majority of the Commons being required to repeal a particular statute. However, this weaker

form of entrenchment seems to fall foul of the rule that the courts cannot enquire in the internal procedures within each House. On the other hand a statute could expressly empower the courts to investigate the internal procedures.

However, judicial support for the redefinition theory is slender. It has been accepted in two commonwealth cases (*A-G for New South Wales* v. *Trethowen* (1931) and *Bribery Commissioners* v. *Ranasinghe* (1965)) (Privy Council) and in a South African case (*Harris* v. *Minister of the Interior* (1952)). *Trethowen* went so far as to suggest that the court could grant an injunction to prevent a bill being submitted for the Royal Assent if it did not comply with the entrenched procedure. This seems unlikely to apply in England since the courts have consistently refused to interfere with the conduct of parliamentary proceedings. The issue would arise in the UK if a court were asked to obey a document that fails to comply with an entrenched provision.

These cases are ambiguous authority. *Trethowen*, *Ranasinghe* and *Harris* have been explained on the basis that the legislatures in these countries were not truly supreme in the same way as the UK Parliament. In *Trethowen* and *Harris* a UK Act had established the powers of the legislatures in question, and in *Ranasinghe* the relevant entrenching power was contained in a written constitution. On the other hand, in *Trethowen*, the relevant UK Act (the Colonial Laws Validity Act 1865) provided that the New South Wales Parliament had complete lawmaking power as far as internal matters were concerned. However, when *Trethowen* reached the Privy Council it was emphasised that the case turned on the fact that a subordinate legislature was involved (see [1932] AC at 526). In *Harris* the Statute of Westminster 1931 had given the South African Parliament unlimited lawmaking power. Moreover the court stressed that its reasoning did not assume that the Parliament was in any sense subordinate. Indeed in both *Trethowen* and *Ranasinghe* there were dicta that the same arguments might apply to the UK Parliament. It was said in *Ranasinghe* (at p. 198) that the entrenched clause argument does not limit parliamentary supremacy, but merely changes the way in which that supremacy must be exercised.

The issue also arose in *Manuel* v. *A-G* (1982). A peculiarity of the Canadian Constitution was that certain changes to it could only be made by the UK Parliament. Canada wished to enact a new constitution free from this remnant of empire. A group of Canadian Indians brought an action in the English courts arguing that the Canada Act 1982 (a UK Act giving effect to Canada's wishes) was invalid because it was passed without the request or consent of the Indian nations of Canada whose consent was arguably required under s. 4 of the Statute of Westminster 1931, a UK statute. Megarry J at first instance applied the traditional principle that no court can refuse to obey an Act of Parliament and struck out the action. However, the Court of Appeal avoided grappling with the problem of parliamentary supremacy by pointing out that s. 4 did not say that that actual consent was required, but only that the Act must 'declare' that the relevant consent had been given. The Canada Act contained the declaration and whether or not it was true was therefore legally irrelevant. The Court of Appeal was prepared at least to recognise the possibility that if an Act stated that a consent must actually be given, then an attempt to pass an Act without that consent could be invalid even from the UK perspective.

It has also been suggested that the UK Parliament has redefined itself several times. Thus, the Parliament Acts 1911 and 1949 provide that in certain circumstances a bill can receive the Royal Assent without the consent of the House of Lords. Under the Regency Act 1937 the powers of the monarch can be exercised by certain other people when the monarch is indisposed or absent. However, none of this legislation places any limitations upon the powers of Parliament. Moreover even if these provisions can be regarded as redefining Parliament, there is no need for a court to follow the logic of this to its conclusion so as to permit any kind of redefinition. On the other hand the argument at least opens the way to the redefinition possibility.

The most formidable challenge to the 'redefinition' argument comes from Professor H. W. R. Wade (1955, 1980, ch. 3). Wade argues that the meaning of 'Parliament' is 'fixed' by a rule which is 'above and beyond the reach of Parliament'. Parliament cannot simply make itself supreme, so there must be some independent explanation of why Parliament is supreme. Wade argues that the explanation lies in the events of 1688 which created the fundamental rule of our constitution, a rule which is unique in character, a 'grundnorm' essentially a political principle standing outside and above the ordinary legal system and giving it its validity. Wade goes on to argue that, because this rule gave Parliament its power, it cannot be altered by Parliament, so that Parliament remains as monarch, Lords and Commons, and any attempt to redefine Parliament, for example, by adding a referendum, would be ineffective. Thus, paradoxically Wade supports the traditional notion that Parliament can do anything by admitting that there is one thing Parliament cannot do, that is to alter its own definition.

Wade regards laws passed under the Parliament Acts 1911 and 1949, as not being truly Acts of Parliament, but special forms of delegated legislation. Therefore the House of Lords could not be abolished under the Parliament Act machinery under which legislation can become law without the consent of the Lords because a delegate cannot enlarge its own powers. Indeed, if Wade's 'higher law' argument is accepted, it may not be possible lawfully to abolish the House of Lords at all.

Wade accepts that the doctrine of parliamentary supremacy could in political reality be abolished, but would regard this as a revolution, that is, the introduction of an entirely new basic principle. How will we know whether such a revolution has taken place? Wade would place the matter in the 'keeping of the courts', so that if the courts were to accept the redefinition theory this would authoritatively signify the 'revolution'. From this Wade concludes (1980, p. 37) that one way to ensure that a bill of rights prevailed over a later statute would be to make the judges swear a new form of judicial oath, one of loyalty to the bill of rights rather than to justice according to law.

There are difficulties with Professor Wade's argument. For example why should there be a single grundnorm at all? In particular why should the meaning of parliamentary supremacy be frozen in time as of 1688? Could the doctrine rather be seen as one of continuous evolution? Moreover, the notion of revolution is usually confined to a change that is either violent or entirely outside the existing framework of law. A change brought about in accordance with the existing rules which is the basis of the redefinition argument, is surely worth distinguishing from a revolution. Indeed, it seems a misuse of language not to do so. Moreover, even if we accept the idea of Wade's 'higher rule' this does not exclude the redefinition theory. Why should the higher rule, supposedly made by those in charge of the 1688 revolution, not authorise its creature – Parliament – to alter the rule itself? Wade believes that the courts can alter parliamentary supremacy and calls this a revolution, but denies that Parliament can do so. Neither logic, nor practical politics, nor indeed historical evidence, point inevitably to this.

Perhaps the difference between Wade's theory and the redefinition theory is really only one of language, so that, although incommensurable, they turn out to be combinable. Both theories agree that the courts could be faced with the choice and would have to resolve it. Both probably agree that, at this rarefied level, politics and law are inextricably intermingled. If the courts accept a 'redefinition of Parliament' Wade would call it a revolution. Others would regard the court as having resolved a basic ambiguity within the existing constitution, sometimes described as 'continuing or self-embracing sovereignty'. It is a matter for you, the reader, to decide which approach is the more helpful.

6.5.4　The European Union

EC law is made by various special bodies appointed by the member states and is locked into the legal systems of each member state in accordance with the laws of that state. However, member states are obliged under the Treaties to give effect to those community laws that are intended to be binding within domestic law. It is sometimes argued that the UK has therefore surrendered part of parliamentary supremacy (see *Blackburn* v. *A-G* (1971)). If this is right then a democratic body has committed the arrogance of trying to bind the freedom of future generations. We shall discuss the matter in more detail in Chapter 7 but will outline the position here.

A treaty as such cannot change English law. The European Communities Act 1972 incorporated EC law into the UK constitution. Another Act of Parliament could repeal the 1972 Act, the question being how strong would be the language required to do so. The European Communities Act 1972 s. 2 (4) states that 'any enactment, passed or to be passed . . . shall be construed and have effect subject to the foregoing provisions of this section'. The provisions referred to require among other things that the English courts must give effect to certain laws made by European bodies (s. 2 (1)).

The effect of this seems to be that a UK statute, even one passed after the relevant EC law, must give way to EC law. This is often described as 'disapplying' an Act. This creates a strong presumption of interpretation to the effect that the clearest language is needed to displace the primacy of a community law and therefore displaces the doctrine of implied repeal which we said earlier is not sacrosanct. It does not seem to affect a statute that unambiguously states that it is to override European law (see *Garland* v. *British Rail Engineering Ltd (BREL)* (1983); *MacCarthys Ltd* v. *Smith* (1979); *Factortame* v. *Secretary of State for Transport* (No. 2) (1991); *Stoke-on-Trent City Council* v. *B&Q plc* (1991)). However, EC law seems to take priority over the Human Rights Act 1998.

6.6　Parliamentary Supremacy and the Rule of Law

Dicey (1915, Ch. 13) tried to reconcile parliamentary supremacy with the rule of law. He claimed that parliamentary sovereignty favours the rule of law for three reasons. Firstly, since Parliament comprises three separate elements – the Queen, Lords and Commons – it can express itself only through the law in the form of an Act of Parliament with each branch checking the others. Secondly, Parliament has no direct executive power and cannot directly appoint or dismiss the officials of the executive government. Thirdly the rule of law 'necessitates' parliamentary sovereignty, in that if the executive wishes to violate someone's rights it must first obtain powers from Parliament and must therefore place itself under the supervision of the courts whose loyalty is to the statute not the wishes of the executive. Thus the courts operate as a check on Parliament at least by interpreting statutes in accordance with rule of law values.

However, Dicey's view of both parliamentary supremacy and the rule of law depended heavily on the pivotal role which Dicey believed was played by the House of Lords as a brake on party politics and custodian of traditional values. Dicey therefore relied on a separation of powers within the sovereign body. He was also committed to the view, which Craig (1994, ch. 2) refers to as 'self-correcting democracy', that the voice of the nation, i.e. the majority of the electorate, should ultimately prevail. Dicey did not therefore tackle the problem of protecting minorities against the majority although he placed faith in the pragmatic spirit of the common law as a means of protecting civil liberties.

When Dicey revised his book on the brink of the First World War, he realised that the emergence of powerful political parties and the broadening of the popular franchise had greatly increased the power of the executive not only over Parliament but also to manipulate the electorate. In particular Dicey realised that the Parliament Act 1911 which prevents the House of Lords from blocking most bills introduced in the Commons would make it more difficult to get rid of a bad government. Moreover government had begun to provide a wide range of services which benefited some groups at the expense of others, so that a uniform public opinion, if it ever existed, could no longer be assumed and the influence of disparate groups within society including vested business interests was increasing.

As we saw in Chapter 5, modern courts will not interpret statutes mechanically but will apply them in context, part of which is respect for fundamental values and individual rights. The difficulty is of course to draw the line between interpretation of and outright disobedience to a statute. *Anisminic Ltd* v. *Foreign Compensation Commission* (1969) is sometimes regarded as a judicial attempt to subvert Parliament under the cloak of interpretation. The applicant challenged a 'determination' of the Commission that it was not eligible for compensation under a statutory scheme. The governing Act stated that a 'determination' of the Commission could not be questioned in any court of law.

Nevertheless the House of Lords allowed the challenge on the ground that a determination which was outside the Commission's jurisidiction in the sense of its area of power was a nullity and therefore it was not a 'determination' within the meaning of the Act. This reasoning has been criticised as collapsing the distinction between interpreting a statute and overriding one. The contrary argument is that Parliament legislates in the knowledge of basic common law values, which, in accordance with the rule of law, it can be taken to accept unless it clearly states otherwise (see *Piersen* v. *Secretary of State* (1997) per Lord Steyn). Far from being radical the *Anisminic* reasoning was fully documented in the old cases. Therefore Parliament could have anticipated the line that the court might take and have used tighter language if it wanted to exclude challenge.

The notions of the rule of law and separation of powers leave a fundamental question unanswered. What happens if there is a conflict between the will of the elected government clearly expressed in a statute and fundamental rule of law values enforced by the courts? Few would doubt that it is for Parliament to decide what is in the general public interest but suppose Parliament passes a statute that for good reasons, for example combating terrorism, suspends elections. There is no rational way of choosing between these incommensurable values but someone must have the last word. Some such as Dworkin (1996), arguing that democracy is more than merely the wishes of the majority, would entrust the courts with the power to overturn or disregard legislation but others such as Waldron (1998) would allow the legislature the last word on the ground that the courts are no better qualified to decide these matters than is Parliament (see Chapter 18).

As we saw in Chapter 5, Allan (2001) argues that it is inconsistent with the political assumptions of a liberal society on which the rule of law is based that the legislature, or indeed any part of the government should be all powerful. Allan claims that, in the common law tradition, the courts have the duty to protect the fundamental values of the society. He does not challenge parliamentary supremacy directly but pushes the courts' power of interpretation to the extreme. Relying on the fact that the court is concerned not with the statute generally but with its application to the individual case, Allan suggests that the court can legitimately hold that a statute which appears to be grossly unjust in the particular context does not apply to the particular case. This approach could be reconciled with parliamentary supremacy on the basis that Parliament cannot foresee every implication of the laws it makes and can be assumed to respect the rule of law. In *Cooper* v. *Wandsworth Board of Works* (1863) Byles J put the matter more strongly when he said that 'the justice of the common law will supply the omission of the legislature'.

Allan's approach might be regarded as a fiction. For example could the court defy the normal understandings of language and logic to disapply a statute which said that a decision of an official could not be challenged in the courts on any grounds whatsoever *including jurisdictional grounds* (e.g. Regulation of Investigatory Powers Act 2000 s. 67 (8)))? Indeed, it has been said that 'whoever hath an absolute authority to interpret any written or spoken laws, it is he who is truly the lawgiver and not the person who just spoke or wrote them' (Bishop Hoadley's sermon preached before the king, 1717).

As a matter of logic and practice, either the court or Parliament could be the ultimate guardian of fundamental values. There is no necessary connection between a set of laws and the question of how disputes rising out of them should be settled. The matter is one of political preference and the moral and practical advantages of different kinds of dispute mechanism. For example Locke, even though he rejected unlimited sovereignty, would give the last word to the legislature subject to a right of rebellion, and there is still controversy in the USA as to whether the Supreme Court in *Marbury* v. *Madison* (1803) was right to hold that a written constitution entitles the courts to rule upon compliance with it.

The judges themselves are equivocal. Some judges have spoken of 'twin sovereignties' between Parliament and the courts, Parliament being supreme in making the law, the court in interpreting it (see e.g. *X v Morgan Grampian Publishers Ltd* [1991] 1 AC1, 48) while others have asserted the supremacy of Parliament over the common law. In *R* v. *Lord Chancellor's Department ex parte Witham* (1993), one of the most influential protagonists of the common law, Sir John Laws, on the one hand suggested that the supremacy of Parliament was 'accorded' to it by the courts but on the other hand emphasised that, although very clear statutory language is required to override a fundamental right, ultimately Parliament could do so. There are also extra-judicial statements by judges suggesting that parliamentary supremacy may be conditional on compliance with fundamental values (see also Woolf, 1995; Sedley, 1995a and in Nolan, 1997, p. 26; Laws, 1993, 1995, 1997; Cook, 1988 but see Irvine, 1996; Steyn, 1997).

6.7 Conclusion

The doctrine of parliamentary supremacy rests on frail foundations. Parliamentary supremacy was a historical response to political circumstances and it does not follow that the same response is appropriate today. The period during which Dicey promoted the doctrine (before the First World War) was one of relative political stability and economic prosperity for the UK. The people, or at least the majority, were benefiting from the spoils of empire, and belief that Parliament backed by consensus values could deliver stability and prosperity was still plausible. Popular revolution as experienced elsewhere had been staved off by cautious reforms. Latterly, different forces, both domestic and international, have arisen which have made parliamentary sovereignty appear parochial, politically unreal and intellectually threadbare. These forces include the global economy, devolution, membership of the European Union and other international obligations, and the increasing powers of the executive over Parliament. There is no longer a political consensus that Parliament should be legally unlimited and no compelling legal reason why it should be.

6.8   Note: Delegated Legislation

The doctrine of parliamentary supremacy concerns Acts of Parliament. In practice, however, most of English law consists of delegated or subordinate legislation. Delegated legislation comprises laws made outside Parliament, usually by ministers but also by the Privy Council, and by statutory bodies such as local authorities. Such lawmaking is possible only under powers which are conferred by an Act of Parliament (the 'parent' Act). It is commonplace for a statute to lay down a general principle and then to confer power upon a minister to make detailed rules fleshing out the principle. Delegated lawmaking powers are sometimes very wide, and often permit the minister to implement or alter other Acts of Parliament (the so-called 'Henry VIII' clause, e.g. Deregulation Act 1994, Local Government Act 2000 s. 5, Pollution Prevention and Control Act 1999).

Delegated legislation has often been criticised on constitutional grounds, and is, of course, an infringement of the strict theory of the separation of powers. Delegated legislation can be made without the public and democratic processes represented, albeit imperfectly, by Parliament. However, it is difficult to imagine a complex and highly regulated society such as our own that could function effectively if all laws had to be made by Parliament itself (see Committee on Ministers Powers (1932), Cmd. 4060). Most delegated legislation is subject to safeguards in the form of a limited amount of parliamentary scrutiny (see Chapter 11). Unlike a statute, delegated legislation can be set aside by the courts if it is outside the powers conferred by Parliament and also if it violates the Human Rights Act 1998.

Delegated legislation comes under many names, including, for example, regulations, orders, directions, rules, bylaws. Little hinges on the precise terminology used. However, a compendium term, 'statutory instrument', applies to most delegated legislation made by ministers and to Statutory Orders in Council (Statutory Instruments Act 1946). Statutory instruments must be formally published, and, in accordance with the rule of law it is a defence in criminal proceedings to show that an instrument has not been published and that it is not reasonable to expect the accused to be aware of it (ibid. s. 4). However, it seems hat failure to publish does not affect validity for other purposes (see *R.* v. *Sheer Metalcraft* (1954)).

Summary

6.1   The doctrine of parliamentary supremacy provides the fundamental legal premise of the UK constitution. It rests only upon general acceptance by the courts. The doctrine means that an Act of Parliament must be obeyed by the courts, that later Acts prevail over earlier ones, and that rules made by external bodies, for example under international law, cannot override Acts of Parliament. It does not follow that Parliament is supreme politically although the line between legal and political supremacy is blurred.

6.2   Parliamentary supremacy rests on frail foundations. Without a written constitution it is impossible to be sure as to its legal basis other than as an evolving practice which is usually said to depend on the 1688 revolution. It is possible to maintain that the common law is really supreme.

6.3   Parliament is itself a creature of the law. The customary and statutory rules which have evolved since medieval times determine that, except in special cases, Parliament for this purpose means the Queen with the assent of the House of Lords and House of Commons. The courts can determine whether any document is an Act of Parliament in this sense, but cannot enquire into whether the correct procedure within each House has been followed.

6.4   The doctrine has two separate aspects: first, that the courts must obey Acts of Parliament in preference to any other kind of legal authority, and second, that no body, including Parliament itself, can place legal limits upon the freedom of action of a future Parliament. The first of these principles is generally accepted, but the second is open to dispute.

6.5   The doctrine is subject to considerable attack.

   (i) the 'redefinition' argument proposes that by altering the basic requirements for lawmaking Parliament can effectively limit itself, just as it could if it abolished itself in favour of a more limited body;

   (ii) grants of independence to dependent territories; these can probably be revoked lawfully in the eyes of UK courts;

   (iii) the possibility that parts of the Acts of Union with Scotland and Ireland are unchangeable: this is probably outside the courts' jurisdiction;

(iv) the idea that Parliament limited the freedom of future Parliaments in relation to certain laws made by the European Communities. The implied repeal principle has been modified but Parliament probably retains the ultimate power to override an EC rule.

6.6   It is difficult to reconcile parliamentary supremacy with the extended version of the rule of law which was discussed in Chapter 5. There is a separation of powers between Parliament and the courts. The courts interpret statutes and can do so according to their own views of what the statute means. These are not necessarily the same as Parliament's views. There is a thin line between interpretation and disobedience which sometimes creates tension between Parliament and judges. More fundamentally it can be argued that parliamentary supremacy was created by the courts who can therefore withdraw it.

6.7   Acts of Parliament must be distinguished from delegated legislation. The latter can be set aside by the courts on the ordinary grounds of judicial review.

Further Reading

Allan, *Constitutional Justice*, Chapter 7.
Allan 'Parliamentary sovereignty: law, politics and revolution', 113 *Law Quarterly Review* 443.
Craig, *Public Law and Democracy*, chapter 2.
Bradley in Jowell and Oliver (eds) *The Changing Constitution*.
Griffith (2001) 'The common law and the political constitution' 117 *Law Quarterly Review* 42.
Munro, *Studies in Constitutional Law*, chapters 5, 6.
Marshall, *Constitutional Theory*, chapter 3.
MacCormick, N. (1978) 'Does the United Kingdom have a constitution? Reflections on *MacCormack* v. *Lord Advocate*', 29 *NILQ* 1.
MacCormick, (1993) 'Beyond the sovereign state' *Modern Law Review* 1.
Mullender, (1998) 'Parliamentary supremacy, the constitution and the judiciary' 45 *NILQ*, 138.
Wade, (1955) 'The basis of legal sovereignty', *Cambridge Law Journal* 172.
Laws Sir J. (1993) 'Is the High Court the guardian of fundamental constitutional rights?', *Public Law* 59.

Exercises

6.1   Trace the development of the doctrine of parliamentary supremacy. Has it a secure legal basis?

6.2   To what extent, if at all, has the doctrine of parliamentary supremacy been affected by the 'redefinition theory'?

6.3   'Every age and generation must be as free to act for itself, in all cases as the ages and generations which preceded it. The vanity and presumption of governing beyond the grave is the most ridiculous and insolent of all tyrannies' (Thomas Paine). Discuss.

6.4   Marshal the arguments for and against the proposition that the UK Parliament cannot repeal the Act of Union with Scotland.

6.5 To what extent is it useful to distinguish between legal and political sovereignty? Do you agree with Dicey's attempt to do so?

6.6 Consider the validity and effect of the following provisions contained in (fictitious) Acts of Parliament:

  (i) Decisions made under this Act shall not be questioned in any court on any ground whatsoever including jurisdictional grounds.

  (ii) 'There shall be a bill of rights in the UK and no Act to be enacted at any time in the future shall have effect, in as far as it is inconsistent with the bill of rights, unless it has been assented to by a two-thirds majority of both Houses of Parliament and no Act shall repeal this Act unless it has the same two-thirds majority.'

  (iii) 'No Bill shall be introduced into either House of Parliament which purports to affect the established Church of England unless it recites on its face that it has the prior approval of the Synod of the Church of England.'

  (iv) 'There shall be no Parliamentary elections for 50 years.'

  (v) 'This Act shall apply notwithstanding any contrary rule of European Community law' (see Chapter 7).

6.7 'The sovereignty of Parliament and the supremacy of the law of the land – the two principles which pervade the whole of the English constitution may appear to stand in opposition to each other, or to be at best countervailing forces. But this appearance is delusive ...' (Dicey). Discuss.

Part II

The Geographical Division of Powers

7 Federalism and Devolution

7.1 Introduction: Federal and Devolved Government

In a federal state such as the USA, the constitution divides power between a central federal government and separate state units in such a way that each is independent within its own sphere and neither can override the other. Federalism is therefore a way of giving effect to republican values as a form of separation of powers. Federalism allows diverse units to retain their distinctive identity while at the same time encouraging unity where there is a common interest. Federalism is practicable where the component units have sufficient in common economically and culturally, for example a shared history or language to enable them to co-operate, while at the same time each unit is sufficiently distinctive to constitute a community in its own right. Thus a delicate balance must be struck. The USA and Australia are relatively successful federations whereas Canada, with its split between English-speaking and French-speaking regions, is less stable. Yugoslavia, with its many ethnic tensions, has been tragically unsuccessful. The relationship between a federal government and the governments within it, is not, therefore in law, one of superior and inferior, but of partnership. Each has its own sphere of activity and its own constitution and courts and it may be unlawful for one to trespass upon the other. This is why the debate about whether the European Union is a federal structure is sometimes confused by those who regard federalism as a kind of overriding government.

Federalism involves certain basic ingredients. There is a single federal citizenship and free movement within the federation. The central government usually represents the country on the international level and exercises defined functions – typically, defence and foreign affairs, currency, postal services and important commercial activities – while leaving residual power sometimes including the basic civil and criminal law with the states. Some versions allocate particular matters to the states with the federal level as the residuary power. Where responsibilities overlap, doctrines such as 'pre-emption' which allows a governmental entity to stake a claim over a particular area of activity, or the 'supremacy' clause of the US constitution provide resolving mechanisms. Representatives of the states may sit in the federal legislature. In the USA for example the lower house (House of Representatives) is elected according to the population of the states, while in the upper house (the Senate) each state has equal representation.

As with any constitution, the actual disposition of power in a federation depends on political and economic reality so that the real balance between centre and state may not be apparent from reading the constitution. It is probably best to regard terms such as 'federal' or 'unitary' not as precise definitions, but as convenient points upon a political spectrum ranging from loose associations of countries for particular purposes to simple one-government states.

On this spectrum the UK's constitution is closer to the latter extreme and is therefore called a 'unitary' constitution. A unitary state has an overriding supreme lawmaker which can devolve power to subordinate units but is free to take the power back. However the UK is not an extreme example of a unitary constitution being a union of what were the separate units of England, parts of Ireland and Scotland. Wales is also part of the UK but has never been a separate political unit in its own right. Moreover certain powers have recently been devolved to elected assemblies in Scotland, Northern Ireland and Wales but without limiting the powers of Parliament.

Dicey strongly opposed federalism in the UK, a factor which influenced his attitude to parliamentary supremacy. He thought that federalism tends to conservatism, creates divided loyalties and that it elevates legalism to a primary value, making the courts the pivot on which the constitution turns and perhaps threatening their independence (Dicey, 1915, p. 171). However, Dicey recognised that federalism might make it possible to unite communities that otherwise would quarrel.

During the late nineteenth century there were some advocates of a federal UK as a way of avoiding home rule for Ireland and also proposals for a federation of the UK and some of its overseas territories. However, on the whole, federalism has not been a serious element of UK politics. The Kilbrandon Report (1973) argued against a federal constitution for the UK on the following grounds. First the units are widely different in economic terms, with England being the dominant member. Any federation is therefore likely to be unbalanced. Secondly a federal regime would be contrary to our constitutional traditions in that it would elevate the courts over political machinery. Thirdly the UK was thought to require central and flexible economic management since its resources are unevenly distributed geographically much of its land area being thinly populated hills. Fourthly, apart from Northern Ireland, regional issues were not high on the agenda of the main parties, which suggested that there was little public desire for federalism.

Before devolution, the internal affairs of Scotland and Wales were governed by the UK central executive with what has been described as overtones of colonialism an echo of which survives in the present devolution arrangements (Rawlings, 1998). This took the form of 'administrative devolution' to ministers for Scotland, Wales and Northern Ireland. There was therefore no specific democratic power base or accountability mechanism linking the ministers to their regions (see Munro, 1999, p. 37 *et seq.*). Indeed the relevant minister might have an English constituency. Scotland and Northern Ireland have separate legal systems but the House of Lords and the Privy Council are final courts of appeal for all the UK jurisdictions.

Nevertheless the Kilbrandon Report asserted that government in the UK was over-centralised and recommended devolved government. In a closely integrated and mobile economy such as that of the UK this can probably not be justified on the basis of more efficient or less corrupt government but rests upon the more intangible claims of local democracy (see Chapter 8). Referendums were subsequently held in Scotland and Wales which foundered because they failed to obtain the required two-thirds majorities in favour of change. Nothing further was done until the Labour government took office in 1997. Following referendums which produced considerable public support for devolution in Scotland and significant but less support for devolution in Wales, legislation was introduced to give both legislative and executive power to a Scottish Parliament and executive and subordinate legislative power to a Welsh Assembly. At the same time the peace process in Northern Ireland included proposals to restore legislative and executive power to the province which had been directly governed by the UK government since 1972. These proposals were also approved by a referendum and the devolved arrangements were put in place subject to the completion of the peace process between the various parties representing Catholic and Protestant communities. The devolution arrangements also include arrangements for 'concordats' between the UK government and the devolved administrations. These put in place conventions for co-ordinating the activities of the governments, for example through a joint ministerial committee and may buttress of the kind of secretive informality that has long bedevilled UK government (see Memorandum of Understanding and Supplementary Agreements (2001) Cm. 4806; Rawlings, 2000).

The devolution arrangements are asymmetrical in the sense that they are different in each region. First, the powers of the three devolved bodies and their relationship with the UK government are different. Secondly, England, comprising 85% of the population of the UK, has no democratic devolved institutions of its own nor indeed a legal identity. Thus Scottish, Welsh and Northern Ireland members of the UK Parliament are entitled to vote in debates affecting exclusively English matters (the 'West Lothian' question, so-called after the constituency of Tam Dalziel, a relentless pursuer of the matter). Thirdly Scottish, Welsh and Northern Ireland voters are represented in the UK Parliament roughly in proportion to their population. This means that the UK Parliament, which retains unlimited power to legislate in relation to Scotland, Wales and Northern Ireland and provides most of the funding for the regional governments, is dominated by English MPs.

There seems to be little public support for devolution within England and the Kilbrandon Report was divided on the matter. Constitutional issues relating to the English regions are divided between the Departments of Transport, Local Government and the Regions (DTLR), the Department of Trade and Industry and the Cabinet Office. There are nine regional offices of central government charged with a co-ordinating role. There are also eight Regional Development Agencies (RDAs) wholly appointed by the Secretary of State and charged only with one group of purposes, that of advancing economic development including related matters of education and training (Regional Development Agencies Act 1998). RDAs are funded by the DTLR but accountable to the Secretary of State for Trade and Industry. However, the government proposes to issue a White Paper in 2002 on devolution in England.

7.2   Scotland

Scotland was a separate nation state from 1010 until 1706. It has a separate legal system which has stronger links with civil law systems than is the case with England. In 1603, as a result of inheritance, the Crowns of England and Scotland were united in James I (England)/ James VI (Scotland). This led to economic and social integration including free trade and common citizenship. In 1689 Scotland offered its Crown to William and Mary on the same terms, the supremacy of Parliament, as in England.

After quarrels between the two Parliaments the Treaty of Union 1706 abolished the separate Scottish and English Parliaments and created a Parliament of Great Britain. The treaty was confirmed by separate Acts of each Parliament (Act of Union with England 1706;

Act of Union with Scotland 1707). The Acts of Union are still in force. They preserve the separate Scottish legal system and church and safeguard the private rights of Scottish subjects (above, p. 130). The Union was unpopular but was brought about by economic interest on the part of Scotland and fear of invasion on the part of England.

Since the sixteenth-century Reformation there had been cultural assimilation between the two countries, but also religious warfare between Catholics and Protestants. There were violent uprisings and government oppression throughout the eighteenth century followed by governmental attempts to instil a distinctive Scottish culture during the nineteenth century. Also during the nineteenth century the large absentee landowners displaced tenant farmers in the notorious 'Highland Clearances' which remains a source of grievance.

Until the Scotland Act 1998 there was administrative devolution in Scotland through the Scottish Office. There are also special committees in Parliament to examine Scottish Affairs. In particular the 'Scottish Grand Committee' deals with bills exclusively relating to Scotland. Before the Scotland Act 1998, Scotland was entitled to at least 71 seats in the UK Parliament, thus making it over-represented in terms of its population. Section 86(1) of the 1998 Act abolishes this entitlement and places Scotland under the same regime as England in terms of the criteria of defining constituencies. This is likely to reduce the number of Scottish MPs in future UK Parliaments.

The Scotland Act 1998 creates a Scottish Parliament elected by the first-past-the-post system, topped up by a regional party list elected by the additional-member version of proportional representation (below, Chapter 10). There are eight regions each having seven seats and currently 73 single-member constituencies. The Scottish Parliament has a general power, subject to restrictions, to legislate by means of Acts which will receive the Royal Assent. The Parliament elects a Presiding Officer and two Deputies (s. 19).

The Scotland Act 1998 (s. 27(7)) preserves the power of the UK Parliament to legislate for Scotland. Indeed s. 37 empowers the UK Parliament to override the Acts of Union. However, as we saw in Chapter 6, it is arguable that the UK Parliament cannot override certain provisions of the Acts of Union. The Scottish Parliament can legislate generally subject to the restrictions in the Act (s. 28, s. 29 sched. 4). These are substantial and make it clear that, in law at any rate, this is devolution rather than federalism. In practice the scope of the Scottish Parliament corresponds to the functions formerly exercised by the Scottish Office. However, given the substantial influence of the Scottish Nationalist Party, Scottish administrations are more likely to be coalitions than is the case in the UK Parliament because of the proportionate element of the electoral system. This might have a de-stabilising effect on the UK as a whole by enabling Scotland to follow different, and more consensual policies than those of Westminster.

The Scottish Parliament cannot, except in minor respects (sched. 4, para. 4), amend the Scotland Act itself. Nor can it alter basic con-stitutional provisions nor the free trade provisions of the Acts of Union. It cannot override European law, nor ECHR rights binding in UK law under the Human Rights Act 1998. It has a limited tax-raising power to vary income tax by up to 3 pence in the pound, so that the government will depend on supply from Westminster.

There is a list of 'reserved matters' on which only the UK Parliament can legislate (sched. 5). They include the main economic levers, foreign policy, defence and national security, border controls security, trans-port safety and regulation, employment and the regulation of key professions and social security (see Cm. 3658 (1997) and s. 30 sched. 5). By virtue of s. 29 (3) the question whether a matter is a reserved matter must be decided by reference to its purpose having regard among other things to its effect in all the circumstances. Legislation will not therefore be invalidated if it incidentally effects matters outside its field (see *Gallagher* v. *Lynn* [1937] AC 863 at 870). There is a variation applicable to Scots criminal law and private law whereby a provision which would otherwise not relate to a reserved matter but does so because it alters these areas of law is treated as a reserved matter unless its purpose is to secure consistency between reserved matters and others (s. 29 (4)). This allows the Scottish Parliament to make general reforms to Scots law. This purposive approach is capable of giving rise to considerable difficulty (see Himsworth and Munro, 1999, p. 37). However s. 101 (2) requires laws to be interpreted narrowly in favour of their competence.

Despite the royal assent, Acts of the Scottish Parliament are tech-nically subordinate legislation owing their validity only to the Scotland Act 1998 (see e.g. Human Rights Act 1998 s. 21). They can be set aside by the courts and will be overridden by inconsistent UK legislation. The validity of proceedings leading to an enactment does not affect its validity (s. 28 (5)), but otherwise Acts of the Scottish Parliament which are outside its competence 'are not law' (s. 28). Indeed it is arguable that, as in the case of other delegated legislation, for example local bylaws, the courts might set aside an Act of the Scottish Parlia-ment on the grounds of unreasonableness or unfairness. However, the democratic character of the devolved law-making process provi-sions suggests that the court will be reluctant to interfere on these grounds. The parliament has no immunity from legal proceedings but has absolute privilege in defamation and protection in relation to contempt of court (ss. 40–42).

There are mechanisms for ensuring that the Scottish Parliament keeps within its powers. 'Devolution issues' can be raised in any court and can be ultimately decided by the Privy Council either on appeal or by way of a reference from a lower court (sched. 6). Where a devolution issue arises before the House of Lords it must be referred to the Privy Council unless the House in all the circumstances thinks that it is more appropriate to decide it itself. The Advocate General (an officer responsible to the UK government), the Lord Advocate or the UK Attorney-General can bring proceedings or require to be made a party to any litigation (s. 33). The court can protect people who may have relied on invalid laws passed by the Scottish Parliament by removing the retrospective effect of the invalidity or suspending the invalidity to allow the defect to be corrected (s. 102).

When a bill is introduced in the Scottish Parliament the Presiding Officer must decide whether it is within the powers of the Parliament (s. 31). The Advocate General, the Lord Advocate or the UK Attorney-General can also require a bill to be referred to the Privy Council (s. 33). The Presiding Officer submits bills for royal assent. However, and somewhat controversially due to the 'colonial' flavour of such a power, the Secretary of State can prohibit a bill from being sent for royal assent where s/he 'has reasonable ground to believe' that the bill would be incompatible with international obligations, or the interests of national security or defence, or would have an adverse effect on the law relating to reserved matters (s. 35) (see also s. 58). The Secretary of State's intervention would be subject to judicial review. The UK government can make subordinate legislation remedying *ultra vires* acts of the Scottish Parliament and the Scottish executive (s. 107).

The Scotland Act 1998 provides for the executive in terms based on, but differing in important respects from, the conventions that apply to the Westminster Parliament. The Parliament elects a First Minister from among its members. The First Minister appoints and removes the other 'Scottish Ministers'. Appointments must be approved by the Parliament (s. 44, s. 47). The Scottish Ministers must also be members of the Parliament but cannot also hold ministerial office in the UK government. Thus Scottish devolution raises political questions about the balance and composition of the UK cabinet and indeed of the political responsibilities of the Secretary of State for Scotland (see Himsworth and Munro, 1999). Additional functions outside devolved matters can be given to Scottish ministers by Order in Council (s. 63), for which they are accountable to the UK Parliament.

The Scottish Parliament is stronger in relation to the executive than is the case with the UK Parliament. The Parliament lasts for a fixed term of four years, so that, unlike the case with the UK prime minister, the first minister cannot request a dissolution. A first minister can resign at any time and must do so if the Scottish executive is defeated on a vote of confidence (s. 45). The first minister ceases to hold office if a person is appointed in his place, as where a new Parliament is formed after a general election (s. 46). Other ministers must also resign if the executive is defeated on a vote of confidence, and automatically lose office on ceasing to be a member of Parliament except in the case of a dissolution where they retain office until removed by the incoming administration.

Suppose an administration finds itself deadlocked because of tensions within a coalition. Under the Scotland Act the Parliament can resolve that it be dissolved. The resolution must be supported by at least two-thirds of the total number of seats. The Presiding Officer must then propose an election and the Queen 'may' dissolve Parliament and call an election (s. 3). It is not clear what advice, if any, the Queen should take or whether she must automatically dissolve Parliament on a request by the Presiding Officer. The same procedure applies if the Parliament cannot agree on the choice of first minister. This procedure seems to mean that a minority can hold a government to ransom. Bagehot's claim for the Westminster system that Parliament can easily get rid of a struggling government would not therefore seem to apply to Scotland.

7.3   Northern Ireland

The history of Ireland is complex and raises fundamental political issues. These centre upon religious divisions between the Catholic and Protestant communities and upon a history of imposed settlement from England and Scotland. Broadly speaking the majority Protestant community prefer to remain an integral part of the UK while the Catholic community would prefer union with the neighbouring Republic of Ireland.

Ireland had been subject to the English Crown since the tenth century, although in practice England originally controlled only an area around Dublin called the Pale. According to English law, laws made by the Irish Parliament had been subject to English statutes and to approval by the King in Council since 1494 ('Poyning's Law'). Henry VIII and Elizabeth I attempted to extend English administration to the whole of Ireland, precipitating rebellion followed by confiscation of land belonging to the Catholic population and extensive settlement by the English and Scots. Cromwell's regime during the 1650s consolidated this policy with large-scale massacres, thus sowing the seeds of current problems. The conquest of Ireland was completed in 1690 when William III, in alliance with France and supported by the Pope, defeated the deposed Catholic king of England, James II, at the Battle of the Boyne.

After a series of violent rebellions against protestant supremacy, the Acts of Union of 1800 joined Britain and Ireland into the UK thus creating the UK Parliament. The Irish Parliament was abolished in favour of Irish representation in the UK Parliament. The Acts of Union declared that the Union was to last 'for ever'. The Acts of Union also protected the United Church of England and Ireland but the repeal of this provision by the Irish Church Act 1879 has been upheld (*Ex parte Canon Selwyn* (1872)).

Unrest punctuated by periods of violence continued throughout the nineteenth and twentieth centuries generated by internal religious discrimination and by the apparent indifference of the UK government to the economic disasters of the 1840s which decimated the Irish population. In the late nineteenth century the question of 'Irish home rule' was among the most important questions in UK politics. It weakened the personal authority of the monarchy which unwisely took sides in the dispute and generated dispute about the most fundamental principles of the constitution including the balance of representation in the UK parliament. No agreement was reached but the notion of parliamentary supremacy became a powerful symbol. Dicey in particular was a strong supporter of the Union and thought that home rule would be possible only by abolishing Parliament.

In 1920 there was a crude compromise. The Government of Ireland Act 1920 partitioned Ireland and established a devolved government in Northern Ireland. Section 75 provided that 'notwithstanding the establishment of the Parliament of Northern Ireland *or* anything contained in this Act, the supreme authority of the Parliament of the United Kingdom shall remain unaffected and undiminished over all persons, matters and things in (Northern Ireland) and every part thereof.' Originally there was proportional representation, thus giving a voice to the Catholic minority, but this was abolished in 1929, allowing Protestant majority rule until 1972. The Irish Free State (Constitution) Act 1922 gave the southern states internal self-government.

However, these measures were ignored in Southern Ireland which created its own constitution based upon the sovereignty of the people.

This constitution extended to the whole of Ireland although it was ineffective in the north. However, according to UK law, the status of Ireland still depended upon the older UK legislation (see *Murray* v. *Parkes* (1942)). There were therefore conflicting legal orders, each being valid from its internal viewpoint. Eventually the UK recognised the independence of the republic (Ireland Act 1949) but provided that '... in no event will Northern Ireland cease to be part of ... the United Kingdom without the consent of the Parliament of Northern Ireland' (ibid. s. 1 (2)).

In 1972 the devolved Northern Ireland Parliament at Stormont was prorogued and direct rule from Westminster imposed. The Ireland Act 1949 was repealed by the Northern Ireland Constitution (Amendment) Act 1973 and a new Assembly with proportional representation was created (Northern Ireland Assembly Act 1973). The entrenchment of the Union in the 1949 Act was replaced by a provision requiring a referendum of the people. However, these arrangements were opposed by unionist politicians and never implemented. The concept of power-sharing led to strikes and disturbances and stringent emergency legislation was imposed on Northern Ireland (Northern Ireland (Temporary Provisions) Act 1972; Northern Ireland Act 1974).

Latterly a series of agreements attempted to engineer a compromise by tackling discrimination, combating terrorism and creating machinery for inter-community negotiations (e.g. the Anglo-Irish Agreement 1985; the 'Downing Street Declaration' (1994), Cm. 2422). These formed the basis of the current accommodation in the 'Good Friday Agreement' (1998 Cm. 3883) between the two governments and the main political parties in Northern Ireland. This provides for the restoration of devolved government, the amendment of the Irish Constitution so as to accept that Northern Ireland is currently part of the UK, the creation of a 'British Island Council' as a consultative forum representing the interests of Ireland and the various parts of the UK and the Channel Islands, and for an extension of cross border co-operation in the form of a NorthSouth Ministerial Council.

The Good Friday Agreement was endorsed by 71% of voters in Northern Ireland and 94% in the Republic of Ireland in referendums. However, because the Good Friday Agreement makes devolution conditional upon the completion of the peace process there are powers to suspend the devolved institutions and to revert to direct rule by the UK government. This occurred for several months during 1999. The main points of contention are the question of the decommissioning of weapons by the IRA which also bedevilled the unsuccessful negotiations in the 1920s, and the organisation of policing in Northern Ireland (see Police (Northern Ireland Act) 2000).

The current legislation, the Northern Ireland Act 1998, repeals the 1920 Act and the 1973 legislation. The Act is designed to reduce the impact of sectarianism and to encourage power-sharing between the political communities. It introduces a system of devolved government which attempts to ensure a balance between the competing communities. In doing so it restricts the political freedom of the chief executive to a greater extent than is the case with other governments in the UK. The overriding power of Parliament to make law for Northern Ireland is not affected (s. 5 (6)).

Section 1 provides that Northern Ireland remains part of the UK and that the status of Northern Ireland will be altered only with the consent of a majority of its electorate. If a referendum favours a united Ireland, the Secretary of State is required to 'make proposals' to implement this by agreement with the Irish government. This less than absolute commitment can be interpreted as reducing the UK's claim to Northern Ireland to the 'one hinge' of the will of the majority, although it can be argued that because the Irish constitution now renounces territorial claim to Northern Ireland the Union is thereby reinforced (see Hadfield, 1998).

The Act creates a Northern Ireland Assembly elected by the single transferable vote (Chapter 10). The Assembly's powers are more circumscribed than is the case with Scotland and the Secretary of State has stronger powers. The Assembly chooses the executive (below), subject to provisions designed to ensure cross-community representation. It also elects a Presiding Officer (s. 39). Acts of the Assembly require the Royal Assent and the validity of proceedings leading to an enactment shall not be questioned in the courts (s. 5 (5)). The Assembly sits for a fixed four-year term but can be dissolved on a resolution supported by two-thirds of its members or if a Chief Minister or Deputy Chief Minister cannot be elected (s. 32).

The Assembly has general legislative power in relation to matters exclusively within Northern Ireland subject to European law, to the rights protected by the Human Rights Act 1998 and to 'excepted matters' (s. 6). Discrimination on the ground of religious belief or political opinion is also outside the competence of the Assembly. The Assembly can raise certain taxes but not the main taxes that apply generally throughout the UK. Provisions of the Assembly outside its competence are not law (s. 6). Where a measure is ambiguous it must be interpreted in favour of its validity (s. 78). If the Presiding Officer thinks that a bill is outside the competence of the Assembly he must refer it to the Secretary of State and it cannot proceed. The Attorney-General can also refer a bill to the Privy Council (s. 11).

Unlike the case in Scotland where this is a matter for the Presiding Officer, the Secretary of State submits bills for Royal Assent. He can refuse to submit a bill if he thinks it is outside the competence of the Assembly or contains provisions incompatible with international obligations, the interests of defence or national security, the protection of public safety or public order, or would have an adverse effect on the operation of the single market within the UK (s. 14).

'Excepted' and 'reserved' matters are listed in schedules 2 and 3. The Assembly cannot legislate on excepted matters unless ancillary to other matters. It can legislate on reserved matters and on ancillary matters only with the consent of the Secretary of State (ss. 6, 8). Excepted and reserved matters include the following politically sensitive matters: criminal law and procedure and fugitive offenders; election law; public order; national security; the police; emergency powers; defence; nationality and immigration; firearms and explosives; weapons of mass destruction; the administration of justice and the appointment and removal of judges; financial, intellectual property and genetic regulation; the activities of social security and child support commissioners; the membership, powers, privileges and immunities of the Assembly. Disputes about the competence of the Northern Ireland Assembly and other public authorities are dealt with in broadly the same way as in Scotland. The courts have jurisdiction over devolution issues culminating in the Privy Council and can declare Acts of the Assembly invalid. However, the Secretary of State can make an order remedying an *ultra vires* Act (s. 80).

Executive power remains with the Queen who is empowered to act through ministers (s. 23). The system lacks the discretionary power available to a UK prime minister to appoint or dismiss other ministers or dissolve the legislature. Instead there is a tightly controlled bi-partisan arrangement. The first minister and deputy first ministers are elected jointly by the Assembly from its members. This requires not only a majority of the Assembly as a whole but also separate majorities of unionists and nationalists (s. 16). The first and deputy first ministers hold office until a new election subject to *both* losing office if either resigns or ceases to be a member of the Assembly. Subject to a maximum of 10, which can be increased by the Secretary of State (s. 17(4)), and to the approval of the Assembly, the first and deputy first ministers jointly decide on the number of Northern Ireland ministers heading departments and forming a cabinet. Northern Ireland ministers are then nominated by the political parties from members of the Assembly in accordance with the balance of parties in the Assembly (s. 18).

A minister can be dismissed by his or her party nominating officer and loses office on ceasing to be a member of the Assembly other than after a dissolution (s. 18). Ministers collectively loose office when a new Assembly is elected, where a party is excluded on a vote of confidence, where a new determination as to the number of ministers is made or as prescribed by standing order (ibid.). There are also junior ministers appointed and dismissed by the chief and deputy chief ministers subject to Assembly approval (s. 19). Ministers and political parties can be excluded for up to 12 months (renewable) by the Assembly on the ground that they are not committed to peace or have otherwise broken their oath of office (s. 30). The motion must have the support of at least 30 members (of a total of between 96 and 108) and must be moved by the first and deputy first ministers jointly or by the presiding officer of the Assembly if required to do so by the Secretary of State. The Secretary of State must take into account the propensity to violence and co-operation with the authorities of the excluded person. The resolution must have cross-party support.

By virtue of s. 16(10) ministers must take a pledge of office which includes a 'Ministerial Code of Conduct' (see sched. 4). The code requires the 'strictest standards of propriety, accountability, openness, good community relations and equality and avoiding or declaring conflicts of interest'. Any direct or indirect pecuniary interests which members of the public might reasonably think could influence their judgement must be registered. The content of the code is similar to that which, following the reports of the Nolan Committee, applies to UK ministers and requires compliance with the Committee's 'seven principles of public life' (above, p. 82). In the rest of the UK the code has not been entrenched into law. In Northern Ireland it might therefore be enforceable in the courts.

There are further provisions designed to encourage peace. Firstly the Assembly and other public bodies cannot discriminate on grounds of religious belief or political opinion. Secondly all public bodies must have 'due regard' to the need to promote equal opportunities between persons of different religious belief, political opinions, races, ages, marital status, sexual orientation, gender, and in relation to disability and people with dependants. Thirdly all public authorities must have regard to the desirability of promoting good relationships between persons of different religions, political opinions or racial groups. There are Human Rights and Equal Opportunities Commissioners with powers to advise government and support legal proceedings.

7.4   Wales

Wales has strong cultural traditions, but unlike Scotland and Northern Ireland has never had its own government or legal system. Wales was never a separate state but consisted of a number of principalities. The largest of these passed into English rule in 1084 (Statute of Wales) and the others were subdued by England by the sixteenth century (see Acts of Union with Wales 1536). A separate Welsh Assembly was abolished in 1689. English law applied throughout Wales and a single court system was introduced in 1830. Within Wales there are markedly differ- ent areas both economically and culturally, so that it is more difficult than in the case of Scotland to regard Wales as a country or a nation. Earlier proposals for Welsh devolution in the Wales Act 1978 were defeated by a referendum and the current proposals were only nar- rowly approved.

The emphasis of the Welsh arrangements is threefold: first the strengthening of democratic accountability within Wales, secondly stimulating economic development; thirdly representing Welsh inter- ests at a national and international level (see *A Voice for Wales: The Government's Proposals for a Welsh Assembly*, 1997, Cm. 3718). Relatively weak and flexible mechanisms have been devised for Wales which leave considerable discretion in the hands of UK ministers. These might form a test-bed for future devolution within England (see Rawlings, 1998).

The Government of Wales Act 1998 gives Wales less power than the other regions. The Act creates an elected Welsh Assembly of 60 members elected by a combination of first-past-the-post and the 'additional member' system similar to that in Scotland. The Welsh electoral system is less proportional than the Scottish system, having a greater proportion of first-past-the-post seats (40/20 compared with 73/56). This gives greater power to the majority party which in Wales is likely to be the Labour party.

The Assembly is a corporate body, and a hybrid between a local government model and a cabinet/parliamentary one. It is a combination of subordinate lawmaking and executive body and a method of scrutinising the executive. Unlike the other devolved bodies it has no lawmaking powers of its own. It can exercise only such legislative or executive powers as are transferred to it by Order in Council from UK ministers. The Assembly exercises the functions that were previously exercised by the Welsh Office. These include agriculture, forestry, fisheries and food, environmental and cultural matters, economic and industrial development, education and training, health, housing, local government, social services, sport and tourism, town and country planning, transport, water and flood defences, and the Welsh language. There is particular concern with economic development, and the Assembly is required to prepare schemes dealing with sustainable development, the sustaining and promotion of local government and the promotion of relevant voluntary organisations.

The Assembly has certain powers of control over Welsh QUANGOs, these being specialised non-elected bodies that have proliferated in Wales in recent years. These powers include in some cases the power of abolition or to transfer functions to the Assembly or a local authority. This is designed to meet widespread concerns about the lack of democratic accountability in Wales. An expanded Welsh Development Agency takes over the functions of the Development Board for Rural Wales and the Land Authority for Wales, both of which are abolished.

The powers exercisable under the Act are vested in the Assembly itself with flexible powers to delegate. This is analogous to a local government system on which is grafted a cabinet style executive structure. The Assembly must elect a first secretary, analogous to a prime minister. The first secretary appoints assembly secretaries analogous to ministers (about eight are proposed of which two will not have Assembly committee functions). The first secretary and the assembly secretaries together comprise the Executive Committee analogous to the Cabinet. The Executive Committee can be made up from one party but there must be representation of minority parties on other committees.

The Assembly must also elect committees, one for each of its functions as it determines, to which the executive will be responsible, and also an Audit Committee, and a Subordinate Legislation Scrutiny Committee. Because of the blurring of functions between executive and legislature the Assembly committees are expected to be more pro-active than committees of Parliament and to be involved at every stage of the decision-making process rather than merely scrutinising after the event.

The Assembly can delegate any of its executive functions to the Executive Committee or to another committee or to the first secretary. The Executive Committee can delegate to the first secretary or to an assembly secretary. Considerable power is concentrated in the first secretary along the lines of a cabinet system. The first secretary can delegate any function to an assembly secretary, who in turn can delegate to officials (s. 63 (1)). However, the process of delegation and the structuring of the executive functions is initially controlled by the Secretary of State in the form of power to make standing orders on the advice of a commission. These can be overridden only by a two-thirds majority of the Assembly (ss. 46, 50, 51).

There is an Auditor General for Wales who reports to the Assembly and a Welsh Ombudsman. The National Audit Office can also scrutinise the Assembly's accounts and must work in co-operation with the Auditor General for Wales. The Secretary of State for Wales will continue to represent Welsh affairs at national level and in the Council of Ministers of the EU. The Secretary of State has a duty to consult the Assembly.

There are no separate Welsh courts or an Attorney-General for Wales, the UK Attorney-General having responsibility also for Wales. It seems that any court can invalidate decisions and legislation made by the Assembly. Nevertheless there are provisions similar to those in Scotland and Northern Ireland, for the Privy Council to deal with challenges to the powers of the Assembly and other Welsh bodies by way of appeal or by a reference from the Assembly or the Attorney-General (Government of Wales Act 1998 s. 109, sched. 7).

7.5   The Channel Islands and the Isle of Man

The Channel Islands and the Isle of Man have special constitutional status, being neither part of the UK nor colonies nor overseas territories. They are subject to the Crown under the royal prerogative. The Channel Islands are subject to the Crown as successor to the Duke of Normandy and have their own legislatures, the 'states', their own courts, and are self-governing as to their internal affairs. The common law does not apply and, subject to prerogative and statutory legislation, the law is local customary law. However, because the Channel Islands and the Isle of Man are directly subject to the Crown, the important protection provided by the judicial review powers of the High Court applies to both (see *Ex parte Brown* (1864); *Ex parte Anderson* (1861)).

Parliamentary supremacy was extended to the Channel Islands by a Prerogative Order in Council of 1806. There is a presumption of interpretation that an Act will not apply to the Channel islands in the absence of express words or necessary implication. The Channel Islands are not members of the European Union but there are special treaty arrangements. Channel Island citizens are British citizens (British Nationality 1981 ss. 1, 11, 50 (1)). The position of the Isle of Man is broadly similar, although the Crown's rights seem to derive from an ancient agreement with Norway confirmed by statute (Isle of Man Purchase Act 1765 (repealed)). Legislation made by its legislature, the Tynewald, must be assented to by the Queen in Council. (See

generally Royal Commission on the Constitution 1969–1973 Part XI
and Minutes of Evidence VI, pp. 7, 13, 227–34; *X* v. *UK* (1981), ECHR.)

7.6   British Overseas Territories

In the majority of former UK overseas territories all ties with UK law
have been severed by particular Acts of Parliament (e.g. Canada Act
1982; Australia Act 1986). The UK retains a handful of dependent
territories (formerly called colonies). In principle these are subject to
the full force of parliamentary sovereignty and can be governed under
the royal prerogative. However, certain rules determine the extent to
which English law applies. If the colony was acquired by settlement,
then the settlers carry the common law with them. If the colony is
acquired by conquest or agreement (cession) so that it had its own
population then, once a representative legislature has been established,
English law does not apply unless the Crown reserved the right to
legislate (*Campbell* v. *Hall* (1774)). Moreover, under the Colonial Laws
Validity Act 1865 all representative legislatures have full lawmaking
power, including the power to alter their own constitution, powers and
procedure subject to the UK Parliament (see *Liyanage* v. *R.* (1967)).
The inhabited dependent territories are Anguilla, Bermuda, British
Virgin Islands, Cayman Islands, Falkland Islands, Gibraltar, Mont-
serrat, the Pitcairn Islands, St Helena, the Turks and Caicos Islands.

Summary

7.1   The UK constitution does not distribute power geographically as a method of
limiting the power of the state or enhancing democracy. It favours a strong
central authority. The UK is therefore not a federal state.

7.2   Legislative and executive power has been devolved to elected bodies in
Scotland and Northern Ireland and executive power has been devolved to an
elected Welsh Assembly subject to central government control. In the case
of Scotland and Northern Ireland the UK Parliament has reserved the power to
legislate in respect of many matters and has a general power to override the
devolved assemblies. The distribution of powers between the UK Parliament
and the devolved assemblies, including the protection of particular interests,
reflects the historical and political circumstances of each area. The courts
culminating in the Privy Council have power to adjudicate in devolution issues.
Elections to the devolved bodies are by proportional representation.

7.3   There is no devolved government in England. Regional Development Agencies
have been created but these are appointed bodies charged only with particular
economic goals thus lacking essential attributes of democratic government.

Further Reading

Bogdanor, V. (1998) *Devolution in the United Kingdom*, Oxford: OUP.

Bogdanor, V. (1999) 'Devolution: decentralisation or disintegration?' 70 *Political Quarterly* 185.

Brazier, R. (1999) 'The constitution of the United Kingdom', 58 *Cambridge Law Journal* 96.

Hazell, R. (1999) 'Re-inventing the constitution: can the state survive?', *Public Law* 84.

Himsworth, C., Munro, C. (1999) *The Scotland Act 1998*.

Jones, T.H. (1997) 'Scottish devolution and demarcation disputes', *Public Law* 283.

Jowell and Oliver, *The Changing Constitution*, chapter 5.

Rawlings, R. (1998) 'The new model Wales', 25 *Journal of Law and Society* 461.

Rawlings, R. (2000) 'Concordats of the constitution,' *Law Quarterly Review* 257.

Walker, N. (2000) 'Beyond the unitary conception of the United Kingdom constitution', *Public Law* 384.

White Paper, *Scotland's Parliament* (1997), Cm. 3658.

White Paper, *A Voice for Wales* (1997), Cm. 3718.

Mitchell, J. (1999) 'The creation of the Scottish Parliament: journey without End', 52 *Parliamentary Affairs* 649.

O'Neill, A. (2001) 'Judicial politics and the judicial committee: the devolution jurisprudence of the Privy Council', 64 *Modern Law Review* 603.

Merinos, J. (2001) 'Democracy, governance and governmentally: civic public space and constitutional renewal in Northern Ireland', 21 *Oxford Journal of Legal Studies* 287.

McAlester, L. (2001) 'Wales: Labour's devolution dilemma', 54 *Parliamentary Affairs* 156.

Bradbury, J. and Mitchell, J. (2001) 'Devolution: new politics for old', 54 *Parliamentary Affairs* 257.

Exercises

7.1   What is a federation? Outline the advantages and disadvantages of a federal structure.

7.2   Compare the arguments for devolution within the UK with those in favour of a federal UK.

7.3   What are the main differences between the devolved powers of Scotland, Wales and Northern Ireland and what are the reasons for those differences? Which region has the greatest degree of autonomy?

7.4   'The Scotland Act 1998 provides for the executive in terms based on but differing in important ways from the conventions that apply to the Westminster Parliament'. Discuss.

8 Local Government

Local government in the UK is characterised by two main features. First it is fragmented with several different kinds of local body, functions conferred by many different statutes and diverse methods of control and accountability. Secondly it has no constitutional protection and is regulated in detail by the central government. Contrary to the classical republican notion of devolved power, there is neither law nor convention protecting local autonomy. As a matter of political practice, local authorities may in fact be given a degree of freedom in particular cases this option being conditional upon conforming to a central agenda. However, this fails to meet the republican criterion of non-domination as a right. More usually local powers are required to be exercised in conformity with the central executive's wishes.

By contrast some constitutions specifically protect local government autonomy. For example the Italian constitution and legislation protects both regional and local autonomy according to the subsidiarity principle (Arts 5, 117, 118, Acts 1990/142, 1997/59). The US federal constitution leaves the residual powers of government at state level with some states devolving 'home rule' powers to local authorities. This gives protection to local government through the principle that state interference must be justified by a 'substantial state interest' (see *White* v. *City of Dallas* (1974)).

Carnwath (1996) lamented the absence of a framework of constitutional principles which structure competing centres of governmental power and in particular the fact that the central government has an inbuilt advantage in that it both makes the rules and implements them. The attitude of the courts to local government law has also been criticised as unprincipled and perhaps hostile towards local government (see Alder, 2001).

Local authorities have a certain political claim to autonomy at least for the following reasons:

(i) They are directly elected and can therefore act as a separation of powers check on central government.
(ii) Some local expenditure (in practice about 20%) is raised by local taxation.

(iii) Services such as housing, education and environmental control should be administered flexibly in accordance with local circumstances.
(iv) It is desirable in the interests of democracy and individual self-fulfillment for people to have closer contact with governmental bodies than is possible at central government level.
 (v) They generate different political perspectives and healthy disagreement and debate.

The flourishing of incommensurable values was one of Aristotle's primary justifications for the existence of local political units, a position also held by Mill. Aristotle regarded the *polis* as embodying the principle of self-sufficiency essential to which was pluralism. Each smaller community that together make up the *polis*, families, villages etc., should have autonomy within its own sphere. In a widely accepted formulation Sharp (1970, XIII *Political Studies* 153) outlined the foundational values of local government in a way that emphasises the incommensurable values involved. Firstly there is autonomy in the sense of enabling those who use local services to decide priorities; secondly there is democratic participation, including voluntary group involvement in public affairs and also in providing a safety valve, which allows electoral opposition to the central government of the day; thirdly there is (allocate) efficiency of service provision.

In support of local autonomy Mill argued that the role of central government should be confined to laying down general principles and acting as a default mechanism. 'The very object of having local representation is in order that those who have any interest in common, which they do not share with the general body of their countrymen, may manage that joint enterprise by themselves' (*Representative Government,* p. 350). Mill's argument for local autonomy is based on the Aristotelian values of civic virtue and individual self-realisation. One implication of this is that where other values are regarded as more important than local autonomy, for example where equality of service provision is especially valued, the service should not be in local government hands except possibly as a clearly identified delegate of the centre. Thus local government should perhaps do less but have greater autonomy in relation to what it does do.

8.1   Local Authority Organisation and Functions

Until the middle of the nineteenth century, much of the detailed work of government was carried out by local bodies – in particular, justices of the peace and specialised *ad hoc* bodies. Indeed it is sometimes claimed that this local tradition rather than any formal separation of powers is the main reason why the British constitution was stable during the eighteenth century. Elected multi-purpose local authorities were introduced during the nineteenth century in parallel with the extension of parliamentary democracy but were set up as statutory corporations dependent on central government. The basic legislation is the Local Government Act 1972 which must be read together with many later Local Government Acts, various Local Government Finance Acts, the Audit Commission Act 1998, the Local Government and Rating Act 1997 and legislation concerning particular local services. The combined effect of these measures is a dense and complex legislative code.

Outside the metropolitan areas (below) there are three principal kinds of local authority, namely county councils, district councils, and unitary authorities. Counties and districts are not in a relationship of superior and inferior but each has its own area of responsibility allocated to it by statute. Under the Local Government Act 1992, a Local Government Commission appointed by the Secretary of State was established to review periodically the structures, boundaries and electoral arrangements of local authorities and to make recommendations to the Secretary of State who has power to make decisions on these matters subject to parliamentary approval. Except in the case of the metropolitan authorities the Commission can recommend that the two levels of local government can be merged in single unitary authorities. As a result of recommendations made in 1996 there are currently 46 unitary authorities. There are at present 318 local authorities in England and Wales.

At present county councils are responsible for education, strategic land-use planning, waste disposal, highways (other than trunk roads and motorways), personal social services, police, consumer protection and transport. District councils are responsible for housing, detailed town and county planning controls, public health, refuse collection, the control of commercial premises and urban passenger transport. Within rural districts there are parishes (in Wales, community councils). These have purely local functions such as footpaths and recreation grounds and must be consulted on land use planning matters. The larger ones have elected councils, others operate through a parish meeting and parish trustees. Scotland has a separate local government system. There are provisions for co-operation, delegation and joint functions between authorities.

Under the Local Government Act 1985 the six 'metropolitan' areas (West Midlands, Merseyside, Greater Manchester, West Yorkshire,

South Yorkshire, Tyne and Wear) have only a single level comprising district councils without there being any authority responsible for the whole area. Until the Greater London Assembly Act 1999 this also applied to London which after 1985 was the only western European capital without a local authority. There are 32 London boroughs plus the City of London which is a chartered corporation responsible for the small largely commercial enclave within central London. There are also special authorities including the Inner London Education Authority and various non-elected specialised bodies (for example, the Port of London Authority, the Metropolitan Police).

Under the Greater London Authority Act 1999 London now has an elected assembly of 25 people and an elected mayor, currently Ken Livingstone. Neither has significant executive power. Subject to central government control, the mayor makes and sets budgets and draws up general plans and policies relating to transport, land use planning, environmental protection and culture. He appoints certain executive bodies relating to transport, policing and fire services, although there are also powers vested in central government and the London boroughs. In particular transport policy is specifically subject to central government power to impose a public/private partnership regime on the railway system (s. 210). The mayor and the authority also have the general functions, but without corresponding general powers, of promoting economic and social development, wealth creation and environmental protection in Greater London. The authority's main functions are to scrutinise and approve budgets, debate policy, question the mayor, participate in the appointment of staff, and comprise part of the police and fire and emergency powers authorities. Most local government powers in London are, however, still exercised by London boroughs over which the Greater London Assembly has no control.

8.2.   Structure and Powers

Except for the City of London Corporation which was created by charter, local authorities are statutory bodies. They are corporations with separate legal personality and are controlled by elected councils. As a statutory body a local authority can only do what is expressly or impliedly authorised by statute thereby embodying a strict version of the rule of law at the expense of local democracy (see *R*. v *Richmond LBC* [2001] 1All ER 436, 447 per Buxton LJ). By this means the courts are able to exercise considerable control over local government activities.

The limits on local authority powers can be illustrated by *R. v. Somerset CC ex parte Fewings* (1995). For different reasons, Laws J and the Court of Appeal held that a local authority was not entitled to ban stag-hunting for moral reasons on land that it owned. The local authority had wrongly assumed that because it owned the land it had the same rights as a private landowner and also argued that democracy entitled it to make the moral judgement to ban hunting. Laws J denied that the moral views of councillors could be relevant. He did not think that local democracy was a factor that could be taken into account unless the governing statute made it clear that this so to be the case. The Court of Appeal took a slightly broader approach being prepared to interpret the particular statute as allowing moral factors to be taken into account but even they were not prepared to adopt a strong principle of local democracy (see Alder, 2001). Other examples of judicial limits on local government powers will be found in Chapter 16.

8.3 Control by Central Government

Local government is protected against central intervention only in as much as the central government must justify any intervention under statutory powers. During the 1980s, when central government considerably extended its powers of control and also cut back local government spending, there was considerable litigation brought by local authorities against ministers. This had mixed success. The courts have been unable to formulate any principles governing the constitutional relationship between local and central government but have relied upon particular statutory contexts.

Apart from its power to legislate, central government control over local authorities takes many forms. They include the following:

(i) Stringent financial controls (below).
(ii) Default powers exercisable by ministers. The circumstances in which default powers can be exercised depends on the particular statute. In some cases 'unreasonable behaviour' is required (e.g. Education Act 1944 s. 88). In *Secretary of State for Education and Science* v. *Tameside MBC* (1976) the House of Lords supported local independence by holding that the Secretary of State could intervene only if the authority's behaviour was unreasonable in the sense of completely irrational. This test was adopted from that used to decide when a court can interfere with a local authority, and is arguably inappropriate as the test for central

government interference, although it does serve to buttress local independence. However, under differently worded legislation the Secretary of State can take over a local activity without the need to find unreasonable behaviour (see *Norwich City Council* v. *Environmental Secretary* (1982), where only Lord Denning treated the matter as one involving the constitutional importance of local autonomy).

(iii) The power to veto local government decisions, for example bylaws, compulsory purchase orders and planning appeals.

(iv) The power to regulate local authority activities by setting performance standards issuing policy advice and regulating the use of money.

(v) Inspections, audits and inquiries under many statutory provisions.

(vi) Jointly funded central/local enterprises such as urban renewal schemes.

The regime introduced by the Local Government Act 2000 could be said to adopt a Millian approach in favour of local autonomy (above p. 36). Unlike Mill, however, the Act favours central discretionary intervention in matters of detail (e.g. s. 5). Section 2 empowers a local authority to do any thing which it considers is likely to promote or improve the economic, social or environmental well-being of its area, but is compromised by s. 3, which gives a power of veto to the Secretary of State. Nor can s. 2, override any existing statutory restrictions. However, the Secretary of State has a wide power to amend and even to disapply legislation (s. 5). The Local Government Act 1999 imposes substantive direction on local authorities in the form of the 'Best Value' regime, which calls for continuous improvement in the delivery of services and 'public service agreements'. These give an opportunity for relative operational freedoms but, on a selective basis, conferred by the Secretary of State in return for commitments to centrally directed goals (ss. 2, 16, 30). From a republican perspective therefore this remains a condition of domination in that the master's non-interference is a matter of goodwill rather than obligation.

8.4   Internal Constitution

Before the Local Government Act 2000 there was no internal separation of powers. Under its corporate structure a local council is both legislature and executive although its legislative functions are limited to the power to make bylaws for 'good rule and government and suppression of nuisances' (LGA 1972 s. 235). These must be confirmed by the Secretary of State. There is no separate representative assembly to which the authority is responsible. Local authority decisions are corporate decisions made mainly through committees comprising a mixture of elected members and appointed officials with decisions often delegated to officials. This entails weak accountability and the influence of unelected officials as policy makers.

The Local Government Act 2000 Part II introduces a new structure with the intention of strengthening local efficiency and accountability. The Act requires local authorities to adopt a governance model that separates the executive function from the role of supervision and scrutiny (ss. 10, 11). Local authorities must adopt one of three models or accept a regime imposed by the Secretary of State. The models are as follows: (i) an elected mayor (elected under the supplementary vote system, see Chapter 11) who cannot be a councillor and a cabinet of up to 10 councillors appointed by the mayor; (ii) a leader and cabinet appointed by the council itself; (iii) an elected mayor and professional manager appointed by the council; (iv) a structure imposed by the Secretary of State, which might be at the proposal of the authority. In the case of the elected mayor models a referendum must first be held (s. 34). Any proposals to the Secretary of State must meet the ideology of the Act by being 'efficient , transparent and accountable' (s. 12 (3)) and in the case of proposals for the operation of the executive must be have regard to 'efficiency', economy and effectiveness' (s. 25 (4)).

The council is to agree the general policy framework and budget, following proposals from the executive, to scrutinise the actions of the executive and to hold the executive to account both before and after the implementation of the policies. For this purpose councils are required to establish overview and advisory committees independent of the executive (s. 21). They must be politically balanced (s. 21 (11) (b), although the executive itself need not be balanced so that as in the case of central government, the executive can comprise only the majority party. The committees can also take outside advice, for example from voluntary or private sector bodies, thus reflecting the notion of 'community leadership' that informs the Act (see *Local Government: In Touch with the People*, Cm. 4014 (1998), para. 8.1 et seq.; DETR, *Modernising Local Government and Community Leadership* (1998)). Open government is not secured. Subject to regulations made by the Secretary of State, the executive and the committees can decide what meetings will be held in public (s. 22 (8)(9)). Written records of meetings must be made available to the public but again subject to regulations made by the Secretary of State who can censor them (s. 22 (6) (7)).

In relation to ethical standards local authority autonomy is not trusted. There is a code of recommended practice issued by the Secretary of State relating to standards of propriety of councillors, for example concerning conflicts of interest. The Local Government Act 2000 Part III strengthens this in the light of the 'Nolan' principles of public life by means of a Standards Board for England appointed by the Secretary of State (s. 57). Anyone can make a complaint to an Ethical Standards Officer of the Board and there is an investigative process which can lead to the suspension or disqualification of a local council member. In addition each local authority must have a Standards Committee, including two outside members which advises upon and monitors the Code of Practice (see DETR, *General Principles of Conduct in Local Government*, 2001). In addition the Local Government and Housing Act 1989 requires local authorities to designate a 'head of paid services' to report to it on the general management and co-ordination of its functions (s. 4) and also a 'monitoring officer' to report on whether the authority is acting lawfully and without maladministration (s. 5). The chief executive but not the chief finance officer can fill both roles (s. 31).

8.5   Party Politics

The local electoral system gives less opportunity for party dominance than is the case with central government. Elections must be held when prescribed by statute (LGA 1972 s. 7) and there is no convention permitting the party in power to dissolve the council and precipitate an election. In the case of county councils, the whole council is elected every four years. In the case of districts, one-third of the members must be elected each year, although a non-metropolitan district can decide to elect the whole council every four years. The rules governing the conduct of local government elections are broadly similar to those for parliamentary elections. However, electors can vote in every local government area in which they have a residence and candidates must have a residential connection with the area (LGA 1972 ss. 79–81 as amended).

The courts have recognised the political dimension of local government. For example a councillor is entitled to be influenced by the policies of his political group provided that he does not completely close his mind to other considerations and does not blindly adopt party policy (see *R. v. Waltham FDC ex parte Baxter* (1988). A local authority can also exclude a person who opposes party policy from a committee (*R.* v. *Greenwich London Borough Council ex parte Lovelace* (1990)); contrast school governor: *Brunyate* v. *ILEA* (1989)).

However, the political dimension of local government has been regulated by statute. During the 1980s the Conservative government was concerned to ensure that local councils did not frustrate the market-orientated policies adopted by the government. The Widdicombe Committee was set up to consider the question of local authority management and politics from the government's perspective. Its report (Cmnd. 9997 (1986)), adopting the position that local government has no constitutional right to exist, restated the well-known vices of party politics, namely corruption, bribery, conflict and bias, and suggested that local democracy be curbed. The Local Government and Housing Act 1989 Part I, therefore introduced restrictions upon party political activity. In as much as these provisions restrict freedom of expression, they may now be challengeable under the Human Rights Act 1998.

 (i) A requirement that committee composition reflects the balance of parties. This can be overridden by unanimous vote (s. 17). However, as we have seen, under the new structures imposed by the Local Government Act 2000, the composition of the executive need not reflect party balance.
 (ii) Forbidding 'twin tracking' and involvement in politics by staff holding 'politically restricted' posts. Twin tracking is where a council member also works for the same or another local authority. Teachers are automatically exempt and other exemptions can be granted by an adjudicator/adviser appointed by the Secretary of State (s. 3). The general criteria for a 'politically restricted' post is a salary level of £19,500 which can be varied by the Secretary of State. Below that level certain jobs which involve giving advice to the authority or dealing with the media are also restricted (s. 2). Certain senior officers are automatically restricted (ibid.).
 (iii) Officers can be appointed and dismissed only 'on merit'. This attacks an obvious abuse. Again the Secretary of State can make detailed regulations (LGA 1989 ss. 7, 8).
 (iv) Local authorities can appoint no more than three political advisers whose posts must be temporary and paid less than £13,500 (although this limit can be raised by the Secretary of State).
 (v) Co-opted (non-elected) committee members cannot vote (except in the case of police committees and education committees in respect of statutory co-optees, magistrates and school governors). Co-option allows an element of direct democracy with its danger of interest-group domination.

(vi) Local authorities are not entitled to spend money on political propaganda (*R.* v. *ILEA ex parte Westminster City Council* (1986)). A local authority may not publish material which appears to be designed to affect public support for a political party (LGA 1986 Part II) or spend money on publicity except incidentally to its other functions. This is intended to prevent local authorities undertaking political campaigns unrelated to local concerns.

(vii) The Secretary of State can impose conditions of employment, including conditions upon publications intended to support the aims of a political party (s. 1 (5); Local Government Officers (Political Restrictions) Regulations 1990 (SI 1990 No. 851)). The meaning of 'political party' is not defined but arguably a pressure group such as Amnesty International, even though it seeks to advance a political cause, is not a political party because it is not seeking election. In the case of the central civil service, restrictions on political activity are more limited and there are wider exemptions (see Chapter 12).

8.6   Finance

The independence of local authorities is directly connected with the extent to which they can raise and spend money. About three-quarters of their income is provided by central government. Local authority income derives from the following sources:

(i) *Local taxes*. There are two kinds of local tax. One is the domestic 'council tax' which is levied on the sale value of domestic property as estimated by the Inland Revenue. The amount raised by this method can be limited by the Secretary of State, subject to an affirmative vote of the Commons (Local Government Finance Act 1992; Local Government Act 1999). The other local tax is the 'uniform business rate' fixed by central government and distributed to authorities according to an equalisation formula (Local Government Finance Act 1988). Businesses have no vote in local elections.

(ii) *Central government grants*. These are payable according to a complex formula the essence of which is to give the Secretary of State a discretion to decide how much local authorities should spend. Grants are currently calculated upon the basis of a 'standard spending assessment' of how much each authority is supposed to spend upon each of its services. Grants are also made under specific statutory powers and earmarked to individual services, for example housing and urban renewal. These earmarked grants are often awarded on a competitive basis (e.g. the 'City Challenge' scheme).

(iii) *Borrowing and investment.* Local authority general borrowing levels are regulated by central government (Local Government and Housing Act 1989 ss. 43, 44) and the power of an authority to speculate on the money market is very limited. Prudent speculation is possible but only for the limited purpose of facilitating borrowing itself, as opposed to managing debts already incurred (*Hazell* v. *Hammersmith and Fulham London Borough Council* (1992) interest rate swaps).

(iv) *Fees, charges and rents.* Local authorities can charge for services only where specifically authorised to do so by statute (see *R* v. *Richmond LBC* (2001). This is because of the basic constitutional principle of no executive taxation. The courts seem to consider that a charge by a public body and tax are the same thing (see *Macarthy and Stone Ltd* v. *Richmond LBC* (1992)). There are provisions which prevent local authorities from setting up subsidiary companies that avoid central controls over public spending (Local Government and Housing Act 1989 Part V).

(v) *Sales of land.* The consent of the Secretary of State is required for a sale at less than market price and in all cases for the disposal of housing land (LGA 1972 s. 103; LGA 1988 s. 25; Housing Act 1985 s. 32).

8.6.1 Legal restrictions on spending

By virtue of its statutory basis, local spending can be directly challenged in the courts on the basis that money can be spent only on activities authorised by statute or reasonably incidental thereto. The courts take a narrow view of what is reasonably incidental thereby discouraging local enterprise and making it difficult for local authorities to raise funds (see *Mcarthy and Stone Ltd* v. *Richmond Borough Council* (1992); *Hazell* v. *Hammersmith and Fulham London Borough Council* (1992)). Many of the cases discussed in Chapter 16 provide further illustrations.

The courts have sometimes held that local authorities have a 'fiduciary' duty to act in the interests of local taxpayers even against those of the public as a whole thereby confounding the normal ideas of democracy. In a general sense, that of Locke (see Chapter 2), the fiduciary principle is fundamental to the nature of government which is often said to hold its power on trust. It signifies that government has no self-interested rights, only obligations which it owes to the people who have agreed to put it into office. However, in the context of local government the courts have created a *fiduciary* duty in a narrower sense based on the private law analogy of the trust between a local authority and just one section of the people, namely local ratepayers or taxpayers. Moreover the *fiduciary* duty is highly instrumental requiring that an authority must act efficiently on business lines in the interests of minimising the burden on the local taxpayer thus contradicting the notion of democratic choice between competing social values.

Until the Local Government Act 1918, the local franchise was dependent upon traditional property qualifications so that conflict between different interest groups was less apparent than is the case today. After the First World War, however, the fiduciary duty in favour of local taxpayers was separated from any duties that might be owed to the electorate or the wider community (see *Roberts* v. *Hopwood* (1925): duty to pay employees the going rate rather than a living wage).

The cases seems to interpret the *fiduciary* principle in different ways. In one sense supported by dicta in *Prescott* v. *Birmingham Corporation* (1955), the principle requires an authority to allocate resources in a non-discriminatory way that does not favour one group of benefici-aries at the expense of another, except for limited charitable pur-poses. In that case the court refused to permit a local authority to provide free transport for old people, a decision that had to be reversed by statute. If correct, this principle subverts any redistributive policies other than those clearly authorised by statute. Another version, was applied by Lord Diplock in *Bromley LBC* v. *GLC* where the House of Lords refused to permit the local authority to subsidise London Transport by raising local rates. His Lordship appeared to take the view that the *fiduciary* duty implies that special weight must be given to local taxpayers' interests in the sense that the authority must act thriftily and must not impose a disproportionate burden on the taxpayer. Giving preference to social purposes without any direct return to the taxpayer therefore becomes problematic. A third version was applied by Lord Wilberforce and Lord Scarman (with whom Lord Brandon agreed) in *Bromley*. According to this version the *fiduciary* principle, although having the same substantive content as Lord Dip-lock's version, is merely part of the context in which a local government statute should be interpreted. Lord Diplock's version would presum-ably apply unless positively excluded by statutory language (of what strength is not clear), whereas Lords Wilberforce and Scarman's principle would be used as one among several indicators without carry-ing any particular priority.

However, the fiduciary principle has never been the sole rationale for a judicial decision and is therefore not strictly binding as precedent. Indeed in *Pickwell* v. *Camden LBC* (1983), Forbes J undermined the fiduciary principle by interpreting it as meaning only that the interests of local taxpayers should be taken into account along with other interests in exercising power, but that the priority to be given to such interests is a matter for the authority. This reflects the separation of powers principle that the courts are not equipped to second-guess government. Ormerod LJ went further holding that the fiduciary duty meant only that powers must be used for lawfully authorised purposes. It may therefore be that the fiduciary duty as such is redundant since it appears to do no work that cannot be done by general judicial review doctrines such as those of relevance and reasonableness (Chapter 16).

8.7 The Local Ombudsman

There are three Local Commissioners for Administration, one for each of England, Scotland and Wales. They are responsible for investigating complaints by citizens against local authorities (Local Government Act 1974 Part II). The Swedish term 'ombudsman', meaning investigator, is usually used to describe this kind of official of which there are many examples including the Parliamentary Commissioner who investigates central government and some NDPDs. A distinctive feature of the ombudsman institution compared with courts or tribunals such as the Commission for Standards is that an ombudsman usually has no enforcement powers but merely reports to the body to which it is responsible although it can publicise its report. This is said to make the ombudsman more effective as an informal investigator.

The local commissioners' powers are limited to allegations of 'maladministration'. Broadly speaking, maladministration concerns the manner in which a decision is taken as opposed to the merits of the decision itself so that the ombudsman cannot interfere merely because she thinks a particular decision is wrong or undesirable (*R.* v. *Local Commissioner ex parte Bradford City Council* (1979)). Maladministration for example includes 'bias, neglect, inattention, delay, incompetence, inaptitude, perversity, turpitude, arbitrariness and so-on' (the 'Crossman Catalogue' (734 HC Deb. Col. 51 (1966)). The concept of maladministration is therefore vague and open ended. It also may overlap with legal wrongs although this does not require the ombudsman to apply the same criteria (*R.* v. *Local Commissioner ex parte Liverpool City Council* (2001)).

Several matters are excluded from the ombudsman's jurisdiction. Among these are personnel matters, commercial transactions (a particularly sensitive area with the increasing privatization of local government functions), and some educational functions. Also excluded are actions affecting all or most of the inhabitants of the area.

Actions against which there is a remedy in the courts or an appeal to a minister are excluded, but the ombudsman has a wide discretion to override this where the citizen cannot reasonably be expected to exercise his right, for example because of cost (s. 5(2)). This proviso is increasingly important in view of the flexible nature of judicial review which is capable of including most kinds of maladministration. Judicial review is expensive and as we shall see is not designed to investigate factual disputes. In *R.* v. *Local Commissioner for Administration ex parte Croydon LBC* (1989) it was held that the relevant test is whether the issues are suitable for resolution by the courts, and not the applicant's chance of success. *R.* v. *Local Commissioner ex parte Liverpool City Council* (2001) concerned an attempt by a group of local residents to challenge a planning permission for a new stand at a football stadium on the grounds that several councillors had season tickets for the stadium and that undue party political pressures had been brought to bear on council members. The Court of Appeal held that because the allegations were serious and the ombudsman's powers of investigation were more likely to be effective than judicial review and because the complainants were not wealthy this was 'a good example of a case where the commissioners investigation and report can provide the just remedy when judicial review might fail to; and can reach facts that might not emerge under the judicial review process' (Henry LJ at 472).

Complaints must be made in writing to a member of the council concerned who can then refer the complaint to the ombudsman. The local ombudsman can be approached directly by a member of the public if the councillor does not refer the complaint. About 50% of cases reach the ombudsman this way, but over three-quarters of all complaints turn out to be outside the ombudsman's jurisdiction. The ombudsman investigates informally but has powers to see documents and require information from councillors and officials. The result of the investigation is sent to the complainant and to the council concerned and must be available for public inspection (including copying) for three weeks. A newspaper advertisement must draw attention to the report (LGA 1974 s. 30). If the Commissioner thinks that the authority has not taken adequate measures to put matters right he or she can make a further report (s. 31). Beyond the political sanction of publicity the local ombudsman has no powers. This has turned out to be a serious problem because a significant number of councils have ignored the findings of the ombudsman. Normally individuals cannot be named in the ombudsman's reports. However, this does not apply where there is a breach of the National Code of Local Government Conduct (Local Government Act 1974 s. 30 (3A)). The local commissioners make an annual report to special 'representative bodies' drawn from local authorities.

Summary

8.1 There are several constitutional arguments in favour of independent local authorities. These include democracy, checks and balances, the efficient use of resources and individual self development. There are also arguments based on efficiency and equity for central control over local government. The courts have not adopted any coherent approach to the place of local government in the constitution.

8.2 Elected local authorities are statutory corporations and can exercise only powers conferred by statute. There are two main levels of local authority: county councils and district councils. In London there is Greater London Assembly, the City of London Corporation, the City of Westminster and Metropolitan Borough Councils. The relationship between local councils within an area is not one of superior and inferior. Each has specific functions designated by statute.

8.3 There are many central government controls over local authorities. Central control over local authorities has increased in recent years.

8.4 Officials play a more prominent role than is the case with central government. There are provisions designed to weaken party political activity.

8.5 The Local Government Act 2000 has departed from the traditional corporate model of local government by requiring a separation between the executive and the accountability and scrutiny functions of local authorities.

8.6 Local authorities have very limited financial powers and these are regulated by central government and subject to independent audit by the Audit Commission.

8.9 Citizens' grievances can be ventilated through Commissioners for Local Administration (the local ombudsman). Their powers are limited to maladministration and there is no method of enforcing their recommendations except political pressure and publicity. However, the resources and investigatory powers of the ombudsman will often make it more effective than the courts.

Further Reading

'Modern local government in touch with the people' Cm. 4014 (1998) 59 *Political Quarterly* 236.
Alder, J. (2001) 'Incommensurable values and judicial review: the case of local government' *Public Law* 717.

Loughlin, M. *Legality and Locality.*
Chandler (1989) 'The liberal justification for local government', XXIV *Political tudies* 604.
Jowl and Oliver, *The Changing Constitution*, chapter 6.
Stewart, J. *The Nature of British Local Government.*
Norton, *The British Polity.*
Vincent-Jones, P. 'Central-Local relations under the Local Government Act 1999: a new consensus? 63 *Modern Law Review* xxx.
Wilson, D. (1999) 'Exploring the limits of public participation in local government,' 52 *Parliamentary Affairs* 246.
Wilson, D. (2001) 'Local government: balancing diversity and uniformity', 54 *Parliamentary Affairs* 289.

Exercises

8.1   Local government has no right to exist.' Discuss.

8.2   To what extent do the courts protect local democracy?

8.3   To what extent is local government a creature of the central executive?

8.4   Do the reforms made to local government by the Local Government Acts 1999 and 2000 amount to a genuine attempt to strengthen local autonomy and accountability?

9 The European Union

9.1 The Nature of the European Union

What were then called the European Communities or the Common Market were created after the Second World War as an aspiration to prevent further wars in Europe and to regenerate the European economies. The prototype was the European Coal and Steel Community created by the Treaty of Paris 1951. The other Communities were created in 1957 by two Treaties of Rome. They are the European Community (EC) (formerly called the European Economic Community), and the European Atomic Energy Community. The EC is by far the most important, and responsible for most of the legal and political activity. The three communities share the same basic institutions. The founder members were France, Germany, Italy, Luxembourg, Belgium and the Netherlands. The UK became a member in 1972 and, by virtue of the European Communities Act 1972, laws made by EC bodies are binding in English law. The other members who joined at various later dates are Austria, Denmark, Finland, Greece, Ireland, Portugal, Spain and Sweden.

As a result of the Treaty on European Union (Maastricht Treaty) of 1992, the communities have been subsumed within the broader structure of the 'European Union', a process which was consolidated by the Amsterdam Treaty in 1997 (TEU). However, since Maastricht there has been substantial political concern that the process of European integration should be restrained, not least because the European Union is widely regarded as undemocratic. Indeed the Amsterdam Treaty introduced safeguards and flexibility arrangements in favour of national governments (Shaw, 1996). Nevertheless the Nice Treaty of 1999 deals with the proposed expansion of the Union to include the following states most of which were previously satellites of the Soviet Union: Bulgaria, Cyprus, the Czech Republic, Estonia, Hungary, Latvia, Lithuania, Malta, Romania, Slovakia, Slovenia. However, the Nice Treaty has not been ratified as required by all member states. In a referendum the Irish electorate rejected it. Turkey also seeks membership. Enlarged membership is likely to require substantial alterations to the EU decision-making process in order to reflect the changed political balance.

The Treaties, which were consolidated after Amsterdam arguably form a crude constitution. In this chapter unless stated otherwise, references to Articles refer to the consolidated Treaty. All EC powers must be authorised by the Treaty in the light of the fundamental values shared by the members. In 1991 the European Court of Justice, which is charged not only with securing compliance with the law but also with advancing the aims of the Communities, described the EC Treaty as a 'constitutional charter' based on the rule of law. It emphasised that individuals as well as states are the subjects of community law although in fact, individuals other than those employed by the EC have only limited rights to instigate proceedings in the court (see *Opinion on the Draft Agreement on a European Economic Area* [1991] ECR 1-6084).

The European Union as such has no legal identity, nor institutions nor lawmaking power, but exercises an overall policy-making role through inter-governmental agreements sometimes 'borrowing' community institutions for the purpose. Binding law is made by the European communities. The objectives of the communities were originally exclusively economic. A fundamental aim was to encourage free trade between member states, but the organisation was heavily influenced by a desire to protect agricultural interests espoused principally by France. This has left the EU with a heavy financial burden in that about 70% of its budget is still devoted to agricultural subsidies.

Since then the interests of the EU have steadily widened, partly by a bureaucratic process of interpreting the existing objectives liberally and partly by the member states formally agreeing to extend the areas of competence of the EC. In particular the Single European Act of 1986 made environmental protection a separate area of competence. The Union has also developed a substantial security and foreign policy perspective endorsed by the Treaty of Amsterdam. There are few areas of UK law that are immune from EC influence which was famously described by Lord Denning as an 'incoming tide' (*Bulmer* v. *Bolinger* (1974)). In terms of legislative imput from Europe there is currently no sign of the tide going out.

The Maastricht Treaty instigated progress towards monetary union, including the creation of an independent European Central Bank. There is now a single European currency, the 'Euro' which is regulated by the European Central Bank (Art. 4). The UK does not participate in this. Those states within the 'eurozone' are subject to central economic regulation by the European Central Bank which has no formal democratic accountability. The possible effect upon the powers of the UK Parliament, of the single currency, is one reason why the decision whether or not to join the Euro is widely regarded as raising important constitutional issues. The current government has promised that the decision will be taken only after a referendum. There is also freedom of movement between the mainland EU states under the Schenken Agreement. The UK is not a party to this. Involvement in the European enterprise is therefore multi-layered, sometimes described as 'variable geometry'.

The EU is said to have three 'pillars'. The first pillar comprises the central economic purposes of the European Communities together with environmental protection. The second and third pillars were introduced by the Maastricht Treaty and operate mainly at the political level. The second pillar is foreign policy; the third pillar is co-operation in police and judicial affairs. Matters relating to immigration and asylum (Art. 63), however, fall within the first pillar. The European Court of Justice has no jurisdiction in relation to the second pillar and has jurisdiction in third-pillar matters only with the consent of the state concerned (TEU Art. 39).

The treaties are 'framework treaties' that allow the institutions created by them to develop laws and policies, and indeed other institutions for the purpose of closer integration between the member states. The aims of the EC set out in Art. 2 of the EC Treaty are as follows 'to promote throughout the Community a harmonious, balanced and sustainable development of economic activities, a high level of employment and of social protection, equality between men and women, sustainable and non-inflationary growth, a high degree of competitiveness and convergence of economic performance, a high level of protection and improvement of the quality of the environment, the raising of the standard of living and quality of life, and economic and social cohesion and solidarity among Member States'.

Under the TEU the broader goals of the European Union include the following:

- To promote economic and social progress and a high level of employment and to achieve balanced and sustainable development, in particular through the creation of an area without internal frontiers, through the strengthening of economic and social cohesion, and through the establishment of economic and monetary union ultimately including a single currency.
- To assert its identity on the international scene, in particular through the implementation of a common foreign and security policy.
- To strengthen the protection of rights and interests of the nationals of its Member States through the introduction of a citizenship of the Union.

- To maintain and develop the Union as an area of freedom, security and justice in which the free movement of persons is assured in con-
- junction with appropriate measures with respect to external border controls, asylum, immigration, and the prevention and combating of crime.
- To maintain in full the *acquis communitaire* (which means the accumulated legal principles values and practices of the community) and to build on it with a view to considering to what extent the policies and forms of co-operation may need to be revised with the aim of ensuring the effectiveness of the mechanisms and the institutions of the Community.

These aims are internally contradictory and are little more than windy rhetoric. However, as we saw in Chapter 1 the incommensurability of many human values and interests means that the task of any political organisation is to manage disagreement between competing goals. In a democracy this means avoiding grand cohesive agendas in favour of pragmatic trade-offs.

9.2   Community Institutions

The community has lawmaking, executive and judicial powers which are blended in a unique way which does not correspond to traditional notions of the separation of powers. There are no clear lines of accountability. Power is divided between institutions some of which share the same functions. Such democratic accountability as there is takes the forms (i) of a limited degree of accountability to an elected 'European Parliament', and (ii) arrangements made under the constitutions of the individual states. The balance between the different bodies, particularly in relation to the Parliament, varies according to the Treaty provision under which a particular issue arises.

The main institutions are as follows (Art. 7):

1. The Council of Ministers including the European Council (periodic meetings of heads of state).
2. The European Commission.
3. The European Parliament.
4. The European Court of Justice (ECJ).

There are other important community institutions. They will not be discussed here in that their impact on the UK constitution is indirect only. They include, the Committee of Permanent Representatives

(COREPER) which comprises senior officials who prepare the Council's business and are very influential, the Court of Auditors, and the European Central Bank (Art. 8). There are also advisory and consultative bodies notably the Economic and Social Committee and the Committee of the Regions.

9.2.1 The Council of Ministers

The Council's main function is to approve or amend laws proposed by the European Commission (although in some cases it can ask the Commission to make a proposal (Art. 208)). It also decides the budget and adopts international treaties and is responsible for ensuring that the objectives of the treaty are attained. The Council is made up of a minister representing each member state who must be authorised to commit the government. The actual membership fluctuates according to the business in hand. A president holds office for six months, each member state holding the office in turn. The Council's proceedings are secret.

The Council is biased towards national interests rather than towards an overall 'community view'. The community view is represented by the Commission creating a distinct kind of separation of powers and a recipe for political tension. The way in which Council decisions are made is therefore all-important. Certain decisions, albeit a shrinking category, must be unanimous, thus permitting any state to impose a veto. An increasing number of decisions are made by a 'qualified majority', whereby votes are weighted according to the population of each state. At present the weighting is as follows (Art. 205): UK, Germany, France, Italy, 10; Spain, 8; Belgium, Portugal, Netherlands, 5; Austria, Sweden, 4; Luxemburg, 2. Under the Nice Treaty which is not yet in force the weighting will be altered to prevent paralysis in the enlarged community. Occasionally a simple majority suffices. There is a convention, known as the Luxembourg Convention, which was agreed in 1966 according to which where very important interests of a member state are in issue the Council should vote unanimously. It is, however, arguable that, given the increasing use of qualified majority provisions in the treaties, this convention is losing its political legitimacy. Moreover the Amsterdam treaty makes increased pressure for majority voting.

The Council is not formally accountable to any other body other than the Court in respect of legal limits on its powers. In the UK, under the normal convention of ministerial responsibility, ministers who attend the Council are accountable to Parliament in respect of their own imput into the Council's proceedings but not of course for Council decisions as such. Council documents are made available to both Houses, ministerial statements are made after Council meetings, questions can be asked, and, in addtion to the ordinary departmental committees, there are select committees in each House to monitor EU activity. The House of Lords Select Committee is particularly well regarded and, in addition to scrutinising new legislation, makes wide-ranging general reports on the EU.

There may be a convention that no UK minister should consent to an EC legislative proposal before a debate has taken place, unless there are special reasons which must be explained to the House as soon as possible hereafter. However, this is not consistently followed. In practice the volume of EC legislation is greater than the time available and much European business is conducted without MPs having the opportunity to consider it in advance (see HC Deb., 30 October 1980, col. 843–4). Ministers in their capacity as members of the Council are probably not bound by resolutions of the House of Commons.

There is one specific constraint. By virtue of the European Parliamentary Elections Act 1978, s. 6, no treaty which provides for an increase in the powers of the European Assembly can be ratified by the UK without the approval of an Act of Parliament. It is perhaps ironic that this provides protection only against the elected element of the EC rather than against the unelected European Commission.

The European Council, which is a meeting of heads of state and the president of the Commission, previously existed outside the treaties but was 'legalised' by the Single European Act (now Art. 4). Its function is to 'provide the Union with the necessary impetus for its development and shall define the general political guidelines thereof'. It must meet at least twice a year. At the end of each meeting it submits a report to the Parliament and must submit a further report at the end of each year on the progress of the Union. The Council as such has no lawmaking power but nevertheless seems to tip the balance of power away from the supra-national elements of Commission and Parliament towards the inter-governmental element.

9.2.2   The European Commission

The Commission represents the interests of the communities as such. It is required to be independent 'beyond doubt' of the member governments (Art. 213). Its 20 members are chosen by agreement between the member governments and currently comprise one member from each of the smaller states and two from the larger states. There are proposals to reconsider the matter when the Union enlarges. Each commissioner is appointed for a renewable term of five years, in order to correspond with the life of a parliament. Prior to the nomination of the other commissioners the president of the Commission is nominated for a two-year term by the member states after consulting the European Parliament. The president has a right to object to individual nominees (Art. 217) and the appointment of the commissioners as a whole must be approved by the Parliament (Art. 214(2)). The president assigns departmental responsibilities (Directorates-General) to the other commissioners who are required to conform to the political direction of the president (Art. 219). Members of the Commission cannot be dismissed by their governments or the president during their terms of office (Art. 214) so that, unlike a head of government, the president has little political leverage. Commissioners can be compulsorily retired by the European Court on the ground of inability to perform their duties (Art. 216) and, the whole Commission can be dismissed by the Parliament (Art. 201). The main functions of the Commission are as follows:

- To propose laws or political initiatives for adoption by the Council. The Council or the Parliament can request the Commission to submit proposals (Arts 192, 208).
- To make laws itself either directly under powers conferred by the treaty or under powers delegated to it by the Council.
- To enforce community law against member states, and the other community instituions. The community has no police or law enforcement agencies. The Commission enforces the law by issuing a 'reasoned opinion', negotiating with the body concerned and, if necessary, initiating proceedings in the court (Art. 226). The judgements of the court are enforced through the laws of member states.
- To administer the Union budget.
- To negotiate with international bodies and other countries (Arts 228, 22931).

9.2.3   The European Parliament

The European Parliament does not make law but was created as an 'advisory and supervisory' body (Art. 189). It injects a limited but increasing democratic element into Union affairs. It has up to 700 seats, these being allocated in proportion to the population of each member state. Elections are held every five years. Since 1979 MEPs have been directly elected by residents of the member states, the detailed electoral arrangements being left to each country (see Chapter 11).

The Parliament is required to meet at least once a year and in practice meets roughly once each month, alternating, expensively, between Strasbourg and Luxembourg. Its members vote in political groupings and not in national units (see Art. 191). Under the Treaty MEPs are required to be independent of national policies and not to act under instructions from any outside source. Freedom of speech and proceedings within the Parliament are protected but, unlike the UK Parliament, the European Parliament does not seem to enjoy privilege against interference from the courts. The European Court of Justice can review the legality of its activities (*Grand Duchy of Luxembourg* v. *Parliament* (1983)).

The Parliament has the right to be consulted by the Council and in an increasing range of cases a right of veto. It can also give advice, and in limited cases can request the Commission to propose legislation (Art. 190). It can question members of the Council and Commission, and call for reports (Art. 197). It approves the Union budget, and approves nominations for the appointment of commissioners and the admission of new member states. It can hold temporary committees of inquiries into misconduct or maladministration by other Union bodies. There is an ombudsman to investigate the Union executive and report to the Parliament. The Parliament also ratifies treaties with non-member countries

In some contexts the role of the Parliament has been significantly strengthened although it must act within strict time limits, usually three months (see Arts 251, 252). There are two procedures. Firstly, applying mainly to monetary union matters, the 'co-operation' procedure permits a parliamentary input at an early stage and requires a unanimous vote of the Council if Parliament either rejects its policy or proposes amendments with which the Commission disagrees. Secondly, relating to most economic, social and environmental matters but not to agricultural matters the 'co-decision' procedure gives the Parliament a veto which it must exercise by an absolute majority. In the event of a deadlock between the Parliament and the Council there is provision for a joint conciliation committee made up of equal numbers of each, with the Commission as mediator. If agreement still cannot be reached the parliamentary veto stands.

The Parliament can amend the part of the Union budget that is not devoted to compulsory Union functions. This means that the Parliament has little control over most of the budget and no realistic control over the overall level of Community spending or its distribution between the member states. It can veto the whole Union budget (Art. 272), and can dismiss the entire Commission but not individual members of it (Art. 201). However, these sanctions are too crude for any but the most extreme cases.

9.2.4 The European Court of Justice

The European Court of Justice comprises 16 judges appointed by agreement between the governments of the member states. Unlike national judges, they have little security of tenure, being appointed for a renewable term of six years and dismissable by the unanimous opinion of the other judges and advocates-general (Statutes of the Court, EC, Art. 6). As well as the judges there are six advocates-generals who provide the court with an independent opinion upon the issues in each case. The opinion of the advocates-general is not binding on the court, but is highly influential.

In practice one judge is appointed from each member state, the extra appointment being held in rotation by nationals of the four largest states. Appointments must be made from those eligible for the highest judicial office in each member state and also from 'jurisconsults of recognised competence' (EC Treaty, Art. 223). This permits such persons as academic lawyers or social scientists to be appointed. There is also a 'Court of First Instance'. This hears cases of kinds designated by the Council (unanimity is required). There are no specific qualifications for appointment to the Court of First Instance other than being a person 'whose independence is beyond doubt and who possesses the ability required for judicial office'. The Court of Justice hears appeals on a point of law from the Court of First Instance.

The court's task is to ensure that 'in the interpretation and application of the EC treaty the law is observed' (Art. 220). The 'law' consists of the treaties themselves, the legislation adopted in their implementation, general principles developed by the court, general principles of law of the member states including the European Convention on Human Rights and also 'soft law' which is not binding but must be taken into account. Soft law includes 'declarations and resolutions adopted in the community framework; international agreements and agreements between member states connected with community activities' (see Europe Documents No. 1790 of 3 July, 1992, p. 3). A European Charter of Rights has also been proposed. the EU, not being a legal entity, cannot be a signatory to the ECHR. It has been suggested that parts of the EU system are 'entrenched' in the sense that not even the Treaty itself could be altered in defiance of them. However, in *Grau Gromis* (1995) the ECJ accepted that 'the Member States remain free to alter even the most fundamental parts of the Treaty'. Shaw (1996, p. 99) points out that the Union is required (Art. 2) to 'maintain in full the *acquis communitaire*, which is the accumulated inheritance of community values', thus introducing an element of stability and irreversibility into the system.

The jurisdiction of the ECJ is as follows:

(i) Enforcement action against member states who are accused of violating or refusing to implement European Law (Art. 226). These proceedings are usually brought by the Commission, but can be brought by other member states subject to having raised the matter before the Commission (Art. 227). The Commission first gives the member state a chance to state its case. The court can award a lump sum or penalty payment against a member state which fails to comply with a judgement of the court that the state concerned has failed to fulfil a treaty obligation (Art. 228). This is an important strengthening of the enforcement powers of the court.

(ii) Judicial review of the acts or the failure to act of Union institutions (Arts 230, 231, 232). This can be brought by other Union institutions, by member states, an individual or private body can bring an action only in special circumstances where that the community act in question is specifically addressed to the person bringing the action (see e.g. *Salamander A-G* v. *European Parliament* (2000)). In contrast to its reluctance to permit indivduals to sue the EC, the court has been liberal in supporting individual rights against national governments (below).

(iii) Preliminary rulings on matters referred to it by national courts relating to the interpretation of the Treaty and the validity and interpretation of acts of Community institutions and of the European Central Bank (Art. 234). This is the lynchpin of the ECJ's role as a constitutional court and is how actions brought by private persons would normally be dealt with. Any national court, where it considers that a decision on the question is necessary to enable it to give judgement, may request the ECJ to give a ruling on a question of Community law (Art. 177). The role of the European Court is confined to that of ruling upon the question of law referred to it. It then sends the matter back to the national court for a decision on the facts in the light of the court's ruling. A court against whose decision there is no judicial remedy in national law (that is, the highest appeal court or any other court against which there is no right of appeal or review) must make such a request (ibid.). All UK courts are obliged to obey any

Community law that is made binding on them by Community law (see European Communities Act 1972 s. 2 (4)) and are required to follow decisions of the ECJ (ibid., s. 3 (1)). The power to give preliminary rulings does not apply to the Court of First Instance.

It may be difficult to decide whether a reference can or should be made. The parties have no say in the matter (*Bulmer* v. *Bollinger* (1974)). A court need not make a reference if it thinks the point is irrelevent or 'reasonably clear and free from doubt' (the *acte-claire* doctrine) or if 'substantially' the same point has already been decided by the ECJ (see *CILFIT SI Ministro de la Sanita* (1982)). In *R.* v. *International Commission of the Stock Exchange ex parte Else (1982) Ltd.* 1 All ER 420 at 422 Bingham LJ said that 'if community law is critical to the decision the court should refer it if it has any real doubt. Furthermore, the court can take into account the convenience of the parties, the expense of the action, and the workload of the European Court (ibid) (*Van Duyn* Ltd v. *Home Office* [1974] 3 All ER 178 at 1986; *Macarthys Ltd* v. *Smith* (1979); *Customs and Excise* v. *Samex* [1983] 1 All ER 1042 at 1055–6).

It may be particularly difficult to decide whether the law in issue is sufficiently clear to entitle the UK court to decide for itself. Much depends upon the extent to which English legal culture responds to the different reasoning methods of the ECJ, that is whether the UK court approaches the problem by way of our traditional 'literal' approach to questions of interpretation, or takes a broader approach, focusing on the 'spirit' as opposed to the letter of the law in the continental manner (see *Henn and Darby* v. *DPP* (1981)). The same applies to the question of whether a decision in the matter is 'necessary' for the resolution of the case. We cannot know this until we know what the relevant Community law means.

(iv) Disputes between the Union and its employees.
(v) Compulsory retirement of members of the Commission.
(vi) Advisory opinions.
(vii) The enforcement of obligations created by the European Investment Bank.

The court has no jurisdiction over second-pillar matters (foreign and defence policy) or in asylum and immigration matters. Its jurisdiction over other third-pillar matters (co-operation in criminal matters) depends on the consent of the state concerned but it has no jurisdiction in respect of the operations of the police and other law enforcement agencies (Art. 35.5). However, in other areas, for example freedom of trade, the court can interfere with police activities (see *R.* v. *Chief Constable of Sussex ex parte International Traders Ferry* [1999] 1 All ER 109 at 155).

It is often said that the glue that holds together the Communities and the member states in a constitutional framework is the rule of law represented by the ECJ. The Treaty itself is not explicit as to the relationship between the ECJ and the law of the member states, but the ECJ has developed several principles which have enabled it to give primacy to EC law over national law. According to some commentators the ECJ has in defiance of the normal values of judicial impartiality taken upon itself the political agenda of promoting European integration. It has attempted to enlist national courts in this enterprise, by requiring them to defer to EC law and by conferring European law rights on individuals enforceable in national courts (see Ward, 1996, Ch. 2; Rasmussen, 1986; Lenz, 1989; cf. Weiler, 1987; Mancini, 1991). Craig (1992) for example argues that the court has responded to the relative impotence of the other European institutions, none of which have direct powers in relation to domestic law, by becoming not only the judge but the police force of the European enterprise in defiance of the separation of powers.

9.3   Democracy and the European Union

Perhaps the most fundamental constitutional problem of the EU is the 'democratic deficit'. Although a democratic governments is a requirement of membership, the EU is dedicated to particular social and economic goals centring upon the protection of free trade. Although the goals of the EU have become progressively wider, they are not compatible with the democratic premise of neutrality between social and economic goals (see *Lochner* v. *New York* (1905) per Holmes J). None of the institutions combine lawmaking or executive power with democratic accountability and accountability is mainly left to national institutions although these have no veto over EC laws.

Some of the founders of the European Communities were idealists who, from a paternalistic stance, had little interest in democratic processes, assuming perhaps that the 'European spirit' could gradually be infused into public opinion by example and propaganda. This is reflected in the authoritarian, secretive and bureaucratic culture that pervades the decision-making bodies of the EU (see Ward, 1996, Ch. 1). When the European Communities Act 1972 was railroaded through the

UK Parliament, the driving forces were the desperate economic plight of the UK, coupled with the romantic adulation of European culture by the then prime minister, Edward Heath. No serious attention was paid to the democratic credentials of the Community structure.

On the other hand Art. 6 states that 'the Union is founded on the principles of liberty, democracy, respect for human rights and fundamental freedoms, and the rule of law', and requires the Union to respect rights guaranteed under the ECHR and 'as they result from the constitutional traditions common to the Member States as general principles of community law'. However, this nebulous provision does not have priority over the specific goals of the Union. In particular Art. 10 provides that 'Member States shall take all appropriate measures, whether general or particular, to ensure fulfilment of the obligations arising out of this treaty or resulting from actions taken by the institutions of the Community. They shall facilitate the achievement of the Community's tasks. They shall abstain from any measure that could jeopardise the attainment of the objectives of the Treaty.' This seems to impose an obligation to place EU obligations and goals above other values. It has been described as imposing a moral obligation on member states and even as 'the sort of spiritual and essentially vacuous clause that is more commonly found in constitutional orders such as that of Nazi Germany or the Soviet Union' (Ward, 1996, p. 65).

The primacy of the economic goals seems to have been accepted by the European Court of Justice when in *Internationale Handesgesellschaft* v. *EVST* [1970] ECR 1105 at 1135 it was said that 'the protection of such rights, whilst inspired by the constitutional traditions common to the Member States ... must be ensured with the framework of the structures and objectives of the Community'. Thus the notion of a lawmaking body created to pursue what one writer has rather chillingly called the EU's 'mission' (Shaw, 1996, p. 9) is incompatible with the democratic principle. In recent years the ECJ has attempted to install democratic values into Community processes but this is by its nature a sporadic and fragmented exercise (see Mancini, 1994). Indeed many writers have argued that the main contribution of the ECJ has been to advance the interests of market integration (see Weatherill, 1995).

There is no general public right of access to Community information. The Maastrict Treaty (1992) declared (Declaration no. 17) that transparency of the decision-making process strengthens the democratic nature of the institutions and the public's confidence in the administration and the Commission was invited to work on improving public access to information held by the institutions. However, in a

Code of Conduct in 1994 adopted by a Decision (94/90), the Commission undertook to make information available to the public albeit subject to large exceptions. An analogous decision was adopted by the Council (93/731). Exceptions where information cannot be disclosed include the public interest in public security, international relations, monetary stability, court proceedings and investigations. The Commission may also refuse to disclose information on the ground of the institution's interest in the confidentiality of its proceedings.

The ECJ has enforced this limited right to information fairly vigorously. In *World Wildife Fund for Nature* v. *Commission* (1997), which concerned information about the Commission's policy regarding the enforcement of environmental law the Court of First Instance of the ECJ held that, although the Decision was a voluntary undertaking, having adopted it, the Commission is bound to respect third-party rights arising under it. The court also held that exceptions should be interpreted restrictively so as not to inhibit the aim of transparency and that the Commission must give reasons for refusing to disclose information. The court has also refused to accept blanket immunity for particular kinds of information and required the Commission to balance the public right to know against a clear public interest in secrecy in the particular case (see *JT's Corporation* v. *Commission* (2000); *Van der Val* v. *Netherlands* (2000)).

9.4 Federalism and the European Union

The EU is difficult to fit into a coherent constitutional structure. In addition to the conflicts already mentioned, there is a conflict between the ideal of European integration and that of national identity. For example, Art. 6 of the EC Treaty requires national identity to be respected. This tension suggests the possibility of a federal model since, as we saw in Chapter 7, federalism is intended to reconcile this kind of tension by marking out spheres of independence for each unit. While some idealists, notably Jean Monnet, pursued the agenda of a federal Europe, the thrust of the original initiative was towards the pragmatic integration of economic policy as the basis of evolution towards what the treaties call 'ever closer union' but with no agreed final destination. The widening membership makes a federal arrangement unlikely and Jean Monnet and his contemporaries are sometimes regarded as communitarian fantasists.

The EU has certain features of federalism in that the powers and purposes of the Communities are defined in the Treaty with the member states having residual autonomy in other areas. Some EC law overrides incompatible domestic law and, under the doctrine of 'pre-emption', member states may not legislate in areas reserved to the Community at least in cases where the Community has actually exercised its powers (see *Commission* v. *UK* (1981)).

On the other hand the Union has no elected government or enforcement arm of its own. It depends on the courts and the executives of the member states to enforce its will. There is a concept of citizenship of the EU (Art. 17) but this gives only limited rights, namely free movement within the Union within the requirements of the Treaty, and the right to stand or vote in local government elections and in elections to the European Parliament on the same terms as nationals. A delicate balance has to be struck between harmonising the law throughout the Community and catering for particular national needs so that individual states can sometimes depart from normal Community requirements. For example individual states can sometimes opt out of EC laws on the basis of special circumstances, there are also transitional provisions ('multi-speed' or 'variable geometry' arrangements) in which a core of members participate leaving others to opt in later if at all, for example monetary union, social welfare provisions and immigration arrangements (see Shaw, 1996. 94 *et seq*).

In these respects the European Union is more like a confederation or an inter-governmental body rather than a genuine supra-national body. Indeed the German Supreme Court has held that ultimate power remains with the member states (see *Brunner* v. *European Union Treaty* (1994)). The EU is therefore best regarded as a unique legal order not reducible into other forms. The idea of a common market and of pooling resources is an attractive way of increasing wealth and minimising the risk of war but the member states are far from equal economically and have widely different cultures. It is therefore doubtful whether there exists in Europe that delicate balance between diversity and unity on which a federal system depends. The policy of widening membership of the EU is likely to increase this problem.

The tension between the interests of the member states and those of the Union is expressed ambiguously through the concept of 'subsidiarity' which was introduced by the Maastricht Treaty. Subsidiarity is a vague term with no agreed meaning which can be used to serve different political interests. Historically subsidiarity is an authoritarian doctrine used by the Catholic Church to legitimise a hierarchical power structure. Subsidiarity can also be regarded as a pluralist liberal principle that decisions should be made at a level as close as possible to those whom they affect.

The version of subsidiarity in the EC Treaty (Art. 5) concerns the distribution of powers between the Community and national governments.

> In areas that do not fall within its exclusive competence, the Community shall take action, in accordance with the principle of subsidiarity, only if and so far as the objectives of the proposed action cannot be sufficiently achieved by the Member States and can therefore, by reason of the scale or effects of the proposed action, be better achieved by the Community ... Any action by the community shall not go beyond what is necessary to achieve the objects of this treaty.

This formulation is vague (e.g. the notions of 'sufficient' and 'better' and the non-sequitur between them). It is unlikely to be directly enforceable in law but, may operate at a political level thereby indirectly influencing the law. However, there is another definition of subsidiarity in Art. A of the Maastricht Treaty which is not only internally contradictory but seems to clash with that in Art. 5 as 'a new stage in the process of creating an ever closer union in which decisions are taken as near as possible to the citizen' (however, Art. 2 seems to give priority to the Art. 5 version). Moreover, doctrines such as those of the supremacy of EC law and pre-emption are difficult to reconcile with subsidiarity.

9.5   Community Law and National Law

The relationship between the UK constitution and the European Union involves a clash of constitutional tradition between the pragmatic, common law, politically driven constitution of the UK with its notion of unlimited legislative power, and the civil law approach driven by general legal concepts familiar to the continental jurists. Given the incommensurables involved, the relationship between UK law and EC law is unlikely to be one of rational coherence.

There are different ways of approaching the relationship between EC law and national law. One is to regard EC law as a distinct system with its own principles and methods of reasoning, in which the courts must participate by applying European methods as if they were federal courts. It could be argued that the relationship derives from a general obligation to interpret domestic law in line with international treaties. Another way would be to regard laws emanating from EC bodies as 'processed' into English law under the authority of the European

Communities Act 1972, to be approached in much the same way as other legislation in the light of the reasoning methods of English law (see e.g. *R.* v. *Poole BC ex parte Beebee* (1991)). The choice between these two approaches influences the extent to which the courts are willing to subordinate UK law to EC ideas.

The courts originally followed the narrower, second approach which fits traditional ideas of parliamentary supremacy, but, as we shall see, may now be accepting the broader rationale. Nevertheless the strict approach remains influential. For example in *Mayne* v. *Ministry of Agriculture, Fisheries and Food* (2000), it was held that UK regulations implementing an EC Directive do not apply to future amendments of the Directive unless they are clearly worded as doing so. There is also a 'spillover effect' whereby rights initially established for European purposes are later extended to domestic contexts on the basis that it would be unjust for domestic law to be more restrictive than EC law. This has led for example to the extension of a right to interim relief against the Crown contrary to the long-established, but often contested, doctrine of Crown immunity (*M* v. *Home Office* (1993)).

Not all EC rules are automatically part of UK law. Many EC measures take effect 'without further enactment' (European Communities Act 1972 s. 2 (1)) and these are automatically part of UK law. These will be discussed below. In other cases there has to be a conversion to UK law, usually in the form of a statutory instrument (ibid., s. 2 (2)). Certain measures including taxation, the creation of new criminal offences, and retrospective laws, can only be implemented by an Act of Parliament (ibid., Schedule 2).

The main kinds of EC legal instrument are as follows:

(i) *The Treaty*, or at least such provisions of it that according to the European Court have 'direct effect' (*Bulmer* v. *Bollinger* (1974); *R.* v. *Secretary of State for Trade ex parte Duddridge* (1995)).

(ii) *Regulations*. Regulations are general rules, which can be made by the Commission or the Council of Ministers, and apply to all member states and persons. By virtue of Art. 249 of the Treaty all regulations are 'directly applicable' and as such are automatically binding on UK courts except where a particular regulation is of a character that is inherently unsuitable for judicial enforcement.

(iii) *Directives*. Most EC law comprises Directives, which can be made by the Commission or the Council of Ministers. A Directive as such is not automatically binding. It is a requirement to achieve a given objective but leaves it to the individual states to specify the means by which that objective is to be achieved by altering their own laws (Art. 249). A Directive may be addressed to all states or to particular states. A time limit is usually specified for implementing the Directive.

(iv) *Decisions.* These are addressed to specific persons or organisations including member states and are 'binding in their entirety on those to whom they are addressed' (Art. 249).

(v) *Opinions and recommendations.* These do not have binding force. However the ECJ has power under Art. 228 (6) to give an opinion at an early stage of a matter, for example in relation to a proposed treaty.

(vi) *International agreements.* The EC has power to enter into international agreements which might be binding if they are intended to confer rights on individuals.

EC law pervades domestic law through various devices created by the ECJ. These are as follows: supremacy, direct effect, indirect effect, state liability. They are underpinned by the general obligation of member states under Art. 10, to give effect to EC obligations. These devices have been transmitted to English law through the European Communities Act 1972 s. 2 and 3, which require UK courts to apply EC law in accordance with the decisions and general principles of the ECJ.

9.5.1 Supremacy

The Treaty does not expressly deal with conflicts between Union law and national law. However, the ECJ has held that EC law prevails over national law (see *Costa* v. *ENEL* (1964); *Internationale Handelsgesellschaft* (1974)). The ECJ therefore made a political value judgement in much the same way as the US Supreme Court did in *Marbury* v. *Madison*. In the UK the matter is more complex, since the court has conflicting duties and must bear in mind that EC law obtains its force only from a UK statute. Debate has therefore focused upon whether the traditional doctrine of parliamentary supremacy has been affected by membership of the EC. As we saw in Chapter 6, the current position seems to be that a UK statute will give way to an EC law that according to EC jurisprudence has priority, unless possibly the statute contains express and unambiguous words forbidding the court to override the statute on EC grounds. The doctrine of implied repeal does not therefore apply to European law. This position has been reached as follows.

The European Communities Act 1972, s. 2 (4), deals with the relationship between EC law and UK statutes as follows: 'any enactment passed *or to be passed* ... [my italics] shall be construed and have effect subject to the foregoing provisions of this section'. The 'foregoing provisions' require (i) that those rules of Community law that according to the Treaty are automatically part of national law shall be enforced as law, and (ii) that other EC laws shall be translated into UK law. Section 3 (1) is also relevant. This provides that: 'for the purpose of all legal proceedings any question as to the meaning or effect of any of the treaties or as to the validity meaning or effect of a community instrument . . . shall be for determination as such in accordance with the principles laid down by . . . the European Court'. We have seen that the European Court endorses the supremacy of Community law over national law.

However, the language of the 1972 Act cannot in itself resolve the matter since the very question at issue is whether any Act is capable of altering the basic principle of the UK constitution, that of parliamentary supremacy. Only once we have answered yes to that question can we then go on to consider whether the language of the 1972 Act is sufficient to do so. We saw in Chapter 6 there is no compelling legal obstacle in the way of altering or abandoning the doctrine of parliamentary supremacy.

However, a court can avoid the issue of parliamentary supremacy by striving hard to interpret a UK statute so as to conform to community law (e.g. *Macarthys Ltd* v. *Smith* (1979); *Garland* v. *BREL* (1983)). In *Garland* Lord Diplock raised the possibility that unless Parliament expressly said otherwise the court would always interpret a statute to comply with an EC law, however much this might violate the language of the statute, short that is of the statute expressly stating that it overrides EC law. Thus the court could 'read in' to any statute the words 'except where EC law applies'. However, 'interpretation' at this point becomes fictitious and political reality is better represented by obeying the Union rule and admitting that the English rule is inconsistent.

In *Factortame* v. *Secretary of State for Transport (No. 2)* [1991] 1 All ER 70 at 108 it was said that 'under the terms of the 1972 Act, it has always been clear that it was the duty of a United Kingdom Court to override any rule of national law found to be in conflict with any directly enforceable rule of union law'. This reflects the Union doctrine of 'disapplying' national law (*Simmenthal* (1978)), but disapplying is not the same as invalidating a statute (cf. Lord Keith in *Equal Opportunities Commission* v. *Employment Secretary* [1994] 1 All ER 910 at 919). For example the statute retains its full effect in other contexts and if the relevant European rule were to be repealed the statute would surely apply in the ordinary way.

9.5.2   Direct applicability and direct effect

'Direct effect' must be distinguished from 'direct applicability' which applies only to EC regulations. The difference between the two concepts is that regulations are always binding, whereas 'direct effect' depends upon the quality of the particular EC instrument. It has been suggested that the ECJ developed the direct effect doctrine in order to make use of domestic law enforcement agencies as a means of compensating for the weak enforcement provision offered at EC level through the Commission (see Craig, 1992; Weatherill, 1995, p. 101 *et seq*).

Where the direct effect doctrine applies, the national court must give a remedy which, as far as possible, puts the plaintiff in the same position as if the directive had been properly implemented. This might for example require national restrictions to be set aside, or national taxes to be ignored or national rules which are stricter than a Directive covering the same ground to be set aside (see e.g. *Defrenne* (1976) – retirement restrictions; *Pubblico Ministerio* v. *Ratti* (1979) excessive labelling requirements).

Direct effect applies to the Treaty itself but mainly relates to EC Directives. A Treaty provision which has direct effect is enforceable against anyone upon whom its provisions impose an obligation (*Defrenne* v. *SABENA* (1976)). Directives, however, can be enforced only 'vertically', that is, against a public authority or 'emanation of the state', but not 'horizontally' against a private person (see *Marshall* v. *Southampton Area Health Authority* (No. 1) (1986); *Faccini Dori* v. *Recreb* (1995)). The reason seems to be that the state, which, as we saw above has the primary duty to implement a Directive, cannot rely on its failure to do so, an argument that it would be unfair to apply to a private body. It also follows that the state cannot rely on an unimplemented Directive against an individual (see *Wychavon DC* v. *Secretary of State* (1994)).

What is meant by an emanation of the state? It will be recalled that the UK has no legal concept of the state but relies on separate bodies linked in a variety of ways to the central government. For the purpose of direct effect, any public body seems to be regarded as an emanation of the state (*Marshall* v. *Southampton Area Health Authority* (1986)). A public body must (i) exercise functions in the public interest subject to the control of the state, *and* (ii) have special legal powers not available to individuals or ordinary companies (see *Foster* v. *British Gas* (1990)). All the activities of such a body, even those governed by private law, e.g. employment contracts, seem to be subject to direct effect. The privatised utilities of gas, electricity and water are probably emanations of the state but it is unlikely whether the privatised railway companies would be, since although they are subject to state regulation and receive state subsidy they have no statutory obligation to perform public duties or significant special powers (see *Doughty* v. *Rolls-Royce* (1992)).

To have direct effect an instrument must be 'justiciable', meaning that it is of a kind which is capable of being interpreted and enforced by a court without trespassing outside its proper judicial role. In essence, the legal obligation created by the instrument must be certain enough for a court to handle.

The tests usually applied are as follows (see *Van Duyn Ltd* v. *Home Office* (1974)):

(i) The instrument must be 'clear, precise and unconditional'. It must not give the member state substantial discretion as to how to give effect to it. For example in *Francovich* (1993) a Directive concerning the treatment of employees in an insolvency was not sufficiently unconditional because it left it to member states to decide which bodies should guarantee the payments required by the Directive (see also *Gibson* v. *East Riding DC* (2000): Directive about paid leave did not make clear what counted as working time). However, the fact that a Directive leaves it to the state to choose between alternative methods of enforcement does not prevent it from having direct effect if the substance of the right is clear from the Directive alone (*Marshall (No. 2)* (1993)). The European Court interprets the precision test liberally, bearing in mind that apparent uncertainty could be cured by a reference to the court (see Craig, 1992).

(ii) The instrument must be intended to confer rights. A problem arises here in respect of purely 'public' interests, such as some environmental concerns, e.g. wildlife conservation. It is arguable that a body with a public law right sufficient to give standing in national law to challenge the government's action, for example a pressure group, could rely on the direct effect doctrine. In other words the 'rights' requirement is no more than an aspect of the general principle that the directive must be justiciable.

(iii) The time limit prescribed by a Directive for its implementation must have expired.

9.5.3 Indirect effect

Even where a European law lacks direct effect, UK courts must still take account of it. Article 10 requires member states to 'take all appropriate measures' to fulfil European obligations, and Art. 249 requires that the objectives of Directives be given effect. This would afford horizontal effect. The traditional attitude of the UK courts has been that domestic legislation should be interpreted to fit European law only where the relevant European rule had direct applicability or direct effect, or where the domestic rule was specifically passed to give effect to European law and then only where the domestic law was unclear (see *Litser* (1990), *Finnegan* (1990), *Duke* (1990), *Webb* v. *EMO Air Cargo (UK) Ltd* [1992] 4 All ER 929 at 940).

Doubt has been cast on this by the decision of the ECJ in *Marleasing* (1992). The court held that all domestic law, whether passed before or after the relevant community law must be interpreted to conform with community law. The earlier ECJ case of *Von Colson* (1984) was applied, but that case involved an ambiguous domestic rule. However, *Marleasing* also involved a law (in the Spanish civil code) which could be interpreted in different ways. It is uncertain therefore whether clear, unambiguous domestic law, which was not meant to implement an EU obligation must give way to a European rule. In *Webb* v. *EMO Air Cargo (UK) Ltd* (1992), Lord Keith said that *Marleasing* applies to laws passed at any time provided that their language is not distorted.

Moreover, according to *Marleasing*, the domestic court is required to interpret '*so far as possible*' in the light of the aims and purposes of the relevant European law. This is a vague obligation replete with escape routes (see Maltby, 1993). It could be suggested that, in as much as it applies to laws passed before the relevant directive comes into effect, the *Marleasing* rule violates rule of law values of settled expectations and non-retrospectivity. On the other hand, given that old cases cannot be reopened, a revised interpretation of an earlier law seems to be no different in principle from the commonplace case of an amendment to a statute. Indeed as we shall see the Human Rights Act 1998 uses a similar device. Moreover *Marleasing* would not presumably apply to *events* that took place before the case was decided.

9.5.4   State liability

Even where a Directive does not have direct effect, an individual may be able to sue the government for damages for failing to implement it. This was established by the ECJ in *Francovich* v. *Italy* (1992) where a Directive which required employees' pay to be guaranteed against the insolvency of the employer was too vague to have direct effect. Nevertheless the court held that damages could be awarded against the Italian government in an Italian court. The court's reasoning was based upon the principle of giving full effect to EC rights. This is a powerful and far-reaching notion. In order to obtain damages: (i) the Directive must confer rights for the benefit of individuals; (ii) the content of those rights must be determined from the provisions of the Directive (a certain degree of certainty is therefore needed); (iii) there must be a causal link between breach of the Directive and the damage suffered (see also *R.* v. *Secretary of State for Transport ex parte Factortame no. 4* (1996); *R.* v. *Minister of Agriculture ex parte Hedley Lomas* (1996)).

In English law, in the absence of bad faith, damages cannot normally be obtained against the government for misusing its statutory powers and duties (*Barnett* v. *Enfield BC* (1999)). The *Francovich* principle, which was subsequently accepted by the House of Lords (*Kirklees MBC* v. *Wickes Building Supplies* (1992)), is therefore of great significance. *Francovich* leaves the procedures for recovering damages to national courts, but any conditions must not make recovery impossible or excessively difficult. There may also be a developing principle that legal remedies must be equally effective in each member state (below).

The *Francovich* principle also avoids the 'vertical' enforcement rule (above). Failure to implement a Directive against a private person would entitle the plaintiff to sue the government.

9.5.5 Effective remedies

There is also an obligation to give effective remedies to protect rights in EC law. The courts originally took the view that this second obligation merely required that the remedies available in European cases should be no worse than in equivalent domestic cases. However, it now appears that the courts must sometimes provide better remedies in relation to European rights than would be available domestically. In *Factortame* (No. 2) (1991), the House of Lords accepted a judgement of the European Court of Justice that required the court to issue an interim (temporary) injunction against the Crown in order to suspend the operation of a statute, which, contrary to a European Directive, prohibited the applicants from fishing in UK waters. At that time, interim relief against the Crown was not possible in UK law. The government argued that the protection given was the same as that which domestic law would give in similar circumstances, i.e. none. The ECJ, however, held that there is an overriding requirement that the remedy must be effective to protect the European right and the court should consider whether in the circumstances an injunction should issue (see also *Johnston* v. *Chief Constable of Royal Ulster Constabulary* (RUC) (1986)).

It remains to be seen how much freedom a member state has in adjusting its remedies to its own circumstances. For example, in *Factortame* the court still had a discretion whether to issue the injunction based upon the justice and convenience of the circumstances. The English courts are very cautious about issuing interim injunctions and will do so only as a last resort (see *R.* v. *HM Treasury ex parte British Telecommunications plc* (1996)). The governing principle is that the remedy must be adequate and effective, but member states can choose among different possible ways of achieving the object of a directive.

Summary

9.1   The EU and within it the EC exist to integrate key economic and increasingly social policies of member states with the aim of providing an internal 'common market', of creating a powerful European political unit, and of reducing the risk of war within Europe. The constitution of the EU is an evolving one aimed at increasing integration between its member states. The EU has three main policy areas or 'pillars', these being economic development, common foreign and security policy and co-operation on justice and home affairs. Only the first pillar, together with immigration matters, is regulated by law, most laws being made by the EC. EC law raises conflicts between democratic values and the existing goals of the community, between the independence of the member states and the integrationist goals of the EU and between the different legal cultures of the common law and civil law traditions.

9.2   EC law has been incorporated into UK law by the European Communities Act 1972, which makes certain EC laws automatically binding in the UK, requires other laws to be enacted in UK law either by statute or by regulations made under the 1972 Act, and obliges UK courts to decide cases consistently with principles laid down by the European Court of Justice. In some cases questions of law must be referred to the ECJ. The ECJ has developed the role of constitutional court and is sometimes regarded as being a driving force for integrationist policies which enlist national courts in the project of giving primacy to European law.

9.3   The other main policy and lawmaking bodies are the Council of Ministers which is the main lawmaking body, the European Council of heads of state responsible for policy direction, the appointed European Commission which proposes laws, makes some laws, supervises the implementation of policy, carries out research and takes enforcement action, and the elected European Parliament which is mainly a consultative and supervisory body but has certain powers of veto. Taken together these bodies are meant to balance the interests of national governments and those of the Union as such, but not to follow strict separation of power ideas. There is only limited democratic input into the EC lawmaking process.

9.4   Law and policy-making power are divided between the Council and the Commission with the balance in favour of the Council. Voting sometimes has to be unanimous but there is increasing use of qualified majorities where voting is weighed in favour of the more populous states. The Parliament does not initiate laws but has certain powers of veto and can sometimes suggest amendments.

9.5   Not all Union law is directly binding on member states. 'Regulations' are binding. Other laws including the treaty itself are binding if they satisfy criteria of 'direct effectiveness' created by the European Court. Directives can have direct effect only against public bodies (vertical direct effect) but not against private bodies (horizontal direct effect). However, the concept of 'indirect effect' which requires domestic law to be interpreted so as to confirm to EC law may alleviate this. The government may also be liable in damages if its failure properly to implement an EC law damages an individual in relation to right created by the EC law in question.

9.6   Membership of the Union may not have fundamentally altered the doctrine of parliamentary supremacy, but the UK courts have accepted that a statute which conflicts with a binding EC rule must be 'disapplied'. There is a general political principle – perhaps an emerging convention – in favour of the supremacy of Union law.

Further Reading

Arnull, A. (1996) 'The European Court and judicial objectivity: a reply to Professor Hartley', 112 *Law Quarterly Review* 411.
Bogdanor in Jowell and Oliver, *The Changing Constitution*.
Craig (1997) 'Directives: direct effect, indirect effect and the construction of national legislation', *European Law Review* 519.
Craig and De Burca, *The Evolution of EU Law*, chapters 1, 2, 5, 7, 12.
Harden, I. (1996) 'Democracy and the European Union' in Hirst and Khilnani (eds).
Harden, I. (1994) 'The constitution of the European Union', *Public Law* 609.
Hartley, (1996) 'The European Court, judicial objectivity and the constitution of the European Union', 112 *Law Quarterly Review* XXX.
Michael, J. (1996) 'Freedom of Information Comes to the European Union', *Public Law* 31.
Munro, C. *Studies in Constitutional Law*, chapter 6.
Shaw, J., More, G. (eds) *New Legal Dynamics of European Union*.
Walter, N. (1995) 'European constitutionalism and European integration', *Public Law* 266.
Ward, *A Critical Introduction to European Law*, chapters 1, 2.
Weatherill, *Law and Integration in the European Union*, chapters 1, 2, 4, 6.
Weiler, J. (1993) 'Journey to an unknown destination: a retrospective and prospective of the European Court of Justice in the arena of political integration', 31 *Journal of Common Market Studies*, 417.
Wincott, in Richards (ed) (1996) 'The Court of Justice and the European policy process'.

Exercises

9.1   Explain the constitutional structure of the EU. To what extent is it federal? It is a requirement of membership of the EU that the member state must have a democratic form of government, but it has often been remarked that the EU would not satisfy the conditions for membership of itself. Do you agree?

9.2   What powers does the UK Parliament possess in relation to EU policy?

9.3   To what extent are (a) the Council of Ministers and (b) the European Commission accountable for their decisions?

9.4   Explain the relationship between UK courts and the European Court of Justice. To what extent is the ECJ a constitutional court?

9.5   (a) What is the purpose of the direct effect doctrine and what are its main limitations?

(b) An EC Directive requires member states to ensure that compensation is paid to part-time workers who are made redundant. The compensation must be paid by the employer. The UK has not implemented the Directive. Jeff, a part-time employee of Dodgy Burgers plc, is made redundant. His employer refuses to pay him compensation. Advise Jeff as to his rights, if any.

9.6   Explain the constitutional implications of the *Marleasing* case.

9.7   Parliament wishes to put right injustices suffered by women. It passes an Act which permits women to be paid more than men for the same work. Assume that a directly effective EU law requires women to be paid the same as men for the same work and discuss the following:

(a) Gail is paid the same as John for the same work and seeks a remedy (a) in an English court, (b) in the European court.

(b) Would your answer differ if the Act said that 'this Act is applicable notwithstanding any decision of the European Court of Justice, or any powers of European Union Law or any powers of the European Communities Act 1972'?

9.8   Gervase has suffered lead poisoning. It has been established that this has been caused by a reaction in a water softener manufactured by Hydros, a Greek company. The retailer from whom it was purchased has gone into liquidation, and it was not insured. The reaction was one not generally known of at the time the water softener was supplied to Gervase, but some six months earlier an article had appeared in a Japanese scientific magazine which described reactions of this kind in laboratory tests of the filter material used in the water softener.

When Gervase sues Hydros under the Purchasers Protection Act 1990 (fictitious), Hydros admit that the water softener was defective, but rely on s. 4(1)(c) of the Act, which provides a defence to such an action where 'the state of scientific and technical knowledge at the time (time of supply) was not such that a producer of products of the same description as the product in question might be expected to have discovered the defect if it had existed in his products while they were under his control'. Section 5 of the Act also limits damages under the Act to £5,000. Gervase claims that he has suffered injuries worth £10,000 due to his being unable to pursue his job as a self-employed taxi driver for six weeks.

The Act was passed to implement the EC Purchasers Protection Directive (fictitious). Gervase wishes to rely on Art. 7(e) of the Directive which provides a defence only where 'the state of scientific and technical knowledge at the time when he put the product into circulation was not such as to enable the existence of the defect to be discovered'. Advise Gervase as to the rules by which any conflict between the Act and Directive will be resolved and the procedures involved.

Part III

Governmental Institutions

10   Parliament

Strictly speaking, Parliament is a meeting, summoned by the monarch under the royal prerogative of the two separate Houses – the House of Lords and the House of Commons – with the purpose of proposing laws to the Crown and consenting to the Crown's requests for money. Today, as a result of the development of conventions favouring democracy the role of Parliament is primarily to sustain the executive, hold the executive to account and to approve legislation. Parliament also acts as a way of translating the popular vote into the appointment of an executive, since, again by convention, whoever commands a majority in the House of Commons is entitled to form a government. As we shall see, by virtue of the distortions of the electoral system, a popular majority does not necessarily translate into a parliamentary majority. In recent years the effectiveness and standing of Parliament has probably weakened in that members of Parliament may lack the will and resources to be independent of the executive and have therefore allowed political power to accrue to the executive.

10.1   Historical Development

The word 'Parliament', which in origin meant merely a parley or conference, entered into official language about the middle of the thirteenth century. It described formal conferences between the king and the elite members of society. Broadly, the history of Parliament is that of a power struggle between the Crown and Parliament and between the two Houses of Parliament. The House of Commons has triumphed over the Crown in the sense of the monarch, and over the House of Lords, but the Crown in the sense of the executive appears for now to be the winner.

    The House of Lords was the earliest part of Parliament. The House of Lords was the king's great council of advisers, summoned and dismissed by the king. The Lords were originally the great landowners of the realm, 'tenants-in-chief', created as such by the monarch and transmitting to their descendants their property and the titles and power that went with it. Membership also included church dignitaries. There was also an 'inner' council of close advisers exercising executive functions. This developed into the Privy Council which retains residual functions today but whose executive role has mainly been taken over by the cabinet which is by convention nominally responsible to Parliament.

The 'pure' feudal system did not survive the thirteenth century. Land became freely disposable, and wealth and influence could be amassed through commerce and professional skills. This made it possible for people other than the hereditary landowners to aspire to political power, and led to the rise of the House of Commons, the origins of which lay in the occasional practice of the king of summoning leading persons from the wider community to assist in settling appeals from local courts, and to provide him with information.

The king increasingly used the Commons to provide support in his continuing disputes with the nobility. In particular the representatives were useful tax-gatherers, and in 1254 Henry III began the practice of summoning the Commons to seek financial support particularly for overseas adventures. The Commons consisted of property owners: the knights from the shires and (after 1265) the burgesses (leading citizens) from the boroughs. During the reign of Edward III (1327–77), parliaments were summoned more regularly and the Commons began the practice of submitting a list of demands and grievances before they agreed to vote taxes to the king. They also began to distance themselves from the Crown and the Lords by meeting separately.

The independence of the Commons owed much to the Crown's need for money to prosecute foreign wars and to finance the dynastic conflicts with the barons that continued until the Tudor period. Although Parliament was not originally a law-making body, by the sixteenth century it became customary for the most authoritative statements of the existing law to be made by the monarch with the advice of the separate Houses of Lords and Commons: the three 'estates' who claimed to represent the realm. From this it was an easy step to Parliament making new law. Nevertheless, Parliament only met when summoned by the king, drastic changes in the law were rare, the Crown had plenty of inherited revenues, and the Commons usually did as it was told (Chrimes, 1967, Ch. 2).

The Tudor period (1485–1603) saw the monarchy at the height of its power and Parliament became largely subservient to the executive. The power and wealth of the great barons had been exhausted by many years of civil wars and inter-family quarrels. The government was efficiently carried on, particularly during the reign of Elizabeth I, through professional civil servants, prerogative bodies such as the Privy Council and its offshoot courts, and a sophisticated network of local officials appointed by the Crown. This sowed the seeds for the struggles of the seventeenth century between Crown and Parliament wherein the king claimed the right to tax and to suspend and dispense with laws. The common law courts equivocated on these matters. In 1642, however, Charles I conceded that English government comprised a mixture of King, Lords and Commons (Answer to the Nineteen Propositions).

During the civil wars of 1642 to 1648 and the ensuing period of republican government the 'Long Parliament' continued in a reduced and frequently interrupted form. In 1660, Charles II was restored under the constitution that was claimed to have existed at the beginning of the civil war, this being a compromise between the Crown and Parliament. His successor James I attempted to renew some of the claims to royal supremacy that had led to the downfall of Charles I. Although James's religious policy was relatively liberal he was suspected of having a pro-Catholic agenda, whereas Parliament was a bastion of protestantism.

James was deposed in 1688 by the threat of a Dutch invasion and a new settlement formalised by the Crown and Parliament Recognition Act 1689. The group that established the 1688 settlement was dominated by commoners but included 10 peers. The position of Parliament was reinforced. Article 4 of the Bill of Rights 1688 forbade the Crown to raise money without Parliament's consent, and Article 9 enshrined the right of freedom of speech of Parliament and its members. The Bill of Rights also required elections to the Commons. The Act of Settlement 1700 outlawed royal pardons for those impeached by the Commons, and forbade persons having offices or places of profit under the king or securing promises from the Crown, from sitting in the Commons. This last provision might have led to a genuine separation of powers, but it was soon repealed to permit ministers to sit in the Commons. The settlement had no need to make special arrangements for the House of Lords, the role of which was generally accepted.

The eighteenth century saw the emergence of the 'balanced constitution' in which monarch, Lords and Commons were supposed to check each other but ended in popular agitation for democratic reform. During most of this period the House of Lords was in practice the dominant political force because its members had significant influence upon elections to the Commons. The Commons was elected from a small number of property owners and in most parts of England the aristocratic landowners were in a position to manipulate elections.

The main developments of this period were the emergence of the conventions of cabinet government and ministerial responsibility. The monarch gradually ceased to run the executive in person and relied upon a cabinet (which he still appointed) drawn from the ranks of Parliament. This helped to ensure stable government in that the cabinet had the confidence both of monarch and Commons. George III (1760–1820) attempted to recover some of the Crown's waning influence and this provoked a response from the Commons which asserted its independence from the Crown. Thereafter the party system grew in strength and cabinets asserted the right to meet without the monarch and to give advice to the monarch. Royal influence diminished and it became established that the monarch must appoint as prime minister the person who can command a majority of the Commons, must act on cabinet advice and must dissolve parliament if a government loses the support of the Commons. Nevertheless the modern convention that the monarch always acts on the advice of ministers was not firmly established until after the First World War.

From the middle of the eighteenth century the House of Commons gradually became the dominant part of the legislature. Hume believed that the Commons refrained from flexing its muscles and so unbalancing the constitution only because its members were easily corrupted by the patronage of the Crown, a sentiment that modern observers might share (*Essays, Moral, Political and Literary*, 25).

However, external observers might have underestimated the unity of interest that connected the House of Lords and the House of Commons. The elected House of Commons was dominated by patronage from the House of Lords. Aristocratic interests ran local affairs and influenced elections by means of bribing or intimidating voters. Heads of families sat in the Lords, their younger sons in the Commons. In the counties the right to vote was limited to relatively wealthy property owners and the seats were often in the gift of the landed families. In the boroughs the number of seats and the right to vote were based on ancient charters bearing no relation to the size of population. For example, the notorious 'rotten borough' of Old Sarum had two buildings and two Parliamentary seats while Manchester with a population of more than 60,000 had no seats (see Paine, 1987, p. 222 *et seq.*). In the boroughs, Parliamentary seats were sometimes attached to particular properties, sometimes to membership of town councils, sometimes to self-sufficient householders ('potwalloper boroughs') or local ratepayers and could sometimes be sold and/or handed down from father to son.

The industrial revolution of the late eighteenth and early nineteenth centuries permanently changed the political scene. Britain escaped the major revolution of France and America but from 1780 to 1832 there was considerable agitation for the reform of Parliament. Universal male suffrage was sought by radical groups of working people, but resisted by Whigs and Tory establishments. By 1831 Britain was near to revolution, although as usual the rulers skilfully achieved a compromise. Respect for tradition and the propaganda of the rule of law may have played a part (see Thompson, 1963, part III).

The first Reform Act of 1832, passed by a reluctant Parliament and monarch to stave off revolution, was more important symbolically than in what it actually achieved. It extended a uniform franchise to certain moderately well-off property owners and new constituencies were created in the growing urban areas. However, the extended franchise was still property-based and reached only the urban middle classes. Lord Grey, the prime minister, said 'there is no one more decided against annual parliaments, universal suffrage and the ballot than I am. My object is not to favour but to put an end to such hopes and projects' (Thompson, 1963, p. 892), and 'it is of the utmost importance to associate the middle with the higher orders of society' (ibid., p. 899).

Further electoral reforms took place gradually over the nineteenth century and the property qualification was progressively removed. In 1867 the urban working class were given the franchise and the Representation of the People Act 1884 extended the franchise to most male householders. The older 'rotten boroughs' were abolished, so that the influence of landlords and the Crown was reduced. This was also due to the introduction of secret ballots (1872), financial controls over election campaigns (1883) and the principle that constituencies should reflect the number of people within them (Franchise Act 1884). However, it was not until 1914 that a universal male franchise was introduced and only in 1928 were women given the franchise on the same basis as men. In 1945 surviving anomalies such as special university votes were abolished and in 1969 the voting age was reduced from 21 to 18.

During the nineteenth century there were many proposals for reform of the House of Lords and throughout the century there was an uneasy stalemate between the Lords and the Commons. The Lords claimed the right to veto legislation but not to amend financial measures, since by convention money could be supplied only by the Commons. There was also a convention that the Lords should give way to the Commons whenever the will of the people was clearly behind the Commons. This gave the Lords the right to precipitate a general election. Thus, it is sometimes claimed that the Lords are the guardians of democracy against the executive.

During the early years of this century the Liberal government introduced a programme of social reform. The Lords opposed much of this, and the uncertain conventions governing the relationship between Lords and Commons became crucially important. Furthermore it was unclear whether the monarch could refuse to accept the advice of the prime minister to appoint sufficient peers to secure a majority in the House of Lords. In 1909–11 there was a major constitutional crisis the result of which, following two general elections, was that the Lords agreed to the passing of the Parliament Act 1911.

The Parliament Act 1911 placed the relationship between Lords and Commons on a legal basis in which the Commons has the last word. The one vital power left to the Lords is that of preventing a government from remaining permanently in office since the Parliament Acts do not apply to a bill to prolong the life of Parliament. Subject to this the role of the House of Lords is the limited one of suggesting revisions to legislation and providing an opportunity for debate and investigation in committee of matters of public concern. Further reforms were made by the Life Peerages Act 1958 which reinvigorated the House by allowing appointed life peers to sit. This made the House of Lords a respected, but still ultimately powerless, debating chamber. The present government proposes to reform the House of Lords. It has commenced the process in a modest way by the House of Lords Act 1999, which reduced the number of hereditary peers able to sit in the House from many hundred to ninety-two. Its further proposals envisage a predominantly appointed House with a small elected element (see Chapter 11).

10.2   The Meeting of Parliament

The foundations of the modern law were established by the 1688 Revolution. The main principles are as follows. They are a mixture of law and convention.

1. 'Parliament ought to be held frequently' (Bill of Rights 1688 Art. 13) and must meet at least once every three years (Meeting of Parliament Act 1694). In fact Parliament meets annually (convention backed by administrative necessity, for example authorising tax and public spending).
2. Parliament must automatically end at the expiry of five years from the date of its writ of summons (see below) (Septennial Act 1715; Parliament Act 1911).
3. Within the five years Parliament may be dissolved by the monarch (law) on the advice of the prime minister (convention). However, it is possible that in certain extreme cases the monarch can exercise personal choice whether or not to dissolve Parliament (see p. 295). A Parliament usually lasts for about four years, dissolution being timed for the political advantage of the prime minister. This is one

of the main sources of prime ministerial power. It is sometimes suggested that Parliament should sit for a fixed term, thus removing a prime minister's power to call an election to suit his own party. This could, however, paralyse a weak government (see *Royal Commission on the Constitution*, Cmnd. 5460, 1969–73). A prime minister whose government is defeated on a vote of confidence in the House of Commons must ask for a dissolution.

4. Dissolution triggers a general election which must be held within 18 working days of the dissolution. The same proclamation dissolves Parliament and summons a new one. If the monarch dies after the proclamation but before the meeting of the new Parliament the meeting is postponed for 14 days (Representation of the People Act 1985 s. 70). In practice Parliament is either prorogued or adjourned (below) a few days before being formally dissolved so as to permit a breathing space during which it technically remains in being.

5. A 'Parliament' is divided into 'sessions'. These are working periods usually running from November until July (about 170 sitting days). Public bills that are not completed by the end of a session lapse. Sessions are 'prorogued' by the monarch under the royal prerogative. Each session is opened by the monarch, with an Address from the Throne which outlines the government's legislative proposals. The event provides an opportunity for a general debate on government policy which takes place immediately afterwards. Within each Session each House can be adjourned at any time by resolution of the House.

6. There is machinery for recalling each House while it stands prorogued (e.g. Meeting of Parliament Act 1870; Emergency Powers Act 1920). An adjourned Parliament can be summoned quickly by the Speaker and the Lord Chancellor (who presides over the House of Lords) at the request of the prime minister. The Speaker can also suspend individual sittings. However, it does not seem to be possible for ordinary MPs to recall Parliament in order to debate any crisis that may arise while Parliament is not sitting. Government has many powers under the royal prerogative, notably to deploy the armed forces and even to declare war, which it can exercise without reference to Parliament.

10.3 The Functions of Parliament

As we have seen, Parliament combined with the Queen is the supreme law-making body. The separate Houses of Parliament each have distinctive functions.

10.3.1 The House of Commons

Today, Parliament is largely a reactive body responding to initiatives from the government, and sometimes from outside bodies. The House of Commons has several functions which in our loose system, unprotected as it is by the separation of powers, may conflict. Indeed the House of Commons is widely regarded as dysfunctional. The main functions of the House of Commons are as follows:

(i) It legitimises the government by financing and supporting it through its majority and providing a training and recruiting ground for government ministers

(ii) It enacts legislation although this normally takes the form of approving or amending legislation made by the government.

(iii) It holds the government to account through debates, questions and committee investigations.

(iv) It provides a forum for ventilating matters of public concern. These can be generated by outside bodies representing particular interests or by the grievances of individuals. While every MP has a duty to represent his or her constituents it is unclear how far MPs are entitled to act as advocates for other interests.

The procedures by which these functions are implemented will be discussed in Chapter 12.

• Our system is a parliamentary system as opposed to the presidential system pioneered by the USA. By this is meant that the government is not directly elected but chosen by Parliament. By convention the prime minister is the person who commands the support of the majority in the Commons. The prime minister then advises the Queen on the appointment of the other government ministers and the Queen must accept the PM's advice. By convention most ministers must be members of the House of Commons thus ensuring that they are fully accountable. There are, however, statutory limits upon the number of ministers who can sit in the Commons (above, p. 112), a principle that reflects the separation of powers. Therefore some ministers notably the Lord Chancellor, sit in the Lords. Some states such as France combine the parliamentary and presidential systems by having a directly elected president who appoints a prime minister and government, the members of which can, but need not be, members of the legislature. The legislature can remove the government. It is not essential to the parliamentary system that ministers are also MPs provided that Parliament can choose and dismiss the government.

- The size and complexity of modern government means that parliamentary control over government cannot be exercised directly. Parliamentary approval of the executive's budget and accounts is largely a formality. Detailed scrutiny and control over government spending takes place mainly within the government itself through the medium of the Treasury. However, a substantial parliamentary safeguard is provided by the National Audit Office, headed by the Comptroller and Auditor General. This is an aspect of a modern tendency to create specialised supervisory bodies while preserving constitutional propriety by making them formally responsible to Parliament.

- Legislation is usually presented to Parliament ready drafted by the executive. Although any group of members can propose a law, in practice, because the Leader of the House who is responsible for the timetable is a member of the government the parliamentary process is dominated by government business. This is why Bagehot thought that the absence of a strict separation of powers made the UK constitution an effective machine for ensuring government by experts. By convention Parliament can dismiss a government by a vote of no confidence and also require a minister to resign. These sanctions are rarely used. The fact that ministers are also MPs weakens Parliament's independence since backbench MPs, who are meant to hold the government to account, may be corrupted by the desire to become ministers themselves.

Executive domination of Parliament must not be overstated. Parliament, although dominated by members of the executive, remains a separate institution with large powers of its own and protection against executive interference which it could use were it so minded. Government proposals must be publicly explained in Parliament and ministers must justify their decisions in public if required to do so by Parliament. The Opposition is a formal institution protected by the law of parliamentary procedure – a government and prime minister in waiting. The Opposition has a duty to oppose government policy, short of actually frustrating the governmental process, and forms a 'shadow cabinet' ready to take office immediately (see Brazier, 1988). The Speaker who presides over the House of Commons has a duty to ensure that the procedure is fair and to protect minorities. In practice, however, recent opposition parties have been extremely weak, as a result of internal conflicts and failure to recover from damaging election defeats.

10.3.2   The House of Lords

The House of Lords currently comprises some 695 persons. It is unusual among legislative chambers in the following respects:

- Its members are not elected. Most of them are peers appointed by the Crown on the advice of the prime minister, or have inherited their seat from ancestors who were so appointed. There are also 26 senior Church of England bishops. Thus in many cases membership is compulsory although attendance is not.
- Members other than the bishops sit for life.
- Members receive no payment other than expenses.
- Members have no constituencies and are accountable to no one. About 25% of the members are independent of political parties.
- By long-standing practice the proceedings of the House are regulated by the House itself without formal rules or disciplinary sanctions, members being treated as bound by 'personal honour'.

The House of Lords could therefore be depicted as a constitutional abomination, as a valuable ingredient of a mixed constitution or as an anomalous relic which from a pragmatic perspective might nevertheless have some useful functions.

A common justification for a second chamber is to represent the different units of a federal system with the first chamber representing the popular vote, as for example in the United States. The conventional justification for the existence of a second chamber in the UK is that it acts as a revising chamber to scrutinise the detail of legislation proposed by the Commons and to allow time for second thoughts so acting as a constitutional safeguard against the possible excesses of majoritarianism and party politics. The Royal Commission on the future of the House of Lords (Wakeham, 2000; see Chapter 11), recommended that the second chamber should be subordinate to the Commons, that it should provide constitutional checks and balances and that it should provide a parliamentary voice for the 'nations and regions of the United Kingdom'.

Particular roles of the second chamber include the following (see Wakeham, 2000; see also *House of Lords Reform* (1968), Cmnd. 3799):

- To provide advice on public policy bringing a range of perspectives to bear which according to Wakeham (2000) should be broadly representative of British society and in particular provide a voice for the nations and regions of the UK and for ethnic minorities and interest groups.

- To provide a forum for general debate on matters of public concern without party political pressures.
- To process relatively uncontroversial legislation or private bills as a method of relieving the workload of the Commons. Any bill other than a financial measure can be introduced in the Lords.
- To provide committees to discuss general topics, such as the European Communities Committee and the Science and Technology Committee. Such reports are highly respected.
- To permit persons who have made a contribution to public life other than party politicians to participate in government. Life peerages provide the mechanism for this.
- To act as a constitutional check by preventing a government from prolonging its own life in respect of which the Lords has a veto. The consent of the Lords is also needed for the dismissal of senior judges (above, p. 84).
- To act as the highest judicial appellate body (although there appears to be no particular reason other than historical continuity and the convenience of existing members why the House of Lords, rather than a separate supreme court, should perform this function).
- To provide a means of patronage for persons seeking a prestigious lifestyle whom the government wishes to bribe or reward. Prime ministers have sometimes being accused of selling peerages to raise election campaign funds, the most notorious example being that of Lloyd George in 1922.

These functions can be pursued in the House of Lords partly because its procedure and culture differ significantly from the Commons. In particular party discipline is less rigorous and the House of Lords is less partisan than the Commons. Members of the House of Lords (other than bishops of the Church of England sitting as such) are life members removable only by statute and are therefore less susceptible to political pressures than MPs. The House as a whole controls its own procedure and is relatively free from procedural constraints and is subject to less time pressure than the Commons. Its members have considerable accumulation of experience and knowledge. The House of Lords cannot therefore easily be manipulated by the government, it is attractive to external lobbyists and can ventilate moral and social issues in an objective way. Occasionally members of the House of Lords will respond to their individual consciences, or to public opinion, and defeat government proposals. Bills are frequently amended, if only in minor respects, after discussion in Parliament.

10.4   Parliamentary Privilege and Standards

It is important that a legislature be protected against disruption and interference both by outsiders and from within its ranks. Interference by the Crown with parliamentary business was an ingredient of the seventeenth-century revolution and at the beginning of every Parliament the Speaker symbolically asserts the 'ancient and undoubted privileges' of the House of Commons against the Crown. The House of Lords also has its privileges which it polices collectively but does not have the power to punish.

Some parliamentary privileges are mainly of historical or symbolic interest. These include the collective right of access of the Commons to the monarch. Members of the Commons also enjoy immunity from civil, as opposed to criminal arrest, during a period from 40 days before to 40 days after every session. In the case of peers, the immunity is permanent and seems to be based on their status as peers rather than membership of the House (*Stourton*, 1963). Now that debtors are no longer imprisoned, civil arrest is virtually obsolete, being concerned mainly with disobedience to court orders. There is no privilege preventing a civil action against an MP in his private capacity (*Re Parliamentary Privilege Act 1770* (1958)). Members and officers of both Houses have automatic exemption from jury service (Juries Act 1974) and the House can exempt members from giving evidence in court.

The two most important privileges are (i) the collective privilege of each House to control its own composition and procedure, and (ii) freedom of speech. We shall discuss these below. We shall also discuss the conflicts that have arisen between Parliament and the courts over parliamentary privilege. At present there is an uneasy stalemate. Parliament has never accepted that the courts have the power to decide what are the proper limits of its privileges. The ordinary courts accept that Parliament has the exclusive power to regulate its own internal affairs, but claim the right to determine the limits of other privileges (that is, those affecting the rights of people outside the House) but not to interfere with how established privileges are exercised.

10.4.1   Contempt of Parliament

Breach of a specific parliamentary privilege should be distinguished from contempt of Parliament. A parliamentary privilege is a special right or immunity available either to the House collectively (for example, to control its own composition and procedure) or to individual members (for example, freedom of speech). Contempt is a general term embracing any conduct, whether by MPs or outsiders, 'which obstructs or impedes either House of Parliament in the performance of its functions or which obstructs or impedes any member or officer of the House in the execution of his duty or which has a tendency directly or indirectly to produce such a result' (May, 1983, p. 143). This is very wide. It includes, for example, abuses by MPs of parliamentary procedure, disruption in the House, improper or dishonest behaviours by MPs, and even harassment of, or allegations against, MPs in newspapers (see, for example, *Daily Graphic* case HC 27 (1956–7); Duffy's case, HC 129 (1964–5)). Contempt not only protects the 'efficiency' of the House but also its 'authority and dignity'.

One controversial aspect of contempt of Parliament concerns public access to parliamentary information which arguably should be unrestricted except where the disclosure would harm the public interest. However, parliamentary committees often sit in private, and 'leaks' of reports of Select Committees have been prohibited since 1837, although action is only likely to be taken if the leak causes 'substantial interference with the function of a Committee' (see *Report of Committee of Privileges*, 1984–5, paras 51–60; and Leopold, 1986). The House of Commons has waived any more general right to restrain publication of its proceedings and has authorised the broadcasting of its proceedings subject to a power to give directions.

Perhaps the most striking feature of contempt of Parliament is that Parliament accuses, tries and punishes offenders itself. The ordinary courts have no jurisdiction in the matter, and there are no independent safeguards for the individual. Parliament is not subject to the Human Rights Act 1998. This means that in any dispute between Parliament and the courts, Parliament in theory can have the last word, for example by imprisoning the litigants and court officials for contempt. However, there is a broad consensus of mutual respect between Parliament and the courts (see *Hamilton* v. *Al Fayed* [1999] 3 All ER 317 at 33–34).

The procedure for dealing with a contempt of Parliament, or a breach of privilege, is as follows (see HC 417, 1976–7):

1. Any member can give written notice of a complaint to the Speaker.
2. The Speaker decides whether to give priority over other business.
3. If the Speaker decides not to do so, the member may then use the ordinary procedure of the House to get the matter discussed. This would be difficult in practice.

4. If the Speaker decides to take up the matter, the complaining member can propose that the matter be referred to the Committee of Standards and Privileges or that some other action be taken, for example, an immediate debate. A select committee can in certain cases refer a contempt against itself direct to the Committee (HC Deb. vol. 94. col. 763–4, 18 March 1986).
5. The Committee (17 senior members) investigates the complaint. Witnesses are examined but there is no right to legal representation. The procedure is entirely up to the Committee. The accused has no legal right to a hearing nor to summon or cross-examine witnesses.
6. The Committee reports back to the House, which decides what action to take. This could range from a reprimand, through suspension or expulsion from the House, to imprisonment for the rest of the session, renewable indefinitely. The House of Lords can imprison for a fixed term and can also impose a fine.
7. The Speaker also has summary powers to deal with disruptive behaviour in the House, or breaches of the rules of debate. He can exclude MPs and others from the Chamber until the end of the session (HC Standing Orders 24–6), and make rulings on matters of procedure. The Lord Chancellor presides over the House of Lords, but has no procedural or disciplinary powers.

The conduct of MPs and the justice and effectiveness of the internal disciplinary process came in the public spotlight during the 1990s when several MPs, notably Neill Hamilton a junior minister, were accused of payments to give favours to outside interests. In 1999 the Joint Committee on Parliamentary Privilege (the Nichols Committee, HL 43-1, HC 214-1 (1998–9)) recommended that the procedure be reformed in favour of stronger procedural rights reflecting contemporary standards of fairness relating to the right to a fair trial.

10.4.2 Composition and procedure: 'exclusive cognisance'

Although the qualifications for being a member of Parliament are fixed by statute, each House has the exclusive right to decide who shall actually sit, to regulate all matters within the House, and to expel members. No legal process is possible in respect of any matter before the House and no one can be prevented from placing a matter before Parliament (see *Bilston Corporation* v. *Wolverhampton Corporation* (1942); *Pickin* v. *British Railways Board* (1974)). Conversely, the courts cannot order a minister to present a matter to Parliament even where a change in the law is required by European law (*R.* v. *Secretary of State for Employment ex parte Equal Opportunities Commission* (1992)).

In *Bradlaugh* v. *Gossett* (1884), Charles Bradlaugh, a well-known freethinker, had been duly elected to the Commons. The House refused to let him take his seat because it deemed that as an atheist he had no statutory right to take the oath. In fact the courts had previously ruled in his favour on this (*Clarke* v. *Bradlaugh* (1881)). The court held that it had no power to intervene since this was a matter exclusively to do with the internal procedure of the House. However, the court emphasised that the Commons has no control over those outside the House itself. Resolutions of the House of Commons cannot alter the general law (*Stockdale* v. *Hansard* (1839); *Bowles* v. *Bank of England* (1913)) and Parliament cannot interfere with court processes (*Ashby* v. *White* (1703)). Conversely, the courts cannot interfere while a matter is before the House, nor prevent the House considering it. However, approval by the House except as part of a statute cannot make valid something unlawful (*Hoffman La Roche Ltd* v. *Trade and Industry Secretary of State* (1974)). This standoff between courts and Parliament could be regarded as an example of the dual sovereignty which it is claimed that the separation of powers requires.

What counts as 'internal'? On one view anything which happens within the precincts of the Houses of Parliament (the Palace of Westminster) is protected. In *R.* v. *Grahame-Campbell ex parte Herbert* (1935) the Divisional Court held that the House of Commons bar was exempt from the liquor licensing laws and so could sell drinks without restriction. However, an explanation of this case is that the Palace of Westminster, a royal palace, enjoys Crown immunity from statute law. Another view is that immunity applies only to the official business of the House. This will be discussed in the next section in connection with freedom of speech. On this view ordinary criminal offences unconnected with parliamentary business taking place in the precincts should fall within the ordinary law, although the Sergeant at Arms may control the entry of law enforcement officials into the Palace of Westminster.

The immunity of Parliament from interference by the courts is reinforced by the Human Rights Act 1998 which provides that Parliament, except the House of Lords in its judicial capacity is not a public body for the purpose of the Act (s. 6 (3)). This prevents an action being brought against Parliament under the Human Rights Act.

10.4.3 Freedom of speech

This is the central privilege of an MP, who must be at liberty to speak and write without fear of interference from outside bodies. On the other hand, as with any liberty, the price to be paid is that some MPs might abuse this freedom to make untrue allegations against persons who cannot answer back or to violate privacy as in the '*Child Z*' case (HC 1995–6, vol. 252, para 9, 10) where a child was named in defiance of an order of the Court of Appeal.

The privilege of freedom of speech is statutory. Article 9 of the Bill of Rights 1688 (introduced as part of the revolution settlement for the purpose of protecting MPS against the Crown) states 'The Freedom of Speech or Debates or Proceedings in Parliament ought not to be impeached or questioned in any court or palace out of Parliament'. Article 9 has been interpreted widely as preventing parliamentary materials from being used as evidence in court proceedings (*Church of Scientology of California* v. *Johnson-Smith* (1972): MP sued for defamation: evidence of his statements in Parliament could not be used). However, the Defamation Act 1996 s. 13 amended the Bill of Rights in order to accommodate Neil Hamilton, a Conservative MP, who wished to sue a newspaper for defamation, relying upon parliamentary material for the purpose. Section 13 permits an MP to use things said in Parliament in evidence provided that the MP waives his or her own immunity. This illustrates the frailty of constitutional principle against party political government. Indeed the Nichols Committee pointed out that s. 13 was a distortion of the constitution in that Art. 9 exists in the public interest to protect Parliament and is not a provision which individual MPs should be able to waive in their own interests. The Committee therefore proposed that Art. 9 should be waived only by each House.

In *Hamilton* v. *Al Fayed* (1999) the Court of Appeal adopted a narrower interpretation of Art. 9. It held that that Art. 9 does not exclude the use of parliamentary material in court but only prohibits the court from penalising or criticising anything said or done in parliamentary proceedings. For example, evidence of something a minister said in Parliament cannot be used to determine whether he is exercising his statutory powers improperly (*R.* v. *Secretary of State for Trade ex parte Anderson Strathclyde* [1983] 2 All ER 233 at 238–9), although it can be used as evidence of what his policy is. In the same way statements made by the proposers of a bill in Parliament may be used by courts to determine the meaning of a statute (*Pepper* v. *Hart* (1993)).

(1) '*Freedom of speech or debates or proceedings*': This includes questions asked by an MP in the House whether written or oral, committee proceedings, and written documents published by Order of the House (Parliamentary Papers Act 1840, s. 2). Extracts from such documents enjoy only 'qualified' privilege, meaning that they must be

made in good faith. Broadcasts of parliamentary proceedings also have qualified privilege (Defamation Act 1952 s. 9) as do other unofficial reports and broadcasts such as press reports or parliamentary sketches provided that they are not merely selective extracts but reasonably comprehensive (*Wason* v. *Walter* (1868); *Cook* v. *Alexander* (1974)).

(2) '*In Parliament*': The meaning of 'in Parliament' has not been settled. In 1688, it was no doubt thought that the phrase was self-explanatory. However, the work of a modern MP is not confined to work within the Chamber or even in committees. Much of an MP's time is spent in writing letters, and attending meetings in the UK and abroad with pressure groups, local authorities, business organisations, foreign officials, etc. The MP also meets or writes to ministers and constituents. To what extent are these activities protected? Anything said in the Chamber as part of the business of the House and in committees or reports related to the business of the House, is certainly protected. Parliamentary committees often visit places around the country, and interference with their proceedings wherever they take place is a contempt of Parliament (for example, disturbance at Essex University, 1969 HC 308, 1968–9).

At the other extreme, speeches by MPs in their own constituencies are not protected, nor are writings in the press, or TV interviews or election matters. It is arguable that speech even within the House itself which is unrelated to parliamentary business enjoys no privilege (see *Re Parliamentary Privilege Act* 1770 (1958)). In 1976, in the Zircon affair, the Committee of Privileges ruled that the showing to MPs within the precincts of a film about a secret security project was not protected by privilege and could therefore be the subject of an injunction (see HC 365, 1986–7). In *Rivlin* v. *Bilankin* (1953) a libellous letter about a private matter was posted in a letter-box within the precincts. It was held in a short unreasoned judgement that the letter was not protected by privilege.

The main area of doubt concerns things said or written by MPs outside the House as part of their duties on behalf of their constituents, for example, a letter complaining to the Secretary of State about a National Health hospital. In the case of *Strauss* (1958), the House of Commons by a tiny majority (218–213) rejected a recommendation by the Committee of Privileges that such letters should be protected by parliamentary privilege. *Strauss* concerned a complaint about the activities of the London Electricity Board. This was not a central government department so the minister to whom Strauss wrote was not directly responsible to Parliament for its day-to-day activities. It is not clear what the reasons for the Commons resolutions were, and the vote may have been on party lines. The *Strauss* view certainly seems narrow and artificial and in later reports the Committee of Privileges has recommended that *Strauss* be overturned. This has not been implemented. On the basis of *Strauss* a letter from an MP is privileged only if it is to do with a matter currently being debated in the House or is the subject of an official parliamentary question. In 1967 a Select Committee on Parliamentary Privilege (1967–8; HC 34) recommended that privilege be widened to include all official communications by an MP but the recent Nichols Committee favoured the narrow view.

(3) *'Impeached or questioned'*: Parliament takes the view that it is contempt even to commence legal proceedings by serving a writ upon an MP in respect of a matter which Parliament considers to be privileged. This is a direct challenge to the courts, since if this view is right then the courts have no power to decide the limits of parliamentary privilege. We shall discuss this later. The rule in *Pepper* v. *Hart* (1993) which in certain circumstances allows the courts to use statements made in Parliament to help them interpret statutes, supports a narrow interpretation of Art. 9. In *Pepper* v. *Hart* the House of Lords took the view that the purpose of Art. 9 was only to prevent MPs from being penalised for what they said in the House (see *Prebble* v. *Television New Zealand* (1993)).

(4) *'Out of Parliament'*: Article 9 prevents interference with the freedom for speech of MPs by any outside body. Legal actions, bribes and threats are the most obvious illustrations (below), but other kinds of pressure also constitute contempt. This could include, for example, publishing MPs' home telephone numbers (*Daily Graphic Case* (1956)), accusing MPs of drunkenness (*Duffy's case* (1964–5)), or even making press allegations of conflict of interest by MPs (*Junor's Case* (1957)). However, Art. 9 has not been used against media criticism of political speeches by MPs. Nor does Art. 9 prevent courts or other bodies from looking into matters which are also before Parliament provided that the parliamentary processes or things said in them are not criticised (see *Hamilton* v. *Al Fayed* (1999)). The Human Rights Act 1998 might also restrain an expansive interpretation of Art. 9. Although an action could not be brought against Parliament itself, the court is required to interpret all legislation including Art. 9, 'if it is possible to do so', in a way that conforms to the rights set out in the Act one of which is freedom of expression (s. 3).

Independently of the Bill of Rights an MP performing his official duties inside or outside the House is protected by qualified privilege (for example, *Beach* v. *Freeson* (1972); complaint to Lord Chancellor about solicitors). This may include media interviews (*Church of Scientology of California* v. *Johnson-Smith* (1972)) but does not apply to party political activities such as election campaigns. Qualified privilege which is an aspect of the general law does not ensure that MPs are entirely free from outside interference. Qualified privilege covers only statements made in good faith and applies only to defamation, whereas full or 'absolute' parliamentary privilege covers every kind of legal action. Also qualified privilege is a defence to an action so that the MP must subject himself to the burden of legal proceedings. Even if he eventually wins, the expense and uncertainty of litigation may discourage an MP from speaking freely. It is apparently a contempt of Parliament even to begin legal proceedings against an MP in respect of a matter protected by full parliamentary privilege.

None of this affects limitations placed upon members' freedom of speech by Parliament itself, for example, by rules of procedure, or by party discipline. Indeed, these restrictions are themselves immune from control by the courts because of the 'exclusive cognisance' privilege (above). The Speaker who presides over the House of Commons has a duty to control procedure impartially. Internal rules exist to prevent MPs misusing their privilege of freedom of speech, for example, by attacking people who cannot answer back, or by commenting upon pending legal proceedings. For example, 'the invidious use of a person's name in a question should be resorted to only if to do so is strictly necessary to render the question intelligible and the protection of parliamentary privilege should be used only as a last resort', and 'in a way that does not damage the good name of the House' (See HC Deb. vol. 94 col. 26, 17 March 1986; Leopold, 1986, PL 368).

10.4.4 Standards of conduct in the Commons

The protection of parliamentary privilege entails the risk that an MP might abuse his or her privilege for personal gain. The traditional role of an MP is to be an independent representative of his or her constituents and to speak in Parliament in furtherance of the general public interest, thus reflecting Rousseau's ideal of the general will. An MP is not bound to follow the views of his or her constituents but is suppose to exercise judgement as to the interests of the public as a whole. Several factors may threaten the independence of an MP.

First and foremost there are party loyalties. Secondly many MPs are sponsored by outside bodies including trade unions and business interests, who may contribute towards their election expenses, research and administration costs and to local constituency expenses. Some

MPs accept employment as paid or unpaid 'consultants' to businesses, and interest groups such as the Police Federation, or hold company directorships. MPs are also frequently offered 'hospitality', or gifts, or invited on expenses-paid 'fact-finding' trips. There are also 'all-party' subject groups of MPs which involve relationships with outside bodies (see HC 408, 1984–5). Except in the case of a private bill a member is free to vote on a matter in which he has a personal interest.

The position is particularly difficult where an MP acts as a paid adviser to an interest group such as a trade union or a drugs company, and is dismissed for not advocating the employer's interests in Parliament. This happened in the *Brown* Case in 1947 – an MP sponsored by a trade union. The Committee of Privileges voted that a contract could not require an MP to support or represent his sponsor's interests in Parliament, nor could the sponsor punish the MP for not doing so. However, it was not contempt to dismiss a consultant if, for whatever reason, the employer or sponsor was unhappy with his services. This somewhat evasive compromise does not seem to take the matter much further. It would be a contempt to threaten to dismiss an MP unless he took a certain line in Parliament, but not, apparently, to dismiss him after the event. Arguably, pressures from local constituency parties would also be contemptuous.

It is often said that sponsorships and consultancies enable MPs to keep in touch with informed opinion outside Westminster and to develop specialised knowledge. They also enable MPs without private means to supplement their parliamentary salaries. The process of enacting legislation is also helped by consultation with interested parties. There is much 'lobbying' of civil servants, and it is desirable that this should be counterbalanced by MPs having their own access to outside interests. There is an increasing tendency for MPs to be career politicians for all their working lives, thus narrowing their perspective. On the other hand, there is a danger that an MP might cease to be independent and become a hired hand, paid to advocate his patron's cause. MPs might also spend time on activities such as sitting in company boardrooms which may generate little understanding of social problems and where the time would be better spent helping their constituents.

Several resolutions and reports of the House have declared that certain kinds of external influence are contempts of Parliament. The basic distinction seems to be between promoting a specific matter which is forbidden and acting as a consultant generally which is acceptable. A Resolution of 1695 stated that paying a member to promote any matter in Parliament is a 'high crime', and one of 1858 makes it improper for an MP to promote any matter for money, even if the money goes to some worthy cause such as a charity. A Resolution of 1969 made a further distinction between 'advocacy for a fee' and 'the advancing of argument based on specialist knowledge' the latter being acceptable, even if the MP is paid by his source of knowledge. In 1974 it was resolved that MPs should disclose any relevant financial interests in debates, committees and communication with ministers and civil servants.

In its latest Code of Conduct and Guidelines the House accepted the Nolan Committee's 'Seven Principles of Public Life' (see p. 82). The House resolved to ban the advocacy or initiation of any matter in Parliament, or urging others to do so for payment or reward of any kind of direct or indirect including payments to a member's family (see HC 637 (1994–5), HC 816 (1994–5), HC 688 (1995–6), HC Deb. Vol. 263, col. 1674, HC Deb. Vol. 265, col. 604, 661, HC Deb. Vol. 282, col. 392, 1995–6).

There are also criminal offences involving members of public bodies. Corruption is a common law offence and there are also statutory offences under the Public Bodies (Corrupt Practices) Act 1889 and the Prevention of Corruption Act 1916, s. 4 (2). These offences seem wide enough to include cases where MPs are offered bribes (but see Royal Commission on Standards of Conduct in Public Life (1976 Cmnd. 6524). However, the MP might be protected by Art. 9 of the Bill of Rights from prosecution. Nevertheless in *R.* v. *Greenaway* (1998) a Conservative MP had accepted a bribe to use his influence to help a person acquire UK citizenship. The court held that parliamentary privilege did not apply because the offence occurred when the bribe was received and therefore the court did not need to investigate what went on in Parliament itself.

MPs are required to enter information about their financial interests in a Register of Members' Interests, a practice which Enoch Powell condemned as unconstitutional, claiming that an unlawful qualification has been added for serving as an MP. The register itself has been held (oddly) not to be protected by parliamentary privilege (*Rost* v. *Edwards* (1990)). The categories of interest required by the register have been strengthened in response to the Nolan Committee and include provision of services such as consultancy, company directorships, employment or offices, professions and trades, names of clients, financial sponsorships, overseas visits as an MP, payments received from abroad, land or property, shareholdings and 'any interest or benefit received which might reasonably be thought by others to influence the member's actions in Parliament'. As a result of the Committee on Standards recommendation, the value of an interest must now be disclosed and in the case of paid employment or sponsorship, the amount of time involved. According to the register only one in five MPs is without an external source of income, endorsing what Sedley (2001a), calls a culture of moonlighting which would be unacceptable in any ordinary job one can think of and affirming the legitimacy of accepting retainers from outside interests.

Following the First Report of the Committee on Standards in Public Life the House of Commons appointed a Parliamentary Commissioner for Standards empowered to investigate complaints of misuse of the Commons register and to report to Parliament (HC Standing Orders (Public Business) (1995) No. 150). The Commissioner can also investigate complaints by MPs and the public concerning the Code of Conduct and give advice to MPs. Its decisions, being subject to parliamentary privilege are not subject to judicial review (*R* v. *Parliamentary Commissioner for Standards* (1998)). The Commissioner cannot investigate the interests of ministers acting as such because the separation of powers requires their activities as ministers to be dealt with separately. The Commissioner has limited independence. It cannot publish its own reports and serves a fixed time renewable by the Commons. In 2001 Elizabeth Filkin did not have her contract renewed. She had attracted a reputation as an assiduous investigator of potential conflicts of interests among MPs.

10.4.5 Standards in the House of Lords

There is a 'custom' that the House of Lords should not be subject to formal rules regulating standards but should rely on the 'personal honour' of members (see Neill, 2000b). The Lords appears to have no disciplinary sanctions and, with the possible exception of treason a member could not be deprived of a peerage or suspended or expelled for misconduct. Indeed the Letters Patent issued by the Crown which create a peerage confer a legal right to sit in the House of Lords, and the Writ of Summons to a Parliament imposes a duty to do so. Furthermore it is customary for membership of the House of Lords not to be regarded as a full-time commitment and many members notably bishops and judges have outside business and professional interests including full-time jobs. The current proposals for reform of the House of Lords have not decided whether the members of the house should be paid. There is a voluntary register of interests but the Lords have resisted a compulsory register.

The Committee on Standards (Neill, 2000b) has recommended that there should be a House of Lords Code of Conduct and a compulsory register of members' interests although both should be laxer than the equivalent House of Commons arrangements. The recommendation was founded on the belief that public confidence should be the overriding concern and that public opinion would not look favourably upon a voluntary register. However, there would be no obligation to disclose the amount of payment and while disclosure of consultancies and lobbying interests should be compulsory, disclosure of other interests should be voluntary the test being interests which 'members consider may affect the public perception of the way in which a member discharges his or her parliamentary duties'.

10.4.6 The courts and parliamentary privilege

As we have seen, the courts are not prepared to intervene in the internal affairs of the House (see p. 175). The Human Rights Act 1998 reinforces this by providing that Parliament is not a 'public authority' (other than the House of Lords in its judicial capacity), thereby excluding parliamentary proceedings from scrutiny (s. 6 (3)). On the other hand, where parliamentary activity involves the rights of persons outside the House, the courts have claimed the power to intervene at least to the extent of deciding whether the privilege asserted by Parliament exists.

For example, in a famous eighteenth-century controversy the courts held that parliamentary officers have no power to deprive citizens of voting rights (*Ashby* v. *White* (1703)) and in *Stockade* v. *Hansard* (1839) it was held that parliamentary privilege did not protect reports published by order of the House from being the subject of libel actions. The subject-matter of these disputes is only of historical interest. Parliament no longer controls elections and *Stockdale* v. *Hansard* was soon reversed by statute (Parliamentary Papers Act 1840). Nevertheless, the general principle about the power of the courts remains valid.

Parliament has never accepted that *Stockdale* v. *Hansard* was correctly decided, and still claims to be the exclusive judge of the extent of its own privileges (see *Paty's Case* (1704)). This separation of powers conflict between courts and Parliament is sometimes called the 'old duality', reflecting the fact that the seventeenth-century revolution did not settle the relationship between courts and Parliament. *Stockdale* v. *Hansard* illustrates that even the service of a writ is regarded by Parliament as contempt, thus preventing the courts from hearing the case at all. In *The Sheriff of Middlesex Case* (1840), which was a sequel to *Stockdale* v. *Hansard*, Parliament imprisoned the two holders of the office of Sheriff for enforcing the court's judgement in *Stockdale* v.

Hansard. Not surprisingly, the Sheriffs applied to the court for release, but the court, including Lord Denman, who had decided *Stockdale* v. *Hansard* itself, held that it was powerless to intervene. Parliament had the undoubted right to commit to prison for contempt and it did not have to give reasons. Unless some improper reason was disclosed on the face of the committal warrant, the court must assume that Parliament was acting lawfully, even though the judges knew otherwise. Therefore, by relying on the *Sheriff of Middlesex Case*, Parliament can arbitrarily imprison anyone it likes. Whether this principle will be taken advantage of in modern times rests with Parliament's, or the courts', political sense. The courts are unwilling to take action that might be considered as trespassing on Parliament's preserves. Parliament too has shown restraint in asserting claims to privilege (for example, the *Strauss* case mentioned above).

The Nichols Committee (1999) suggested the enactment of a code of parliamentary privilege to include modest reforms largely intended to clarify the relationship between Parliament and the courts. In addition to the recommendations already mentioned they include the following:

- 'Place out of Parliament' for the purposes of Art. 9 should be defined to include courts and tribunals empowered to take evidence on oath but not tribunals of inquiry if both Houses so resolve.
- There should be a criminal offence of abuse of public office which should include MPs.
- MPs should be subject to the criminal law relating to corruption.
- Members of the Lords should be compellable before Commons committees.
- Parliament's 'exclusive cognisance' should be confined to 'activities directly and closely related to the business of the House'.
- Contempt by non-members should be dealt with by the ordinary courts.
- Freedom from arrest should be abolished.

Summary

10.1   The House of Lords originated as the king's council of leading landowners of the realm. It subsequently evolved into a lawmaking body in partnership with the Commons. After the 1688 settlement the House of Lords was regarded as holding the constitutional balance of power, but by the twentieth century it had become subordinate to the elected House of Commons. The Lords were given a new lease of life by the introduction of Life Peers in the 1960s, but the Constitutional role of the House remains controversial. By convention and law the Lords must ultimately defer to the Commons. We mentioned the House of Lord's functions as a limited but relatively independent constitutional check and balance.

10.2 We sketched the historical development of the House of Commons, starting with its medieval origins in the practice of the king seeking advice from trusted local representatives, and concluding after the First World War when the Commons became a fully representative chamber. We emphasised the development of the relationship between the House and the Crown, pointing out that the executive and the party system now dominate the Commons.

10.3 There is a network of laws and conventions to ensure that Parliament meets annually and that it can remove the government. However, the government can dissolve Parliament subject to the possibility of the overriding powers of the Crown, which are discussed in Chapter 11 and MPs cannot hold the government to account during the long periods when parliament is not sitting.

10.4 We outlined the functions of Parliament, these being not to initiate legislation but to scrutinise legislation, provide the executive with finance, hold the executive accountable, debate matters of public concern and redress grievances. We pointed out that the executive is usually too powerful and complex for Parliament to be effective. However, at least Parliament is a public forum in which the executive can be forced to justify its actions.

10.5 The functions of the House of Lords include:
   (i) revising and delaying legislation introduced in the Commons (other than financial legislation);
   (ii) dealing with relatively uncontroversial legislation, and with business overflowing from the Commons;
   (iii) providing a forum for debate of matters of general concern;
   (iv) providing a political base for government ministers who do not possess seats in the Commons;
   (v) providing a method of rewarding those deemed meritorious by the government;
   (vi) acting as a constitutional safeguard should a government attempt to extend its own life or dismiss the judiciary;
   (vii) acting as a final appellate court.
   Because of the control over the Commons exercised by the executive, a second chamber is desirable but there is no agreement as to how the hereditary element in the Lords should be replaced. At present the House of Lords is accountable to no one.
   The rules of procedure and of party discipline in the House of Lords are more relaxed than is the case with the Commons.

10.6 We examined Parliament's power to protect itself against interference from without and within through the law of parliamentary privilege and its powers to punish for contempt. Parliament can enforce its own privileges free from interference by the ordinary courts.

10.7 We discussed the parliamentary privileges, based on the separation of powers of exclusive control over its own procedures and freedom of speech drawing attention to its possible limits in terms of what counts as parliamentary proceedings and to the separate matter of qualified privilege in the law of defamation.

10.8 We discussed the safeguards against conflicts of interest by MPs including the Register of Interests and the Parliamentary Commissioner for Standards.

We referred to the difficulty of distinguishing between lobbying on behalf of an interest and using specialist knowledge to present a case in the public interest.

10.9   We discussed the relationship between the courts and parliamentary privilege drawing attention to the unresolved conflict as to who decides whether a claimed privilege exists. This conflict may depend on the extent of Parliament's power to commit for contempt.

Further Reading

Dickson, B. and Carmichael, P. (eds) (1999) *The House of Lords: Its Parliamentary and Judicial Roles*.

Lock, Joint Committee on Parliamentary Privilege HC 2/4–I (1999) *Parliamentary Privilege and the Courts* [1985] PL 64.

Munro, *Studies in Constitutional Law* Ch. 7.

Norton, *Does Parliament Matter?*

Oliver, D. and Drewry, G. (eds) *The Law and Parliament*.

Shell, D. *The House of Lords* (3rd edn).

Weston, C. C. (1965) *English Constitutional Theory and the House of Lords*.

Archer, P. (2000) 'The House of Lords, past, present and future', 70 *Political Quarterly* 396.

Riddall, P. (2000) 'The second chamber: in search of a complementary role', 70 *Political Quarterly* 404.

Exercises

10.1   'The House of Commons is essentially a method of choosing a government. It has no other effective constitutional role.' Discuss.

10.2   'Parliament is not really a lawmaker but is nevertheless separate from the executive.' Discuss.

10.3   What is the constitutional justification for the House of Lords?

10.4   'It is not unduly idealistic to regard the integrity of Members' judgement, however constrained it may be by the party system, and the devotion of their time to the job to which they have been elected, as fundamental values worth not only protecting but insisted on' (Sedley). Discuss in relation to the outside interests of MPs and peers.

10.5   To what extent can the courts rule on matters related to parliamentary privilege?

10.6   In what circumstances is an MP immune from legal action in respect of things he says or writes?

10.7   Outline the arguments for and against (i) abolishing the convention that ministers must be members of Parliament; (ii) introducing fixed-term parliaments. To what extent are these two proposals interrelated?

10.8   How are MPs' conflicts of interest policed and how satisfactory are the current arrangements?

10.9 Rat, a member of Parliament, is employed on a salary by the Institute of Top Executives, a right-wing pressure group, to represent the Institute in Parliament. During a debate, Rat makes a speech calling for higher taxation of executives' salaries, and accusing various members of the Institute of tax evasion. He later circulates copies of this speech to members of his local constituency party.

Dog, the Chairman of the Institute, who is one of those accused of tax evasion, seeks your advice as to whether the Institute can dismiss Rat as its parliamentary representative, and as to whether he should bring a libel action against Rat. Advise Dog.

10.10 George is a member of Parliament. A constituent sends George a letter accusing the management of a local nuclear power station of negligence in relation to safety standards. George, who is employed as a consultant by a company involved in the nuclear power industry, passes on the letter to the minister responsible. The manager of the power station hears about the letter and issues writs for libel against (i) the constituent, and (ii) George.

The manager also alleges that George has taken bribes to ask questions in the House slanted towards the interests of a rival power company.

Discuss the relevance of these events to parliamentary privilege.

10.11 Bulldog, MP, asks Fox, the Minister of Health, in the House of Commons, a question in which he strongly criticises the manner in which the National Health Board deals with the problem of 'lengthy waiting lists for hospital treatment and allocation of hospital beds'.

Bulldog, in a later letter to Fox, makes further and more serious allegations concerning the conduct of the National Health Board (NHB).

The solicitor to the NHB advises the Board that Bulldog's letter is defamatory. Acting on this advice, the NHB issues a writ for libel against Bulldog while Parliament is in session.

Contending that this is a matter of parliamentary privilege over which the court has no jurisdiction, Bulldog refuses to enter an appearance or to defend the action.

Meanwhile the House of Commons resolves that any judge, counsel or party who takes part in such proceeding will be guilty of contempt.

Discuss the position of Bulldog and any possible action that may be taken against (i) the members of the National Health Board, and (ii) any solicitor or counsel who proceeds with the libel action against Bulldog.

11 The Composition of Parliament and Parliamentary Elections

11.1 The House of Lords

Almost anyone can be a member of the House of Lords. Aliens (Act of Settlement 1701 s. 3), persons under 21 (SO no. 2), undischarged bankrupts (Insolvency Act 1986 s. 427 (1)) and persons convicted of treason until their sentence is served (Forfeiture Act 1870 s. 2) cannot sit in the House of Lords. Members can apparently be removed only by statute.

There is no legal limit on the size of the House of Lords. Before the House of Lords Act 1999 there were about 1,349 members making the House of Lords the largest legislative chamber in the world. The 1999 Act reduced this to 695 by ejecting 654 of the 746 hereditary peers. The numbers will remain similar if the current proposals for reform (below) take effect. This makes the House of Lords one of the largest second chambers in the world, eclipsed, according to Kellner (*Evening Standard*, 8 Nov. 2001), only by Kazakhastan and Burkino Faso. By contrast Germany's Bundesrat has 69 members and the US Senate 100. In Europe, Italy, with 326 comes nearest to the UK. Small upper chambers could be justified on the basis that, having more limited powers than the lower house, they can be more cohesive and more focused (Russell, 2000). A large body is, however, a useful source of patronage for those desperate for personal recognition.

The dominant feature of the House of Lords is that none of its members are elected all being chosen by the executive in one form or another. Protocol 3 of the ECHR requires states to hold free elections to the legislature. In *Mathieu-Mohin* v. *Belgium* (1987), the ECHR held that this requires at least one chamber to be elected. However, one of the judges went further and stated that the elected element must comprise a majority of the legislature and the non-elected element must not have greater powers than the elected element. The present House of Lords seems to violate the majority requirement there being currently 659 members of the House of Commons. The reformed House may at least comply since it is proposed that 20% will be elected.

The membership of the House of Lords comprises the following.

236

11.1.1 The Lords Spiritual: church and state

The Lords Spiritual comprise the archbishops of Canterbury and York, the bishops of London, Durham and Winchester, and 21 other diocesan bishops of the Church of England, these being the senior in order of appointment. Bishops are appointed by the Queen on the advice of the prime minister, the practice being that he chooses one from a list of nominations provided by the church authorities. The bishops vacate their seats in the Lords on ceasing to hold office. They are not peers and can vote in parliamentary elections. Dignitaries from other faiths can be appointed to the House of Lords as ordinary peers.

The presence of Church of England bishops in the House of Lords is a manifestation of the principle that the Church of England is the 'established church' and an integral part of the state machinery. The Queen is the head of the Church. Given that the Church of England may be a less significant social and moral force in the UK than other religions such as Islam and Roman Catholicism, this privileged position seems difficult to justify. It is sometimes defended on the basis that the Church of England provides spiritual facilities open to everyone.

11.1.2 Hereditary peers

Until the House of Lords Act 1999, the hereditary peers formed a majority of the House of Lords, thereby biasing it in favour of conservative interests and being difficult to justify on the basis of democratic principles. Hereditary peers are persons on whom, or on whose ancestors, the monarch latterly on the advice of the prime minister has conferred various ranks, namely dukes, duchesses, marquises, earls, viscounts and barons, specifying that the peerages can be inherited by the peer's descendants. No reason need be given for the conferring of a peerage and it is unlikely that the conferring of honours or titles by the Crown is subject to judicial review. Allegations are made from time to time that peerages are used to bribe supporters or to get rid of dead wood in the House of Commons or even sold to wealthy businessmen.

Peers of the UK derive their titles from grants made after the Acts of Union with Scotland and Ireland. Peers of England were created before the union with Scotland in 1706 and peers of Great Britain were created between 1707 and the union with Ireland in 1801. Scottish peerages are those created before 1707 (Peerage Act 1963 s. 4). Irish peers as such cannot sit in the Lords but can be elected to the

Commons (*Earl of Antrim's Petition* (1967)). A peeress in her own right can sit in the House of Lords but only since the Peerage Act 1963.

At common law a peer cannot surrender his or her peerage (*Re Parliamentary Election for Bristol South East* (1964)). However, under the Peerage Act 1963 an hereditary peerage can be disclaimed for life. The peerage must be disclaimed within 12 months of succeeding to it (one month if the new peer is a member of Parliament) or within 12 months of coming of age. The succession to the peerage is not affected. A peer who disclaims his or her title cannot again become a hereditary peer but could be appointed a life peer.

The government is currently proposing to reform the composition of the House of Lords although the details and timing of this are far from clear (below). As an initial measure the House of Lords Act 1999 provides that no one shall be a member of the House of Lords by virtue of a hereditary peerage. This is subject to an exception, negotiated to prevent the peers from rejecting the Act. Under the exception the House elects 90 peers together with the Earl Marshall and the Lord Chamberlain who are royal officials. The elected peers comprise 75 peers elected on the basis of party balance (currently 42 conservatives, 28 cross-benchers without party membership, 3 Liberal Democrats and 2 Labour), together with 15 elected as deputy speakers and committee chairs. The elected peers sit for life. Peers who are not members of the House of Lords can stand for and vote in elections to the House of Commons. Apart from this rump of hereditary peers most of the other members of the House of Lords are effectively appointed by the executive.

11.1.3   Life peers

Life peers are appointed by the Crown on the advice of the prime minister, with the rank of baron. Originally life peers could not sit in the House of Lords, but under the Life Peerages Act 1958, enacted in order to regenerate the House of Lords, they can now do so. Life peerages are intended to enable hand-picked people to play a part in public life without having to be elected and also as a way of countering the apparent conservative bias represented by the hereditary peers. In practice a radical element has not emerged. Life peerages are often bestowed on retired public officials who have served loyally or on retired members of the House of Commons, particularly those who have held high government office. They are used more as a reward for past services, or as a device for ridding the Commons of unwanted

members than as means of infusing the House with new blood. Occasionally a life peerage is created for a person such as a businessman
who has performed party political services or whom the prime minister
wishes to appoint as a minister. This may cause political problems
arising out of a lack of perceived legitimacy. There are currently about
470 life peers in the House of Lords. A life peerage can be terminated
only by statute.

It is uncertain whether in an extreme case, where for example a
prime minister attempts to flood the Lords with his or her cronies,
the monarch could reject the prime minister's advice. Where a prime
minister seeks to act undemocratically it is arguable that the monarch
has a duty to act as the ultimate constitutional check. On two important occasions the monarch reluctantly agreed to appoint sufficient
peers to secure a government majority. These were the Reform Act
1832 which extended the parliamentary franchise, and the Parliament
Act 1911 which reduced the powers of the House of Lords. In both
cases the House of Lords was threatening to obstruct the Commons.
In the case of the 1911 Act, George V agreed to appoint the peers only
if the government's policy was submitted to a general election.

Pending reform of the House of Lords the prime minister's
conventional power to appoint life peers is subject to a non-statutory
House of Lords Appointments Commission. Appointed by the House
(see Hansard (HL) 4 May 2000 Col. 181w), the commission vets all
proposals for appointment as a life peer and also administers a new
process for non-party political appointments (the so-called 'people's
peers'). However, its decisions are no more than advisory. The commission comprises a cross-bench peer as Chair, together with three
peers nominated by the main parties and three 'independent' persons.
Its terms of reference embody the Nolan principles of impartiality,
integrity and objectivity. Any British or Irish citizen over 21 can apply
for appointment to the House of Lords. The criteria for appointment
are a record of 'significant achievement', 'independence of political
parties' and 'an ability to contribute to the work of the House' (see
http//www.houseoflordsappointmentscommission.gov.uk).

The last of these criteria invites preference to be given in the manner
of a private club to those with whom the existing members feel personally comfortable. Most of the life peers appointed under the new
regime have been persons of orthodox opinions prominent in public
life and likely to be personally known to members of the appointing
committee. As a result of the 1999 Act and the appointment of life
peers it seems that the political balance of the House of Lords is now
held by liberal democrats and cross-benchers (Neill, 2000b).

11.1.4   Lords of Appeal in Ordinary

These currently comprise 12 judges specifically appointed for the purpose from which are drawn the highest appellate tribunal as the Appellate Committee of the House of Lords. The same judges also sit as members of the Judicial Committee of the Privy Council which is strictly part of the executive. They are life peers and can sit and vote in the House after they give up their judicial office from which they must retire at 70 (Judicial Pensions and Retirement Act 1993). By convention the law lords do not participate in party political debate while holding judicial office but often speak on questions of law reform. Other peers who hold or who have held high judicial office, notably the Lord Chancellor in defiance of the separation of powers, can also be members of the Appellate Committee. This dual role is a violation of the separation of powers and may also threaten the right to a fair trial under the European Convention of Human Rights. However the Wakeham Committee on reform of the House of Lords was content with the status quo although it failed to provide reasons for this preference. Given the increasing importance of constitutional powers both under the Human Rights Act and arising out of devolution there is much to be said for the creation of a genuine supreme court such as exists in most civilised countries (see www.ucl.ac.uk/constitution-unit/reports).

11.1.5   Attendance in the House of Lords

Many members of the House of Lords, particularly the hereditary and business elements, have little interest in politics and do not regularly sit. This may introduce unpredictability. Members can claim daily expenses for attendance and there is no guarantee that a flood of members may not descend on the House on a particular occasion in search of personal advantage. The influence of erratic attenders can be decisive, as was the case in 1987 when the House was flooded with Conservative peers to support the abolition of local taxes on landed property in favour of a 'poll tax' on individual residents (subsequently abolished). Standing Order 20 enables a peer to apply for leave of absence. The Order requires a peer to state an affirmative intention to attend. Peers granted leave of absence are not expected to attend for the remainder of that Parliament, although one month's notice can be given of termination of leave of absence. There are, however, no sanctions against peers who disregard the attendance rule.

11.2   House of Lords Reform

Attempts to reform the Lords have foundered, partly because of disagreement as to what the role of the House should be as well as its composition, and partly because the matter has not had high political priority. The problem is intractable. The most obvious solution is an elected House. In a federal system this might work well in that one House can represent the units within the federation while the other represents the population as a whole. In a unitary system such as that of the UK, a wholly elected house might either duplicate or rival the House of Commons thereby weakening the accountability or dominance of the government. On the other hand an appointed Chamber would lack public credibility and reinforce the patronage that currently undermines the constitution. Furthermore there is no consensus as to who should make appointments to the House and on what basis. The hereditary element is said to have the advantage of independence but at the price of legitimacy. An attractively democratic possibility would be random selection from the whole adult community, as is currently the case with jury service. However, this raises many practical and economic problems and is probably unrealistic.

The Parliament Act 1911 began the process of reform by removing the power of the House of Lords to veto public bills introduced in the Commons other than a bill to prolong the life of a Parliament. The Bryce Conference of 1917–18 (Cd. 9038) attempted to tackle the problem of the composition of the House of Lords but was unable to agree. In 1958 the introduction of life peers reinvigorated the House to a certain extent particularly in relation to the work of its committees, enabling the House, according to Wakeham (2000), to become an 'efficient' rather than a 'dignified' part of the constitution. In 1968 an all-party conference proposed removed voting rights from most of the hereditary element and introduced the concept of 'working peers', mainly life peers, who would form a permanent nucleus of the House. The bill to introduce these reforms was abandoned because of backbench opposition from both sides of the House.

The present Labour government is reforming the House of Lords in two stages. Stage 1 comprised the House of Lords Act 1999 (above). Stage 2 remains unrealised. The report of the Royal Commission on the future of the House of Lords (Wakeham, 2000) has been broadly accepted by the government (Hansard (HL) 7 March 2000, Col. 919), but attracted widespread criticism for its conservatism and lack of rigour. The members of the Commission did not include radical opinion and looked at the House of Lords in isolation from wider questions of constitutional reform. The Commission did not therefore question the role and powers of the House of Commons nor those of the executive. Wakeham endorsed the existing roles of the House of Lords, as subordinate to the Commons, as providing limited checks on the executive, a revising mechanism for legislation and a 'constitutional long-stop' to persuade the government to have second thoughts. Wakeham's governing principles seems to be 'the capacity to offer council from a range of sources, . . . broadly representative of society in the UK at the beginning of the 21st century. . . . It should give the UK's constituent nations and regions, for the first time a formally constituted voice in the Westminster parliament.' (Wakeham, 2000, p. 31): The electorate is not to be trusted to produce these outcomes but must be paternalistically protected against itself.

Wakeham rejected the extremes of an all-elected second chamber and one comprising 'experts', the former because of the risk of unbalancing the relationship with the Commons, the latter because Wakeham recognised that government is about accommodating disagreement and is necessarily political rather than a 'council of the wise'. Perhaps updating the classical 'mixed constitution' Wakeham therefore proposed a House comprising representatives from the main interests in the community. Wakeham though that a wholly elected second chamber might produce the wrong sort of people, reinforce party political control, result in 'voter fatigue' and either conflict with or rubber-stamp the Commons. Wakeham rejected random selection because of the risk of attracting undesirables.

The government White Paper (7 Nov. 2001, Cm. 5291) broadly adopted Wakeham's proposals but weakened them in favour of a larger element of government control over the House of Lords. The government's proposals are as follows:

1. The second chamber should comprise about 600 members with 120 of them being elected in regional constituencies based on those for the European Parliament under the closed party list system (below). The link with the peerage should be entirely removed. Wakeham had recommended that elections should be on a 12–15-year cycle with one-third elected each time thus ensuring continuity and strengthening independence. This recommendation was not followed.

2. An appointments commission appointed by the House itself and comprising a mix of politicians and others should appoint another 120 members on the basis of applications from the public. Wakeham had proposed that the Commission appoint all other members. The aims of making appointments should be: i) representation of

all parts of British society with a minimum of 30% of each gender and representation of ethnic groups in proportion to the presence in the general population; ii) a breadth of experience and range of skills; iii) a strong independent element.

3. The Law Lords should remain as now.
4. The Church of England bishops should remain but their numbers reduced to 20. Wakeham had proposed representatives from other religions.
5. The remainder of the House should be nominated by political parties in accordance with their share of the vote at the last election as determined by the Commission. While no one party will have an overall majority the government will have the largest single voice particularly as the element chosen by the Commission itself may well include a preponderance of individuals whose careers have been advanced by sycophancy to those in power.
6. Existing life peers should remain thereby unbalancing these arrangements for many years.
7. The government has not decided the important question of whether members should be full-time salaried or part-time unpaid. Under the system of patronage proposed, both are likely to attract undesirables. Nor is it clear how long the appointed members would serve. If this is a short period the dominance of the government of the day is strengthened. On the other hand, in the case of party placemen, a long period would be unrepresentive.

The proposals are therefore a pragmatic accommodation, informed by a desire to maintain the traditional constitution and preserve the supremacy of the government. The democratic argument for this is the need for clear accountability. On the other hand the proposals risk producing a two-tier House with the minority of elected members having a superior status and the appointees being treated with contempt. There is also a problem in ensuring that the political appointees reflect the changing balance of party support after each general election. The government's proposals allow considerable patronage and for that reason have been almost universally condemned. There is a strong body of opinion in favour of a largely elected chamber.

11.3 Membership of the House of Commons

Anyone can be a member of the House of Commons other than the following:

- aliens other than citizens of Ireland;
- people under 21 (Family Law Reform Act 1969 Schedule 2 para. 2);
- mental patients (Mental Health Act 1983) – there are provisions for removing MPs under the Mental Health Act 1983;
- members of the House of Lords;
- clergy ordained by bishops in the Churches of England and Ireland, ministers of the Church of Scotland and Roman Catholic priests (see *Re MacManaway* (1951));
- debtors made bankrupt, until five years after discharge unless the discharge certifies that the bankruptcy was not caused by the debtor's misconduct;
- persons convicted of election offences (below);
- persons convicted of treason, until expiry of the sentence or pardon (Forfeiture Act 1870);
- persons convicted of an offence and sentenced to prison for more than one year while actually in prison or unlawfully at large (Representation of the People Act 1981) – this was designed to prevent convicted terrorists in Northern Ireland from standing;
- persons holding certain public offices (House of Commons (Disqualification) Act 1975).

The last of these disqualifications is an example of the separation of powers. One element of the seventeenth-century conflict between Crown and Parliament was the fear of the Commons that the Crown might bribe members by giving them jobs. The Act of Settlement 1700 therefore provided that nobody who held Crown office or place of profit could sit in the Commons. This would of course have prevented ministers from sitting, and the UK Constitution would have had a strict separation of powers. This part of the Act was repealed by the Succession to the Crown Act 1707. However, there are limits upon the number of ministers who can be members of the Commons, thus giving the Commons a degree of independence. These are as follows:

(i) Under the House of Commons (Disqualification) Act 1975 not more than 95 ministers may sit and vote.

(ii) The Ministerial and Other Salaries Act 1975 (as amended) fixed the salaries of the various grades of minister, and limits the number of paid ministers of the government to 83 plus about 30 other specialised political office-holders such as whips; and also four Law Officers. However, a government can increase its loyalists in the House by appointing unpaid parliamentary secretaries.

(iii) The House of Commons Disqualification Act 1975 debars certain other holders of public office from sitting in the Commons. The main examples are as follows:

- full-time judges of various kinds;
- regulators of privatised utilities;
- civil servants;
- members of the regular armed services and police (other than specialised forces such as railway police);
- members of foreign legislatures. However, by virtue of the Disqualification Act 2000, a member of the Irish legislature (the Oireachtas) can be a member of the Commons;
- members of certain public boards and undertakings;
- holders of the offices of Steward or Bailiff of the Chiltern Hundreds or of the Manor of Northstead. These are meaningless titles in the gift of the Chancellor of the Exchequer. There are no specific rules entitling MPs to resign or retire but a successful application for one of these offices has the same effect.

In the event of a dispute about a disqualification the Judicial Committee of the Privy Council may make a declaration on the application of any person (s. 7). The House may also refer a matter to the Privy Council for an opinion (Judicial Committee Act 1833 s. 4). The House has the statutory power to disregard a disqualification if it has been subsequently removed (for example, by the MP resigning from a disqualifying post (s. 6 (2))).

11.4 The Electoral System

11.4.1 The purpose of elections

There is a divergence between the theory of the electoral process and practical politics. The theoretical basis of democracy in the United Kingdom is that the electorate chooses the legislature as an assembly of representatives for each local community. The legislature in turn chooses the executive. In reality the party political system encourages voters to vote essentially for an executive. Coupled with the prime minister's conventional right to dissolve Parliament, this means that effectively the executive controls and legitimates the legislature. Dicey, however, believed that a 'parliamentary executive must by the law of its nature follow, or tend to follow, the lead of Parliament' (1915, p. 484). We can assess the electoral system only in relation to its aims.

Is it (a) to secure democratic local representation; or (b) to produce effective government; or (c) to produce 'accountable' governments? No electoral system has yet been thought up that successfully combines all of these aims.

The European Convention on Human Rights (First Protocol Art. 3) requires 'free elections, at reasonable intervals by secret ballot, under conditions which will ensure the free expression of the people in the choice of the legislature' but does not confer any specific right to vote. This does not require any particular kind of voting system or method of electoral boundaries, thus endorsing the principle that elections may have different aims. An electoral system must not discriminate against particular groups of citizens although a particular political party cannot apparently challenge the electoral system on the basis that it is at a disadvantage (see *Lindsey* v. *UK* (1979); *Mathieu-Mohin* v. *Belgium* (1987); *Liberal Party* v. *UK* (1980)). The courts are likely to adopt a low level of review in relation to electoral machinery because of sensitivity to the separation of powers.

Election law is found primarily in the Representation of the People Act 1983 and the Parliamentary Constituencies Act 1986. Important changes were made by the Representation of the People Act 2000 and the Political Parties, Elections and Referendums Act 2000. This chapter will assume that the relevant provisions of the Act are in force.

11.4.2   The Electoral Commission

The Electoral Commission was a response to the concerns of the Fifth Report of the Committee on Standards in Public Life (Cmnd. 4057, 1998) relating to the financing of political parties. It was created by the Political Parties, Elections and Referendums Act 2000 with a wide-ranging remit to supervise the conduct of elections and the financial affairs of political parties thereby bringing what had previously been regarded as private concerns into the open. The Commission registers political parties and keeps records of their accounts and of donations to them. It reports and advises upon the conduct of elections and referendums and provides for public access to information relating to the financial affairs of political parties. It is empowered to facilitate public education relating to current electoral systems in the UK and the European Union. The Electoral Commission will also take over the functions of the Boundary Commissions (below) in relation to parliamentary and local government constituencies. Finally the Electoral Commission is empowered to arrange schemes for alternative methods of voting such as for example making voting facilities available in shops or exrtending voting times. This applies at present only to local government elections where some pilot schemes have already been tried out (see www.norwich.gov.uk).

The Electoral Commission is appointed by the Queen on an Address from the House of Commons which must have the support of the Speaker after consultation with the party leaders (s. 3). Its members must not be members, officers or employees of political parties or holders of elective office. Nor must they have had such connections or been registered party donors (below) within the last 10 years (s. 3 (4)). The Electoral Commission is supplemented by an advisory Speaker's Committee which comprises relevant ministers and back-bench MPs (s. 2) and an advisory Parliamentary Parties Panel comprising persons appointed by the parties who must include at least two MPs (s. 4).

11.4.3   General elections and by-elections

A general election must be held after a new Parliament has been summoned by royal proclamation. Writs are sent from the Crown to designated returning officers in each constituency. The returning officers are responsible for the election, but registration officers, who are normally local authority chief executives, make the detailed arrangements. There are detailed rules for designating returning officers, but where a constituency is a whole county or a whole district the returning officer is the sheriff of the county or the chairman of the district council (s. 24 (1)). In England this is one of the few remaining duties of the sheriff, who prior to Tudor times was the representative of the Crown in local areas. A by-election takes place when there is an individual vacancy in the House. The House itself decides whether to fill the vacancy, and by convention the motion is proposed by the party to which the former member belonged. Unfortunately there is no time limit for this. When the House is not sitting the Speaker can issue the writ (Recess Elections Act 1975).

11.4.4   Candidates

Subject to the disqualifications above anyone can stand for Parliament who can provide a deposit of £500 (to be forfeit if one-twentieth of the total vote is not won), and is supported by 10 signatures (Representation of the People Act 1983 Sched. 1). However, no one can be nominated unless their nomination paper states either that they stand in the name of a qualifying registered party under Part II of the Political Parties, Elections and Referendums Act 2000 or that they do not purport to represent any party (s. 22). The latter applies to candidates standing either as independents, or the Speaker seeking re-election or if the nomination paper provides no description. For the purposes of the Act a political party is any organisation or person that puts up candidates for electoral office (s. 40). There can therefore be a one-person party.

Each political party must be registered with the Electoral Commission. In order to qualify for registration the party must provide its name, its headquarters address and the names of its leader, treasurer and nominating officer although these can be the same person. It can also provide the name of its campaign officer and if it does so the campaign officer will have some of the responsibilities of the treasurer (s. 25). It must also have a scheme approved by the Commission for regulating its financial affairs. The Commission can refuse to register a party on the following grounds: duplication of or confusion with existing names, names having more than six words, names being obscene or offensive or where publication would be an offence, names in a script other than roman, or containing words prohibited by the Secretary of State (s. 28). This seems to create a significant possibility of executive censorship. Similar rules apply to party emblems (s. 29).

A registered political party is also subject to accounting and audit requirements (Political Parties, Elections and Referendums Act 2000 Part III). Its accounts must be lodged with the Electoral Commission and must be available for public inspection (s. 46). For the first time the law has acknowledged that political parties are more than private clubs and that they should be subject to external financial controls. On the other hand, this creates a risk of state interference with political freedom. Hence, despite a substantial body of opinion in favour, there is no public funding of political parties election campaigns. However, grants of up to two million pounds are available from the Electoral Commission to parties represented in Parliament by at least two members to develop policies (Political Parties, Elections and Referendums Act 2000 s. 12). There are also parliamentary grants to opposition parties for their parliamentary work ('Short Money' named after the MP who proposed it).

11.4.5   Qualifications to vote

To be eligible to vote, a person must: i) be 18 years of age on the date of the poll: ii) be either a British citizen or a 'qualifying' Commonwealth citizen: iii) not be subject to any legal incapacity (below); iv) be registered on the electoral register for the constituency

(Representation of the People Act 2000 s. 1). A qualifying Commonwealth citizen is one who either does not require leave under immigration law to enter the UK or who has leave.

To qualify for registration a person must be:

- 18 years of age or due to be 18 within 12 months beginning on the first of December following the date of the application for registration.
- Resident in a dwelling in the constituency on the date of the application for registration.

'Residence' means the person is normally living at the address in question as his or her home. This is a question of fact and seems to focus on whether the dwelling is the applicant's home for the time being as opposed to being a guest or a lodger for some particular purpose (see *Hipperson* v. *Newbury Electoral Officer* (1985) – temporary residents). According to s. 3(2) of the Representation of the People Act 2000 'regard shall be had in particular to the purpose and other circumstances, as well as to the fact of his presence at or absence from the address on that date ... for example, where at any particular time a person is staying at any place other than on a permanent basis he may in all the circumstances be taken to be at that time (a) resident there if he has no home elsewhere, or (b) not resident there if he does have a home elsewhere.'

Temporary absence in performance of a duty arising out of work or attendance on a course at an educational institution does not interrupt residence if the applicant either intends to return to actual residence within six months and will not be prevented from doing so by performance of that duty or where the dwelling would otherwise be his permanent residence and he would be in actual residence (s. 3(3)). Temporary periods of unemployment can be ignored for this purpose (s. 3(4)). Detained offenders are not resident where they are detained but remand prisoners, and mental patients unless detained as offenders, can be resident where they are detained (ss. 4, 5).

There are special registration provisions for the benefit of certain people who have to be absent from their normal residence for long periods. These include overseas electors who have been resident in the UK during the last 20 years (Representation of the People Act 1985), mental patients both voluntary and compulsory, unconvicted prisoners, merchant seamen, members of the armed forces (service voters) and certain other public employees. Moreover under the Political Parties, Elections and Referendums Act 2000 s. 6, mental patients other than offenders, unconvicted prisoners and the homeless, as an alternative to establishing residence on normal principles, can make a 'declaration of local connection' in relation to any constituency. In general the law relating to eligibility to vote has become progressively more liberal partly in response to a steady decline in turnout at general elections. For example at the election of 2001 the turnout was less than 60%, the government being elected by only 25% of the electorate thus raising serious questions of legitimacy.

Incapacities
Even if they are on the electoral register, the following have no right to vote:

- Members of the House of Lords other than bishops sitting *ex officio*.
- Convicted prisoners and mental patients detained as offenders including persons unlawfully at large (Representation of the People Act 2000 s. 2).
- Persons convicted of election offences (corrupt practices – five years; illegal practices – five years in the particular constituency).
- Persons lacking the mental capacity to vote.
- Illegal immigrants and asylum seekers waiting for a decision (Political Parties, Elections and Referendums Act 2000 s. 2).

11.4.6 The voting system

There are problems with the workings of voting systems as reflections of democratic values. First a system which always produces a genuine majority government may be impossible to achieve. Kenneth Arrow showed that, unless the vote is between only two alternatives, it is impossible to rank preferences to achieve a pecking order on which a majority will certainly agree. For example, in an election where there are three candidates, different majorities might prefer A to B, B to C and C to A. This has serious consequences for those who believe in the idea of the 'general will' (but see Waldron, 1999, ch. 5).

Secondly both majority and plurality systems are defective in democratic terms in that they ignore all minority votes. Complex systems of proportional representation can alleviate this but have the disadvantages that a minority party may hold the balance of power in forming a government, and in versions where voters vote for a 'closed party list' of candidates, the direct link between the voter and the MP is lost. The choice between voting systems therefore involves a choice between the incommensurables of strong government, giving effect to the general will, and protecting minorities. The electoral systems that have recently been introduced in Scotland, Wales, Northern Ireland, London and for the European Parliament are based on proportional representation.

The 'first past the post' system
The voting system used in elections to the UK Parliament and in local government elections is the 'relative majority' or 'plurality' system. There are single-member constituencies and the candidate with the largest number of votes is elected, irrespective of the total number of votes cast for that candidate. The plurality system has been much criticised and different voting methods are used in the newer election systems in the UK, including elections to the European Parliament, the devolved governments, the Mayor and Assembly of London and possibly other local authority mayors (Local Government Act 2000 s. 42).

- It is not representative. Runners-up get no credit, however many votes they earned. It is sometimes said that small parties are unfairly treated but large parties suffer equally. The main reason why small parties often have less seats than their share of the national vote would indicate (for example in 1983 the Liberals won 25.4% of votes but only 3.5% of seats) is because of geographical and class factors. The two main parties, Conservative and Labour, each attract massive support in particular geographical areas from economic interests which predominate in those areas. There are therefore numerous 'safe seats' for each party where the MP is effectively chosen by party activists. Roughly 120 out of 650 seats are genuine contests at a general election. Support for the smaller parties is scattered throughout the country so that, except in a few 'marginal' constituencies, their votes are not sufficiently concentrated to win seats.
- Except in a straight two-party fight, the winner is unlikely to command a majority. For example, the Labour government elected in 1974 had only 37% of the popular vote, and the present government with a majority of over 170 has only 44% of the popular vote, which is much the same as it had in the previous election which it lost. In Parliament itself the members always vote by simple majority in a straight, yes/no way between two propositions. The combination of these two forms of voting means that any particular law may command the support of only about 20% of the public. In 1951 Labour won more votes than the Conservatives, but lost the election. In 1974 the opposite happened. In 1976 the Blake Commission on Electoral Reform (Hansard Society) castigated the voting system

as producing flagrant 'minority rule' and at the same time suppressing other minorities.

- The plurality voting system is said to encourage mindless party solidarity and to encourage swings between the two main parties, with each seeking to reverse the policies of the other, thus producing instability. However, one of the main objectives to proportional representation (PR) is the risk of instability in that PR might produce constantly shifting coalitions of minorities.
- The plurality voting system accentuates divisions between different parts of the country, notably the north and the south.

The present system can be defended on the following grounds:

- It produces governments which enjoy reasonably substantial support. A more representative system might lead to coalitions of small parties, none of which enjoys much support.
- It is transparent and encourages accountable governments bound together by collective responsibility. A party stands or falls as such at an election and it must answer on its own record. It cannot blame any minority parties, and governments cannot change, without the consent of the electorate.
- It offers voters a clear choice. They know what they are voting for. It usually produces strong, stable government. This argument is not altogether convincing and the experience of other European countries with different voting systems is a mixed one. The existence of many or few parties seems to be due more to social factors than to the electoral system as such. For example, the Netherlands has enjoyed greater governmental stability than has Britain while France has enjoyed less. It may be that the electoral system is a symptom, not a cause.
- It is simple. This is particularly important in England where the electorate, in comparison with those of most other European countries, is poorly educated.

Other voting systems
Proportional representation (PR) is used in most European countries and for elections to the EU Parliament. Within the UK, PR is used for elections to the devolved bodies in Scotland, Wales and Northern Ireland. There are several variations of PR. They have in common the use of mathematical and procedural techniques to make the outcome correspond more closely to the distribution of the vote. Some have safeguards to prevent extremist minority parties from holding the

balance of power. All have advantages and disadvantages. The main forms of PR are as follows:

- *The party list.* This has several variations. The method applied in Scotland and Wales (see Scotland Act 1998 ss. 1–8, Government of Wales Act 1998 ss. 1–8) is the additional member system in which a proportion of candidates are first elected on the first-past-the-post principle in constituencies which are the same as those for elections to the UK Parliament. This is then topped up by a second vote for other candidates to represent eight regions in Scotland and five regions in Wales. In Scotland each region has seven seats, in Wales four. There are a total of 129 seats in the Scottish Parliament and 60 in the Welsh Assembly. The second vote can be either for an individual candidate or for a registered political party. Each party lists its candidates in order of preference. Each region is allocated an 'electoral region figure'. In the case of individual regional candidates this is simply the total number of votes cast for that person. In the case of a party the electoral region figure is the number of votes won by that party divided by one plus the number of seats won by the party in the constituency elections. The candidate or party with the highest electoral region figure wins the first seat. The second and subsequent seats are awarded on the same basis in each case after a recalculation to take account of seats already won. Thus the fewer the seats won by a party in the constituency elections the better the chances of winning a seat in the top-up election.

  Elections to the EU Parliament in Britain are on the basis of a closed party list (European Parliament Act 1999). There are 87 seats divided into electoral regions (nine for England, one each for Scotland, Wales and Northern Ireland with 71, eight, five and three, members, respectively). Each party lists its candidates in order of preference and votes can be cast either for a party or for an individual standing separately. The party list system is crude and has been said to destroy the principle of local representation in favour of authoritarian party control. In Germany a party must secure at least 5% of the overall vote or win three constituencies to gain 'list' seats. Thus extremist minorities are prevented from holding the balance of power.

- *The single transferable vote.* This is probably the method that is most capable of reflecting voting preferences but loses the single-member constituency. It is used for elections in Northern Ireland where, as we have seen, the desire to neutralise conflicting political forces dominates the constitutional arrangements (see Northern Ireland

Act 1998 ss. 8, 28, 34). Ministers and members of Committees of the Northern Ireland Assembly are elected by the Assembly in a similar way (ibid.). Each constituency can elect a given number of members. Votes are cast for candidates in order of preference. There is an 'electoral quota' for each constituency calculated according to a formula based on the number of voters divided by the number of seats. The quota is the winning post. A candidate who obtains the quota based on first preferences is elected. Any surplus votes over the quota are transferred to other candidates according to the second preference expressed on the winning candidate's voting slips. This may produce more winners who reach the quota. The process is repeated until all the seats are filled. If no candidate reaches the quota the candidate with the lowest number of votes is eliminated and his votes distributed among the other candidates. This system enables voters to choose between different candidates within the same party since all seats within a constituency could be fought by each party. It also prevents wasted votes and protects minorities.

There are also voting systems which do not achieve PR but which attempt to produce a candidate with majority support where there are three or more candidates. The main examples are:

- *The single alternative vote.* This was recommended for Britain as long ago as 1910 by the Royal Commission on Electoral Systems. The candidates are voted for in order of preference and there are several rounds until a winner with a clear overall majority emerges. After each round the candidate with the lowest vote is eliminated and his votes distributed among the others.
- *The supplementary vote.* Voters have two votes, a first preference and a second preference. If when the first preference votes are counted no candidate obtains a majority, all but the leading two (or more if there is a tie) are eliminated. The second preference votes for the surviving candidates are then counted. If there is still a deadlock a winner might then be chosen by lot. This system is used for elections for the Mayor of London and, for part of the Greater London Authority (Greater London Authority Act 1999 s. 4).

In 1998 the Independent Commission on the Voting System chaired by Lord Jenkins, a Liberal Democrat victim of the simple majority system, recommended the introduction of a voting system which combined the alternative vote in single-member constituencies, topped up from a party list according to the proportion of votes gained by each party. It appears, however, that the first-past-the-post system will remain for elections to the UK Parliament for the foreseeable future. It is unlikely to be in the interests of an incumbent government to change the electoral system for the sovereign assembly.

Voting procedure

Voting is normally in person at a designated polling station. However, 'absent voters' are permitted to vote by post or proxy (Representation of the People Act 2000 Sched. 4). Any person otherwise qualified to vote can apply for a postal vote and there appear to be no further requirements. A person who is on the register but no longer resident in the constituency can also have an absent vote (Representation of the People Act 1990 s. 1). A proxy vote applies only in special cases. These include service and overseas voters, disabled people, people with work or education commitments and people who would have to make an air or sea journey.

The ballot is secret in the sense that the vote itself is cast in privacy. However, by comparing the registration number on the voting slip with the register of electors it is possible for officials to discover how a voter cast his vote. Indeed this is necessary to prevent multiple voting. The Act contains provisions intended to prevent ballot papers being examined, except for the purpose of detecting election offences (see Representation of the People Act 2000 Sched. 1).

11.4.7 The constituencies

The outcome of a general election is usually determined by a relatively small number of 'marginal constituencies' in which no one party has a substantial majority. Voting patterns in the UK are significantly influenced by geographical considerations so that the boundaries of the constituencies are crucial, as is the number of constituencies in each region. Moreover the population is not evenly dispersed. Therefore some constituencies will contain more voters than others, so that each vote does not carry equal weight.

There is semi-independent machinery for fixing electoral boundaries (Parliamentary Constituencies Act 1986). This requires the Electoral Commission working through boundary committees to make proposals for altering constituency boundaries (Political Parties, Elections and Referendums Act 2000 s. 14). Previously four Boundary Commissioners for England, Wales Scotland and Northern Ireland carried out this function. A wide range of criteria are used and the Commission has considerable discretion. The House of Commons has a veto, although it can neither initiate nor amend proposals.

There must be a review of the number and boundaries of constituencies at intervals of between 10 and 15 years. A review may take several years to complete and once made could well be out of date. A report is submitted to the Home Secretary who is required 'as soon as may be' to lay the report before both the Houses of Parliament together with a draft Order in Council giving effect to it. (s. 2 (5)). Each House must approve the Order which is then submitted to the Queen in Council. It then becomes law.

The criteria are as follows (Sched. 2):

1. The total number of seats in the UK but excluding Northern Ireland must not be substantially greater or less than 613.
2. Scotland must have at least 71 constituencies, Wales at least 35 and Northern Ireland between 16 and 18, but normally 17. The effect is that Scotland and Wales are represented more generously than in England and Northern Ireland in terms of population.
3. There must be a separate 'City of London' constituency.
4. Each country has an 'electoral quota'. This is a rough average of voters per constituency. It is calculated by dividing the total electorate by the number of constituencies on the date when the Commission begins its review. It cannot be updated during the course of a review. For England the quota is roughly 65,000. The electoral quota is one factor to be taken into account but because of the many factors which have to be balanced few constituencies correspond exactly to the quota although in recent years the extent of variation has become less.
5. Other factors to be taken into account are as follows:
    (i) conformity to local government boundaries;
    (ii) local ties;
    (iii) the inconvenience involved in altering boundaries except to comply with local government boundaries;
    (iv) special geographical considerations including the size, shape and accessibility of a constituency.

These factors may point in different directions and it is a matter for the commission how to rank them. The Commission is not required 'to aim at giving full effect in all circumstances to the rules' (Sched. 2, para. 7). However, the rules relating to the number of constituencies seem to have the highest priority. Inconvenience and local ties can be balanced against any of the rules, but 'special geographical considerations' are related only to the 'local government boundary' and the 'electoral quota' factors.

The report and the Order in Council can be challenged in the courts but the chances of success are small. The time factor is important. As we have seen, no court can interfere with parliamentary procedure, so that the Home Secretary could not be prevented from laying an order before the House (see *Harper* v. *Home Secretary* (1955)). A court could perhaps require a Home Secretary to lay an order, in order to prevent him delaying a report which does not favour the government party.

A court could review the completed Order in Council since approval by Parliament as such cannot save something which is unlawful. However, by virtue of s. 4(7) the validity of any Order in Council which purports to be made under the Act and which recites that approval was given by each House 'shall not be questioned in any legal proceedings'. The effect of 'ouster' clauses of this kind is controversial and is affected by the Human Rights Act 1998 (see Chapter 17). This form of words would, because of the word 'purports', probably prevent the court from setting aside the Order in Council.

An applicant must therefore challenge a report before it is submitted to the Home Secretary. Even here the chances of success are slim because of the Commission's wide discretion. The court will defer to the subjective judgement which the Commission is required to make. Indeed even if the Commission does act improperly, for example by ranking the various factors capriciously, the court would not normally make an order that prevents the report from going to Parliament. At most it would make a declaration (a non-binding opinion, see *R.* v. *Boundary Commission for England ex parte Foot* (1983)).

11.5 The Conduct of Campaigns

This chapter is concerned with parliamentary elections but the same principles apply to the various other elections that are now held in the UK, namely local government elections, elections to the European Parliament, and elections to the Scottish Parliament, Welsh Assembly or Northern Ireland Assembly. The election conflict at constituency level has always been closely regulated by law designed to ensure fairness between the candidates campaigning in their local arenas. The law was open to the charge that it does not allow for national party politics with its massive financial backing from private donors or for modern methods of campaigning including the intensive use of the national and international media. The Political Parties, Elections and Referendums Act 2000 attempts to bring the law up to date by addressing this reality (see *The Funding of Political Parties in the United Kingdom* Cm. 4443, 1999). Reflecting the Nolan principles of public life, the Act attempts in particular to bring greater openness and accountability to the financing of political parties and national campaigns.

11.5.1   Campaign expenses

There are controls over the money spent on campaigning during the election period. The law is designed to ensure that no candidate has an unfair advantage or can buy votes. In the USA, restrictions upon election expenses have been held to violate freedom of speech (*Buckley* v. *Valeo* (1976)). The counter-argument is that equality of resources in elections is a better safeguard of free speech in the long run. The main principles are as follows:

- Every candidate must have an election agent who is accountable for the conduct of the candidate's campaign. A candidate can appoint himself as agent. There are controls over receipts and expenses out of the candidate's own pockets (Representation of the People Act 1983 ss. 73, 74).
- No expenditure over 50p can be incurred 'with a view to' promoting a candidate without the authority of the candidate or his agent (s. 75(1)). Breach of this is a corrupt practice, the more serious of the two kinds of election offence (below). There are exceptions for newspapers and broadcasting. In *Bowman* v. *UK* (1998) the ECHR held that s. 75 violated the right to freedom of expression because it prevented a pressure group from distributing leaflets in support of a candidate. The right to freedom of expression must be balanced against the right to a free election. The court held that a state could lawfully take measures to ensure equality between candidates but in this case the pressure group had no other reasonable means of contributing to the debate. The position of third parties is now to some extent regulated by the 2000 Act (below).
- There is a maximum limit upon the amount that can be spent on behalf of the candidate. At present the limit is £1,000,000 (Political Parties, Elections and Referendums Act 2000 s. 132). Candidates are entitled to use schools and public buildings for meetings (ss. 95, 96). Each candidate can also send one election address to each voter post-free. Reasonable personal expenses can be incurred (s. 18). Some expenditure, for example to canvassers, on posters (except to advertising agents), on hiring vehicles to take people to vote, and on broadcasting from abroad, is banned completely (ss. 101–12).

- Controls apply to expenditure made during the 365 days before the date of the poll (Political Parties, Elections and Referendums Act 2000 Sched. 10 para. 3). For the purpose of broadcasting restrictions the relevant date is the announcement of the dissolution of Parliament, that is, when the election date becomes 'official' (1983 Act s. 93). The same applies to controls over donations made during the campaign under the Political Parties, Elections and Referendums Act 2000 (s. 63 (6), see also Sched. 10).

11.5.2 Party expenditure

The Political Parties, Elections and Referendums Act 2000 extended controls over expenditure by registered political parties at national level. Thus the artificiality of distinguishing between promoting the party and promoting the individual candidate that surfaced in earlier cases may no longer arise (see *Grieve* v. *Douglas-Home* (1965); *R.* v. *Tronah Mines Ltd* (1952); *DPP* v. *Luft* (1977)). First all expenditure must be authorised by the party treasurer, his or her deputy, or other responsible officer delegated by the treasurer (s. 75). Secondly there are overall limits on expenditure based on the number of constituencies contested (s. 79). The treasurer must deliver a return of expenditure to the Electoral Commission (s. 83) which must be made available for public inspection (s. 84).

11.5.3 Donations

There are also controls over substantial expenditure by third parties. The Political Parties, Elections and Referendums Act 2000 has introduced the concept of 'controlled expenditure'. Controlled expenditure is the production or publication of material which can reasonably be regarded as intended to promote any candidate (including prejudicing another candidate) even if the material serves some other purpose as well (s. 85). For example, a leaflet put out by a pressure group in favour of banning hunting might be controlled expenditure if one of the candidates was associated with the issue of hunting.

It is an offence to incur controlled expenditure above certain limits unless it is made by a 'recognised third party' (s. 94). The limits are £10,000 for England and £5,000 for the other regions. A recognised third party can incur expenditure up to £793,500 for England, £108,000 for Scotland, £60,000 for Wales, £27,000 for Northern Ireland (Sched. 10). There are certain exceptions to these limits. They include newspaper editorial matter, broadcasts, personal expenses and the value of services provided free by individuals (s. 87).

A recognised third party must be an individual resident in the UK or on the electoral register, or a registered political party, company, trade union, building society, friendly society, partnership, or unincorporated association, for example a pressure group (s. 88). A recognised third party must register with the Commission (s. 89). All spending on controlled expenditure must be made on the authority of a designated 'responsible person' (who is liable for any breach). The responsible person must make a return of controlled expenditure to the Commission (s. 96). This must be available for public inspection (s. 100). Returns of more than £250,000 in any registration period must be independently audited (s. 97).

Similar controls apply to donations to political parties. These controls are not intended to outlaw donations as such but to bring them into the open and ensure accountability. Suspicions concerning secret donations particularly from overseas sources have tainted both main parties. 'Donation' is widely defined to include gifts, sponsorship, subscriptions, fees, expenses, non-commercial loans and the provision of non-commercial services (s. 50). A registered party cannot accept a donation if it is not made by a 'permissible donor' or if it is anonymous (s. 54 (2)). However, trusts established before 27 July 1999 are exempt (s. 55 (5)).

A permissible donor must be registered to vote in the UK or be a business, trade union or registered political party based in the UK. In the case of a company the shareholders must have approved the donation and the amount must be disclosed in the Directors' Report (s. 140, Sched. 19). There are some exceptions to the duty of disclosure. These include voluntary services provided by an individual, donations of not more than £200, various payments made under statute, payments to MPs by the European Parliament, and the hire of stands at party conferences for a payment deemed reasonable by the Commission.

The party must report relevant donations to the Electoral Commission, in the case of donations of over £5,000, on a quarterly basis and weekly during an election campaign if the party is fielding a candidate (ss. 63, 65, 68, 96). In addition the donor must report multiple small donations which make an aggregate of more than £5,000 in a reporting period (s. 68). The Electoral Commission keeps a register of donations although this must not include the address of a donor who is an individual (s. 69). Impermissible donations must be returned or if the donor cannot be identified, given to the Commission (s. 56). The court can order a donation to be forfeited (s. 58). Similar controls apply to donations to recognised third parties (Sched. 11).

11.5.4 Broadcasting and the press

It is widely believed that modern elections are won or lost on television. There are therefore rules which attempt to ensure that the parties are treated fairly. These work reasonably well in the traditional two-party context. Indeed they are in some respects very stringent.

1. Political advertising is unlawful except for party political broadcasts made by agreement between the British Broadcasting Corporation (BBC), the Independent Broadcasting Authority (IBA), and the main parties. This prevents the worst excesses of wealthy parties. Only registered political parties can make party political broadcasts (Political Parties, Elections and Referendums Act 2000 s. 37). Political broadcasting programmes are excluded from counting as election expenses (s. 75 (1)).
2. There is a general duty imposed by statute on the Independent Broadcasting Authority to preserve balance and impartiality in all political broadcasting (Broadcasting Act 1990 ss. 6 and 90). The BBC is not governed by statute but operates under a Royal Charter and a licence from the Home Office. In theory the BBC could lawfully be operated as an instrument of government propaganda. Its duty of impartiality stems only from an informal undertaking given by the BBC to the government. The licence itself forbids the expression of editorial opinion about matters of public policy excluding broadcasting matters. It is arguable that these duties could be enforced by the courts as public duties. On the other hand the idea of political impartiality is both vague and complex and the courts are reluctant to interfere in party political matters. For example, must there be balance within the context of every specific subject? How much coverage should minority parties enjoy? (See *R.* v. *Broadcasting Complaints Commission ex parte Owen* (1985).) It is unlikely that a court would intervene with the IBA's decision except in a case of bad faith or complete irrationality (see *Wilson* v. *IBA* (1979)).
3. There are further controls over broadcasts about particular constituencies. Given the general framework we have just outlined perhaps these are unnecessarily strict. An item in which any candidate 'takes part' (which means 'actively participate' (*Marshall* v. *BBC* (1979)) cannot be broadcast without all the candidates' consent (s. 93 (1)).

4. It is an illegal practice for a person to 'use or aid, abet, counsel or procure' the use of broadcasting stations outside the UK for electoral purposes except where the matter is to be retransmitted by one of the domestic broadcasting companies (s. 93). This may not prevent overseas stations from directly broadcasting to voters via satellite television.

11.6   Election Disputes

There is an Election Court comprising two High Court judges. Either a voter or a candidate may within three months of the election lodge a petition to the court. The court can disqualify a candidate, order a recount or scrutiny of the votes, declare the result of the election, void the election and order a fresh election (s. 159). The court's decision takes the form of a report to the Speaker which the House is bound to accept (s. 144 (7)).

There are election offences called 'corrupt' or 'illegal' practices. These involve the offender being disqualified as a candidate or prevented from sitting in Parliament. The extent of the disqualification depends upon whether it is a corrupt practice (10 years everywhere) or an illegal practice (five years in a particular constituency). 'Innocent' illegal practices can be overlooked (s. 167). A corrupt practice involves dishonesty, improper pressure on voters, or excessive expenditure. Illegal practices concern breaches of various statutory requirements relating to agents, premises, advertising, broadcasting and other matters. Where an election offence is involved, separate criminal proceedings may be taken in an ordinary court in relation to the offence. Conviction disqualifies a person from membership of the House, and the Speaker must declare the seat vacant.

Summary

11.1   The House of Lords is unelected and with nearly 700 members is one of the largest legislatures in the world. This is thought to be inappropriate to its functions. It currently comprises 92 hereditary peers, 12 law lords, 26 senior Anglican bishops *ex officio* and a potentially unlimited number of life peers appointed by the prime minister on the advice of an independent Commission. The composition of the House of Lords is to be further reformed. The government has proposed that the House mainly remain unelected but with an elected element of one-fifth. A further one-fifth should be chosen by an independent commission but most of the House should be nominated by the political parties and appointed by the prime minister. As yet no further reforms have been made.

11.2   The voting system for parliamentary elections is currently the simple plurality 'first-past-the-post' system. Voting systems must cater for the incommensurables of effective government, accountable government and democratic representation. We asked whether the electoral system is adapted to its modern task of choosing governments, whether it is truly representative of public opinion and whether it is fair to all the candidates. We briefly compared different kinds of voting system including the alternative vote and PR. Variations of PR are used in elections to the regional legislatures and to the European Parliament. This is likely to create political tensions within the UK.

11.3   We discussed the machinery for regulating constituency boundaries. This is given a certain amount of protection against political interference but proposals for changes must be approved by the House of Commons. It is difficult to challenge decisions made by this process in the courts.

11.4   The law governing the conduct of elections, which had previously ignored national politics in favour of the individual election at local level, has recently been reformed to regulate campaign expenditure at national level including spending by third parties on election material and donations to and sponsorship of political parties. The independent Electoral Commission has wide responsibilities in relation to the finances of political parties and the conduct of elections. This is intended to bring greater openness and accountability to political parties.

11.5   We discussed controls over broadcasting. These are designed to ensure fairness between the parties in accordance with their popular support and are more stringent than are restrictions over the press.

11.6   We outlined the provisions made by the Political Parties, Elections and Referendums Act 2000 for regulating referendums. These attempt to ensure equality between the contenders and to focus the issues.

Further Reading

5th Report of the Committee on Standards in Public Life The Funding of Political Parties in the United Kingdom (1998) Cm. 4057–I.

Bogdanor, V. (1999) 'Reforming the Lords: a sceptical view', 70 *Political Quarterly* 375.

McClean, I. (2000) 'Mr Asquith's unfinished business', 70 *Political Quarterly* 382.

Shell, D. (2000) 'The future of the second chamber', 70 *Political Quarterly* 390.

Jowell and Oliver, *The Changing Constitution,* chapter 11.

Munro, *Studies in Constitutional Law,* chapter x.

Report of the Independent Commission on Electoral Reform (Jenkins Report) (1998).

Reports of the Electoral Commission; www.electoralcommission.gov.uk.

Wakeham (2000) *A House for the Future,* Report of the Royal Commission on the House of Lords.

Russell, M., Cornes, R. (2001) 'The Royal Commission on the House of Lords: a house for the future?' 64 *Modern Law Review* 82.

Lardy, H. (2000) 'Democracy by default: the representation of the People Act 2000' 64 *Modern Law Review* 63.

Webb, P. (2001) 'Parties and party systems: modernisation, regulation and diversity', 54 *Parliamentary Affairs* 308.

Exercises

11.1 'The Government's half-baked plans for a largely unelected House of Lords will lead to a bloated, unworkable second chamber' (Peter Kellner). Explain and critically discuss.

11.2 'The UK electoral system penalises minority parties'. Discuss.

11.3 Explain the basis on which parliamentary constituencies are designated. Do the present arrangements contain adequate safeguards against party political manipulation?

11.4 'There is now an overwhelming case for legislation regulating expenditure on a national (election) campaign' (Rawlings); 'Restriction on the conduct of elections violate basic rights of free expression'. Do you consider that the Political Parties, Elections and Referendums Act 2000 has adequately addressed these competing concerns?

11.5 What controls does the law provide over election broadcasting. Do you consider these to be adequate and fair?

11.6 What problems are created by private donations to political parties and how successfully has the law addressed them?

11.7 'Reforms of the electoral system through the introduction of a single transferable vote ... would revitalise the operation of political processes and make a major contribution to the development of a more accountable, effective system and a more influential citizenry' (Oliver). Discuss.

11.8 The Association for Transexuals' Rights promotes a national publicity campaign in favour of its aim of giving transexuals full legal status. It spends two million pounds on the campaign, much of it raised from donations by American supporters which includes leaflets, TV advertisements and its own journal. Six months into the campaign a general election is called. Several of the candidates at the election had previously appeared on television voicing strong objections to the aims of the Association. Advise the association as to its position under electoral law.

12 Parliamentary Procedure

12.1 Introduction

Although the legal supremacy of Parliament probably remains in place, the political power and prestige of Parliament has declined in recent years. This is the result of an accumulation of factors, some new, others long standing which together raise doubts as to whether Parliament is still the most important institution of the constitution. These factors include the following:

- the increasing influence of international lawmaking which in practice restricts national governments, making the notion of state sovereignty an anachronism. Examples are the European Union, NATO, the World Trade Organisation and World Bank, and the European Convention on Human Rights;
- at the other end of the scale the devolution of powers, albeit to differing extents, to the nations within the UK;
- the increase in the power of the executive at the expense of the legislature;
- a more assertive and activist judiciary;
- the increasing but still limited use of referendums, see Political Parties, Elections and Referendums Act 2000.

Parliamentary procedure has four main purposes: first to enable different interests to combine in a single outcome such as a statute; second to make the executive accountable; third to provide for the raising of grievances on behalf of the public; and fourth to prevent outside interference. Parliamentary procedure is based upon standing orders, customs and conventions and rulings by the Speaker who presides over the House of Commons. The authoritative manual of parliamentary procedure, *Erskine May* (1989), contains the standing orders and other rules of the House as well as collating the mass of customs and practices.

The underlying ethos of parliamentary procedure is firstly that it is adversarial, presupposing a government and opposition constantly in conflict. The rectangular layout of the Chamber, and indeed of the Palace of Westminster itself, reflects this. Other European legislative chambers are characteristically semi-circular in layout representing a more conciliatory ethos with the parties, usually elected by proportional representation merging into each other.

The adversarial nature of Commons procedure is to some extent mitigated by what are known as 'usual channels'. These involve informal co-operation between the parties so as to ensure that the procedures operate smoothly and fairly. For example, legitimate absences from votes may be arranged in 'pairs' so as to maintain party balance. Whips have the responsibility of enforcing party discipline and liaising between the government and backbench MPs. The Government Chief Whip, although not a cabinet member, frequently attends cabinet meetings. The Chief Whip also advises the prime minister upon the careers of ministers and MPs.

Secondly the government is usually able to dominate the business of the House of Commons. In some countries the doctrine of separation of powers subjects parliamentary procedure to special machinery in order to prevent the procedure from being controlled by the executive. In the UK the reverse applies. The parliamentary timetable is determined by the government under Standing Order 13 which usually gives priority to government business. The government also exercises considerable influence over MPs through party discipline and patronage and through influencing the membership of committees. Apart from the day-to-day pressures imposed by the whips, the government can appoint an unlimited number of unpaid parliamentary private secretaries who are required under the convention of collective responsibility to support the executive. This device can also be used to remove an unwanted individual from a departmental select committee, membership being limited to backbenchers.

A recent report from a Hansard Society Commission (*The Challenge for Parliament: Making Government Work* (Newton, 2001)), suggested that there are 'serious gaps in the working of accountability to Parliament'. The Commission recommended in particular that departmental select committees should have greater freedom from government interference and that backbench MPs should have their own career structure to make them independent of government patronage. An attempt by the government in 2001 to remove two independently minded select committee members was defeated by the House as a whole, illustrating that ultimately the House does have the power needed to preserve some independence from the executive.

The quorum is 40. Parliamentary debates consist of a motion and question proposed by the Chair in the same form as the motion. Following debate the question is put and voted upon, the result being expressed as a resolution or order. At any stage there may be amendments proposed but in all cases issues are presented to the House one at a time for a yes or no vote by a simple majority. This reflects the confrontational nature of Parliament and also ensures that the voting is on a majoritarian basis.

The House of Lords regulates its own procedure which is less adversarial and less dominated by the political parties than is the case in the Commons. There is less reliance on formal procedural rules than in the House of Commons. The Lord Chancellor presides over the House of Lords as well as speaking for the government. The Lord Chancellor does not have the disciplinary powers available to the Speaker his only power being to put a question to the vote (SO 18). The House of Lords has no power to suspend or expel a member. The House of Lords is subservient to the Commons but the limits of this are not clear. Under the Parliament Acts 1911 and 1949 the Lords can delay most bills introduced in the Commons for a certain time (below, p. 273) and this gives them a certain measure of legitimacy. By convention, the Lords are not entitled to oppose the will of the Commons certainly in relation to financial measures, nor it appears where a Commons proposal gives effect to a commitment in the government's election manifesto or possibly to other important government policies.

The Wakeham Report (see Chapter 11) did not propose major changes in the constitutional role of the second chamber. It emphasised that the House of Commons should remain the superior body and that the holding of government to account in the context of the second chamber meant no more than requiring government to explain and justify its actions. Wakeham rejected extending the powers of veto of the second chamber to constitutional matters. Instead it recommended that the committees of the second chamber be strengthened by the addition of a Constitutional Committee perhaps with a human rights sub-committee.

12.2 The Speaker

The office of Speaker of the Commons symbolises the historical development of the House, particularly in the seventeenth century. The Speaker presides over meeting of the Commons and is the intermediary between the House and the Crown. The Speaker represents the rights of the House against the Crown, keeps order and is responsible for protecting the rights of all groups within the House, particularly those of minorities. The Speaker makes rulings on procedure and has summary powers to suspend members or to terminate a sitting. He or she has considerable discretion in terms of the conduct of particular proceedings, choice of amendments, whom to call in debates and in the keeping of order and need not normally give reasons for decisions (see SO 31, 42, 45).

The Speaker, the 'first commoner', is elected from its membership by the House at the beginning of each Parliament. The 'father of the house', the longest-serving member runs the election. Traditionally a newly elected Speaker has to be dragged to the chair, reminding us that this was once a dangerous post . The Speaker is required to be impartial between the political parties. He cannot therefore represent his constituency in debates nor does he fight elections under a party banner. The Sergeant at Arms is the enforcement agency responsible to the Speaker. There is also a deputy Speaker and deputies to him. One of these presides when the House is sitting as a Committee.

12.3   Legislative Procedure

The main distinctions are between public bills and private bills. There are also special arrangements for financial measures.

12.3.1   Public bills

A public bill is a bill intended to alter the general law. The formal procedures in the House are only the tip of the iceberg. Any member can propose a bill but almost all public bills are promoted by the government and introduced by ministers. Private members' bills are unlikely to get beyond first reading without government support. Twelve Fridays are provided in each session to private members' bills (SO 13 (4)). Priority is determined by a ballot held annually for which only backbenchers are eligible. Only the first six in the ballot have a realistic chance of success because, of the twelve Fridays, six are devoted to bills in their later stages. Sometimes the winners adopt bills proposed by others, for example outside pressure groups or the executive. A private member can also get a bill debated under the '10-minute rule' (SO 19). This involves a motion twice a week that leave be given to present a bill. A short debate takes place at peak time for publicity purposes. There is little prospect of the matter going any further, the essential aim being to publicise an issue. Nevertheless, some important social reforms were achieved before 1979 by private members' bills, including abortion legislation, the abolition of the death penalty and divorce reform. However, all had government support in the form of time allocation and drafting assistance.

Before their formal introduction, public bills go through various processes within the administration involving the formulation of policy and principles. When these have been completed the bill is sent to Parliamentary Counsel for drafting. Some bills, particularly those dealing with commercial matters, are drafted with the aid of outside lawyers. The relationship between the draftspeople and the government is similar to that of lawyer and client. The draftspeople work under considerable pressure of time and there is continuous consultation with government departments (see *Report of Renton Commission: The Preparation of Legislation* (1975) Cmd. 6053; Kent, 1979). Outside bodies may also be consulted, although there is no convention to this effect. Some bills relating to reform of the general law are prepared by the Law Commission.

Important bills may be foreshadowed by Green Papers which are consultation documents or by White Papers which state the government's concluded opinions. Both are published. The final version of a bill is approved by the Legislation Committee of the Cabinet and then introduced into Parliament. A reform that is often suggested is that there be a general debate on a draft bill before it is formally introduced. Except for financial measures, which must be introduced by a minister in the Commons, a bill can be introduced into either the House of Lords or the House of Commons. The same stages apply in each House, subject to the special procedures required by the Parliament Acts 1911 and 1949. Relatively uncontroversial bills are likely to be introduced in the House of Lords.

The stages of a public bill are as follows:

1. *First Reading.* This is a formality which ensures that the bill is printed and published.
2. *Second Reading*, at which the main principles of the bill are discussed. In theory once a bill has passed this stage its principles cannot later be challenged. However, 'wrecking' amendments are sometimes introduced (for example by addition of the word 'not') with a view to neutralising a bill. Manipulating fine dividing lines is part of the parliamentary art. Occasionally second reading is dealt with by a special committee.
3. *Committee Stage.* Where the bill is examined by a standing committee, with a view to suggesting detailed amendments. Unlike a select committee which exists for the whole of a Parliament, a standing committee is set up only for the purpose of a particular

bill. Its membership of around 50 is based upon the strength of each party in the House so that it is difficult for amendments to be made against the wishes of the government. Opponents of a bill sometimes deliberately cause delays by discussing matters at length in committee. However, the chairman has power to decide which amendments should be discussed and a 'business sub-committee' allocates time for discussion. The parliamentary draftsperson may be present and civil servants can be called to give evidence. Sometimes a bill is referred to a committee of the whole House. This might happen for example when the bill is uncontroversial or at the opposite extreme where it is of profound political significance. Special procedures requiring a committee of the whole House are required for financial measures (see below).

4. *Report Stage*. The result of the committee's deliberations is returned to the House which can then vote upon the amendments and consider further amendments. The Speaker can select the amendments to be debated. The report stage can be dispensed with where the bill has been discussed by a committee of the whole House.

5. *Third Reading*. This is the final vote on the bill. Only verbal amendments are usually possible at this stage but the bill as a whole can be opposed.

12.3.2   Private bills

A private bill is a bill directed to particular persons or places, for example a bill to build a new section of railway line, or a reservoir, or a bill to permit persons to marry who would be disqualified from so doing under the general law. It is a somewhat antiquated notion and today most powers directed to specific persons or places are exercised by the executive either by delegated legislation or under discretionary powers. Delegated legislation is usually subject to annulment by Parliament but private bill procedure allows Parliament to amend proposals and is therefore suitable for very large private schemes.

The private bill procedure involves the following:

 (i) Advertisement of the proposals in the locality.
 (ii) A petition and a copy of the bill to be lodged in Parliament by 27 November each year. This is the equivalent of first reading.
(iii) Notification to persons affected. The bill's promoters must do this and persons affected are entitled to petition against the bill.
(iv) Second reading. This is to discuss whether the bill is contrary to national policy.

(v) The committee stage before a special committee of the Commons or the Lords. At this stage those who petitioned against the bill can appear represented, if they wish, by counsel. The procedure is similar to that of a court and evidence can be called and witnesses cross-examined. Public bill procedure is therefore slow and expensive.

(vi) Report stage and third reading and royal assent are similar to those for public bills.

A bill that is basically a public bill but with a private element is called a 'hybrid bill'. For example, the Aircraft and Shipbuilding Bill 1976 nationalised these industries and was, as such, a public bill but it exempted certain named firms from its proposals. A hybrid bill is subject to the public bill procedure until the committee stage when it is examined by a select committee in the same manner as a private bill. Although a private bill procedure involves outside elements it is still wholly within parliamentary privilege. Therefore the courts cannot intervene on the ground that the procedure has not been properly followed or even that there has been fraud (*Pickin* v. *British Railways Board* (1974)).

Private bill procedure has been much criticised, not only because it is slow but because it fails to provide opportunities for the public to be directly involved in debating schemes which may have serious environmental impact, for example new railway lines. There is, however, a range of alternative procedures with less and sometimes no parliamentary imput. These enable public bodies such as local authorities or utility companies to obtain powers to override private rights. The main examples are as follows:

- The Transport and Works Act 1992 applies primarily to large rail and waterway projects. The Act allows a Secretary of State to authorise projects after consulting local authorities and affected parties and including an environmental assessment. A public inquiry must be held into objections. The Secretary of State can also refer proposals of national importance to Parliament for debate.
- Provisional Orders made by Ministers, again following a public local inquiry, are confirmed by a Provisional Order Confirmation Bill, the committee stage of which involves a select committee at which interested parties can be heard. Thus there is an element of detailed parliamentary scrutiny.
- 'Special parliamentary procedure' involves a ministerial order which is subject to a public inquiry and also to a hearing before a special

parliamentary committee. It can be debated on the floor of the House. This procedure is less cumbersome than private bills or provisional order confirmation bills but gives the authority of Parliament to sensitive proposals (for example, the sale of certain National Trust land).

- Many projects such as new highways can be authorised without Parliament by ministerial order made under general legislation, usually following a local public inquiry (for example Acquisition of Land Act 1981). It has been held that, because these procedures are political rather than judicial, they do not violate the right to a fair trial under the European Convention on Human Rights, provided that the safeguard of judicial review is available (see *Alconbury Developments* v. *Secretary of State for the Environment, Transport and Regions* (2001)).

12.3.3   Cutting short debate

If a public bill has not become law by the end of a session it lapses. There are procedural devices available to both Houses but most importantly in the Commons to cut short the time spent on debate. The devices to cut short debate usually depend upon a vote of the House and in the Commons are therefore under the control of the government. Procedure in the Lords is under the control of the House collectively and is more consensual.

The main procedural devices are as follows:

- *Closure*: a motion that the question be now put (SO 35). If there is a division at least 100 members must support the motion. In a committee a quorum must support it. The Speaker can also cut short debate when (s)he thinks there has been adequate discussion (SO 67). Except in the case of private members' bills closure motions are rare.
- *Guillotine*: a minister may propose a timetable for a bill. The debate on a guillotine motion cannot be longer than three hours. A similar procedure exists within committees. If the motion succeeds, the bill is then divided up by the Business Committee (which is nominated by the Speaker in accordance with party strengths), each part being given a specified time for discussion. The guillotine procedure may prevent parts of a bill being discussed at all. Conversely, where a government is weak a defeated guillotine motion can destroy a bill.
- *'Kangaroo'* (SO 41): the Speaker at report stage or the chairman of a committee select clauses or amendments for discussion.

- There are also procedural devices available in specific contexts (see Griffiths and Ryle, 1989, p. 219).

12.3.4 House of Lords legislative procedure

Bills other than those involving government taxation or expenditure can be introduced in the House of Lords. A bill introduced in the House of Commons and passing all its stages goes to the House of Lords. The procedure is broadly similar except that the committee stage usually takes place before a committee of the whole House. If the Lords proposes amendments or vetos any provision the Bill is returned to the Commons.

Under the Parliament Acts 1911 and 1949 the House of Lords can delay most legislation only for two successive sessions, that is for roughly one year. After the second session the bill can receive the Royal Assent without the consent of the Lords. If the Commons amend a bill after it has come back from the Lords in the first of the two sessions, then it may not count as the same bill, unless the amendments were suggested by the Lords. One year must elapse between the second reading of the bill in the Commons in the first session and its third (the final) reading in the second session.

In the case of a 'money bill' the Lords can delay only for one month provided that the bill is sent to them at least one month before the end of a session. A 'money bill' is a public bill which deals *exclusively* either with central government taxation or central government spending, borrowing or accounts. The certificate of the Speaker that a bill is a money bill is conclusive for all purposes (1911 Act s. 3). This definition is fairly narrow since few bills deal exclusively with these matters. The Speaker must certify that the Parliament Act's procedure has been followed and his certificate cannot be challenged. The Parliament Act procedure has been little used (see Welsh Church Act 1914; Government of Ireland Act 1914, Parliament Act 1949). In practice, while the Lords sometimes delay bills, they have in the end given way to the Commons.

The Parliament Acts do not apply to certain kinds of legislation. These are as follows:

- local and private bills;
- bills confirming Provisional Orders (above);
- bills introduced in the House of Lords;
- a bill to prolong the life of Parliament. Because of this exemption the House of Lords retains the key constitutional role of preventing a government from avoiding an election by prolonging its own life.

The Parliament Act procedure may possibly not apply to a bill to abolish or to reduce the powers of the House of Lords. This argument assumes that a law passed by the Queen and Commons alone under the Parliament Act is no more than a special kind of delegated legislation and a delegate cannot enlarge its own powers without statutory authority. It is therefore arguable that the Parliament Act 1949, which reduced the delaying power of the Lords, is void because it was passed under the 1911 Act procedure without the assent of the Lords. The Wakeham Commission (Wakeham, 2000) proposed that it be made clear by a simple amendment to the Parliament Acts that the Parliament Acts should not apply to a bill that affects the composition or powers of the House of Lords. Wakeham rejected any other extension of the Lords' power of veto on the ground that this might risk upsetting the supremacy of the Commons. Wakeham emphasised that, in the context of the House of Lords, the vague concept of accountability means primarily that the Lords should provide a mechanism to make the government think again, rather than to overrule the government.

12.3.5   The Royal Assent

The Royal Assent is not usually given by the monarch in person but through commissioners who notify the assent to each House separately (Royal Assent Act 1967). Some bills are assented to at the Prorogation ceremony that ends each session when the Commons attend the Lords in accordance with long-standing practice. By convention the monarch must always assent, except possibly in the unlikely event of the prime minister advising to the contrary. In this case, however, the government would be at odds with the Commons and so required to resign. The monarch's function in such a case will be discussed later.

Once a bill has received the Royal Assent it becomes law. However, it is often provided that the Act, or specific parts of it, shall not take effect until a minister so orders. A minister's decision whether or not to bring an Act into effect is subject to judicial review (see *R. v. Secretary of State for the Home Department ex parte Fire Brigades Union* (1995)). It is also common for an Act to confer power on ministers to make detailed regulations without which the Act itself cannot operate. These might include a 'Henry VIII clause' under which a minister is empowered to alter other statutes.

12.4 Financial Procedure

It is a fundamental principle embodied in both law and convention that the House of Commons controls public finance. On the other hand, modern government finance is so large and complex that such control may be unrealistic. In practice the most substantial control over government finance particularly in advance of spending is exercised internally by the Treasury, which is itself accountable to Parliament. Parliament is also assisted, particularly in relation to the scrutiny of past expenditure, by the National Audit Office which is independent of the executive.

The dependence of the executive on money voted by the people is an essential feature of a democratic constitution. The constitutional theory is that the Crown comes to the Commons to ask for money. Hence financial measures can be proposed only by the Crown and the Commons can reduce the estimates but not increase them (see SO 46). The survival of a government depends upon the Commons voting it funds, and the refusal of the Commons to do so is the equivalent of a vote of no confidence so that the government must resign. By convention the House of Lords cannot amend measures relating to central government finance and, as we have seen, can delay money bills only for one month.

By virtue of the Bill of Rights 1688 the Crown cannot raise taxation without the consent of Parliament. Payments into the consolidated fund, the government's bank account, require statutory authority (Exchequer and Audit Act 1866 s. 11). Moreover it seems that central government expenditure is unlawful unless authorised by statute although this need not be in detail and usually consists merely of global departmental estimates (*Auckland Harbour Board* v. *R.* (1924), *R.* v. *Secretary of State ex parte World Development Movement* (1995)).

The main financial measures are embodied in three kinds of Act passed each year. Firstly, the Finance Act deals with taxation. The Royal Assent to a taxation measure is expressed in the words: '*La Reyne remercie ses bons sujets, accepte leur benevolence et ainsi le veult*' (The Queen thanks her good subjects, accepts their kindness and thus assents), as opposed to the normal '*La Reyne le veult*'. Secondly, the annual Appropriation Act authorises the spending programmes of each government department. Thirdly, Consolidated Fund Acts authorise government drawing from its bank account supervised by the Treasury. In addition there is a principle that taxation and expenditure must first be authorised by a resolution of the House of Commons (SO no. 48).

The resolution is proposed by a minister before the committee stage which is usually taken before the whole House. Amendments cannot be made outside the terms of the resolution, thus strengthening the government's hand.

12.4.1   Taxation procedure

The key taxation event is the annual 'budget' resolution proposed by the Chancellor usually in March. This includes the Chancellor's views on the economy and overall strategy and proposals for tax changes. It therefore sets the general economic framework of government policy. The budget resolution is followed by the annual Finance Bill. This includes taxes (notably, income tax) that must be authorised afresh each year. These annual taxes are enforced and administered under permanent legislation (Income and Corporation Taxes Act 1988). Some taxes mainly indirect taxes such as customs duties are authorised by permanent legislation although their rates can be changed at any time. Constitutional principle is preserved in the case of EC law by the requirement in the European Communities Act 1972 that EC laws affecting taxation, e.g. VAT, must be implemented by a statute.

The effect of the budget resolution is that the budget's main tax proposals become law with immediate effect, but lapse unless embodied in a Finance Act that becomes law by a specified time. This is 5 August if the speech is in March or April, otherwise within four months (Provisional Collection of Taxes Act 1968). This procedure illustrates the basic constitutional principle that resolutions of the Commons cannot by themselves change the law but need statutory backing (*Bowles* v. *Bank of England* (1913)).

Central government money does not come exclusively from taxation. Governments borrow large sums of money in the form of bonds and on the international money market. Money is also raised from landholding, investments both in the UK and overseas, and from trading activities. These sources of finance are not subject to detailed parliamentary scrutiny although statutory authority is required in general terms for borrowing (National Loans Fund Act 1968).

12.4.2   Spending procedure

Most public expenditure must be authorised annually by the Appropriation Act which approves the government's estimates. These include 'votes' setting out the government's proposed allocation of funds between departments. Thus the Commons approves not only the global sum but also the executive's broad priorities. The annual Appropriation Act and Consolidated Fund Acts (which authorise temporary borrowing in advance of approval of the estimates) are usually passed without debates. Debates on the estimates have been replaced by 20 'opposition days' which allow the opposition parties to raise anything they wish, and by special 'adjournment debates' following the passage of the Acts. The latter allow issues to be discussed without a vote.

Some items of expenditure are permanently authorised. These are called consolidated fund services. They include judicial salaries, royal expenses, European Community payments and interest on the national debt. In practice, however, most government spending is the subject of long-term commitments (e.g. National Insurance), thus leaving little flexibility.

12.4.3 Supervising expenditure

Money raised by the central government goes into the 'consolidated fund'. The control of spending from the consolidated fund is the responsibility of the Commons, but given the size and complexity of modern government this is clearly an impossible task for an elected assembly. In practice, direct parliamentary control over expenditure is very limited. The Public Accounts Committee admitted in 1987 that parliamentary control over the estimates is largely a formality (HC 98 (1986–7) para. 2). In medieval times the Court of Exchequer supervised government spending, but the modern courts have relinquished this responsibility in favour of Parliament. The courts are therefore reluctant to interfere with central government spending decisions which are subject to parliamentary scrutiny (see *Nottinghamshire CC* v. *Secretary of State* (1986)).

However, in *R. v. Secretary of State for Foreign and Commonwealth Affairs ex parte World Development Movement* (1995) a Foreign Office decision to give a large grant to the Malaysian government for the Pergau Dam project was set aside by the Court of Appeal on the basis that the project had no economic justification and that there was an ulterior political motive. In that case the governing legislation specifically required that the decision be based on economic grounds, which, crucially, the court equated with 'sound' economic grounds (see Harden *et al.*, 1996) and parliamentary approval was not required. In the case of local government, the courts are more willing to police financial decisions, using the concept that a local authority owes a fiduciary duty analogous to that of a trustee to the local ratepayer (see *Bromley LBC* v. *GLC* (1983)).

The most effective controls are, in characteristically English fashion, imposed within the government machine itself by the Treasury and are an example of the importance of internal rules base on the inherent power of any employer to administer its workforce. Harden *et al.* (1996) describe this as a 'self-regulatory system relying on trust and elite consensus' (see *Government Accounting*, 1989). Each department and agency has authority from the Treasury to spend within prescribed limits and has an accounting officer, appointed by the Treasury, who is responsible for administering the financial controls prescribed by the Treasury and can be questioned by parliamentary committees. The Treasury exercises statutory control over the form of government accounts, in particular in relation to public, private partnerships and in the allocation of expenditure between different years (Government Resources and Accounts Act 2000).

Public expenditure of central departments and other public bodies related to the centre is scrutinised by the Comptroller and Auditor General supported by the National Audit Office. The Comptroller is appointed by the Crown on a motion from the House of Commons proposed by the prime minister with the Agreement of the Chair of the Public Accounts Committee (Exchequer and Audit Depts Acts 1866–1957, NAA 1983 s. 1). The Comptroller is an Officer of the Commons and has security of tenure similar to that of a High Court Judge (see Exchequer and Audit Dept Act 1866). The Comptroller is supported by the National Audit Office (NAO) which is responsible for scrutinising the accounts of central government departments and also those of some outside bodies dependent on government money, such as universities. The NAO carries out two kinds of audit. 'Certification Audit' is based on financial accounting practice. 'Value for Money Audit' is based on the wider concerns of the 'economy, efficiency and effectiveness' of government expenditure (National Audit Act 1983 s. 6). This is not meant to include the substantive merits of government policy, although the line between them may be difficult to draw. The NAO is also concerned with matters of 'regularity, legality, propriety and probity'. Again it may not be clear how far accounting officers and the NAO should go into questions of legality (see Hardin *et al.*, 1996).

The Comptroller reports to the Public Accounts Committee of the House of Commons. This committee carries out an annual scrutiny of government accounts and its report is debated by the Commons. It thus provides a key mechanism for the control of government finance and for government accountability in general. The Comptroller and Auditor General are not directly concerned with the merits of government policy but only with the efficient and economical use of money (National Audit Act 1983 ss. 6 and 7).

12.5 Supervision of the Executive

This depends upon the doctrine of ministerial responsibility and relies in the last resort upon the convention that the House of Commons can require the government to resign. In modern times the role of Parliament has been weakened by the party system and the difficulty of obtaining information from the government. It should also be remembered that not all government activity requires formal parliamentary authority. This includes royal prerogative powers, including the making of treaties and other matters concerning foreign affairs, commercial and property transactions carried out under private law powers, national security and the use of the armed forces where additional expenditure is not involved. Parliamentary scrutiny is also limited by the practice of conferring decision-making power to semi-independent bodies outside the central government.

The main procedures for scrutiny of the executive are as follows:

Questions (SO 50)
About 45 minutes each day are allowed for questions to ministers. Any MP can put down a question. The prime minister has two 30-minute question sessions each week. Three ministers are available per day but members must ballot for the privilege of asking an oral question. Except in the case of prime minister's questions, advance notice must be given but a member may ask one unscheduled supplementary question. Civil servants who brief ministers are skilled in anticipating possible supplementaries. A supplementary need only bear a tenuous relationship to the main question. For example: Q. 'What are the prime minister's engagements for the day?'. S. 'Why is he not visiting X where another hospital has been closed?'. Conversely sycophantic questions by government supporters are frequently asked.

By convention, ministers must provide the information requested but can refuse to answer on various grounds. and cannot be pressed upon a refusal to answer. Moreover answers can be perfunctory and incomplete although ministers must not 'knowingly' mislead Parliament and must correct any inadvertent error at the earliest opportunity (see Ministerial Code). Apart from the prime minister, ministers have about two weeks' advance notice. Questions can be put in writing without limit and the answers are recorded in *Hansard*, the official parliamentary journal.

The Speaker has no power to call a minister before the House and a common contemporary abuse of Parliament is for ministers to give information to the press before making a statement in Parliament. However, 'Private Notice' questions can be asked by any member without prior warning, which requires a minister to answer. This must, however, be of an 'urgent character' and relate either to matters of public importance or to the arrangement of business (SO 17(3)). Questions are unlikely to reveal detailed information but do have the advantage of putting ministers under pressure and exposing weaknesses in public.

Debates
There are various opportunities for debating general matters. All involve limited time, sometimes at the tail-end of a sitting in the late evening.

(i) *Adjournment debates*: these can be on any matter for which a minister is responsible. The most common is a half-hour daily adjournment debate which can be initiated by a backbencher. There is a weekly ballot (SO 9). There can also be all-night adjournment debates following the passage of a Consolidated Fund or Appropriation bill (above), emergency adjournment debates (which are rarely permitted), and 'recess' debates in which miscellaneous topics can be debated for up to three hours. Amendments cannot be moved to adjournment motions, so adjournment motions can be used by the government to restrict the opposition. Adjournment debates do not result in a formal vote, and a minister's response cannot be questioned.

(ii) *Opposition days* after the proceedings on the annual Appropriation Act (above).

(iii) *Emergency debates*: to open the debate the support of 40 members or a vote of the House is required (SO 20). The Speaker must hold that the matter is urgent and relates to the responsibilities of ministers. Only three minutes are allowed for the application.

(iv) The debate following the Queen's Speech at the opening of a session.

(v) *Censure motions*: by convention a government is expected to resign if defeated on a censure motion (also called a no-confidence motion). The government must provide time to debate the motion. Until the 1970s the convention also seemed to include other government defeats on important matters, but the latter seem no longer to require resignation (870 HC Deb. 71–2 (1974)). The possibility that a government can be defeated on a major part of its programme but also remain in office strengthens a weak government by providing a safety valve for dissidents within its party. Since 1964 a government has resigned only once following a censure motion (1979). On that occasion the government was a minority government, again a rare event. A no-confidence motion has no particular form. Either government or opposition can declare any vote to be one of confidence. In today's conditions the procedure seems to be essentially a publicity stunt. However, such a vote does require the government to publicly defend itself.

(vi) The budget debate.

(vii) Ministerial statements which can be followed by questions and discussion.

12.5.1 Scrutiny of delegated legislation

The practice of delegating lawmaking powers to the executive is necessary, given the complexity of modern government and the pressure upon parliamentary time. Most delegated legislation is detailed and highly technical. It would be impracticable to subject all delegated legislation to detailed democratic scrutiny so that the law is necessarily a compromise. Thus delegated legislation is subject to a limited degree of parliamentary control by being laid before one or both Houses for approval. Unlike a bill, Parliament cannot usually amend delegated legislation.

Originally the laying process was haphazard, but as a result of public concern about 'bureaucratic tyranny' (see *Report of Committee on Ministers' Powers*, 1932, Cmnd. 4060) limited reforms were made by the Statutory Instruments Act 1946. Most delegated legislation takes the form of a statutory instrument which subjects it to the Act. A statutory instrument made after the 1946 Act came into force is defined as such if it is made by Order in Council or if the parent Act expressly provides. Thus there is no legal obligation on governments to comply with the controls in the 1946 Act. Moreover a statutory instrument has to be laid before the House only if its parent Act so requires. The 1946 Act also requires that statutory instruments must be published 'as soon as may be' unless there is a special excuse for not doing so (s. 3). Failure to publish may not make the instrument invalid but provides a statutory defence to prosecution, provided that the accused was unaware of the instrument and that no reasonable steps had been taken to publicise it (s. 3 (2); see *R. v. Sheer Metalcraft Ltd* (1954)).

The laying procedures typically require only that the statutory instrument be 'laid on the table' of the House in draft or in final form for 40 days subject to annulment by a vote of the House – the 'negative' procedure. The fate of the instrument therefore depends upon the chance of a member seeing the document and securing a debate. Some instruments are required to be laid for information only, Parliament having no power to annul them. A small number of important statutory instruments are made subject to an 'affirmative' procedure under which there must be a positive vote in order to bring them into effect.

The Parliament Acts do not apply to delegated legislation so that the House of Lords has the power to veto a statutory instrument. It has done so only once in the last 30 years when it vetoed a measure that would deny free mailing for candidates in the election for the Mayor of Greater London (Hansard (HL) 20 Feb. 2000 Col. 136). The Wakeham Committee and the government have proposed that this power be removed in favour of a delaying power only (Wakeham, 2000).

The Joint Committee on Statutory Instruments is responsible for scrutinising statutory instruments laid before Parliament. The scrutiny committee is not concerned with the political merits of the instrument but is required to draw the attention of Parliament to specified constitutional matters. These are as follows:

(i) Does the instrument impose taxation or other forms of charge?
(ii) Does it exclude control by the courts?
(iii) Is it retrospective without the express authority of the parent Act?
(iv) Has there been unjustifiable delay in laying or publishing it?
(v) Is there doubt as to its legal validity or does it appear to make some unusual or unexpected use of the powers under which it was made?
(vi) For any special reason does its form or purport call for elucidation?
(vii) Does its drafting appear to be defective?
(viii) Any other ground other than those relating to policy or merits.

12.5.2   Select committees

A select committee is appointed for the whole Parliament, by convention mainly from backbenchers. Its task is to investigate and report to the House. It can investigate matters referred to it, or on its own initiative. In an attempt to strengthen Parliament's control over the executive, departmental select committees were introduced in 1979

(SO 130). Each committee is responsible for investigating the activities of a government department and reporting to the House. There is however no select committee for the Lord Chancellor's department nor for the prime minister's office. There are also functional select committees dealing with contemporary issues. These committees include 'modernisation', broadcasting, deregulation and regulatory reforms, environmental audit, European scrutiny, information, and standards and privileges. There are joint committees of the two Houses on human rights, parliamentary privilege, tax simplification and statutory instruments. The Public Administration and Public Accounts committees of the House of Commons exercise broad scrutiny functions.

The Liaison Committee selects the members in proportion to party representation in the House. In practice, however, it appears that the membership is selected according to instructions from party whips. The chairmanship is a matter for negotiation between government and opposition. Select committees may also recruit outside advisers such as academics. They interview witnesses but have little real power to probe. Time, the doctrine of ministerial responsibility and the rules of parliamentary privilege combine to frustrate their activities. In principle, a select committee has power to call for 'persons and papers' at any time, even when Parliament is not sitting, and failure to attend or refusal to answer questions could be a contempt of the House. However, enforcement would require a resolution of the House and the committee can do little on its own (see HC 353 (1991-2) paras 20-21). Particular problems are as follows:

- Members of the House of Lords, being protected by their own privilege, cannot be required to attend.
- Members of the Commons, including ministers can probably not be required to attend or to answer questions without an Order of the House. In particular there may be a convention that the prime minister does not appear before select committees.
- Committees have no power to demand papers from government departments. An address to the Queen (in respect of a secretary of state) or a formal Order from the House is required.
- Select committees have no independent research resources.
- Ministers have relied on traditional notions of ministerial responsibility as a means of shielding the inner workings of government from parliamentary scrutiny, slightly tempered by a general undertaking by ministers to co-operate with committees, for example by explaining why evidence cannot be given. Civil servants are protected by ministerial responsibility and cannot be required to

attend. Even where they do attend, their evidence has been limited to describing their 'actions' taken on behalf of ministers as opposed to their 'conduct' generally. Thus civil servants cannot give evidence about cabinet matters, or the consultation process within government, or the advice they gave to government, or policy alternatives.

Indeed ministers have sometimes forbidden civil servants from appearing, in particular on the grounds of national security, 'good government' and 'excessive cost'. However, this remains controversial. In 1986 the Defence Select Committee claimed the absolute right to secure attendance from civil servants (HC 519 (1985–6)), and in 1994 the permanent secretary in the Overseas Development Department disclosed to the Public Accounts Committee that ministers had over-ridden his advice (*Times*, 18 January 1994, see also Civil Service Code, HC 588 (1977–8) paras 7.5–7.27; HC 92 (1982–3); HC 100 (1986–7); 123 HC Deb. 572–5 (1987); HC 353 (1991–2) paras 201; see Chapter 14).

Select committees have drawn public attention to important issues and have exposed weaknesses in governmental policies and procedures. Their capacity to do this may have a deterrent effect on government departments. On the other hand, their reports do not necessarily lead to action or even to debate in Parliament and they are not tools for extracting information. To this extent the view of the Procedure Committee that select committees have been a modest success in requiring government to explain itself is perhaps a little sanguine (HC 19 (1989–90) paras 356–7). On the other hand the backbench composition of select committees and their practice of seeking consensus have given them a certain independent status.

Except for committees of the whole House and some minor committees all House of Lords Committees are select committees who can therefore accumulate expertise. Select committees in the House of Lords deal with subjects rather than departments reflecting the role of the Upper House as a forum for the detailed discussion of important issues free of immediate party pressures. The Science and Technology Committee, the European Committee and the Environmental Committee are particularly well regarded.

12.6   Redress of Grievances

Overlapping with Parliament's duty to supervise the executive is the duty of members of Parliament and the right of Parliament collectively to seek the redress of the grievances of subjects of the Crown. Procedurally this depends upon opportunities being made available to backbench members to raise individual grievances. One problem is the possibility of conflicts with party interests, another is the lack of resources including time. No parliamentary time is reserved for the redress of grievances as such. An MP is able to give publicity to a grievance by placing it on the parliamentary record. Apart from that, the process is haphazard.

The main procedures available are parliamentary questions, adjournment debates, and, perhaps most effectively, informal communications with ministers, although, as we have seen, the latter are not always protected by parliamentary privilege. All these suffer from the inability of an individual MP to force disclosure of information. Early Day Motions can also be used. This procedure allows an MP to put down a matter for debate without a fixed date. Early Day Motions are hardly ever debated. Their function is to draw public attention to a particular issue. They may be supported by a large number of members across parties, amounting in effect to a petition.

There are other miscellaneous opportunities by way of business questions and points of order, both of which allow members briefly to draw attention to matters which concern them. These must, strictly speaking, relate to the internal procedures of the House, but the Speaker customarily gives considerable latitude. These devices have the advantage of being available in the well-publicised middle of the parliamentary day. Finally, there are public petitions which members can present on behalf of their constituents. These are published in *Hansard*.

These examples suggest that a sophisticated knowledge of the procedures of the House can be used tactically to some effect. On the other hand it is easy for a member of Parliament to avoid following up a complaint from a constituent, by passing it to another agency. There is, however, considerable evidence that members habitually deal with grievances outside the formal parliamentary framework, acting in effect as generalist welfare offices (see Rawlings, 1986). A letter from an MP is likely to be dealt with at a higher level in the civil service hierarchy than would otherwise be the case. On the other hand, MPs lack the expertise and resources to be in a position to follow up complaints in detail.

12.6.1 The Parliamentary Commissioner for Administration

The Parliamentary Commissioner for Administration (PCA) investigates on behalf of Parliament complaints by citizens against the central government and certain other bodies (Parliamentary Commissioner Act 1967; Parliamentary and Health Services Commissioners Act 1987; Parliamentary Commissioner Act 1994). Popularly known as the 'ombudsman', the PCA enjoys similar salary and security of tenure to a superior court judge. The PCA has a discretion whether or not to investigate any particular case although this is subject to judicial review (see *R*. v. *Parliamentary Commissioner ex parte Dyer* (1994)).

Individuals who claim to have suffered 'injustice in consequence of maladministration' can enlist the aid of the ombudsman. In this respect and others the Parliamentary Commissioner's powers are similar to those of the local commissioners (Chapter 8). There are considerable limitations on the powers of the PCA as follows:

(i) Important areas of central government activity are excluded from his jurisdiction. These include foreign affairs, state security (including passports), legal proceedings, criminal investigations, government contracts, commercial activities other than compulsory purchase of land (but statutory powers exercised by contractors under privatisation arrangements are within the ombudsman's jurisdiction), civil service employment matters and the granting by the Crown of honours, awards and privileges.

(ii) Complaints must be in writing within 12 months of the decision complained of.

(iii) Complaints must be made to a member of Parliament. It is up to the MP whether to request the ombudsman, to intervene and the ombudsman cannot be approached directly by the citizen. There has been considerable criticism of this rule. MPs, it has been suggested, prefer to take the credit for redressing grievances themselves and may therefore be reluctant to refer to the ombudsman. Conversely, MPs may be unclear about the ombudsman's power and refer inappropriate cases, or even pass the buck by referring cases indiscriminately (see Drewry and Harlow, 1990). A bill to allow direct citizen access to the ombudsman was introduced in 2000 but did not become law.

(iv) The ombudsman cannot normally investigate cases where the citizen has a legal remedy but he has a discretion to do so. The position is similar to that of the local ombudsman (Chapter 8).

(v) The ombudsman has no power to enforce his findings. Unlike the local ombudsman he does not have the sanction of publicity. His only power is to report to the MP who enlisted his aid. If he has found injustice caused by maladministration and considers that it has not been remedied he may also lay a report before Parliament.

There is a select committee of the House of Commons to oversee the ombudsman's work. Reflecting the convention of ministerial responsibility, it is for the minister concerned to decide whether to give effect to the recommendations, for example by compensating the victim of the injustice, or improving departmental procedures. Government departments have usually accepted the ombudsman's recommendations but much depends on the attitude of the House of Commons (see for example HC Deb., 6 August 1975, Col. 532).

(vi) The ombudsman's investigations are private (s. 7 (2)). The ombudsman can see documents and interview civil servants and other witnesses and the normal plea of government confidentiality cannot be used against him (s. 8 (3)). However, cabinet documents can be excluded (s. 8 (4)) and the ombudsman must not name individual civil servants in his report.

Summary

12.1 Procedure in the House is regulated by standing orders and by the Speaker who has a duty to safeguard all interests. We outlined the lawmaking procedure as it applies to public bills and private bills. We then looked at the procedural framework within which the Commons attempts to control public finance, to supervise the executive and to redress citizens' grievances. The timetable is largely under the control of the government as well as procedural devices for cutting short debate. However, there are opportunities such as 'opposition days', parliamentary questions, adjournment and emergency debates for backbenchers and the opposition to intervene.

12.2 There are mechanisms for approving government spending and taxation proposals and for scrutinising government expenditure, notably the office of Comptroller and Auditor General who scrutinise past government expenditure and report to the Public Accounts Committee of the Commons. In general, however, the House of Commons is not equipped for the detailed control of government expenditure. In recent years the emphasis has switched to internal controls over expenditure through the Treasury, through prescribing 'targets' or limits on spending and by delegating financial responsibility to individual officials. These devices have implications for the constitutional doctrine of ministerial responsibility.

12.3 Other devices for parliamentary control of the executive include specialist select committees and the Parliamentary Commissioner for Administration who investigates citizens' grievances and reports to the House of Commons. These devices have implications for ministerial responsibility. This is because (i) they involve investigating the activities of civil servants; and (ii) they raise questions about the relationship between ministers and the House of Commons. Select committees provide a valuable means of publicising issues but have weak powers and are subject to influence by the executive. The extent to which select committees can scrutinise the activities of executive agencies is unclear.

12.4   Delegated legislation is often required to be laid before the House although unless the affirmative procedure is used it may not get serious scrutiny. The Joint Committee on Statutory Instruments monitors delegated legislation on constitutional grounds.

12.5   The House of Lords regulates its own procedure. The Lord Chancellor presides but does not have the disciplinary powers available to the Speaker. Subject to these considerations, procedure in the Commons is dominated by the government through its power to propose business and its control of a majority of votes. Government proposals take up most of the available time. Government business is so large and complex that detailed scrutiny by the House is impossible. Members of Parliament have no privileged access to government information so that their debate is not especially well informed.

12.6   The conventional assessment of Parliament is that it has become subservient to the executive, primarily because its members have capitulated to party loyalty reinforced by the electoral system and by the dual role of ministers as members of both executive and Parliament. Parliament, according to this view, is at its worst as a method of controlling government finance, poor at supervising the executive and lawmaking but better at redressing individual grievances, although this owes a lot to the work of members outside the formal parliamentary procedures and to the statutory Parliamentary Commissioner who investigates citizens' grievances on behalf of Parliament.

12.7   On the other hand, Parliament provides a forum where the executive must defend itself in public and expose the strengths and weaknesses of its leaders. The possibility of defeat in an election may encourage members to distance themselves from an unpopular government and act as a limited constitutional check.

Further Reading

Brazier, *Constitutional Practice*, chapters 8, 11, pp. 204–31, 243–62.
Brazier (1988) 'The financial powers of the House of Lords' *Anglo American Law Review* 131.
Clothier, C. (1986) 'The value of an ombudsman' *Public Law* 204.
Harden *et al.*, Audit, *Accounting Officers and Accountability: The Pergau Dam Affair* [1994] PL 526.
Harden (1993) 'Money and the constitution: financial control reporting and audit' 13 *Legal Studies* 16.
Hennessy, *The Hidden Wiring*, chapter 6.
Jowell and Oliver, *The Changing Constitution*, chapter 8.
Leyland and Woods, *Administrative Law, Facing the Future: Old Constraints and New Horizons*, chapters 3, 4.
Silk, Wallers, *How Parliament Works*.
Turpin, *British Government and the Constitution, Text, Cases and Materials*, chapter 7.
Waldron, *Law and Disagreement*, chapters 2, 3, 5.
White, Harden, Donnelly, *Audit, Accounting Officers, and Accountability, the Pergau Dam Affair* [1994] Public Law 526.

Exercises

12.1   Explain and illustrate the difference between a public bill, a private bill and a hybrid bill. What parliamentary procedures apply in each case?

12.2 To what extent does Parliament supervise the making of delegated legislation?

12.3 'The key to democracy is the power to control public finance'. Is the UK constitution democratic in this sense?

12.4 Explain the extent to which the government of the day can control the parliamentary process.

12.5 Examine the strengths and weaknesses of select committees and parliamentary questions as a means of controlling the executive.

12.6 Compare the procedures of the House of Commons and House of Lords. To what extent do these reflect the different constitutional functions of the two Houses?

12.7 Explain the constitutional similarities and differences between the Parliamentary Commissioner for Administration and the Parliamentary Commissioner for Standards.

12.8 The government proposes to introduce the following measures at the beginning of the parliamentary session 2002–3. The House of Lords has declared its firm opposition to all of them. Advise the government.

- A bill to extend the life of the present Parliament to 2008. This bill has the support of 70% of the public in an opinion poll.
- A bill to ban foxhunting and to increase the taxation on country houses. In order to comply with an EC Directive the bill must become law by the end of 2003.
- A bill to replace hereditary peers by persons elected by the readers of the *Sun* newspaper.
- A statutory instrument imposing restrictions upon rural fishing rights.

13 The Crown

13.1 The Nature of the Crown

We saw in Chapter 4 that UK law has no concept of the state as an entity and sometimes uses the notion of the Crown as a substitute. However, the Crown is an obscure concept, particularly as to whether the Crown and the Queen are the same. The Queen/Crown is (i) part of the legislature; (ii) the formal executive of the UK as a whole and of the devolved governments of Wales, Scotland and Northern Ireland; (iii) head of the Church of England; (iv) head of the armed forces; (v) source of the authority of the judiciary; (vi) prosecutor. The Queen also has primitive ceremonial and symbolic functions representing Bagehot's 'dignified' constitution as a focus of authority.

There may be conflicts between different aspects of the Crown. In *R.* v. *Preston* [1993] 4 All ER 638 at 663 Lord Mustill said 'the Crown is an ambiguous expression often used to denote those who conduct prosecutions on behalf of the state but on other occasions denoting the state as an indivisible entity'. In that case there was a conflict between the Crown's duty as prosecutor to disclose relevant material to the defence and its wider security duties involving secret surveillance.

There is not one Crown but many (*R.* v. *Secretary of State for Foreign and Commonwealth Affairs ex parte Alberta Indian Association* (1982)). Australia, New Zealand and Canada and several other former UK territories recognise the Crown as their Head of State. The office happens for historical reasons to be held by the Queen of the UK, but in each case she has a separate title and responsibilities. This is probably not the case in relation to the few remaining UK dependent territories. The Queen is also Head of the Commonwealth, a title of symbolic importance which carries no legal powers, but probably still has political significance. Indeed, a conflict could arise between the Queen's role as Head of the Commonwealth and her duty to accept the advice of the British government. For example in the mid-1980s the commonwealth, contrary to the wishes of the UK government, wanted to ban sporting and trade links with South Africa because of apartheid.

The legal nature of the Crown is unclear. When speaking of the head of state we refer to the Queen, but when speaking of the executive we refer to the Crown. It may be that there is no legal significance in this terminology. For example the Scotland Act 1998 refers to the executive power as vested in 'Her Majesty' (s. 52). However, the Crown in its official capacity must be separated from the Queen since, under the Crown Proceedings Act 1947, the Crown can be sued but not the Queen in her personal capacity. The Crown is often said to be a corporation sole (Maitland, 1901). A corporation sole is an office being a legal entity separate from the individual who holds the office at any given time and which therefore exists permanently, not being affected by the death of the office holder. A bishop, for example, is a corporation sole.

An alternative view which accommodates the reality of modern government is that the Crown is a corporation aggregate akin to a company. In *Town Investments Ltd* v. *Department of the Environment* (1977) the question arose whether an office lease taken by a minister was vested in the minister or the Crown since in the latter case it would benefit from Crown immunities from taxation. The House of Lords held that the lease was vested in the Crown on the basis that a minister was part of the Crown. Lord Diplock thought that the Crown was a fiction describing the executive. Lord Simon of Glaisdale explained (at 831) that the expression 'the Crown' symbolises the powers of government that were formerly wielded by the wearer of the crown, and reflects the historical development of the executive as that of offices hived off from the royal household. He stated (at 833) that the legal concept best fitted to the contemporary situation was to consider the Crown as a corporation aggregate headed by the Queen and made up of 'the departments of state including ministers at their heads'. His Lordship added two riders: 'First the legal concept still does not correspond to the political reality. The Queen does not command those legally her servants. On the contrary she acts on the formally tendered collective advice of the Cabinet'. Secondly, 'when the Queen is referred to by the symbolic title of "Her Majesty" it is the whole corporation aggregate which is generally indicated. This distinction between "the Queen" and "Her Majesty" reflects the ancient distinction between "the King's two bodies", the "natural" and the "politic"' (see *Duchy of Lancaster Case* (1567) 1 Plow 325 at 327). Sir Robert Armstrong, a former Cabinet Secretary, said that 'for all practical purposes, the Crown is represented by the government of the day' (see Hennessey, 1989, p. 346).

On the other hand, where statutory powers are conferred specifically upon individual ministers as is normally the case, ministers have no special immunity. In *M*. v. *Home Office* (1993), the Home Secretary attempted to rely on Crown immunity in order to deport an immigrant in defiance of a court order. The House of Lords held that he was liable in his official capacity for contempt of court. In that case Parliament had conferred the power in question directly upon the Secretary of State, whereas in *Town Investments* the lease had been made 'for and on behalf of her majesty'. Similarly, while the Crown itself retains certain immunities, a Crown servant who commits a legal wrong is personally liable, thus vindicating the rule of law.

13.2   The Queen

13.2.1   Succession to the Crown

Under the 1688 settlement Parliament conferred on itself the power to appoint the sovereign. The Act of Settlement 1701 provides that the Crown is to be held by the direct descendants of Princess Sophia (the grand-daughter of the deposed James II). The holder of the Crown must be a Protestant and must not marry a Catholic. The rules of descent are based upon the medieval law governing succession to land. Preference is given to males over females and to the elder over the younger. The land law rules required sisters to hold land equally (co-parcenaries). However, in the case of the Crown the first-born prevails (although the matter has not been litigated). Since the point of these rules is that they are arbitrary, in the sense that personal merit or public choice is irrelevant, we need not pursue them further. The succession has been altered only once when Edward VIII abdicated in 1936 (His Majesty's Declaration of Abdication Act 1936). By convention the consent to abdication is required from the independent commonwealth countries of which the Queen is head of state. It is not settled whether the monarch has the power to abdicate without an Act of Parliament. Since monarchy is a status conferred by law and without a voluntary act, the answer is probably not. The Crown's titles are also determined by statute (Royal Titles Act 1953).

When the monarch dies, the successor immediately and automatically becomes monarch. A special Accession Council, composed mainly of members of the House of Lords, proclaims this. The proclamation is later confirmed by the Privy Council. Whether these bodies have a power of veto is unclear. Certainly the subsequent coronation ceremony has no legal significance being purely symbolic and theatrical. If the monarch is a minor, ill or absent abroad, the royal functions are exercised by a regent or councillors of state (see Regency Acts 1937–53). In such cases certain bills cannot be assented to, most importantly a bill for altering the succession to the Crown.

13.2.2 Financing the monarchy

Even in her private capacity the Queen is exempt from taxes unless statute specifically provides otherwise. The Queen has, however, entered into a voluntary agreement to pay tax on current income and personal capital. Many of the royal expenses are funded by government departments, such as the upkeep of Crown buildings, travel and entertaining political dignitaries. The basic expenses of the monarchy and of those members of the royal family who perform what they regard as public duties are funded from the Civil List. This is an amount granted by Parliament at the beginning of each reign. It consists of an annual payment that can be increased by statutory instrument made by the Treasury subject to veto by the House of Commons (Civil List Acts 1952–72).

13.2.3 The functions of the monarchy

Since 1688 the functions and personal powers of the monarchy have gradually been reduced. The 1688 revolution left the monarch in charge of running the executive but dependent upon Parliament for money and lawmaking power. The monarch retained substantial personal influence until the late nineteenth century, mainly through the power to appoint ministers and to influence elections in the local constituencies. Until after the reign of George V (1910–1934) monarchs occasionally intervened in connection with ministerial appointments and policy issues. The abdication of Edward VIII (1936) probably spelt the end of any political role for the monarch. Moreover the office of prime minister, which was originally that of chief minister, is now becoming confused with that of head of state, thus putting the legitimacy of the monarchy into question.

The modern functions of the monarchy can be outlined as follows:

1. To symbolise the nation, participating for this purpose in ceremonies and public entertainments. It is often said that the popularity and public acceptance of the monarchy is directly related to the fact that the monarch has little political power and is primarily an entertainer. It is not clear why a modern democracy requires a personalised 'leader'. There is a strong element of superstition inherent in the notion of monarchy, hence the importance of the link between the monarch and the Established Church.
2. To 'advise, encourage and to warn' (Bagehot, Crossman (ed), 1963, p. 111). The monarch, supported by a private secretary has access

to all government documents and regularly meets the prime minister. The monarch is entitled to express views in private to the government but there is no convention as to the weight to be given to them.

3. Certain formal acts. The monarch must normally accept the advice of ministers. These include:

  (i) assent to statutes. Today this function is usually performed on the Queen's behalf by a commission;

 (ii) consents to Orders in Council;

(iii) appointments of ministers, ambassadors, bishops, judges, and other officials;

(iv) royal proclamations, for example dissolving and summoning Parliament or declaring a state of emergency;

 (v) ratifying solemn treaties;

(vi) granting charters to universities, professional bodies, etc. These bestow the seal of state approval and also incorporate the body in question so that it can be treated as a separate person in law;

(vii) awarding peerages, honours and medals. The Queen has certain personal powers in this respect.

13.2.4   Personal powers of the monarch

In a few cases it is believed that the monarch can and indeed must exercise personal power. This is a matter of convention with little precedent. There are internal cabinet office guidance documents on the matter but the fact that unpublished sources have any weight at all is a sad reflection on the culture of those who exercise power. The governing principle seems to be that the head of state is the ultimate guardian of the constitution and must intervene where the normal machinery of government has broken down. Important occasions calling for the intervention of the monarchy are as follows:

- The appointment of a prime minister. The Queen must appoint the person who can form a government with the support of the House of Commons. This usually means the leader of the majority party as determined by a general election. Nowadays each party elects its leader. In the unlikely event of the electoral process not producing a clear winner the existing prime minister must probably be permitted to attempt to form a government. Failing that, the Queen should summon the leader of the next largest party. If that fails there is disagreement as to what should happen, and in particular as to whether the monarch has any personal discretion. On one view the Queen should attempt to find someone else capable of commanding a majority, but it is not clear whom, if anyone, she should consult. For example, should she consult the outgoing prime minister? According to another view the Queen should automatically dissolve Parliament causing another election. The guiding principle seems to be that she must try to determine the electorate's preference.

- The dismissal of a government and the dissolution of Parliament. If a government is defeated on a vote of confidence in the House of Commons but refuses to resign or to advise a dissolution the Queen could probably dismiss the government. This has not happened in Britain since 1783, but happened in Australia in 1975. In such a case the opposition, if it could form a majority, could be placed in office or the Queen could dissolve Parliament, thus putting the case to the people through an election. It has been suggested that the Queen could dismiss a government that violates a basic constitutional principle, for example by proposing legislation to abolish elections. In order to dissolve Parliament the Queen would require a meeting of the Privy Council. It would therefore be convenient as a temporary measure for her to appoint the Leader of the Opposition as prime minister who would then formally advise her in favour of a dissolution (see *Adegbenro* v. *Akintola* [1963] AC 614 at 631).

- Refusing a dissolution. This possibility arises because of the convention that the prime minister may advise the monarch to dissolve Parliament. The Queen might refuse a dissolution if the prime minister is acting clearly unconstitutionally, for example if a prime minister whose party lost a general election immediately requested a second dissolution or where a prime minister falls personally foul of his party. Unfortunately there are no clear-cut precedents. It is likely that the Queen could refuse a dissolution only where there is a viable alternative government and a general election would be harmful to the national interest, although it seems difficult for anyone, let alone the Queen, to make such a judgement. A dissolution has not been refused in Britain this century but one was refused by the Governor-General of Canada in 1926. The Governor-General's decision was later rejected by the electorate.

- The Queen might refuse a prime ministerial request to appoint peers to the House of Lords where the reason for the request is to flood the Lords with government supporters. The precedents (1832 and 1910–11) suggest that the monarch would have to agree to such a request but only after a general election. This matter is therefore closely connected with the power to dissolve Parliament.

- The royal assent. The monarch has not refused assent to legislation since 1709. It appears to be a strong convention that royal assent must always be given. However, the Queen might refuse royal assent where the refusal is on the advice of the prime minister, for example in the unlikely event of a private member's bill being approved by Parliament against the wishes of the government. Here two conventions clash. It is submitted that the better view is that she must still give assent because the will of Parliament has a higher constitutional status than that of the executive.

13.3   Crown Immunities

The Crown has certain privileges in litigation. At common law no legal action would lie against the Crown in respect of its property rights and contracts, or in respect of injuries caused by the Crown (torts). Nor was the Crown bound by Acts of Parliament. This obvious gap in the rule of law was avoided by the Crown's practice of voluntarily submitting to the jurisdiction of the courts. In the case of actions involving property and contract this was through a procedure called a 'petition of right'. In the case of a tort, the individual Crown servant who committed the tort could be made liable and, where it was not clear who was responsible, the Crown would nominate a defendant, for example where a visitor to military premises was accidentally injured. In either case the Crown would pay the damages. Dicey did not regard Crown immunity as seriously threatening the rule of law, pointing out that the individual Crown servant could always be held liable and that in practice the Crown would usually be willing to stand behind its employees. This seems a little flimsy and indeed is counter to the republican ethics according to which it is offensive to rely upon voluntary forbearances.

The maxim that 'the king can do no wrong' is a common law principle that goes beyond the procedural rule that the king cannot be sued in his own courts. It means that wrongdoing or bad faith cannot be attributed to the Crown. The monarch has no power to do or authorise a wrong. For example, the Crown at common law could not be liable for wrongs committed by its employees because unlawful acts of its employees were necessarily committed without its authority. The maxim has never prevented the courts from deciding whether a particular action falls within the lawful powers of the Crown. Invalid acts are not the same as wrongful acts (see *Dunlop* v. *Woollahra City Council* (1982)).

13.3.1 The Crown Proceedings Act 1947

This Act was intended to make the Crown liable as if it were a private person for breaches of contract, for the wrongs of its servants and for injuries caused by defective Crown property, etc. Section 1 permits action for breach of contact against the Crown; s. 2 permits action in tort, but only where a private person would be liable in the same circumstances. However, the Act still leaves the Crown with several special privileges. The most important are as follows:

1. *No court order can be enforced against the Crown*, so that the plain-tiff's right to damages depends upon the Crown voluntarily paying up. Similarly no injunction lies against the Crown nor against a Crown servant acting on behalf of the Crown (Crown Proceedings Act 1947 s. 21). However, where a function is conferred by statute on a minister directly, an injunction will lie and the protection of the Crown cannot be claimed (*M*. v. *Home Office* (1993)).
2. *In an action for breach of contract the Crown can plead 'executive necessity'*. This means that it can refuse to comply with a contract where it has an overriding power to take some action in the public interest (see the *Amphitrite Case* (1921); *Commissioners of Crown Lands* v. *Page* (1960)). It is unlikely that a court would challenge a minister's view of executive necessity, provided that a plausible justi-fication is given. However, it is not correct to state that the Crown cannot be bound by any contract that hinders its freedom of action, since all contracts do this. There must either be some definite pre-rogative power that overrides the contract, or the contract must con-flict with a statutory duty. For example, governments cannot cancel contracts without compensation merely because of policy changes.
3. In the case of action in tort the 1947 Act contains several restric-tions. The main ones are as follows:
   (i) The Crown is not liable for the acts of its 'officers' unless the individual officer was appointed directly or indirectly by the Crown and paid wholly from central government funds (s. 2 (6)). (The term 'officer' includes all Crown servants and ministers.)
   (ii) The Crown is not in any circumstances liable for wrongs com-mitted by 'judicial' officers (s. 2 (5)): that is, judges or members of tribunals. A person exercising judicial functions also enjoys considerable personal immunity (see Chapter 17).
   (iii) Until 1987 a member of the armed forces who was injured on duty by another member of the armed forces or while on

military property could not sue the Crown if the injury was pensionable under military regulations (s. 10). This sometimes caused injustice because it was irrelevant whether or not the victim actually qualified for a pension. The Crown Proceedings (Armed Forces) Act 1987 abolishes this rule but authorises the Secretary of State to restore it in times of war or national emergency (see below 15.4).

4. *The Crown is not bound by an Act of Parliament unless it expressly or by necessary implication binds the Crown.* Necessary implication is a strict notion. It is not sufficient to show that the Crown is likely to cause unfairness and inconvenience or even that the exemption is against the public interest (*Lord Advocate* v. *Dumbarton District Council* (1990)). It has to be established that the statute would be unworkable unless the Crown were bound (see *Cooper* v. *Hawkins* (1904) – speed limit did not bind Crown). It is debatable whether the Crown can take the benefit of statutes, even though it is not bound by them. For example, the Crown can evict a tenant free of statutory restrictions, but could the Crown as a tenant resist eviction by a private landlord by relying on the same statutory rights that it can ignore as a landlord?

5. The Queen cannot be prosecuted or sued in her personal capacity.

13.3.2   Act of State

The Crown is not liable for injuries caused in connection with bona fide acts of government policy, provided that the action is authorised or subsequently ratified by the Crown (for example, *Nissan* v. *A-G* (1970) – British troops billeted in Cyprus hotel – not an Act of State); *Buron* v. *Denman* (1848) – British naval officer setting fire to barracks in West Africa in order to liberate slaves – Crown subsequently confirmed the action). The defence of Act of State is of little modern significance, being largely a product of the days of imperial aggression. Indeed when the Human Rights Act 1998 comes into force the defence of Act of State may fall foul of Art. 6 of the ECHR – the right to a fair trial (see *Osman* v. *UK* (1999); Chapter 15).

As it stands at present the defence of Act of State cannot apply within the UK except against 'enemy aliens', that is, citizens of countries with which we are formally at war (*Johnstone* v. *Pedlar* (1921) – US citizen maltreated – Crown liable). This is because the Crown owes a duty to protect everyone who is even temporarily on British soil. Indeed the defence may not be available against a British subject anywhere in the world. In *Nissan*'s case (above) the House of Lords expressed divided views on the point. It is not whether this means any British passport holder or a British citizen under the British Nationality Act 1981 or includes citizens of dependent territories. The underlying principle is that British subjects owe allegiance (loyalty) to the Crown, whether they wish to or not, and therefore the Crown has a duty to protect them (see also *Walker* v. *Baird* (1982)); *Johnstone* v. *Pedlar* (above)). On the other hand it seems unfair to favour people with no substantial link with the UK merely because they happen to hold British passports. As against this, a person with a British passport, even one who has never visited Britain, owes sufficient allegiance to the Crown to be hanged for treason (see *Joyce* v. *DPP* (1946)).

It is sometimes said that there are two kinds of 'Act of State'. One is the defence mentioned above. The other consists of recognised kinds of high-level policy acts directed at other countries: for example, making treaties, declaring war, annexing or giving up territory, recognising new governments or granting diplomatic immunity (see Diplomatic Privileges Act 1964). All these are examples of sovereign powers with which the courts will not interfere. British subjects along with others may be incidentally affected by this kind of Act of State. For example, in *Cook* v. *Sprigg* (1899) the Crown annexed Pondoland and refused to honour railway concessions granted to British subjects by the former government (see also *West Rand Central Gold Mining Co.* v. *R.* (1905)).

Indeed this kind of Act of State may affect rights in domestic law. For example a formal declaration by the Crown as to the existence of a state of war (*R.* v. *Bottril ex parte Kuchenmeister* (1947)), the recognition of a foreign government (*Carl Zeiss Stiftung* v. *Rayner & Keeler Ltd (No. 2)* (1967)), the conferring of diplomatic immunity (*Engelke* v. *Musmann* (1928); *Mighell* v. *Sultan of Johore* (1894)), or military needs (*Chandler* v. *DPP* (1964)) would be conclusive declarations and not challengeable in the courts. They might invalidate existing obligations or prevent legal actions or create criminal liability.

13.4 The Royal Prerogative

The Royal Prerogative is the residue of special powers, rights and immunities vested in the Crown under the common law. There is little democratic control over officials claiming to act under the prerogative since parliamentary approval is not required. Medieval legal theory did not regard the Crown as either the source of law or as above the law, but did confer special rights on the monarch. Some of these were based upon the position of the monarch as chief landowner within the feudal system. Others derived from the responsibility of the monarch as the 'fount of justice' to keep the peace and to defend the realm. Thus the most significant prerogative concerns declaring war and deploying the armed forces. This duality may have corresponded to the distinction drawn in seventeenth-century cases between the 'ordinary' and the 'absolute' prerogatives, the latter being discretionary powers vested in the king and arguably beyond the reach of the courts (see *Bates Case* (1606)).

13.4.1   Historical sketch

During the sixteenth century, theories of absolute monarchy became dominant in Europe, but were less influential in England. Nevertheless, absolutist theories – the intellectual fashion of the day – strengthened the Crown's hand in asserting prerogative power. The Tudors (1485–1603) governed successfully and without seriously antagonising Parliament, through 'prerogative courts' including the notorious Star Chamber. Much law was made by royal proclamation and it is controversial as to when statute was regarded as necessary. A statute had at that time the status of an authoritative court judgement concerned with declaring rather than changing the law. Social regulation fell within the prerogative; for example, a proclamation of 1546 closed London brothels, and one of 1530 prohibited the publication of unauthorised religious books. Another proclamation of 1530 required 'vagabonds and beggars' to be stripped and beaten. It could, however, be argued that these exercises of power were not examples of true lawmaking but concerned the enforcement of existing law.

In 1611 it was made clear that the King can legislate only within areas of prerogative allowed to him by the general law (*Case of Proclamations* (1611)). The debate therefore shifted to exploring the limits of the prerogative. The Stuarts attempted to extend the prerogative and to impose taxes and override the ordinary law. However, even they submitted themselves to the courts and, in a series of famous cases punctuating the political conflicts of the time, the scope of the prerogative was inconclusively argued (for example, *Bates Case* (1606); *R.* v. *Hampden* (1637); *Godden* v. *Hales* (1686)).

The short-lived settlement of 1641 between Charles I and Parliament saw the abolition of the prerogative courts. One legacy of these events was a deep-seated distrust among English lawyers of the idea of a separation between 'public' and 'private law', 'public law' being associated with prerogative courts. This led to Dicey's belief that the subjection of government and governed alike to the ordinary law was an essential part of the 'rule of law'. As we saw in Chapter 4, the conflict between King and Parliament was resolved in 1688. The Bill of Rights outlawed certain aspects of the prerogative including the power to suspend laws without parliamentary consent. The power to dispense with laws (that is, to free individuals from penalties) was abolished only 'as it hath been assumed and exercised of late', thus preserving the prerogative of mercy which is exercised in modern times by the Home Secretary. The Bill of Rights also banned taxation under the Royal Prerogative. Modern judges have taken this further by refusing to imply a power to tax directly or indirectly without very clear statutory language (see *A-G* v. *Wilts United Dairies* (1921); *Congreve* v. *Home Office* (1976); *Macarthy and Stone Ltd* v. *Richmond LBC* (1991)).

The 1688 settlement provides the framework of the modern law. This can be summarised as follows:

- In principle the Royal Prerogative remains but must give way to statute.
- No new prerogatives can be created (see *BBC* v. *Johns* (1965)) but new applications of existing prerogatives are possible.
- The prerogative can be controlled by the courts, although the extent of such control depends upon the type of prerogative power in question and the context.

13.4.2 Prerogative or prerogatives?

Influenced by Locke's *True End of Civil Government* and Blackstone's *Commentaries*, Lord Denning in *Laker Airways Ltd* v. *Department of Trade and Industry* (1977) considered that the Crown had a general discretionary power to act for the public good in certain spheres of governmental activity for which the law had otherwise made no provision (at p. 192). This suggests that the state may benefit from a single, over-arching power to interfere in private rights where it perceives an important public benefit may result, especially in times of emergency. This interpretation is, however, inconsistent with *Entick* v. *Carrington* (1765). Here the court emphatically rejected a claim of 'executive necessity' that officers of the state had a general power to enter and search private property in the absence of express statutory or common law powers (see also *IRC* v. *Rossminster* (1980)). Lord Denning's views were not supported by the other members of the Court of Appeal. They are also inconsistent with ideas of limited government. The better view is that, although the Crown has certain discretionary powers in relation to emergencies, such as the requisitioning of ships, the prerogative comprises a finite number of powers rather than one general power to act for the public good (Vincenzi, 1998).

13.4.3   Modern prerogative powers

Prerogative powers are exercised either directly by ministers or by prerogative orders in council. The latter requires a formal meeting of the Privy Council (a quorum of four) in the presence of the monarch. Many prerogative powers remain of central importance. Prerogative orders in Council, although laws, are not published in an easily accessible form, thus violating an important aspect of the rule of law. Prerogative powers include the making of treaties, the waging of war, and indeed most matters concerned with foreign affairs, defence and national security although the security services are now subject to a loose statutory regime. Control over the civil service and armed forces is based on prerogative powers, although, particularly in respect of the army, intermingled with statute. There is an uncertain and potentially threatening area of prerogative power concerned with 'keeping the peace' and defending the realm. This has been used to justify arming the police (*R.* v. *Secretary of State for the Home Department ex parte Northumbria Police Authority* (1988)) and may justify entry to private property (see *Burmah Oil Co. Ltd* v. *Lord Advocate* (1965)). The ancient writ of *ne exeat regno* prevents persons from leaving the country. Although *ne exeat regno* is sometimes regarded as obsolete there is no doctrine of obsolescence in English law (see *Felton* v. *Callis* (1969); *Parsons* v. *Burke* (1971)). Other important prerogatives include the following:

- the monarch's powers in relation to the appointment of ministers and the summoning and dissolving of Parliament (above);
- various Crown immunities (below);
- the prerogative power to pardon offenders resides with the Home Secretary;
- the Attorney-General has a prerogative power to institute legal proceedings in the public interest. There is also a prerogative power to stop criminal proceedings by issuing a *nolle prosequi*;
- powers relating to the Church of England;
- '*parens patriae*': the care of children and other vulnerable groups although this is now largely regulated by statute;
- the administration of charities and trusts through the courts again subject to statutory regulation;

- the award of peerages and other titles, medals, etc., the Crown being the 'fount of honour';
- the granting of Royal Charters to bodies such as universities, learned societies, charities or professional associations which gives the body the status of a legal person and signifies state approval of its activities;
- the appointing and receiving of ambassadors and the issue of passports.

13.4.4   Two kinds of prerogative power?

There is ambiguity as to what a prerogative power is. Blackstone, the eighteenth-century authority, whose view seems to be technically correct, regards the prerogative as confined to the special powers which the Crown preserves 'over and above all other powers and out of the ordinary course of the common law' (1 *Bl. Comm.* 239). A century later, however, Dicey described the prerogative as including all the non-statutory powers of the Crown including the 'private law' powers of ownership, contracting, etc., possessed by the Crown as a person in common with everyone else (1915, p. 429).

Professor Wade has endorsed Blackstone's view arguing, for example, that the control of civil servants is not really a matter of prerogative since anyone can employ others (Wade, 1980, pp. 46–53). This does not seem to be the best example. The Crown's overriding right to dismiss a civil servant or member of the armed forces is surely sufficiently 'special' to put that matter in the prerogative camp. Orders in Council relating to the civil service are legally enforceable, whereas private employment depends on either contract or statute. Wade would also exclude the power to issue passports and the power to make treaties from being prerogative powers since these are voluntary executive acts that do not in themselves have legal consequences.

Blackstone's distinction seems unreal in that all these Crown powers are important politically, and involve wide discretion which can be exercised independently of Parliament. There is much to be said for Dicey's view and for treating all non-statutory powers of the Crown alike. Indeed the modern cases seem to support Dicey. In *CCSU* v. *Minister for Civil Service* (1985), the House of Lords treated the control of the civil service as part of the Royal Prerogative holding that they could review the validity of an Order in Council varying the terms of employment of certain civil servants. Lord Diplock expressed the view that the distinction between special and ordinary powers of the Crown is artificial and would regard all common law powers of the

Crown as part of the prerogative. In *R. v. Criminal Injuries Compensation Board ex parte Lain* (1967) a government scheme to pay compensation to the victims of crime was treated as a matter of prerogative, thus enabling the court to review errors of law made by the board which was set up to run the scheme. The scheme was financed out of money provided by Parliament but was not then statutory. Since anyone can give away money, this scheme would not count as Royal Prerogative under the Blackstone/Wade definition.

13.4.5   Parliamentary scrutiny

The exercise of some (but not all) prerogative powers can be subject to parliamentary scrutiny. However, in practice, effective scrutiny is limited (Syrett, 1998; Munro, 1999, pp. 275–8). In part this is because of the general weakness of parliamentary scrutiny of ministerial action. Another reason is that, by convention, the prime minister cannot be questioned about advice given to the sovereign concerning her personal prerogative powers, such as the grant of honours, the appointment and dismissal of privy councillors and the dissolution of Parliament. Whether their exclusion is justifiable upon any basis other than the mystique that has traditionally attached to the prerogative is debatable. They involve wide discretionary powers, but that in itself is an argument for rather than against political accountability.

Most prerogative powers, such as the deployment of the armed forces, do not need formal parliamentary approval, so that opportunity for debate is limited. Other prerogative powers relate to foreign relationships, national security matters and the prerogative of mercy on which ministers sometimes refuse to be questioned. However, Parliament, if it wished, could insist on investigating. Parliament also retains ultimate power because of its control over government spending although in the case of the prerogative the exercise of this in any detail is unrealistic.

13.4.6   Judicial control over the prerogative

In the past the courts exercised only limited control over the prerogative. If a prerogative power was disputed a court could determine whether it existed, and (if it existed) what it empowered the executive to do, but the monarch (that is, a minister) was the only judge of how to exercise the power. An example includes *Prohibitions del Roy* (1607) 12 Co Rep 63 in which the court decided that the king did not have a prerogative power personally to sit as a judge in court. Another example is the *Saltpetre* case (1607) in which the king was held to have the power in an emergency to enter private land and to be both the sole judge of whether an emergency existed and what measures to take (see also *R.* v. *Hampden* (1637); *A-G* v. *de Keysers Royal Hotel Ltd* (1920)). The courts' approach was contradictory. A power limited to emergencies (as in *Saltpetre*) was not really limited at all if its holder can conclusively decide what counts as an emergency.

In *CCSU v Minister for the Civil Service* (1985) the courts asserted a jurisdiction over prerogative powers. A decision made under a pre-rogative power is in principle reviewable on the same basis as a decision made under a statutory power. But this does not mean that this jurisdiction will always be exercised. The power must be of a 'justiciable' nature, which means that it must be suitable for the courts' intervention. This is no longer resolved by looking at the source of the power (statute or prerogative) but upon its subject matter. If the subject matter is amenable to judicial review (i.e., a matter which, under the separation of powers, the courts are entitled to consider) the matter is open to judicial review.

If the subject matter of the decision concerns the rights or legiti-mate expectations of individuals the decision is more likely to be reviewable. For example, reviewable powers now include the power to issue a passport (*R.* v. *Secretary of State for Foreign and Common-wealth Affairs ex parte Everett* (1989)); the power to grant a pardon (*R.* v. *Secretary of State for the Home Department ex parte Bentley* (1993); *A-G of Trinidad and Tobago* v. *Phillips* (1995)), the power to make *ex gratia* payments to the victims of crime (*R.* v. *Criminal Injuries Compensation Board ex parte P* (1995)); the issue of warrants for telephone tapping (*R.* v. *Secretary of State for Home Department ex parte Ruddock* (1987), the policy of discharging homosexuals from the armed service (*R.* v. *Ministry of Defence ex parte Smith* (1996)).

The courts accept that the subject matter of some prerogative powers means that they are not suitable for review. For example, the court will not entertain an application that asserts that a treaty-making power has been unlawfully exercised, nor review the content of a treaty (*R.* v. *Secretary of State for Foreign and Commonwealth Affairs ex parte Rees-Mogg* (1994); *Blackburn* v. *A-G* (1971)). The dichotomy between reviewable and unreviewable powers compels the courts to address the question of which issues are amenable to the judicial process under the separation of powers. This poses questions about the functions of the courts. The reasons for a power being deemed non-justiciable are many and various. These include (i) defer-ence to matters of high policy and to Parliament; (ii) lack of judicial knowledge and effectiveness; (iii) the absence of objective standards; (iv) the need to trust the executive in an emergency; (v) the existence of other remedies; and (vi) worries about hampering government efficiency (see the American case of *Baker* v. *Carr* (1962) for a useful general discussion). A non-justiciable power can in principle be statutory or prerogative but is more likely to be prerogative. Prerogative powers are usually exercised at the highest political levels; many of them concern foreign affairs and emergencies and most of them involve wide subjective discretion.

An indicative but not comprehensive list of non-justiciable powers was offered by Lord Roskill in the *CCSU* case ([1985] AC 374, at 418). The making of treaties and other high-level political decisions involving foreign governments, the disposition of the armed forces, and the Attorney-General's powers to commence legal actions have all been held to be unreviewable (see *Blackburn* v. *A-G* (1971); *Chandler* v. *DPP* (1964); *Gouriet* v. *UPOW* (1978)). To these can be added the appointment and dismissal of ministers, the grant of honours and the summoning and dissolution of Parliament. Lord Roskill's list also included the prerogative of mercy. However, this power has subsequently become reviewable (ex parte *Bentley*, above). Thus the courts are still developing the boundary between justiciable and non-justiciable powers. It is unlikely, however, that other powers mentioned by Lord Roskill would be justiciable in the absence of a fundamental remodelling of the separation of powers.

13.4.7 Prerogative and statute

Parliament being sovereign, statute can abolish a prerogative power although the courts may require express words or necessary implication (*British Coal Corporation* v. *R.* (1935); *De Morgan* v. *Director General of Social Welfare* (1998)). Sometimes an exercise of prerogative power is needed to repeal a statute. For example, the Import, Export and Customs Powers (Defence) Act 1939 was to continue in force until an Order in Council declared that the 'emergency' (the Second World War) was over. No such Order was made and thus the Act continued in force notwithstanding the end of hostilities (*R.* v. *Blackledge, The Times*, May 29th 1995).

If a matter is subject to both a statutory and a prerogative power, the statutory power may supersede the prerogative power (see *A-G* v. *de Keysers Royal Hotel Ltd* (1920); *Laker Airways Ltd* v. *Department of Trade and Industry* (1977)). Whether or not it does so is a matter of interpretation of the statute in question. First, it depends on whether the statute is intended to bind the Crown (see above), and secondly, whether the statute is intended to replace the prerogative.

Where the statute co-exists with a prerogative power it seems the government cannot choose whichever power is most favourable to it but must apply the statute *Laker Airways* suggests that, for statute to prevail, the prerogative and statute do not have to be inconsistent. It is enough that the statute covers the same ground as was formerly regulated by prerogative. In that case the Department of Trade and Industry was held to be bound by a statute regulating the licensing of civil airlines which required an element of competition. It could not therefore rely on its prerogative power to make a treaty for the purpose of preventing Laker from setting up a cut-price airline between London and New York. This broad view seems to conflict with the general principle that the Crown cannot be bound by statute without clear words or necessary implication.

More recently the courts have taken a different approach. The prerogative was not put into abeyance where an apparently comprehensive system of statutory powers existed. In *R.* v. *Secretary of State for the Home Department ex parte Northumbria Police Authority* (1988)) it was held *obiter* that the Home Secretary could use a prerogative power to supply the police with weapons, even though statute placed local authorities in charge of providing police resources. The court said that the prerogative power was suspended only when its exercise was inconsistent with a statutory power. *De Keyser's* case was treated as an example of inconsistency. Purchas LJ suggested that the *De Keyser* principle is qualified where executive action is designed to benefit or protect the individual. In such cases the exercise of prerogative power will be upheld unless statute unequivocally prevents this.

This decision was somewhat surprising since the relevant statute contained no saving for the prerogative. Vincenzi (1998) is critical of it, arguing that the decision is an unprecedented example of the courts permitting the Crown to disregard statutory provisions in its perception of the public interest. He identifies a tension with the Bill of Rights that prohibits the Crown from suspending or dispensing with statute. *R.* v. *Secretary of State for the Home Department ex parte Fire Brigades Union* (1995) seems to support Vincenzi's view. The Secretary of State had statutory power to make a commencement order bringing legislation into force that was intended to establish a particular regime for compensation for victims of crime. It was held that he could not refuse to bring the statute into effect in order to establish a different scheme under the prerogative, since this would frustrate the intention behind the statute, which would become almost impossible to bring into effect (cf. above p. 108). The prerogative power is therefore subject to the important limitation that it must not be exercised in a manner which conflicts with the intention of Parliament. What if the relevant statute is repealed? Does the prerogative power spring to life again, freed from its statutory confinement? Logically the answer should be yes, unless the repealing statute states otherwise (see *A-G* v. *de Keysers Royal Hotel Ltd* at 539; *Burmah Oil Co. Ltd* v. *Lord Advocate* (1965) AC 75 at 143).

13.4.8   Prerogative and human rights

The Human Rights Act 1998, s. 21 enacts that an Order in Council made under the Royal Prerogative is 'primary legislation' for the purposes of the 1998 Act. This means that the court cannot set aside an exercise of the prerogative made by an Order in Council that conflicts with a right protected under the European Convention of Human Rights (Chapter 18). A further consequence of s. 21 is that a public authority is only bound to act in accordance with convention rights unless conflicting primary legislation requires it to act otherwise (s. 6). Since an Order in Council is deemed by s. 21 to be primary legislation, a public authority that acts in accordance with its terms would appear to act lawfully even if in breach of a convention right (see Billings and Ponting, 2001).

Summary

13.1   In this chapter we first discussed the meaning of the term Crown. The Queen as head of state must be distinguished from the Crown as the executive. It is not clear whether the Crown is a corporation sole or a corporation aggregate.

13.2   Succession to the throne depends entirely on statute, thus reinforcing the subordinate nature of the monarchy.

13.3   The monarch has certain personal political powers which should be exercised in times of constitutional crisis. These include the appointment of a prime minister, the dissolution of Parliament and the appointment of peers.

13.4   At common law the Crown was immune from legal action. Some of this immunity has been reduced by the Crown Proceedings Act 1947, but the Crown is still immune from enforcement and has certain special defences including 'Act of State' and 'executive necessity' in contract. There is, however, no general doctrine of state necessity as justifying interference with private rights. Certain acts of the Crown give rise to immunity from legal liability.

13.5 The Crown's executive powers derive from three sources:
- Statutes.
- The Royal Prerogative – that is, the residue of special common law powers peculiar to the monarch. While many prerogative powers have been surrendered or are obsolete, some, notably in foreign affairs, remain important. The prerogative must give way to statute and cannot be used to make law or raise taxation. No new prerogative powers can be created. Prerogative powers can be reviewed by the courts unless they concern a 'non-justiciable' subject matter such as foreign relationships. In practice, political control over prerogative power is limited.
- Powers possessed by virtue of the fact that the Crown is a legal person with basically the same rights and duties as an adult human being. The Crown can therefore make contracts, own property, distribute money, etc. There is a dispute as to whether this kind of power is part of the Royal Prerogative.

Further Reading

Billings and Ponting (2001) 'Prerogative powers and the Human Rights Act: elevating the status of Orders in Council' *Public Law* 21.
Brazier, *Constitutional Practice*, chapter 9.
Harris, B.V. (1992) 'The third source of authority for government action', 109 *LQR* 626.
Hennessy, *The Hidden Wiring*, chapter 2.
Jowell and Oliver (eds), *The Changing Constitution*, chapter 8.
Loveland, *Constitutional Law, a Critical Introduction*, chapter 4.
Munro, *Studies in Constitutional Law*, chapter 8.
Nairn, T. (1988) *The Enchanted Glass: Britain and its Monarchy*.
Turpin, 137–54, chapter 6.
Vincenzi, *Crown Powers, Subjects, Citizens*.

Exercises

13.1 Compare the Royal Prerogative with parliamentary privilege (see Chapter 10) with reference to (i) its purposes; (ii) its history and sources; and (iii) the extent to which it can be controlled by the courts.

13.2 Define the Royal Prerogative and discuss the extent to which Royal Prerogative powers can be politically and legally controlled. How does judicial control of the prerogative relate to the separation of powers?

13.3 To what extent do government contracts differ from ordinary contracts?

13.4 To what extent does the Crown enjoy special privileges in litigation?

13.5 Explain the legal effect of a treaty in UK law. In what circumstances must a treaty be confirmed by statute?

13.6 What is the significance of constitutional convention in relation to the Royal Prerogative (see also Chapter 3).

13.7 There has just been a general election in the UK. The existing government has obtained the largest number of seats in the Commons but without an overall majority. The opposition is negotiating with a minority party to form a government. The prime minister refuses to resign. Advise the Queen.

What would be the position if the opposition had obtained the largest number of seats in the Commons, and the government was negotiating with the minority party?

13.8   The government is defeated in a vote on the Annual Finance Act. The prime minister refuses to resign. Advise the Queen.

13.9   The prime minister has just been sacked as party leader. However, due to an agreement with the opposition and a minority party, he could still command a small majority in the Commons. Advise the Queen.

13.10   The prime minister wishes to enact legislation transferring the powers of the monarch to the president of the European Commission. Opinion polls suggest a bare majority of public support for this proposal, but a minority within his party are depriving him of a Commons majority. He asks the Queen to dissolve Parliament and to call a general election. Advise the Queen.

13.11   The government of Carribia, an independent commonwealth island, is overthrown by a rebel force, 'The People's Front'. Cane, the displaced prime minister of Carribia, requests the aid of the British government. British troops are sent to Carribia and are authorised under an agreement between the British government and Cane to 'use all necessary measures to restore the lawful government of Carribia'. During the British troops' campaign on the island they requisition buildings owned by Ford, an American citizen, for use as a military depot, and destroy the home of Austin, a British citizen, in the belief that it is being used as a base by the rebels. Ford and Austin sue the British government for compensation. Discuss.

13.12   Ruritania is a self-governing member of the commonwealth. The Queen is the Queen of Ruritania. Last week a military coup in Ruritania succeeded in capturing the palace occupied by the Governor-General who represented the Queen. The military commander requests the Queen to abdicate in favour of himself as King. The situation in Ruritania is currently uncertain, and forces loyal to the Queen are attempting to secure control. The British government advises the Queen not to abdicate. The commonwealth Secretary-General advises her to abdicate. What would you advise?

14 Ministers and Departments

14.1 The Prime Minister

The office of prime minister is a creation of convention and the main powers of the prime minister are conventional. The prime minister also holds the formal office of first lord of the Treasury (No. 10 Downing Street is the first lord's official residence) and is the minister for the Civil Service. The Chancellor of the Exchequer is actually in charge of the Treasury. The prime minister is appointed by the Queen. By convention the Queen must appoint the person who can command a majority in the Commons. This usually means the leader of the largest party, but could involve a coalition of parties. The Queen usually has no discretion in the matter.

14.1.1 The powers of the prime minister

The powers of the prime minister have evolved gradually since the middle of the eighteenth century, corresponding to the decline in the powers of the monarch. The office was originally that of cabinet chairman deputising for the monarch, and intermediary between the monarch and the government (*primus inter pares*).

The extent of the power of a modern prime minister is controversial. The powers of a prime minister are scattered in convention, custom and practice, royal prerogatives and 'nods and winks'. The prime minister also has statutory powers in sensitive political areas (e.g. Police Act 1997 s. 9; Intelligence Services Act 1994 s. 2; National Minimum Wages Act 1998; National Audit Act 1983 s. 1). Except for (i) the unlikely event of intervention by the monarch and (ii) the almost equally remote possibility of rejection by the House of Commons, there is no formal machinery to curb the power of a prime minister who has support of a majority government. Moreover there is no convention that the prime minister can be removed by a vote of no confidence in the Commons. Such a vote can only bring down the government as a whole. Everything therefore depends upon the political balance between the particular holder of the office, the cabinet and party solidarity. The influence of senior backbench MPs may be significant, particularly where the cabinet is divided.

The main conventions that secure the pre-eminent power of a prime minister are as follows:

1. The prime minister must be a member of and enjoy the support of the House of Commons. This was originally designed to limit the power of governments, but modern party discipline and the domination of the House of Commons by paid career politicians whose elections are financed by party funds means that, given a majority of seats, the support of the Commons is usually automatic.
2. The prime minister appoints and dismisses all government ministers and determines their status and pecking order. S/he also has powers of appointment in relation to senior judges and many other important public posts (a mixture of statute and convention). The prime minister is also the minister responsible for the civil service.
3. The prime minister controls the cabinet agenda, formulates its decisions and allocates cabinet business. In this way cabinet discussion can be bypassed and matters entrusted to smaller groups of ministers or civil servants. Loyalty is secured through the principle of collective responsibility.
4. The cabinet is serviced by a secretariat. The cabinet secretary, a permanent official, is also head of the home civil service and reports to the prime minister. This gives the prime minister unique access to the government machine since the cabinet office co-ordinates the work of all government departments and is responsible for the training and deployment of the civil service.
5. The prime minister may advise the Queen to dissolve Parliament without consultation with the cabinet. Thus the prime minister can choose the date of a general election, holding his or her colleagues' careers to ransom.
6. Ministers' energies are centred upon their own departmental interests. Few have the time or knowledge to concentrate upon issues outside their departmental concerns.
7. The prime minister is head of the internal security services.
8. The prime minister is the channel of communication between Queen and government.
9. The prime minister is the main spokesperson for the nation and as such has unique access to the media. The prime minister's press office holds a key position. There is a danger that, in terms of public perception and therefore legitimacy, the prime minister is perceived as a president, in other words as a head of state thereby eclipsing the monarchy.

14.1.2   Limits on prime ministerial power

The main limits upon the power of a prime minister lie in the checks and balances that prevent the prime minister using his or her powers arbitrarily. These include:

1. The Queen's power to intervene in extreme cases (see Chapter 13).
2. The risk of dismissing cabinet ministers who may enjoy political support in their own right. In practice, a prime minister's freedom to appoint ministers may be limited by party considerations. The cabinet is full of rivals for power.
3. There are similar risks in bypassing or overruling cabinet discussion and in advising a dissolution.
4. The absence of a separate prime ministerial department (apart from a small but growing private office). However, prime ministers may have a staff of independent policy advisers brought in from outside the regular civil service.
5. A prime minister could be deposed as party leader and therefore lose the support of the Commons.
6. A prime minister could not impose his or her will over a united cabinet that enjoys substantial support in the Commons. The resignation of Margaret Thatcher in 1989 provides an example.

14.2   The Cabinet

In theory the cabinet is the policy-making body which is collectively responsible to Parliament and co-ordinates the work of government departments (see Haldane Committee (1917) Cmnd. 9230). The cabinet is a creature of convention and has no legal powers. Statute law recognises the status of the cabinet by protecting cabinet secrecy (Health Service Commissioners Act 1983 s. 12; Parliamentary Commissioner Act 1967 s. 8 (4)) and sometimes powers can be exercised only by a minister of cabinet rank (Data Protection Act 1984 s. 27; Telecommunications Act 1984 s. 45).

The cabinet originated in the seventeenth century as a group of privy councillors called together to give confidential advice to the monarch. An attempt was made in the Act of Settlement 1700 to prevent 'inner caucuses' of ministers from usurping the functions of the Privy Council, but the provisions were never implemented and were later repealed. The term 'cabinet' was originally one of abuse and referred to the King's 'closet' or anteroom. George I (1714–27) leaned particularly heavily on party leaders, and from his reign on the monarch ceased to attend cabinet meetings. During the reign of George III (1760–1820) the convention emerged that the monarch should generally consult the cabinet.

Eighteenth-century cabinets served the dual purpose of ensuring that the executive could command the support of the Commons and as a means of presenting the monarch with a united front, and from a mid-nineteenth-century perspective Bagehot regarded the cabinet as the pivot of the constitution and its driving force. Today we are less sure of this because of the rival power centres of the prime minister, civil servants and influential groups of ministers, and media and political advisers appointed by individual ministers.

By convention the prime minister advises the Queen on all cabinet appointments and dismissals. The Queen has no power of veto. In theory the prime minister may appoint anyone to the cabinet, but in practice the selection is confined to members of the prime minister's own party. A majority should be members of the House of Commons. Under the Ministers of the Crown Act 1975, the Lord Chancellor and three other cabinet members must be drawn from the House of Lords. Cabinets usually comprise between 20 and 30 ministers including the heads of the main government departments and certain other senior office-holders. Other ministers and civil servants often attend cabinet meetings for particular purposes, notably the Chief Whip who forms a link between the government and its backbench supporters.

Cabinet business is frequently delegated to committees and sub-committees or even to informal groups of ministers and other persons such as civil servants and political advisors. This is an important method by which the prime minister can control the decision-making process. Nevertheless, the use of committees and delegation seems to be an inevitable consequence of the size and complexity of modern government. There are two kinds of formal cabinet committee: (i) *ad hoc* committees set up on a temporary basis to deal with particular problems and (ii) named permanent committees, for example defence and overseas policy, economic strategy and legislation. The names and membership of these committees are published (http://www.cabinet. office.gov.uk). However, even these could be bypassed in favour of informal groups of prime ministerial cronies.

Collective cabinet responsibility (below) ensures that the cabinet is bound by committee decisions, whether or not the full cabinet has discussed them. Thus it is sometimes said that the full cabinet has become merely a rubber stamp or 'dignified' part of the constitution, the key decisions being made elsewhere. The secrecy surrounding the workings of the cabinet is also an aspect of collective responsibility and makes objective analysis difficult. Other practical limits upon cabinet power are that its meetings are relatively short (about two hours per week), its members have departmental loyalties, and its agenda and procedure are controlled by the prime minister.

Cabinet committees are 'shadowed' by committees of civil servants. The cabinet secretariat services and co-ordinates the work of the cabinet including the crucial and sensitive task of recording its decision for implementation by departments. The deputy prime minister is currently the minister responsible for the cabinet office. The cabinet secretariat comprises about 100 civil servants headed by the cabinet secretary who is also head of the home civil service and chief adviser to the prime minister. The cabinet secretariat also co-ordinates other Whitehall committees and designates most of their chairmen. It therefore plays a central role in the practice of the constitution. Arguably the three roles of the official concerned create fundamental conflicts of duty.

14.3   Ministers

A minister is defined by the Ministers of the Crown Act 1975 as an office holder under Her Majesty. It is for the Queen on the advice of the prime minister to designate the number and titles of ministers. Some ministers have separate legal personality as corporations sole. By convention a minister must be a member of Parliament. In theory this strengthens parliamentary control over the executive. As we saw in Chapter 5, there are statutory limits on the number of paid ministers who can sit in the Commons so as to prevent a prime minister flooding the House with his or her supporters. In practice, however, party political pressures and patronage have combined to make the Commons usually subservient to the executive. There are about 100 ministers, ranked as follows.

- *Cabinet ministers.* Most cabinet ministers head the largest and most important departments but some offices are traditionally without departments and can be assigned to special or co-ordinating work by the prime minister. These include the Chancellor of the Duchy of Lancaster and the Lord President of the (Privy) Council. The Leader of the House of Commons is also a member of the cabinet and is responsible for managing government business in the House. The most important departments are headed by secretaries of state. These are the successors of the powerful officials created by Henry VIII to control the central government. In theory any secretary of state can exercise the powers of any other secretary of state unless statute says otherwise (see Simcock, 1992, p. 535).

- *Ministers of state.* These are the second in command within departments and are usually allocated particular areas of responsibility.
- *Parliamentary under-secretaries of state* (where the head of the department is a secretary of state).
- *Parliamentary secretaries.* These are mainly recruited from the House of Commons and assist departmental heads with political and administrative work.
- *Parliamentary private secretaries.* These are members of Parliament who act as unpaid assistants to individual ministers. They do not count as ministers for the purpose of counting the number of ministers who may sit in the House of Commons.
- *Whips.* These control party discipline and provide a channel of communication between government and backbenches. The Chief Whip is not a member of the cabinet but attends cabinet meetings and consults with the prime minister on matters such as the appointment of ministers.
- *The law officers.* The Attorney-General is the chief law officer, and is assisted by the Solicitor-General. There are corresponding Scottish law officers. As party politicians the law officers raise questions about the separation of powers. The Attorney-General and the Solicitor-General are members of the House of Commons. They are entitled to consult other ministers but by convention act independently. The Attorney-General has the following specific functions in relation to the judicial process:
  - (i) representing the government in civil proceedings either as plaintiff or defendant;
  - (ii) prosecuting in important criminal cases. By statute his consent is needed for the prosecution of some offences;
  - (iii) independently of his role as government lawyer, instituting legal proceedings on behalf of the general 'public interest', either on his own initiative or on the application of any member of the public (a relator action). This might include an action against a public authority. The Attorney-General's decision whether or not to intervene cannot be challenged in the courts (*Gouriet* v. *Union of Post Office Workers* (1978));
  - (iv) intervening in any legal proceedings to put the government's view and referring questions of law to the Court of Appeal where an accused person has been acquitted of a criminal offence.

The extent to which the Attorney-General is influenced by the wishes of the government is obscure. For example in a case involving government attempts to suppress newspaper reports about matters of national security, his two roles as government lawyer and representative of the public interest are inseparable. We have only the predictable assertions of successive attorney-generals that they can be trusted. In 1924 the government fell because the attorney acted on instructions from the government (see Edwards, 1984, pp. 206–12).

14.4 Government Departments

By convention a minister must head each department in order to preserve ministerial responsibility. There are no constitutional requirements relating to the organisation of government departments. They can freely be created, abolished or amalgamated by the government. The matter is sometimes regarded as one of 'royal prerogative' but could also be the right of the Crown, as of any private organisation, to organise itself as it wishes thus illustrating a possible weakness in our non-statist constitution. In the nineteenth century committees of the Privy Council or special bodies were set up to deal with new governmental responsibilities but, as the work of government increased, separate permanent departments headed by ministers were created. These were expanded, abolished, split up or combined as circumstances dictated. Flexibility is facilitated by statutory provisions allowing functions, property, etc. to be transferred between departments and also to outside bodies (see Ministers of the Crown Act 1975, Civil Service (Management Functions) Act 1992; Deregulation and Contracting Out Act 1994). For purposes of litigation a list of appropriate departments is maintained by the Treasury. In cases of doubt the Attorney-General represents the Crown (Crown Proceedings Act 1947 s. 17).

Some government departments and ministers, notably the Treasury and the Lord Chancellor, trace their origins back to medieval times. The Treasury is an overlord and co-ordinating department in the sense that it is responsible for the economy as a whole and finances the other departments. The Home Office and the Foreign Office are nineteenth-century creations without a statutory basis. The Home Office exercises a mixed bag of responsibilities, being essentially a receptacle for domestic matters not allocated elsewhere. Its responsibilities include, for example, law and order, prisons, the electoral system, immigration, drugs and explosives.

A perennial problem for modern governments is that many policy programmes, for example urban regeneration do not fit neatly within departmental boundaries, and yet the civil service is organised on departmental lines and ministers' careers depend upon departmental success. Thus internal rivalries are a feature of the governmental process. As long ago as 1918 the Haldane Committee recommended that government business should be reorganised upon broadly functional lines, for example finance, commerce, defence, policing. This was not implemented as such. However, there are many inter-departmental and co-ordinating committees and the Treasury and cabinet office have important co-ordinating functions.

14.5   Ministerial Responsibility

We have frequently referred to the doctrine of ministerial responsibility. This is a central principle of the constitution that defines both the relationships between ministers and Parliament and that between ministers and civil servants. It has two aspects which are not entirely consistent, namely collective and individual responsibility. 'Responsibility' is sometimes used interchangeably with 'accountability'. Both terms have a range of meanings. They include duties of at least the following kinds: explanation, information, acknowledgement, review, redress and punishment. The particular combination appropriate to any given case depends on the circumstances (see Barberis, 1998).

Ministerial responsibility does not mean that Parliament (except in its capacity as lawmaker) can give orders to ministers or lay down policies. Parliament does not itself govern and to this extent we have a separation of powers. It means only that the government and individual ministers must usually explain and justify themselves to Parliament and, if the Commons so votes, the government or an individual minister must resign. Ministers must discharge their duties in a manner which has the continued support of the Commons which can influence ministers in their decisions, exert pressure for changes in government policy, and obtain information about governmental action. Ministerial responsibility may also provide information to arm opponents in the adversarial conduct of British political debate.

The doctrine of ministerial responsibility developed during the eighteenth and nineteenth centuries, corresponding with the rise of the House of Commons and the decline in the power of the Crown. Its original purpose was as a weapon against the monarch. According to one view, the convention can be acclaimed as a device to ensure accountability of government in the sense that an elected person has to take responsibility. An alternative view is that the convention favours 'strong' government because, given the domination of the House of Commons by the executive, it allows ministers to govern with little effective supervision or interference.

It can also be argued that the doctrine of ministerial responsibility is out of line with the practices of modern government in particular the fact that much of modern government is carried out by unelected officials especially through contemporary techniques of devolved public management. The chain of accountability through Parliament to the electorate has been broken and ministerial responsibility serves to strengthen the executive and to reinforce the tradition of secrecy that pervades government in the UK. This is reinforced firstly by the convention that civil service advice to ministers cannot be disclosed nor can whether that advice was accepted, a convention that is reflected in the Freedom of Information Act 2000 (see Chapter 22), and secondly by the convention that civil servants appear before parliamentary committees only with the permission of ministers (see *Civil Service Code* (January 1996); *Notes of Guidance on the Duties and Responsibilities of Civil Servants in Relation to Ministers* (the Armstrong Memorandum) 1985; Oliver, 1994).

14.5.1 Collective responsibility

Collective responsibility applies to the cabinet and probably to all government ministers. It was developed originally so that government and Parliament could put up a solid front against the king. It suggests a misleading picture of collegial government and has three aspects:

 (i) Solidarity. All ministers must be loyal to the policies of the government, whether or not they are personally concerned with them.
 (ii) It requires the government as a whole to resign if defeated on a vote of confidence in the House of Commons or if the Prime Minister resigns.
 (iii) It requires that cabinet and government business be confidential.

Collective responsibility is often said to be important for the Hobbesian purpose of ensuring that the government speaks with a single voice even though there may be no single solutions. Ministers can also discuss policy differences in private confident that all will support the decision which is eventually reached. The presentation of a single view also adds authority to the government's position because it disguises the coalition nature of many governments.

The drastic sanction of a vote of confidence is the only method by which Parliament can enforce collective responsibility, but governments have rarely been defeated in this way in modern times. In 1924 Ramsey MacDonald's Labour government resigned, and in 1979 so did James Callaghan's Labour government. Both were minority governments.

Collective responsibility is also important as a method of asserting prime ministerial power and protects secrecy within the government since cabinet discussions are confidential (see *Ministerial Code*, Cabinet Office 2001, para 17). Indeed, the cabinet is not recognised as a public authority for the purposes of the Freedom of Information Act 2000 (see Chapter 22). A minister is not entitled to disclose what went on in cabinet nor to disclose any disagreement he may have with his colleagues (see *A-G* v. *Jonathan Cape* (1975)). Resignation is also required before a minister can speak out on a particular issue. Collective responsibility applies even though many important decisions are made by informal groups or subcommittees and are not fully discussed by the cabinet as a whole. Nevertheless, as a convention, it may be adapted to new circumstances. The prime minister can apparently modify it over a particular issue (for example, membership of the EEC (1975)).

The relationship between the prime minister and cabinet can be obscure. There are tensions between a collegial style and a prime ministerial style of government. The collegial model of government, which emphasises the participation of all cabinet ministers in decision making, disguises the dominance of the prime minister in the formulation of policy. This is so notwithstanding that the prime minister has few formal powers. The prime minister controls the agenda of the cabinet and appoints members of it to cabinet subcommittees and, perhaps more important, informal working groups the most important of which he chairs (and where he does not, he may choose who does). The power to appoint loyal colleagues as ministers and dismiss opponents also strengthens the Prime Minister's position and may be seen as the prime minister's most significant power. It has become notorious that collective ministerial responsibility does not function so as to permit all policy issues to be openly debated in cabinet. It serves to require ministers to lend unswerving loyalty to policies formulated elsewhere.

The extent to which the prime minister can exercise an authoritarian style depends on the composition and mood of the cabinet, the attitude and cohesion of the party, and that of the Commons, the temper of the electorate and not least the personal style of the prime minister. If undue reliance is placed on a select group of senior ministers, if too many 'private deals' are struck with individual ministers, or if too many controversial policies are effectively formulated outside the cabinet, ministers may be reluctant to express loyalty to policies in the discussion of which they had not participated and with which they do not sympathise. Some consensus amongst ministers would seem to be necessary if only to avoid political embarrassment or ministerial resignations over policy differences. Serious embarrassment can result where senior ministers resign having concluded that the workings of the cabinet have strayed unacceptably far from the collegial model. Michael Heseltine resigned during the Westland affair in 1986. Similarly, Geoffrey Howe's resignation over EC policy in 1990 was closely related to his perception of the manner in which the prime minister appeared to disregard collective decision making. This resignation played a pivotal role in ending Mrs Thatcher's tenure of No. 10 Downing Street.

It is uncertain how far collective responsibility applies to junior ministers and whips who have no legal status as ministers of the Crown, and who do not even nominally participate in the decision in question. It would appear, however, that the same 'conform or go' rule can be applied by a prime minister. Thus the government is assured of the 'payroll vote' from about 100 MPs who hold government office and from the whips. It seems that a junior minister cannot accept individual responsibility for departmental errors, because this is a responsibility that lies with the Secretary of State. Junior ministers account to Parliament on behalf of the minister. However, a constitutional duty binds even junior ministers to resign in the event of serious personal misjudgement (e.g., Edwina Currie and the salmonella affair).

It could be argued that collective responsibility is no different from the solidarity expected within any organisation. This argument begs the question whether government can be compared with, say, a large private sector company. Governments exist on behalf of and for the benefit of the people and in that sense has no 'rights' only 'duties'. Constitutional doctrines should therefore be assessed only in the light of their advantage to the public. From this perspective, collective responsibility can be defended on the ground that it strengthens both the authority and the accountability of the government who stand or fall together.

14.5.2 Individual responsibility

The conventional formulation of the doctrine of individual ministerial responsibility is as follows, 'Each minister is responsible to Parliament for the conduct of his or her department, and for the actions carried out by the department in pursuit of government policies or in discharge of responsibilities laid upon him or her as a minister. Ministers are accountable to Parliament in the sense that they have a duty to explain to Parliament the exercise of their powers and duties and to give an account to Parliament of what is done by them in their capacity as ministers or by their departments. This includes the duty to give Parliament, including its select committees, and the public, as full information as possible about the policies, decisions and actions of the government and not to deceive or mislead Parliament and the public' (Questions of Procedure for Ministers, Cabinet Office, 1992).

In fulfilment of the convention ministers provide information to Parliament by means of answers to parliamentary questions, formal ministerial statements and letters to MPs. As we shall see, there have been many recent reforms to the convention, but it was not felt to be appropriate to go further and give the new Parliamentary Commissioner for Standards a responsibility in respect of ministerial conduct.

The scope of individual ministerial responsibility to Parliament, and the relationship between ministers and civil servants, has recently been subjected to close scrutiny. It was at issue in the Scott Inquiry into arms sales to Iraq (1996), in which ministers were found to have given inaccurate, incomplete or misleading answers to Parliament, and in the Nolan Inquiry into Standards in Public Life (1995) as well as in the controversies surrounding such events as the dismissal of the Head of the Prison Services Agency, Derek Lewis, and the Westland affair in 1986. The major restructuring of government involving the creation of Executive or Next Steps Agencies has also prompted criticism and debate concerning the convention.

The classical doctrine emphasises that a minister must always answer questions and give a full account of the actions of his department. This is so whether or not the minister is personally at fault for what has gone wrong. The classical doctrine does not, however, satisfactorily resolve the question of when, as a constitutional requirement, a minister's 'responsibility' entails a duty to take the blame for departmental errors, if necessary by resignation. One interpretation of the convention is that resignation is required for every serious departmental error regardless of the personal blame of the minister. As we shall see, with the possible exception of Lord Carrington's resignation as foreign secretary following the Argentinean invasion of the Falkland Islands, modern practice does not support this ministerial vicarious liability. The burdens of government have become so extensive and so complex that ministers have been unwilling to resign, even for serious errors by their officials. Direct personal involvement is almost certainly now required.

Ministers have attempted to limit their responsibility to 'policy' mistakes as opposed to 'operational' errors, which are deemed to be failures properly to implement policy. This has particularly been evident following the radical restructuring of government, with the majority of civil servants working in semi-detached Executive or Next Steps Agencies under the day-to-day direction of chief executives with only limited departmental control. The distinction between policy and operation has been accompanied by a dichotomy between 'accountability' and 'responsibility' (Scott, below). This seems to be to divorce the circumstances in which a minister must give to the House an explanation of the actions of their department (accountability) from cases in which a minister must accept the blame for departmental mistakes and resign (responsibility), thereby restricting the scope of ministerial responsibility. In *Taking Forward Continuity and Change* (Cm. 2748, pp. 27–8) the government stated that Parliament can always call a minister to account for all that goes on his department, but it added that a minister cannot be responsible in the sense of having personal knowledge and control of every action taken, and cannot be personally blameworthy when delegated tasks are carried out incompetently or errors of judgement are made at an operational level (see also the *Armstrong Memorandum* of 1st December 1987).

The accountability/responsibility distinction was in substance accepted by the Scott Inquiry (1995–6) Section K Vol. IV (Scott, 1996a). It appears to mean that a minister, regardless of personal blame, and with only limited exceptions (related *inter alia* to commercial confidence, national security and some macro-economic issues) cannot escape from the constitutional duty to answer questions, not intentionally to mislead, and to give an account of the actions of his department. Ministers must be prepared to offer a complete explanation of any error to Parliament. The duty embraces an obligation to offer reasons by way of justification in the face of criticism.

Even this restricted version of the convention has not been applied consistently. The forthright conclusion of the Scott Inquiry (Scott, 1995–6), was that numerous examples came to light of ministers failing to give full information about the policies, decisions and actions of government regarding arms sales to Iraq (K8.1 para. 27) and that this had undermined the democratic process (D4.56–D4.58). Answers to parliamentary questions in the affair had been 'designedly uninformative' because of a fear of adverse political consequences if the truth were revealed (D3.107).

Following revelations of this kind about the manner in which both ministers and civil servants had interpreted their constitutional functions, it became clear that there should be a renewed commitment to the doctrine of individual responsibility combined with a need to clarify the obligations entailed by it and, in particular, to ascertain the matters about which ministers must answer questions. One fundamental dimension of this reform concerned the Resolutions of the House of Commons and House of Lords on ministerial accountability (1997). The Resolutions are in similar but not identical terms. The Resolutions led to the adoption by the then newly elected Labour government of the *Ministerial Code* (2001). This incorporates the Resolution of each House (para. 1, sub paras (ii)–(v)). As amended, Section 1 of the *Code* reminds ministers that they can only continue to hold office for as long as they have the support of the prime minister. The *Code* then states that the prime minister (and not the respective Houses of Parliament) 'is the ultimate judge of the standards of behaviour expected of a Minister and the appropriate consequences of a breach of those standards'. This suggests that the *Code* envisages that the prime minister is both a setter of standards and responsible for their enforcement. For that reason the statement reads rather oddly in the context of the Resolutions. The *Code* then expresses the following principles of ministerial conduct (which are mostly in the terms of the Resolutions).

1. Ministers of the Crown are expected to behave according to the highest standards of constitutional and personal conduct. In particular they must observe the following principles of ministerial conduct:
   (i) Ministers must uphold the principle of collective responsibility;
   (ii) Ministers have a duty to Parliament to account, and be held to account, for the policies, decisions and actions of their Departments and Next Steps Agencies;
   (iii) It is of paramount importance that Ministers give accurate and truthful information to Parliament, correcting any inadvertent error at the earliest opportunity. Ministers who *knowingly* mislead Parliament will be expected to offer their resignation to the Prime Minister; (emphasis supplied)
   (iv) Ministers should be as open as possible with Parliament and the public, refusing to provide information only when disclosure would not be in the public interest, which should be decided in accordance with relevant statute, and the Government's *Code of Practice on Access to Government Information*
   (v) Similarly Ministers should require civil servants who give evidence before Parliamentary Committees on their behalf and under their directions to be as helpful as possible in providing accurate, truthful and full information in accordance with the duties and responsibilities of civil servants as set out in the *Civil Service Code*.

These Resolutions are of fundamental importance because minister-ial responsibility is arguably no longer an unwritten convention which can be varied at will by the government of the day but is now part of the law of Parliament although not of course enforceable in the courts. The terms of the Resolutions are not, however, without difficulty.

As Woodhouse observes (1997), satisfying the terms of the resolu-tions may not be unduly burdensome. Ministerial judgement will still govern what it means to be 'as open as possible' and when disclosure 'would not be in the public interest'. This means that the problems of interpretative ambiguity still remain, and that the doctrine of min-isterial responsibility remains somewhat elusive. It can also be asked whether a minister who deliberately misleads Parliament has sufficient integrity to offer resignation to the prime minister? And what is the effect of the statement that the prime minister is the ultimate judge of the appropriate standards of behaviour? Does this merely re-state the political reality that loss of office inevitably follows the loss of prime ministerial support for a beleaguered minister or does it hint at a diminished role for Parliament?

The *Code of Practice on Access to Government Information* (1994) was revised in 1997 to create a clear statement of the presumption in favour of disclosure of information. The need for this had been effect-ively heralded by Scott who stated that the accountability/responsi-bility divide was only constitutionally acceptable provided that there was a 'consequent enhancement of the need for ministers to provide ... full and accurate information to Parliament' which is vital to effective accountability (K8.16). There were also revisions to limit the scope of the exemptions under which information could be withheld. Moreover, a new official document, *Guidance to Officials on Drafting Answers to Parliamentary Questions* (1996–7) emphasises that if information is to be withheld, and a parliamentary question cannot be fully answered, the answer must itself make this clear and explain the reasons in equiv-alent terms to those in the *Code of Practice*.

The *Code* which, at the time of writing continues to apply, includes exemptions in Part II which permit information to be withheld (e.g. defence, security and international relations, immigration and nationality, information of economic sensitivity, and internal discus-sion and advice such as cabinet papers). Under a further reform, and contrary to previous practice, the Table Office now only prevents the tabling of parliamentary questions if the minister has refused to answer it in the same session. The block is only applied to the terms of the question and not the broader subject matter of it (Erskine May, 1997, pp. 298–301). There is a range of issues about which ministers do not answer questions (ibid., pp. 291–306). A list of questions which ministers declined to answer in the 1995–6 session was presented to the Public Service Committee (see First Report, 1996–97, *Ministerial Accountability and Responsibility*, HC 234, pp. 18–34).

The responsibility/accountability distinction continues to be controversial. The Public Service Committee rejected the bifurcation of accountability and responsibility and doubted whether in practice the distinction could be made ((2nd Report, 1995–6, HC 313, para. 21). The Committee concluded that the essence of ministerial responsibility is that it ensures that government explains its actions. It concluded that ministers are obliged to respond to parliamentary criticism in a manner which will satisfy it, including, where appropriate, by resignation (para. 21). But this may be no more than acknowledgement of both political and constitutional obligations. The government, which maintains the validity of the accountability/responsibility dichotomy, has not accepted the Committee's views. This illustrates the absence of any authoritative way of identifying the meaning of a convention.

There remains a problem of an 'accountability gap'. The dichotomy between responsibility and accountability means that accountability can break down where a minister blames a civil servant for some failure and subsequently directs that individual not to appear before a select committee (this is permitted under the cabinet office document *Departmental Evidence and Response to Select Committees* (1997) which replaced the so called Osmotherly Rules). Notoriously, the Secretary of State for Trade and Industry refused to allow the civil servants involved in aspects of the Westland affair to appear before the Commons Defence Select Committee (see HC 519, 1985–6, Cmnd. 9916 (1986)). This problem has in part been addressed in the parliamentary Resolutions. Although civil servants still give evidence to select committees under the direction of ministers, the minister must impress civil servants to be as helpful as possible in providing accurate, truthful and full information. (HC resolution para (iv) above). Ultimately, however, Parliament still lacks power to compel ministers to answer questions and cannot require civil servants to give evidence to select committees.

14.5.3   Resignation

The issue of ministerial resignation engages both collective and individual responsibility. This is so because where resignation takes place it saves fellow ministers from having to offer support for the beleaguered minister under the principle of collective ministerial responsibility. The question of ministerial resignation may now be regarded as having received undue emphasis; more weight is now attached to other facets of responsibility which embrace a duty to provide information to Parliament as well as a duty to provide an explanation and redress where errors are made. Nevertheless the issue of resignation remains of importance.

When the issue of ministerial resignation is considered, it may be necessary to separate a *constitutional* duty to resign from *political* pressures to resign (Scott, 1995–6). It seems that resignation is only *constitutionally* required in two categories of case: (i) where a minister has knowingly misled Parliament (except in the very limited cases where this is justified: see Public Service Committee, 2nd Report, 1995–6 HC 313, para. 32; Scott, 1996a, p. 421); or (ii) the minister is personally to blame for a serious departmental error (Woodhouse, 1994; Sir Richard Butler in evidence to Scott, 9 Feb. 1994, Transcript pp. 23–24).

In cases falling within category (i), both the *Ministerial Code* and Resolutions of the Houses of Parliament emphasise that resignation is only demanded of ministers who *knowingly* misled Parliament. One recent resignation suggests the possibility that loss of office may also result where a minister has not volunteered a full disclosure of information to a ministerial colleague who has then unwittingly misled Parliament (see Hammond, 2001, para. 5.128 and further below although, in this case, wider issues of political embarrassment complicate any assessment).

An honest but unreasonable belief in the accuracy of information given to Parliament can be a lifeline to beleaguered ministers. Scott found that Mr Waldegrave clung to the view that government policy governing the sale of arms to Iraq had been reinterpreted but that it had not changed – a view which Scott found unconvincing to the point where it was unsustainable in serious argument (Scott, 1995–6, D3.123–124). Waldegrave did not resign. Did this suggest that a minister was not constitutionally responsible for incompetence? If not, who was? Similar questions arise after Lord Falconer's refusal in 2001 to resign in respect of the funding and sale of the Millennium Dome.

The second case where resignation is required embraces both serious personal misjudgement and serious error in the minister's department in which the minister is implicated. Examples of the former include the case of Peter Mandelson who, in 1998, did not disclose that he had received a substantial private loan from a fellow minister whose business affairs were subject to investigation by Peter Mandelson's department. Edwina Currie's remarks on salmonella in eggs in 1988 also revealed personal misjudgement.

Major failings of policy for which a minister bears the ultimate responsibility should also lead to resignation. There does not now seem to be a general duty requiring resignation for departmental errors caused by officials. Crichel Down, which was once thought to have required resignation in such cases, is not now considered to support such a wide proposition. Sir Thomas Dugdale's resignation probably owed more to political misjudgement and a lack of parliamentary support, rather than self-sacrifice as a direct consequence of mistakes of officials.

The circumstances in which a minister will bear responsibility for major failings is not easy to identify where Executive Agencies have been established, because here the issue is blurred by the uncertain dichotomy between policy and operation. Ministers seem reluctant to resign where the fault lies in management failings (e.g. James Prior and Kenneth Baker after escapes from prisons. Michael Howard also refused to resign after the breakout from Parkhurst prison and more recently Lord Falconer has not resigned over the troubled Millennium Dome). But it is not clear where the boundary between policy and management failings can be drawn.

Calls for ministerial resignation are also part of an adversarial debate, and the interplay of politics and convention cannot be ignored. Some ministers have not tendered their resignation until the lack of political support has become clear (e.g., David Mellor in 1992 following adverse publicity about his private life). Even in cases of personal misjudgement or serious policy failure, resignation will be influenced by pragmatic issues touching upon the gravity of the issue, party support for the beleaguered minister, including that of senior backbenchers, the timing of the discovery of the error, the support of the prime minister and cabinet and the public repercussions of the fault. Norman Lamont kept his post as Chancellor of the Exchequer after sterling was withdrawn from the exchange rate mechanism in 1992 notwithstanding that this amounted to a serious reversal of a central strand of government macro-economic policy. James Callaghan, his predecessor during the 1967 devaluation crisis, was less fortunate. Parliament was not, however, sitting during the 1992 crisis. A minister may be *politically* (as opposed to conventionally) obliged to resign in other cases if he or she can no longer command political support, most notably the support of the prime minister. Political embarrassment, as much as the misleading of Parliament, appears to explain Peter Mandelson's resignation during the Hinduja Passport affair (Hammond, 2001). The extent to which a minister's behaviour sidetracks newspapers from other news favoured by party managers is also important. Raw politics may thus force a minister from office, and this, rather than constitutional obligation, may explain why resignation sometimes occurs following public criticism of the private lives of some ministers. However Woodhouse (1994, p. 33) asserts that cases of personal indiscretion can also fall within the ambit of conventional requirements because they affect the public credibility of the minister affected.

14.6 Civil Servants

14.6.1 Legal status

There is no legal definition of a civil servant. As with other basic institutions, the position of a civil servant is governed largely by tradition and a pragmatic mixture of prerogative, convention, parliamentary practice and statute. Thus the relationship between politicians and the permanent and supposedly impartial civil service is a delicate and vulnerable one. The Tomlin Commission (Cmnd. 3909 (1931)) defined civil servants as 'servants of the Crown, other than holders of political or judicial office who are employed in a civil capacity and whose remuneration is paid wholly and directly out of moneys voted by Parliament'. The police, for example, are not civil servants and are paid partly out of local funds.

The relationship between the Crown and a civil servant is usually said to be governed by the royal prerogative. According to this view a civil servant has no contract of employment and cannot enforce the terms of his employment other than those laid down by statute (*Civil Service Code*, para. 14). At common law the Crown can dismiss a civil servant 'at pleasure', that is, without notice and without giving reasons (*Dunn* v. *R.* (1896)). This is consistent with the view that there is no contract. On the other hand, it has been held that there can be a contract between the Crown and a civil servant but that as a matter of public policy the contract can be overridden by the Crown's power to dismiss the civil servant at pleasure (*Riordan* v. *War Office* (1959), but see *Reilly* v. *R.* (1934)). On this second analysis other terms of the employment such as pay and conditions are enforceable against the Crown.

Modern cases have stressed that there is no inherent reason why the relationship cannot be based on contract (see *Kodeeswaren* v. *A-G for Ceylon* (1970); *R.* v. *Civil Service Appeal Board ex parte Bruce* (1988); *R.* v. *Lord Chancellor's Department ex parte Nangle* (1992)). The Employment Act 1988 s. 30, deems there to be a contract between the

Crown and a civil servant for the purpose of making a civil servant liable for industrial action. Whether or not there is a contract it seems clear that the Crown can still dismiss at pleasure and that a contractual term which says otherwise is not enforceable (*CCSU* case (below) at 950 per Lord Diplock). This can be regarded as a matter of public policy. Rules controlling the civil service are sometimes made by prerogative Orders in Council which have the status of primary law but also take the form of instructions issued by the Treasury.

Civil servants, like other citizens may be protected by judicial review although in *Nangle* (above) it was held that judicial review did not apply to internal disciplinary matters (cf. *Bruce* (above) and *R. v. Civil Service Appeals Board ex parte Cunningham* (1991)). Most civil servants are also protected by statutory unfair dismissal rules administered by industrial tribunals (Employment Rights Act 1996 s. 191). 'Unfair dismissal' is not the same as unlawful dismissal and the only enforceable order that an industrial tribunal can make is one of compensation.

Special machinery applies to security issues. A minister can by issuing a certificate remove any category of Crown employee from the employment protection legislation on grounds of national security (Employment Rights Act 1995 s. 193). A civil servant who is suspected of being a security risk is given a special hearing, but without the normal rights of cross-examination and legal representation, before a panel of 'three advisers'. These usually comprise two retired senior officials and a High Court judge.

14.6.2   Civil service impartiality

Since the Northcote–Trevelyan Report (1854), civil servants have been regarded as politically neutral. The constitutional justification for this is to provide continuity and stability and a source of accumulated knowledge and experience. However, the notion that political neutrality is possible is contested and elected politicians may regard civil servants as frustrating the democratic process, famously satirised in the television series *Yes Minister*. Civil servants are, however, under a duty to obey ministers in relation to the implementation of policy and, in return for impartiality, are not subject to accountability to Parliament without the permission of ministers. Their advice to ministers is confidential (see *Notes of Guidance on the Duties and Responsibilities of Civil Servants In Relation to Ministers*, Cabinet Office, 1987).

Most countries have politicised their civil service. In the USA for example the 'spoils' system operates under which about 3000 senior civil servants are appointed by the incoming president thus securing commitment to the elected regime. It is, however, widely recognised that co-ordination between the political and permanent elements of the public service is necessary. In the UK this is attempted by the appointment of special advisers attached to ministers and holding office for the duration of a government. Although they are civil servants paid from public funds, special advisers are not required to be politically impartial. They are relatively few (currently about 83, 25 of which are in the prime minister's office) but are gradually increasing in number. In recent years concern has been expressed because of their involvement in government news management. This was illustrated in 2002 by the simultaneous resignation of two civil servants in the Transport Department, one a special adviser, the other the regular head of the department's press office.

Although there is a model contract for special advisers and a Special Advisers' Code, the scope and limits of the role of special advisers is not clear. In particular, the constitutional balance may have been upset when the government used prerogative powers to confer executive powers on special advisers to give instructions to regular civil servants. The Wicks Committee on Standards (Civil Service (Amendment) Order in Council 1999) is currently reviewing the position of special advisers. Both main parties support a Civil Services Act entrenching the non-political status of the Civil Service.

The political activity of civil servants is restricted according to the status of the individual. The majority are unrestricted except while on duty or in uniform or on official premises. An 'intermediate' group can take part in political activities with the consent of their head of department. This includes officials performing non-political jobs. A 'restricted' group of senior officials directly involved in policy-making cannot take part in national politics but can indulge in local politics with the consent of their head of department. However, whole departments can be exempted (see *Civil Service Pay and Condition of Service Code*). There is also a code of practice prohibiting civil servants from taking gifts or doing other things that could create a conflict between their private interests and their official duties. A retired civil servant requires government approval before accepting employment with private sector organisations that are likely to have dealings with the government.

14.6.3 Civil service functions

A Civil Service Code (1999) emphasises the role of the civil service as that of giving independent and objective advice to government, of providing information without deceit and of impartially carrying out the policies of governments of whatever political complexion. The code also emphasises that the duty of a civil servant is to ministers and not to Parliament. Apart from the day-to-day task of running government departments and administering public services, civil servants have the following general functions.

1. *To advise ministers upon policy matters.* This includes attending committees, drafting speeches, preparing answers to parliamentary questions and preparing legislation. In theory there is a distinction between party-political advice, which is not the civil servant's concern, and government advice as such. However, the line between the two is often blurred. For example, in recent years there has been emphasis upon the achievement by departments of positive political goals. The idea that senior civil servants should be 'politicised' is not generally accepted, although ministers are entitled to play an active part in choosing senior civil servants. It is often believed that because ministers, being temporary, necessarily rely upon the accumulated knowledge and experience of the civil service, the civil service forms policies of its own which it persuades ministers to adopt. The influence of civil servants may reach ministers through the cabinet office and through the private office of each departmental minister. The private office is staffed by regular civil servants and has been described as 'the gear box' between ministers and their departments (Thompson, 1987, 50 *MLR* 498). It is arguable that the hierarchical civil service machine works most effectively by responding to initiatives from the top.

2. *To manage the use of government resources.* The head of each department – the permanent secretary – is the departmental accounting officer. The accounting officer's activities can be directly examined by Parliament by means of the Public Accounts Committee and the Comptroller and Auditor General (see Chapter 12).

3. *To make decisions in individual cases under powers conferred by particular statutes upon ministers.* Most decisions are made by civil servants in the name of the minister, for example determining planning appeals, allocating grants and other benefits, dealing with immigration and deportation matters. Under the *Carltona* doctrine (see *Carltona Ltd* v. *Commissioner of Works* (1943)), a minister can lawfully exercise any of his statutory powers through a civil servant in his department and need not personally exercise any power, unless statute specifically so requires. It is not clear whether the

courts can control the delegation arrangements made by a minister. In *Olahinde* v. *Secretary of State* (1990) the House of Lords held that a deportation decision could be made by an immigration officer on behalf of the Secretary of State. However, Lord Templeman remarked (at 397) that the person exercising the power must be 'of suitable seniority in the Home Office for whom the minister accepts responsibility' (cf. *Re Golden Chemical Products Ltd* (1976)). In law and by convention the decision remains that of the minister (see also *Bushell* v. *Secretary of State for the Environment* (1981); *R. (Alconbury)* v. *Secretary of State* (2001). Occasionally a statute states or assumes that a minister shall personally exercise a power (see, for example, Immigration Act 1971 s. 13 (5); Regulation of Investigatory Powers Act 2000).

4. *To carry out the day-to-day administration of government departments.* The overwhelming majority of civil servants are concerned with this, in many cases operating within quasi-autonomous executive agencies. In *Williams* v. *Home Office (No. 2)* (1981) the Court drew a distinction between acts done by civil servants in the exercise of statutory functions conferred on ministers, and routine management matters, saying that the latter are not to be regarded as the act of ministers. This is questionable in terms of the traditional doctrine of ministerial responsibility, but perhaps represents a more realistic view of the nature of modern government. In particular it is questionable whether the *Carltona* principle should apply to civil servants working in executive agencies who are not directly under the control of a minister (see Freedland, 1994). The 6th Report of the Committee on Standards in Public Life (2000a) has recommended placing the civil service on a statutory basis in order to protect its distinctive role as a permanent aspect of the executive.

14.6.4 Civil servants and ministerial responsibility

The classical doctrine has been that there is no direct link between civil servants and Parliament. Civil servants are responsible to their permanent secretary who is responsible to the minister. Sir Edward Bridges, the Permanent Secretary to the Treasury, expressed this in 1954 after the *Crichel Down* affair (quoted in the Second Report of the Public Service Committee, 1995–6, HC 313, para. 8). He stated that a minister is responsible to Parliament for the exercise of all executive powers and every action taken in pursuance of those powers. As civil servants have no powers of their own, and so cannot take decisions or do anything except and in so far as they are subject to the direction and control of ministers, a civil servant has no direct responsibility to Parliament and cannot be called to account by Parliament (although ministers were never expected to defend official action of which they either disapproved or had no prior knowledge.

In particular advice given to ministers by civil servants cannot be disclosed without the permission of ministers and civil servants appear before parliamentary committees only with the consent of their ministers. Ministers therefore shield civil servants from Parliament. In return, civil servants are loyal to ministers and owe no other allegiance thus emphasising the minister's own accountability to Parliament (see 7th Report of Treasury and Civil Service Committee (19856) HC 92 and Cmnd. 9841 (1986) – government's reply). Where issues of propriety or conscience arise, a civil servant may appeal to the independent Civil Service Commissioners, who report directly to the Queen (see www. cabinet-office.gov.uk/OCSC). The Commissioners also monitor senior civil service appointments.

The Scott Inquiry revealed how civil servants have sometimes acted independently of ministers, or in the expectation of subsequent ministerial ratification of their actions (Scott, para. D3.40). Civil servants concealed important questions from ministers and may even have defied ministerial instructions (Scott, paras D2.398, Lewis and Longley, 1996). In these circumstances the classical doctrine of ministerial responsibility masked where real responsibility for governmental decisions lay. Moreover, as we saw above, ministers have attempted to limit the doctrine of ministerial responsibility, firstly by distinguishing between policy and operational matters and secondly by distinguishing between 'accountability' as a duty to explain and 'responsibility' as liability to take the blame (5th Report from Treasury and Civil Service Select Committee, HC 27, 1993–4, para. 120).

Select committees cannot force civil servants to attend to answer questions, but should they do so they appear subject to ministerial direction (para. 37, *Departmental Evidence and Response to Select Committees* (Cabinet Office, January 1997) which replaced the so called 'Osmotherly Rules'). This document exhorts civil servants to be as forthcoming as possible in providing information under the *Code of Practice on Access to Government Information*. Information can, however, be withheld, in the public interest, which should be determined in accordance with the law and the exemptions set out in the *Code*. On the other hand it has long been accepted that, as accounting officer, the permanent head of a department must appear before the relevant parliamentary committee.

14.7 Executive Agencies and the 'New Management'

In recent years the delivery of many public services has been restructured by hiving off executive agencies ('next-steps' agencies) from the central executive. These remain part of the civil service but are free-standing structures with substantial operational independence and each with its own chief executive. The devolved decision makers are therefore outside the traditional heirarchical mechanism of political accountability through ministers to Parliament. Nevertheless it appears to be assumed that executive agencies do not raise constitutional issues (see *Next Steps*, Cm. 524). However, as with other decentralising changes, executive agencies cast doubt on the role of Parliament as the ultimate source of accountability and make it difficult to identify clear lines of responsibility.

As we have seen, the traditional view that civil servants only provide advice to ministers was seriously questioned after the Scott Inquiry. The reorganisation of government has further placed the classical model under strain. This is most notably the case in the relationship between ministers and chief executives of EA. Framework agreements made between the agency and the sponsoring department (sometimes with the Treasury as a party) constitute the relationship between the two. The framework agreement contains the corporate strategy and financial arrangements under which the agency will work. The Citizen's Charter sets standards for service delivery against which the actual performance of the Executive Agency will be monitored as part of the drive for efficiency and value for money. A chief executive is appointed (as a temporary civil servant) to be responsible for the day-to-day management of the agency, which is staffed by civil servants.

The principle underlying the respective functions of the agencies and the departments is that autonomy for service delivery should reside with the agency, whilst policy matters should be reserved for the department acting under ministerial control. According to the government, the minister remains responsible for general policy, and the chief executive for operational matters, which are essentially matters of implementation. This is a significant realignment of the traditional doctrine of ministerial responsibility. However, ministerial responsibility was intended to apply equally to the work of Executive Agencies which remain subject to the scrutiny of the PCA and the relevant select committees. The chief executive is responsible to the minister but, as accounting officer, also appears before select committees to answer MPs' questions about the functioning of the agency over which they have day-to-day management. Controversially, this suggests that a convention *may* have been emerging under which agency chief executives are directly responsible to Parliament in their own right (but see below). This possible dual line of responsibility would radically have altered their position as civil servants.

Diverse forms of accountability have been introduced although they are weak because they have no enforceable sanctions and are mainly policed within the executive itself (see Lewis, 1994). These are mainly copied from the practices of private businesses. Regulatory controls under the new public management take the form of performance standards or targets, contracts, financial mechanisms and incentives, audits and disclosure duties (see Willet, 1996, Ch. 4). In the case of the privatised utilities and railway companies, statutory regulators appointed by ministers but not directly accountable to Parliament have the power to impose penalties and negotiate. The government has also published a series of 'Citizen's Charters' which attempt to set out standards of service which citizens, envisaged as individualistic customers, are entitled to expect from government but these have no legal status as such (see White Paper, *The Citizen's Charter. Raising the Standard* (1991) Cm. 1599).

In principle, the extent of ministerial control depends on the terms of the framework agreement. In practice, chief executives are often required to take management initiatives independently of ministers. The traditional assertion that civil servants advise ministers and act on their behalf has been radically altered. MPs have also been encouraged to approach chief executives directly on behalf of their constituents, and chief executives answer written parliamentary questions. The answers are published in *Hansard* to avoid the bypassing of Parliament which might have occurred if chief executives responded direct to individual MPs (see, e.g., Fifth Report of the Treasury and Civil Service Committee, *The Role of the Civil Service*, HC 27 (1993–4) col. 53 para. 170).

In the context of the agencies (just as in former nationalised industries from which the dichotomy originates) the policy/operational dichotomy has been exposed as problematic. Indeed, the two are often so inextricably interconnected that they cannot be distinguished. The effect has been to make it more difficult for Parliament to find out who is to blame when problems arise. For example, is prison overcrowding policy or operation? Further, even if a matter can be classified *ab initio* as 'operational' as soon as adverse political consequences arise the same matter may mutate into one of policy, causing confusion as to whether (and if so when) responsibility shifts from a chief executive to a minister. An example of this concerned the computer problems at the Driver and Vehicle Licensing Agency which caused unexpected failures in producing driving licences. The involvement of ministers when the matter acquired a political dimension converted an apparently operational failure into a policy matter. The example of the Child Support Agency illustrates some ministerial reluctance to accept blame where inadequate agency performance is partly attributable to such matters as inadequate funding (a matter for ministers under *Taking Forward Continuity and Change*). This exposes a fundamental gap in accountability.

Moreover, ministers can exploit confusion over these vague labels by categorising any political embarrassment as 'operational', or by intervening in 'operational' matters where there are electoral risks in not being sufficiently involved. This has been identified as a problem in the prison service and in particular emerges from the events leading up to the dismissal of Derek Lewis. (See the Learmont Report, Cm. 3020, Oct. 1995; the House of Lords Public Service Committee Session (1997–8) 55 para. 341.) Ministers may also interfere in 'operational' matters whilst declining to answer questions about them, claiming that such matters fall within the responsibility of the chief executive. Moreover, since it is the minister who decides what is policy and what is operation, ministers can effectively determine the extent of their constitutional responsibilities.

The House of Lords Select Committee on Public Service recently concluded that it was not possible effectively to separate policy from operations and that such a division was not desirable (ibid. para. 348). The Committee identified a need for a re-examination of the relationship between ministers and civil servants, but expressed their own clear view that there should be no distinction between the constitutional responsibilities of chief executives and other civil servants. This would mean that when they answer written parliamentary questions or appear before select committees they do so on behalf of their ministers. The Committee stated emphatically that ministers remain accountable for what goes on in agencies just as in their departments. However, there remain concerns that when chief executives appear before select committees they are subject to the direction of their minister under the *Departmental Evidence and Response to Select Committees* (Cabinet Office, January 1997) which would limit their competence as witnesses and Parliament's ability to investigate.

14.8 Non-Departmental Public Bodies

Contemporary political fashion favours the devolution of many governmental functions to specialist bodies including private bodies outside the central government framework thereby further weakening constitutional accountability but ostensibly reducing government expenditure. Under the Deregulation and Contracting Out Act 1994 a minister can authorise the transfer of any of his or her functions to any other body and can authorise a local authority to do likewise. This does not apply to the jurisdiction of courts or tribunals which exercise 'the judicial power of the state' nor to functions which affect individual liberty or involve the power of search, entry to or seizure of property (subject to exceptions mainly concerned with the lucrative insolvency business), nor to the making of subordinate legislation (s. 71).

Non-departmental public bodies (NDPDs), sometimes called 'Quangos' (quasi-autonomous non-governmental organisations) are usually created by statute although some are voluntary bodies. They are controlled by ministers through various devices, the extent and nature of control depending on the particular body. Typically a minister appoints and dismisses the boards of non-departmental bodies (although some, such as the utilities and rail regulators have a certain amount of security of tenure). Such appointments are therefore a valuable lever of patronage attracting as they are likely to do, the sycophantic and the conformist.

Following the recommendations of the Nolan Committee (below) (see 6th Report of the Committee on Standards in Public Life; Neill, 2000a), an independent Commissioner for Public Appointments has been created under the royal prerogative with the power to regulate and oversee appointments made by ministers to NDPDs and to deal with complaints (Order in Council, 23 Nov. 1995). Ministers are bound by its general principles and code of practice (see http://www.ocpa.gov.uk). These principles follow the Nolan Principles of Public Life and emphasise openness, fair competition and proportionality in the process of making appointments. Characteristically, there are no legal sanctions other than the general law of judicial review. The Commission has no enforcement powers of its own, responsibility being political and probably vesting in the prime minister.

An important question is whether a particular body is part of the Crown, and so subject to certain immunities and special rights and accountable directly to Parliament. Legislation establishing a public body usually specifies whether or not that body is part of the Crown (e.g. Utilities Act 2000 s. 1: the gas and electricity regulator is part of the Crown), but failing this, the test is the extent to which the Crown, through ministers, is entitled *in law* to exercise detailed control over the body in question (see e.g. *Tamlin* v. *Hannaford* (1950)). By virtue of particular statutes ministers can usually give directions or guidance to

NDPDs (the latter not being strictly binding), and also provide finance. Thus in practice NDPDs have little significant independence from central government but the extent to which ministers are formally accountable for them is blurred (below). NDPDs must be distinguished from (i) 'ministerial public bodies', such as the Inland Revenue and the NHS for which a minister is fully accountable; and (ii) 'non-ministerial departmental bodies' such as the Charity Commissioners, (Charities Act 1996), and the Gas and Electricity Markets Authority (Utilities Act 2000), who exercise functions wholly on behalf of the Crown but over which ministers have only limited powers.

NDPDs are not usually part of the Crown and comprise a large and variegated category (see *Executive NDPDs,* Cm. 4657 (1999)). They are usually subdivided into executive bodies such as the Higher Education Funding Council and the Environment Agency, advisory bodies such as the Committee on Standards in Public Life (which is non-statutory) and tribunals exercising judicial functions, for example the Immigration Appeals tribunal. However, many non-judicial bodies, for example English Nature, exercise both executive and advisory functions. Moreover in recent years regulatory bodies have been created or their powers increased in order to exercise governmental control over the activities of private bodies exercising functions that had previously been carried out by government. In defiance of the separation of powers some of these bodies exercise a mixture of judicial and executive functions acting as police force, judge and executioner in one (e.g. Housing Act 1996 – The Housing Corporation). These arrangements may fall under the scrutiny of the Human Rights Act 1998 in respect of whether they afford a fair trial before a sufficiently independent tribunal. However, provided that judicial review is available conflicts of function will probably not violate Art. 6 at least in the case of policy-making bodies (see *R. (Alconbury)* v. *Secretary of State* (2001; *Adam* v. *Newham BC* (2002) (below p. 430)).

There are also numerous voluntary bodies such as housing associations that carry out functions on behalf of government and, in doing so, have surrendered the independence that is arguably important in a democracy. These bodies are collectively known as 'public service organisations', a term which has no legal significance. Many activities, notably professional sports, are subject to regulation on a voluntary basis by bodies which have no formal links with government or special powers but nevertheless act to protect the public. Profit-making bodies have also contracted with government to provide public services, notably in the case of prisons and trunk roads. Under the Private Finance Initiative private enterprises finance government projects either as loans or in return for benefits such as leases or shares in revenue (see Government Resources and Accounts Act 2000 ss. 16, 17). The fact that a given body exercises functions under an agreement with government or is funded by government is not sufficient in itself to make that body a public body for example for Human Rights Act purposes. However, its functions may be regarded as public functions if they are enmeshed with those of a government body (see *Donoughue* v. *PHARCA* (2001)).

The dispersal of power to private bodies raises problems of accountability. Ministers will not formally be accountable to Parliament for their activities except to the extent that a minister exercises his or her own powers. Indeed, apart from the courts and statutory agencies such as the Charity Commission, the Financial Services Authority and the Housing Corporation, which regulate some of these bodies, there is no method of formal accountability. In 1918 the Haldane Committee on the machinery of government warned about dangers in creating governmental bodies without the 'safeguards' of ministerial responsibility to Parliament. Moreover where a private company runs a service on behalf of the government it will owe dual and perhaps conflicting loyalty to its shareholders and to the government but without clear accountability mechanisms. There might also be accountability problems where private bodies claim commercial confidentiality for their decisions or where they seek the protection of contractual rights against public interest concerns.

Summary

14.1   As a body the cabinet has been reduced in power in recent years, with decisions being effectively made by smaller groups within and outside the cabinet and by departments of the executive.

14.2   There are few constitutional laws or conventions concerning the detailed distribution of functions between departments. Political and administrative considerations rather than constitutional principle determine the number, size, shape and interrelationship of government departments. The creation of bodies outside the framework of the Crown is of greater constitutional and legal significance.

14.3   The convention of ministerial responsibility is central to the UK constitution. We discussed its two limbs with their several branches. Collective responsibility means that all members of the government must loyally support government policy and decisions and must not disclose internal disagreements. Individual responsibility means that each minister is answerable to Parliament for all the activities of the department under his control. It also means that civil servants are not personally accountable. From these principles follow: (i) the traditional notion of the civil service as anonymous and politically neutral having a duty to serve with unquestioning loyalty governments of any political complexion; (ii) the secrecy that pervades the British system of government.

14.4 Many people believe that the traditional doctrine of ministerial responsibility is out of line with the practices of modern government and effectively shields the government from accountability. In particular: (i) cabinet decisions are rarely made collectively; (ii) many government bodies are not directly controlled by ministers, the creation of executive agencies reinforcing this; (iii) civil servants are increasingly expected to make political decisions and to be responsible for the financial management of their allotted activities, (iv) public functions are increasingly being given to special bodies or private bodies. Thus the traditional chain of accountability between Parliament, ministers and civil servants is weakened.

14.5 In law, civil servants are servants of the Crown. They can be dismissed 'at pleasure', that is, without notice and without reason being given. However, the modern cases suggest that there can be a contractual relationship between the Crown and a civil servant and that a civil servant can be protected by the law of judicial review.

14.6 Civil servants are regarded as servants of the government of the day with an absolute duty of loyalty to ministers. Their advice to ministers is secret and they appear before Parliament only with the consent of ministers. They are supposed to be non-political and neutral, responsible for giving ministers objective advice and for carrying out ministerial orders, thus providing stability and continuity. The neutrality of the civil service has been affected by the appointment of politically partisan special advisers.

14.7 The internal arrangements for the carrying out of government business involve entrusting individual civil servants with considerable decision-making responsibility and in recent years with financial accountability within the government machine. Many civil servants work in executive agencies, hived off from the central departmental structure and outside the direct control of ministers. This has led to tensions between traditional ideas of ministerial responsibility and the actual channels of accountability and has raised problems in connection with the supposed distinction between policy and operational matters. Ministerial responsibility is also weakened by the practice of entrusting public functions to specialised NDPDs operating to varying extents independently of the central government.

14.8 The civil service is torn between competing duties, that of giving impartial advice to ministers and that of carrying out the goals of the elected government. In particular there is the moral dilemma faced by 'whistleblowers' who wish to expose misconduct by ministers and also by civil servants who are sometimes required to conduct inquiries in politically sensitive areas.

Further Reading

Barberis, P. (1998) 'The new public management and a new accountability', 76 *Public Administration* 451.
Brazier, *Constitutional Practice*, chapters 5, 6, 7.

Dowding, K. and Wun-Taek, K. (1998) 'Ministerial resignations', 76 *Public Administration* 411.

Hennessy, *The Hidden Wiring*, chapters 3, 4, 5, 8.

Jowell and Oliver, chapters 5, 6.

Lewis (1994) 'Reviewing change in government. New public management and next steps', *Public Law* 105.

Lewis, N. (1998) 'A civil service act for the United Kingdom', *Public Law* 463.

Lewis, N. and Longley, D. (1996) 'Ministerial responsibility. The next steps', *Public Law* 490.

McEldowney, *Public Law*, chapters 10, 13.

Marr (1995) *Ruling Britannia*, Michael Joseph.

Oliver and Drewry, (1996) *Public Service Reforms*, Pinter.

Rhodes, R. (1994), 'The hollowing out of the state: the changing nature of the public service in Britain', 65 *Political Quarterly* 158.

Tomkins (1998) *The Constitution After Scott*, OUP.

Willet (ed.), *Public Sector Reforms and the Citizen's Charter*, chapters 4, 5.

Woodhouse (1997) *In Pursuit of Good Administration, Ministers, Civil Servants and Judges*.

Woodhouse (1994) *Ministers and Parliament*, Clarendon Press, Oxford.

Exercises

14.1   Consider whether the relevant laws and conventions support Bagehot's view that the Cabinet is the central institution of the UK constitution.

14.2   Draft a bill which defines the powers of the prime minister and strengthens his accountability.

14.3   'Ministerial responsibility is, in practice, an obstacle to the availability of information and to the holding of government to account' (Oliver). Discuss.

14.4   To what extent can powers conferred on a minister be exercised (a) by another minister? (b) by a civil servant?

14.5   How does the 'Next Steps' initiative affect the accountability of the executive?

14.6   To what extent can Parliament and the public scrutinise the activities of a civil servant? (see also Ch. 2).

14.7   What is the distinction between accountability and responsibility? Has this distinction limited ministerial responsibility?

14.8   When should a minister resign?

14.9   The government creates an executive agency to regulate motorway service areas. The Secretary of State for Consumption delegates to the agency his statutory powers to ensure the 'adequate provision of motorway services'. Under a contract made with the Secretary of State, the agency promises to achieve certain 'targets', including the provision of high-quality catering and a clean environment. The agency is given power to approve all catering outlets at service areas. The agency informs George that it proposes to approve his ice-cream stall at the Naff Service Area on the M6. George thereupon purchases several thousand gallons of low-grade ice-cream made from petroleum by-products. George is subsequently told by the agency that it has revised its food quality standards in the light of an EC Directive and that he must therefore sell ice-cream made only from milk. George sells his ice-cream to a local garage at a considerable loss.

The agency makes a contract with Grasper to provide a cleaning and waste disposal service at the Naff Service Area. Due to cuts in its funding from the Secretary of State, the agency does not check Grasper's performance but increases its chief executive's annual 'performance bonus' by 100%. Jane, a regular user of the service area, writes to the agency stating her view that the standards of cleanliness are inadequate and are likely to create a health risk. She receives a reply stating only that the agency is committed to 'fazing in Nolan Standards of Excellence in all our Missions' and apologising for the delay in 'actioning her application'.

George and Jane now write to Crawler, their MP (who is a government loyalist), complaining about their treatment. Explain to them their chances of obtaining redress by this means.

15 The Police and the Armed Forces

15.1 Introduction

The police and the armed forces together constitute the enforcement arm of the community authorised to use violence. However, the constitutional position of each of them is different. In the case of the armed forces the overriding imperative in a democracy is to ensure that they are subordinate to the civilian power and that there is political accountability. It is also important to accommodate the need for special powers and disciplines with the values of the rule of law so as to ensure that the military are not only subject to the law but also protected by it. In the case of the police the issues are more complex, because the police are closely connected with the judicial arm of government having the dual responsibilities of keeping order and investigating crime. As well as the need to subject police powers to the rule of law there is the concern to accommodate political accountability with police independence.

15.2 Police Organisation and Control

The organisation of police forces in the UK rests upon three incommensurable concerns. These have led to complex and tension-ridden arrangements for police governance and accountability. First there is the traditional status at common law of the constable as an independent officer owing duties directly to the Crown and the rule of law to keep the peace. All police officers and also prison officers are constables. The office of constable is an ancient office of the Crown with inherent common law powers, although many powers, particularly those concerned with arrest, search and detention, have been superseded by statute. A constable has no immunity from liability for wrongful acts, thus reflecting Dicey's version of the rule of law. Today the police have a wide range of statutory powers and are subject to considerable administrative regulation.

A constable is not, strictly speaking an employee of anyone (although under regulations made by the Home Secretary many of the conditions of work are similar to those of employees) and the powers and duties of a constable derive from the general law (*Fisher* v. *Oldham Corporation* (1930)). According to dicta in *Fisher*, the status of a constable is that of 'a servant of the state', and a police officer has been held to be 'a person holding office under her Majesty' so as to be bound by the Official Secrets Act (*Lewis* v. *Cattle* (1938)). This means only that the police officer's legal powers derive ultimately from the Crown and it does not follow that the Crown can control the day-to-day activities of the police. Police premises provided by the Crown may attract Crown immunities and this may also apply to police officers while on duties on behalf of the Crown, such as guarding prisoners in court (see also *A-G for New South Wales* v. *Perpetual Trustee Co. Ltd* (1955); *Enever* v. *R.* (1906); *R.* v. *Metropolitan Police Commissioner (MPC) ex parte Blackburn* (1968); *R.* v. *Chief Constable of Devon & Cornwall ex parte Central Electricity Governing Board* (1982)).

Second there is fear of unaccountable power. Dating from the Metropolitan Police Act 1829 this has led to local police forces rather than the centralised agency beloved of the police state, and to attempts to make these forces accountable to the local community. Local police forces are answerable to their local police authority which comprises a mixture of local councillors and justices of the peace. The inclusion of the latter is an illustration of the blurring of the separation of powers, in that JPs have an uneasy mixture of judicial and administrative functions among which an interest in police work may be regarded as undesirable.

Third there are concerns for efficiency and, again, accountability, this time for the spending of government money. The technical support required by the police is too expensive to be provided without substantial central government funding with its inevitable con-commitment of central control. Moreover modern crime is no respecter of local or even national boundaries and electronic communications require rapid co-ordination between local police areas.

Under the Police Act 1996, which consolidates the Police Act 1964, and subsequent legislation, counties are the basic police unit in England and Wales. The organisation of the London police has historically been governed by special provisions under which the police authority was the Home Secretary and the Commissioner of Police of the Metropolis, who is the equivalent to a chief constable, and Assistant Commissioners were appointed by the Crown on the advice of the Home Secretary. By virtue of the Greater London Authority Act 1999 there is now a separate police authority for Greater London with a similar composition and powers as other police authorities although the senior appointments remain with the Home Secretary. There is also a special City of London Police Force limited to the square mile that technically comprises the City. Its police authority is the City local authority, the Court of Commons Council.

The 1996 Act provides for the alteration of local police areas (s. 32). This requires the consent of the Home Secretary either after proposals from individual forces, or on his own initiative following a local inquiry. Many forces have been amalgamated. In 1961 there were 123 separate police forces in England outside London whereas there are now 43. There is provision for co-operation between forces (s. 53).

In recent years the search for efficiency and the interdependence of local police forces has led to the creation of central organisations such as the National Police Data Bank, and the Mutual Aid Co-ordinating Centre. The recent creation of the National Criminal Intelligence Service and the National Crime Squad Service may constitute an embryonic national police force (see Police Act 1997). These bodies carry out police operations directly operating formally by agreement with local forces. They are regulated by central boards the membership of which strikes a balance between a minority of independent persons appointed by the Secretary of State, and nomination by chief officers and local police authorities from among their members. There is also provision for appointment of a 'crown servant' and a member of the security services (see Police Act 1997 as amended by Criminal Justice and Police Act 2001). Their operational directors, are the equivalent of chief constables. They are appointed by the boards from a list approved by the Secretary of State and can be removed with the approval of the Secretary of State who can also order their dismissal. A Central Police Training and Development Authority has also been created (Criminal Justice and Police Act 2001) the objectives of which are decided by the Secretary of State who can also give it detailed guidance and directions.

The regulation of local forces is split three ways. The chief constable is in charge of day-to-day policing. The police authority, in London the metropolitan police authority, provides funds and exercises a limited policy and strategy function. The Home Secretary exercises policy, funding and supervisory powers and controls senior appointments. Thus the police authority must respond both to the chief constables' operational requirements and to the policy requirements of the central government. It therefore acts as a transmission belt between the two.

15.2.1   The chief constable

Day-to-day 'direction and control' is vested in the chief constable (in London the metropolitan police commissioner), whose powers and duties have been said to be owed only to the law itself (Police Act 1996 s. 10; *R.* v. *Metropolitan Police Commissioner ex parte Blackburn* [1968] 2 QB 118 at 136). It appears that no one is politically accountable for operational decisions taken by the chief constable although, as we shall see, the central government has substantial power to direct policing priorities. The relationship between a chief constable and an individual police officer is not that of employer and employee. As we have seen, the powers and duties of a constable derive from the general law and not even the chief constable can order police officers how to exercise their powers, for example of arrest, in a particular case.

The chief constable has operational discretion but must have regard to the objects and targets set out in an annual plan made by the police authority under s. 8 of the Police Act 1996. This plan includes policing priorities and expected financial constraints. The chief constable must also report to the police authority annually and whenever required (s. 20).

15.2.2 The police authority

Each police force has a local 'police authority'. This is a committee or joint committee of the relevant local authority. It normally comprises 17 members including nine local councillors, three magistrates, and five appointed by the local authority from a short list made by the Home Secretary. Thus elected persons form a bare majority over the recipients of patronage. The political balance of the elected members must reflect that of the council as a whole (Criminal Justice and Police Act 2001 s. 105). The functions of the police authority depend entirely on statute.

(i) The police authority must maintain an efficient and effective police force (Police Act 1996 s. 6 (1)). This is a crucial but ambiguous provision. Some argue that it gives the police authority political control in the sense that it allows it to specify how policing priorities should be ordered. The more widely held view is that it only requires the authority to provide material resources and to fix the budget for whatever policing policies are determined by the chief constable. However, s. 7 enables a police authority to impose 'objectives' on its force consistent with any objectives imposed by the Home Secretary (below). The police authority is required by s. 8 to make an annual plan setting out its strategic priorities, its expected financial resources and its proposed allocation of resources. The plan must also have regard to national objects and performance targets set out by the Home Secretary under ss. 37 and 38 of the 1996 Act.

(ii) The police authority appoints, retires and dismisses senior police officers, that is, chief constables and assistant chief constables. The consent of the Home Secretary is required (Police Act 1996 ss. 11, 11A, 12). In London, the metropolitan commissioner and deputy commissioner are appointed by the Crown on the advice of the Home Secretary. They can be removed by the metropolitan police authority with the consent of the Home Secretary (Greater London Authority Act 1999 s. 315, 318; Police Act 1996 ss. 9E, 9F). Other appointments, dismissals and disciplinary decisions are for the chief constable or metropolitan police commissioner. There is an appeal to a tribunal against decisions to retire and dismiss whether by the police authority or the chief constable (s. 85).

(iii) The police authority receives an annual report from the chief constable and can also require special reports. However, the chief constable can refuse to provide information if he believes that it would either be contrary to the public interest or outside the functions of the authority (Police Act 1996 s. 22). Disputes are settled by the Home Secretary. Here again there is room for debate as to whether the police authority should be concerned with matters of policing policy.

(iv) The police authority administers the police fund (ibid. s. 14).

15.2.3 The Home Secretary

Under the Police Act 1996 the Home Secretary has a range of important statutory powers over individual forces and broadly similar powers under the Police Act 1997 over the National Criminal Intelligence Service (NCIS) and National Crime Squad (NCS) (above). These powers do not include the giving of direct operational orders but could be indirectly used to achieve considerable central control. The main powers are as follows:

- Consent to the appointments and dismissals of the chief constable and deputy chief constables. In the case of the NCIS and NCS the directors are appointed by the boards from a list approved by the Secretary of State (Police Act 1997 ss. 6, 52).
- To require a police authority to dismiss a chief constable in the interests of 'efficiency and effectiveness' (s. 42).
- To set objectives (s. 37), and performance targets (s. 38), to issue codes of practice (s. 39).
- To make regulations about pay, discipline, uniforms, organisation, training, duties and equipment, welfare and housing.
- To require reports from chief constables, police authorities (s. 43 (1)).

- To give grants to police authorities (s. 46). Central government grant amounts to about 70% of the cost of running a local force.
- To inspect individual forces. For this purpose there is an Inspectorate of Constabulary which makes an annual report which is laid before Parliament. The Home Secretary can require the inspectorate to hold an inspection into any force (s. 40). The Home Secretary can also appoint any person to hold an inquiry into the efficiency or effectiveness of a force and can give directions as the result of the inquiry (s. 49). For example the Macpherson Inquiry into the death of Stephen Lawrence which reported in 1999 found widespread 'institutional racism' within the force and made numerous recommendations for changes in the law and practice of policing.
- To alter police areas (s. 5).
- To provide and maintain 'such organisations, facilities and services as he considers necessary or expedient for promoting the efficiency and effectiveness of the police' (s. 57).
- To control the Central Police Training and Development Authority (Criminal Justice and Police Act 2001).

Apart from these statutory powers the Home Secretary can invoke the Royal Prerogative to enable him to influence police policies, thus clashing with local independence. In *R.* v. *Secretary of State for the Home Department ex parte Northumbria Police Authority* (1988), the Home Office had made plastic bullets and tear-gas available to individual police forces without the consent of the local police authority. It was argued that this kind of decision is the exclusive responsibility of the local police authority. It was held by the Court of Appeal that nothing in the governing legislation made the police authority the exclusive provider of police resources and that the prerogative power of the Crown to keep the peace permits the Home Office to equip the police. Moreover the Court held that the Police Act 1964 also authorised the Home Secretary to supply weapons to the police as a 'central service'. These powers apply only to the supply of equipment and cannot be used to direct a chief constable how to deploy any equipment so provided.

15.3 Police Accountability

The question of police accountability raises three main constitutional issues. They relate to the separation of powers and raise the conflict between liberal and communitarian values. (i) Should the police be subject to political control and accountability? (ii) Should police forces be national or local bodies? (iii) To what extent should detailed police decisions be subject to independent scrutiny by the courts? The efficiency advantages of a national police force are obvious, as are the corresponding dangers. The argument in favour of local accountability is attractive but raises the danger of bias. There are considerable practical difficulties with operationally separate local forces, given the expensive technology required for police activities and the indifference of criminals to geographical boundaries. The liberal perspective would favour an independent police force but one in which efficiency is sacrificed to clear legal restrictions on police powers.

15.3.1   Political accountability

The police spend large amounts of public money that has to come from the same purse as other government services. Arguably they should be subject to principles of political accountability in the same way as, say, education and health services. Furthermore the resources available to the police are unlikely to be adequate to enable them to perform all their many tasks to the ideal extent. Therefore hard choices may have to be made and priorities balanced. This, it is often argued, requires political judgements and therefore calls for democratic mechanisms. In particular, it is argued, in communitarian style, that the police should be responsive to the priorities of their local communities.

The contrary argument focuses upon traditional ideas of the rule of law, in particular the need for the police to be unbiased and politically impartial, and upon the specialised professional expertise needed to make policing judgements. The arguments are confused if we do not distinguish between different kinds of 'accountability': that is, between control over decision making, and the need to explain and justify action after the event. We might also distinguish between responsibility for operational decisions in individual cases – which few would want to be within political control and responsibility for general policies and priorities, although this distinction is a more difficult one.

The allegedly independent status of constable is one of the reasons why the problem of controlling the police is difficult and controversial. There are no clear lines of accountability since neither central nor local government are directly accountable for the exercise of police powers in individual cases. This emphasises the independence of police officers but is sometimes regarded as artificial and undesirable because it ignores the political and financial framework within which the police operate (Lustgarten, 1986, Ch. 4). It does not follow, it is said, that because a police officer has certain powers directly conferred on him by law, that he should not be subject to any kind of political control. It is for the constable to decide how to exercise his powers, but this is not the same as deciding the question of general priorities – dividing resources between traffic regulation or sex offences, for instance.

Local accountability is through the local police authority. The police authority cannot interfere with operational decisions but is responsible for allocating resources, and the chief constable must have regard to the police authority's annual plan (above). As a result of the report by Lord Scarman into the Brixton riots in 1981, the Police and Criminal Evidence Act 1984 s. 106, provides for 'arrangements for obtaining the views of the community on policy and for obtaining their co-operation in preventing crime in the area'. These arrangements must be made by the police authority after consulting the chief constable. In the case of the Metropolitan police, the arrangements must be made by the commissioner, taking into account 'guidance' from the Secretary of State and after consulting each London local authority. No timetable or procedure is laid down, but the Home Secretary has the power to oversee the arrangements made. However, this does not include a power to direct an authority to make any specific arrangements, but only to refer the matter back to the authority if he is dissatisfied. The outcome of whatever arrangements are made has no binding effect.

The Sheehy Report (*Inquiry into Police Responsibilities and Rewards*, Cmnd. 2280 (1993)) concerned the internal structure and management of the police. It recommended strengthening internal accountability mechanisms by using what has become a standard device in private industry: fixed-term contracts and 'performance standards'. The obvious threat that these pose to the independence of a police officer as an officer of the law is dealt with by recommending a right of appeal to the Home Secretary and that appointments be terminable only upon the grounds of misconduct, inadequate performance, structural consideration and medical and related grounds. However, the government has rejected fixed-term contracts except in the case of the most senior ranks.

15.3.2 The courts and the police

A basic difficulty in relation to police accountability arises from the English 'adversarial' system of criminal justice. This treats a trial as a contest between two supposedly equal parties, the prosecution (the Crown) and the accused person. This can be compared with the continental 'inquisitorial system' where the process is one of official investigation, the aim being to discover the truth. In Britain the aim is for the prosecution to 'prove' its case according to the rules of the trial, which some people compare with a contest or game (see Lustgarten, 1986). The adversarial procedure encourages the police to be partisan and to measure success in terms of convictions, thus encouraging the abuse of police powers.

Originally the police themselves conducted most prosecutions. The Director of Public Prosecutions (DPP) and the Attorney-General also had prosecution powers. However, the Prosecution of Offenders Act 1985 created a separate Crown Prosecution Service which is under the control of the Director of Public Prosecutions. Crown prosecutors in local areas have powers to prosecute and conduct cases subject to discretion given by the DPP under the Act. The DPP is appointed by the Attorney-General who is answerable in Parliament for the Crown Prosecution Service. The DPP makes an annual report to the Attorney-General which is laid before Parliament. The DPP is required to issue a code for Crown prosecutions, laying down general guidelines and this must be included in the annual report. The Attorney-General can also prevent a prosecution of any indictable (meaning jury trial) offence by issuing a 'nolle prosequi' – an order not to prosecute under the Royal Prerogative.

The Crown prosecutor has power to take over most criminal prosecutions (s. 3) or to order any proceedings to be discontinued (s. 23). Except where an offence can only be prosecuted by a person named in the relevant statute (for example the Attorney-General, or a specified public authority), any individual may bring a private prosecution, but the Crown Prosecution Service can take over such a prosecution (s. 6 (2)).

Operational decisions taken by the police can be reviewed by the courts. In particular, an order of *mandamus* can be made to require a chief constable to enforce the law or perform some other legal duty. Conversely, an injunction can be obtained to restrain an excess of power. However, the courts are reluctant to interfere with what they consider to be matters of professional judgement against a background of limited resources. They will interfere with the discretion of the chief constable only if it is exercised irrationally, even if it means that the law is not fully enforced and legal freedoms are compromised.

This is the normal *Wednesbury* ground of judicial review (see Chapter 14) but seems to be applied particularly cautiously in this context (see Lord Slynn in *R. v. Chief Constable of Sussex ex parte International Traders Ferry Ltd* [1999] 1 All ER 129 at 137). It is not unlawful for a chief constable to take into account competing calls upon limited resources although this may be subject to priorities determined by EC law or the Human Rights Act. *R.* v. *Chief Constable of Sussex ex parte International Traders Ferry Ltd* (1999): inadequate resources available to police demonstrations by animal rights protesters, police restricted number of lorries using docks). It is also lawful for the police not to take action against particular lawbreakers as part of a strategy of community relations. For example in *R.* v. *Chief Constable of Devon & Cornwall ex parte Central Electricity Generating Board (CEGB)* (1982) the Court of Appeal accepted that it had no power to interfere with the policy of the chief constable not to evict anti-nuclear campaigners from a site, even though they had committed at least one criminal offence. It would, however, be unlawful for a chief constable not to enforce the law in respect of a particular offence because he disagreed with the wisdom of the law itself (see *R.* v. *Metropolitan Police Commissioner ex parte Blackburn* (1968)).

Ordinary civil actions for damages can also be brought against the police. The chief constable is made statutorily liable as if he was the employer of the wrongdoer, and any damages are payable from police funds (Police Act 1996 s. 88). Police officers are probably Crown servants (above), but by virtue of the Crown Proceedings Act 1947 the Crown is not liable for their wrongs because police officers are not appointed or paid wholly by the Crown. In relation to the standard of police liability there is a distinction between cases where a police officer has a general discretion, for example whether or not to arrest at that time, and cases where the law requires the police officer to have a 'reasonable' belief that some state of affairs exists, for example that an offence has been committed. In the former case the standard is the minimal one of *Wednesbury* unreasonableness appropriate to judicial review. In the latter case a higher standard is required and the police officer's grounds must be objectively reasonable in the view of the court (see *Holgate-Mohammed* v. *Duke* (1986) p. 375; *Castorini* v. *Chief Constable of Surrey* (1988)).

It has been held that the police are not generally liable for negligence in respect of policy decisions (*Hill* v. *Chief Constable of West Yorkshire* (1987)) although the European Court on Human Rights has recently condemned such blanket immunity (see *Osman* v. *UK* (1998)). There could, however, be liability in respect of purely operational duties with limited discretion, such as guarding offenders (see *Home Office* v. *Dorset Yacht Company* (1970)) or where considerations of the public interest, for example the need to protect informers, call for liability (see *Swinney* v. *Chief Constable of Northumberland Police* (1996)).

15.3.3   Complaints against the police

We have seen that the 'ombudsman' device is sometimes used to reinforce political controls over important government bodies. In the case of the police, the tradition has long been maintained that the police themselves investigate complaints against their peers on the ground that expertise and efficiency are regarded by UK governments as more important than impartiality. The inquiry may result in a criminal prosecution or internal disciplinary proceedings these being separate matters. Independently of any police proceedings a civil action can be brought against the individual officers concerned thus reflecting the rule of law principle that the police have no special immunities. An advantage of a civil action is that the co-operation of the police themselves is not required. Moreover the burden of proof in civil proceedings, that of balance of probabilities, is lower than the standard required in disciplinary and criminal proceedings, that of 'beyond reasonable doubt'.

One of the recommendations of the MacPherson Report (1999) into the police failure properly to investigate the murder of Stephen Lawrence was that there should be an independent procedure for investigating complaints against the police. Moreover in *Belilos* v. *Switzerland* (1988), the European Court of Human Rights held that the existence on a police board of a member who was in fact independent was not enough and that public confidence requires that there be organisational independence when serious allegations are investigated.

The present complaints procedure is only partly independent. The Police and Criminal Evidence Act 1984 created an independent Police Complaints Authority appointed by the Crown (s. 83 and Sched. 4). However, the Authority's main function is to supervise internal investigations and it has no independent staff to carry out investigations itself. Minor matters are dealt with by the chief constable by negotiation. Complaints against senior officers (officers above chief superintendent rank) are submitted to the police authority. Investigations into more serious complaints are investigated by an officer of at least chief inspector rank, usually from another force. The Police Complaints Authority either monitors or supervises the complaints process, its involvement increasing in proportion to the gravity of the matter. In cases involving death or serious injury it must supervise the investigation itself. However, the procedure is secretive and remains dependent upon the police investigating each other. There is no public right of direct access to the Police Complaints Authority. Indeed it is unlawful for members, or former members, officers or servants of the

Authority to disclose information to outsiders except in the form of a summary or general statement made by the Authority itself (s. 98).

If a complaint is established there may be disciplinary proceedings with a right of appeal to the Home Secretary who must usually refer the appeal to a special three-person inquiry. If a possible criminal charge is involved the report goes to the DPP whose consent is necessary for a prosecution. The Police Complaints Authority can refer the case to the DPP itself, or can order disciplinary charges to be brought. It can also set up a special disciplinary tribunal comprising the chief constable and two of its own members, but only in exceptional circumstances (s. 94).

15.4 The Armed Forces

In Britain there is a political consensus that the armed forces are subordinate to the Crown and to Parliament. Historically there is a distinction between the navy and the other forces. The navy was originally raised under the inherent royal prerogative power of the Crown to defend the realm. Armies, by contrast, were raised by feudal landlords, amongst whom was the Crown, to defend their own interests. Under the Bill of Rights 1688 a standing army cannot be raised or maintained within the realm in peacetime without the consent of Parliament. Thus, funding, the life blood of the executive is in principle under democratic control. Accordingly Armed Forces Acts which must be periodically reviewed are required to keep the army and air force (historically an off-shoot of the army), in being, together with the funding authorised by the annual Appropriation Acts. A similar arrangement for naval discipline and finance is governed by the Naval Discipline Act 1971.

The control of the armed forces is part of the Royal Prerogative and the courts are unlikely to interfere with matters concerning the deployment of the armed forces (*Chandler* v. *DPP* (1964)). Parliamentary control is also limited, for example in the case of the government's decision to deploy troops in Afghanistan. The discipline of members of the armed forces is governed by a statutory code derived from the Armed Forces Acts 1955 and 1986. Apart from statute, a soldier, sailor or airman has the same rights and duties as any other citizen, thus reflecting Dicey's rule of law (see *Grant* v. *Gould* (1792)). For example, force can only be used in self-defence and must be reasonably proportionate to the attack. This causes difficulties in cases where soldiers are operating under conditions of great stress requiring swift reactions. Furthermore it is no defence to claim obedience to the orders of a superior. Unlawful orders must not be obeyed. However, there is authority, although it is unreliable, that a reasonable belief that an order is lawful is a defence (see *R.* v. *Smith* (1900); *Keighley* v. *Bell* (1866) 4 F and F 763 at 790). The matter probably depends upon the particular legal context, in particular the extent to which intention or negligence is an ingredient of the offence.

Military law includes a code of offences triable by courts martial. Courts martial follow a procedure analogous to that of an ordinary court and there is a right to legal representation. However, their members and prosecutors are internally appointed. Courts martial are supervised by the ordinary courts (*Grant* v. *Gould* (1792)). There is also a Courts Martial Appeal Court composed of ordinary civil judges. Thus military law is integrated into the general system of justice (see Courts Martial (Appeal) Act 1968).

The Armed Forces (Discipline) Act 2000 has increased the protection given to persons accused under military law. This includes limits on the power to detain without charge, a right to elect a proper court martial rather than an informal hearing by the commanding officer and a right of appeal to an independent appeals court in respect of summary offences tried by the commanding officer. These measures were necessary in order to comply with the European Convention on Human Rights, particularly Art. 6 which confers a right to a fair trial before an impartial judge, illustrating that the rule of law is an overiding concern, at least in non-combat circumstances. For example in *Findlay* v. *United Kingdom* (1997) it was held that the organisation of a court martial did not offer adequate impartiality where the members of the court were appointed by the convening officer and there was an internal review of the sentence. Thus the Act does not go far enough to satisfy the Convention and there seems to be a structural deficit of independence in the court martial system (see *Morris* v. *UK* (2002)).

Military law overlaps with the general criminal law in that some offences will be covered by both regimes. The more serious offences are tried by the ordinary courts, and there are provisions preventing 'double jeopardy' that is, being tried twice for the same offence (see Armed Forces Act 1966, ss. 25, 26, 35). In certain cases civilian employees or dependants of members of the armed forces are subject to military law.

There is authority that rights conferred by military law, for example actions against officers for improper disciplinary actions, cannot be enforced in the ordinary courts even if the officer acts maliciously (see *Dawkins* v. *Lord Rokeby* (1866); *Dawkins* v. *Lord Paulet* (1869)). However, these cases concerned the exercise of disciplinary powers by officers acting within their powers and so would not be actionable in any event. If an officer commits a legal wrong, there is no reason in principle why the court should not intervene. On the other hand, the courts are likely to give weight to the need to preserve internal discipline and therefore to defer to the internal decision maker (see *Leech* v. *Parkhurst Prison Deputy Governor* [1988] 1 All ER 485 at 498–501; *R.* v. *Ministry of Defence ex parte Smith* (1996)). Where it is alleged that a soldier has been denied a fair hearing in disciplinary proceedings the courts are more willing to interfere (see e.g. *R.* v. *Army Board ex parte Anderson* (1992)). Moreover the Human Rights Act 1998 is likely to require the courts to take a more interventionist stance. For example the decision in *Smith* (above) where the Court of Appeal refused to interfere with a decision to ban active homosexuals from serving in the army has been condemned by the European Court of Human Rights (below p. 386).

By virtue of s. 10 of the Crown Proceedings Act 1947, a member of the armed forces could not sue in respect of injuries which the Secretary of State certified were attributable to service for pension purposes, whether or not the victim qualified for a pension. This covered injuries on active service, injuries on military premises and injuries caused by other military personnel. This clear injustice was remedied by the Crown Proceedings (Armed Forces) Act 1987 but without retrospective force and giving the Secretary of state power to restore the immunity in war time. This left a large area of immunity in respect of injuries incurred before 1987, a period during which health and safety standards were not especially stringent. However, in *Matthews* v. *Ministry of Defence* (2002), it was held that s. 10 violated the plaintiff's right to a fair trial under Art. 6 of the European Convention on Human Rights. There was no strong policy reason in favour of the immunity so that the interference failed the proportionality test and the court made a declaration of incompatibility. This was a procedural immunity in that it depended on the Secretary of State's certificate thereby engaging Art. 6. It is less clear whether Art. 6 applies to a substantive immunity, where a public body is made automatically exempt from liability. (see *Osman* v. *UK* (1999)).

Summary

15.1 The police are organised upon a local basis. There is no national police force but about 49 local or regional forces, each one in theory independent. In practice they share resources and work closely together, confined by central government controls. Police powers derive from the general law and are vested in each individual constable. Managerial and financial controls are divided between individual chief constables, local authorities and the Home Office. Central government control over the police generally has been increased by recent legislation.

15.2   There is no formal method of rendering the police subject to political or demo-cratic control or accountability. It is controversial whether this is desirable. There are disputes about whether accountability should be national or local and whether there should be democratic accountability at all. As in every area of government, limited resources must be balanced and priorities established.

15.3   There is provision for public consultation about policing matters, but this is left to the police themselves to arrange and detailed machinery is not prescribed.

15.4   The courts exercise a limited degree of control over police decisions. This is based upon the law of judicial review but in some cases a higher level of civil liability is imposed, reflecting Dicey's notion of the rule of law. On the other hand the police have a degree of immunity in the law of negligence.

15.5   There is an independent Police Complaints Authority which monitors the investigation of complaints against the police and in serious cases super-vises the investigation. The procedure is not public and open, and the actual investigation is carried out by the police themselves.

15.6   The armed forces are servants of the Crown and are under the direct control of the elected government. Historically, control over the armed forces was based largely on the Royal Prerogative particularly in the case of the navy. The Bill of Rights 1688 placed the army under parliamentary control and in modern times all the armed services are regulated by statute as far as organisation and discipline is concerned but not as regards deployment. There is a special system of military law with its own courts, but it is subject to control by the ordinary courts. The rights of members of the armed forces have been strenghened by the Human Rights Act 1998. Members of the armed forces have no special legal immunites but the extent to which the courts will interfere depends on the sensitivity of the particular issue and in particular the extent and urgency of the need to deploy force.

Further Reading

Lustgarten, *The Governance of the Police*.
Clayton and Tomlinson, *Civil Actions Against the Police*.
Jowell and Oliver, *The Changing Constitution*, chapter 11.

Exercises

15.1   Explain the legal position of a police constable as regards control over his or her activities.

15.2   To what extent is policing in Britain a local responsibilty? Would a national police force desirable?

15.3   Do you think that the police are adequately protected against political interference?

15.4   To what extent are local police forces subject to democratic control?

15.5   You believe that you are being subject to unreasonable harassment by the police because

    (i) The public house of which you are the manager has been selected for police surveillance every weekend.

    (ii) Your son, who is black, claims that a policeman beat him up and smashed his portable radio because he refused to step into the gutter to allow the policeman to pass by.

    (iii) Your wife, who is a civilian caterer at the local police station, is subject to verbal sexual harassment at her place of work.

    What remedies are available to you in the courts and elsewhere?

15.6   The Chief Constable of Denton announces that his force can no longer patrol wealthy residential areas after dark because of a shortage of funds, and that residents should employ private security guards. This policy is contrary to central government advice. Your client, who lives in a wealthy residential area tells you that her house is regularly burgled and that she wishes to compel the local police force to change this policy.

    (i) Advise her.

    (ii) Advise the local police authority what steps, if any, they can take to change this policy.

    (iii) Advice the Home Secretary whether he can compel a change of policy.

15.7   To what extent are members of the armed forces subject to a special legal regime?

Part IV

The Citizen and the State

16 Judicial Review of the Executive: The Grounds of Review

16.1 Introduction: Constitutional Basis of Judicial Review

Judicial review, sometimes called the supervisory jurisdiction, is the High Court's power to police the legality of decisions made by public bodies. A right to binding judicial review is required under Art. 6 of the European Convention on Human Rights (the right to a fair trial, see *Bentham* v. *Netherlands* (1985)), although the level of review depends on the context (*Zumbotel* v. *Austria* (1993)). An accommodation must be struck between competing concerns. The rule of law requires at least that the government justify its powers by reference to statute or the royal prerogative and may also require the government to conform to basic procedural standards of justice and equality. On the other hand, parliamentary supremacy prevents the courts from overriding a statute. Both the separation of powers and the European Convention on Human Rights requires the courts to check misuse of power by the executive but also to avoid trespassing into the political territory of the government. At least in cases where a decision maker is politically accountable to the electorate, the courts claim not to be concerned with the 'merits' of government action, that is whether it is good or bad, but only whether governmental decisions fall within their authorising legislation and meet legal standards of fairness and 'reasonableness' (see e.g. *R. (Alconbury)* v. *Secretary of State* (2001) particularly Lord Hoffmann's speech, *R.* v. *Somerset CC ex parte Fewings* (1995) per Laws J). However, we shall see that these legal standards shade into questions of merits and that there is considerable room for debate as to the proper limits of the courts' powers.

The separation of powers also requires the court to respect bodies of equal status to itself. We saw an example of this in the context of parliamentary privilege. For example the High Court cannot review another superior court decision (Re *Racal Communications* (1981)). The High Court can review all executive bodies including ministers and local government, police and military decisions, inferior courts including magistrates courts, the county court and the many hundreds of statutory tribunals and non-departmental public bodies. It is not clear how far judicial review extends to powerful private bodies such as educational institutions, sporting and professional associations which make decisions affecting the individual and sometimes act on behalf of the government (see Chapter 17).

Judicial review covers a wide range of matters. In the CCSU case it was suggested that some matters are non-justiciable in the sense of inappropriate for judicial review. This might be because of their political sensitivity or because the courts lack relevant powers or expertise to deal with them. Examples include the dissolution of Parliament, the appointment of ministers, the granting of honours and the making of a treaty and other matters concerning relationships with overseas governments. However, Allan (2000, Ch. 6) argues that, as a blanket principle, this violates the rule of law. He suggests that any exclusion from review should have reasoned justification and that the matter should depend on the circumstances of the particular case. The extent of the decision-maker's discretion, the political nature of the issues, alternative remedies, the court's expertise and effectiveness are factors which must be set against the gravity of the interference with individual rights and the public interest in protecting the rule of law.

Thus, while the principles of judicial review are of general application, the way they are applied in the sense of the intensity of review, the range of grounds available or the selection of remedies, varies with the context. We will meet examples throughout this chapter and the next. In particular the courts apply strict standards to judicial bodies, such as tribunals which determine legal rights (e.g. *R.* v. *Army Board ex parte Anderson* (1992)) but are less willing to interfere with a decision which involves the discretionary allocation of scarce resources for example whether or not to treat an NHS patient (see *R.* v. *Cambridge Health Authority ex parte B* (1995)). The courts also respect the sphere of accountability of the executive to Parliament although some judges are more deferential to this than others (see the disagreement in *R.* v. *Secretary of State for the Home Department ex parte Fire Brigades Union* (1995)). As early as 1911 one judge at least was expressing doubts about ministerial responsibility (see *Dyson* v. *A-G* (1911)).

Similarly the court may defer to specialist expertise. For example in *Clarke* v. *University of Lincolnshire and Humberside* (2000), it was held that matters of academic judgement in a university such as the award of degree classifications or prizes were not normally reviewable by the courts but other aspects of the relationship between the university and the student were justiciable, in particular allegation of breaches of the university regulations. The courts usually defer to a minister's opinion as to what national security requires but will ensure that the matter is genuinely one of national security (CCSU v. *Minister for the Civil*

Service (1985)). Other cases where the courts are cautious include electoral matters (*R.* v. *Boundary Commission for England ex parte Foot* (1993), child care (*R.* v. *Harrow LBC* (1990)) and voluntary regulatory bodies (*R.* v. *Panel on Takeovers and Mergers ex parte Datafin plc* (1987)), although there is usually no protection for unfair procedures.

The legal basis of judicial review is disputed. One perspective bases judicial review upon broad common law notions that powerful bodies must act in accordance with basic values of fairness and justice, respect for rights and rationality (*Dr Bonham's Case* (1610); *Cooper* v. *Wandsworth Board of Works* (1863)). During the late nineteenth century, however, the democratic basis of both central and local government had led to a shift in the justification for judicial review. The assumption was that, because most government powers are created by statute, the courts' role should be confined to ensuring that powers were exercised as Parliament intended. The '*ultra vires*' doctrine ('beyond powers') became widely accepted as the constitutional basis of judicial review. For a time from the First World War until the early 1960s the *ultra vires* doctrine was used to justify a low level of judicial review according to which, a government decision falling within the language of the statute that created the power could not be challenged (see *Local Government Board* v. *Arlidge* (1915); *Liversidge* v. *Anderson* (1942); *Franklin* v. *Minister of Town and Country Planning* (1948)).

More recently, heralded by *Ridge* v. *Baldwin* (1964) (below), the courts have taken a more active role in controlling government. This was recognised by Lord Mustill in the *Fire Brigades* case (above) where he explained that a perception that parliament accountability has failed, leaving the citizen without remedy has stimulated the courts to fill the 'dead ground'. However, in the same passage Lord Mustill warned of the danger of violating the separation of powers. The courts have developed broad grounds of review including unfairness, unreasonableness and error. They have also extended judicial review to the royal prerogative and to bodies which do not derive their powers from statute (e.g. *R.* v. *Panel on Takeovers and Mergers ex parte Datafin plc* (1987)) and have begun to invoke the common law as underpinning judicial review (e.g. *R.* v. *Secretary of State ex parte Piersen* [1997] 3 WLR 492, 518). These developments have made the *ultra vires* doctrine questionable as the basis of judicial review.

Some writers have therefore suggested that the judicial review principles are free-standing common law principles even if they are displaced by clear words in a statute (see Allan, 2000, p. 207; Craig, 1998; Oliver, 1987). In *Council of Civil Service Unions* v. *Minister for the Civil Service* (1983), Lord Diplock famously classified the grounds of judicial review independently of *ultra vires* under three broad but not exhaustive principles, these being 'illegality, irrationality and procedural impropriety'. On the other hand there are dicta that the basis of judicial review remains the *ultra vires* doctrine at least in relation to statutory powers (*Boddington* v. *British Transport Police* [1998] 2 WLR 639 at 650, 655, 662; *Credit Suisse* v. *Allerdale DC* [1996] 2 All ER 129 at 167; *Page* v. *Hull University Visitor* [1993] 1 All ER 97 at 107; *O'Reilly* v. *Mackman* [1982] 3 All ER 1124 at 1129).

The two approaches could be reconciled by claiming that it is Parliament's intention that principles of judicial review be implied into the exercise of statutory powers because Parliament can be assumed to respect the rule of law (see Forsythe, 1996; Elliott, 1999a, b; cf. Craig, 2001). However, this could be regarded as a fiction and indeed as undermining the integrity of the rule of law. It turns the *ultra vires* doctrine into an empty vessel for whatever happens to be the prevailing orthodoxy, whether in terms of human rights, as is currently the case or the 'principles of good administration' which flourished in the 1980s (see *R.* v. *Lancashire County Council ex parte Huddlestone* [1986] 2 All ER 941 at 945; *R.* v. *Monopolies and Mergers Commission ex parte Argyle Group plc* [1986] 2 All ER 257 at 266). The *ultra vires* doctrine is certainly an important aspect of judicial review but not the whole story. In particular it cannot easily rationalise judicial review of royal prerogative and other non-statutory powers.

An important function of judicial review is the protection of individual rights. On the other hand judicial review goes beyond the protection of legal rights as such. For example a member of the public can sometimes seek judicial review even if he or she has no rights at stake and judicial review might be invoked between government agencies such as central government and a local authority or between the UK government and the devolved governments. Moreover, even where the rights of the individual are at stake, the court has a discretion whether or not to intervene and might in principle refuse to give the citizen a remedy for reasons of the public interest (see Chapter 17).

16.2   Appeal and Review

Judicial review must not be confused with an appeal. An appeal is a procedure which exists only under a particular statute or, in the case of a voluntary body, by agreement. An appeal allows the appellate body to decide the whole matter again, unless the particular statute or agreement limits the grounds of appeal (e.g. Tribunals and Inquiries

Act 1992 s. 11, questions of law). An appeal therefore may involve a thorough reconsideration of the whole decision whereas judicial review is concerned only with ensuring that legal standards are complied with. Depending on the particular statute, an appellate body might be a court, tribunal, minister or indeed anyone. A claim for judicial review is possible only in the High Court.

An appellate body can usually substitute its decision for the first instance decision, although in some cases its powers are limited to sending the matter back to be decided again by the lower body. In judicial review proceedings the court cannot make a decision on the merits but must send the matter back to the decision maker with instructions as to its legal duties.

Unlike a right appeal of appeal which can be raised only in the body specified, the invalidity of government action can be raised not only in the administrative court but, by way of 'collateral challenge' in any proceedings where the rights of a citizen are affected by the validity of government action (e.g. *Boddington* v. *British Transport Police* (1998), prosecution for smoking contrary to railway bylaws alleged to be *ultra vires* as a defence). This is because an unlawful government decision is of no effect in law (void/nullity) and can be ignored thus vindicating the rule of law (*Entick* v. *Carrington* (above)). In the case of an appeal the offending decision is fully valid until the appeal body changes it.

This concept of nullity does not always lead to a just solution. For example in *Credit Suisse* v. *Allerdale BC* (1996) a local authority successfully relied on the argument that a guarantee which it has given was *ultra vires* so as to prevent the guarantee being enforced against it, and in *DPP* v. *Head* (1959) a man charged with having sexual relations with a patient 'detained' under the mental Health Acts was able to argue that because the patient's detention order had not been made according to the required formalities, she was not detained under the relevant Acts.

Under the Human Rights Act 1998 the question arises whether the availability of judicial review is a sufficient safeguard to comply with the right to a fair trial before an independent tribunal under Art. 6 of the European Convention on Human Rights. There is a problem where the government decision that is being challenged does not itself provide for an independent decision maker. For example many decisions involving the compulsory acquisition of land or planning restrictions on the use of land are made by ministers who are predisposed in favour of government policies and lack the independence of a judge. In *R. (Alconbury)* v. *Secretary of State* (2001), the House of Lords, held that, although such decisions impact on individual rights, the law must recognise that the minister has a political discretion intended to implement a public goal. On the other hand, where a decision is a direct adjudication about the existence of a right and where the decision maker has no discretion, for example a decision by a tax tribunal, it may be that nothing short of a full right of appeal would satisfy the right to a fair trial (below p. 430).

16.3   Classification of the Grounds of Review

Unfortunately there is no general agreement as to how to classify the grounds of review and the text books take different approaches. The grounds themselves are broad and vague and overlapping a conspicuous example of this being *Wheeler* v. *Leicester City Council* (below p. 383). In the following sections I shall organise the grounds of judicial review on the basis of Lord Diplock's classification in *CCSU* v. *Minister for the Civil Service* (1985) (above) that is, under the three heads of 'illegality, irrationality and procedural impropriety'. However, the Diplock categories tell us little in themselves and do not avoid overlaps. Indeed the House of Lords has emphasised that the heads of challenge are not watertight compartments but run together (*Boddington* v. *British Transport Police* [1998] 2 All ER 203, 208). It might be helpful at this point to provide a checklist.

1. 'Illegality'
   - 'Narrow' *ultra vires* or lack of jurisdiction in the sense of straying beyond the limits defined by the statute.
   - Errors of law, and (in certain cases) errors of fact.
   - 'Wide' *ultra vires* in the sense of acting for an ulterior purpose, taking irrelevant factors into account or failing to take relevant factors into account.
   - Fettering discretion.
2. 'Irrationality'
   - '*Wednesbury*' unreasonableness. This could stand alone or be the outcome of taking an irrelevant factor into account.
   - Proportionality.
3. Procedural impropriety
   - Violating important statutory procedures.
   - Bias.
   - Lack of a fair hearing.
   - Failure to give reasons for a decision.

16.4   Illegality

16.4.1   Narrow *ultra vires*

A decision is *ultra vires* if it is outside the language of the statute. In the case of courts and judicial tribunals the terminology of 'lack' or 'excess' of jurisdiction means the same as *ultra vires* although a distinction is sometimes made between lacking jurisdiction at the outset and straying outside jurisdiction by some subsequent defect. In most cases, however, this distinction does not matter (*Aninsminic Ltd* v. *Foreign Compensation Commission* (1969)) (a possible exception being personal liability (below p. 406)). An example is *A-G* v. *Fulham Corporation* (1921). A local authority had power to provide a 'wash-house' for local people It interpreted this as authorising the provision of a laundry service for working people who could leave washing to be done by staff and delivered to their homes. This was held to be unlawful in that 'wash-house', according to the court, means a place where a person can do their own washing. More recently in *Bromley LBC* v. *GLC* (1983) the House of Lords held that an obligation to provide an 'efficient and economic' public transport service meant that the council could not subsidise the London Underground for social purposes. Among other lines of reasoning it was held that 'economic' meant that there was an obligation to break-even financially.

These cases raise questions as to the assumptions that the courts bring to the task of interpreting statutes. For example, if the court in *Bromley* had adopted a principle in favour of local democratic freedom the outcome might have been different. Where the scope of a statute is unclear, the courts rely on presumptions of interpretation which protect the rights of the individual. These presumptions are applied unless overridden by express statutory language and probably also by necessary implication (see *R.* v. *Secretary of State for the Home Department ex parte Simms* [1999] 3 All ER 400 at 412 per Lord Hoffmann). One such presumption is that a citizen shall not be taxed or charged without clear statutory language (e.g. *Congreve* v. *Home Office* (1976): increase in TV licence fee). Another presumption is against excluding access to the courts (e.g. *Anisminic Ltd* v. *Foreign Compensation Commission* (1969); *R.* v. *Lord Chancellor ex parte Witham* (1997): increase in the charge for instituting court proceedings excluded the poor). There is also a presumption in favour of personal freedom. In *Raymond* v. *Honey* (1993) it was held that prisoners retained their legal rights except in as far as the governing legislation necessarily excluded them. A prisoner therefore had a right to write to a solicitor and to the confidentiality of correspondence with his lawyer (see also *Simms* (above), *Pierson* v. *Secretary of State* (1997), *R.* v. *Secretary of State for the Home Department ex parte Leech* (1993)). These presumptions have been strengthened by the Human Rights Act 1998 which requires government action to conform to the European Convention on Human Rights unless a statute renders this impossible (see Chapter 18). They have often been criticised on the basis that they might favour individualistic values at the expense of social welfare (e.g. *Fulham* and *Bromley* (above)).

There is further leeway in the *ultra vires* doctrine. The courts will permit an activity that, although not expressly authorised by the statute, is 'reasonably incidental' to something that is expressly authorised (e.g. *A-G* v. *Crayford UDC* (1962): voluntary household insurance scheme reasonably incidental to power to manage council housing because it helped tenants to pay the rent). However, the courts take a strict approach which impacts particularly on local authority freedom. For example in *Macarthy and Stone* v. *Richmond LBC* (1991) a charge for giving advice in connection with planning applications was held not to be incidental to the authority's planning powers. The giving of advice was not expressly authorised and was therefore itself an incidental function. The House of Lords took the view that something cannot be incidental to what is itself incidental. In *Hazell* v. *Hammersmith and Fulham BC* (1991), it was held that interest swap arrangements made by several local councils to spread the risk of future changes in interest rates were not incidental to the council's borrowing powers because they concerned debt management rather than borrowing as such.

16.4.2   Errors of law

The question whether the court can review decisions on the ground of legal or factual errors has caused problems. There seems to be a clash of principle. On the one hand, if the court can intervene merely because it considers that a decision is wrong it would be trespassing into the merits of the case (see *R.* v. *Nat Bell Liquors* (1922)). On the other hand the rule of law surely calls for a remedy if a decision maker misunderstands the law. After many years of groping towards an accommodation the courts have adopted a compromise. The outcome appears to be that almost all errors of law and some errors of fact can be challenged. This would conform to the European Convention on Human Rights, Art. 6 which requires a high level of review in relation to matters of law (*Bryan* v. *UK* (1995)).

A rationale which was popular in the nineteenth century is the doctrine of the 'jurisdictional' or 'collateral' or 'preliminary' question. According to this doctrine, if a mistake relates to a state of affairs which the court thinks that Parliament intended should exist objectively before the official has power to make the decision, then the court will interfere on the ground that the authority has acted *ultra vires* if the court thinks that the required state of affairs does not exist. For example in *White and Collins* v. *Minister of Health* (1939), the Secretary of State had power to acquire land 'other than a garden or parkland'. It was held that the court could interfere if it thought that the minister had wrongly decided whether the plaintiff's land was parkland. This can be justified on the rule-of-law ground that a minister should not be allowed to expand his own powers (see Farwell J in *R.* v. *Shoreditch Assessment Committee* [1910] 2 KB 859 at 880). However, there seems to be no logical way of deciding which of many issues that a decision maker has to decide are preliminary in this sense.

A second device which flourished during the 1960s but has largely been superseded is the doctrine of 'error of law on the face of the record' or patent error (*R.* v. *Northumberland Compensation Appeal Tribunal ex parte Shaw* (1952)). This allows the court to quash a decision if a mistake of law can be discovered by reading the written record of the decision without using other evidence. This could not be squeezed into the *ultra vires* doctrine. Thus decisions tainted by patent error are valid unless and until formally quashed by the court. This provides a practical compromise by allowing obvious mistakes to be rectified without reopening the whole matter. Many bodies were required to give written reasons for their decisions as part of the record (now Tribunals and Inquiries Act 1992 s. 10), and the courts were liberal in what material they regarded as part of the record.

As a result of the speeches of the House of Lords in *Anisminic Ltd* v. *Foreign Compensation Commission* [1969] 2 AC 147, notably that of Lord Reid, the older doctrines have been made largely redundant in relation to errors of law. *Anisminic* appears to have made all errors of law reviewable at least in principle. In *Anisminic* the FCC had wrongly interpreted the criteria for awarding compensation to the victims of an Arab–Israeli conflict. The governing statute purported to prevent challenge in the courts to a 'determination' of the FCC. However, the statute did not protect an act that was not in law a 'determination' at all, that is, where the commission had acted outside its jurisdiction so that its decision was a complete nullity. A majority of the House held the FCC's mistake meant that a factor was taken into account that Parliament did not intend which therefore took the FCC outside its jurisdiction. *Anisminic* has been widely taken as deciding that any mistake of law makes a decision *ultra vires* thereby giving narrow *ultra vires* a powerful extension. It is not clear that their Lordships intended to go so far (see *South East Asia Fire Brick Sdn BHD* v. *Non-Metallic Mineral Products Manufacturing Employees Union* (1981)). However, the wide reading of *Anisminic* has been confirmed, albeit *obiter*, in *Re Racal* (1981), *O'Reilly* v. *Mackman* (1983), and *Page* v. *Hull University Visitor* (1993)).

The courts have to some extent drawn back. They have used two main devices.

- In *Re Racal Communications* (1981) Lord Diplock suggested that *Anisminic* did not apply to decisions of courts which could be trusted to decide questions of law for themselves although this was later denied (*R.* v. *Manchester Coroner ex parte Tal* (1984)). In *Page* v. *Hull University Visitor* (1993) it was held that the specialised rules of universities could be conclusively interpreted by the University Visitor.

- They have manipulated the difficult distinction between questions of law and questions of fact. *Anisminic* has not been applied to mistakes of fact which arguably should not be reviewable because the primary decision maker is usually in a better position than the court to discover the facts. It is not always easy to distinguish between questions of law, questions of fact and questions of opinion. A question of law basically involves the meaning and usually the application of a rule. A question of fact involves the existence of some state of affairs or event in the world outside the law and depends on evidence. A question of opinion is where on the same evidence more than one view can reasonably be taken (*Luke (Lord)* v. *Minister of Housing and Local Government* [1968] 1 QB 172). It has been held that the courts should not interfere where the question involves a broad subjective or political concept or a term in everyday use unless the decision-maker's interpretation is unreasonable. The courts may treat some apparently legal questions of interpretation as matters of fact or opinion where they concern broad everyday notions or involve value judgements or matters of degree (see e.g. *Pulhoffer* v. *Hillingdon BC* (1986), 'homeless'; *R.* v. *Monoplies and Mergers Commission ex parte South Yorkshire Transport* (1993), 'substantial' part of the UK; *Edwards* v. *Bairstow* (1956), trade; *Brutus* v. *Cozens* (1973), 'insulting'; *R.* v. *Radio Authority ex parte Bull* (1997), 'political nature'. In these cases the initial question as to whether the statutory meaning requires this approach is of course a question of law (*Shah* v. *Barnett LBC* [1983] 2 AC 309, 341 – ordinarily resident).

16.4.3 Errors of fact

We have seen that errors of fact are not normally reviewable but there are exceptions (see Jones, 1990). The doctrine of the preliminary question (above) applies to errors of fact where it is sometimes called the 'precedent fact' doctrine. This allows the court to decide the question of fact for itself. For example in *Kawahaja* v. *Secretary of State for Home Affairs* (1983) the Home Secretary could deport an 'illegal immigrant'. The House of Lords held that the court could decide whether the appellant was in fact an illegal immigrant and was not limited to deciding whether the minister's decision was unreasonable. The problem is to decide what kind of case falls within the doctrine. This depends upon the statutory context. In *Kawahaja* the court was influenced by the fact that the decision involved personal freedom, so that a high level of judicial control was required. By contrast, in *Bugdaykay* v. *Secretary of State* (1987) the question was whether the applicant was a genuine asylum seeker. Here the decision was heavily laden with subjective political judgement and the court was not prepared to treat the matter as one of precedent fact.

Judicial review does not include a reinvestigation of disputed facts unless the decision is perverse (*Adam* v. *Newham BC* [2002]). However, in *R.* v. *Criminal Injuries Compensation Board ex parte A* [1999] 2 AC 330, 344–5, Lord Slynn said that 'misunderstanding or ignorance of an established and relevant fact' is reviewable, but emphasised that this is no more than an application of ordinary review principles. (See also *Secretary of State for Education and Science* v. *Tameside MBC* [1977] AC 1014 at 1017.) This principle also complies with Art. 6 of the ECHR which requires a right to challenge findings of fact, but not necessarily a full re-investigation of the facts, as an aspect of the right to a fair trial (see *R. (Alconbury)* v. *Secretary of State* (2001); *Bryan* v. *UK* (1995); *Chapman* v. *UK* (2001)). However, where the decision is directly concerned with a citizen's legal rights or entitlements, as opposed to a decision taken in the public interest which incidentally affects rights, if there is a dispute on the primary facts, Art. 6 may require a full appeal on the facts, unless the decision maker is independent (see *Adam* v. *Newham BC* [2002], below p. 430).

16.4.4 'Wide' *ultra vires*: improper purposes and irrelevant considerations

These aspects of illegality arise in the context of discretionary powers and are sometimes labelled abuse of discretion. Even though the decision maker keeps within the express language of the statute its motive may be improper or it may be influenced by irrelevant factors or it may overlook relevant factors. This applies even where the statute appears to give the decision maker an unrestricted subjective discretion using such expressions as 'if the minister thinks fit' since even the widest discretionary power is in principle reviewable (*Padfield* v. *Minister of Agriculture* (1968): a minister acting under a particular statutory power must not be influenced by wider political considerations that do not advance the policy of the Act).

The court will not set aside a decision if the irrelevant consideration would not have made any difference to the outcome. In this sense the line between legality and merits is blurred (see *R.* v. *ILEA ex parte Westminster City Council* (1986); *R.* v. *Secretary of State for Social Services ex parte Wellcome Foundation* (1987)). In the context of improper purposes this is sometimes expressed as the 'dominant purpose' test. For example in *Westminster Corporation* v. *London and North Western Railway* (1905) the local authority had power to construct public lavatories. It incorporated a subway into the design of its lavatories. This was held to be lawful on the basis that the subway was merely incidental to the lavatory. Although it could be used by people to cross the street it was also an appropriate method of reaching the lavatory. By contrast in *Webb* v. *Minister of Housing* (1965) the local authority had power to construct coast protection works. It incorporated a promenade into their scheme compulsorily acquiring a number of houses for the purpose. This was held to be unlawful on the ground that more land was acquired than was needed for an adequate coast protection barrier. The whole scheme was invalid and the good part could not be separated from the bad. Similarly in *R.* v. *Lewisham LBC ex parte Shell UK Ltd* (1988), the council decided to boycott Shell's products on the ground that Shell had interests in South Africa which, at the time, was subject to apartheid. It was held that the policy itself could have been lawfully justified on the ground of promoting good race relations in the borough. However, as the council had tried to persuade other local authorities to adopt a similar policy it had gone too far, its broad purpose being to put pressure on Shell.

In a borderline case the court is able to scrutinise in considerable depth the actual motives of the decision maker. In *Porter* v. *Magill* (2002), a local authority had embarked upon a policy of selling off its housing. It concentrated sales in marginal electoral wards with a view to attracting votes. The House of Lords held that, while political reality must be accepted, the policy could not be justified on the basis of legitimate housing purposes. A democratic body can hope for an electoral advantage as the outcome of its policies (and probably choose between alternative legitimate policies for electoral reasons), but it cannot *distort* policies in order to seek electoral advantage.

The starting point as always is the language of the particular statute. For example in *R.* v. *City of Westminster Housing Benefit Review Board* (2001), legislation required the housing benefit authority to reduce a claim when it considered that the rent was unreasonably high, 'having regard in particular to the cost of suitable accommodation elsewhere'. The board interpreted this as preventing it from taking into account the claimant's personal circumstances including his wife's pregnancy and his reduced income as an asylum seeker. The House of Lords held that personal circumstances were relevant pointing out that the phrase 'in particular' invited other factors to be considered and that a matter is legitimate provided that it was reasonably (or properly) regarded as relevant.

The scope of a statutory power may not be clear from the statutory language. The court must therefore infer from all the circumstances what are proper purposes and relevant considerations. Indeed, in *Westminster* (above) Lord Bingham said that '(i)n the absence of very clear language I would be very reluctant to conclude that the ... board were precluded from considering matters which could affect the mind of a reasonable and fair minded person'. This requires them not only to draw on rule of law values, but also to make political and moral judgements. For example the Town and Country Planning Act 1990 s. 70 (2) requires land use planning authorities 'to have regard to the provisions of the development plan ... and any other material considerations' leaving it to the courts to decide what these are. In *Stringer* v. *Minister of Housing* (1971) it was held that any factor relating to the use of land can be relevant. Thus in *Tesco Stores* v. *Secretary of State for the Environment* (1993) the House of Lords held that a local planning authority could adopt a policy that those who profit from planning permission should pay something back into the community.

What is 'relevant' may change in the light of changing community values to which the courts should be sensitive (see *Pickwell* v. *Camden*

BC (1987)). In *R. (Bulger)* v. *Secretary of State* (2001) the court, drawing on international obligations held that in fixing the length of time a convicted child offender must serve, the Secretary of State must take into account the welfare of the child and keep its progress and rehabilitation under review. In *R.* v. *Secretary of State for the Home Department ex parte Venables* (1997) it was held that public opinion, in the shape of an opinion poll in *The Sun* newspaper, was not relevant where the Secretary of State was charged with the judicial duty of reviewing the sentence in a notorious child murderer case since his judicial function must be exercised by his independent judgement. The courts have also held that local authorities should concern themselves with local issues as opposed to general issues of national or international politics (see *R.* v. *ILEA ex parte Westminster City Council* (1986); *R.* v. *Lewisham LBC ex parte Shell UK Ltd* (above)). It has also been held that local authorities should be guided by business principles in fixing wages, fares and prices (*Roberts* v. *Hopwood* (1925); *Prescott* v. *Birmingham Corporation* (1955); *Bromley LBC* v. *GLC* (1983)).

The courts are therefore policing the boundaries of the democratic process and in doing so imposing their own constitutional values (see Alder, 2001). In cases where a very wide range of factors might be relevant, the court may leave it to the official to decide what is relevant, interfering only if the decision is perverse. For example in *R.* v. *Somerset CC ex parte Fewings* (1995) a majority of the Court of Appeal thought (*obiter*) that a local authority might be entitled to take into account moral attitudes towards hunting in exercising a power to manage land for the 'benefit of the community,' but would not be required to do so (see also *CREEDNZ Inc.* v. *Governor-General* (1981)). However, Laws J at first instance took the view that moral factors could be taken into account only if clearly authorised by the governing legislation.

In *R.* v. *Foreign Secretary ex parte World Development Movement* (1995) the court perhaps went too far into the merits of government action. The government had statutory power to give financial aid to other countries for 'economic' purposes. It decided to give a grant to Malaysia for the Pergau Dam project. The Court of Appeal held that Parliament must have intended the word 'economic' to include only 'sound' economic decisions so that the court was entitled to infer that the decision had been made primarily for an ulterior purpose (perhaps of facilitating an arms sale arrangement). This seems to come very near to interfering with the merits of the decision since the court could deepen its investigation into any statutory function by saying that Parliament must have intended that function to be carried out 'soundly'. On the other hand, parliamentary scrutiny of public spending did not expose the misdeeds in this case so that the court's role may be justifiable as the only available constitutional check.

16.4.5 Fettering discretion

An official fetters his or her discretion by applying a rigid rule without being prepared to consider departing from it review (*ex parte Kynoch* (1919)). An official must be prepared to be flexible in the circumstances of the particular case. Officials can of course follow general rules or policies generated within government. Indeed government would be impracticable without them. Moreover the principle of fairness requires that people be treated equally thereby generating rules. Nevertheless, unless a rule is laid down by or under statute, officials must always consider whether in any given case an exception should be made. As Lord Reid put it in *British Oxygen Co.* v. *Ministry of Technology* [1971] AC 610, 625 'a Ministry or large authority may have had already to deal with a multitude of similar applications and then they will almost certainly have evolved a policy so precise that it could well be called a rule. There can be no objection to that, provided that the authority is always willing to listen to anyone with something new to say.'

This is a vital protection for the individual against official intransigence. For example in *R v. Secretary of State for the Home Department ex parte Hindley* (2000); a 'whole life tariff' set by the Home Secretary for a convicted murderer was lawful, provided that it was open to periodic review. On the other hand the courts are not normally concerned with the weight to be given to any particular factor so that, short of tying their hands completely, officials can give preference to policies or rules departing from them only in exceptional cases. Examples of unlawful fetters include the following:

- Rigid application of government policies or party political policies without making an independent judgement (*R.* v. *Waltham Forest DC ex parte Baxter* (1988); *R.* v. *Local Commissioner for Administration ex parte Liverpool City Council* (2001)).
- Electoral mandates (*Bromley LBC* v. *GLC* (1983)).
- Agreements and contracts (*Ayr Harbour Trustees* v. *Oswald* (1883); *Stringer* v. *Minister of Housing* (1971)). Given that a contract necessarily ties the hands of the body that makes it, the courts will intervene only if the contract is clearly contrary to a statutory obligation (see *R.* v. *Hammersmith and Fulham LBC ex parte Beddoes* (1987)).

- Advice given by officials (*Western Fish Products* v. *Penwith District Council* (1981)); thus the doctrine of estoppel, under which in certain circumstances a person is bound by a promise or statement on which another relies, does not apply to governmental decisions made under statute.
- Acting under the dictation of another body (*Lavender* v. *Minister of Housing* (1970)) but consulting another body and even relying on another body unless an objection raised is lawful (see *R.* v. *GLC ex parte Blackburn* (1976)).

16.4.6   Legitimate expectations

The fettering discretion doctrine sometimes protects the citizen. It may also work the other way in that it enables a public body to go back on promises or assurances that it has given to a citizen. The concept of 'legitimate expectation' confronts the fettering discretion doctrine. First recognised by Lord Denning in *Schmidt* v. *Home Secretary* (1969), a legitimate expectation arises where the citizen has been led to believe by some action of the government that he will obtain some benefit or advantage. This might be generated by a promise or assurance either announced generally (*A-G for Hong Kong* v. *Ng Yuen Shiu* (1983): interview would be given before deportation), *R.* v. *Secretary of State for the Home Department ex parte Khan* (1985) or given, specifically to an individual (*Preston* v. *IRC* (1985)). However, a legitimate expectation cannot be inferred merely from the general context (*Re Westminster City Council* (1986)) but might be generated by a practice whereby people in the same position as the applicant have been given a benefit in the past (*CCSU* v. *Minister for the Civil Service* (1985) but see *R.* v. *Secretary of State for the Environment ex parte Kent* (1988): practice of informal consultation on planning applications going beyond statutory requirements not sufficient). It is doubtful whether a general announcement in Parliament can generate a legitimate expectation and there is apparently no legitimate expectation that the government will honour an international treaty obligation (*R.* v. *DPP ex parte Kebelene* (1999)). The statement that gives rise to the expectation must be clear and unambiguous and it must be reasonable for the claimant to rely upon it (see *Preston* v. *IRC* (above)). Furthermore, where an assurance is given to an individual, the individual must have disclosed all relevant information (*R.* v. *IRC ex parte MFK Underwriting* (1990). Moreover where the individual is relying on a general government policy, the purpose of that policy might not be consistent with a legitimate expectation (e.g. *Re Findlay* (1985), parole policy).

It is clear that a legitimate expectation cannot confer an absolute right and that a legitimate expectation can be withdrawn (*CCSU* (above), *O'Reilly* v. *Mackman* (1982). The question is whether the expectation confers a heightened claim to the benefit in question and how is this enforced. Sometimes, as in *Shiu*, and *CCSU* (above) the expectation itself may be only *procedural*, that is of being consulted or given a hearing before a decision is made. In other cases it may be *substantive*, that is of an actual benefit or permission. In *Khan* (above) where the government stated by letter that certain policies concerning overseas adoptions would be followed, Lord Parker CJ suggested that 'vis-à-vis the recipient of such a letter, a new policy can only be implemented after such recipient has been given a full and serious consideration whether there is some overriding public interest which justifies a departure from the procedures stated in the latter' (at 48). This is ambiguous. On the one hand, even where the expectation is substantive, the claimant might be entitled only to a hearing. Apart from this, the court would intervene only if the government could offer no rational reason for its change of policy. On the other hand it might require the government, not merely to provide a reason for changing its policy but to advance a strong justification for doing so. This would take the courts into the merits of the case.

The cases are conflicting. The possibility of a substantive legitimate expectation was accepted in *R.* v. *Secretary of State for the Home Department ex parte Ruddick* (1987) where it was held that the minister had in fact complied with the expectation. It was rejected in *R.* v. *Secretary of State for Health ex parte United States Tobacco International Inc.* (1992). In that case the government had encouraged the company to manufacture snuff in the UK. After the company had incurred expense on its investment the government withdrew its permission on medical advice. It was held that any legitimate expectation could not override the government's statutory power. However, the company was entitled to a hearing on the health issue and an opportunity to persuade the government to change its mind. In *R.* v. *Minister of Agriculture ex parte Hamble Fisheries* (1995) Sedley J gave stronger effect to a substantive legitimate expectation. This concerned a claim to retain the benefit of a fishing licence in the face of a change in a policy designed to conserve fishing stocks. Sedley J suggested that a legitimate expectation creates a binding obligation that could only be overridden, if the objectives of the statute could not otherwise be achieved, a matter to be assessed by the court. However, in *R.* v. *Secretary of State for the Home*

Department ex parte Hargreaves (1997) the Court of Appeal condemned the 'heretical' doctrine of Sedley J, holding that a legitimate
expectation did not prevent a change of policy being no more than a
factor which the decision maker should take into account. Nevertheless in *R.* v. *North Devon Health Authority ex parte Coughlin* (2000), the
Court of Appeal held that a severely disabled resident of a local
authority nursing home could hold the local authority to a previous
assurance that it would be her home for life. The authority proposed to close the home in order to transfer nursing care to the local
authority. The Court of Appeal held that the assurance created an
enforceable legitimate expectation which only an overriding public
interest could displace. The scope of this is not clear. In particular the
right to respect for home and family life (European Convention on
Human Rights Art. 8) was in issue thereby raising the threshold of
review. Moreover, although the decision to close the home had financial consequences for the authority, it was not the application of a
government policy.

In *Coughlin* Lord Woolf took the view that an enforceable legitimate expectation should be confined to one or a few people. This
relates to the issue of equality. Where the undertaking in question is
given to particular individuals there is a strong argument that these
deserve special consideration. However, the expectation is often generated by a general policy announced in a circular, or a general practice.
In this kind of case the legitimate expectation doctrine, in as much as it
singles out the claimant for special treatment, may be regarded as
unfair. It is arguable that, where the claimant relies on an announcement or practice directed to the public at large, the claimant must show
that s/he has acted on the expectation so as to incur expense or other
detriment (see *R.* v. *Jockey Club ex parte RAM Racecourses* [1983] 2 All
ER 225 at 236–240). However, in *Hamble* (above), which concerned
a general policy, Sedley, J held that detriment was not required to
enforce a legitimate expectation.

The legitimate expectation debate sets the individual claim to
respect against the majoritarian public good. The law cannot combine
these goods and so reaches an untidy accommodation by offering the
individual a hearing which might persuade the authority to change its
mind. Legitimate expectations must therefore also be considered under
the head of procedural impropriety. Another rough and ready solution would be to pay compensation to the victim. Unfortunately there
is no right to compensation in UK law for unlawful administrative
action as such.

16.4.7 Duty and discretion

The reverse problem to that of fettering discretion sometimes arises. This is where an authority claims to have a discretion when the statute itself appears to impose an absolute duty and arises most frequently when a local authority fails to provide a benefit, for example a welfare payment, medical treatment or a school place, on the ground that it does not have sufficient resources and must prioritise between different kinds of need. If the court were to order the authority to perform the duty, the rule of law would be asserted and political pressure put on the government to come up with the necessary resources. On the other hand the court cannot command the impossible and the claimant would be merely a stalking horse for a broader political agenda. Moreover the imposition of a duty inhibits democratic choice. The courts are required to interpret the particular statute in order to determine whether the duty intended to be absolute (mandatory) or permissive. Words such as 'shall' or 'must' or 'may' are indicative but not conclusive and the whole statutory context must be examined. There appears to be no general principle and the judges often disagree.

For example in *R. v. Gloucestershire County Council ex parte Barry* (1997), the House of Lords by a bare majority held that the duty created by s. 2 of the Chronically Sick and Disabled Persons Act 1970 to 'make arrangements ... if satisfied ... that these were 'necessary' in order to meet the needs of a chronically sick and disabled person' gave the authority a discretion to choose between competing demands. The majority controversially held that the concept of need was relative to the cost of providing the service whereas Lord Lloyd and Lord Steyn (dissenting) were concerned by the inequity of different standards being applied in different local areas. In *R. v Birmingham City Council ex parte Mohammed* (1998) Dyson J suggested that the courts should be slow to downgrade a duty into a discretion. (See also *R. v. East Sussex CC ex parte Tandy* (1998); *R. v. Sefton MBC ex parte Help the Aged* (1997).)

Where the claim falls within the Human Rights Act 1998, for example if it involves respect for the home and family life (European Convention on Human Rights Art. 8), the duty might well be treated as mandatory. However, in *R. v. Newham London Borough Council ex parte Begum* (2000), the local authority had failed to ensure that suitable accommodation was provided under the Housing Act 1996 s. 193 for a homeless family. Collins J adopted a compromise approach which depends on the court's discretion. He took the view that a duty will not be unreasonably enforced against a local authority but it must show that it is doing all it can to comply with its legal obligations.

16.5   Irrationality/Unreasonableness

Irrationality or unreasonableness can be used to challenge the exercise of discretion or findings of law and fact. The notion of 'unreasonableness' is so vague that it seems to invite the court to impose its own opinion of the merits for that of the decision maker. However, it has a special and limited meaning. This ground of review is usually called 'Wednesbury unreasonableness' after Lord Greene's speech in *Associated Provincial Picture Houses Ltd* v. *Wednesbury Corporation* (1948). Lord Greene MR emphasised that the court will interfere only where a decision is so unreasonable that no reasonable authority could have made it, not merely because they think it is a bad decision. Another way of putting it is that the decision must be 'beyond the range of responses open to a reasonable decision maker' (*R.* v. *Minister of Defence ex parte Smith* [1996] 1 All ER 257 at 263–4; see also *R.* v. *Chief Constable of Sussex ex parte International Traders Ferry Ltd* [1999] 1 All ER 129 at 157).

This is sometimes equated with 'perversity' or 'irrationality'. In *CCSU* v. *Council of Civil Service Unions* [1984] 3 All ER 935 at 951, Lord Diplock said that the courts will interfere only where a decision has no rational basis or 'is so outrageous in its denial of ... accepted moral standards that no sensible person who has applied his mind to the question to be decided could have arrived at it.' For example in *Brind* v. *Secretary of State for the Home Department* (1991) the government banned live media interviews with supporters of the IRA. The House of Lords held that, although the ban was probably misguided, it had some rational basis as a means of denying publicity to terrorists and was therefore valid (see also *R.* v. *Radio Authority ex parte Bull* [1997] 2 All ER 561, 577).

Perversity therefore produces a low level of review to the point almost of non-existence. However, although successful challenges for unreasonableness are rare, they are not confined to perversity. For example in *Hall* v. *Shoreham Urban District Council* (1964) a local authority planning condition required the plaintiff to dedicate a road to the public. This was held to be unreasonable because it amounted to the confiscation of property without compensation. The condition was hardly perverse or immoral given that the plaintiff stood to make considerable profit out of the permission. Moreover unreasonableness may overlap with other grounds. In *Wheeler* v. *Leicester City Council* (1985), a local authority refused to allow a rugby club to use its playing field. This was because the club had not approved certain of its members from touring in South Africa during the apartheid era. The House of Lords held that the Council had acted unlawfully. This could be regarded as unreasonable infringement of individual freedom, or as a decision based upon an improper political purpose, or as an unfair decision in that the matter had been prejudged. Today *Wheeler* would probably be explained on human rights grounds, a perspective which was raised in the Court of Appeal but the House of Lords avoided.

A more flexible approach to unreasonableness is to ask whether a reasonable decision maker in the light of the material properly before him could reasonably justify his decision. This enables the court to apply different levels of scrutiny in different contexts, what Laws LJ in *R. (Mahmood)* v. *Secretary of State* [2001] 1 WLR 840 called a sliding scale: 'the graver the impact of the decision upon the individual the more substantial the justification that will be required'. In particular an 'anxious scrutiny' is required for a decision that impacts on human rights' (below). This approach therefore requires the court to consider the weight given to the relevant factors.

At the other end of the scale, where a decision depends on social, economic or political factors or matters 'remote from ordinary judicial experience' the court should, as a matter of practical reality, be cautious in interfering perhaps falling back on Lord Diplock's rationality test. For example it has been held that the courts will not interfere with a decision concerning the allocation of public resources in sensitive political contexts for irrationality except in extreme cases (*Nottinghamshire CC* v. *Secretary of State for the Environment* (1986): central grants to local government; see also *Hammersmith and Fulham LBC* v. *Secretary of State for the Environment* (1990); *R. (Asif Javed)* v. *Secretary of State for the Home Department* (2001)). National security cases are also subject to a low level of review (see Chapter 22).

R. v. *Cambridge Health Authority ex parte B* (1995) illustrates the difference between the two approaches. The courts were asked to review a NHS decision not to allocate funds to an experimental but possibly life-saving treatment to a child suffering from leukaemia. Laws J invoked the right to life under the ECHR, holding that a specially strong justification was required to override the right to life. The Court of Appeal, overruling Laws J, applied the 'rationality' standard according to which it is not for the court to weigh the competing considerations.

A deeper level of review is required in cases governed by the Human Rights Act 1998. Contrary to the normal principle, this may require the court to assess the *weight* of the evidence not merely to decide that a rational basis exists. Interference with a right protected by the European Convention on Human Rights must be 'necessary' to meet to a pressing social need of a kind stipulated in the Convention (see Chapter 18). It is debatable whether this is a matter for the court or for the minister since it is essentially a political judgement having no objectively correct answer. The prevailing view is that the matter is primarily for the minister within what is often called the 'discretionary' area of judgement. However, the courts will ensure a rigorous scrutiny by requiring the minister to give especially strong justification backed by convincing evidence. 'When anxiously scrutinising an executive decision that interferes with human rights the court will ask the question, applying an objective test, whether the decision maker could reasonably have concluded that the interference was necessary to achieve one or more of the legitimate aims recognised by the Convention' (per Lord Phillips MR in *R. (Mahmood)* v. *Secretary of State* (2000) at para. 32; see also *R.* v. *Secretary of State for the Home Department ex parte Simms* [1999] 3 All ER 400 at 411).

For example, in *R.* v. *Secretary of State ex parte Daly* (2001), government policy was that a prisoner's confidential correspondence with his lawyer could be examined in the absence of the prisoner in order to ascertain that it was genuine. The House held that, although the policy satisfied the bare rationality test, it was contrary to Art. 8 of the European Convention on Human Rights (respect for correspondence). A reasonable minister could not have concluded that the policy was necessary for the legitimate goal of keeping order in prisons. The House emphasised that in human rights cases the rationality threshold was not enough and that the court must 'anxiously scrutinise' the decision to ensure that the minister gave proper weight to the right at stake.

Lord Bingham went further. He based his reasoning firstly on the common law approach that there was no reasonable justification for the policy. However, he also said that, under the Human Rights Act, 'domestic courts must go beyond the ordinary *Wednesbury* standard and themselves form a judgement whether a convention right has been breached (conducting such an inquiry as is necessary to form that judgement' ([2001] 3 All ER at 455). Lord Bingham could be interpreted as saying that, at least in some cases, the court will not defer to the minister's discretion but will decide for themselves that the interference was justified (see below, 18.5.3).

Lord Cooke (para. 32) went beyond the human rights context. He described the *Wednesbury* case as 'an unfortunately retrogressive decision in English administrative law, in so far as it suggested that only a very extreme degree (of unreasonableness) can bring an administrative decision within the scope of judicial invalidation'. He emphasised that the level of interference should vary with the subject matter. 'It may well be, however, that the law can never be satisfied in any administrative field merely by a finding the decision under review is not capricious or absurd.'

The intensive human rights level of review and the orthodox approach sometimes produce the same outcome. By contrast in *R. (Farrakhan)* v. *Secretary of State* (2001), it was held that a decision to ban a leader of an anti-semitic group from entering the UK was an unlawful restriction upon freedom of expression in that the Secretary of State had no concrete evidence that the visit would result in violent disturbances. The Secretary of State's decision, like that in *Brind* (above) would probably have satisfied the *Wednesbury* test.

16.5.1 Proportionality

The level of review required in a human rights case can be expressed in the doctrine of proportionality, which in different manifestations is an important feature of the laws of many other countries and of EC Law and the European Convention on Human Rights. Proportionality broadly requires that government action must be no more intrusive than is necessary to meet an important public purpose. As Lord Diplock rather ponderously put it in *R.* v. *Goldsmith* [1983] 1 WLR 151 at 155, proportionality 'prohibits the use of a steam hammer to crack a nut if a nutcracker would do.' In *De Freitas* v. *Permanent Secretary* (1999) endorsed by Lord Steyn in *R.* v. *A.* (2001) the Privy Council outlined the proportionality test as follows. Whether:

(i) The legislative objective is sufficiently important to justify limiting a fundamental right. The court will not normally decide this question itself, since this would be entrenching on democracy but will satisfy itself that a reasonable minister could have reached this conclusion.

(ii) The measures designed to meet the legislative object are rationally connected with it.

(iii) The means used to impair the right or freedom are no more than is necessary to accomplish the objective. This is the most important factor.

English courts have sometimes objected to proportionality on the ground that it takes the court too far into the political merits (see *Hone* v. *Maze Prison Visitors* [1988] 1 All ER 321 at 327–9; *Brind* v. *Secretary of State for the Home Department* (1991); *Tesco Stores* v. *Secretary of State for the Environment* (1994); *R.* v. *Chief Constable North Wales Police ex parte AB* (1998)). Therefore English law has sometimes fallen foul of the ECHR because it has failed to reach the standard of necessity required by the proportionality doctrine. In *R.* v. *Minister of Defence ex parte Smith* (above), which concerned a decision to ban active homosexuals from the army the court reluctantly refused to intervene even though a human right was in issue on the ground that a court did not have sufficient expertise to assess the importance of military requirements. *Smith* was later rejected by the European Court of Human Rights which, in *Smith and Grady* v. *UK* (1999), held that the *Wednesbury* threshold of unreasonableness was too high to satisfy the European Convention because it excluded any consideration of whether the interference with the applicant's rights answered a pressing social need or was proportionate to the national security and public order aims pursued (see also *Sunday Times* v. *UK* (1979); *Observer and Guardian Newpapers* v. *UK* (1991); cf. *Vilvarrajah* v. *UK* (1991) 14 ECHR 248 at 292).

It is not clear whether proportionality would apply outside the Human Rights Act and EC contexts. In *R. (Alconbury)* v. *Secretary of State* [2001] 2 All ER 929 at 976 Lord Slynn stated that proportionality was different from *Wednesbury* but emphasised that 'the difference in practice is not as great as is sometimes supposed'. He thought that proportionality and *Wednesbury* should not be kept in separate compartments and that 'even without reference to the 1998 Act the time has come to recognise that this principle is part of English Administrative law, not only in when judges are dealing with community acts but also when they are dealing with acts subject to domestic law' (see also *Council of Civil Service Unions* v. *Minister for the Civil Service* [1984] 3 All ER 935 at 950 per Lord Diplock, and Lord Cooke in *Daly* (above)). Proportionality will be discussed further in Chapter 18.

16.6   Procedural Impropriety

16.6.1   Statutory procedural requirements

This topic illustrates the elastic nature of contemporary judicial review. Failure to comply with a procedural requirement laid down by

statute (such as time limits, consultation or giving required information or notice) could make a decision invalid. However, the courts are
reluctant to set aside a decision on purely technical grounds. Traditionally the courts have tried to rationalise this by distinguishing
between 'mandatory' (important) and 'directory' (unimportant) procedural requirements by reference to the language of the governing
statute. Recently they have abandoned this approach in favour of a
flexible response to the particular context. Using their discretionary
power to withhold a remedy, the courts will set a decision aside for
procedural irregularity only if the harm or injustice caused to the applicant by the procedural flaw outweighs the inconvenience to the government or to innocent third parties in setting the decision aside (see e.g.
Coney v. *Choice* (1975); *London and Clydesdale Estates Ltd* v. *Aberdeen
District Council* (1979); *R.* v. *Immigration Appeal Tribunal ex parte
Jeyeanthan* (1999)). However the courts may not be willing to allow
administrative efficiency to override a statutory right of the public to
be consulted. In *Berkeley* v. *Secretary of State for the Environment*
(2000), the House of Lords held that a local authority was required to
make environmental information relating to a planning application
for a football stadium available to the public even though the council
successfully argued that it already had adequate environmental evidence before it. Lord Hoffman in particular, reflecting the broad
concept of democracy suggested that public consultation was an end in
itself and not merely an instrument of effective decision making.

Another important statutory procedural requirement is the rule
against delegation. An official (or indeed anyone) who is entrusted with
power to make a decision should not in principle transfer that power to
someone else (*delegatus non potest delegare*). Applying this principle
strictly would cause administrative gridlock and many exceptions have
been made. Its only strict application is to judicial tribunals who adjudicate upon disputes in accordance with legal rules (*Barnard* v. *National
Dock Labour Board* (1953)). Exceptions to the principle are as follows:

- The *Carltona* doctrine that a minister can act through a civil servant
  in his department (above, p. 332). This can be rationalised as not a
  true exception in that constitutionally the minister and civil servant
  are one (see *R. (Alconbury)* v. *Secretary of State* (2001)).
- Many local authority functions can be delegated by statute to
  committees, sub-committees, officers and other authorities but not
  to individual councillors or to outside bodies unless authorised by
  statute (see Local Government Act 1972 s. 101; *R.* v. *Port Talbot BC
  ex parte Jones* (1988)).

- Many governmental functions can be transferred to private bodies (Deregulation and Contracting Out Act 1994 ss. 61, 69).
- Functions involving little discretion can be delegated, and the courts seem ready to imply statutory authority to delegate in cases where it would be inconvenient for the decision maker to do everything himself (*Provident Mutual Life* v. *Derby Corporation* (1981); *Nelms* v. *Roe* (1969)).
- Fact finding, making recommendations and giving advice can be delegated, but the decision maker must not merely 'rubber stamp' the advice he is given. He must have enough information before him, e.g. a summary of evidence, to make a genuine decision (*Jeffs* v. *New Zealand Dairy Board* (1967)).

16.6.2　The right to a fair hearing

This ground of review is of ancient common law origin and is central to the idea of the rule of law. Until the First World War the courts applied a broad principle, traceable to the seventeenth century and usually labelled 'natural justice', namely that anyone whose rights were affected by an official decision was entitled to a fair hearing before an unbiased judge (e.g. *Dr Bonham's Case* (1610), *Cooper* v. *Wandsworth Board of Works* (1863)). However, the contraction of judicial review that took place between the 1920s and the mid-1960s saw natural justice being withdrawn from government decisions other than those which the courts labelled 'judicial'. For this purpose 'judicial' means the impartial application of rules to settle a dispute about the parties' existing rights narrowly defined; essentially what a court does.

Thus the courts were taking a crude separation of powers approach in order to define the limits of judicial review. This excluded natural justice from political, discretionary and policy orientated areas of government activity which the court labelled 'administrative'. It excluded much of the welfare state since the conferring of benefits such as education and housing do not strictly affect existing rights. It also excluded government powers such as planning, compulsory purchase and other forms of licensing which although they affect rights are usually discretionary. The main area left for natural justice was where a formal tribunal or inquiry determined a specific dispute but even this caused problems in the case of public inquiries held as part of a larger discretionary process leading to a political decision, for example to build a new road (see e.g. *Franklin* v. *Minister of Town and Country Planning* (1948).

However, in *Ridge* v. *Baldwin* (1964) the House of Lords reviewed the history of natural justice and returned the law to its older rationale. The Chief Constable of Brighton had been dismissed by the local police authority without a hearing. The authority had statutory power to deprive him of his position for incapacity or misconduct but not otherwise. The House of Lords held that he was entitled to a hearing for two reasons: (i) he had been deprived of a public office (not just an ordinary job); and (ii) the power to dismiss was limited by statute so that the authority did not have a complete discretion. Lord Reid emphasised that a government decision which causes serious harm to an individual ought in principle to attract the right to be heard. *Ridge* is generally taken as freeing natural justice from its dependence on judicial functions although as we shall see the concept of judicial remains relevant.

Since *Ridge* v. *Baldwin* the courts have extended the right to be heard into most areas of government, including for example prison management (*R.* v. *Hull Prison Visitors ex parte St Germain* (1979); *Leech* v. *Parkhurst Prison Deputy Governor* (1988)). Although the expression natural justice is still sometimes used it has become interchangeable with 'fairness' (see *Re HK* (1967)). However, fairness means whatever the court thinks fair in the circumstances of the particular case so that general principles are difficult to establish (see *Lloyd* v. *McMahon* [1987] 1 All ER 1118 at 1161). Perhaps the law has become too flexible, with the disadvantage that 'fairness' does not necessarily imply a definite right to a hearing.

For example in *Calvin* v. *Carr* (1980), the plaintiff, a racehorse trainer, was suspended from the course because of accusations of tampering. The Privy Council held that a combination of factors meant that he was not entitled to be heard. These included the need to act quickly to preserve the integrity of the sport, the fact that he could appeal when he would be given a full hearing, and the fact that he had agreed to the regulations under which the decision was made. It is noteworthy that their Lordships rejected the strict rule-of-law argument that failure to give a hearing at first instance makes a decision void so that any appeal is also void. This argument had been accepted in *Ridge* v. *Baldwin* (above).

However, the courts have also introduced limits to the right be heard. These are based on pragmatic factors and include the following:

- 'Fairness' concerns the protection of persons who are adversely affected by government action, and not the idea of democratic participation in government. Thus the right to be heard may not include access to policy information (see *Bushell* v. *Secretary of State for the Environment* (1981); *Hammersmith and Fulham LBC* v. *Secretary of State for the Environment* (1990)). Similarly, advisory or preliminary governmental decisions do not attract a right to be heard unless the decision has direct adverse consequences for the individual's rights (*Norwest Holst* v. *Trade Secretary* [1978] Ch. 201 – decision to start an investigation: no right to be heard, compare *Furnell* v. *Whangarie High School Board* [1973] AC 660: suspension of teacher pending investigation, hearing required).

- The notion of a judicial decision remains significant in the sense that a decision to remove existing legal rights usually attracts a hearing, but the refusal of a discretionary benefit in the public interest, without any specific entitlement, may not (see *Schmidt* v. *Home Secretary* (1969): extension of immigration permit; *McInnes* v. *Onslow-Fane* (1978): refusing a referee's licence, *Re Findlay* (1985): parole, change in policy). However, a decision to refuse a benefit which can only be made on limited ground or which involves accusations of misconduct or bad character will probably attract a hearing (see *R.* v. *Gaming Board ex parte Benaim and Khaida* (1970); *R.* v. *Army Board ex parte Anderson* (1992); *R.* v. *Secretary of State for the Home Department ex parte Fayed* (1997)), as perhaps will other cases where it would be unfair to deny a hearing, e.g. where important property or environmental interests are in issue.

- Other factors might override the right to a hearing. In particular, national security (*CCSU* v. *Minister for the Civil Service* (1985)). The need to act in an emergency will also exclude at least a prior hearing (*R.* v. *Secretary of State for Transport ex parte Pegasus Holdings Ltd* (1988): air safety). A hearing might be excluded where a decision affects many people so that a hearing would be impracticable, or where large numbers compete for scarce resources, for example applications for University places or in respect of general decisions such as school closures which do not concern the interests of the persons affected. On the other hand where a policy decision, for example to close an old people's home directly relates to the interests of the persons concerned, there may be a collective right to be consulted, although not necessarily a hearing in individual cases (see *R.* v. *Devon County Council ex parte Baker* (1995).

- A hearing may be excluded when the court thinks that the outcome of the decision was not affected. There have been judicial warnings against this which seem to violate the basic principle that the courts are concerned with legality, not merits (see *John* v. *Rees* (1969); *R.* v. *Environment Secretary ex parte Brent LBC* [1983] 3 All

ER 321 at 357; *Cheall* v. *Apex* (1983); cf. *Cinnamond* v. *British Airports Authority* (1980)).

16.6.3 The content of a fair hearing

A flexible concept of 'fairness' also determines the ingredients of a hearing. There are no fixed requirements. Everything depends on the particular circumstances. It is sometimes suggested that 'fairness' applies only to non-judicial decisions with fixed standards to judicial decisions. However, in both cases the overriding test is what is required in the particular circumstances to enable the citizen to know the case he has to answer and to answer it (see *Lloyd* v. *McMahon* [1987] 1 All ER 1118 at 1161). The following factors seem to be particularly important.

- Article 6 of the European Convention on Human Rights (fair trial) applies to decisions which affect 'civil rights and obligations'. A fundamental aspect of the right to a fair trial is 'equality of arms', in the sense that the parties must be on a equal footing. However, it has been emphasised that, although the right to an overall fair trial is absolute, particular ingredients such as disclosure of information are not absolute and that a 'fair balance ' based on proportionality must be struck between the public interest and the rights of the individual. This is similar to the domestic approach (see *Brown* v. *Stott* (2001): requirement to give incriminating information and below, 18.3.1).
- The more serious the consequences for the individual the higher the standard of hearing that is required. To this extent the notion of a judicial decision remains important. At one end of the scale, preliminary or advisory investigations at best entitle a person to be told only an outline of any accusations against him and to answer them (*Maxwell* v. *Trade Department* (1974); *R.* v. *Commission for Racial Equality ex parte Cotterel and Rothon* (1980)). At the other end of the scale, a person accused of misconduct leading to deprivation of a public office or other valuable right is normally entitled to see all the evidence and to cross-examine witnesses (*R.* v. *Army Board ex parte Anderson* (1991)). Administrative convenience cannot justify refusing to permit a person to call witnesses although the tribunal does have a residual discretion in the matter.
- Fairness is a minimum standard to be balanced against the government's right to decide its own procedure. For example there is no right to legal representation unless skilled legal support is absolutely necessary (*Hone* v. *Maze Prison Visitors* (1988)), and formal rules

of evidence are not required (*Mahon* v. *Air New Zealand* (1984)). Indeed an oral hearing is not necessarily required (*Lloyd* v. *McMahon* (1987)). On the other hand, those where existing rights are affected by a decision must be given an opportunity to be heard. Moreover, if an enquiry is held, as is the case with planning and other land use decisions, the decision maker cannot take new factual material into account without giving the parties an opportunity to comment (see *Elmbridge BC* v. *Secretary of State for the Environment* (2002).

- As we have seen a *legitimate expectation* might confer a right to be heard as an aspect of fairness (see e.g. *CCSU* v. *Minister for the Civil Service* (1985); *R.* v. *Secretary of State for Transport ex parte Richmond BC* (1994) and cases above 16.4.6). However, the courts will give effect to a legitimate expectation only where do so would be fair in all the circumstances. For this reason it is questionable whether the notion of legitimate expectation adds anything to the general concept of fairness. For example the claimant must disclose all relevant facts (*R.* v. *IRC ex parte MFK Underwriting Ltd* (1990)).

16.6.4   Natural justice and the ECHR

The common law is re-enforced by Art. 6 of the European Convention on Human Rights which states that 'in the determination of his civil rights and obligations or of any criminal charge against him, everyone is entitled to a fair and public hearing within a reasonable time by an independent and impartial tribunal established by law'. Article 6 covers much of the same ground as the common law although it requires particular rights in criminal cases. However, the common law does not necessarily require a public hearing (see *Bentham* v. *Netherlands* (1985); *R.* v. *DPP ex parte Kebilene* (1999)). It is also arguable that under the Human Rights Act 1998 the right to a fair trial would require legal representation at least in the case of judicial decisions.

The relationship between the common law and the European Convention on Human Rights is determined firstly by what is meant by 'civil rights and obligations' and secondly by the fact that statute can exclude the right to a fair hearing but under the Human Rights Act 1998 only where this is the only possible interpretation of the Act. According to the ECHR an administrative decision does affect civil rights and obligations in cases where it interferes with existing rights, for example tax or land use decisions, or where the citizen has particular entitlements, for example to social security payments. In other cases, involving the conferring of discretionary benefits, such as some immigration cases, Art. 6 would not necessarily apply. In *R. (Alconbury)* v. *Secretary of State* (2001), Lord Hoffmann regretted this relatively broad approach. He would have preferred an approach based on the separation of powers, that Art. 6 should not apply to policy decisions taken in the public interest for which the decision maker is responsible to an elected body such as land use planning decisions, even though these affect property rights but should be confined to private law adjudication, the direct purpose of which is to determine individual rights in other words to judicial decisions in the traditional sense. However, as *Alconbury* makes clear, the jurisprudence of the ECHR takes a broader approach.

Nevertheless there is a distinction between policy decisions and judicial decisions. This relates to conflicts of interest (below 16.6.5) and, in cases involving political discretion, allows a more limited right to be heard. This reflects political and administrative realities and does not necessarily follow the equality of arms principle Thus Art. 6 seems to reflect the common law approach (see below 18.3.1, *R. (Alconbury)* v. *Secretary of State* (2001)).

16.6.5 Bias

The idea of an impartial and independent judge is a fundamental aspect of the rule of law. However, complete impartiality is impossible to realise since bias is inherent in human nature. The law has to compromise, and has done so by distinguishing between different kinds of decision and different kinds of bias. The decision maker need not actually be biased (this would fall under the head of irrelevant considerations). The bias rule has traditionally been concerned with the risk or appearance of bias, hence the well-known dictum of Lord Hewart in *R.* v. *Sussex Justices ex parte McCarthy* [1924] 1 KB 256 at 259 that justice must not only be done but must manifestly and undoubtedly be seen to be done. The rationale is not only that of fairness to the parties but also public confidence in the integrity of the decision- making process. The main principles are as follows:

- A direct personal financial interest, however small, will automatically disqualify the decision maker, the law conclusively presuming bias (*Dimes* v. *Grand Junction Canal Co.* (1852); Lord Chancellor held shares in company appearing before him; *R.* v. *Hendon (RDC) ex parte Chorley* (1933) – councillor had financial interest in development for which planning permission was sought. See also *Hesketh*

v. *Braddock* (1776) 3 Burr 1847, *R.* v. *Camborne Justices ex parte Pearce* [1955] 1 QB 41 at 47). One exception is where no other decision maker is qualified to act, in which case Parliament must be taken to have impliedly authorised the bias (*Wilkinson* v. *Barking Corporation* (1948); see also Supreme Court Act 1981 s. 11 – judges as taxpayers). Also an insignificant (*de minimis*) interest might be ignored (*Locobail (UK) Ltd* v. *Bayfield Properties Co.* [2000] 1 All ER 65, 71).

- In *R.* v. *Bow Street Magistrates Court ex parte Pinochet* (No. 2) (1999), the House of Lords extended automatic disqualification to a case where a judge has a personal non-financial connection with one of the parties. Lord Hoffman, a Law Lord, was an unpaid director of a charitable subsidiary of Amnesty International, a human rights pressure group, which was a party to an appeal before the House of Lords. Although Lord Hoffmann had no financial interest in the outcome he was a supporter of a cause that might be advanced by the case. *Pinochet* has been criticised on the ground that there is an important distinction between 'interest' where the judge stands to gain personally so that he is a judge in his own case and 'favour' where the judge might prefer a particular outcome (Olowofoyeku, 2000). *Pinochet* seems to be a case only of favour. In the case of favour a more flexible approach may be more appropriate. Other common law jurisdictions have confined automatic disqualification to strictly financial interests (ibid.).

- A decision of a *judicial* body such as a court or a tribunal will be quashed if there is a 'real danger' of bias. This arises in many circumstances. Examples include *R.* v. *Liverpool Justices ex parte Topping* (1983): justices had print-out of the accused's previous convictions; *Locobail (UK) Ltd* v. *Bayfield Properties Co.* (2000): judge in an insurance case had written articles in the legal press criticising insurance companies in the context of similar issues; *Metropolitan Properties* v. *Lannon* (1968): rent tribunal chair advised his father in a dispute with the same landlord; *Hannam* v. *Bradford Corporation* (1970): member of a local authority committee adjudicating on a teacher's disciplinary case was also a governor of the school in question where the governors had previously considered the case.

Cases in which a person plays multiple roles are particularly vulnerable. In *Hannam* for example, it made no difference that the governor in question had not attended the relevant governors' meeting because group loyalty was enough to raise a possibility of bias. At the other end of the scale, political views as such do not disqualify nor does loyalty to an organisation whose rules the claimant is accused of breaking unless in both cases the decision maker actually behaves unfairly (*Re S (a barrister)* (1981)).

It is not clear how high the threshold should be. Different formulations such as 'real likelihood' or 'real suspicion' of bias have been used but without general acceptance. There seems to be two crucial differences between these formulations. According to the 'reasonable suspicion' test which was favoured for example in *Hannam* (above), the test is not whether the reviewing court think there was bias but whether a reasonably well-informed ordinary person might do so. Secondly, according to the reasonable suspicion test, the decision is made in the light of facts known to the claimant even though there may be other facts not so known that might dispel the suspicion, for example the decision maker's explanation or an internal practice. The reasonable suspicion test therefore emphasises the appearance of bias in the context of public perception. Under the 'real likelihood' test the court itself decides whether bias is likely in the light of all the circumstances.

In *R*. v. *Gough* (1993) the Court of Appeal applied a compromise which it labelled the 'real danger' test (or 'real possibility' or 'real risk'). According to this test the court itself asks whether there is a chance of bias in the light of all the circumstances the hypothetical informed outsider being dispensed with. In *Gough* the accused was a neighbour of a jury member who did not, however, recognise him. The decision was held valid. It was perhaps a crucial factor that the accused had accepted the jury-person's explanation.

Gough was followed for a time in the UK but was rejected in some commonwealth jurisdictions as weakening the element of public confidence (see Olowofoyeku (above)) and may also be less stringent than the ECHR Art. 6 requires. In *Medicaments and Related Classes of Goods, in Re* (2001) the Court of Appeal, having reviewed the ECHR cases, suggested a 'modest adjustment' to *Gough*. This required the court to decide, on the basis of all the circumstances known to it as in *Gough*, not whether there was a real danger of bias but whether the hypothetical informed outsider could reasonably so believe. In *Medicaments* a lay member of the Restrictive Practices Court was applying for a job with a firm one of whose members was an expert witness before the court. The Court of Appeal held that she was disqualified even though she had taken steps to minimise the conflict of interest. The *Medicaments* test was endorsed by the House of Lords in *Porter* v. *Magill* (2002).

● In the case of administrative decisions taken by politicians a less stringent approach is taken because conflicts of interest arising out of political policies or out of the competing duties of decision makers may be built into the system by statute. In this kind of case bias does not invalidate the decision unless the decision maker acts unfairly (*R. v. Frankland Prison Visitors ex parte Lewis* (1986): prison visitors having judicial and investigatory roles; *R. v. Secretary of State for the Environment ex parte Kirkstall Valley Campaign Ltd* (1996): local authority had interest in developing land for which it also had to decide whether to grant planning permission).

According to the House of Lords, this relaxed approach satisfies Art. 6 of the ECHR at least in the context of policy decisions taken by ministers. In *R. (Alconbury)* v. *Secretary of State* (2001) a variety of decisions made by the Secretary of State were challenged on the ground of incompatibility with Art. 6. These included decisions to 'call-in' planning appeals which would otherwise be decided by independent inspectors and to confirm compulsory purchase orders relating to road and rail schemes in which the government had an interest. It was common ground that the Secretary of State was not an independent and impartial tribunal. The question was whether the process as a whole, including the protection given by judicial review, satisfied Art. 6.

The House of Lords, overruling the lower courts, held unanimously that the process satisfied Art. 6. They held that the jurisprudence of the European Convention supported a fundamental distinction between policy or political decisions for which the minister is answerable to Parliament and judicial decisions made by courts and similar bodies. It would be wrong for policy decisions to be second guessed by the courts. Therefore, provided that there is judicial review in relation to the legality and fairness of the decision 'a government minister can be both a policy maker and a decision taker without violating Art. 6 (1)' (per Lord Hutton [2001] 2 All ER 929 at 1018), The position might be otherwise where a decision turns on findings of law or disputed facts as opposed to policy, where further safeguards such as independent fact finding might be necessary. This depends on the circumstances (see Lord Hoffmann at 992 and *Adam* v. *Newham BC* (2002), below p. 430). Thus the House of Lords endorsed the traditional common law approach.

16.6.6   Reasons for decisions

There is no general duty to give reasons for decisions, although many statutes impose such a duty (see *R. v. Criminal Injuries Compensation board ex parte Moore* (1999); *Stefan* v. *GMC* (1999); Tribunals and Inquiries Act 1992 s. 10). This has been justified on the grounds of cost, the danger of excessive formality, the difficulties of expressing subjective reasons, and because, in the case of collective decisions, it may be impossible to identify specific reasons (see *McInnes* v. *Onslow-Fane* (1978); *R.* v. *Higher Education Funding Council* (1994); *Stefan* v. *GMC* (1999)). However, these concerns do not meet the main justi-fication for the giving of reasons, which lies in the value of respect for human dignity and equality so that those who purport to exer-cise power are accountable. Even an admission that a decision is based on subjective judgement fulfils this requirement. The giving of reasons also strengthens public confidence in the decision-making process, strengthens the rationality of the process itself, supports accountability and helps challenge, a factor regarded as essential by the ECHR. However, the ECHR has confined itself to holding that courts, as the citizen's last protection, must give reasons for their decisions (*Van de Hurk* v. *Netherlands* (1984)). The ECHR has also held that reasons need not be detailed and comprehensive provided that they enable the parties to understand the basis of the decision (*Helle* v. *Finland* (1997)).

However, the courts do require reasons to be given in a wide range of cases, drawing upon the general principle of fairness which allows the court to take all the circumstances into account. In *R.* v. *Secretary of State for the Home Department ex parte Doody* (1993) 3 All ER 92 at 107 Lord Mustill referred to 'a perceptible trend towards an insist-ence upon greater openness in the making of administrative decisions'. Indeed in *R.* v. *Lambeth LBC ex parte Walters* (1993) it was suggested that reasons should be given unless there was some special justification for not doing so. However, the dominant view seems to be that a duty to give reasons must either be expressed or implied in the relevant statute or there must be some special justification for giving reasons. In *R.* v. *Higher Education Funding Council* (above), Sedley J held that arguments which applied to all cases were not sufficient, for example the difficulty of challenging a decision in the absence of reasons. Never-theless, the cases where reasons must be given may be sufficiently wide ranging to come close to a general duty. Examples of cases where there is a duty to give reasons include the following:

- Judicial decisions analogous to those of a court (*R.* v. *Minister of Defence ex parte Murray* (1998).
- Cases which involve very important interests, where, if reasons were not given, the individual would be at a disadvantage (e.g. *Doody*

(above): fixing of minimum sentence for life prisoner; *Stefan* (above): risk of loss of livelihood, unrepresented defendant).

- Cases where the particular decision is aberrant or unusual or where a severe penalty is involved (e.g. *R.* v. *Civil Service Appeals Board ex parte Cunningham* (1991): compensation award out of line with that given in analogous cases by industrial tribunal; *R.* v. *DPP ex parte Manning* (2000), decision not to prosecute after coroner's finding of unlawful killing).

- A legitimate expectation might also generate a duty to give reasons for overriding the expectation (*R.* v. *Secretary of State for Transport ex parte Richmond BC* (No. 4) (1996)).

- If an appeal is provided this may point to a duty to give reasons where the appeal would otherwise be pointless (*Stefan* (above)). On the other hand, a comprehensive appeal that reopens the whole case may point *against* a duty to give reasons at first instance.

- In *Padfield* v. *Minister of Agriculture* (1968), the House of Lords suggested that if a minister refuses to give reasons the court can infer that he has no proper reasons for his decision. However in *Lonrho* v. *Secretary of State for Trade and Industry* (1989) the House took the view that a failure to give reasons does not in itself justify the drawing of an adverse inference but is at most supportive of other evidence that the decision is improper.

- Failure to give reasons concerns the decision *after* it is made and should be distinguished from failing *before* the decision is made to disclose *grounds* in the sense of allegations against the applicant. Failure to disclose such grounds would normally be unfair as a breach of the right to a hearing. There is also the 'cards on the table' doctrine (*R.* v. *Lancashire County Council ex parte Huddlestone* (1986)). Once an applicant has obtained leave to apply for judicial review the authority must then assist the court by disclosing the reasons for its decision but only in as far as the reasons relate to the particular ground of challenge.

Summary

16.1   The courts' task of ensuring that public bodies keep within their powers is an important aspect of the rule of law and of the separation of powers. On the other hand, the separation of powers also requires the courts not to trespass upon the sphere of other branches of government. The law of judicial review attempts to steer a middle course between these ideals. It is sometimes said that judicial review is concerned to ensure that powers are exercised in a fair and proper manner but not with whether a government decision is right or wrong. Another popular formulation is that judicial review concerns 'illegality, irrationality and procedural impropriety'. The latter includes the rules of natural justice.

16.2 Since the late nineteenth century judicial review has been based on the theory that the government has acted beyond its powers (*ultra vires*). In theory an *ultra vires* decision is a nullity. This is often regarded as unreal because, unless successfully challenged in the courts, even illegal government action is in practice effective. The courts have sometimes departed from the theory of strict nullity in the interests of doing justice. The *ultra vires* doctrine may no longer be adequate to explain the law of judicial review. The common law and in some cases the Human Rights Act 1998 provide alternative foundations for judicial review.

16.3 Particular problems are raised in relation to whether the courts should be able to correct errors made by government bodies. Most errors of law and clear errors of fact are probably reviewable. However, some broad terms in statutes are regarded as analogous to questions of fact so that the court will only interfere if the decision-maker's approach is unreasonable.

16.4 Notions of improper purposes and irrelevant considerations may invite the courts to enter into the merits of government action. An improper purpose or an irrelevant consideration will invalidate a decision if it has an impact on the outcome and where the statute confers wide discretionary powers the courts limit democratic decision making by deciding what factors should be taken into account.

16.5 Conversely, a statutory discretion cannot be fettered whether by a policy, an undertaking or any other commitment although the courts cannot normally interfere with the relative importance an official gives to the various factors to be taken into account when exercising a discretion.

16.6 The doctrine of legitimate expectation gives some protection to a citizen where government goes back on a commitment. However, the extent to which this is a *substantive* right going beyond a *procedural* right to a reasoned explanation and a hearing is unclear.

16.7 It may be difficult to distinguish between a discretionary power and an absolute duty particularly in cases where demands on local authorities have to be met from limited resources.

16.8 The doctrine of *Wednesbury* unreasonableness also comes near to interfering with the merits of a decision. The threshold of unreasonableness varies with the context on a sliding scale determined by the impact of the decision on the individual and whether the decision involves political factors with which a court should not interfere. At one extreme a bare 'rationality' test is applied. At the other extreme, where the Human Rights Act 1998 applies, the court itself may weight the competing considerations exercising what is effectively an appeal function. Between these extremes the test appears to be whether the outcome is within the range of reasonable responses to the particular context. In effect the court is drawing upon widely shared social and moral values.

16.9 The doctrine of proportionality is applied in the human rights context and may extend to other contexts. This requires the court to weigh the competing factors on the basis that the interference with the right must be no greater than is necessary to achieve a legitimate objective, (in the case of some rights protected by the European Convention on Human Rights, 'a pressing social need'. Proportionality is discussed further in Chapter 18.

16.10   The rules of natural justice or procedural fairness are also underpinned by the Human Rights Act 1998 although what amounts to a fair trial depends on the context, and in particular the extent to which the decision is a policy orientated political decision. The doctrine of legitimate expectation may also confer a right to a hearing but the courts have disagreed as to whether there can be 'substantive' legitimate expectations which bind government to honour a previous undertaking or at least require an exceptional justification to override. In this context and in others courts are increasingly requiring reasons to be given for decisions.

Further Reading

Elliott (1999) 'The *ultra vires* doctrine in a constitutional setting: still the central principle of administrative law', 58 *Cambridge Law Journal* 129.

Craig (1992) 'Legitimate expectations: a conceptual analysis', *Law Quarterly Review* 79.

Craig (1999) 'Competing models of judicial review', *Public Law* 428.

Craig and Bamforth (2001) 'Constitutional principle, constitutional analysis and judicial review', *Public Law* 763.

Irvine (1996) 'Judges and decision makers: the theory and practice of *Wednesbury* Review', *Public Law* 59.

Jowell (2000) 'Beyond the rule of law: towards constitutional judicial review', *Public Law* 671.

Jowell (1999) 'Of *vires* and vacuums: the constitutional context of judicial review', *Public Law* 448.

Jones (1990) 'Mistake of fact in administrative law', *Public Law* 507.

Laws (1995) 'Law and democracy', *Public Law* 72.

Oliver (1998) 'A negative aspect to legitimate expectations', *Public Law* 558.

Olowofoyeku (2000) 'The Nemo Judex rule: the case against automatic disqualification', *Public Law* 456.

Richardson and Genn (eds), *Administrative Law and Government Action*, Part 1.

Richardson, G and Sunkin, M. (1996) 'Judicial review: questions of impact', *Public Law* 79.

Walker, P. (1995) 'What's wrong with irrationality?', *Public Law* 556.

Wong, G. (2000) 'Towards the nutcracker principle: reconsidering the objections to proportionality', *Public Law* 92.

Woodhouse, D. (1995) 'Politicians and the judiciary: a changing relationship', *Parliamentary Affairs* 401.

Exercises

16.1   To what extent is the law of judicial review adequately explained on the basis of the *ultra vires* doctrine?

16.2   How far does the law of judicial review prevent judges interfering in politics?

16.3   Explain the significance of legitimate expectations in relation to the rule against fettering discretion.

16.4 'I think the day will come when it will be more widely recognised that the *Wednesbury* case was an unfortunately retrogressive decision in English administrative law' (Lord Cooke in *R.* v. *Secretary of State ex parte Daly* (2001). What does he mean and do you agree?

16.5 'The difference in practice (between *Wednesbury* unreasonableness and proportionality) is not as great as is sometimes supposed ... even without reference to the 1998 Act the time has come to recognise that this principle is part of English administrative law, not only in when judges are dealing with community acts but also when they are dealing with acts subject to domestic law' (Lord Slynn). Do you agree?

16.6 Does the bias rule strike a reasonable balance between efficiency and justice?

16.7 'What may not have been recognised back in 1974 was the emergence of judicial review to the point where most if not all matters which could form the basis for a complaint of maladministration are matters for which the elastic qualities of judicial review might provide a remedy' (Henry LJ in *R.* v. *Local Commissioner ex parte Liverpool City Council* (2001)). Discuss.

16.8 Jack and Jill are law students. Each has obtained a place at the College of Law to study for the Solicitors' Final Examination. Jack applies to Meanshire County Council for a grant for this course under a statute which requires the authority 'to have regard to the manpower needs of the community and all other material factors'. He is informed by letter that 'owing to the current surplus of solicitors we are unable to entertain any applications from law students.' Jill makes a similar application to Greedshire County Council and is told that her application 'will be considered on its merits but it is the policy of the Council to award grants to law students only of exceptional ability.' Jill who has no financial resources is invited to submit a written statement, and having done so is informed that her application has been refused. No reasons are given. Jill wishes to have a personal hearing before the council to impress upon them her personal circumstances although a council officer had told her that personal circumstances are irrelevant. Advise Jack and Jill as to the grounds, if any, on which they can challenge these decisions in the courts.

16.9 Under the Sports Act 2002 (fictitious), the Minister of Sport has power, 'where he considers it necessary in the interest of public safety and good order, to require the admission of paid spectators to any sporting event to be subject to showing membership cards at the entrance'. The Minister also has power to revoke any such membership cards. The Minister, interpreting 'sport' as including any activity which is competitive, has made an order requiring entrance to chess competitions to be subject to the showing of membership cards. There has been some evidence of disorder at the events. The Minister has been advised that chess events are an important source of the opposition party's finances. In another case, a civil servant has revoked the membership cards of all the members of a football club because the club has failed to provide an all-seating stadium. The club is in the third division and the present stadium is very rarely more than half full. Discuss.

16.10 Sam a pupil at a sixth form college was ordered by the head teacher to remove a tattoo across his forehead which expressed support for vegetarianism. Having refused to do so Sam was suspended. He appealed to the college governing body but his appeal was rejected without reasons being given. One of the members of the appeal committee was a parent governor and a neighbour of Sam but had deliberately absented himself from the governors' meeting that considered Sam's case. Another member of the committee was the manager of a local meat packing company. Advise Sam.

17   Judicial Review Remedies

It could be argued that the courts provide the only open and universal means by which the individual can challenge governmental action. Ministerial responsibility to Parliament is of little use to the citizen directly in that it operates within a political framework and can be called upon only by Members of Parliament. The various commissions that have been established as a result of the work of the Committee on Standards in Public Life play a valuable monitoring role but again the citizen cannot obtain a decision from them as a matter of right. Nor do they deliberate in public. The ombudsman has a useful role overlapping with that of the courts and is cheaper and its powers of investigation more flexible than those of the courts but has limited jurisdiction, investigates in private and has no enforcement powers (see *R. v. Local Commissioner for Administration ex parte Liverpool City Council* (2001)).

Judicial review applies within the UK the Channel Islands and Isle of Man and to the UK's remaining overseas territories. However, unlike most other types of legal action, judicial review is not a matter of right. The claimant must obtain the permission of the court to commence proceedings (below) although this will be granted if the claimant has an arguable case and has not abused the process, for example by delay. The leave mechanism is a safeguard against using the courts as a surrogate political process in order to ventilate political causes even where the claimant has a hopeless legal case (see Harlow, 2000a).

17.1   The Range of Remedies

The grounds of judicial review discussed in Chapter 16 emerged from the various remedies which the courts deployed against the excess or abuse of official power. This gave the law the practical strength emphasised by Dicey as part of the rule of law (see Chapter 5). From the seventeenth century the courts developed the 'prerogative orders' (called such because in theory they issue from the Crown) of *mandamus*, *prohibition* and *certiorari* that enable the High Court to police the powers and duties of 'inferior bodies', i.e. lower courts and government officials. *Mandamus* ordered a body to perform its duty. *Prohibition* was issued in advance to prevent a body from exceeding its jurisdiction.

Certiorari summoned up the record of an inferior body to be examined by the court and the decision to be quashed if it was invalid.

These orders remain the basis of the modern law of judicial review but are now called, mandatory orders, prohibiting orders and quashing orders, respectively. In relation to a quashing order the court can also send the matter back to the decision maker to decide again and where it considers that there is no point in sending it back can take the decision itself (Civil Procedure Rules (CPR) 54.19). This would apply in the rare case where there is only one possible decision that could lawfully be made.

The judicial review procedure *must* be used when applying for the above remedies (CPR 54.2). A claimant *may* also apply for the remedies of declaration, injunction and damages which are also available in an ordinary legal action (CPR 54.3). A declaration is a statement of the legal position which declares the rights of parties for example, 'X is entitled to a tax repayment'. Declarations are not enforceable but a public authority is unlikely to disobey one. Indeed a declaration is useful where an enforceable order would be undesirable, for example a government order before it is considered by Parliament or an advisory government opinion. The former prerogative orders do not lie against the Crown as such, but the declaration does. However, this is relatively unimportant because most statutory powers are conferred on ministers and the prerogative orders lie against individual ministers.

An injunction restrains a person from breaking the law or orders a person to undo something done unlawfully (a mandatory injunction). An interim injunction can restrain government action pending a full trial. In *M*. v. *Home Office* (1993) the House of Lords held that an injunction can be enforced against a minister of the Crown (see also *R*. v. *Minister of Agriculture ex parte Monsanto Plc* (1998). This overturns a long tradition that the Crown and ministers cannot be the subject of enforceable orders (see Crown Proceedings Act 1947, s. 21). However, it was stressed that injunctions should be granted against ministers only as a last resort. Injunctions cannot be granted against the Crown itself. The court also has a general power under s. 31 of the Supreme Court Act 1981 to stay the government action complained of pending the trial. Claimants often apply for more than one of the remedies which may well overlap. For example, a quashing order has the same effect as a declaration that the offending decision is void. A claimant cannot seek damages alone but must attach it to a claim for at least one of the other remedies (CPR 54.3(2)). Other financial remedies such as restitution of money paid as a result of an unlawful demand are not available in judicial review proceedings but can be sought in an ordinary action (*Woolwich Building Society* v. *IRC* (No. 2) (1993)). A mandatory order in judicial proceedings to return the money might also be available.

17.1.1 Damages against public bodies

Claims for damages are rare in judicial review proceedings. Damages cannot be awarded in respect of unlawful government action as such. Damages can be awarded only in respect of conduct and losses which are not authorised by statute and which would be actionable in an ordinary civil action (Supreme Court Act 1981 s. 31 (4), see *Metropolitan Asylum District* v. *Hill* (1881)). Damages might also be awarded in respect of the negligent performance of governmental functions which cause damage to persons or property, for example allowing a prisoner to escape (*Home Office* v. *Dorset Yacht Company* (1970)). This type of claim would normally be pursued in an ordinary civil action rather than judicial review proceedings because damages would be the only remedy sought.

It is sometimes claimed that there should be blanket immunity from damages for policy decisions taken by public authorities exercising regulatory powers in the public interest. This is because the risk might inhibit the decision maker from exercising its powers independently. There is no general immunity as such although the threshold is very high. Indeed in *Osman* v. *UK* (1999), the European Court of Human Rights held that a blanket immunity based on public interest grounds would violate the right to a fair trial under Art. 6 of the European Convention on Human Rights. An authority exercising a policy discretion conferred by statute is liable for negligence only if it exercises its powers in a way that is *Wednesbury* unreasonable and therefore not a valid exercise of its powers (see *X* v. *Bedfordshire County Council* (1995), decisions relating to child care and education). Moreover, it may not be not clear what injury has been suffered. For example, in the case of a decision to refuse a licence, which is void because of failure to take a relevant factor into account, the effect of the invalidity is to require the decision maker to make a new decision, the outcome of which might still be to refuse the licence.

In the case of what are sometimes called operational functions, even though some discretion may be involved, in principle an authority is liable for a negligent exercise of its powers (*Barratt* v. *Enfield Borough Council* (1999), failure to look after a child after taking him into care).

However, the difference between policy and operational functions may be unclear. For example, the neglect of a child due to a shortage of resources in a local authority residential home may be the result of a policy decision to spend money elsewhere. Moreover, the courts are reluctant to impose in respect of purely financial loss arising from the negligent exercise of statutory powers (see *Murphy* v. *Brentwood DC* (1991)).

There is also a distinction between damage which an authority fails to prevent and damage that it causes. In *Kane* v. *New Forest District Council* (2001) the Court of Appeal held that a local planning authority could be liable for creating a danger by granting planning permission for a development without first ensuring that an associated footpath which the council required the developer to construct was safe. However, where a public authority fails to exercise a power to prevent some existing danger there may be a higher threshold. In *Stovin* v. *Wise* (1996), the House of Lords held that the authority's failure to act must firstly be *Wednesbury* unreasonable and secondly that there must be exceptional reasons for requiring compensation to be paid. By contrast, where the authority fails to perform a statutory *duty* to prevent a danger it might be liable although the courts have still been reluctant to impose liability to prevent harm caused by the wrong-doings of others (see *X (Minors)* v. *Bedfordshire County Council* [1995] 2 AC 633, 751). In relation to liabilty for nuisance, however, it has been held that a landowner, including a public body, is required to act reasonably to remove nuisances, however they arise (*Marcic* v. *Thames Water* (2002)).

Judges have special immunities from personal liability. Superior court judges, that is, the Crown Court when it is dealing with trials on indictment, the High Court, the Court of Appeal and the House of Lords, are immune unless they knowingly act outside their jurisdiction in that they are not then acting as judges. Most inferior court judges and tribunals are immune if they act within their jurisdiction but liable in respect of acts outside jurisdiction (see generally *Re McC*. (1985)). Magistrates, however, while immune for acts within their jurisdiction, are liable for acts outside jurisdiction only if they act in bad faith, i.e. knowingly (Courts and Legal Services Act 1990, s. 108). For this purpose acting outside jurisdiction probably has a narrow meaning being confined to 'narrow *ultra vires*' in the sense mentioned in 16.4.1 (*Re McC*. (above)). Magistrates and their clerks can be indemnified against liability, for example for costs, unless they act in bad faith (Access to Justice Act 1999, s. 99).

In three kinds of cases damages may be awarded on the basis of unlawful government action independently of the private law of tort.

1. Under the *Francovich* principle in EC law (see Chapter 9).
2. The tort of 'abuse of public office' where an authority acts maliciously or knows that it is acting unlawfully (*Dunlop* v. *Woolahra City Council* (1982); *Calverley* v. *Chief Constable of Merseyside Police* (1989); *Racz* v. *Home Office* (1994)).
3. Where a right conferred by the European Convention on Human Rights is infringed. Under the Human Rights Act 1998 s. 8 a person can apply for 'just satisfaction' to a court which has power to award damages in civil proceedings. The court must take into account the principles applied by the European Court on Human Rights. For example in *Z* v. *UK* (2001) and *T.P. and K.M.* v. *UK* (2001) the children who failed to recover damages in *X* v. *Bedfordshire County Council* (above) which was decided before the Human Rights Act 1998 came into force, recovered on the same facts in the European Court for breaches of Art. 8 of the European Convention on Human Rights (respect for home, privacy and family life; see also *Marcic* v. *Thames Water* (2001)). However, the approach of the European Court is less generous than a domestic court and it is rare for non-financial loss to be compensated (see below 18.4.5).

Where an action for damages under the Human Rights Act is brought in respect of a judicial act, meaning in this context an act of a court, there is no liability in respect of an act done in good faith except for an unlawful arrest or detention. The action must be brought against the crown with the judge concerned being made a party (HRA 1998 s. 9 (3) (4)).

17.2 The Judicial Review Procedure

Before 1977 there was no single legal process that combined all the remedies. The old prerogative orders had developed separately from the other ('ordinary') remedies. Each group of remedies had to be sought in a different court, each generating an overlay of confusing technicality. In 1974 the Law Commission recommended that all the remedies be brought together into one procedure and that pointless differences between them be removed. This was implemented by rules of court in 1977, confirmed by the Supreme Court Act 1981, s. 31 and revised by the Civil Procedure Rules 2000 Part 54 (see Practice Direction [2000] 1 WLR 1654). A claim for judicial review is made in what is now called the Administrative Court (formerly the Crown Office List), and means 'a claim to review the lawfulness of – (i) an enactment; or (ii) a decision, action or failure to act in relation to the exercise of a public function' (CPR 54.2 (*a*)). The court can issue any of the remedies in any combination and is not limited to those for which the claimant has applied (Supreme Court Act 1981 s. 31 (5)).

There is also the ancient prerogative writ of *habeas corpus* ('produce the body') which, according to Dicey (1959, p. 199), is 'worth a hundred constitutional articles guaranteeing civil liberty' but may be of little practical importance today (see Le Sueur, 1992, cf. Shrimpton, (1993)). *Habeas corpus* is not part of the judicial review procedure although the grounds for issuing it are probably the same as those of judicial review (see Law Commission, 1994). It requires anyone detaining a person to bring the prisoner immediately before a judge to justify the detention. However, judicial review can also provide a speedy way of challenging unlawful detention.

17.2.1 Standing

The applicant must show that he has 'sufficient interest' in the matter to which the application relates (Supreme Court Act 1981 s. 31(3)). The question of standing must be considered not only at the threshold stage of permission to apply but also at the full hearing when it is examined in depth (see *IRC* v. *National Federation of Self-Employed and Small Businesses Ltd* (1981)). The courts take a broad approach to standing which is not confined to persons whose legal rights are directly in issue. They have, for example, given standing to pressure groups, at least where they have a specific involvement with the matter as representatives of people directly affected by the decision or where they have showed serious involvement by investing money or expertise (*R.* v. *Pollution Inspectorate ex parte Greenpeace* (No. 2) (1994)). Groups and individuals representing the general public interest have also been given standing at least where there is no other way of challenging the decision (*R.* v. *HM Treasury ex parte Smedley* (1985); *R.* v. *Foreign Secretary ex parte World Development Movement* (1995); *R.* v. *Secretary of State for Foreign and Commonwealth Affairs ex parte Rees-Mogg* (1994)). Indeed the contribution of pressure groups has been welcomed as adding a valuable dimension to judicial review (*R.* v. *Secretary of State ex parte Greenpeace* (1998) Envir. LR 415). It has been suggested that anyone who is not a mere busybody with no connection with the issues should have standing (*R.* v. *North Somerset DC ex parte Dixon* (1998)).

On the other hand in *R.* v. *Secretary of State for the Environment ex parte Rose Theatre Trust Ltd* (1990), a case that has been much criticised, it was held that a campaigning interest in protecting the site of the Shakespearian Rose Theatre was not sufficient in itself. It was also emphasised that individuals cannot give themselves standing merely by forming a group. Perhaps this could be contested on the communitarian basis that group involvement is a manifestation of democratic legitimacy? A restrictive approach was also taken in *R. (Bulger)* v. *Secretary of State* (2001) where it was held that the father of a baby murdered by two boys in horrific circumstances did not have standing to challenge the Lord Chief Justice's recommendation to the Home Secretary of the length of the punishment element of their sentence. The court stressed that there was no need for a third party to intervene since the Crown and the boys could both challenge the decision and raise all the relevant issues. According to Rose LJ a low threshold of standing can be justified because of the importance to the rule of law that someone should be able to call decision makers to account but this was not the case here. The particular remedy is also a factor. For example in *R.* v. *Felixtowe Justices ex parte Leigh* (1987) a newspaper editor had standing for a declaration that magistrates should not hide behind anonymity but not *mandamus* to reveal the identity of magistrates in a particular case.

However, in many cases including *Bulger* and *Rose Theatres*, even where the claimant lacks standing the court considers the substantive issues. It seems therefore that the court has a broad discretion. At the permission stage, standing is likely to be generous, so as to filter out only hopeless cases. At the full hearing, those whose legal rights are in issue would always have standing, while in other cases the court will balance the extent of the applicant's interest against the public importance of the issues involved and the particular remedy sought. Moreover, even where a person has no standing in their own right, the court has a discretion to hear any person thereby broadening the scope of the process and allowing interest groups to have a say (CPR 54.17).

17.2.2 Government protection

An important feature of the application for judicial review is the amount of discretion it gives to the court. This is designed to make the procedure speedy and effective but also to protect the public interest against malicious or futile challenges to government. The main provisions are as follows:

- As we have seen permission to apply is required from a judge before proceedings can be commenced (SCA 1981 s. 31 (3), CPR 54.4). This is sometimes depicted in the media as having 'obtained a judicial review'. However, at this stage the applicant merely shows that he has a chance of success. The procedure is *ex parte*, that is, the government side does not have to appear. Moreover there need not be a formal hearing (CPR 54.12). There is a right to renew the application for permission before another judge in open court or, in the case of a refusal in open court, before the Court of Appeal.

- The court has a discretion in relation to procedural matters. The case is normally decided on the basis of affidavits (sworn written statements), but the court may allow discovery of documents, witnesses and cross-examination if this is needed to do justice (see *O'Reilly* v. *Mackman* (1982)).

- There is a time limit. The present Rules seens to have rationalised the somewhat incoherent provisions that were originally made. The claim must be filed (a) promptly; and (b) not later than three months after the ground to make the claim first arose. In the case of a quashing order this means the date of the decision (CPR 54.5 (1) (*b*)). The time limit can be extended by agreement and is subject to any shorter time limit in a particular statute (CPR 54.6). The time limit can also be extended by the court. However, even within three months the court may refuse leave to make the application or refuse to give a remedy if 'undue delay' results in 'substantial hardship to any person, substantial prejudice to the rights of any person, or would be detrimental to good administration' (Supreme Court Act 1981 s. 31 (6) (7)); see *Caswell* v. *Dairy Produce Quota Tribunal* (1990)).

- The court can refuse to grant a remedy even when a decision is *ultra vires* and strictly speaking void (*Credit Suisse* v. *Allerdale DC* (1996)). The court will not set aside a decision where, for example, no injustice has been done, or where the interests of third parties would be prejudiced or where intervention would cause serious public disruption (e.g. *R.* v. *Secretary of State for the Home Deptartment ex parte Swati* (1986); *R.* v. *Secretary of State for the Environment ex parte Association of Metropolitan Authorities* (1986); *Coney* v. *Choice* (1975)). The court might also prefer a declaration to an enforceable order where enforcement might be impracticable or hinder the governmental process (see e.g. *R.* v. *Panel on Takeovers and Mergers ex parte Datafin plc* (1987); *Chief Constable of North Wales Police* v. *Evans* (1982); *R.* v. *Boundary Commission for England ex parte Foot* [1983] 1 All ER 1099, 1116). An important reason not to intervene is where the applicant has an alternative and equally appropriate remedy such as a right of appeal or an internal means of redress.

Judicial review is intended to be a last resort (see e.g. *R.* v. *Chief Constable of the Merseyside Police ex parte Calverley* (1986)).

17.3 Choice of Procedure: Public and Private Law

The special features of the application for judicial review raise two questions: (i) When is the procedure available? (ii) When must it be used in place of other methods of approaching the courts? As we have seen, before the judicial review procedure was created in 1977, the prerogative orders were available only in the Divisional Court of the Queen's Bench Division, but the other remedies, declaration, injunction and damages, were, and still are, available in any court. Decisions of governmental bodies and powerful private bodies such as trade unions were also challengeable in the ordinary courts.

Until the 1980s the citizen could apply to any court for a declaration or injunction. Indeed free access to the courts is a constitutional principle which the leave procedure seems to deny. Nevertheless in *O'Reilly* v. *Mackman* (1982) the House of Lords held that a 'public law' case must normally be brought under the application for judicial review procedure. It will be remembered that a major plank of Dicey's rule of law was the idea that English law does not recognise any distinction between public and private law. *O'Reilly* v. *Mackman* has therefore caused problems. Two distinct questions must be separated. Firstly, what is a public law matter? If a matter is not one of public law then the application for judicial review procedure is irrelevant. Secondly, the 'exclusivity' question, that is, what 'exceptional cases' fall outside the special procedure in a public law matter?

17.3.1 Public law matters – scope of the judicial review procedure

Although it is often suggested that powerful private bodies should be subject to the judicial review (see Craig, 1998), the judicial review procedure applies only to 'public functions' (CPR 54.1). Not all disputes involving public officials concern public functions. The issues involved may be the same as arise in a private context (for example, dismissal of a clerk in a government office). The Court of Appeal has decided that a public law function depends upon a combination of factors. First, the power must have some governmental underpinning. Where a power is conferred directly by statute, royal prerogative, or even governmental rules of practice, this test will normally be satisfied (see *Scott* v. *National Trust* (1998)). In other cases the position is more difficult. It was held in *R.* v. *Panel on Takeovers and Mergers ex parte Datafin plc* (1987) that the Takeover Panel, a self-regulating voluntary body which acted as a city 'watchdog', was exercising public law functions. This was because it was set up in the public interest, it reported to the government, and although not having statutory powers itself, was supported by the statutory powers of the Department of Trade (see also *Donoughue* v. *Poplar Housing and Regeneration Community Association Ltd* (2001)). Another test is to ask whether, if the body in question did not exist the government would have to intervene (see *R.* v. *Chief Rabbi ex parte Wachman* (1993)). However, this is not reliable since there is no agreement on what functions are necessary in this sense.

The Court of Appeal has also said that a power which is based exclusively on agreement or contract, for example, the disciplinary power exercised by sport or professional associations is a private law power (see *R.* v. *Disciplinary Committee of the Jockey Club ex parte the Aga Khan* (1993); *R.* v. *East Berkshire Health Authority ex parte Walsh* (1985); *R.* v. *Home Secretary ex parte Benwell* (1985)). This seems somewhat rigid since many contractual regulatory bodies, such as professional associations, exercise their powers for the purpose of protecting the public in much the same way as the Takeover Panel. However, in *Donoughue* (above) the contractual power of a housing association to evict a tenant was regarded as a public function for the purpose of the Human Rights Act, because the activities of the association were enmeshed with those of a local authority (see also *McLaren* v. *Home Office* (1990); *R.* v. *Legal Aid Board ex parte Donn & Co.* (1996); *R.* v. *Disciplinary Committee of the Jockey Club ex parte the Aga Khan* (1993) per Hoffman LJ). Agreement may therefore be relevant but not conclusive.

The judges are not in agreement about the nature of a public function and have expressed concerns about the state of the law. Indeed, if as was suggested in Chapter 16, the basis of judicial review is to protect against abuses by powerful bodies it is arguable that a non-governmental power such as that of a trade union, or large company or private school should be reviewable where it has serious consequences for the individual (see *R.* v. *Disciplinary Committee of the Jockey Club ex parte the Aga Khan* (1993) per Lord Bingham MR). The position of charitable bodies that are obliged to act only for public purposes is uncertain. In *RSPCA* v. *A-G* (2001), Lightman J stated that a charity might in theory be subject to judicial review (see also *Scott* v. *National Trust* 1998). However, his Lordship pointed out that the appropriate forum would normally be charity proceedings in the Chancery division with the approval of the Charity Commissioners. A charity as such is not 'public' for the purpose of the Human Rights Act 1998 (below Ch. 18).

17.3.2 Exclusivity

Assuming that a decision is one of public law, must the judicial review procedure always be used? Because the judicial review procedure is more restrictive than an ordinary action, there is a school of thought that the rule of law is threatened by forcing people to use it. As against this, the judicial review procedure is geared to the special concerns of challenging government action so that it would be inefficient if people could circumvent it.

In *O'Reilly* v. *Mackman* (1982), a group of prisoners sought to challenge a decision not to give them remission for good behaviour. They were outside time for judicial review and attempted to bring an ordinary civil action for a declaration. The House of Lords struck out their claim as an abuse of the court's process. Lord Diplock said that the judicial review procedure should normally be used because of its safeguards which protected the government against 'groundless, unmeritorious or tardy harassment'. However, Lord Diplock accepted that an ordinary action might sometimes lie although he did not fully explain when. He did, however, stress that a prisoner has no legal right to remission, which was an 'indulgence' from the government but at most a legitimate expectation that his case would be considered fairly. In *Cocks* v. *Thanet DC* (1983) the House of Lords applied *O'Reilly* to hold that a claimant under homelessness legislation must use judicial review rather than a more convenient action in a local county court. This was because the legislation gave no absolute rights but required a discretionary government decision before a claimant became entitled to housing.

Perhaps recognising its potential for injustice, the courts subsequently backed away from a strict application of *O'Reilly*. In particular it was decided that a citizen can raise a defence in any relevant proceedings against an unlawful government claim (*Wandsworth BC* v. *Winder* (1985); *Boddington* v. *British Transport Police* (1998)). In *Roy* v. *Kensington, Chelsea and Westminster Family Practitioners Committee* (1992) this was taken further. A doctor was seeking a discretionary 'practice allowance' from the National Health Service. He had established entitlement to some kind of allowance, but not as to how much. The House of Lords suggested that whenever a litigant was pursuing or defending a 'private law right' whether as a defence or as a claim s/he need not use the judicial review procedure. Their Lordships defined 'private right' widely to include any case where a person could establish even part of a definite claim against the government.

These cases seem to leave *O'Reilly* v. *Mackman* little to bite on, because in the absence of a 'private law right', judicial review with its flexible standing requirement would in any event be the only possible procedure (see *Gouriet* v. *UPOW* (1975); *Lonrho* v. *Tebbit* (1992); *Mercury Communications* v. *Director General of Telecommunications* (1996); *Trustees of the Dennis Rye Pension Fund* v. *Sheffield City Council* (1997)). Indeed Feldman (1999) suggests that the *O'Reilly* rule might violate Art. 6 of the ECHR, the right to a fair trial.

Since new Civil Procedure Rules were introduced in 2000, the ordinary civil procedure has become more flexible and the differences from the judicial review procedure less substantial. In particular Part 24 of the Civil Procedure Rules contains safeguards to protect the public interest in pointless litigation by allowing the court to strike out a civil action at an early stage if the defendant can show that it has no reasonable chance of success. (In judicial review proceedings however, the *claimant* must establish a reasonable chance of success.) In *R. (Balbo)* v. *Secretary of State* (2001) the court refused to allow judicial review to challenge a government demand for a penalty against a transport company that had, apparently inadvertently, carried asylum seekers. This was because the issue were factual for which a defence in ordinary civil proceedings would be more appropriate. In *Clark* v. *University of Lincolnshire and Humberside* (2000) a student brought an ordinary action, in breach of contract against a decision by the university to fail her. It was argued that she should have brought a judicial review claim within the three-month time limit. The Court of Appeal held that she was entitled to bring a civil action. Even if judicial review were appropriate, as was the case here because the university also had statutory powers, the court would not strike out a claim merely because of the procedure that had been adopted unless the court's processes were being misused or the procedure chosen was unsuitable. Moreover the court can transfer a case from the Administrative Court to an ordinary procedure at any time (CPR 54.20).

17.4   The Exclusion of Judicial Review

Sometimes a statute attempts to exclude judicial review. The courts are reluctant to accept this and construe such statutes narrowly. For example, a provision stating that a decision shall be 'final' does not exclude review but merely prevents the decision maker from reopening the matter and excludes any right of appeal that might otherwise apply (*Ex parte Gilmore* (1957)). Even a provision stating that a 'determination of the tribunal shall not be questioned in any court of law' is ineffective to prevent review where the tribunal exceeds its 'jurisdiction' (powers) on the basis that the tribunal's act is a nullity and so not a 'determination'. Given that a government body exceeds its jurisdiction whenever it makes an error of law, this neatly sidesteps the 'ouster clause' (*Anisminic Ltd* v. *Foreign Compensation Commission* (1969)).

A sufficiently tightly drafted 'ouster clause' would surmount *Anisminic*. A clause often found in statutes relating to land-use planning and compulsory purchase allows challenge within six weeks and then provides that the decision 'shall not be questioned in any court of law'. The courts have interpreted this provision literally, on the ground that review is not completely excluded and that the policy of the statute is to enable development of land to be started quickly (see *R.* v. *Cornwall CC ex parte Huntingdon* (1994)).

A provision stating that a particular act such as entry on a register or a certificate shall be 'conclusive evidence' of the matters stated may also be effective since it does not exclude review as such but makes it impossible to prove invalidity (*R.* v. *Registrar of Companies ex parte Central Bank of India* (1985); see also Anti-Terrorism and Investigatory Powers Bill 2000, clause 29(3): certificates that person is an international terrorist). However, this clause may not protect against a challenge for unfairness.

Statutes dealing with the surveillance and the security services feature a clause stating that a decision cannot be challenged even on jurisdictional grounds (e.g. Security Services Act 1989 s. 5(4); Regulation of Investigatory Powers Act 2000 s. 67(8)). The purports to exclude judicial review of a decision to detain a non-British citizen under the Act and against a certificate of the Home Secretary to exclude the Refugees Convention under the Act. However, apart from the conclusive evidence provision (above) the language appears to create the weaker form of ouster that did not survive *Anisminic* (see clauses 29, 30, 33). Moreover there is a right of appeal to the Special Immigration Commission (clauses 25, 26) and on a point of law to the Court of Appeal (see Special Immigration Commission Act 1997). Article 6 of the ECHR may be invoked on the ground that an ouster clause prevents a fair trial. There are no overrides in the ECHR to the right to a fair trial and there must arguably always be provision for judicial review even though the level and scope of this may vary with the particular context. For example decisions based on political policy or national security can be subject to a lower level of review (see *R. (Alconbury)* v. *Secretary of State* [2001] 2 All ER 929).

Summary

17.1   There is a special procedure for challenging decisions of public bodies. This is called the Application for Judicial Review and is highly discretionary. The procedure provides the citizen with a range of remedies including damages, but also provides machinery for protecting government against improper or trivial challenges. Leave to apply is required and judicial review will be refused where there is an equally convenient alternative remedy.

17.2   Standing is flexible and increasingly liberal although a third party may not be given standing where others are in a better position to challenge the decision.

17.3   The Application for Judicial Review applies only to public law functions which usually include powers exercised by a wide range of bodies connected to the government or exercising statutory powers but do not usually include exclude powers derived exclusively from contract or consent. In some cases the citizen may challenge public law powers outside the judicial review procedure on the basis of the rule of law principle that, where private rights are at stake, unlawful government action can be ignored.

17.4   The remedies and procedure for judicial review are discretionary so that even though an unlawful government decision is strictly speaking a nullity, the court may be refuse to intervene. Delay, misbehaviour, the impact on third parties and the absence of injustice may be reasons for not interfering. Public inconvenience or administrative disruption are probably not enough in themselves but they might be relevant to the court's discretion coupled with another factor such as delay.

17.5   Sometimes statutes attempt to exclude judicial review. The courts are reluctant to see their powers taken away and interpret such provisions strictly. The Human Rights Act 1998 reinforces this.

Further Reading

Cane, P. (1995) 'Standing Up for the Public', *Public Law* 276.

Fredman S. and Morris, G. (1995) 'The costs of exclusivity: public and private re-examined', *Public Law* 68.

Law Commission (1994) *Administrative Law: Judicial Review and Statutory Appeals*, Law Com. No 226, HC 669.

Le Sueur (1992) 'Applications for judicial review: the requirement of leave', *Public Law* 102.

Richardson and Genn (eds), *Administrative Law and Government Action*, Part 1.

Richardson, G and Sunkin, M. (1996) 'Judicial review: questions of impact', *Public Law* 79.

Taggart (ed.), *The Province of Administrative Law*, chapters 1, 2, 10.

Woolf, H. (1990) *Protection of the Public: A New Challenge*, 24 *et seq.*

Exercises

Note: material in Chapter 16 may also be relevant to some of these questions.

17.1 What are the advantages and disadvantages of the application for judicial review procedure from the point of view of the citizen? When may government action be challenged in the courts by means of an ordinary action?

17.2 The distinction between public private powers is too uncertain and artificial to define the court's judicial review jurisdiction. Discuss.

17.3 This case is 'a good example of a case where the commissioner's investigation and report can provide the just remedy when judicial review might fail to; and can reach facts that might not emerge under the judicial review process' (Henry LJ in *R. v. Local Commissioner ex parte Liverpool City Council* (2001)). Explain and compare judicial review with the ombudsman (Chapters 8, 12) as a method of protecting the citizen.

17.4 Snobville District Council has statutory power to acquire within its area, land which in its opinion it 'is desirable to set aside as a public park'. The Council makes a compulsory purchase order in respect of a row of houses owned by Fred, who lets them at a low rent and who has frequently been prosecuted by the Council under public health legislation for offences involving overcrowding in the houses. The governing statute provides that a compulsory purchase order may be challenged in the High Court within six weeks of its confirmation by the minister on the ground of *ultra vires*, but 'thereafter a Compulsory Purchase Order shall not be questioned in any court of law'. Fred does not challenge the order, but, nine months after its confirmation by the minister, John, one of the residents in Fred's houses, learns that the Council had agreed with another landowner, X, to acquire Fred's land rather than X's on the ground that 'since Fred's houses were unhealthy this would kill two birds with one stone'. John also believes that there is already adequate provision for public parks in Snobville. Advise John.

17.5 Forever Open Housing Association provides sheltered accommodation for vulnerable people. It is a charity and is registered with the Housing Corporation, a government agency that funds and regulates housing providers. Mary lives in a residential home owned by Forever Open, her accommodation being paid for by the local authority under its statutory obligation to arrange for care provision for the elderly. When Mary took up residence, Forever Open told her that she 'now has a home for life'. Forever Open now proposes to close the home in order to concentrate its resources upon housing teenage drug addicts as advised by the Housing Corporation. Advise Mary whether and how she can challenge this proposal.

17.6 By statute (fictitious) the NHS is required to provide 'an effective health care service for all UK citizens'. The statute also provides that decisions made by any NHS hospital in relation to the provision of any service to the public shall not be questioned in any court. St Tony's hospital is short of money and trained staff due to government financial cuts. The Secretary of State has issued a circular to all hospitals stating among other things that no further patients be admitted for sex-change operations, and that hip-replacement operations should normally be performed only on patients who play an active part in the economic life of the community.

(a) The Holby Transsexual Rights Society, a local pressure group, objects to the circular. They discovered its contents six months after it came into effect. Advise the Society as to its chances of success in a claim for judicial review.
(b) Frank, who is an unemployed resident in a hostel for the homeless is refused a hip replacement operation. Advise him.

18 Human Rights and Civil Liberties

18.1 Introduction: The Bill of Rights Debate

Human rights disputes require the decision maker to decide the limits of the law in the sense of when the legal rights of individuals should give way to the public welfare. It has been debated for many years whether the UK should enact a 'bill of rights' (see, e.g. Griffith, 1979; Brennan, 1989; Dworkin, 1996, ch. 18. The gist of the argument in favour of doing so is that the modern executive-dominated Parliament is unable to afford adequate protection to the citizen. A bill of rights would impose consistency upon the judges, would ensure that statutes are drafted with civil liberties in mind and would educate public opinion possibly even changing the political culture (see White Paper, 1997a).

Arguments against a bill of rights are concerned with the high political content of human rights disputes and the fact that disputes involving human rights typically raise incommensurable values that cannot be resolved by the application of an established general principle but only by a provisional accommodation that commands sufficient public support (see Chapter 2). Human rights disputes require the decision maker to decide the limits of a law in the sense of the extent to which a right should be sacrificed to some important public goal, for example personal freedom against the suppression of terrorism. Either Parliament or the courts could do this probably using the same arguments but, in a democracy, is there any convincing reason in favour of an unelected court having the last word?

There are three interrelated issues. The first is whether there are such things as fundamental rights or are they anything other than political claims on behalf of competing interests (Griffith, 1979; Campbell, 1999)? In favour of rights Dworkin (1996) argues that certain interests, such as freedom of expression, and the right to a fair trial are non-negotiable conditions of a democratic society because they underpin equality, this being the nearest we can get to a bedrock principle (see also Lord Hoffmann in *R. (Alconbury)* v. *Secretary of State* (2000)). It is only by identifying and protecting these rights that a democratic community can be sustained.

The second issue concerns what counts as a fundamental right in practical terms and what are its limits? The UK has decided to rely on the European Convention on Human Rights (ECHR), which has, through the European Court, developed a substantial jurisprudence. The ECHR concentrates upon freedom from state interference and is not directed to 'positive rights' such as the right to work or rights to health. However, rights of this kind might sometimes fall within the scope of ECHR rights (e.g. Art. 8 (family life) includes a healthy environment (*Guerra* v. *Italy* (1999)). Reliance on the ECHR has drawbacks. As an international agreement the Convention is something of a bland compromise with many exceptions and vague language.

As regards conflicts between different rights and between rights and other interests, the ECHR has recognised the political sensitivity of human rights by including devices that attempt to mediate between conflicting concerns. These include a list of particular exceptions or overrides to many of the rights, and a right to derogate from the Convention in emergency situations. The European Court has also developed concepts that can dilute the protected rights. These include 'margin of appreciation', 'fair balance' and 'proportionality' (below). Despite lengthy judicial expositions (e.g. *Gough* v. *Chief Constable of the Derbyshire Constabulary* (2001)), these concepts lack overarching rationality because they require a choice to be made between incommensurable values.

This raises the third issue. Who should have the last word in disputes relating to fundamental rights? In particular should a bill of rights be protected against being overridden by the democratic lawmaker? Even if we accept that the concept of human rights is meaningful and should be imbedded in the law, nothing follows automatically from this as to what is the best mechanism for protecting them. The ultimate decision maker might, for example, be a court as in the USA, an elected lawmaker as in the UK or a special body, such as an ombudsman, a parliamentary committee or a commission possibly including nongovernmental organisations (NGOs).

It is often claimed that the courts are most likely to produce the 'best' outcome (Dworkin, 1996). However, this is question begging. There is profound disagreement about every aspect of human rights. As we do not agree as to what counts as a best outcome we could not agree what mechanism is most likely to produce it. Arguments about what is the best outcome merely repeat the disagreement. The appropriate question is therefore what mechanism can most appropriately manage disagreement irrespective of outcomes. Many would argue, following

Locke, that this should be a democratic assembly in which the whole community can participate on equal terms (Waldron, 1999, Part III). According to William Cobbett (ibid., p. 232), '(t)he great right of every man, the right of rights, is the right of having a share in the making of the laws to which the good of the whole makes it his duty to submit.'

Both sides recognise that fundamental rights cannot be directly applied as rules, but, like morality, provide abstract principles which guide decision making See *R. v. DPP ex parte Kebelene* [1999] 4 All ER 801, 843. They translate into concrete outcomes in accordance with the changing attitudes of society in ways that the original drafters may not have anticipated. Contrary conclusions can be drawn from this. It might be argued that the kind of legalistic mechanisms depending on verbal formulae that judges are good at (e.g. is abortion an aspect of 'privacy'?) are an unacceptably narrow way of addressing a problem which requires political and moral choice. On the other hand it might be argued that the complexity and open-endedness of the issues requires the careful, 'objective' scrutiny, that courts are also good at.

The main argument in favour of a court is based on the checks-and-balances aspect of the separation of powers namely that 'democracy' is more than just the will of the majority but entails certain basic principles of equality and freedom which must be protected against the volatility, corruption or foolishness of the majority (see Dworkin, 1996, Allan, 1999). Our democracy is necessarily imperfect since the people cannot act directly but must elect representatives. We can only vote for the kind of people who put themselves forward for election. We recognise that government is an untidy accommodation between competing values. Why should there therefore not be safeguards? After all, a court is independent, relatively impartial and required to justify its decisions publicly by reasoned argument. It can protect unpopular minorities. By contrast, if the majority were allowed to decide the limits of its own power it would be judge in its own case and lack public confidence particularly as the 'majority' under the British electoral system often represents the will of a minority political party.

Another argument in favour of the courts is that, according to the founders of the US Constitution, the courts 'lacking ultimate 'influence over either the sword or the purse' ... may truly be said to have neither force nor will but merely judgement and may thus be expected to remain the least dangerous branch' (Tribe, 1988, p. 10). It is also argued that handing over power to a court is not anti-democratic but a prudent 'pre-commitment' chosen by a majority anxious to guard against its own weaknesses of pandering to the mob or panicking under the pressure of events. Just as Ulysses ordered the crew to bind him to the mast and to ignore his subsequent pleas to unbind him so that he would not give way to the temptations of the Sirens or a smoker may ask a friend to hide the cigarettes, by removing fundamental rights from its control the majority lessens the risk that it will abuse its power, for example by introducing draconian laws as a panic response to a terrorist outrage (see Waldron (1999, p. 257).

Waldron (1999, ch. 11) is not convinced by the above. He argues that, assuming we wish to be a democracy, the people through an elected body should decide the limits of fundamental rights. Despite its risks and weaknesses, representative democracy is the nearest we can get to equal participation. Waldron suggests that, while judges may be good at applying laws, conflicts between fundamental rights and other important interests go beyond legal rules into territory where judges have no special expertise. Because disagreement is all pervasive in relation to human rights, it demeans us as autonomous rational beings to defer to judges in areas in which they are not experts and makes our constitution aristocratic rather than democratic. For example in *R.J.B. MacDonald Inc.* v. *Canada (A-G)* (1995) the Canadian Supreme Court was divided as to whether the undoubted public interest in combating ill health justified overriding freedom of expression by banning tobacco advertising. It is difficult to see why a judge is better placed than a democratic assembly to decide such an issue.

Moreover, judges are not directly accountable for their actions, a fact which might tempt the legislature to be irresponsible and to shuffle hard choices to the judges. There is no reliable way of discovering what are the values of the community. A judge might be forced to rely on his personal opinions or be swayed by the circumstances of the case before him. Politicians might appoint judges whose views reflect those of the very politicians whom the judges are supposed to protect us against. In the UK, contrary to the separation of powers, judges are not appointed by a formal independent process but are nominated privately by the Lord Chancellor who is a member of the executive dependent on the support of the Prime Minister.

Furthermore, according to Waldron, the Ulysses and cigarette analogies (above) are misplaced. Ulysses and the smoker voluntarily submit to external *impersonal* constraints to meet a specific problem about which there is no disagreement whereas in the human rights context, we are surrendering our power to decide controversial matters to the personal judgement of others in an objectionably paternalistic way. The 'judge in its own cause' analogy (above) is also misplaced. The problem of bias arises when an individual or faction purports to decide a dispute concerning its own interests. It has no application where the decision concerns the whole community, since, unless the decision is made by someone wholly external such as an overseas court, the decision maker is a judge in its own cause whatever mechanism is used. Moreover, we all like to be right so that any final decision maker is a judge in its own cause as to whether its decision is right.

The Human Rights Act recognises this irreducible disagreement. The Act tries to accommodate both sides by using the advantages of the courts in applying law in the shape of the European Convention on Human Rights, even to the extent of scrutinising statutes for compatibility with the Convention. On the other hand the Act upholds democracy by leaving the final word with Parliament while empowering the court to put pressure on Parliament thereby creating an accommodation in accordance with the separation of powers.

18.2 The Common Law

English lawyers have traditionally used the negative terminology of civil liberties rather than the more positive language of rights. This is because the common law embodies the liberal perspective that everyone is free to do whatever the law does not specifically prohibit. In Hobbes's language, 'freedom lies in the silence of the laws'. However, in a constitution such as that of the United Kingdom which lacks political checks and balances and where the lawmaker can be easily controlled by a single political party, the problem lies in ensuring that the laws are indeed silent.

To the modern reader therefore the following remarks of Dicey (1915, p. 500) may appear complacent. 'English law no more favours and provides for the holding of public meetings than for the giving of public concerts ... A man has a right to hear an orator as he has a right to hear a band or eat a bun'. Similarly Dicey was content to assert that the press has no special protection but merely the freedoms of ordinary citizens. Thus press freedom from censorship was, according to Dicey triumphantly restored in 1695 merely by not renewing the legislation that had empowered the Crown to licence printing presses (ibid., p. 257).

The common law's residual or negative approach therefore depends on trusting the lawmaker, the executive and the police not to enact or enforce intrusive laws and on trusting the courts to interpret laws in a way sympathetic to individual liberty. In connection with judicial review, for example, we met the presumption of statutory interpretation, known as the 'principle of legality', that clear language or necessary implication is required to override fundamental rights (see *R.* v. *Secretary of State ex parte Piersen* (1997) per Lord Steyn and Lord Browne-Wilkinson; *R.* v. *Secretary of State for the Home Department ex parte Simms* [1999] 3 All ER 400 at 411, 412).

The common law approach might overlook the creeping erosion of liberty by the accumulation of statutes which, taken individually, are relatively innocuous but which add up to a formidable armoury of state powers. For example, over 200 statutory provisions authorise officials other than the police to enter private property so that the residual freedom promoted in *Entick* v. *Carrington* (1765) is somewhat frail (see *R.* v. *IRC ex parte Rossminister Ltd* (1980)). Public order law is especially vulnerable to this kind of erosion in that particular threats, such as football hooliganism, harassment and anti-social conduct in residential areas can be combated by draconian legislation which is more likely to be overinclusive than precisely targeted. Thus the rule of law's insistence on general principles might be counter productive. In this respect the Anti-Terrorism, Crime and Security Act 2001, which is aimed at the legitimate target of terrorism contains provisions, concerning for example intimidation and powers to require identification, that go well beyond the case of terrorism. Similarly, the Treason Felony Act 1848 remains on the statute book. Intended to deal with violent threats to the constitution s. 3 outlaws any writing advocating the abolition of the monarchy, thus restricting debate about republicanism. Moreover legislation enacted to deal with a particular urgent problem is rarely repealed but remains in force to be used in other contexts.

The courts' record has been mixed. In some contexts notably the defence of property rights they have on the whole been libertarian. In other contexts, notably political dissent, they have been less protective and readily deferred to government claims based on confidentiality, national security and public order (see Whitty *et al.*, 2001, p. 39 et seq.). Moreover there has been no consensus as to what liberties are fundamental in the common law. Sometimes the very notion of a constitutional right has been rejected. In *Home Office* v. *Harman* (1983), the question arose whether the defendant, (who is currently the Solicitor General), could be punished for revealing information to a journalist that had been read out in court but which the judge had asked not to be further published. Lord Diplock said (at 543) '[The case] is not about freedom of speech', whereas Lord Scarman commented that [the case] must recognise 'the important constitutional right to freedom of expression' (543), see also *Secretary of State* v.

Guardian Newspapers Ltd [1984] 3 All ER 601 at 603 and 615), *A-G* v. *Associated Newspapers Ltd* (1994).

Although the UK has been a party to the European Convention on Human Rights since 1952 and indeed played a major role in its drafting, Convention rights have become binding in English law only after the Human Rights Act 1998 came into force in November 2000. Before the 1998 Act, it was not clear how far our treaty obligations under the European Convention on Human Rights should be taken into account in domestic courts. However, in recent years there has been a trend in favour of interpreting the law in the light of international obligations. This is of great importance in relation to treaties such as those relating to genocide, terrorism, the environment and the rights of the child that have not been formally incorporated into the law.

Even before the Human Rights Act, the courts had begun to place greater emphasis on fundamental rights, notably in relation to prisoners and press freedom (e.g. *Derbyshire County Council* v. *Times Newspapers Ltd* (1993), *Piersen* v. *Secretary of State* (1997), *R.* v. *Secretary of State for the Home Department ex parte Simms* (1999), cf. *R.* v. *Secretary of State for the Home Department ex parte Hindley* (2000)). Judges have also written extra-judicially, in favour of fundamental rights, and of incorporating the European Convention on Human Rights into English law or of interpreting the law to give effect to fundamental rights (e.g. Browne-Wilkinson, 1992; Laws, 1993, 1998; Bingham, 1993, cf. Hooper, 1998; Hoffmann, 1999).

Judges sometimes claim that the ECHR reflects the common law. For example, in *R.* v. *Secretary of State ex parte Brind* [1990] 1 All ER 469 at 477, Lord Donaldson said that 'you have to look long and hard before you can detect any difference between the English common law and the principles set out in the convention at least if you view the convention through English judicial eyes.' It is also claimed that the reasoning methods in UK law are essentially the same as those of the ECHR in that in both cases freedom can be overridden only in specified circumstances. In *A-G* v. *Guardian Newspapers Ltd* (No. 2) [1988] 3 All ER 545 at 660, Lord Goff, said: 'I can see no inconsistency between English law (freedom of expression) and (the ECHR). This is scarcely surprising, since we may pride ourselves on the fact that freedom of speech has existed in this country perhaps as long if not longer than anywhere else in the world. The only difference is that (the convention) ... proceeds to state a fundamental right and then to qualify it, we in this country (where everyone is free to do anything subject only to the provisions of the law) proceed rather on an assumption of freedom of speech, and turn to our law to discover the established exceptions to it.' Similarly in *Derbyshire County Council* v. *Times Newspapers* (1993) and *R.* v. *Secretary of State for the Home Department ex parte Simms* (1999), both concerning freedom of expression, Lord Keith and Lord Steyn regarded the common law as complying with the ECHR. In *Simms*, Lord Hoffman suggested that the Human Rights Act confirms the existing state of English law (below p. 433).

However, the two approaches are significantly different. Firstly, the European Convention requires the special justification of proportionality to override a right, whereas in the common law any clearly worded statute and even a discretionary power will do. Secondly the common law, sometimes described as unprincipled, is multi-factoral in the sense that it depends on accumulating factors pointing to or against a particular conclusion, without necessarily organising these within a formal hierarchy of principles. These factors include precedent, logical coherence, social policy and morality. However, some values or interests may be given greater weight than others and in this respect the common law method overlaps with that of the ECHR.

Proponents of the Human Rights Act argue that it has several advantages (Irvine, 1998, White Paper (1997, 1–13)). These include the following:

(i) The common law is too weak and vulnerable.
(ii) Most other European states have enacted human rights legislation so that the UK appears to be a persistent offender in the European Court.
(iii) Minimise delays and costs.
(iv) A distinctively British approach to the development of human rights jurisprudence.
(v) Encouraging closer scrutiny of new laws and policies.
(vi) Enhancing awareness of human rights among the people and making remedies more directly accessible.

On the other hand the principle of equality means that powerful companies as well as individuals can claim the protection of the Act (e.g. *R.J.R. MacDonald Inc.* v. *Canada (A-G)* (1995): freedom of expression for tobacco advertising *Wilson* v. *First County Trust* (below)). Furthermore, litigation is likely to become longer, more complex and therefore more expensive, and judicial opinions more prolix (see Ford, 1999). Confidence in the judiciary might be eroded by the overtly political nature of the issues involved. On the other hand, a more informed public might become more confident in the judiciary as important issues are openly debated.

18.3 The European Convention on Human Rights

The European Convention on Human Rights was created by the Council of Europe which currently has 41 members. It was a response to the atrocities of the fascist era of the 1930s and 1940s. It therefore concentrates upon the protection of individual freedom against state interference rather than what are known as second- and third-generation human rights, these being respectively social claims such as housing, and community claims such as environmental quality.

The European Court of Human Rights sits in Strasbourg. The judges are elected for six years by the Parliamentary Assembly of the Council of Europe, there being one judge from each member state. Originally there was a two-stage process involving an initial filtering by a Commission partly on political grounds with some cases being sent to the Committee of Ministers for resolution. Litigation was very slow with cases often taking more than five years to be resolved and the court's workload has steadily increased. For example in 1976 it decided five cases and in 1997 145 were pending.

The 11th Protocol abolishes the Commission and gives states, individuals and groups a permanent right to apply directly to the Court. The Committee of Ministers retains a role in supervising the execution of the court's rulings (Art. 46 (2)). The Court, now full-time, sits in Chambers of seven judges and a Grand Chamber of 17 judges, the latter dealing with cases that raise important general principles. Applications are referred to a committee of three judges to decide on admissibility. Remedies in the domestic courts must first be exhausted. A decision that an application is inadmissible must be unanimous and there is no appeal. This procedure is likely to speed up the process. However, the absence of a political element might reveal flaws in the notion of subjecting human rights to adversarial judicial determination by a large and disparate international tribunal.

The Court can make a declaration as to the rights of the individual and award 'just compensation'. However, its decisions are not legally enforceable but depend on the political will of the member states. The UK has long accepted the right of individuals to take proceedings in the Strasburg Court, but unlike the other signatories, did not incorporate the Convention into its own law. One result of this was that the UK was one of the most persistent defaulters in the European Court since we had no domestic remedies. The Human Rights Act 1998 has partially rectified this.

18.3.1   Convention rights

]The following rights embodied in the European Convention on Human Rights are incorporated into UK law by the Human Rights Act 1998 s. 1.

- *Article 2*: *right to life*: except for capital punishment following criminal conviction, defence against unlawful violence, lawful arrest or prevention of unlawful escape, lawful action for quelling riot or insurrection. The right to life does not apparently include a right to die (see *R. (Pretty)* v. *DPP* (2002) (below).
- *Article 3*: *torture or inhuman or degrading treatment or punishment.* This cannot be overriden (see *Tyrer* v. *UK* (1978), *Costello-Roberts* v. *UK* (1993) – corporal punishment; *Soering* v. *UK* (1989) – extradition to USA with risk of long delays on death row; *Ireland* v. *UK* (1978) – interrogation of suspected terrorists).
- *Article 4*: *slavery, forced or compulsory labour.* Exceptions are prison or parole, military service, emergency or calamity, 'normal civic obligations'.
- *Article 5*: *liberty and security of person.* The main exceptions are criminal convictions, disobedience to a court order, control of children, infection, mental health, alcoholics, drug addiction or vagrancy. There are safeguards to ensure a speedy trial and adequate remedies against unlawful detention. A person arrested must be informed promptly of the reasons for the arrest and be brought promptly before a court (see *Brogan* (below)). The court proceedings must be fair and reasonably speedy. This overlaps with Art. 6 (below) and is similar to the flexible common law rules of natural justice (above Chapter 16). However, Art. 5 includes matters such as bail and parole which do not strictly fall within Art. 6 (see *R. (DPP)* v. *Havering Magistrates Court* (2001), *Hirst* v. *United Kingdom* (2001)).
- *Article 6*: 'In relation to civil rights and obligations and the determination of any criminal charges against him there is a right to a fair trial in public before an independent and impartial tribunal established by law.' Civil rights include administrative law rights, at least where the existing rights of citizens are at stake (see *Bentham* v. *Netherlands* (1985)). However, it is not sufficient that a decision disadvantages the claimant. It must actually affect a legal right or entitlement as opposed to a discretionary benefit (see *R.* v. *Secretary of State for Social Services ex parte C* (2000); *McLellan* v. *Bracknell*

Forest BC (2002)). Article 6 requires procedural safeguards associated with the rule of law, namely the right to silence, 'equality of
arms' between the parties as regards time, access to witnesses
and information, legal representation, and sometimes legal aid (see
Rowe v. *United Kingdom* (2001), *Airey* v. *Ireland* (1979), *Van Der
Musselle* v. *Belgium* (1983), *Brown* v. *Stott* (2001)).

Article 6.2 requires a presumption of innocence where a person is
charged with a criminal offence although this does not rule out
a burden to prove particular facts being placed on the accused
(*R.* v. *DPP ex parte Kebelene* (1999), *R.* v. *Lambert* (2001)). In a
criminal case there must be further safeguards. These include a right
'to be informed promptly and in a language he understands and in
detail, of the nature and cause of the accusation', adequate time and
facilities to prepare a defence, a right to choose a lawyer and free
legal assistance 'when the interests of justice so require', a right to
call witnesses and to examine opposing witnesses on equal terms, a
right to an interpreter. However, 'charged with a criminal offence'
has been defined narrowly to exclude matters relating to sentencing
and bail. These are protected only by the general provisions of
Arts. 5 and 6 (*Phillips* v. *United Kingdom* (2001), *R.* v. *Havering
Magistrates Court* (2001)).

The right to a fair trial as such is not subject to exceptions and
cannot be overridden by public interest concerns such as blanket
claims to immunity (see *Osman* v. *UK* (1998)). However its *individual
ingredients* such as a right to see information held by the other side
can be overridden. The matter depends on the political circumstances. The process as a whole must be looked at and the scope of
any appeal or judicial review will be taken into account. For example
in *Brown* v. *Stott* (2001), the Privy Council held that the requirement
of the Road Traffic Act 1998 s. 172 (2), to disclose the name of the
driver was not in breach of the right against self-incrimination. The
reason for this was the clear public interest in reducing the high rate
of death and injury on the roads. Nevertheless any shortfall in one
respect should either be compensated by scrupulous fairness in
others (e.g. *Phillips* v. *United Kingdom* (2001): onus of establishing
facts on accused must be subject to safeguards) or heard by an appeal
or judicial review (see *McLellan* v. *Bracknell Forest BC* (2002)).
However, in *Porter* v. *Magill* [2001] 1 All ER 465, 501, Lord Hope
asserted that Art. 6 breaks down into distinct rights so that a failure
in one cannot be compensated by the others. These include, a fair
hearing, a public hearing, a hearing within a reasonable time and
a hearing before an independent tribunal established by law.

Article 6 applies differently in relation, on the one hand to political decisions such as land use planning matters which are are usually taken by politicians sometimes following a public hearing, and on the other hand to judicial decisions, the primary purpose of which is to determine the legal entitlements of individuals (*Zumtabel* v. *Austria* (1993)). In the case of political decisions, individual rights may be affected, for example in the case of a compulsory purchase order to build a new road but this is part of a larger public interest concern.

In the case of a political decision, where the decision maker is unlikely to be impartial, the primary decision need not satisfy Art. 6's requirements of independence and equality of arms, although even here there must be safeguards for the individual in relation to factual and legal issues. Judicial review may suffice to comply with Art. 6 (see *R. (Alconbury)* v. *Secretary of State* (2001)). In the case of a judicial decision, either the initial decision maker must be independent or, if the decision depends on establishing particular facts, there must be provision for a full rehearing on appeal. Independence is particularly difficult to establish in the context of military tribunals and other disciplinary bodies within an organisation (see *Ghosh* v. *GMC* (2001); *Findlay* v. *UK* (1997) and in cases involving 'internal review' of decisions (see *Adam* v. *Newham BC* (2002); *McLellan* v. *Bracknell Forest DC* (2002)).

Judgement shall be pronounced publicly. The press and public may be excluded from all or any part of the proceedings in the interests of morals, public order, national security in a democratic society, where the interests of juveniles or the protection of the private lives of the parties so require, or the extent strictly necessary in the opinion of the court in special circumstances where publicity would prejudice the interests of justice (see *R.* v. *Bow County Court ex parte Pelling* (1999)).

- *Article 7*: no retrospective criminal laws except in respect of acts which were criminal when committed according to the general principles of law recognised by civilised nations.
- *Article 8*: respect for privacy, family life, home and correspondence. This seems to be treated as worthy of a 'less high degree of constitutional protection' than at least freedom of expression and access to the courts, and is therefore more easily overridden (see e.g. *R. (Samaroo)* v. *Secretary of State for the Home Department* (2000)). Privacy and family life are vague open-ended concepts so that, in addition to concerns with state and media surveillance and intrusion, there is room for considerable development into the

areas of personal identity and relationships, life-style and cultural matters and environmental pollution (see Feldman, 1997, 1999a). The eviction of local authority tenants both on social grounds and because of anti-social behaviour may also override Art. 8 (*R.* (*McLellan*) v. *Bracknell Forest DC* (2002)).

- *Article 9*: freedom of thought, conscience and religion.
- *Article 10*: freedom of expression. This is given an especially high level of protection particularly in respect of the media.
- *Article 11*: freedom of assembly and association. This should also be given high protection being closely related to freedom of expression. However, public order issues are related to freedom of association, in respect of which the executive is often conceded a wide discretion (below).
- *Article 12*: the right to marry and found a family according to national laws governing the exercise of the right. This has been interpreted as referring only to traditional marriages between biological men and women (*Rees* v. *UK* (1987); transsexuals).
- *Article 13*: effective remedies before a national authority (not included in the Human Rights Act).
- *Article 14*: the rights under the convention must be secured without discrimination on the grounds of sex, race, colour, language, religion, opinion, national or social origin, association with a national minority, property, birth or other status. However, there is no general right against discrimination (see e.g. *Abdulaziz* v. *UK* (1985)). The Court of Appeal has interpreted Art. 14 widely. In *Aston Cantlow and Wilmcote with Billesley Parochial Church Council* v. *Wallbank* (2001) it was held that a duty imposed under ecclesiastical law on the owner of glebe land (land originally part of a clergyman's benefice) in the form of an obligation to pay for the upkeep of a church was discriminatory in that it was an unfair burden compared with burdens imposed on property owners generally.
- *Article 15*: states can derogate or reserve from most of the Convention in times of war or other public emergency threatening 'the life of the nation'. Article 2, the right to life, cannot be derogated from except in respect of deaths resulting from lawful acts of war, nor can Arts. 3 (torture), 4(1) (slavery), or 7 (retrospective punishment). The state must show firstly that the threat is current or imminent, secondly that the threat must affect the whole population involving a breakdown in the normal machinery of law and order, thirdly that the measures must be intended as a necessary response to the needs of the situation and fourthly there must be the safeguard of judicial review. This is stricter than the 'fair balance' approach

taken in other contexts (see *Lawless* v. *Ireland* (1961), *Brannigan and McBride* v. *UK* (1994), *Askoy* v. *Turkey* (1996)). However, protection ultimately depends on the extent to which the Court is prepared to accept the government's word as to the needs of the situation. Both the UK courts and the European Court give considerable deference to the government in relation to emergency and security matters (see *R.* v. *Secretary of State for the Home Department ex parte McQuillan* (1995); Marks, 1995).

- *Article 16.* Articles 10, 11 and 14 shall not prevent a state from imposing restrictions on the political activities of aliens.
- *Article 17 (abuse of rights)*: 'Nothing in this Convention may be interpreted as implying for any State, group or person any right to engage in any activity or perform any act aimed at the destruction of any of the rights and freedoms set forth herein or at their limitation to greater extent than is provided for in the Convention.' This intended to prevent for example racist groups from exploiting Convention rights such as freedom of expression or association in order to damage other rights such as religious freedom or privacy (see *Lawless* v. *Ireland* (No. 3) (1961), *Gough* v. *Chief Constable of the Derbyshire Constabulary* (2001)).
- *Article 18*: 'The restrictions permitted under this Convention ... Shall not be applied for any purpose other than those for which they have been prescribed.'
- *Protocol 1, Article 1*: 'Every natural or legal person is entitled to the peaceful enjoyment of his possessions. No one shall be deprived of his possessions except in the public interest and subject to the conditions provided for by law and by the general principles of international law. The preceding provisions shall not, however, in any way impair the right of a State to enforce such laws as it deems necessary to control the *use* of property in accordance with the general interest or to secure the payment of taxes and or other contributions or penalties.' This protects property rights against confiscation without compensation, including the right to dispose of property, but does not confer a positive right to acquire property (see *Marckx* v. *Belgium* (1979)). It also protects against restrictions on the use of property, even if they take the form of other property rights, which are confiscatory because they are uncertain in extent (see *Aston Cantlow and Wilmcote with Billesley Parochial Church Council* v. *Wallbank* (2001)). Lesser restrictions on the use of property, for example planning and rent controls, are valid without compensation although the line between use and confiscation may be difficult to draw (*Mellacher* v. *Austria* (1989), *Fredin* v. *Sweden* (1991)).

- *Protocol 1, Article 2*: education – including parental choice in relation to religious and philosophical convictions. (The UK has made a reservation in respect of this, namely, 'only so far as compatible with 'the provision of efficient instruction and training and the avoidance of unreasonable public expenditure'.)
- *Protocol 1, Article 3*: free elections to the legislature at reasonable intervals by secret ballot.
- *Protocol 6, Articles 1 and 2*: outlaws the death penalty except in times of war or where there is an imminent threat of war. The Human Rights Act 1998 s. 21 (5) abolished the last remaining death penalty provisions in the UK.

18.4 The Human Rights Act 1998

18.4.1 The structure of the Human Rights Act 1998

The Human Rights Act does not incorporate the ECHR as such into UK law but, by virtue of s. 1, gives the main rights embodied in the European Convention on Human Rights the status of 'Convention rights' having specific consequences in UK law. According to Lord Hoffmann, (*R.* v. *Secretary of State for the Home Department ex parte Simms* [1999] 3 All ER 400 at 412), the Act has three aims. These are firstly to provide a specific text much of it, in his view, reflecting existing common law principles, secondly to enact the existing 'principle of legality' according to which fundamental rights can be overridden only by explicit statutory language or necessary implication, thirdly to force Parliament to face squarely what it is doing. Lord Hoffmann's approach is relatively cautious, reminiscent of the 'power-sharing' constitution mentioned in Chapter 1.

The Act has increased the political power of the judges and may stimulate a wider political culture of rights although not necessarily of a radical kind. For example in *Gough* v. *Chief Constable of Derbyshire Constabulary* [2001] 4 All ER 289 at 321, Laws LJ said, adopting a communitarian philosophy, that 'rights are divisive, harmful, ultimately worthless, unless their possession is conditional upon the public good.' This is rather stronger than the widely accepted proposition that rights are rarely absolute but must sometimes yield to a greater public good.

In *R. (Pretty)* v. *DPP* (2002) the House of Lords also took a cautious approach in which the right to life was interpreted in a narrow way so as not to include a right to assisted voluntary euthenasia.

Lord Steyn explained that the ECHR was intended to embody a body of values that commanded wide international acceptance and not to invite the judges to embark upon morally and politically controversial lawmaking. In *Brown* v. *Stott* (2001) paras 834, 839, 841, it was emphasised that Convention rights foster democracy in that they require compromise between competing claims.

If the view that English law already substantially conforms to the European Convention on Human Rights is correct, successful challenges are likely to be relatively few. In one respect however the Act has already made a difference, namely in intensifying the traditional *Wednesbury* level of judicial review in favour of an a approach based on proportionality. However, even this reinforces a trend that already existed (above 16.5).

Convention rights do not include rights from which the UK has derogated or reserved (s. 14). Nor does the Act include the duties under Art. 1 to secure to everyone within the jurisdiction the rights and freedoms under the Convention, and Art. 13 which requires effective domestic remedies for breach of the Convention. These duties would be relevant, for example, to an argument whether the police must protect freedom of expression and assembly at a public meeting. However, Arts. 10 and 11 may themselves imply positive duties to protect freedom of expression and assembly (see Chapters 19 and 20). Moreover adequate safeguards and remedies are implicit in the overall requirement that inroads on convention rights must be prescribed by law.

18.4.2   The interpretative obligation

The Act does not affect the validity of any incompatible primary legislation thus preserving parliamentary supremacy (s. 3 (2) (*b*)). However, 'So far as is possible to do so, primary legislation and subordinate legislation must be read and given effect in a way which is compatible with Convention rights' (s. 3 (1)).

For this purpose the traditional method of seeking the purpose of the legislative does not apply. According to Lord Woolf CJ in *Donoghue* v. *Poplar Housing and Regeneration Community Trust* (2001), the effect of s. 3 is as if conflicting legislation is amended to comply with Convention Rights. If, of course, the statute can be interpreted on ordinary principles as permitting a 'fair balance' to be struck between the right in question and the public interest (below 18.5.2), then the special s. 3 interpretative obligation is not triggered at all. It is therefore a last resort. In the case of legislation passed *after* the Human Rights Act, the interpretative obligation is a strong one because if such legislation conflicted with the Act it would normally impliedly repeal the Human Rights Act (above ch. 6). Under the Human Rights Act this applies only if it is impossible to reconcile the two. However, in the case of *earlier statutes* the Human Rights Act is relatively weak in that s. 3 prevents the Act impliedly repeating the earlier legislation.

Primary legislation includes not only statutes but also Prerogative Orders in Council, Measures of the Church Assembly and the General Synod of the Church of England, and delegated legislation which brings into force or amends primary legislation. Subordinate legislation includes other delegated legislation and Acts of the Scottish Parliament and Northern Ireland Assembly (s. 21). The court can set aside subordinate legislation that is incompatible with the Convention just as it can on ordinary judicial review grounds.

The obligation to interpret in conformity with Convention rights is weaker than, for example the European Community Act 1972, which appears to make EC law overriding (see Chapter 9). Nevertheless s. 3 (1) was apparently intended to be a strong provision (see Cmd. 3782, 2.7, 8). However, it is not clear how far, if at all, it goes beyond the existing law. For example in *R.* v. *Radio Authority ex parte Bull* [1997] 2 All ER at 578 Brooke LJ said that a statute must be construed in accordance with the ECHR if it is 'reasonably capable of bearing such a meaning'.

How far does the phrase 'so far as it is possible to do so' justify distorting the language of a statute? A strong view is that a Convention right should prevail unless the statute expressly or by necessary implication excludes the possibility. On the other hand the White Paper specifically rejected a 'notwithstanding' clause of the kind used in Canada under which a statute must expressly state that it overrides the Bill of Rights (Cmnd. 3782, 2.10). Indeed, the phrase echoes the language of the *Marleasing* case (above p. 202) in the context of EC law. In *Webb* v. *EMO Cargo Ltd* [1992] 4 All ER at 939 Lord Keith took the view that the *Marleasing* obligation did not extend to distorting the language of the statute.

In *R.* v. *Lambert* (2001) the question was whether a person arrested with a bag containing cocaine in his possession had to prove that he did not know that the bag contained cocaine. Under s. 28 of the Misuse of Drugs Act 1971 it is 'a defence for the accused to prove that he neither knew of nor suspected nor had reason to suspect some fact alleged by the prosecution'. This conflicts with the presumption of innocence (Art. 6 (2)). The House of Lords read s. 28 as referring to an 'evidential' burden rather than to a legal burden of proof. In order to do so the House had to give the phrase 'to prove' the unusual but not distorted meaning of 'to give sufficient evidence'.

Lambert can be compared with *R.(H.)* v. *Mental Health Review Tribunal* (2001). Sections 72 and 73 of the Mental Health Act 1983 provide that a tribunal must release a patient if the requirements according to which the patient was detained no longer apply. This places the burden of proof on the patient contrary to Art. 5. The Court of Appeal held that ss. 72 and 73 were incompatible with the Convention. While the Human Rights Act entitles the court to limit the meaning of a statute, the court could not read the statute in a way that contradicts its natural meaning. Similarly, in *Wilson* v. *First County Trust Ltd* (2001) s. 127 (3) of the Consumer Credit Act 1974 provided that the court 'shall not' make an order enforcing a regulated credit agreement unless a document containing all the prescribed terms had been signed by the debtor. The Court of Appeal held that this was contrary to Art. 6 (fair trial) and Protocol 1 (protection of property). However, it was held that s. 127 (3) could not be interpreted as Convention compatible. The court took the view that it could not give words a meaning they cannot bear nor imply a qualification, such as 'if reasonable', into clear language. Similarly in *Donoghue* v. *Poplar Housing and Community Regeneration Association* (2001), the Court of Appeal refused to read a limitation into a provision that required the court automatically to evict certain categories of social tenant on the ground that such a limitation would radically change the purpose of the Act and defeat Parliament's objective. According to Lord Woolf CJ, this would be legislation, rather than interpretation. This was followed in *Adam* v. *Newham BC* (2002) where a majority of the Court of Appeal refused to qualify a right of appeal on a point of law to include questions of fact where justice required. Hale LJ, however, was pepared to do so.

These cases can be contrasted with the more radical approach of Lord Steyn in *R.* v. *A* (2001). He stated that the interpretative obligation is not confined to cases where the legislation is ambiguous nor does it require the court to look for the intention of Parliament. He indicated that the court might be required to distort language or imply exceptions and qualifications. Indeed he came near to suggesting that nothing short of clear and express limitation on a Convention right would give rise to impossibility. In the particular case, a statutory ban on the giving of certain kinds of evidence in a rape trial, although linguistically absolute was held not to apply where the right to a fair trial would be seriously infringed.

The Act seems to take the meaning of Convention rights as a given, providing a template against which UK law is interpreted. However, interpretation is a two-way process and it might be possible to interpret the Convention down to fit a narrow reading of existing English law as opposed to reading English law up to fit a more expansive view of the Convention. Decisions and opinions of the European Court of Human Rights are not binding on the court although they must be taken into account (s. 2 (1)).

As regards the courts' general approach to the Human Rights Act, it is too early to make a firm analysis. There are considerable differences of emphasis between individual judges. The most liberal but rejected approach (see e.g. *R. (Pretty)* v. *DPP* (2002)) is that the decisions of the European Court provide an international lowest common denominator but that UK courts should strive for a higher standard. A narrower but still liberal approach is that the courts should interpret the Convention generously without preconceptions as to the existing law. For example in *R.* v. *DPP ex parte Keblene* (1999), Lord Hope emphasised that a generous approach should be taken to the scope of fundamental rights and freedoms. In *R.* v. *Lambert* [2001] 3 All ER 577 at 581, Lord Slynn remarked that 'it is clear that the 1998 Act must be given its full import and that long or well entrenched ideas may have to be put aside, sacred calves culled'. Lord Steyn has also taken a liberal approach (above).

At the other extreme, it has been suggested that English law should form the baseline and be assumed to confirm to the convention unless clearly incompatible. Lord Hoffman (1999) has suggested a cautious approach arguing that UK culture is more communitarian than, for example, that of the USA (see also his speeches in *R. (Alconbury)* v. *Secretary of State* (2001) and in *R.* v. *Secretary of State for the Home Department ex parte Simms* [1999] 3 All ER 400, 413). Sir John Laws (1998) has also proposed a cautious approach based on the common law. In *R.* v. *Lambert* [2001] 3 All ER 577 at 603 Lord Hope emphasised 'the need (a) to respect the will of the legislature so far as this remains appropriate and (b) to preserve the integrity of our statute law so far as this is possible.' In *R.* v. *Secretary of State for Social Services ex parte C* (2000), Lord Hoffmann remarked that the Human Rights Act 1998 'was no doubt intended to strengthen the rule of law but not to inaugurate the rule of lawyers' (see also Scott Baker J in *Gunn-Russo* v. *Nugent Care Housing Society* (2001), para. 65).

A middle position is that the decisions of the European court are taken as the primary guidance unless there is some important feature of our constitutional arrangements, legislation or case law that requires us to differ (see *R.* v. *Togher* [2001] 3 All ER 463, 472 per Lord Woolf, *R. (Alconbury)* v. *Secretary of State* [2001] 2 All ER 929, 969 per Lord Slynn. This approach carries with it the danger of a 'race to the bottom' because international human rights jurisprudence tends towards bland compromise (see Gardner in McCrudden and Chambers, 1994).

18.4.3   Declaration of incompatibility

This is a last resort. The court has a duty to interpret primary legislation in line with a Convention right. Where this is not possible a higher court (High Court and above) may, but is not required to, make a 'declaration of incompatibility' (s. 4). This is at the heart of the accommodation between law and democracy. A declaration of incompatibility has no effect on the validity of the law in question and is not binding on the parties (s. 4(6)). A declaration of incompatibility invites Parliament to consider whether to change the law. Additionally s. 10 creates a 'fast-track' procedure applicable in special circumstances. This enables a minister by statutory instrument subject to the approval of Parliament to make such amendments as he considers necessary to remove the incompatibility. The fast-track procedure can be used where a declaration of incompatibility has been made or where an incompatibility arises because of a ruling by the ECHR and a minister considers that there are 'compelling reasons' for proceeding. It does not apply to Measures of the Church of England. Subordinate legislation which conflicts with a Convention right can be quashed by the court and reinstated in amended form under this procedure.

In *Wilson* v. *First County Trust Ltd* (above) the Court of Appeal took the view that a declaration of incompatibility should be made, firstly because the point had been fully argued, secondly because a formal declaration gives legitimacy to the court's order overriding the human right and thirdly in order to provide a basis for the responsible minister to consider making a remedial order (see also *R.* v. *Mental Health Review Tribunal* (above)). The court did not express a view as to whether the law should be changed thereby avoiding making an overt political value judgement. Ministers are not bound to obey a declaration of incompatibility and judicial review may not lie in respect of a refusal to do so (below 18.4.5).

18.4.4   Statement of compatibility

Under s. 19, a Minister of the Crown in charge of a Bill in either House of Parliament must, before the Second Reading of the Bill: (a) make a statement to the effect that in his view the provisions of the Bill are compatible with the Convention rights (a 'statement of compatibility');

or (b) make a statement to the effect that although he is unable to make a statement of compatibility the government nevertheless wishes the House to proceed with the Bill. The statement must be in writing and published in such manner as the minister making it considers appropriate. Apart from putting political pressure on the government, the statement might be used by the courts along with other evidence of the government's intentions to help them interpret legislation. The main purpose of the statement of compatibility is to ensure that the promoters and drafters of all legislation give attention to human rights aspects. There is a Joint Parliamentary Committee on Human Rights and the government is considering whether to introduce a Commissioner to monitor the working of the Act.

18.4.5 Remedies

By virtue of s. 6(1) 'it is unlawful for a public authority to act in a way which is incompatible with a Convention right' except where: (a) 'as a result of one or more provisions of primary legislation, the authority could not have acted differently'; or (b) 'in the case of one or more provisions of, or made under, primary legislation which cannot be read or given effect in a way which is compatible with the Convention rights, the authority was acting so as to give effect to or enforce those provisions.' For this purpose an 'act' includes a failure to act but does not include a failure to introduce or lay before Parliament a proposal for legislation nor make any primary legislation or remedial order (s. 6(6)). A failure to respond to a declaration of incompatibility may therefore not be reviewable unless it is unreasonable on ordinary grounds.

Section 7 entitles a 'victim' to bring proceedings in respect of an act which is unlawful under s. 6, and also to rely on Convention rights in 'the appropriate court or tribunal or any legal proceedings such as defence against a criminal charge or administrative action or an appeal. However the Secretary of State can make rules designating an appropriate court or tribunal for particular purposes (s. 7(1)(a), s. 9(1)(c); see below p. 570).

'Victim' has the same meaning as in cases brought before the ECHR (s. 7(7)). The claimant or a close relative must be directly affected, or at least very likely to be affected, by the action complained of (see *Klass* v. *Federal Republic of Germany* (1978), *Open Door and Dublin Well Woman* v. *Ireland* (1992)). There is no standing for NGOs representing the collective or public interests (*Director General of Fair Trading* v. *Proprietary Association of Great Britain* (2001)). In a judicial review case an NGO would be able to challenge a decision only on domestic grounds while a victim could join the same proceedings on human rights grounds (s. 7(3)). However if the common law claims to recognise human rights irrespective of the Act, then an NGO might have standing in a representative capacity. The Act does not create criminal liability (s. 7(8)).

Under s. 8 the court can award any of the remedies normally available to it 'as it considers just and appropriate'. Damages can be awarded only by a court which has power to award damages or order compensation in civil proceedings (e.g. not by the Crown Court) and then only if the court is satisfied that 'the award is necessary to afford just satisfaction to the person in whose favour it is made' (s. 8(4)). The phrase 'just satisfaction' is part of the jurisprudence of the ECHR and the court must take into account the principles applied by the ECHR (under Art. 41) in awarding compensation (ibid.). Under the jurisprudence of the ECHR, compensation is based on restoring the victim as far as possible to his original position, including an award of legal costs, and also includes compensation for non-pecuniary loss such as humiliation. Compensation can also be given in relation to anticipated future breaches (*Marcic* v. *Thames Water Utilities Ltd* (No. 2) (2001)). Compensation is discretionary and the applicant's conduct can be taken into account (see e.g. *Halford* v. *UK* (1997), *Campbell* v. *UK* (1992), *Kruslin* v. *France* (1990); cf. Mowbray, 1997). Awards made by the ECHR tend to be low.

In relation to the judicial functions of a court or tribunal, proceedings must be by way of appeal or judicial review or otherwise as provided for by rules made by the Lord Chancellor or Secretary of State. Damages cannot be awarded against a court or tribunal in respect of action taken in good faith except in respect of arrest or detention contrary to Art. 5(5) of the Convention (s. 9).

By virtue of s. 11 (*b*), a person's reliance on a convention right does not restrict his right to bring other proceedings.

18.4.6   Public authorities

The European Convention on Human Rights applies to states and their agencies. Similarly the Human Rights Act can be directly enforced only against a public authority (s. 6(1)). For the purposes of the Act, 'public authority' includes a court or tribunal (s. 6 (3)). A public authority also includes any body 'certain of whose functions are functions of a public nature (ibid.). However, Parliament or a person exercising functions in connection with proceedings in Parliament is not a public authority (s. 6 (4)). Thus the separation of powers is acknowledged in the form of parliamentary privilege except the House of Lords in its judicial capacity is not a public authority.

There are therefore two kinds of public authority. First there are bodies such as central and local government and the police which are inherently public. All the activities of these bodies fall within the Act. Secondly, there are 'functional' public authorities. These are more difficult to identify. Functional public authorities may perform some functions on behalf of government but also perform private functions. The 'private acts' of bodies of this kind do not fall within the Act (s. 6 (5)). The issue is particularly important given the current popularity of various forms of privatisation.

The European Court of Human Rights has not addressed the question directly of what is a public function. However, it has hinted at an approach which asks whether the particular act is carried out under the control of the government or on behalf of the government (see *Sigur Jónnson* v. *Iceland* (1993)). In *Donoghue* v. *Poplar Housing and Regeneration Community Association Ltd* (2001) the Court of Appeal followed this approach. A housing association had evicted a tenant who claimed that this violated her right to home and family life under Art. 8 of the Convention. The Court of Appeal held that whether such a body was a public authority depended on the particular function that it was carrying out in relation to the claimant. Lord Woolf emphasised that it was not sufficient in itself that the body was carrying out functions in the public interest, nor that it was publicly funded, nor that it was subject to regulation by the government as opposed to being subject to government direction. The association was a public body in connection with its treatment of former local authority tenants because it had been established by the local authority to take over its housing stock, its activities were significantly influenced by local authority policy and there were local authority representatives on its governing board. The test therefore seems to be that the body is 'governmental' rather than public in a broad sense. This is analogous to the test for deciding whether a body exercises public functions for judicial review purposes (above Chapter 17). However, the Court held on the merits that the public interest in ensuring that there was sufficient housing for those in need outweighed the tenant's right to a home.

18.4.7   Horizontal effect

It is controversial whether the Act should have 'horizontal effect' in the sense that private persons as well as public bodies should be required to respect human rights. On the one hand it is arguable that human rights should pervade all law. Even private legal relationships are created and defined by the state which could therefore be regarded as responsible for ensuring that the law meets the minimum standards appropriate to a democratic society. For example it would be anomalous if there were a right of privacy against a NHS hospital, a state school and the BBC and not a private hospital, school, newspaper or television company. On the other hand the ECHR itself is enforceable only against a state (Art. 34) and the Human Rights Act does not grant right directly to an individual but imposes obligations on courts and other public authorities to comply with the specified Convention rights. Moreover the Act does not include Art. 1 of the ECHR which requires states to 'secure to every one within their jurisdiction' the rights and freedoms conferred by the Convention.

However, the Act might have 'indirect' horizontal effect. By virtue of s. 6, the courts are public authorities. Wade (1998, 2000) therefore suggests that a court would act 'unlawfully' if it did not apply Convention rights in every case before it, even between private persons. The victim's right would be against the court itself not directly against the other private party. A less extreme view is that, while the Act cannot create a new cause of action against a private body, the Convention might still be used as a shield so as to prevent the court from granting a remedy or making an order in proceedings between private parties and also as a way of developing existing common law rights (Hunt, 1998). The matter would therefore have to arise in the course of ordinary legal proceedings in the form of a claim in domestic law in which a human rights dimension could be implied.

Examples of indirect horizontal effect in this more limited sense are as follows:

- The court's duty under s. 3 to interpret legislation in line with Convention rights is not limited to cases involving public bodies. It would be odd if the same statute had to be interpreted differently depending on whether a public or private body was relying upon it.
- Using human rights as a shield. A private person might be denied the assistance of the court in enforcing a claim contrary to a Convention right against another private entity. In particular a court order for damages or an injunction, or an enforcement order might

be opposed on human rights grounds. For example a court might refuse an injunction against a newspaper in order to protect freedom of expression against a competing right of privacy (Chapter 20), or to give a possession order to a landlord who attempted to evict a tenant from her home (*R. McLellan*) v. *Bracknell Forest DC* [2002] 1 All ER 899, 913; see also *Venables* v. *News Group Newspapers* (2001)).

* Developing existing rights under the common law. In *Douglas and Zeta-Jones* v. *Hello! Ltd* (2001) the Court of Appeal used s. 6 as the basis for recognising a common law right of privacy (below Ch. 20) although they did not commit themselves fully to endorsing Hunt's argument for horizontal effect. The courts sometimes relied on human rights even before the Act (see e.g. Rantzen v. *Mirror Group Newspapers* (1994)).

There are, however, strong arguments against horizontal effect (see Buxton, 2000; Phillipson, 1999). In particular, in ECHR jurisprudence Convention rights are, *as a matter of substance*, rights only against the state and its emanations. For example, a tenant has no Convention rights against a private landlord. If this correct then there is nothing for the court's own duty to bite on. In *Donoghue* v. *Poplar Housing and Regeneration Commmunity Association Ltd* (2001), Lord Woolf CJ seemed to accept this when he said that the argument based on the court itself being a public authority only avails the defendant if there is a contravention of Art. 8. From this perspective, the court's duty as a public authority to comply with Convention rights refers only to its own procedures in relation to Art. 6 (fair trial). Nor, according to Buxton is there any general indication in the Act itself or the parliamentary debates of so radical a change (see also *Wainright* v. *Home Office* (2002), *RSPCA* v. *Attorney General* [2001] 3 All ER 530 at 547).

A compromise can be found in ECHR jurisprudence. Some rights are especially vulnerable to abuse so that the state has a positive duty to ensure that even private bodies comply with them (see *Kroon* v. *Netherlands* (1994) A 297-C). The ECHR has held under Art. 8 (privacy), even though this is expressly limited to the acts of public authorities, Art. 9 (freedom of religion), Art. 10 (freedom of expression), Art. 11 (freedom of association) and Art. 12 (right to marry), that the state must take positive protective action even in the sphere of private relationships (see *X and Y* v. *Netherlands* (1985): child abuse; *A* v. *UK* (1998), parental chastisement: *Rees* v. *UK* (1986): facilitating transexualism). This might for example subject the press to a duty under the Act to respect privacy, (see *A* v. *B* (2001)).

18.4.8   Retrospective effect

The Act applies to legislation made both before and after it came into force (s. 3 (2) (*a*). However, the Act is not fully retrospective. In the case of a defence to 'proceedings brought by a public authority' it applies whenever the act in question took place but otherwise applies only where the particular act complained of took place or is continued after the Act came into force (s. 22 (4)), see *Venables* v. *News Group Newspapers* (2001), *R.* v. *DPP ex parte Kebelene* (1999), *Wilson* v. *First County Trust Ltd* (2001)). It may not be clear what counts as the particular act. In this context *R.* v. *Lambert* (2001) provides a good illustration of different judicial approaches. The question was whether the Act applied to an appeal made by the victim to the House of Lords after the Act came into force against a conviction before the Act. The House held that English law's traditional presumption against retrospectivity should apply and that the relevant act complained of was the conviction. However, Lord Steyn argued firstly that the court should try and advance the broad purpose of the Act and secondly that the plain words of the Act impose a duty on all public authorities, including the House of Lords in its judicial capacity, to apply Convention rights (see s. 6 (1)). He thought that the relevant act was the appeal itself so that the protection of the Human Rights Act applied.

18.4.9   Derogation

Under s. 14 the Secretary of State can make a 'designated derogation' order which excludes from the Act any part of the Convention from which the UK has derogated (s. 1 (2)). The order can be made in advance of a proposed derogation (s. 14 (6)) and must be laid before Parliament (s. 20). If not withdrawn earlier, a designated derogation lapses after five years (s. 16). In 2001, following the attack on the World Trade Center in New York, the UK derogated from Art. 5 in order to detain foreign terrorist suspects without trial (see Anti-Terrorism, Crime and Security Act (2001)) and in 1988 derogated in respect of the length of detention of terrorist suspects in Northern Ireland.

18.5   Restrictions on Protected Rights: Reasoning Methods

Any workable code of fundamental rights must be expressed in general language and with sufficient exceptions to permit governments to act in the public interest or to resolve conflicts with other rights. It is tempting to seek an overarching principle that would combine the human right with the competing interest under some overall concept of the common good (see McHarg, 1999). However, the whole point of human rights is that they are not only an instrument of the community good but are entitlements of the individual and, as such, are valued for their own sake irrespective of any contribution they make to some greater good. Moreover, as we saw above, fundamental rights disputes raise incommensurable values so that the imposition of a general principle threatens to suppress other goods.

The main concepts which I shall discuss in the following sections structure decision making to a certain extent. They do not avoid the need to make a subjective political judgement but at least make it clear that in human rights cases the state has a particular burden to justify its intrusion. In other cases it is presumed that state action is lawful unless the citizen can show otherwise.

The interpretative obligation in s. 3 (above) arises only where the statute in question would otherwise violate the Convention. A Convention issue can therefore be structured in four stages as follows.

  (i) Does the matter concern a protected right at all? This is entirely for the court taking into account the jurisprudence of the European Court.
 (ii) Does the justification for infringing the right strike a 'fair balance' between the right and another relevant concern? This involves the doctrines of 'proportionality'. The primary decision maker here may not be the court which will sometimes exercise a review function by allowing the legislature or the executive a 'margin of discretion' (below). If the Convention is violated because of an act or a decision which is not required by statute the claimant will be entitled to a remedy at this stage.
(iii) If the Convention is violated because of the terms of a statute, is it possible to interpret the statute as Convention compliant? (above). If so the claimant will be entitled to a remedy.
 (iv) It it is not so possible the court may make a declaration of incompatibility this being the only remedy.

18.5.1 Overrides

Some Articles of the Convention, notably Art. 8 to 11, give more specific guidance. The rights concerned can be limited in accordance with such law are 'necessary in a democratic society' for specified purposes. The purposes vary with the particular article but in all cases include public safety, public order, the prevention and detection of serious crime, the protection of health and morals and the protection of the rights of others. The overrides have been strictly interpreted and the onus is on the state to establish them (*Sunday Times* v. *United Kingdom* (1979)). Nevertheless the choice between the right and the override may still be incapable of rational justification. For example, in *A-G* v. *Guardian Newspapers Ltd* (1987) both majority and dissenting law lords thought that the European Convention supported their views. Lord Templeman thought that the restrictions on freedom of speech involved in banning *Spycatcher* (the memoirs of a British security agent) were 'necessary in a democratic society in the interests of national security' whereas Lord Bridge preferred freedom of expression.

Before applying an override there are certain threshold requirements. First the restrictions must be 'prescribed by law' or 'in accordance with the law', terms which apparently mean the same (*Malone* v. *UK* (1984)). This is akin to Dicey's version of the rule of law. Indeed the 'rule of law' is referred to in the Convention's preamble. The restrictions must be clear (for example, the vague terms used in UK public order legislation may be vulnerable), must not involve wide discretion and must be made in accordance with a regular and accessible law-making process (see *Sunday Times* v. *UK* (1979); *Klass* v. *Federal Republic of Germany* (1978)). Taking into consideration the circumstances of the domestic law, the applicant must be able reasonably to foresee that the conduct in question would be unlawful and there must be adequate safeguards including independent and accessible courts (see *Open Door and Dublin Well Woman* v. *Ireland* (1992); *Kruslin* v. *France* (1990); *Benthem* v. *Netherlands* (1985); *Leander* v. *Sweden* (1987); *Airey* v. *Ireland* (1979); *Brogan* v. *UK* (1989)). Secondly the restrictions must be 'necessary in a democratic society'. The concept of 'necessary in a democratic society' is loose. It means only that there must be a 'pressing social need' which is more than merely 'useful', 'reasonable' or 'desirable' (see *Handyside* v. *UK* (1976); *Fayed* v. *UK* (1994)).

18.5.2   Fair balance and proportionality

In *Sporrong* v. *Sweden* (1982, 5 EHRR 35, 52) it was said that 'the Court must determine whether a fair balance was struck between the demands of the general interests of the community and the requirement of the protection of the individual's fundamental rights ... the search for the balance is inherent in the whole Convention.' 'Balance' is of course an unfortunate metaphor in that the problem at the heart of human rights is that there is no objective measure against which the competing interests can be 'weighed'. All that is meant by fair balance seems to be the lame proposition that rights must be accommodated with other rights and with public welfare concerns. As Laws LJ said in *Gough* v. *Chief Constable of Derbyshire Constabulary* [2001] 4 All ER 289, 320), 'it is inherent in the nature of the right itself that that the individual who claims its benefit may have to give way to the supervening weight of other claims ... the right's practical utility rests upon the fact that there can be no tranquility within the state without a plethora of unruly individual freedoms.' Thus Laws LJ acknowledged the inevitability of disagreement and the need to protect rival views of the good (see also Lord Steyn in *Brown* v. *Stott* [2001] 2 All ER 97 at 118). In *R.* v. *Secretary of State ex parte Samaroo* (2001), Dyson LJ listed factors that are taken into account in the 'balancing' exercise. They include the following:

- Is the right absolute or subject to overrides? 'Absolute' rights have a higher status but, by implication, even these might sometimes be compromised.
- The extent to which economic, social or political factors are involved which would require the court to defer to the government on democratic grounds.
- The extent to which the court has special expertise, for example in relation to criminal matters.
- Whether the right claimed is of special importance requiring a high level of protection. This applies to torture, freedom of expression, a fair trial, and also probably personal liberty, but less to the more nebulous rights to home and family life. (See also *Brown v Stott* (2001): self-incrimination justified to meet the serious social evil of drunken driving, Lord Steyn in *R.* v. *Lambert* (2001), Laws LJ in *Gough* v. *Chief Constable of Derbyshire Constabulary* [2001] 4 All ER 289, 321.)

Proportionality (above 16.5) is the way in which the fair balance is struck. Proportionality, it will be recalled, means that 'the right in question is not to be interfered with save on substantial and objective grounds of public interest and that the state, if it decides that the right must be interfered with, has to choose a means judged to constitute the least interference consistent with the policy aim in view' (per Laws LJ in *Gough* v. *Chief Constable of Derbyshire Constabulary* [2001] 4 All ER 289 at 321). This operates both at the macro-level of the general restriction and the micro-level of the particular case. In *Gough* it was held that the serious threat of football hooliganism justified drastic restrictions on freedom of movement. But in *McVeigh* v. *UK* (1981) the European Court held that anti-terrorist restrictions did not justify a refusal to let the claimants contact their wives. In *R.* v. *Oakes* (1986) 26 DLR (4th), 200), Dickson CJ seems to have gone further. He said (at 227–228) 'there must be a proportionality between the *effects* of the measures ... and the objective which has been identified as of sufficient importance' (ibid.). This would require a cost benefit analysis of the competing interests, a matter that does not seem appropriate to a court. Proportionality also requires that the restrictions must not be discriminatory in the sense that like cases must be treated alike (*Marckx* v. *Belgium* (1979)).

The English courts seem to be approaching proportionality in a way that gives a substantial 'margin of discretion' to the executive. In *R. (Saadi)* v. *Secretary of State for the Home Department* (2001), the Court of Appeal held that it was lawful to detain asylum seekers for up to 10 days to enable inquiries to be made into their claims so that they would be decided more quickly. Even though detention for administrative purposes was not justified under any specific override, the extent of the problem of processing applications for asylum justified this measure. The Court recognised that this went further than the European Court might have done. In *Samaroo* (above) the Court of Appeal held that the Secretary of State had struck the correct balance between respect for family life and the prevention of crime and disorder. He deported the claimant, who had lived with his wife and children in Britain since 1988, on his release on parole after the claimant had served six years of a 13-year sentence for drug dealing. There was no evidence that the claimant would re-offend. The Court held that the Secretary of State did not have to show that law and order would actually be undermined if the applicant were not deported, only that the justification be 'convincingly established'. In *Daly* (2001) where the decision was held to be disproportionate, it was also irrational in the traditional *Wednesbury* sense (16.5.1 above). However, Lord Steyn emphasised, at 27, that the intensity of scrutiny is deeper than the *Wednesbury* approach and is based on proportionality.

Proportionality cannot therefore avoid subjective choice since few public interests are monolithic. Proportionality requires that a protected right be interfered with to the smallest extent 'necessary' to meet a competing 'pressing social need' or another important right. However what is 'necessary'? Even pressing social needs might be met to a greater or lesser extent. The question is how much of the right or the public interest should give way and this cannot be answered rationally. For example in *R.J.R.-MacDonald* v. *Canada (A-G)* (1995) the Canadian

Supreme Court was divided over the extent to which tobacco advertising should be restricted in order to meet the public interest in health (see also the cases in 16.5.1 above). Why should anything less than a total ban be proportionate? Moreover, where the competition is between two individual protected rights for example privacy and freedom of expression, the proportionality test cannot easily be applied since the burden will depend on whoever happens to be the claimant. Here the court may be forced to prioritise one right over the other which again is a subjective political choice. This will be discussed in Chapter 20.

18.5.3   Margin of appreciation/discretion

Proportionality therefore requires the exercise of subjective political judgment. The concept of the margin of appreciation, sometimes called the discretionary area of judgement, reflects this. It was developed by the European Court of Human Rights in order to accommodate national differences in political, religious or moral values or practices. When it applies the margin of appreciation the ECHR will not substitute its views for those of the state but asks itself only whether the national authorities were reasonably entitled to think that the interference complained of was justifiable, see *Handyside* v. *UK* (1976); *Open Door and Dublin Well Woman* v. *Ireland* (1992), *Buckley* v. *UK* (1996)). This is another important aspect of incommensurability (see Chapter 2). Different communities may have different but justifiable blends of values and attitudes and if an international tribunal intervened it might forfeit respect.

It is arguable therefore that the doctrine of margin of appreciation as such should play no part in domestic cases. However, by whatever name, the courts are leaving a discretionary area of judgement to ministers. In *R.* v. *DPP ex parte Kebelene* [1999] 4 All ER 801, 843. Lord Steyn, quoting Lester *et al.* (1999), spoke of: (an) 'area of judgement within which the judiciary will defer, on democratic grounds, to the considered opinion of the elected body or person whose act or decision is said to be incompatible with the Convention ... It will be easier for such an area of judgement to be recognised when the Convention itself requires a balance to be struck, much less so when the right is stated in terms that are unqualified. It will be easier for it to be recognised where the issue involves questions of social and economic policy, much less so where the rights are of high constitutional importance or are of a kind where the courts are especially well placed to assess the need for protection' (see also *Gough* v. *Chief Constable of Derbyshire Constabulary* [2001] 4 All ER 289 [72] [78]).

In *R.* (*Mahmood*) v. *Secretary of State for the Home Department* (2001) Lord Phillips MR emphasised that even where human rights are at stake the role of the court is supervisory or secondary. The court would only intervene when the decision fell outside the range of responses open to a reasonable decision maker. 'The court will bear in mind that, just as individual states enjoy a margin of appreciation which permits them to respond, within the law, in a manner that is not uniform, so there will often be an area of discretion permitted to the executive of a country before a response can be demonstrated to infringe the Convention ... The court will ask the question, applying an objective test, whether the decision maker could reasonably have concluded that that the interference was necessary to achieve one or more of the legitimate aims recognised by the Convention.'

The margin of distinction will be strongest in relation to the question of the importance of the public interest that is being asserted, but might also apply to the question of whether the interference is necessary. In *Gough* (above) it was said (para. 78) that the margin of discretion is greater, perhaps akin to the *Wednesbury* test, when the decision maker is the primary legislator. In *Donoughue* v. *PHARCA* (2001) the Court of Appeal refused to condemn s. 21 (4) of the Housing Act 1988 which gave social landlords an automatic right to possession of a dwelling house in certain circumstances. Lord Woolf LCJ remarked, (para. 69) that 'the economic and other implications of any policy in this area are extremely complex and far reaching. This is an area where in our judgement the courts must treat the decisions of Parliament as to what is in the public interest with particular deference.' At the other end of the spectrum, where the right interfered with is very important, and the issues are closely related to the court's own expertise, for example the right to a fair trial, the court might do the balancing exercise itself (see Laws LJ in *Mahmood* (above), Lord Steyn in *R.* v. *A* [2001] 3 AU ER 1, 15 and Lord Bingham in *R.* v. *Secretary of State ex parte Daly* (2001), above 16.5).

The concept of the margin of appreciation both internationally and domestically has the problem of being both negative and vague. It offers a court a reason not to intervene but fails to specify when intervention is appropriate. As we saw in Chapter 16, the *Wednesbury* threshold of rationality is probably too high for human rights cases. Another approach might be to seek a lowest common denominator of consensus standards. However, this is unlikely to giver clear guidance in individual cases, since one reason why they reach the court at all is the absence of consensus, few government decisions being entirely out of line with widely held beliefs. In practice the courts are likely to prefer a procedural approach limited to ensuring that the decision maker has applied the proportionality test.

However, the government must provide a justification supported by evidence of its assertion as to the importance of its goals and of the need to override the right in issue. The court may go beyond traditional interpretative materials and look at for example parliamentary debates, government papers and evidence from civil servants. In *Wilson* v. *First County Trust* (2001) for example the government was unable to show a clear reason why the there should be an absolute ban on the enforcement of a credit agreement. In *Matthews* v. *Ministry of Defence* (2002) the government was unable to explain why there was a pressing social need to deny a legal remedy to a soldier injured on duty (see also *R. (Asif Javed)* v. *Secretary of State for the Home Department* (2001) and *Farratham* v. *Secretary of State for the Home Department* (2001)).

18.5.4 Terrorism and the margin of discretion

There is a wide margin of discretion in relation to national security and anti-terrorism measures (*R.* v. *DPP ex parte Kebelene* (1999)). Terrorism is different from ordinary crime in its consequences, in its uncertainty and complexity, its international dimension and in the difficulty of obtaining a conviction. Terrorism therefore puts the rule of law under particular strain. *Brogan* v. *UK* (1989) illustrates the kind of balance that the European court strikes. Suspects were detained under the anti-terrorism legislation in force in Northern Ireland, questioned and released after four and a half days without being brought before a court. It was held firstly that 'administrative' detention for the purpose of questioning was unlawful under Art. 5 of the Convention and that there must be an intention to bring the suspect promptly before a court in connection with a specific offence. The offence could, however, be widely defined, in this case 'acts of terrorism'. On the other hand the questions of intention and of outcome are distinct and it did not matter that the suspect was not in fact brought before a court. However, the accused had not been brought 'promptly' before a court because the language of Art. 5 gives little flexibility in this respect. This reasoning shows firstly that the question of independent judicial supervision is of high importance and secondly that, while there is some flexibility in meeting the needs of government, the language of the Convention is strictly applied in cases where there is a high risk of abuse (see also *Murray* v. *UK* (1994)).

The Terrorism Act 2000 adopts a wide definition of terrorism which might be considered disproportionate. This is as follows. 'the use or threat, for the purpose of advancing a political, religious or ideological cause, of action which: (a) involves serious violence against any person or property; (b) endangers the life of any person; or (c) creates a serious risk to the health or safety of the public or a section of the public' (s. 1). This might include for example computer hackers, civil liberties campaigners and those protesting against repressive overseas regimes. The Act gives wide power to the Secretary of State to proscribe terrorist organisations (s. 3), extends 'stop and search' powers and powers of arrest and detention for questioning before being taken before a court (up to seven days) and gives power to seize cash where there are reasonable grounds to suspect that it is connected with terrorism (Anti-Terrorism, Crime and Security Act 2001 Part 1). It is an offence to incite terrorism anywhere (ss. 59–61) and to help to organise a meeting which will be addressed by someone who professes to belong to a proscribed organisation (s. 12). This might also be disproportionate. There are safeguards such as the introduction of video recordings of police interviews in holding centres (s. 100) and the introduction of judicial consent for extended periods of detention (Sched. 8).

The Anti-Terrorism, Crime and Security Act 2001 substantially extends powers of detention of suspected foreign terrorists and confers powers to freeze the assets of persons who are reasonably believed to be involved with external threats to the UK's economy or to the life or property of UK residents or nationals.

Section 21 authorises the Home Secretary to certify a person as a suspected terrorist if he has reasonable ground to believe (a) that the person's presence is a risk to national security and (b) to suspect the person to be a terrorist. Suspicion is of course a lower threshold than belief. The Home Secretary can detain a certified person indefinitely as an alternative to deportation (s. 27). This required a derogation from the ECHR thus preventing challenge under the Human Rights Act (see SI 2001 no. 3644). The derogation itself could be challenged in the European Court, perhaps on the ground that there is no national emergency. The derogation can also be challenged under the Human Rights Act. However, this can only be before SAIC, the Special Immigration Appeals Commission (s. 30). SIAC can also hear an appeal against certification on the merits (s. 25) but not against the decision to detain. SAIC must also review every certificate initially after 6 months then every 3 months.

SIAC was created in 1997 as a result of the case of *Chahal* v. *UK* (1997) where it was held that the previous system of informal non-statutory advisors was not an adequate safeguard in national security cases (see SIAC Act 1997). SIAC's decisions are binding and it has the status of the High Court with full judicial review powers (s. 35). There is an appeal to the Court of Appeal. SIAC's three members include a high court judge and one other member must either be a chief adjudicator or a legally qualified member of the Immigration Appeals Tribunal. However, its procedure is specialised. Most significantly the person detained is not entitled to full particulars of the case against him (SAIC 1997 s. 5 (3) (a)). Although judicial review is not excluded, the derogation coupled with the margin of discretion normally given to national security matters makes a successful challenge unlikely. The detention powers of the Act lapse after 15 months but can be renewed.

18.5.5 Other principles of interpretation

* The Convention has been described as a 'living tree' meaning that the rights themselves and their ranking against other factors change with the times (e.g. *Soering* v. *UK* (1989) – present-day attitudes to death penalty mean that extradition to death row in USA would violate Art. 3). This is, however, limited by the language of the convention (*Brown* v. *Stott* [2000] 2 WLR 817, 835). For example in *Johnston* v. *Ireland* (1996) it was held that the language of the convention meant that the right to marry does not include a right to divorce.
* '*Systematic interpretation*', according to which the Convention must be read as a whole (e.g. *Abdulaziz* v. *UK* (1985) specific treatment of immigration in Protocol 4 did not exclude other parts of the Convention from protecting immigration rights).
* *Internal aids to interpretation*. Article 16 permits states to restrict the movement of aliens notwithstanding Arts. 10, 11 and 14. Article 17 (abuse of rights) prevents the convention being interpreted so as to authorise acts intended to destroy or limit the exercise of other Convention rights, for example by anti-democratic groups or terrorists (see *Lawless* v. *Ireland* (1976); *Purcell* v. *Ireland* (1991)). Article 18 prevents the restrictions permitted by the Convention on its rights and freedoms being used for purposes other than those prescribed.
* *Teleological interpretation*, according to which the court looks at the purpose intended to be served by the Convention of protecting liberal and democratic values and the rule of law and can take account of changing state practices and attitudes (*Soering* v. *UK*

(1989); *Handyside* v. *UK* (1976); *Golder* v. *UK* (1975)). The court can look at the preparatory documents (*traveaux preparatoirs*) used in drafting the Convention (*Marckx* v. *Belgium* (1979), compare *Pepper* v. *Hart* (1993)).

- *The consensus principle.* Widely shared state practices may be called in aid. Conversely, divergent state practices may persuade the court to allow a margin of appreciation particularly in respect of cultural and religious practices (*Cossey* v. *UK* (1990), refusal to endorse transexual marriage). The court may also take into account international instruments and general principles of international law, for example sovereign immunity, the 1966 United Nations Covenant on Civil and Political Rights and the International Convention on the Elimination of All Forms of Racial Discrimination (1965), (see *Jersild* v. *Denmark* (1994), *McElhinney* v. *Ireland* (2001)).

Summary

18.1   The human rights debate involves attempts to accommodate fundamentally competing and incommensurable values without any coherent overarching principle to enable a choice to be made. It is therefore arguable that an elected body rather than a court should have the last word. The Human Rights Act 1998 has attempted a compromise by leaving Parliament the last word but giving the court power to influence Parliament.

18.2   Freedom in the common law is residual in the sense that one can do anything unless there is a specific law to the contrary. I suggested that this is an inadequate method of safeguarding important liberties. There is a debate as to the extent to which the common law embodies the principles of the ECHR and it is suggested that there are important differences in the approach of the two systems.

18.3   The ECHR as such is not strictly binding upon English courts but can be taken into account where the law is unclear or where a judge has discretionary powers.

18.4   The Human Rights Act 1998 while not incorporating the convention as such has given the main rights created by the ECHR effect in domestic law. UK legislation must be interpreted to be compatible with Convention rights, and public bodies other than Parliament must comply with Convention rights. The courts must take decisions of the ECHR into account but are not bound by them. It is unlawful for public authority to act in a way that is incompatible with a Convention right. Victims can bring proceedings under the Act against a public authority and rely on Convention rights in any legal proceedings.

18.5   The Act can be directly enforced only against public authorities and by a 'victim' defined in accordance with the case law of the European Court. 'Public authority' includes all the activities of government bodies proper and courts and tribunals but in relation to bodies that have a mixture of public and private functions (e.g. social landlords) only to their public 'acts'. The courts seem to be taking a similar approach to the question of what is public function as in judicial review cases.

18.6 'Horizontal effect' may be direct, where the court is required to enforce a right against a private person, or indirect, where the state is required to protect against violations by private persons. It is not clear how far the Act has horizontal effect although there are several devices that might enable it to do so.

18.7 Parliamentary supremacy is preserved in that Convention rights must give way where they are incompatible with a statute. The courts have taken a moderate approach in relation to the obligation to interpret statutes, 'so far as it is possible to do so', to be compatible with Convention rights. However, there are differences of emphasis between judges as to the assumptions on which interpretation should be approached, in particular the extent to which established English law should be respected.

18.8 Where primary legislation is incompatible the court can draw attention to violations by making a declaration of incompatibility. There is a 'fast-track' procedure available in special circumstances to enable amendments to legislation to be made. The government must be explicit as to any intention to override Convention rights.

18.9 The accommodation between Convention rights and competing factors depends on the circumstances of the particular case and cannot be formulated in general terms. The courts are guided to some extent by concept of 'fair balance', established in accordance with proportionality. The balance, or more accurately accommodation, must be struck between Convention rights and public interest concerns and between competing Convention rights. While these devices help to structure and rationalise decision making they do not remove the need for the court to make a subjective political judgement.

18.10 The courts have also applied the notion of 'margin of appreciation' or margin of discretion in the context of decisions made by elected officials. The width of the margin of appreciation depends on various factors chief among which is the importance and extent of the particular right that is violated in relation to the seriousness of the public harm if the right were not overridden and to extent to which the matter involves controversial political, social or economic choices.

Further Reading

Buxton, R. (2000) 'The Human Rights Act and private law' 116 *Law Quarterly Review* 8.

Ewing, K. (1999) 'The Human Rights Act and parliamentary democracy' 62 *Modern Law Review* 79.

Feldman (1999) 'The Human Rights Act and constitutional principles' 19 *Legal Studies* 165.

Hoffman, Lord (1999) 'Human Rights and the House of Lords' 62 *Modern Law Review* 159.

Hope, Lord (2000) 'Human Rights – where are we now' *European Human Rights Law Review* 443.

Hunt, M. (1998) 'The "horizontal effect" of the Human Rights Act' *Public Law* 423.

Klug (2000) htttp://www.charter88.org.uk/pubs/reinven/reincomm.html.

Klug, F., Staner, K. (2001) 'Incorporation through the "front door": the first year of the Human Rights Act' *Public Law* 654.

Laws, Sir J. (1998) 'The limitation of human rights' *Public Law* 254.

Leigh, I., Lustgarten, L. (1999) 'Making rights real: the courts, remedies and the Human Rights Act' 58 *Cambridge Law Journal* 507.

McHarg, E. (1999) 'Reconciling human rights and the public interest: conceptual problems and doctrinal uncertainty in the jurisprudence of the European Court of Human Rights' 62 *Modern Law Review* 671.

Oliver, D. (2000) 'The frontiers of the state: public authorities and public functions under the Human Rights Act 1998' *Public Law* 476.

Pannick, D. (1998) 'Principles of interpretation of Convention rights under the Human Rights Act and the discretionary area of judgement' *Public Law* 45.

Steyn, The Rt. Hon. Lord (2000) 'The new legal landcape' *European Human Rights Law Review* 549.

Wade, W. (1998) 'Human rights and the judiciary' *European Human Rights Law Review* 520.

Wade, W. (2000) 'Horizons of horizontality' 116 *Law Quarterly Review* 217.

Waldron, *Law and Disagreement*, Part III.

Waldron, J. (1993) 'A rights based critique of constitutional rights' *Oxford Journal of Legal Studies* 132.

Exercises

18.1 'This is the trouble with fundamental values. Whichever one you take with you as a guide, another one is waiting round the corner with a sock full of sand' (Sedley). Explain and discuss.

18.2 'The (Human Rights) Bill is a key component of our drive to modernise our society and refresh our democracy in a way that will strengthen representative and democratic government' (Jack Straw). Do you agree?

18.3 'The striking of a fair balance lies at the heart of proportionality' (Dyson LJ in *R. (Samaroo) v. Secretary of State* (2001)). Discuss critically.

18.4 'The court will bear in mind that, just as individual states enjoy a margin of appreciation which permits them to respond, within the law, in a manner that is not uniform, so there will often be an area of discretion permitted to the executive of a country before a response can be demonstrated to infringe the Convention' (Phillips LJ *in R. (Mahmood) v. Secretary of State* (2001). Discuss critically.

18.5 Explain the constitutional significance of the Declaration of Incompatibility.

18.6 'For the constitutionalist, the explicit subjection of all law to the law of fundamental human rights represents a further important step in the gradual process whereby private law, instead of constitutionalising our entire legal system by its all-pervasive influence on general principles of interpretation, is itself becoming constitutionalised by generally applicable norms of public law' (Hunt). Explain and discuss.

18.7 'It may be that the cases that have been decided under the Human Rights Act 1998 (below) would have been decided in the same way even if the Act did not exist.' Discuss. Consider whether *Brind* v. *Secretary of State* (1991) and *A-G.* v. *Associated Newspapers Ltd* (1994) would be decided the same way today.

18.8 Mary lives near a large factory owned by a private company. She claims that the incessant noise and pollution which the factory emits 24 hours per day violates her rights to the peaceful enjoyment of property and respect for family life. Advise Mary.

18.9 The 'Road traffic (Zero Tolerance) Act 1999' (imaginary) provides that a constable may arrest "any person in charge of a motor vehicle whom he has reason to suspect has recently driven in excess of a statutory speed limit". The defendant is guilty of an offence "unless he can prove that he was not driving the vehicle in question at the relevant time". In the Parliamentary debates on the bill, a government spokesman declared that the need to combat speeding is so important that even basic legal safeguards should be overridden. In September 2000, Will was arrested but was subsequently acquitted of an offence under the 1999 Act. In November 2000 the Attorney-General successfully appealed and Will was convicted. Will now appeals to the House of Lords. Will argues that his arrest is contrary to the Human Rights Act 1998. How would you decide the appeal?

19 Freedom of Political Expression

19.1 Introduction: Justifications for Freedom of Expression

Freedom of expression (including freedom of the press) has long been identified as important by judges, politicians and commentators on the constitution. Blackstone, for example, saw a free press as essential to the nature of a free state (Blackstone, 1825; see also Dyzenhaus, 1991, p. 201). This may explain why it is commonly assumed that the UK is a country in which there have long existed adequate protections of freedom of expression. This perhaps rather complacent view was encouraged by Lord Goff where he declared that 'freedom of expression has existed in this country perhaps as long, if not longer, than it has existed in any other country in the world' (*A-G* v. *Guardian Newspapers Ltd* (No. 2) (1998) p. 660.

Similarly in *Derbyshire County Council* v. *Times Newspapers* (1993), the House of Lords relied on the common law independently of the ECHR to protect press freedom, Lord Keith in particular being pleased to discover that English law conformed to the ECHR (see also *Simms* v. *Secretary of State* 1999 per Lord Steyn at 408).

This view is not universally endorsed. Professor John Griffith describes Britain as a country in which a lacklustre commitment to freedom of expression has been the norm (Griffith, 1997, p. 299). The weight of historical evidence provides considerable support for this view (Ewing, 2000). Consider Dicey's writing on the constitution. He did not regard freedom of expression as a fundamental right. Rather, he saw it as a residual liberty that could be abrogated by the sovereign legislature, subject only to the non-legal constraint of political opinion.

Thus we encounter a gap between the assumption that freedom of expression has long enjoyed protection in Britain and constitutional reality. This gap has prompted commentators in recent years to argue for greater legal protection for freedom of expression (e.g., Feldman, 1993, p. 34 and p. 555). In other jurisdictions which embody rights-based protection of expressive activity there has been considerable judicial elaboration of the law. This point can perhaps best be exemplified by reference to the law of the USA. The right to freedom of expression is guaranteed by the First Amendment to the US constitution. It provides that 'Congress shall make no law . . . abridging the freedom of speech'. This provision has provided the basis for judicial development of the law relating, *inter alia*, to expression in the electoral process, offensive and provocative expression, and non-verbal conduct that has symbolic significance. These developments have, moreover, spawned a considerable academic literature on, *inter alia*, the moral significance of freedom of expression.

Now that the UK courts have to give effect to Article 10 of the ECHR, judges are beginning to close the gap referred to above and are giving much greater consideration than in the past to the rationales for freedom of expression (see, for example, *R.* v. *Secretary of State for the Home Department ex parte Simms* (1999), p. 126, per Lord Bingham and *McCartan-Turkington Breen* v. *Times Newspapers Ltd* (2001), pp. 296–7, per Lord Bingham). A range of arguments can be advanced in support of freedom of expression (Greenawalt, 1989; see *R.* v. *Secretary of State for the Home Department ex parte Simms* (1999), p. 408, per Lord Steyn). These include, self-fulfillment, the testing of truth, democratic debate, checking the abuse of power and exposing error in government. Freedom of expression reinforces the fundamental principle of equality. These arguments can be placed in two broad groups (Dworkin, 1996, pp. 199–200). Arguments in the first group identify freedom of expression as *intrinsically* valuable (cf. Fish, 1994, pp. 14–15, where it is argued that free expression cannot plausibly be regarded as intrinsically valuable). By contrast, those in the second group identify freedom of expression as *instrumentally* valuable: i.e., valuable as a means by which to pursue some other valuable end. Dworkin has recently argued that freedom of expression is valuable in itself. On Dworkin's account: [F]reedom of speech is valuable ... because it is an essential and 'constitutive' feature of a just political society that government treat all its members, except those who are incompetent, as responsible moral agents (Dworkin, 1996, p. 201).

This argument can be a little elusive. One way of capturing its gist is by regarding provisions such as Article 10 of the European Convention as encoding a message about the intrinsic significance of granting the right to freedom of expression. This message can be stated thus: those upon whom the right to freedom of expression is conferred are regarded as capable of 'making up their own minds about what is good or bad in life or in politics, or what is true and false in matters of justice and faith' (Dworkin, 1996, p. 201; see also p. 205). This is because measures such as Article 10 give expression, *inter alia*, to the view that those who enjoy the right to freedom of expression are properly entitled to 'participate in politics' and to 'contribute to the formation of [their] moral or aesthetic climate' (Dworkin, 1996, p. 201; see also Freeden,

1991, pp. 8–9, on the 'worth' or 'status' conferred on those who are identified as rights-bearers).

Dworkin's argument can easily be conflated with two arguments in which freedom of expression is identified not as intrinsically valuable but, rather, as a means to a valuable end. According to the first of these arguments, freedom of expression is a means to the end of democracy. According to the second, it is a means to the end of human self-actualisation. Let us examine the first of these arguments. When we speak of 'democracy' we refer to a mode of government in which the people as a whole participate. Such participation can only occur in circumstances where people are free to advance their views (Feldman, 1993, p. 550). Moreover, it can reasonably be argued that democracy can only flourish in circumstances where the press are free to disseminate information on and offer comment concerning matters of political significance. A particularly strong defence of the view that the right to freedom of expression is a means to the end of democracy was set out by the American commentator Alexander Meiklejohn (Meiklejohn, 1960; cf. Richards, 1999, pp. 18–22). Writing with regard to the First Amendment, he argued that the framers of the US constitution were interested in political freedom and in making democracy work. Hence, they put in place a constitutional guarantee of free expression on matters of political significance. A corollary of Meiklejohn's argument is that commercial expression (e.g., advertising) and artistic expression particularly of a pornographic kind merit less protection. Expressive activity concerning matters of public concern can, of course, take a wide variety of forms. It may involve the articulation of a new vision of social organisation (as set out in a political party's election manifesto). More modestly, it may involve the articulation of views critical of the way in which public officials are conducting themselves. In this latter connection, one commentator has identified free expression as having a 'checking function' (Blasi, 1977).

Let us now turn to the argument that freedom of expression provides a means to the end of self-actualisation. This argument has been advanced by, *inter alia*, J.S. Mill and Thomas Emerson. Its starting point is the proposition that the proper end of man is the realisation of his character and potentialities as a human being' and that freedom of expression is a necessary condition of self-actualisation. Without it, we cannot, on this analysis, flourish. In this argument, we hear echoes of the Romantic movement. According to the Romantics, 'we find truth within us' and come to understand it in the course of giving expression to our 'inner voice' (Taylor, 1989, Ch. 21; see also Berlin, 1996, p. 178). More recently, a variation on this theme has been advanced by Joseph Raz. He argues that freedom of expression provides a means by which the styles of life we adopt can, through public portrayals and representations, be validated (Raz, 1991, p. 311).

A further argument advanced in support of freedom of expression is that it facilitates the pursuit of truth and the acquisition of knowledge. This argument has a lengthy lineage. We find it being set out in the seventeenth century by John Milton in his *Areopagitica*. In the twentieth century, the same line of argument has been advanced by Oliver Wendell Holmes. In his dissenting judgement in *Abrams* v. *United States* (1919, p. 630), Holmes stated that 'the best test of truth is the power of a [given] thought to get itself accepted in the competition of the market [place of ideas]'. Holmes's point is that, in circumstances where a plurality of arguments are advanced, the stronger can be expected, other things being equal, to drive out the weaker. This is a view that coheres with the thinking of the late Professor Karl Popper (Popper, 1966, pp. 224–5. According to Popper (who was a philosopher of science), critical discussion provides a means by which to eliminate errors in our thinking and thus to move towards ever more plausible working hypotheses (but never incontrovertible truths).

A narrower variation on the pursuit of truth rationale for freedom of expression is to be found in the US Supreme Court case of *Whitney* v. *California* (1927). In a concurring opinion, Brandeis J wrote that: 'freedom to think as you will and to speak as you will are means *indispensable* to the discovery and spread of *political truth*' (at pp. 375–6 (emphasis added)). Here, we find Brandeis J identifying freedom of expression as means by which to identify not truth generally but rather 'political truth'. In his opinion, Brandeis J does not offer a definition of 'political truth'. However, it seems reasonable to suppose that he understood it to include, *inter alia*, models of human association that conduce more, rather then less, satisfactorily to human welfare. (This narrower form of the pursuit of truth rationale intersects, of course, with the democracy rationale discussed above. For further discussion of this point and Brandeis J's opinion, see White, 1996.)

The pursuit of truth rationale described above conjures up a picture of discursive processes in which participants, while disagreeing with one another, exhibit a tolerant disposition. Bollinger has argued that freedom of expression facilitates 'the development of [a] capacity for tolerance' (Bollinger, 1990, p. 984). A capacity for tolerance is, on Bollinger's account, desirable for, *inter alia*, the three following reasons. First, it works to weaken 'a general bias against receiving or acknowledging new ideas' (p. 983). Secondly, it is particularly valuable in 'large and complex societies' containing people with 'varied beliefs and interests'. This is because a readiness to tolerate views other than one's own facilitates coexistence by serving to check 'the wish to establish an overly homogenised society' (ibid.). Thirdly, in circumstances where people are willing to tolerate views other than their own, they may be more ready than would otherwise be the case to tolerate non-verbal modes of activity that they regard as objectionable (p. 984). This is, moreover, a point that can be regarded as having particular relevance in plural societies.

As can be seen from the above, a wide range of arguments support the view that we should enjoy considerable freedom of expression. We must now examine the bodies of law noted above. They are, of course, informed by purposes that could be thwarted, or at least compromised, in circumstances where people enjoy broad expressive freedom.

19.2   The Status of Freedom of Expression

Among the rights protected by the European Convention on Human Rights, freedom of expression has an especially high status (see Laws LJ in *R. (Mahmood)* v. *Secretary of State* (2001)). In *R.* v. *Central Independent Television plc* [1994] 3 All ER 641 at 652 Hoffmann LJ said that 'freedom of speech is a trump card that always wins'. However, rights are rarely if ever absolute and, as Sedley LJ pointed out in *Douglas and Zeta-Jones* v. *Hello! Ltd* [2001] 2 All ER 289 at 323–4, Lord Hoffmann was speaking in a context where there was no competition with the exceptions in the ECHR. Even freedom of expression must sometimes give way to a 'pressing social need' and must be accommodated with other rights such as privacy. Thus Art. 10 confers the right of freedom of expression, subject to 'duties and responsibilities' (see *Handyside* v. *UK* (1974)). These duties and responsibilities entitle the state to limit freedom of expression in a manner 'prescribed by law' and 'necessary in a democratic society' for the following purposes:

- national security;
- territorial integrity or public safety;
- for the prevention of disorder or crime;
- for the protection of health or morals;
- for the protection of the reputation or rights of others. In particular, freedom of expression may have to be compromised by the right to a fair trial (Art. 6), privacy (Art. 8, below Ch. 20), and freedom of religion (Art. 9);

- for preventing the disclosure of information received in confidence;
- for maintaining the authority and impartiality of the judiciary.

Article 11 confers a right to freedom of assembly with overrides for national security, public safety, the prevention of disorder or crime, the protection of health or morals and the protection of the rights and freedoms of others.

Some forms of expression are regarded as more important than others. Political speech is widely regarded as especially important so that attacks on the government are subject to restriction only in extreme cases (see *Castells* v. *Spain* (1992)). Therefore freedom of the press is regarded as particularly important because the press (including for this purpose the broadcast media) is a watchdog over government on behalf of the public (see *Jersild* v. *Denmark* (1994); *Lingens* v. *Austria* (1986)). In *Hector* v. *A-G of Antigua and Bermuda* [1990] 2 All ER 103 at 106, Lord Bridge said that 'in a free democratic society ... those who hold office in government must always be open to criticism. Any attempt to stifle or fetter such criticism amounts to political censorship of the most insidious and objectionable kind'.

The common law has recognised the importance of press freedom by limiting the rights of public bodies to sue for defamation (*Derbyshire County Council* v. *Times Newspapers Ltd* (1993). In *R.* v. *Secretary of State for the Home Department ex parte Simms* (1999) the House of Lords held that a prisoner has a right to a visit from a journalist in order to campaign for his conviction to be quashed. In *Richmond LBC* v. *Holmes* (2000) a newspaper was permitted to publish a report on the child-care policies of a local authority which the authority claimed to be confidential although the balance would probably fall against publication if the interests of an individual child were at stake.

US law and probably the ECHR, is less sympathetic to artistic expression. The Supreme Court has denied that pornography was protected at all, being in the view of the court without redeeming social benefit (*Roth* v. *US* (1957)). This instrumental approach which makes freedom conditional contrasts with the liberal stance that the harm of pornography must be set against freedom as an end in itself as well as the literary or artistic merit that some pornography may possess. 'Commercial speech' is likely to enjoy the least protection of all although interference must still be justified (see *R.J.R.-MacDonald Inc.* v. *Canada (A-G)* (1995): tobacco advertising).

Freedom of expression includes a right not to say anything. The law does not normally *require* anyone to provide information. However, the ECHR has held that that the public have a right to receive information, ideas and opinions, so that the state has a corresponding duty to safeguard the free-flow even of undesirable information and opinion. Thus in *Plattform 'Arzte fur das Leben'* v. *Austria* (1988), it was held that the state should take positive measures to protect freedom of expression, by policing arrangements at public meetings. However, this was under Art. 13 (duty to provide adequate remedies), which is not incorporated by the Human Rights Act (see also *Farrakhan* v. *Secretary of State for the Home Department* (2001)). Sometimes freedom of expression is protected by statute. For example, universities have a positive obligation to 'take such steps as are reasonably practicable to secure that freedom of speech within the law is secured for members, students and employees of the establishment and for visiting speakers' (Education (No. 2) Act 1986 s. 43).

Government claims to confidentiality or demands for information from the press are closely scrutinised although this has not always been the case (below, 22.4.2). In *R.* v. *Central Criminal Court ex parte Bright, Alton and Rushbridger* (2001) the Court of Appeal quashed a production order sought by the Crown against the editors of the *Guardian* and the *Observer* to disclose information received from Derek Shaylor, a former MI5 agent, whom the government were seeking to prosecute under the Official Secrets Act. It was held that disclosure would inhibit press freedom without there being a compelling reason for the disclosure. The Contempt of Court Act 1981 s. 10 gives some protection to journalistic sources (below).

The protection of free expression against state intrusion has its dangers. Some argue that these dangers have been realised in the USA, where considerable reverence is attached to the First Amendment of the Constitution as a protection against the state (e.g. *Brandenburg* v. *Ohio* (1969)). It has been suggested that this gives free reign to oppression by powerful private interests and facilitates indirect censorship through social and economic forces generated for example by commercial, ethnic and religious interests which are intolerant of dissenting opinions. According to this view American society is polarised between a deeply conformist majority and marginalized dissenters and the protection of minorities might be improved through greater state intervention (see Abel, 1994a, b; Fish, 1994; cf. Paton, 1995).

19.3   'Prior Restraint' and Censorship

Blackstone promoted the distinction in the eighteenth century between censorship of speech in advance by requiring government approval, and punishing the speaker after the event. Prior restraint is regarded as violation of freedom of expression because it removes from the public sphere the possibility of assessing the matter whereas punishment may be regarded as a legitimate compromise between competing goods. Prior restraint should therefore be resorted to only as a last resort. The ECHR subjects prior restraint to a high level of scrutiny, particularly in the case of news 'which is a perishable commodity' (see *Observer and Guardian Newspapers* v. *UK* (1992)). Indeed in *Open Door* v. *Ireland and Dublin Well Woman* (1992), five judges thought that prior restraint should never be tolerated.

Since the abolition in 1695 of state licensing of printing presses, English law has no general censorship powers over the printed word although in characteristically British fashion there are voluntary mechanisms presided over by committees of insiders for the purpose of encouraging self-censorship (the 'D' Notice Committee) and remedying intrusive practices (the Press Complaints Commission). There is, however, state censorship over advertising, broadcasting and the cinema (Broadcasting Act 1990; Wireless Telegraphy Act 1949 – BBC licence agreement; Cinemas Act 1985 – local authority licensing). The police have wide prior restraint powers in the interests of public order (below). The Local Government Act 1988 s. 28 forbids local authorities from publishing material with the intention of promoting homosexuality and from promoting 'the teaching in any maintained school of the acceptability of sexuality as a pretended family relationship'.

19.3.1 Press freedom

The European Court has said that the press have not only a right but an obligation to impart information and ideas on matters of public interest, and the public have a right to receive such material. The press therefore enjoy a high level of protection under the ECHR (see *Castells* v. *Spain* (1992) para. 43; *Lingens* v. *Austria* (1986) para. 41; *Goodwin* v. *UK* (1996)). *Jersild* v. *Denmark* (1994) concerned a television interview with representatives of an extremist political group. The interview was edited to highlight abusive remarks made about ethnic groups within Denmark. The TV interviewer, who did not challenge the racist remarks, was charged with aiding and abetting the offence of 'threatening, insulting or degrading a group of persons on account of their race, colour, national or ethnic origin or belief'. The court held, with seven dissenters, that the interview was protected by Art. 10 because of the duty of the press to report controversial opinions in its role of public watchdog, and the corresponding right of the public to be informed. It was not for the court to decide how journalists presented their material provided that, taken in its whole context, the broadcast did not support the views put forward. In these circumstances restricting the press was not necessary in a democratic society as required by Art. 10. However, in *Purcell* (1991), and *Brind* (1991) the Commission held that the UK and Irish governments' ban on live interviews with IRA supporters and other groups were lawful. These cases might be distinguished from *Jersild* in that they concerned terrorism, which is an area where the state enjoys a wide margin of appreciation.

The courts have prior restraint powers in the form of an injunction, disobedience to which attracts imprisonment for contempt of court. The Attorney-General can seek an injunction in the name of the public interest, most notably in the case of publications that risk prejudicing legal proceedings such as newspaper comments on matters related to pending litigation (contempt of court) and in the interests of national security (breach of confidence or under official secrets legislation; below, Chapter 18). A temporary injunction can readily be granted on the basis of an arguable case since once material is published there is no turning back (see *A-G* v. *Guardian Newspapers Ltd* (1987)). The effect of a temporary injunction is drastic in that it prevents anyone, whether a party or not, who is aware that the injunction is in force from publishing the material (see *A-G* v. *Observer Ltd* (1988); *A-G* v. *Times Newspapers Ltd* (1991)). However, under the ECHR once the material becomes public, even if unlawfully, the press has a duty to disseminate it, and to comment on, and further restraint cannot be justified (see *Observer and Guardian Newspapers* v. *UK* (1991)).

UK law has also fallen foul of the European Convention on Human Rights because the power to grant an injunction has been used in a manner disproportionate to the risk of harm. In *A-G* v. *Times Newspapers Ltd* (1974) the House of Lords held that it was a contempt for a newspaper to comment on the merits of civil litigation concerning the victims of thalidomide, for the reason that 'trial by newspaper' was undesirable in itself, irrespective of the possibility that the publication might influence the outcome of the trial. However, in *Sunday Times* v. *UK* (1979) the ECHR held that contempt law could inhibit freedom of expression only where this was necessary to ensure a fair trial, for example if there was a risk of a jury being influenced.

The Contempt of Court Act 1981 was a response to this. Section 2 introduces a test for strict liability contempt of 'substantial risk' that the course of justice could be seriously impeded or prejudiced. This applies while the proceedings are 'live'. In *A-G* v. *English* (1983) the House of Lords weakened s. 2 by holding that 'substantial' merely means genuine or not remote. This is unlikely to satisfy the proportionality doctrine of the ECHR (but see *A-G* v. *News Group Newspapers* (1987); *Re Lonrho* (1990); no substantial risk). There is also a common law offence of contempt of court. This requires an intention to influence court proceedings and can apply even before the proceedings have started, indeed even perhaps where it is not certain that they will take place (see *A-G* v. *News Group Newspapers* (1988), doubted in *A-G* v. *Sport Newspapers Ltd* (1992)).

The importance of freedom of expression in relation to the press is now reinforced by s. 12 of the Human Rights Act 1998. Section 12 provides firstly that a court order limiting the 'Convention right of freedom of expression' cannot normally be granted in the absence of the respondent. This affects interim injunctions which might be sought as an emergency measure against the media. Secondly s. 12 prevents an interim order being made unless the applicant is likely to establish that publication should not be allowed. Thirdly s. 12 requires the court to have particular regard to freedom of expression and, 'where the proceedings relate to material which the respondent claims or which appears to the court to be journalistic, literary or artistic material (or to conduct connected with such material), to (a) the extent to which

(i) the material has, or is about to, become available to the public; or
(ii) it is, or would be, in the public interest for the material to be published;

and (b) any relevant privacy code' (e.g. that made by the Press Complaints Commission).

It is sometimes argued that s. 12 has the effect of privileging freedom of expression above other Convention rights. However, in *Douglas and Zeta-Jones* v. *Hello! Ltd* (2001), the Court of Appeal held that s. 12 does not have this effect. According to the Court of Appeal, s. 12 merely ensures that the competing rights in question are taken into account even at the interim stage whereas traditionally an injunction has been granted where there is a serious issue to be tried (see *American Cyanamid* v. *Ethicon* (1974)).

A 'fair balance' has probably been struck in relation to the reporting of court proceedings. Section 4 of the Contempt of Court Act 1981 empowers the court to postpone but not to prohibit publication 'where it appears to be necessary for avoiding a substantial risk of prejudice to the administration of justice'. In *R.* v. *Beck ex parte Daily Telegraph* (1993) a court had ordered that the reporting of the trial of three alleged child abusers should be postponed. It was held that the order was invalid because the matter was of serious public concern and the public fear of a possible cover-up outweighed the interests of justice in the particular case. The Court of Appeal stressed that gagging orders must be justified on the basis of a strong necessity. Section 11 of the Contempt of Court Act 1981 deals with the prohibition of publication of information given in court proceedings. It assumes but does not confer such a power by enabling the court ('having the power to do') so to give direction for the purpose. There are also statutory powers which enable the court to prohibit publication (e.g. Domestic and Appellate Proceedings (Restriction of Publicity) Act 1968; Magistrates Courts Act 1980 s. 71). The court can order witnesses to remain anonymous but only where publicity is likely to lead to serious harm (see *R.* v. *Chief Registrar of Friendly Societies ex parte New Cross Building Society* (1984); *A-G* v. *Leveller Magazine Ltd* (1979)).

Privacy and respect for family life are protected by Art. 8 of the ECHR thus clashing directly with freedom of expression without any apparent means of deciding which to prefer (below Ch. 20). There is a general principle that the convention is enforceable only in respect of violations by public bodies, but the ECHR has held that Art. 8 may impose a positive obligation on the state to ensure that private bodies such as the press protect privacy (see *X and Y* v. *Netherlands* (1985)). Article 17, which prevents the abuse of convention rights, might also be used against press intrusion.

19.3.2   Morality

There are substantial censorship powers in relation to pornography. This area of the law seems to be geared to the moral values of the majority without the need to show any special interference with particular rights or interests (see *Knuller* v. *DPP* (1973)). The thrust of the law of obscenity and indecency seems to be to accommodate pluralism up to the point where it threatens the stability and order of the community.

Article 10 of the ECHR extends its protection to matters which 'offend, shock or disturb' on the ground that 'such are the demands of that pluralism, tolerance and broadmindedness without which there is no democratic society' (*Handyside* v. *UK* (1976)). However, under Art. 10 the state is entitled to license 'broadcasting, television or cinema enterprises' and can override freedom of expression for the protection of 'morals' to the extent to which this is 'necessary in a democratic society'. The fact that the protection of morals is in itself a legitimate object of state concern, has caused differences of opinion within the European Court. Although there have been strong dissents the court seems to be less favourably disposed to artistic expression than to political expression. It has urged the notion of restraint upon artists in the interests of public feelings and the moral well-being of the community (see *Muller* v. *Switzerland* (1988), *Otto Preminger Institut* v. *Austria* (1994) (below)).

As we have seen, there is a violation of convention rights if the state's protective measures are disproportionate to the evil, but the ECHR gives a margin of appreciation where moral attitudes vary between the different European states. In *Open Door and Dublin Well Woman* v. *Ireland* (1992) the Irish government banned a voluntary body from advertising in Ireland abortion services available in England. Although abortion was then unlawful under the Irish constitution it was not unlawful under Irish law for an Irish person to have an abortion in England. The ban was held by a majority of fifteen to eight to be contrary to Art. 10. The majority held that the ban was for a legitimate purpose, namely the protection of morals, but that it went well beyond what was necessary for that purpose even given the margin of appreciation. The court therefore avoided ruling on the broader question whether banning abortion was contrary to the convention. This would have involved the right to privacy and might have raised the question of the right to life. However the majority rejected the argument that protecting the life of an unborn child outweighed all other interests.

In *Dudgeon* v. *UK* (1981) the court was split on the question whether Northern Ireland could outlaw homosexual acts between consenting adults in private. A majority held that this went beyond what was reasonably necessary in a democratic society to preserve order and morality while the minority deferred to the predominant moral view in the province, arguing that a shared morality was a legitimate concern of the state.

It is unlikely that the Human Rights Act 1998 will substantially affect English law in relation at least to obscenity. Not only is there the specific public morality override but it is also arguable that public displays of pornography violate the right to privacy in Art. 8 and may also be discriminatory (see *R.* v. *Butler* (1992), Canadian Supreme Court). It is an offence to publish an 'obscene' article (including films and videos, and placing obscene material on the Internet: Obscene Publications Act 1959 s. 2, Criminal Justice and Public Order Act 1994 s. 168). There is a similar offence under the Theatres Act 1968 in relation to live performances, and the Video Recordings Act 1984 as amended by the Criminal Justice and Public Order Act 1994 makes it an offence to supply a video that has not been classified by the British Board of Film Censors.

The statutory meaning of obscene is that the article taken as a whole has a tendency to 'deprave and corrupt' a significant proportion of those likely to see, hear or read it (s. 1(1)). The meaning of deprave and corrupt has been left to the jury or magistrate and is therefore subject to public opinion as to the limits of acceptable behaviour. Anti-social behaviour is not required (see *DPP* v. *Whyte* (1972); *DPP* v. *A&BC Chewing Gum Ltd* (1968)). The emphasis on those likely to have access to offending material is an important element of ECHR jurisprudence. For example, an exhibition open to the public at large without warning as to its contents may lawfully be controlled (see *Muller* v. *Switzerland* (1988)). The same applies to material targeted at vulnerable groups (*Handyside* v. *UK* (1974)).

There is a defence of 'public good' (s. 4) where the publication, although obscene, is in the interests of science, literature, art or learning or other objects of general public concern and in the case of films, drama, opera, ballet or any other art (see *DPP* v. *Jordan* (1977)). A similar defence applies under the Theatres Act 1968. The defence of public good is a classical example of an attempt to 'balance' incommensurables. Being corrupted is an evil, but is it possible rationally to decide when the evil is outweighed by literary merit?

The police have power under s. 3 of the Obscene Publications Act 1959 to seize under a magistrate's warrant any 'article' (including books, magazines, pictures, films, tapes and disks) which they have reason to believe is obscene. The magistrates may then make a forfeiture order to destroy the article. This might be regarded as disproportionate under the Convention in relation to property rights. Customs officers have an even wider power to confiscate materials which are 'indecent' or obscene (Customs and Excise Management Act 1979). It seems that indecent material is something that is capable of causing offence whether or not it depraves and corrupts (see *R.* v. *Stanley* (1965)). There is also a common law offence of indecency which requires only public offence (see *R.* v. *Gibson:* (1990)). This might be challenged under the Human Rights Act 1998 as disproportionate.

There are many statutory offences connected with obscenity and indecency which are designed to protect particular interests such as those of children (Protection of Children Act 1978, Criminal Justice and Public Order Act 1994 s. 57(7), indecent photography and computer images) or which apply to particular outlets (Indecent Displays (Control) Act 1981; Local Government (Miscellaneous Provisions) Act 1982). The latter statute which gives local authorities draconian powers to regulate sex shops has survived considerable challenge (see *Quietlynn Ltd* v. *Southend on Sea BC* (1990); *McMonagle* v. *Westminster City Council* (1990); *R.* v. *Birmingham City Council ex parte Sheptonhurst* (1990)).

19.3.3 Hate speech

Blasphemy

This is an ancient common law offence the gist of which is an attack upon religion. Until the nineteenth century, church and state were closely related, so blasphemy could be used as a political weapon. The modern law claims to be neutral as to religious faith so religious belief can be denied or questioned provided that 'the decencies of controversy are observed' (see *Bowman* v. *Secular Society* (1917); *R.* v. *Ramsey & Foot* (1883)). However, the offence is a wide one and is committed by conduct which seriously offends the ordinary Christian by 'insulting or vilifying the deity, God or Christianity' (see *R.* v. *Lemon* (1979); poem depicting Christ as homosexual). The offence seems to apply only to the Christian faiths and is not related to public order (*R.* v. *Chief Metropolitan Stipendiary Magistrate ex parte Choudhury* (1991); cf. *R.* v. *Gott* (1922); *R.* v. *Gathercole* (1938)). Reformers are divided between those who would abolish blasphemy and those who would extend it to other religions in order to reflect our multi-cultural society.

The European Convention gives considerable importance to protecting freedom of religion particularly in the case of dominant religions. Moreover the Human Rights Act 1998 s. 13 requires the court to have particular regard in matters involving religious organisations to the importance of freedom of thought, conscience and religion. This could be read as authorising religious organisations to violate other rights such as privacy or to discriminate on religious grounds.

In *Otto Preminger Institut* v. *Austria* (1994) the state seized a film which offended the Roman Catholic sensibilities of most of the people of the Tyrol. Among other things the film depicted Christ and his mother as in league with the devil. The ECHR held that the seizure was lawful for the purpose of protecting the rights of others. However, it is difficult to see how an insult that does not prevent the practice of a religion can be regarded as interfering with rights, particularly as the film in question was limited to a small specialist cinema. Any harm lay merely in knowing that the film existed.

Recognising that there are differences in religious sensibilities between states and regions, the Court conceded a wide margin of appreciation to the state. Similarly in *Wingrove* v. *UK* (1996) the Court upheld a decision of the UK film censors not to grant a distribution certificate to a video on the grounds of blasphemy. Indeed in *Otto Preminger Institut* the court seems to have gone further by saying that 'in the context of religious opinion and beliefs ... may legitimately be included an obligation to avoid as far as possible expressions that are gratuitously offensive to others and thus an infringement of their rights, and which therefore do not contribute to any form of public debate capable of furthering progress in human affairs.' This seems to run counter to at least one of the rationales for protecting freedom of expression by allowing the state to decide what is a worthy purpose of speech.

The Anti-Terrorism, Crime and Security Bill proposed offences relating to religious hatred by the device of extending the law relating to racial hatred (below) to religious hatred including lack of religious belief. This would be a significant restriction upon freedom of expression in that unlike racial characteristics, religious beliefs are held voluntarily and there seems no reason why these should be especially privileged over, for example political beliefs. However, in return for a smooth passage for other provisions in the bill, this extension was severely curtailed (below p. 474).

Sedition

This consists of publishing material, for example speeches, leaflets, books or electronic messages, with one or more of the following intentions (see *R.* v. *Burns* (1886); *R.* v. *Aldred* (1909); *R.* v. *Caunt* (1947)):

- to bring into hatred or contempt the monarch or the government;
- to excite subjects to attempt to alter the established order by unlawful means;
- to raise discontent or disaffection among Her Majesty's subjects;
- to promote ill-will or hostility between different classes of Her Majesty's subjects.

During the eighteenth century seditious libel was used as a tool of state control in that the judges had a wide power to decide what was seditious. Under Fox's Libel Act (1772) this was made a matter for the jury, thus providing a safeguard for the individual in that judges cannot direct a jury to convict and juries do not have to give reasons for their decisions.

The accused must intend to incite violence or disorder but this need not it seems be immediate. In *R.* v. *Chief Metropolitan Stipendiary Magistrate ex parte Choudhury* (1991) it was held that sedition applies only to incitement against the state and not to attacks on religious groups. Moreover 'the limits of permissible criticism are wider with regard to the government than in relation to a private citizen or even a politician' (*Castels* v. *Spain* (1992) para. 46) and there may be no margin of appreciation in such cases. Therefore, if prosecution is limited to cases of serious disorder it is unlikely that a proportionate response would fall foul of the Human Rights Act 1998. On the other hand, given the availability of other public order powers, sedition may be regarded as unnecessarily draconian (cf. above p. 424).

Racism
Racism has been so widely condemned throughout Europe as to amount to a special case. Freedom from discrimination as such is not protected under the convention which expressly prohibits discrimination only in respect of the other protected rights (Art. 14). However, the International Convention on the Elimination of All Forms of Racial Discrimination (1965) (CERD) has been ratified by most members of the Council of Europe (not Ireland, Lithuania or Turkey). Article 4 of the convention requires signatories to create offences in relation to 'all dissemination of ideas based on racial supremacy or hatred, incitement to racial discrimination, as well as acts of violence or incitement to such acts against any race or group of persons of another colour or ethnic origin'. Article 4 also requires states to have 'due regard' to (*inter alia*) the right to freedom of opinion and expression.

Racist speech is not entirely outside the protection of Art. 10 but has a low level of protection, usually being outweighed by the need to protect the rights of others and to prevent disorder (but see *Farrakhan* v. *Secretary of State for the Home Department* (2001): right to hear even extreme opinions). In *Jersild* v. *Denmark* (above) the objective reporting by the media of racist abuse was held to be protected by Art. 10. The reason for this is the role of the media as a watchdog against obnoxious elements in society. This reflects the 'search for truth' rationale of freedom of expression. In *Jersild* the court expressed the view that deliberate racist abuse would not be protected and that racism is a substantial threat to democracy. Measures to combat racism are reinforced by Art. 17 which aims at preventing reliance on a convention right in order to undermine another. It is unlikely therefore that UK law contravenes the ECHR. The main anti-racism offences are as follows.

- *Incitement to racial hatred.* Sections 18 to 23 of the Public Order Act 1986 extend earlier provisions. The gist of the main offence is the use of 'threatening, abusive or insulting words or behaviour either with intention to stir up hatred in circumstances in which such hatred is likely to be stirred up'. Race includes colour, race, nationality, ethnic or national origins (s. 17). An ethnic group can be defined by cultural as well as physical characteristics (see *Mandla* v. *Dowell-Lee* (1983) – Sikhs; *Commission for Racial Equality* v. *Dutton* (1989) – gypsies but not other travellers). The offence applies to the display of written material including pictures (s. 29), but not to broadcasting, for which there are separate provisions (s. 18 (6)). The racial group need not be present at the time, although there must be at least one person among the audience or readership likely to be stirred to racial hatred.

Incitement to racial hatred can be committed in public or private places except exclusively within a dwelling. Thus the offence applies even to activities within a private club or other association. Public disorder is not relevant; for example the offence could apply to an academic paper read to an audience in a university with which the whole audience agrees. The accused is not guilty if he did not intend to stir up racial hatred and if he was unaware that his words or actions might be threatening, abusive or insulting (s. 18 (5), s. 18 (2)).

- Similar provisions apply to a public performance of a play (s. 20), to distributing, showing or playing recordings, and to broadcasting or cable services, except from the BBC and ITC (s. 22 (7), s. 23 (4)). Broadcasts by the BBC and ITC are governed by their own internal systems of regulation and the Home Secretary has power to ban any broadcast (see *Brind* v. *Secretary of State for the Home Department* (1991)).
- It is an offence to possess racially inflammatory material (s. 23), and the police have wide powers of entry and search (s. 26).
- Under the Crime and Disorder Act 1998 ss. 28, 31, the penalties for the offences of 'fear or provocation of violence' and 'harassment alarm and distress' under the Public Order Act 1986 (below) are increased where there is a racial motivation. The Anti-Terrorism, Crime and Security Act 2001 s. 39 extends this to case of religious motivation.

19.4   Public Order: Demonstrations and Meetings

Public demonstrations and meetings are an important expression of democracy. However, there are many statutory restrictions imposed for the purpose of public order and the police have wide discretionary powers. The law has developed as a series of pragmatic responses to particular problems and political agendas. This illustrates the weakness of the traditional residual approach to liberty. The Human Rights Act 1998 may subject our untidy law to a more principled analysis which will at least require its anomalies to be justified under the ECHR.

The emphasis of the law is often upon the circumstances and the setting of the conduct complained of, rather than upon the content of speech as such; Art. 11 (freedom of assembly) therefore becomes important. A similar distinction is drawn in US law between the content of speech which probably cannot be restricted, and its mode of expression which can be restricted where there is a 'clear and present' danger of serious injury (see Feldman, 1993, pp. 813–14; cf. *Brandenburg* v. *Ohio* 395 US 444 (1969); *Edwards* v. *South Carolina* 372 US 279 (1963)). It is sometimes said that modern methods of communicating – mass circulation newspapers, TV and radio – make it less important to worry about public space than was the case 50 years ago when much of the case law was generated by fascist and communist demonstrations. Nevertheless, meetings, demonstrations or processions in the open air remain the only means by which people without money or influence can express their views.

It has been held that under Art. 11 states should take positive measures to protect freedom of assembly by attempting to control troublemakers before banning a meeting, although the state will be given a margin of appreciation as to what measures are reasonable in the circumstances (*Plattform 'Arzte fur das Leben'* v. *Austria* (1988)). As we shall see, English law may not comply with this.

Dicey's notion that everything is permitted unless forbidden is particularly ironic in the case of public meetings. All meetings and processions take place on land. All land, even a public highway, is owned by someone, either a private body, a local authority or the Crown or government department. Therefore holding a meeting without the consent of the owner may be a trespass and can be prevented by an injunction or compensated by an action for damages (see *Harrison* v. *Duke of Rutland* (1893)). The offences of 'aggravated trespass' under s. 68 (1) of the Criminal Justice and Public Order Act 1994 and 'trespassory assembly' under s. 70 take advantage of this, putting a powerful weapon into the hands of the police to remove trespassers from land.

In the case of both offences the essential question is what are the public's rights in relation to the highway (which includes roads and their verges, footpaths, bridleways and waters over which there is a public right of navigation)? The traditional view has been that the public has a right only to 'pass or repass' on a highway (that is, to travel) and also to stop on the highway for purposes which are reasonably incidental such as 'reasonable rest and refreshment' (*Hickman* v. *Maisy* (1900)). In *Hubbard* v. *Pitt* (1976), for example, a majority of the Court of Appeal held that peaceful picketing by a protest group who distributed leaflets and questionnaires was not a lawful use of the highway. Dicey thought that a procession, but not a static meeting, would usually be lawful because processions comprise a large number of individuals exercising their right to travel at the same time. However, the owner of the highway could sue for trespass if the procession paused to allow a speech to be made. If this is right, then if highways are obstructed, however minimally, the police could treat the matter as one of aggravated trespass or even without an obstruction, if a group of people are involved, as a trespassory assembly.

In *DPP* v. *Jones* (1999) a majority of the House of Lords upheld the right of peaceful demonstration in a public place although the limits of this are not clear. The defendant was part of a group of environmentalists who were arrested during a demonstration at Stonehenge. The demonstration was peaceful, and nobody was obstructed. Taking into account Art. 11 of the ECHR Lord Irvine LC held that the law should now recognise that the public should have a right to enjoy the highway for any reasonable purpose whether the land was public or private provided that the activities did not constitute a nuisance and did not obstruct other people's freedom of movement. Lord Hutton and Lord Clyde agreed, but took a narrower approach emphasising that not every non-obtrusive and peaceful use of the highway is necessarily lawful. Lord Hutton said 'the common law recognises that there is a right for members of the public to assemble together to express views on matters of public concern and I consider that that the common law should now recognise that this right, which is one of the fundamental rights of citizens in this country, is unduly restricted unless it can be exercised in some circumstances on the public highway.' Lord Hope and Lord Slynn dissented, Lord Hope because of the effect of such a right on property owners who were not before the court to defend their interests, Lord Slynn because of a reluctance to unsettle established law. *Jones* therefore illustrates the range of concerns generated by human rights jurisprudence.

Under the Highways Act 1980 s. 137, it is an offence to obstruct the highway. It is not necessary that the highway be completely blocked or even that people are inconvenienced. The accused's intentions are also irrelevant (*Arrowsmith* v. *Jenkins* (1963); *Homer* v. *Cadman* (1886); *Hirst* v. *West Yorkshire Chief Constable* (1987)). However, as a result of *Jones*, a reasonable peaceful demonstration would probably not be unlawful. There are also numerous local statutes and bylaws regulating public meetings in particular places. Rights of public meetng cannot apparently be acquired by custom.

19.4.1 Police powers

The police have wide powers to regulate public meetings and processions. These are supplemented by powers relating to particular places (e.g. Seditious Meetings Act 1817 s. 3: meetings of 50 or more people in the vicinity of Westminster when Parliament is sitting). There are also common law powers to prevent a breach of the peace. The main general police powers are as follows.

- The 'organiser' of a public procession intended (i) to demonstrate support for or opposition to the views or actions of any person or body of persons; (ii) to publicise a campaign or cause; and (iii) to mark or commemorate an event must give advance notice to the police. There are certain exceptions. These include (i) processions commonly or customarily held in the area; (ii) funeral processions organised by a funeral director in the normal course of his business; and (iii) cases where it is not reasonably practicable to give advance notice (for example a spontaneous march) (s. 11).
- If a 'senior police officer' reasonably believes (a) that any public procession may result in serious public disorder, serious damage to property, or serious disruption to the life of the community, or (b) that the purpose of the organisers is to intimidate people into doing something they have a right not to do, or not doing something they have a right to do, he can impose such conditions as appear to him to be necessary to prevent such disorder, damage, disruption or intimidation, including conditions as to the route of the procession or prohibit it from entering any public place specified in the directions (s. 12). A senior police officer is either the chief constable, Metropolitan police commissioner, or the senior officer present on the scene (s. 12 (2)). Intimidation requires more than merely causing discomfort and must contain an element of compulsion (*Police* v. *Reid* (1987)).
- All public processions, or any class of public procession, can be banned if the chief constable or Metropolitan police commissioner reasonably believes that the power to impose conditions is not adequate in the circumstances (s. 13). The decision is for the local authority, with the consent of a secretary of state (in practice the Home Secretary).

- There are powers to impose conditions upon public assemblies for the same purposes as in the case of processions (s. 14). For this purpose a public assembly is an assembly of 20 or more people in a public place which is wholly or partly open to the air (s. 16). Unlike processions, the police have no power to ban a lawful assembly but can control its location, timing and the numbers attending. However, the Criminal Justice and Public Order Act 1994 s. 70 (inserting ss. 14 A, B, C into the Public Order Act 1986), confers power on a local authority with the consent of the Secretary of State to impose a blanket ban upon certain assemblies in a place to which the public have no right of access or only a limited right of access. This includes private land and buildings where the public is invited, for example ancient monuments such as Stonehenge, meeting rooms, shops, sports and entertainment centres and libraries. The chief constable must reasonably believe that an assembly:
  - (a) is a trespassory assembly, being likely to be held without the permission of the occupier or to exceed the limits of his permission or of the public's rights of access, and
  - (b) may result in serious disruption to the life of the community or, where the land or a building or monument on it is of historical, architectural or scientific importance, may result in significant damage to the land, building or monument. A ban can last for up to four days within an area of up to five miles. The ban covers all trespassory assemblies and cannot be confined to particular assemblies.

  The Terrorism Act 2000 imposes further wide restrictions on meetings because of its broad definition of terrorism. This includes the use or threat for the purpose of advancing a political, religious or ideological cause, of action which ... involves serious violence against persons or property ... or ... creates a serious risk to the health or safety of the public or a section of the public (s. 1). The Secretary of State can proscribe organisations within this definition (s. 3). By virtue of s. 12, a person commits an offence who arranges or helps to arrange a meeting (of three or more persons) which he knows supports or furthers the activities of a proscribed organisation or which is addressed by a person who belongs to or professes to belong to a proscribed organisation, irrespective of the subject of the meeting. Vague concepts such as 'ideological', 'violence' and 'safety' mean that the law might include campaigning organisations such as parents groups and campaigners against human rights violations overseas.
- A police officer (and indeed any citizen) has a common law duty to prevent a breach of the peace. Where a breach of the peace is taking

place or reasonably anticipated the police have a summary power to arrest anyone who refuses to obey their reasonable requirements. A charge of obstructing the police is also possible (Police Act 1996 s. 89 (1)). The meaning of breach of the peace may be confined to violence or the likelihood of violence (see *R.* v. *Howell* (1982)). However, in *R.* v. *Chief Constable of Devon and Cornwall* (1981) 3 All ER 826 at 832 Lord Denning MR thought that there is a breach of the peace 'wherever a person who is lawfully carrying out his work is unlawfully and physically prevented by another from doing it' – protesters lying in front of a drilling machine. Thus passive resistance might be a breach of the peace. Lord Denning also thought that in deciding whether to intervene the police did not need to go into the rights and wrongs of the matter and could clear the site irrespective of who is to blame.

The power to prevent a breach of the peace includes for example a right of entry to private premises (*Thomas* v. *Sawkins* (1935)), a right to control the number of pickets on a picket line (*Piddington* v. *Bates* (1960)) and even a right to prevent people from travelling to a demonstration held several miles away (*Moss* v. *McLachlan* (1985)). It is not clear how 'imminent' or likely a breach of the peace must be. In *Moss* v. *McLachlan* the court emphasised that the matter is for the judgement of the policeman on the spot, who must consider on the basis of some evidence that there must be a 'real risk' of a breach of peace 'in the sense that it is in close proximity both in space and time'. The statutory power to ban processions (above) is in one respect wider because it allows bans to be imposed well in advance. In other respects the common law power is considerably broader.

All the above powers are characterised by wide discretion and there are no specific safeguards for freedom of expression or assembly. The courts are reluctant to interfere with police discretion and have applied the minimal '*Wednesbury*' test of unreasonableness according to which they will interfere only where the police decision is irrational. The main consideration seems to be that of efficiency in giving the police the power to control the disturbance as they see fit within the resources reasonably available to them (see *R.* v. *Chief Constable of Devon and Cornwall* (1981); *R.* v. *Chief Constable of Sussex ex parte International Traders Ferry Ltd* (1999)).

Furthermore the principle in *Beatty* v. *Gillbanks* (1882) seems to have been discarded according to which someone peacefully demonstrating on the highway cannot be penalised for a disturbance unlawfully created by opponents. In *Beatty*, a temperance march by the

Salvation army was disrupted by a gang, known as the Skeleton Army sponsored by brewery interests. *Beatty* concerned the obsolete offence of unlawful assembly, and the question of the powers of the police to prevent an imminent breach of the peace was not raised. Therefore, even where a peaceful and lawful meeting is disrupted by hooligans or political opponents, the police may prevent a likely breach of the peace by ordering the speaker to stop in preference to controlling the troublemakers (*Duncan* v. *Jones* (1936)) or by removing provocative symbols from the speaker (*Humphries* v. *Connor* (1864)).

Although the police must act even-handedly (*Harris* v. *Sheffield United Football Club* [1988] QB 77 at 95) there is a risk that they will exercise their discretion in favour of interests supported by the government or at least supported by majoritarian opinion. For example, during the miners' strike of 1983 the police restricted the activities of demonstrators in order to protect the 'right to work' of non-strikers, going as far as to escort non-strikers to work and spending vast sums of money on police reinforcements (see also *Coventry City Council ex parte Phoenix Aviation* (1995)). A cheaper and less provocative policy would have been to restrain the non-strikers.

The Human Rights Act 1998 may require *Beatty* to be reinstated in order to show that the response is proportionate. We saw earlier that the ECHR has held that the state has a positive duty to attempt to protect freedom of expression and assembly. Moreover, because it is indefinite, the police common law power may fall foul of the principle that a violation of Convention Rights must be 'prescribed by law'. On the other hand in *R.* v. *Chief Constable of Sussex* (1999), Lord Hoffmann said that there is no difference in the wide margin of appreciation that is required both in domestic law and under the 'superimposed' ECHR. The case concerned a police ban on lorries entering a port at times when the police had insufficient resources to provide security against disruption caused by animal rights demonstrators. The ban was upheld on the basis that the matter is one of police discretion. *Beatty* was distinguished on the familiar basis that police discretion was not involved in that case (but see *Redmond-Bate* v. *DPP* (1999)). Trespassory assembly may also be challenged on the ground of proportionality. However, the main police powers to regulate meetings and processions are probably sufficiently certain and proportionate.

19.4.2　Public order offences

There are a number of specific public order offences. Even minor punishments or disciplinary measures might be condemned under the

ECHR as disproportionate or uncertain and so 'chilling' the right of assembly (*Ezelin* v. *France* (1992)). The offences strike primarily at people who intentionally cause violence, but sometimes go beyond that. Moreover the offences overlap allowing police discretion in relation to the penalties.

The Public Order Act 1936 was a response to fears of fascism and communism. Much of it has been replaced by the Public Order Act 1986 which was provoked by race riots. Further legislation has been aimed at miscellaneous targets of the government of the day. These included anti-nuclear weapon, environmental and animal rights activists, hunt saboteurs, travellers, anti-social behaviour in residential areas, 'stalkers' and football hooligans (see Criminal Justice and Public Order Act 1994, Protection from Harrassment Act 1997, Crime and Disorder Act 1998, Football (Offences and Disorder) Act 1999, Football (Disorder) Act 2000). Whether or not all of these are legitimate causes for concern, the legislation may be drafted loosely enough to include wider political activities thereby attracting human rights arguments based on uncertainty, proportionality and discrimination. The development of this subject is an example of creeping erosion of civil liberties of a kind that Dicey did not anticipate.

Section 1 of the 1936 Act survives. This prohibits the wearing of political uniforms in any public place or public meeting without police consent, which can be obtained for special occasions. 'Uniform' includes any garment which has political significance, for example a black beret (*O'Moran* v. *DPP* (1975)). Political significance can be identified from any of the circumstances, or from historical evidence. The 1986 Act creates several offences, replacing a clutch of ancient and ill-defined common law offences (rout, riot, affray and unlawful assembly). They are as follows (in descending order of seriousness).

- *Riot* (s. 1). Where 12 or more people act in concert and use or threaten unlawful violence for a common purpose each person using violence is guilty of the offence.
- *Violent disorder* (s. 2). At least three people acting in concert and using or threatening unlawful violence.
- *Affray* (s. 3). One person suffices. Using or threatening unlawful violence is sufficient, but threats by words alone do not count.

All three offences may be committed in public or in private and the accused's conduct must be such 'as would cause a person of reasonable firmness present at the scene to fear for his personal safety'. No such person need actually be on the scene. The accused must either intend to threaten or use violence or be aware that his conduct may be violent or threaten violence (Public Order Act 1986, s. 6).

- *Fear or provocation of violence* (s. 4). This offence is somewhat wider and places a political speaker at the mercy of the susceptibilities of the audience. A person is guilty who uses towards another person 'threatening, abusive or insulting words or behaviour or distributes or displays any writing, sign or visible representation that is threatening, abusive or insulting'. The offence can be committed in a public or a private place except exclusively within a dwelling or between dwellings (see s. 8). The meaning of threatening, abusive or insulting is left to the jury (see *Brutus* v. *Cozens* (1973)) but the accused must be aware that his words are threatening, abusive or insulting (s. 6 (3)).

  The act must be aimed at another person with the intention either to cause that person to believe that immediate unlawful violence will be used or to provoke that person into immediate unlawful violence. Alternatively the accused's conduct must be likely to have that effect even though he does not so intend. In *R.* v. *Horseferry Road Magistrate Court ex parte Siadatan* (1993), Penguin books were prosocuted under s. 4 in relation to the publication of Salman Rushdie's book *Satanic Verses*. It was alleged that the book was likely to provoke future violence because it was offensive to Muslims. It was held that the violence must be likely within a short time of the behaviour in question. However, whether the other person's reaction is reasonable is irrelevant, so that the principle that a speaker 'takes his audience as he finds it' seems to apply. Thus, provoking a hostile or extremist audience, as in *Beatty* (above) would be an offence, provided that the words used or act performed are, to the knowledge of the accused, threatening, abusive or insulting to that particular audience (*Jordan* v. *Burgoyne* (1963)).

- Under s. 4A (inserted by the Criminal Justice and Public Order Act 1994), it is an offence to use threatening, abusive or insulting behaviour or disorderly behaviour with intent to cause harassment, alarm and distress where harassment, alarm or distress is actually caused. Violence is not involved.

- *Harassment, alarm, or distress* (s. 5). This is the widest offence and applies not only to threatening, abusive or insulting words or behaviour but also to 'disorderly behaviour', an expression which is not defined. Section 5 does not require an intent to cause harassment etc., but only that a person who actually sees or hears the conduct must be *likely* to be caused 'harassment, harm or distress'. The defendant has the defences (i) that he had no reason to believe that any such person was present; (ii) that he did not intend or know that his words or actions were threatening, abusive or insulting, or disorderly, as the case may be; (iii) that his conduct was 'reasonable'. For example in *DPP* v. *Clarke and others* (1992), the accused was protesting against abortion outside an abortion clinic by displaying upsetting images. It was held that although her conduct was threatening, abusive or insulting and was not reasonable and she was aware that her conduct was likely to cause distress, she was nevertheless not guilty because she did not subjectively believe that her actions were threatening, abusive or insulting. This is a safeguard of a kind, but may not suffice to meet the concerns of freedom of expression (cf. *DPP* v. *Fidler* (1992)).

The police have a summary power of arrest in relation to all the above offences but under s. 5 must first warn the accused to stop. The conduct before and after the warning need not be the same.

It is unlikely that ss. 1–4 are contrary to the ECHR in that they aim at preventing a 'clear and present danger'. Sections 4A and 5 are more vulnerable. In addition to 'threatening' behaviour, they target abusive, insulting and disorderly behaviour which leads to no more than distress. This arguably runs counter to the view of the European Court that conduct which shocks and offends is a price that must be paid for democracy (*Handyside* v. *UK* (1974)). In *Plattform 'Arzte fur das Leben'* v. *Austria* (1988) the ECHR held in the context of an anti-abortion demonstration that a peaceful demonstration should be protected even though it may annoy or give offence to persons opposed to the ideas and claims which it is seeking to promote.

- *Aggravated trespass.* Trespass is not in itself an offence. However, under s. 68 of the Criminal Justice and Public Order Act 1994, the offence of aggravated trespass occurs where a person who trespasses on land in the open air does anything (such as shouting threats, blowing a horn or erecting barricades) which, in relation to any lawful activity which persons are engaging or about to engage in on that land or on adjoining land, is intended to have the effect:
  (a) of intimidating those persons or any of them so as to deter them or any of them from engaging in that lawful activity;
  (b) of obstructing that activity; or
  (c) of disrupting that activity.

For this purpose a lawful activity is any activity that is not a criminal offence or a trespass (s. 68 (2)).

Section 68 is aimed at anti-hunting protesters. It would not seem to cover passive protests such as refusing to move, although it would cover the forming of a human barricade. It is unclear whether the act of assembling on land in order to demonstrate would be an aggravated trespass. There is no defence of reasonableness and violence is not an ingredient. The police have a power of arrest. Moreover the police can order a person committing or who has committed or who intends to commit an offence to leave the land (s. 69). The police can also order two or more people who are present with the common purpose of committing the offence to leave the land. In both cases it is an offence to return within three months.

- Under s. 1 (2) of the Protection from Harassment Act 1997 a course of conduct which amounts to the 'harassment' of another is an offence. 'Under s. 4 (1) a person whose course of conduct causes another to fear, on at least two occasions, that violence will be used against him is guilty of an offence if he knows or ought to know that his course of conduct will cause the other so to fear on each of those two occasions.' In both cases the test is whether a reasonable person in possession of the same information as the accused would think the conduct likely to cause fear or harrassment (s. 1 (2), s. 4 (2)). Harassment includes alarm and distress (s. (7) (2)) and can also include 'collective' harassment by a group (Criminal Justice And Police Act 2001, s. 44). There are defences of preventing or detecting crime, and acting under lawful authority. In the case of fear of violence there is also a defence of reasonable protection for persons or property. In the case of harassment there is a broad defence of 'reasonableness'. This would allow the press to claim that its duty to inform the public overides the victim's right of privacy.

19.5   Justices' Powers of Prior Restraint

Binding over
Magistrates can make orders binding people over to keep the peace or be of good behaviour even though no offence has been committed or threatened. The penalty is to forfeit a sum of money called a recognisance. This is very vague, going well beyond the commission of a definite offence. However, the penalty must not be so excessive as to inhibit the exercise of legal rights (*R. v. Central Criminal Court ex parte Boulding* (1984)). The binding-over procedure permits a magistrate to act upon his personal views of the worthiness of the citizen's motives and contains no effective safeguards for freedom of expression. Anyone brought before or in the court can be bound over, so that the normal safeguards of a criminal charge do not apply. The binding-over power probably fall fouls of the requirement of the ECHR that exceptions to

Art. 10 rights must be prescribed by law (*Hashman and Harrup* v. *UK* (1999); *Steel* v. *UK* (1999)).

Anti-social behaviour orders

Section 1 of the Crime and Disorder Act 1998 creates 'anti-social behaviour' orders. A local authority can apply to the magistrates court if it 'appears' to it that the following conditions are fulfilled: namely that, that the person has acted in a manner that causes or is likely to cause harassment, alarm or distress to one or more persons not of the same household, and that an order is 'necessary' for the purpose of protecting persons in the same local government area or an adjoining area from further anti-social acts. On the application of the local authority, to whom anyone can complain in confidence (an advantage for those intimidated by their neighbours), a magistrates court can make an order lasting for at least two years if it is 'proved' that the conditions are fulfilled.

Disobedience to an order carries imprisonment for up to five years. There is a defence of reasonableness. Although couched very broadly, anti-social behaviour orders as such are unlikely to fall foul of the ECHR in that they serve the legitimate purpose of protecting vulnerable people. Anti-social behaviour order proceedings are civil rather than criminal proceedings since their purpose is not to punish but to protect the public (*R. (McCann)* v. *Manchester Crown Court* (2001)). They are therefore subject to less procedural protection under Art. 6 of the ECHR, for example permitting tolerance of an uncertain scope of liability, the use of hearsay evidence and the civil standard of proof of balance of probabilities.

Summary

19.1 We first examined the justifications for freedom of expression and its general problems. These justifications concern the advancement of truth, the protection of democracy and the rule of law and also personal dignity. However, other values which may compete with freedom of expression also advance these goals.

19.2 Freedom of expression involves the state not only abstaining from interference but in some cases taking positive steps to protect freedom of expression. We distinguished between prior restraint (censorship) and punishments after the event. UK law has some direct censorship by the executive but further powers of censorship are available by applying to the courts for an interim (temporary) injunction. We discussed the court's wide powers of direct and indirect censorship by granting injunctions and in relation to s. 10 of the Contempt of Court Act 1981. These may be too broad in the light of the Human Rights Act 1998.

19.3   We touched on various areas of law intended to protect morality, particularly obscenity and indecency law which confers powers on magistrates, and Customs and Excise officials, to confiscate materials. We drew attention to the communitarian nature of the concepts of obscenity and indecency, to the margin of appreciation given in this area by the ECHR, and to the defence of public good, pointing out the impossibility of reconciling the incommensurables in this area.

19.4   We discussed 'hate speech' including blasphemy, sedition and racism pointing out that even in these cases there must be some tolerance of freedom of expression. In relation to blasphemy English law is anomalous.

19.5   We discussed the law relating to public order. This is characterised by broad police discretion and there is not always a duty to protect lawful activities against disruption. A range of statutes responding to perceived threats have created various offences that restrict freedom of expression and give the police extensive powers to regulate public gatherings, and protests and lobbying by individuals and groups. The police also have wide common law powers to prevent breaches of the peace. These may fall foul of the ECHR unless freedom of expression is given special weight in their exercise. In some cases there are uncertainty issues.

Further Reading

Card, R. (2000) *Public Order Law*.

Harris, O'Boyle and Warbrick, *Law of the European Convention on Human Rights*, chapters 10, 11, 12.

Lester, 'Freedom of expression', in MacDonald et al. (eds), *The European System for the Protection of Human Rights*.

McCrudden, C., Chambers, G., *Individual Rights and the Law in Britain*, chapters 2, 5, 8.

Nicolson, D., Reid, K. (1996) 'Arrest for breach of the peace and the ECHR', *Criminal Law Review*, 764.

Shorts, E., de Than, C., *Civil Liberties*, chapters 3, 5.

Turpin, *British Government and the Constitution, Text, Cases and Materials*, pp. 135–164.

Whitty, Murphy and Livingstone, *Civil Liberties Law: The Human Rights Act Era*, chapters 2 and 8.

Williams, D.G.T. (1987) 'Processions, assemblies and the freedom of the individual', *Criminal Law Review*, 167.

Exercises

19.1   'Freedom of speech is a trump card that always wins.' Lord Hoffmann. Does this reflect the present state of the law?

19.2   ' – In the context of religious opinion and beliefs – may legitimately be included an obligation to avoid as far as possible expressions that are gratuitously offensive to others and thus an infringement of their rights, and which therefore do not contribute to any form of public debate capable of furthering progress in human affairs'. *Otto Preminger Institut* v. *Austria* (1994). Discuss the implications of this for freedom of expression.

19.3   'The common law recognises that there is a right for members of the public to assemble together to express views on matters of public concern and I consider that the common law should now recognise this right which is one of the fundamental rights of citizens in this country is unduly restricted unless it can be exercised in some circumstances on the public highway' (Lord Hutton in *DPP* v. *Jones* (1999)). Discuss whether there is such a right and what are its limits.

19.4   To what extent do 'prior restraint' powers enable the courts to censor the media?

19.5   'A function of free speech is to invite dispute. It may indeed best serve its purpose when it induces a condition of unrest, creates dissatisfaction with conditions as they are and even stirs people to anger' (Mr Justice Douglas in *Terminiello* v. *Chicago* 337 US 1 (1949)). To what extent does English law protect 'hate speech'?

19.6   Frank, the leader of the Tactical Voting Action Group (TAG), organises a meeting in a church hall to which members of the public are invited by ticket only. He also invites a television crew. At the meeting Frank makes a speech urging the audience to vote for 'any party that will keep the Tories out'. Among the audience are members of the League of Gentlemen, an extreme right-wing organisation. They constantly interrupt Frank's speech and call upon the audience to 'keep England for the English'. Joe, a policeman, hearing the commotion, enters the hall despite the protests of the doorman and orders the television crew to leave. They refuse to do so and Joe arrests them for obstruction. Joe also arrests Frank, informing him that he is to be charged with 'breach of the peace'. Discuss what offences have been committed, if any, and by whom.

19.7   Newcottage University Genetics Society proposes to hold a lecture on university premises addressed by Professor Plumb, a well-known South African geneticist. The Society announces that Professor Plumb's paper will argue that certain ethnic groups have an inherited propensity to cannibalism. A large contingent of the ethnic group in question are currently students at Newcottage and propose to disrupt the lecture. Advise the university and the local police as to whether they can prevent the lecture from taking place and as to what offences will be involved if it does take place.

19.8   Animal rights protesters are holding a continuous vigil outside Tynbury docks. They threaten to prevent any vehicle carrying live animals from entering the docks. The local chief constable announces on television that his force has insufficient resources to police the docks and that any animal rights protester who approaches within one mile of the docks will be arrested. Discuss the legal implications of this announcement.

19.9   The *Daily Gleaner* has agreed to publish the memoirs of Sir Arthur Loudmouth, a recently retired senior judge now living in the USA. It announces that the memoirs include intimate details of Sir Arthur's sex life and also of discussions between Sir Arthur and senior politicians about female appointments to the judicial bench. The media are eager to discuss the memoirs. Advise the British government what steps, if any, it can take to suppress the publication and discussion of Sir Arthur's memoirs.

19.10   The *Daily Rag* has prepared an article based upon interviews with a civil servant which accuses government ministers of taking bribes from city institutions. One of the ministers serves a writ for libel upon the publishers of the *Rag*. The minister requests the court to order the *Rag* to disclose the name of its informant, and also seeks an injunction preventing publication of the article on the ground that it will prejudice his proposed legal action. Advise the *Rag*.

20 Freedom of Expression and Competing Private Interests

20.1 Introduction

We saw in the previous chapter that judicial decisions are having a noticeable effect on areas concerned with public order and the criminal law. In this chapter we examine two areas of private law, namely the law of defamation (which protects reputation) and the law of confidence (which protects confidences reposed in others). In each of these areas judges have made decisions that assume that the Human Rights Act has indirect horizontal effect (above p. 442). In the course of this discussion, we also examine the relationship between Art. 10 of the ECHR and Art. 8, which establishes a qualified right to privacy. Now that further effect has to be given to this latter right in domestic law, the judiciary are able to develop private law as a means by which to protect privacy-related interests.

The main private interests with which freedom expression is likely to clash are the interests in reputation, the interests in confidentiality and the interest in personal privacy. While distinct interests are protected by the law relating respectively to defamation, confidentiality and privacy, each of these bodies of law can be regarded as affording protection to human dignity. This is because attacks on reputation, breaches of confidence, and invasions of privacy evince a lack of respect for those who suffer them. (See *Reynolds* v. *Times Newspapers Ltd* (2001), p. 201, per Lord Nicholls (on '[r]eputation [as] an integral and important part of the dignity of the individual').) To the extent that the law protects the various interests noted above, it does so by placing restrictions on expressive activity. This being so, the right to freedom of expression stands in an uneasy relationship with our interests in reputation, confidentiality and privacy. One way of thinking of the relationship between, for example, freedom of expression and the law of defamation is in zero-sum terms. To the extent that we protect freedom of expression, we reduce the level of protection given to reputational interests and vice versa (Scruton, 1982, p. 498). This sort of analysis is, for example, helpful vis-à-vis issues like the proper scope of a defence in the law of defamation. To broaden the defence is *simultaneously* to give greater protection to freedom of expression and to reduce the protection given to reputation. But this zero-sum view does not capture the full complexity of the areas of law under discussion. For both a good reputation and freedom of expression serve to secure the personal autonomy of individuals. Those who are well regarded are, other things being equal, more likely than those with a tarnished reputation to enjoy access to a range of valuable options wide enough to make personal autonomy a possibility. And the right to freedom of expression provides protection against arbitrary interference on the part of the state, groups and individuals and thus works to secure autonomy. (See Raz, 1996, pp. 373–8 on access to valuable options and freedom from arbitrary interference as necessary conditions of autonomy.)

Both freedom of expression and reputation are, of course, widely regarded as valuable. Hence, those who have the task of accommodating them within the law must make agonising and politically controversial choices. The same point can, of course, be made, *mutatis mutandis*, regarding the relationship between, on the one hand, freedom of expression and, on the other, the law concerning confidentiality and invasion of privacy.

20.2   Defamation

20.2.1   Cause of action

In order successfully to mount a defamation claim, a claimant must prove that the relevant material is (i) defamatory, (ii) has been published and (iii) refers to him or her (Markesinis and Deakin, 1999, pp. 606–21). To satisfy the first of these conditions, a claimant must show that the relevant published material falls within one of the definitions of defamation that have been elaborated by the judiciary at common law. Three such definitions typically feature in accounts of this area of the law. According to these definitions, material can be categorised as defamatory if it:

  (i) reflects on the claimant's reputation so as to lower him or her in the estimation of right-thinking members of society generally (*Sim* v. *Stretch* (1936)); or

 (ii) would tend to cause the claimant to be shunned or avoided (*Youssoupoff* v. *Metro-Goldwyn-Mayer Pictures Ltd* (1934)); or

(iii) would bring the claimant into ridicule or contempt (*Dunlop Rubber Co. Ltd* v. *Dunlop* (1921)).

Defamatory publications are identified by the law as taking one of two forms: namely, libel and slander (Markesinis and Deakin, 1999, pp. 604–6). Material is libellous if it is published in a permanent form: e.g., writing. It is slanderous if it takes a less than permanent form: e.g., the spoken word. While protecting reputation, defamation law also affords a significant measure of protection to freedom of expression. To this end, both the judiciary and more recently Parliament have established a range of defences that may afford defendants with means by which to escape the imposition of liability.

20.2.2 Defences

Prominent among the defences that can be pleaded by defendants in this area of the law are the following:

(i) *Truth* (or justification): a defendant can escape liability by proving the truth of the statements that he or she has made. This defence can (subject to one exception) be pleaded even in circumstances where a defendant has been actuated by malice (i.e., spite or ill-will). (The relevant exception concerns truthful, but malicious, statements vis-à-vis those who have 'spent' convictions. See the Rehabilitation of Offenders Act 1974, s. 8.)

(ii) *Absolute privilege*: liability for defamation cannot be imposed in respect of expressive activity in the course of:
   (a) Parliamentary proceedings (see the Bill of Rights 1688 and *Ex parte Wason* (1869));
   (b) judicial proceedings (*Dawkins* v. *Lord Rokeby* (1875));
   (c) official communications (as between, for example, ministers of the Crown (*Chatterton* v. *Secretary of State for India* (1895)).

(iii) *Qualified privilege*: this defence can be successfully pleaded in circumstances where a defendant, who honestly believes what he or she says to be true, can (notwithstanding the factual falsity of his or her statement(s)) meet the following two requirements (which are set out in *Adam* v. *Ward* (1917), p. 334, per Lord Atkinson and *Reynolds* v. *Times Newspapers Ltd* (2001), pp. 194–5 and p. 200, per Lord Nicholls):
   (a) the defendant has an interest or a duty (legal, social, or moral) to communicate the relevant material to another or others;
   (b) the recipient of the material must have a corresponding interest or duty to receive it.
      The rationale for making this defence available (in circumstances where the above requirements can be met) has long been

said to be 'the common convenience and welfare of society' (*Toogood* v. *Spyring* (1834), p. 193, per Parke B and *Davies* v. *Snead* (1870), p. 611, per Blackburn J).

(iv) *Fair comment*: this defence protects honest expressions of opinion on matters of public interest. In cases in which the fair comment defence has been invoked, it is common to find judges identifying it as a bulwark of free expression (see, for example, *Slim* v. *Daily Telegraph Ltd* (1968), p. 170, per Lord Denning MR). While fair comment protects expressions of opinion, defendants have to establish that their views were based on a substratum of fact that was true at the time of publication (*Cohen* v. *Daily Telegraph Ltd* (1968)). This defence has been identified as protecting comment on the behaviour of public institutions and officials, the behaviour of public figures, and items submitted for public criticism (including books, public exhibitions and theatrical performances). As with qualified privilege, a plea of fair comment can be defeated by a showing that the defendant was actuated by malice.

20.2.3   Two further protections for freedom of expression

Just as the defences described above are supposed to protect freedom of expression, so too are two further features of the law. First, the institution of the jury and, secondly, the limited availability of the remedy of an injuction. Defamation actions (which are heard in the High Court) are usually tried with a jury. Juries are widely employed in this context in that they are seen as providing a basic guarantee of free speech (see Fox's Libel Act 1792). But defamation law's commitment to the jury is qualified. Relevant in this connection is *Grobbelaar* v. *News Group Newspapers Ltd* (2001). In this case, the Court of Appeal took the [apparently] ground-breaking step of overturning a jury's findings of fact on the ground that they were perverse and unreasonable.

The judiciary have long exhibited, in the defamation context, considerable reluctance to grant the remedy of an injunction This is because they fear introducing, vis-à-vis both threatened and repeated expression, controls amounting to censorship. Hence, this remedy will not be granted unless the plaintiff can satisfy a number of exacting conditions. He or she will, for example, have to show that there is no real ground for supposing that the defendant may avoid liability by pleading the defences of truth, privilege or fair comment (*Bonnard* v. *Perryman* (1891)). Further, judges are particularly grudging in their readiness to grant interim (or interlocutory) injunctions (ibid.). Such injunctions are only granted where (i) a court is satisfied that publication will result in immediate and irreparable injury and where (ii) damages would not provide an adequate remedy (see *Monson* v. *Tussauds Ltd* (1894)). The position on injunctive relief staked out by the judiciary at common law has been reinforced by s. 12 of the Human Rights Act (see above p. xxx). This section applies 'if a court is considering whether to grant relief which, if granted, might effect the exercise of the Convention right to freedom of expression' (s. 12 (1)). Moreover, courts are required to have 'particular regard to the importance of the Convention right to freedom of expression' (s. 12 (4)). These features of the Human Rights Act were the upshot of successful press lobbying, the aim of which was to ensure wide press freedom. See Phillipson and Fenwick (2000), p. 670 and p. 674.

The various features of the law detailed above bespeak an ongoing effort to establish a defensible accommodation of the reputational and expressive interests that feature in this area of the law. This effort has long been described as involving both judges and legislators in seeking to establish 'a proper balance' between the two sets of interests (Franks, 1975, para. 19). The search for balance can be expected to intensify with the incorporation of European Convention rights. This is because the European Court of Human Rights has repeatedly emphasised the importance of establishing a 'fair balance' between these rights and countervailing concerns (see, for example, *Fayed* v. *UK* (1994), para. 65).

In recent years, three features of defamation law have been modified by the judiciary with a view to establishing such a balance. They are examined below.

20.2.4   Local authorities, political parties and defamation law

(a) *Local authorities (and government departments)*
Local authorities cannot maintain actions in defamation. But as recently as the early 1990s, such bodies could sue in defamation in order to vindicate their 'governing reputation'. The acceptability of such claims had been confirmed in *Bognor Regis UDC* v. *Campion* (1972). In this case, the defendant was a ratepayer who had circulated a pamphlet strongly critical of Bognor Regis Urban District Council. Browne J held that an action in defamation could lie and the plaintiff local authority was awarded both compensation and costs. Two decades later, the *Campion* decision was overruled by the House of Lords in *Derbyshire County Council* v. *Times Newspapers Ltd* (1993).

In the *Derbyshire* case, the Council sued following the publication in *The Sunday Times* of an allegation of impropriety vis-à-vis the management of pension funds. While the trial judge held that the Council could sue in defamation, both a unanimous Court of Appeal and the House of Lords held that it could not. In the House, Lord Keith explained their Lordships' decision by reference to the aim of ensuring that defamation law did not inhibit criticism of local authorities. In this connection, he stated that: '[i]t is of the *highest public importance* that a democratically elected body ... should be open to *uninhibited public criticism*' (p. 1017 (emphasis added)). Hence, the law could not be allowed to exert on expressive activity what Lord Keith (following US law (discussed below)) characterised as a 'chilling effect'. Such an effect manifests itself in circumstances where liability rules encourage writers and other commentators to censor themselves rather than risk the (potentially negative) consequences of litigation. (On 'chilling effects', see Gibbons, 1996, p. 609 and Wright, 2001, p. 161 (and materials cited therein)) Further, while the House of Lords (like the Court of Appeal) decided to overrule *Campion*, it did not (unlike the Appeal Court) base its decision on the ECHR. Rather, the House found support for its decision in 'the common law of England'. Lord Keith did, however, conclude that English common law was 'consistent' with the ECHR's requirements.

The importance attached by Lord Keith in *Derbyshire* to 'uninhibited public criticism' of local authorities suggests a strong commitment to the end of promoting democratic discourse. So too does a further feature of his speech: namely, his stating (in an *obiter dictum*) that the proposition of law he and his colleagues were enunciating applied to central government departments. But two other features of the House's decision in *Derbyshire* expose their Lordships to the criticism that their commitment to freedom of expression is rather half-hearted. First, the House held that councils can maintain actions in the tort of injurious falsehood (which provides a remedy vis-à-vis false statements that are made maliciously and prove to be harmful). Secondly, Lord Keith indicated (*obiter*) that *individual* public officials can sue in defamation on the same basis as private individuals.

Lord Keith prayed in aid two US authorities: namely, *City of Chicago* v. *Tribune Co.* (1923) and *New York Times* v. *Sullivan* (1964). In the first of these cases, the Supreme Court of Illinois held that governmental bodies could not, when subjected to political criticism, respond by advancing claims in defamation or injurious falsehood. The effect of, and rationale for, this decision were summed up by Thompson CJ of the Illinois Supreme Court in robust terms: '[E]very citizen has the right to criticise an inefficient or corrupt government without fear of civil ... prosecution. This *absolute* privilege is founded on the principle that it is *advantageous for the public* that the citizen should not be *in any way* fettered in his statements' (pp. 606–7 (emphasis added)). This absolute privilege was, of course, partially adopted by the House of Lords in *Derbyshire County Council*. While it does not, in the UK, extend to injurious falsehood, it does apply to defamation.

In the second of the US cases cited by Lord Keith, the First Amendment to the American constitution was identified as limiting the range of circumstances in which public officials could successfully sue in defamation. The Supreme Court held that such actions could only succeed where the plaintiff could prove that the defendant had acted with 'actual malice'. By 'actual malice' the Court meant either knowledge that the statement made was false or reckless disregard as to whether it was true or not (Tribe, 1988, p. 864). The Supreme Court saw the introduction of this requirement into the law as a means by which to forestall the danger of a 'chilling effect' being exerted on politically significant expression. This was because the 'actual malice' rule relieved defendants of the need to prove the truth of their statements in order to avoid the imposition of liability. The relationship between the innovation made in *Sullivan* and the aim of protecting politically significant expression from legal sanction was emphasised in the opinion of Brennan J. He characterised the actual malice rule as a means by which to protect 'citizen critics' from the operation of defamation law. Moreover, he saw the rule as giving effect to '[a] profound national commitment to the principle that debate on public issues should be uninhibited, robust, and wide-open'.

The use made by the House of Lords in the *Derbyshire* case of the US authorities described above has attracted criticism. In following the *Chicago* case, by introducing into defamation law an absolute privilege vis-à-vis criticism of local authorities, *Derbyshire* has been characterised as overly protective of free speech interests. This is because 'it . . . gives *carte blanche* to an opposition party or the . . . press *knowingly* to publish the most *flagrant lies* in an attempt – *by deceit* – to persuade voters not to support the governing party' (Loveland, 1998, p. 634 (emphasis added)); cf. *Gertz* v. *Robert Welch* (1974), p. 340, per Powell J: '[t]here is no constitutional value in false statements of fact'). The House of Lords has also been criticised for failing to follow the US Supreme Court's lead in the *New York Times* case by introducing the actual malice rule into UK defamation law (Loveland, 1998, p. 634). Introduction of this rule would have had at least three (closely related) virtues. First, it would have meant that public officials would find it harder than private individuals to advance defamation claims.

Hence, it would (as the Supreme Court recognised in *Sullivan*) have worked to protect politically significant expression. Secondly, the House would have insulated itself against the criticism that, in allowing public officials to sue on the same basis as private individuals, its commitment to freedom of expression is half-hearted. Thirdly, it would have brought the law of defamation into closer alignment with the jurisprudence of the European Court of Human Rights. This is because the European Court has read Art. 10 of the ECHR as requiring a tripartite set of distinctions in the defamation law of signatory states (*Lingens* v. *Austria* (1986); *Castells* v. *Spain* (1992); *Oberschlick* v. *Austria* (1991)). According to the European Court, political figures should receive less protection from defamation law than private individuals. Further, governmental bodies (and political parties) should receive even less protection from the law than political figures. This tripartite set of distinctions reflects the European Court of Human Rights' commitment to the view that political expression merits particularly strong protection (see Wright, 2001, p. 150). But this distinction does not, of course, feature in the House's decision in the *Derbyshire* case. Rather, their Lordships draw a bipartite distinction: no protection for councils, etc., while private individuals and public officials enjoy the same level of protection.

(b) *Political parties*

The proposition of law established by the House of Lords in the *Derbyshire County Council* case extends, as we have noted, both to local authorities and (*per* Lord Keith) to central government departments. This proposition has subsequently been extended to political parties. This extension in the proposition's scope was made in *Goldsmith* v. *Bhoyrul* (1997). This case concerned a newspaper article that appeared in *Sunday Business*. In the article it was stated that the plaintiff's political party was preparing, due to unpopularity, to withdraw many of its candidates from the 1997 General Election so as to avoid humiliation at the polls. At trial, Buckley J held that political parties could not maintain defamation claims. Further (and in line with the House's decision in *Derbyshire*), he justified his decision by reference to the public interest in uninhibited expression concerning matters of political significance. Moreover, in one other respect, Buckley J's decision is strongly reminiscent of that reached by the House in the *Derbyshire* case. He stated that, while political parties cannot bring defamation claims, 'any individual candidate, official or other person connected with the party who was sufficiently identified could sue' (p. 271). He thus established a distinction between parties (unprotected by defamation law) and individual candidates for office, etc., who can bring claims on the same basis as private individuals. For the reasons given above vis-à-vis the *Derbyshire* case, a further distinction between candidates, etc., and private individuals will have to be drawn to bring defamation law into line with the European Court's jurisprudence.

While the *Derbyshire* and *Bhoyrul* cases might be taken as suggesting judicial insensitivity to the requirements of the ECHR, another group of cases create a contrary impression. They concern the law relating to damages for defamation, and it is to an examination of them that we turn.

20.2.5   Defamation law and damages

(a) *Compensatory damages*
Damages are the principal remedy for defamation (Fleming, 1998, p. 657). Plaintiffs are entitled to damages for both reputational and economic injury (e.g., loss of employment). Ceilings have never been placed, either at common law or by statute, on the quantum of damages that can be recovered in defamation actions (Loveland, 1996, p. 193). Juries determine the sum of compensation to be awarded, and, until recently, they were not furnished with clear guidance as to the appropriate sum to award. This sometimes led to awards of compensation being made that were excessive (Jones, 1998, pp. 495–6). Such awards are open to objection on at least two grounds. First, they are a disproportionate response to a defendant's wrongdoing and, hence, can be regarded as unjust. Secondly, the prospect of having to pay such a sum may exert a powerful 'chilling effect' on expressive activity.

Objections such as the two noted above have prompted change in the law. In the 1960s, the Court of Appeal conferred on itself the power to order a new trial when it considered a jury's compensation award so large as to be 'divorced from reality' (*McCarey* v. *Associated Newspapers Ltd* (1964)). But juries continued to award very large sums of compensation to plaintiffs. Hence, Parliament addressed itself to this matter in the Courts and Legal Services Act 1990. Under s. 8 of this Act, the Court of Appeal has the power, where a jury has awarded 'excessive' compensation, to substitute a lower sum (instead of ordering a new trial). This power was first exercised by the Appeal Court in *Rantzen* v. *Mirror Group Newspapers* (1993). In this case, the Court substituted an award of £110,000 for the jury's award of £250,000. While the Court of Appeal based its decision on the Act of 1990, it also justified it by reference to Art. 10 of the ECHR. Neill LJ stated that the Convention required that damages in cases such as

Rantzen should not exceed the level 'necessary to compensate the plaintiff and re-establish his reputation' (p. 994). The Court of Appeal thus staked out a position that is in line with Art. 41 of the European Convnetion. Article 41 identifies 'just satisifaction' as the criterion by reference to which damages awards should be assessed (see Wright, 2001, pp. 39–42).

At the time of the Court of Appeal's decision in *Rantzen*, the ECHR was not, of course, a feature of domestic law. Hence, one commentator has described that decision as an 'anticipatory invocation' of the Convention (Loveland, 1996, p. 193). Further, the same commentator has identified the *Rantzen* decision as having been 'vindicated' by the later decision of the European Court of Human Rights in *Tolstoy Miloslavsky* v. *UK* (1995) (ibid.). This case concerned a pamphlet in which Lord Abingdon was accused of having perpetrated war crimes. In the domestic courts, the pamphlet was held to be defamatory and Lord Abingdon was awarded £1.5 million. Thereafter, Tolstoy Miloslavsky appealed to the European Human Rights Court. It held that the compensation sum awarded against him was a violation of his right to freedom of expression as guaranteed by Art. 10 of the ECHR. This was because the compensation recovered was in excess of the amount necessary in order to re-establish Lord Abingdon's reputation.

More recently, the Court of Appeal has staked out a position vis-à-vis compensation for defamation that is in line with the stance of the European Court in *Tolstoy Miloslavsky*. In *John* v. *Mirror Group Newspapers Ltd* (1996), the Court of Appeal stated that judges could, in defamation actions, draw a jury's attention to the level of awards made in personal injury cases (p. 54, *per* Lord Bingham MR). The Court took this step with a view to curbing the impulse among jurors to make excessive awards. In this connection, the Master of the Rolls stated that '[a]ny legal process should yield a successful plaintiff *appropriate compensation*, that is, compensation that is neither too much nor too little' (p. 51 (emphasis added); see also p. 49). While this statement coheres with the decision reached by the European Court in *Tolstoy Miloslavsky*, the Appeal Court based its decision not on the ECHR but, rather, on the common law (p. 58, *per* Lord Bingham). The Court did, however, identify the Convention as 'reinforcing and buttressing' its decision (p. 58, *per* Lord Bingham). Moreover, the Court found further support for the position it was staking out in the Australian High Court's decision in *Carson* v. *John Fairfax and Sons Ltd* (1993), in which it was held that juries in defamation cases could have their attention drawn to conventional awards for personal injuries.

(b) *Exemplary damages*

In the *John* case, the Court of Appeal also restricted the range of circumstances in which a plaintiff can recover exemplary or punitive damages. The purpose of such awards is, as their name suggests, to punish wrongdoers (p. 56, *per* Lord Bingham (and authority cited therein); see also Cane, 1997, pp. 114–15). The Court stated that awards of this sort could only be recovered where the plaintiff offers 'clear' proof of the two following things (p. 58, *per* Lord Bingham). First, the defendant knowingly or recklessly published untruths. Secondly, the defendant proceeded to publish the relevant untruths having cynically calculated that the profit accruing from the publication would be likely to exceed any damages award made against him or her. As with the position it adopted vis-à-vis compensatory damages, the Court buttressed its decision by reference to the ECHR. Article 10, Lord Bingham noted, requires that '[f]reedom of expression should not be restricted by awards of exemplary damages save to the extent shown to be *strictly necessary* for the protection of reputations' (ibid. (emphasis added)).

The above decisions reveal considerable judicial sensitivity to the requirements of the ECHR. So too does the House of Lords' recent decision in *Reynolds* v. *Times Newspapers Ltd* (2001), which concerned, *inter alia*, the defence of qualified privilege. In *Reynolds*, Lord Steyn stated that, 'in considering the issues before the House and the development of English law, the House *can and should* act on the *reality* that the Human Rights Act 1998 will soon be in force' (pp. 207–8; see also Wright, 2001, p. 24). Before examining the House's decision in *Reynolds*, some general comments must be made on the defence of qualified privilege.

20.2.6 Qualified privilege

In our earlier discussion of qualified privilege, we noted that in order to plead this defence successfully defendants must be able to prove (a) that they had an interest or duty (legal, social or moral) to communicate with another (or others) and (b) that the recipient(s) of the material had a corresponding interest or duty to receive it ((a) and (b) as here described correspond to the two conditions described above). In circumstances where (a) and (b) can be proved, judges typically characterise the defendant and the person(s) with whom he or she has communicated as standing in a relationship of 'reciprocity' (see, for example, *Adam* v. *Ward* (1917), p. 334, *per* Lord Atkinson).

One subset of defendants who have experienced difficulty in establishing reciprocity are newspapers vis-à-vis material communicated to the public at large. The judiciary have long set their face against the acceptance of a qualified privilege plea in such circumstances. This is because they have been of the view that to accept such a plea would be to bestow on newspapers and other media organs an open-ended 'public interest' defence (see Jones, 2000, p. 510). The judicial reluctance to accept such a defence can be illustrated by reference to *Blackshaw* v. *Lord* (1983). In this case, the Court of Appeal conceded that, in some circumstances, communication to the general public *may* be in the public interest. But this concession was accompanied by a further observation. Statements did not attract the protection of qualified privilege simply because they concerned 'a matter of public interest believed by the publisher to be true in relation to which he has exercised reasonable care' (p. 327, *per* Stephenson LJ; see also Faulks, 1975, paras 211–15).

In *Reynolds* v. *Times Newspapers Ltd* (2001), the House of Lords held that qualified privilege can, in some circumstances, be pleaded where political material is disseminated to the general public. Their Lordships were, however, at pains to point out that such material would not fall within an extended (or, as they termed it, 'generic') qualified privilege defence (p. 200 and p. 204, *per* Lord Nicholls). Rather, it would fall within the defence as described by Lord Atkinson in *Adam* v. *Ward* (1917). This being so, their Lordships rejected the gloss placed on the qualified privilege defence by Lord Bingham LCJ when *Reynolds* (1998) was before the Court of Appeal. In the Appeal Court, the Lord Chief Justice stated that a condition over and above the two in *Adam* would have to be satisfied in order to plead qualified privilege in the circumstances under discussion. This condition was what Lord Bingham termed 'the circumstantial test' (p. 909). To satisfy this test, defendants were required to show that 'the nature, status and source of the material and all the circumstances of its publication' were such that the publication should 'in the public interest' be protected (p. 912). The circumstantial test was rejected by the House. But their Lordships (rather equivocally) identified 'circumstances' as a highly relevant consideration when determining whether qualified privilege could be successfully pleaded. In this connection, Lord Nicholls made the following observation: '[th]rough the cases runs the strain that, when determining whether the public at large had a right to know the particular information, *the court has regard to all the circumstances. The Court is concerned to assess whether the information was of sufficient value to the public that, in the public interest, it should be protected by the privilege in the absence of malice' (p. 195 (emphasis added)). To this his Lordship added a (non-exhaustive) list of considerations relevant to the question whether the qualified privilege defence should be available: viz: (i) the seriousness of the allegation(s); (ii) the nature of the information, and the extent to which the matter is a matter of public concern; (iii) the source of the information; (iv) the steps taken to verify the information; (v) the status of the information; (vi) the urgency of the matter; (vii) whether comment was sought from the claimant; (viii) whether the relevant publication contained the gist of the claimant's side of the story; (ix) the tone of the article; and (x) the circumstances of the publication (p. 205).

The position staked out by the House in *Reynolds* on the applicability of the qualified privilege defence to politically significant material is open to at least two criticisms. First, in circumstances where judges draw on the considerations listed by Lord Nicholls, they will (where newspaper defendants are concerned) be defining standards of good journalistic practice. It is far from obvious that this is a task that they are well equipped to undertake. Secondly, the House's decision in *Reynolds* can be expected to engender uncertainty among newspaper editors. This is because Lord Nicholls' (non-exhaustive) list of relevant circumstances embraces a wide range of factors. Moreover, the weight or significance that should properly be attached to factors such as those enumerated by his Lordship is not specified with any degree of precision (see p. 205). One way of avoiding such uncertainty and the chilling effects it may generate might be to adopt the approach of the New Zealand courts on the question whether politically significant material should enjoy qualified privilege. In *Lange* v. *Atkinson and Consolidated Press NZ Ltd* (1998), the New Zealand Court of Appeal held that defendants can plead qualified privilege *vis-à-vis* politically significant material communicated to the public. As well as expanding the qualified privilege defence, the Court also sought to forestall the danger of chilling effects. To this end, it stated that plaintiffs must, in order to defeat a plea of qualified privilege, prove that the defendant lacked an honest belief in the truth of his or her statements. Further, the New Zealand Court found support for the position it adopted in Art. 10 of the ECHR. (The New Zealand Court of Appeal's decision in *Lange* was subsequently appealed to the Privy Council. The Privy Council remitted the case to New Zealand for rehearing, thus affording the New Zealand Appeal Court the opportunity to consider the House of Lords' decision in *Reynolds* (2000). While prepared to 'amplify' its earlier decision, the New Zealand Appeal Court declined to follow the House's approach in *Reynolds* (2000). One of the reasons it gave for this decision was the greater readiness of the New Zealand press, as compared to the British press, to behave responsibly (p. 398).)

There are reasons for thinking that at least some of the 10 considerations listed by Lord Nicholls could have relevance to the public interest defence as it features in the action for breach of confidence. Before explaining why this may be so, something must be said about breach of confidence and invasion of privacy.

20.3   Breach of Confidence

The cause of action for breach of confidence – which has been fashioned by the judiciary – serves to protect secrets and personal information (Gurry, 1984, pp. 6–21). A plaintiff can secure a remedy (damages and/or injunctive relief) for breaches of confidence in circumstances where the following three conditions (which were approved by the House of Lords in *Attorney-General* v. *Guardian Newspapers (No. 2)* (1990)) can be satisfied:

1. The information is confidential in character: i.e., it must not be something that is public property or public knowledge.
2. The information must have been imparted in circumstances imposing an obligation of confidence: e.g., it was imparted (either explicitly or implicitly) for a limited purpose.
3. Thirdly, there must be an unauthorised use of the relevant information by the confidant: e.g., use of the information by the confidant for a purpose other than that for which it was imparted.

While protecting secrets and confidences, the law of confidentiality also affords protection to the expression-related interests of, *inter alia*, the press (in disclosure of information) and the public (in the free flow of information) (see Toulson and Phipps, 1996, Ch. 15). In circumstances where the three requirements described above have been satisfied, defendants may be able to avoid the imposition of liability by establishing that disclosure of the relevant material was in the public interest (Feldman, 1993, p. 438, *et seq.*). In order to invoke this defence successfully, defendants must establish that the public interest served by disclosing the relevant information outweighs the interest in preserving confidentiality (*Riddick* v. *Thames Board Mills Ltd* (1977)).

In recent years, the judiciary have broadened the range of circumstances in which liability for breach of confidence can arise. Prior to the case of *Stephens* v. *Avery* (1988), it had been thought that an obligation of confidence could only arise where there had been a pre-existing relationship between plaintiff and defendant. The decision in *Stephens* has, however, been read as supporting the proposition that such a relationship does not have to be established in order to secure relief. Plaintiffs can succeed in a confidentiality claim simply by establishing that the relevant information was acquired in circumstances where a reasonable person would have realised that it was confidential. This is a test that can be used to establish breaches of confidence in a wider range of circumstances than was the case when a pre-existing relationship had to be established. This point can be illustrated by reference to *HRH Princess of Wales* v. *MGN Newspapers Ltd and Others* (1993). In this case, the defendants had no pre-existing relationship with the plaintiff. Nonetheless, the information that they acquired concerning her (i.e., photographs of the plaintiff exercising in a semi-public gymnasium) was held to be subject to a duty of confidentiality. This was because it would have been obvious to a reasonable person that the plaintiff did not wish the information to be obtained.

The developments described above bespeak a growing judicial readiness to protect confidences and secrets. Hence, a basis exists for suggesting that the judiciary may have to modify the public interest defence described above in order to ensure that the competing interest in freedom of expression is adequately protected.

20.4 Invasion of Privacy

Prior to the incorporation of the ECHR, no legal ground existed for asserting an invasion of privacy claim (*Malone* v. *Metropolitan Police Commissioner (No. 2)* (1979); *Kaye* v. *Robertson* (1991)). (Some privacy-related interests have, however, been protected by, *inter alia*, the law of confidentiality and a number of causes of action in the law of tort, including trespass to land, private nuisance, and injurious falsehood.) A basis upon which to bring invasion of privacy claims is now, however, provided by Art. 8 of the ECHR. It provides, in Art. 8 (1), that '[e]veryone has the right to respect for his private and family life, his home and correspondence'. Further, Art. 8 (2) identifies a range of considerations that serve the public interest and that can be invoked as a basis upon which to limit or override the right enunciated in Art. 8 (1). They include public safety, the prevention of disorder or crime, the protection of health or morals, and the protection of the rights and freedoms of others. Numbered among these rights is freedom of expression (which protects, *inter alia*, press freedom and the associated public interest in the free flow of information). Article 8 (2) also specifies that '[t]here shall be no interference by a public authority with the exercise of [the right enunciated in Art. 8 (1)], except as is in accordance with the law and *necessary* in a democratic society' (emphasis added).

With a view to determining how effect might be given to the Art. 8 right in this country, members of the judiciary have sought guidance from the law of a number of other jurisdictions (see, for example, Bingham, 1998, where German law is discussed). One such jurisdiction is the United States of America. In the USA, the law of tort has been used to fashion a cause of action for invasion of privacy. On one very influential account of US law, tortious invasions of privacy are identified as taking four distinct forms (Prosser, 1960; cf. Bloustein, 1964). They are:

(i) *Intrusion*: e.g., incursions into a person's private sphere that outrages his or her sense of modesty and security (Fleming, 1998, p. 666).

(ii) *Appropriation of personality*: e.g., the unauthorised use of a person's name or picture in aid of advertising or other commercial purposes (Fleming, 1998, p. 668).

(iii) *Disclosure of private facts*: e.g., disclosure by the media of disreputable incidents from the depths of a person's past (Fleming, 1998, p. 670).

(iv) *False light invasion of privacy*: e.g., use of a person's picture to illustrate an article concerned with criminal activity with which he or she has no connection (Prosser and Keeton, 1994, pp. 863–6).

In the account of US law summarised above, it is frankly acknowledged that invasion of privacy can take a variety of forms. This acknowledgement provides a basis for suggesting that those whose task it is to define 'invasion of privacy' may find themselves faced with intractable difficulties. Some support for this view can be found in an essay by David Feldman, in which it is stated that '[*a*]*ny attempt* to identify a single interest at the core of privacy is *doomed to failure*' (Birks, ed., 1997, p. 21 (emphasis added)).

The difficulty pointed up by Feldman notwithstanding, judges are (with the coming into force of the Human Rights Act) exhibiting a readiness to develop private law actions relating to invasions of privacy. The Act's impact can be illustrated by reference to two recent cases: *Douglas and Zeta-Jones* v. *Hello! Ltd* (2001) and *Thompson and Venables* v. *News Group Newspapers Ltd* (2001). In *Douglas*, Michael

Douglas and Catherine Zeta-Jones sold the exclusive rights to publish their wedding photographs to *OK!* magazine. Thereafter, *Hello!* magazine obtained unofficial photographs of the wedding. The claimants sought to restrain publication of these photographs. While identifying an injunction as an inappropriate remedy on the facts, the Court of Appeal stated (unanimously) that English law should now, in the light of Art. 8, protect privacy. Moreover, both Keene and Sedley LJJ recognised that private law could be developed in ways that would serve to protect the Art. 8 right to privacy. They also identified such development as being required by s. 6 of the Human Rights Act. This provision, of course, places courts and other 'public authorities' under a duty to act compatibly with Convention rights. Of the two judges Keene LJ staked out the less adventurous position. He identified the existing action for breach of confidence as affording a means by which to protect the Art. 8 right. He was, however, unsure as to '[w]hether this duty extends to creating a new cause of action'. Sedley LJ, by contrast, entertained the possibility that a new cause of action could be fashioned in order to protect at least some privacy-related interests unprotected by existing causes of action. He characterised such an 'innovation' as 'precisely the kind of incremental change for which the [Human Rights] Act is designed'. Such a process of case-by-case change would not, on his analysis, undermine the 'measure of certainty that is necessary to all law'. Sedley LJ also discussed the relevance of s. 12 of the Human Rights Act to invasion of privacy claims. This section (as already noted) governs the issuing of remedies and requires courts to have particular regard to freedom of expression. (See s. 12, ss (3) and (4).) Section 12 was relevant to *Douglas* since the claimants were seeking injunctive relief. Moreover, both s. 12 and s. 6 were identified by Sedley LJ as supporting the conclusion that judges are now under a duty to establish a new common law cause of action for invasion of privacy. (This analysis supports the view that Convention Rights now have (indirect) horizontal effect in private law. See Hare, 2001.)

In *Thompson and Venables* v. *News Group Newspapers Ltd* (2001), the claimants (the notorious killers of James Bulger) sought an indefinite continuation of injunctions restraining the press from disclosing their (new) identities on release from custody. Since the circumstances of the case were 'exceptional', Dame Butler-Sloss granted the injunction. But she took a rather less expansive view than Sedley LJ (in *Douglas*) of private law's potential as a means by which to protect privacy. While recognising that courts are under a duty to act compatibly with Convention rights, she identified this duty as extending only to existing causes of action. Moreover, she identified both Art. 10 of the ECHR and s. 12 of the Human Rights Act as sharply circumscribing the range of circumstances in which privacy-related interests can be protected. With respect to Art. 10, she stated that it will only be necessary to grant injunctive relief where it can be 'convincingly demonstrated' that the requirements of Art. 10 (2) can be satisfied. On Dame Butler-Sloss's account, s. 12 enhances the protection given to freedom of expression and, hence, works to limit the range of circumstances in which injunctive relief will be granted. This view of the law is open to criticism on the ground that the injunction is the only effective remedy where invasion of privacy is threatened.

In both *Douglas* and *Thompson and Venables*, we encounter judges (Keene J in the former case and Dame Butler-Sloss in the latter) identifying breach of confidence as the only private law means by which to afford protection against invasions of privacy. There is, however, good reason to regard this view as unduly restrictive. The action for breach of confidence affords a means by which to address the threats posed by disclosure of information. But it does not afford a means by which to address the problems that can arise when publicity is given to information that is in the public domain. If problems of the latter sort are properly regarded as falling within the purview of Art. 8, it will be necessary to fashion a new cause of action. Support for this can be found in the writing of Wacks (1995, p. 56). He argues that breach of confidence does not deal adequately with 'the archetypal "privacy" claim because the action is largely concerned with: (a) disclosure or use rather than publicity, (b) the source rather than the nature of the information, and (c) the preservation of confidence rather than the possible harm to the plaintiff caused by the breach'.

While the action for breach of confidence is too narrow to address invasions of privacy arising from publicity, there is reason to suppose that it could produce uncertainty thus inhibiting the press. Some support for this suggestion can be found in the recent case of *A* v. *B plc and another* (2001). In this case, which conceived the liaisons of a premier league footballer, Jack J held that sexual partners owe a duty of confidentiality to one another that can be overridden only if the disclosure can be shown to be in the public interest. The difficulty here is to determine when the public interest is sufficient to displace the confidence. In *A*. v. *B*. the Court of Appeal, overruling Jack J, permitted the press to disclose the identity of the footballer. One way of addressing this problem would be for the judiciary to provide clearer guidance on the range of circumstances in which the public interest defence can be pleaded. In this connection, at least some of the considerations listed in *Reynolds* (2001) by Lord Nicholls (vis-à-vis the applicability of the qualified privilege defence in defamation) would be relevant. But even if this step were taken, uncertainty would remain a problem for the reasons given earlier.

Guidance as to how at least some of the chilling effects on free expression contemplated above might be reduced, if not eliminated, can be found in US Supreme Court's decision in *Time Inc.* v. *Hill* (1967). In this case, the defendant published a description of a new play adapted from a novel that fictionalised the experiences of the plaintiff and his family while being held hostage in their home by a group of escaped prisoners. The plaintiffs successfully sued in the state of New York for false light invasion of privacy. In a subsequent action before the US Supreme Court, the First Amendment guarantee of freedom of expression was identified as placing a constraint on the scope of the tort of invasion of privacy. The Court stated that, in order to advance their claim successfully, the plaintiffs would have to prove actual malice. The Court's aim in taking this step was to protect expression that served the public interest by throwing light on an actual incident. In placing this constraint on the law relating to invasion of privacy, the Court applied, in a new context, the approach it adopted to defamation law in *New York Times* v. *Sullivan* (1964).

In *Time Inc.* v. *Hill*, we see public law (in the form of a fundamental right) being mobilised in order to place a constraint on the private law of tort. Assuming that tort law is used to elaborate the right established by Art. 8 of the ECHR, we can expect to see Art. 10 being used in much the same way as the First Amendment in *Hill*. If it is used in this way, the upshot can, for reasons given below, be expected to be tension in the law.

20.5 Tension in the Law

Defamation law prioritises reputational interests, while accommodating freedom of expression. Article 10, by contrast, prioritises freedom of expression, while accommodating, *inter alia*, reputational interests. It is this clash of priorities that gives rise to tension in this area of the law. This tension arises because a single system of law cannot simultaneously prioritise the protection of reputation *and* the protection of reputation. These priorities are uncombinable. Consequently, primacy has to be accorded either to reputation or to free expression. With the incorporation of Art. 10 into domestic law, priority will, it seems reasonable to suppose, be given to free expression rather than to reputation. Support for this view can be found in *Reynolds* v. *Times*

Newspapers Ltd (2001), where Lord Nicholls identifies freedom of expression as an appropriate 'starting point' for deliberation in defamation cases (p. 200). (See also pp. 207–8, *per* Lord Steyn.)

While Art. 10 provides a ground for prioritising expression over reputational interests, it should not be supposed that tension will be banished from the law. We attach high value both to free expression and to the maintenance of an untarnished reputation. Further, it is not obvious how we might rank bodies of law that prioritise either reputation or freedom of expression. This being so, we may be faced with options that are incommensurable. And, if this is the case, disputes between the proponents of free expression and reputation can be expected to rumble on interminably. Further, while the law does not provide a clear route out of the impasse here contemplated, it does, at least, provide a device that serves to mute the tension described above: namely, the proportionality principle.

20.6   Proportionality: a Mediating Principle

Proportionality affords a mediating principle. Such principles yield guidance on the question as to how competing interests can be accommodated in ways that afford some measure of protection to each (Mullender, 2001, pp. 181–5). Proportionality does this by specifying conditions (above, Chapter 18) that require adjudicators to take seriously and offer reasoned arguments concerning their efforts to accommodate competing interests. These reasons will, of course, provide a basis upon which to justify the decision reached both to litigants and to the broad aggregates of people whose interests are indirectly touched by legal disputes. This being so, proportionality can be regarded as affording a means by which to pursue the ideal of distributive justice: i.e., a fair allocation of benefits and burdens across society (Blackburn, 1994, p. 203). But even where competing interests are accommodated in the way here contemplated, judges will still be making controversial choices as to the circumstances in which expression-related interests should yield to reputational ones. Relevant to this point is the writing of the political philosopher, John Rawls. In his *Political Liberalism*, Rawls discusses what he terms 'burdens of judgement' (Rawls, 1993, pp. 54–8). On his account, such burdens are encountered in circumstances where a range of views can reasonably be taken vis-à-vis the significance to be attached to 'cherished values' that compete with one another. Such burdens will be encountered by judges in circumstances where they use the proportionality principle in the way contemplated above. They will have to judge whether the protection of reputational interests is generally beneficial. Likewise, they will have to judge whether limitations placed on the right to free expression are strictly necessary in order to protect reputational interests.

Burdens of judgement will also be a feature of judicial attempts to accommodate, on the one hand, expression-related interests and, on the other, confidentiality- and privacy-related interests. On some occasions these burdens are likely to be regarded as even greater than those that will arise when reputational and expression-related interests compete. This may be the case when judges find themselves having to mediate interests that are protected by fundamental rights. This would be the case where, for example, expression-related interests (protected by Art. 10(1)) and privacy-related interests (protected by a body of civil law grounded on Art. 8(1)) clash with one another. There are at least two ways of dealing with such difficulties, to which we now turn.

20.7 A Hierarchy of Rights and the Contingencies of Litigation

One way of addressing the difficulties described above would be to establish a hierarchy of Convention rights (in which, for example, freedom of expression was identified as more significant than protection from invasions of privacy). The European Convention does not establish a formal hierarchy of rights (Feldman, 1993, p. 554). But against this point must be set three considerations. First, the jurisprudence of the European Court of Human Rights identifies freedom of expression as a particularly important right (see *Handyside* v. *UK* (1976), para. 49). Secondly, s. 12 of the Human Rights Act 1998 accords (as noted above) particularly high importance to freedom of expression. Thirdly, under the influence of the Human Rights Act, senior British judges have (as already noted) begun to identify freedom of expression as the 'starting point' for deliberation in cases concerning defamation (see, for example, *Reynolds* (2001), p. 200, *per* Lord Nicholls). On this view, freedom of expression should *always* be accorded priority over countervailing private interests of the sort examined in this chapter.

However there is a problem with this view. This concerns what might be termed the contingencies of litigation. Consider a claimant who seeks a remedy against invasion of privacy. Where his or her claim rests (ultimately) on Art. 8 of the Convention, that provision becomes the starting point for judicial deliberation. In other words privacy should be protected against all but an invasion, whether by freedom of expression or by some other countervailing concern, that meets the test of proportionality. On this basis privacy is the stronger concern. Conversely where a plaintiff relies on freedom of expression, the countervailing concern raised by the defendant of privacy is weaker, since this time it is privacy that must be submitted to the proportionality test. Take for example a dispute between neighbours. A claims that freedom of expression entitles him to hold a hymn singing meeting in front of his house, B claiming that this causes undue disturbance in a quiet neighbourhood. The outcome might well be different according to whether B is seeking an injunction against A or A is suing B for assault.

Summary

20.1   Historically, the protection given, in the UK, to freedom of expression has been modest. On Dicey's account, freedom of expression had the status of a residual liberty that could be abrogated by the legislature. This state of affairs has been altered by the incorporation of the European Convention on Human Rights (ECHR), which establishes a qualified right to freedom of expression.

20.2   The right to freedom of expression enunciated in Art. 10 stands in an uneasy relationship with two bodies of private law: defamation law and the law relating to breach of confidence. The protection of reputation and confidences necessarily entails the restriction of expressive activity. Hence, the uneasy relationship mentioned above. A similarly uneasy relationship can be expected to exist between Art. 10 and civil law-based protections against invasion of privacy grounded on Art. 8 of the ECHR.

20.3   Freedom of expression can be regarded as intrinsically valuable since it is a 'constitutive' element of a just political order. Free expression can also be regarded as valuable in that it provides a means to a variety of significant ends. These ends include self-actualisation, the pursuit of truth, and the promotion of tolerance.

20.4   In recent years, a number of features of defamation law have been modified with a view to extending the protection given to freedom of expression. Local authorities, government departments and political parties can no longer maintain claims. The availability of damages (both compensatory and exemplary) has been limited. The scope of the qualified privilege defence has been extended to embrace the communication by the press to the public of politically significant material.

20.5   Public officials and politicians can bring defamation claims on the same basis as private individuals. To bring defamation law into closer alignment with the European Court of Human Rights' Article 10 jurisprudence, it will be necessary to reduce the level of reputational protection afforded to public officials and politicians.

20.6 Both the judiciary and Parliament have sought to establish a defensible balance between expression-related interests and the various interests protected by private law that have been discussed in this chapter. In, for example, the sphere of defamation law, a variety of institutional means have been employed to this end. They include, *inter alia*, the specification of a number of defences (e.g., fair comment), the use of jury trials, and a restrictive approach to the granting of injunctive relief.

20.7 Article 10 of the European Convention on Human Rights and the law of defamation law each prioritise an interest (free expression in the case of Art. 10 and reputation in the case of defamation law) that brings each into a relationship of tension with the other. This is because the respective priorities of the relevant areas of law are uncombinable.

20.8 The proportionality principle affords a means by which judges can seek to establish a defensible accommodation of expression-related and competing interests in, *inter alia*, reputation. But, in using this principle, judges will bear considerable burdens of judgement. They will have to determine when limitations on expressive activity are (a) strictly necessary in order (b) to pursue a generally beneficial goal. (Burdens of judgement are also borne by judges when applying many of the other norms discussed in this book. A prominent example is provided by the *Wednesbury* standard of unreasonableness (which features in the law relating to judicial review). See Chapter 14.)

20.9 The action for breach of confidence has been identified by members of the judiciary as affording a means by which to secure some of the privacy-related interests embraced by Art. 8 of the European Convention on Human Rights. See *Douglas* v. *Hello! Ltd* (2001) and *Thompson and Venables* v. *News Group Newspapers Ltd* (2001).

20.10 While the action for breach of confidence provides protection against disclosure of information, it does not provide protection against the adverse consequences that may from from publicity being given to information that is publicly available. This being so, the common law will have to be further elaborated in order to ensure that domestic law complies with Art. 8 of the European Convention on Human Rights.

Further Reading

D. Feldman, *Civil Liberties and Human Rights in England and Wales* (Oxford: Clarendon Press, 1993), chapters 12 and 13.

K. Greenawalt, 'Free speech justifications' (1989) 89 *Columbia LR* 119.

I. Hare, 'Vertically challenged: private parties, privacy and the Human Rights Act' (2001) 5 *European Human Rights Law Review* 526.

I. Loveland, 'The constitutionalisation of political libels in English common law?' [1998] *Public Law* 633.

G. Phillipson and H. Fenwick (2000) 'Breach of confidence as a privacy remedy in the Human Rights Act era' 63 *Modern LR* 660.

Exercises

20.1 Freedom of expression has been regarded as a residual liberty. With the incorporation of the ECHR, it now enjoys more extensive legal protection. How should this protection be characterised?

20.2 The reputational interests of public officials and politicians are protected by defamation law to an extent that does not comport with the requirements of Art. 10 of the ECHR. Discuss.

20.3 Why do the right to freedom of expression as protected by Art. 10 of the ECHR and the bodies of private law discussed in this chapter stand in a relationship of tension?

20.4 A UK statute provides that any person who publishes material that impinges on the privacy of any member of the Royal Family is guilty of an offence. Your client is a newspaper editor who wishes to challenge this provision. Advise her as to the possible courses of action available to her and as to the possible outcomes including getting the law changed. What would be the position if she published personal photographs of a member of the royal family and were charged under the statute?

20.5 Paul is the leader of the 'Sunday Welcomers' a group of Evangelical Christians that meet every Sunday afternoon at Paul's house to hold a rally that includes the extensive singing of hymns to the accompaniment of a brass band. Paul has recently moved to a house next to that occupied by Melanie who spends Sunday afternoon watching television and drinking wine. Melanie, incensed by the noise from Paul's house, turns up the volume of her television to the point where Paul complains that the hymn singing is becoming difficult to pursue. Advise Paul and Melanie as the legal position under the Human Rights Act 1998.

21 Police Powers of Arrest and Search

21.1 Introduction

The days are long gone when a police constable was viewed as little more than a citizen in uniform, having few powers peculiar to that office. Influences such as, for example, demographic changes, the increase in regulatory legislation and the developing nature of crime in an industrial and technological society, have engendered demands that special and extended powers be granted in order that the police may effectively carry out their work. Nevertheless, the policing of labour disputes and civil unrest during the 1980s, and animal rights and environmental protests in the 1990s combined with increasing revelations of miscarriages of justice and racism, have greatly tarnished the image and reputation of the profession. The discernible movement away from a consensus and reactive approach towards proactive policing, the insatiable attention of the media and the highly politicised nature of law and order, have also served to highlight concerns about civil liberties. Accordingly, a compromise is constantly being sought between the seemingly inevitable extension of police powers and the accountability of those who are to exercise them. The traditional Dicean approach, however, still remains dominant. This entails that police action is unlawful unless it is specifically justified by law. For example, if someone is detained beyond the period prescribed by law or even beyond the time specified for a review of the detention, then, from that moment, the prisoner can sue for false imprisonment (*Roberts* v. *Chief Constable of Cheshire Police* (1999)). Moreover, the Human Rights Act 1998 (which makes the European Convention of Human Rights part of English law) expressly recognises that a violation of convention rights by the police is unlawful.

As illustrated recently by the Criminal Justice and Police Act 2001, developments tend to be somewhat one-sided. Police powers have been extended but without a corresponding increase in safeguards for the suspect. The 2001 Act, for example, allows the police to impose 'on the spot' penalties for disorderly behaviour, to close licensed premises immediately as a result of drink-related offences, to confiscate alcohol from young persons and to impose child curfew schemes. Other legislative developments include, for example, wide powers to stop and search for weapons and to take DNA samples under the Criminal Justice and Public Order Act 1994; phone tapping and other forms of intrusive surveillance (Police Act 1997); increased rights to take non-intimate body samples (Criminal Evidence (Amendment) Act 1997; and additional stop and search and detention powers (Terrorism Act 2000, Knives Act 1997, Anti-Terrorism Crime and Disorder Act 2001).

21.1.1   The Human Rights Act 1998

Importing the European Convention of Human Rights into domestic law entails that disputes as to breaches of Convention Rights can be dealt with by national courts. Those Convention Rights which will effect police powers are:

- Article 3 which provides that 'no one shall be subjected to torture or to inhuman or degrading treating or punishment'. This gives an absolute right which cannot be restricted in any circumstances. 'Inhuman treatment' is defined as treatment which causes intense physical and mental suffering whereas 'degrading treatment' is treatment which arouses feelings of fear, anguish and inferiority capable of humiliating and debasing the victim. Accordingly, in *Ireland* v. *UK* (1978) the sensory deprivation and disorientation of detainees violated Art. 3.
- Article 5 which promotes the right to liberty and security of an individual, subject to lawful powers of arrest and detention. This offers a test for the legality of a person's detention and sets out a list of safeguards which include the rights to be informed of the reasons for the arrest, taken promptly before a court and either tried within a reasonable time or bailed, and to compensation if the detention contravenes Art. 5. The Terrorism Act 2000, for example, was framed so as to comply with Art. 5.
- Article 6 which confers a right to a fair trial and a presumption of innocence. This contains a list of basic rights activated once an accused has been charged with a criminal offence. These include the rights to have a court interpreter, to have adequate time and facilities for the preparation of a defence and, when the interests of justice require it, to receive free legal assistance.* Article 8 offers everyone 'the right to respect for his private and family life, his home and his correspondence'. This can be overriden 'in accordance with the law' and when in the public interest (for example, to ensure public safety and/or the economic well-being of the country; to

prevent crime, to protect health and morals, and/or to protect the rights and freedoms of others). This article covers policing methods such as surveillance, telephone tapping and obtaining medical or financial data.

21.1.2 The Police and Criminal Evidence Act 1984

The Police and Criminal Evidence (PACE) Act represents the first major attempt to codify and clarify police powers (unless the contrary is expressed, all statutory references within this chapter are to this Act). The underlying purposes of the Act are to foster an overall strategy in the fight against crime, to abolish anomalies in the pre-existing law, to provide the police with adequate and clear powers, and to offer strengthened safeguards against potential abuse. These safeguards primarily concern the clearer definition and communication of the rights and entitlements of suspects, the formalisation of the supervisory role of senior police officers, and the maintenance of detailed records concerning how and why the police exercise their powers. Despite the statistical data, empirical research and commentary which have now been published, the extent to which the objectives of the Act have been achieved remains open to debate.

21.2 Violation of PACE and Codes

The Police and Criminal Evidence Act 1984 embodies an uneasy tension between state powers and individual freedoms. The legislation is supplemented by a series of Codes of Practice which are designed to explain and amplify the statutory provisions. The Codes regulate stop and search (Code A); search and seizure (Code B); the treatment of detainees (Code C); the identification of suspects (Code D); and the tape-recording of interviews (Code E). Each contains 'Notes for Guidance' which, although technically not part of their respective Code, provide further guidance as to the application and interpretation of the substantive provisions. The Codes are admissible in evidence and their provisions must be taken into account, where relevant, in determining any issue (fact or law) which arises in criminal or civil proceedings (s. 67 (11); *R.* v. *Kenny* (1992)).

A breach of the Act or the Codes may make an officer liable to disciplinary action (s. 67 (8)) and, although it does not *per se* give rise to any criminal or civil liability (s. 67 (10)), the breach could also provide the basis for subsequent litigation (e.g. habeas corpus, assault, battery, false imprisonment and misfeasance in public office). Ironically, those who are most vulnerable to abuse are perhaps those who are the least equipped to pursue a complaint or to commence litigation. A violation may offer a tactical advantage in subsequent dealings with the Crown Prosecution Service appertaining to, for example, the discontinuance of a prosecution or plea-bargaining. Although such sanctions may provide an encouragement to the police to exercise their powers properly, they clearly offer no guarantee that the rights of a suspect will be observed. This is particularly so in the case of stop and search powers where the existence of Code A appears to have made little difference to traditional modes of policing.

21.2.1 Exclusion of evidence

Perhaps the most effective incentive to conduct investigations properly, however, is that evidence obtained in contravention of the statutory provisions or the Codes may be excluded where 'the admission of the evidence would have such an adverse effect on the fairness of the proceedings that the court ought not to admit it' (s. 78). In order to ensure a fair trial there is also a residual discretion where the probative value of the evidence is outweighed by its prejudicial effect (s. 82(3); *R. v. Sang* (1980)).

No guidance is given by the Act as to when it would be unfair to the accused or when that discretion is to be exercised. The discretion will be interfered with only when it can be said that no reasonable judge could reach that conclusion (*R. v. Quinn* (1997)). If the evidence is admitted the jury must be directed that it was not obtained in accordance with PACE (*R. v. MacMath* (1997)). Instances of where exclusion has occurred are varied, and include, for example, where the detainee has been wrongly denied access to legal advice (*R. v. Samuel* (1988)); when the breaches of the Codes were 'flagrant', 'deliberate' and 'cynical' (*R. v. Canale* (1990)); when the detainee was unadvised as to his rights under the Act (*R. v. Beycan* (1990)); where a DNA sample was obtained by deception (*R. v. Nathanial* (1995)); and when the sole identification evidence arose after the witness saw the accused in handcuffs (*R. v. Bazil* (1996)) and when the interpreter for the accused was called as a prosecution witness (*Bozkurt* v. *Thames Magistrates* (2001)).

Exclusion does not automatically follow on from a breach of the Act or Codes and is governed by the judge's conception of 'justice' and 'fairness' as rooted in the facts of a particular case. In *R. v. Hassan* (1995), for example, an officer's interview notes were admitted even

though the subject had been denied the rights to a lawyer and to contact a third party. Similarly in *R.* v. *Barker* (1996) evidence obtained
by an unlawful search was admissible. As a rule of thumb, the operation of s. 78 will require there to be 'bad faith' on the part of the police
(*R.* v. *Anderson* (1993)). For example, in *R.* v. *Ridley* (2000) evidence
was excluded because the police interview was conducted in a tendencies, persistent, aggressive and prurient manner. It is, therefore, for the
court to balance the interests of justice in prosecuting criminals with
the need to discourage abuses of process by the police. As a general
rule, therefore, significant and substantial breaches of PACE are likely
to lead to the exclusion of evidence and this is particularly so when an
admission is obtained subsequent to such breaches (*R.* v. *Allen* (2001)).
Although the appellate courts are reluctant to interfere with the findings of an experienced trial judge, the same confidence does not extend
to magistrates, who are advised only to exclude evidence in the clearest
case and in exceptional circumstances (*R.* v. *Kings Lynn Justices ex
parte Holland* (1992)).

The ECHR appears to take a similar view to UK law on the question whether improperly obtained evidence is admissible (see *Schenk* v.
Switzerland (1998)). In *Khan* v. *UK* (2000), it was held that, despite a
breach of ECHR Art. 8 (privacy), evidence obtained by a bugging
device was admissible. The overriding concern is whether the criminal
proceedings are unfair. Although issues of evidence are primarily matters for the domestic courts, judges have now to consider whether Art. 6
requires them to exercise their discretion to exclude evidence. Problems
have already arisen concerning entrapment which, although no defence,
does invoke issues of fairness. If the police act as agents provocateur,
that is, they create a criminal intention on the part of the accused, then
any evidence so obtained will be tainted under Art. 6. To admit such
evidence would be an affront to the public conscience. If, however,
the police entrap the defendant in circumstances where the defendant
already has a criminal intention, and freely takes the opportunity to
break the law, the evidence is admissible (*R.* v. *Elwell* (2001)).

Confessions, self-incrimination and the right to silence
Unsound confessions, that is those induced either by oppression
(which usually entails physical intimidation or inhumane treatment:
see *R.* v. *Fulling* (1987)) or, even where there is no police impropriety,
as a consequence of 'anything said or done' which makes them unreliable (see *R.* v. *Harvey* (1988)), are subject to mandatory exclusion
under s. 76, such confessions are also likely to offend Art. 3 and
Art. 6 of the ECHR. The unreliability ground operates particularly to

prevent the conviction of weak-minded and suggestible persons solely on the basis of their own admissions (*R.* v. *Heaton* (1993)). Otherwise the trial judge has a discretion, but not a duty, to exclude evidence. In *R.* v. *Walker* (1998), for example, a confession by a person with a severe personality disorder was inadmissible. In *DPP* v. *Cornish* (1997), by contrast, a confession made by a mentally handicapped person was allowed even in the absence of an appropriate adult, in that the absence did not itself make the confession unreliable. These evidential safeguards, protect only those who plead not guilty. The danger remains that defendants who are not legally represented may plead guilty on the basis of a confession which might otherwise be inadmissible evidence. On the entry of a guilty plea, the court will not be concerned with how evidence underlying the plea was obtained.

It is a widely accepted principle that nobody should be forced to answer police questions nor to incriminate themselves in court, and the common law has traditionally recognised a right to silence (*Rice* v. *Connolly* (1966)). Prior to the Criminal Justice and Public Order Act 1994, juries and magistrates could not draw adverse inferences from an accused's silence in interview or court. Indeed, it could not even be commented upon by the prosecution. Sections 34–38 of the 1994 Act, however, allow the court or jury to draw such inferences 'as appear proper' from an accused's failure to mention any fact relied on in his defence in certain circumstances. These circumstances arise when the accused is being questioned under caution before being charged or where the accused is being charged, or formally warned that he might be prosecuted and where the fact in question was one which it would be reasonable to expect him to have mentioned. It has been held that remaining silent on legal advice is not itself sufficient (*Condron* v. *UK* (2000); see also *R.* v. *Argent* (1997)). Section 34 (2A) does, however, prevent an adverse inference to be drawn when the detainee at a police station had been denied the opportunity to consult a solicitor prior to interview. Section 35 of the Act allows the court or jury to draw inferences from an accused's failure to give evidence at the trial itself, but only when a prima facie case exists: *Murray* v. *UK* (1996). It cannot, therefore, be the sole basis of a conviction. This ability to draw inferences does not operate where the physical or mental condition of the accused makes it undesirable for him to give evidence: *Condron* v. *UK* (2000), (heroin addicts experience withdrawal symptoms).

The ECHR regards the right to silence as fundamental. Article 6 (2) contains the presumption of innocence which impliedly reinforces the right against self-incrimination. Such protection is thought to ensure a fair trial. Hence, domestic attempts to exclude or modify the right to silence might fall foul of the Human Rights Act. Following *Brown* v. *Stott* (2001) (above p. 429) a national court, when faced with an alleged derogation from Convention Rights, should test whether it can give an interpretation of the statutory provision which is compatible with the ECHR. If not, the provision offends s. 6 (1) of the 1998 Act and is to be disapplied. A declaration of incompatibility may then be issued under s. 4 (see above pp. 434–8).

In certain cases, notably the Companies Act 1995 s. 432 (2) (see also Criminal Justice Act 1987 s. 2), and Road Traffic Act 1988 s. 172 (2) a person is required to give information. It may be that such powers violate the ECHR (see *Saunders* v. *UK* (1997); *R.* v. *Chauhan* (2000)), but this is not necessarily the case (see *DSS* v. *Wilson* (2001)).

21.3 Pre-Arrest Questioning

A police officer, just as any person, has the right to attract the attention of any individual and, in doing so, may make reasonable (i.e. trivial) physical contact (short of restraint) without incurring civil liability for trespass to the person (*Collins* v. *Wilcox* (1984)). Questions may be put to that individual but, in the absence of some specific statutory provision (e.g. as under the Road Traffic Act 1972 or Terrorism Act 2000) there is no common law obligation to answer them (*Rice* v. *Connolly* (1966)). If, however, a false story is concocted by that person, it could amount to the offence of obstruction of a police officer under s. 51 (3) of the Police Act 1964. Short of lawful arrest, the police enjoy no common law power to detain for the purposes of questioning (*Kenlin* v. *Gardiner* (1967)). If the questioning elicits sufficient information to suspect the individual of committing an arrestable offence, it then becomes an interview and the suspect must be cautioned and the subsequent dialogue noted down.

21.4 Stop and Search

Stop and search is traditionally a contentious issue and is often viewed as a provocative, random and unproductive aspect of policing. It is nevertheless prized by the police for its alleged deterrence value. On a practical level, the appeal to the police officer is that such powers provide the opportunity to establish the commission (or otherwise) of an offence without making an arrest and on the basis of intangible suspicion rather than proof. The inherent danger is that their exercise also offers scope for the potential harassment and victimisation of individuals and may be easily directed at the law-abiding citizen. There is much evidence suggesting that racial prejudice and stereotyping influence who is likely to be stopped and searched.

Part I of PACE has to some extent recognised the dangers associated with pre-arrest stop and search and has attempted to keep the exercise of such powers on a tight rein. Although creating for the first time a national power to stop and search persons or vehicles for certain unlawful items, the Act (and also Code A) contains safeguards and procedures which are specifically designed to protect the rights of the citizen. This power is also subject to Art. 5 of the ECHR which requires that a deprivation of liberty must be justified within the terms of the Convention (see below).

In outline, the general power conferred by s. 1 allows a police officer to stop and search any person or any attended or unattended vehicle, in any place to which the public have access, if there are reasonable grounds for suspecting that the officer will find stolen articles, equipment to be used for theft, or weapons. This is echoed in Art. 5 (1) (c) of the ECHR which permits the deprivation of liberty on reasonable suspicion that the individual has committed a criminal offence. As demonstrated in *Murray* v. *UK* (1994) the level of suspicion need not be sufficient to justify the charging of the detainee with an offence. Although the co-operation of the suspect should be sought in all cases, reasonable force may be used if necessary, and as a last resort, to detain and to search (A: 3.2). Any such items found may be seized (s. 1 (6)). Note, however, the Terrorism Act 2000 which allows the police to stop and search persons or vehicles in order to prevent terrorism without any need for suspicion. All that is necessary is that an officer of at least the rank of Assistant Chief Constable considers it 'expedient' for the prevention of terrorism.

21.4.1　Reasonable grounds for suspecting

Before considering s. 1 in more detail it is necessary to examine the requirement of reasonable suspicion. This is of relevance not merely to stop and search, but (alongside the concept of 'reasonable belief') represents a safeguard against arbitrary exercise applicable to many other powers, including, for example, search, arrest and seeking a warrant. While incapable of precise definition, it is clear that 'suspicion . . . is a state of conjecture or surmise where proof is lacking: "I suspect but I cannot prove" ' (per Lord Devlin (*Hussein* v. *Chong Fook Kam*

(1970))). The term 'belief', however, imposes a higher degree of confidence than 'suspicion' (*Baker* v. *Oxford* (1980)).

Not surprisingly, nowhere in the Act or Codes is any attempt made to define these illusive terms. Nevertheless, some important guidance is to be found within the revised Code A. It is made clear that the existence of 'reasonable suspicion' will depend on the circumstances of each case and, moreover, must be capable of objective evaluation (A: 1.6). Mere instinct or hunch will not suffice and no power exists which allows the police to stop and search in order to discover grounds for suspicion (A: 2.1). There is, however, nothing which prevents an officer questioning any person provided no compulsion is present (A: 1B), and the grounds for justifying a subsequent restraint and search can emerge from such voluntary questioning.

The grounds for a reasonable suspicion may arise from the nature of the article thought to be carried, coupled with other factors such as, for example, time, place and behaviour (A: 1.6). Situations which may indicate the likelihood that an article of a certain kind will be found are illustrated in the Code. These include where relevant information has been received by that officer; where the suspect is behaving covertly or warily or is attempting to hide something; or when the individual is carrying a certain type of article at an unusual time or in a known area of criminal activity (A: 1.6). In order to outlaw the crude stereotyping of suspects, the Code makes it clear that the colour, dress, appearance and previous convictions of a person are no justifications for stop and search (A: 1.7). Nevertheless, it remains likely that such matters will continue as operating factors in the initial suspicion of an individual, and the cynic may fear that the police will persist with broad categorisations of potential suspects and merely look harder for objective reasons after the event so as to validate their actions. This is a seemingly inevitable price to be paid for street policing. The targeting of male members of the Black and Asian community would, however, contravene Art. 14 of the ECHR. Article 14 requires that Convention Rights (here against an unjustified deprivation of liberty) be enjoyed without discrimination on any ground such as sex, race, colour, language and religion.

21.4.2 Search under section 1

The stop and search may be initiated only for the purposes of detecting 'stolen or prohibited items' or those items listed within s. 1 (8A). For these purposes, a 'stolen' article will include any item dishonestly obtained, whereas, a 'prohibited article' is either an offensive weapon (i.e. something designed to injure or intended to do so) or an item designed or intended for use for stealing, burglary, deception or taking a motor vehicle (s. 1 (7) (*a*), (*b*)). This enables the police to carry out a search for a flick knife, jemmy, picklock or bunch of duplicate car keys, for example. The additional basis for stop and search concerns an article, other than a pocket knife, which has a blade or is sharp-pointed or a pocket knife where the cutting edge of the blade exceeds three inches. These latter items need not be 'offensive' or 'made or adapted' for committing a criminal offence.

The stop and search power may be exercised in any place where the public have access, whether as of right (the highway, public park or public toilet, for example), or by virtue of express or implied permission (for example, cinema, pub car park or private grounds); or any other place (except a dwelling) where people have ready access (an unfenced building site or open frontage to an industrial unit, for example). Although a search of a dwelling is not allowed under s. 1, someone who is in the yard or garden of a dwelling may be searched if the constable does not reasonably believe that person to be the resident or a guest of the resident. Except for the stopping of a moving vehicle (s. 2 (9) (*b*)), there is no requirement that the officer be in uniform.

21.4.3   Proprieties: sections 2, 3

Although there is no need for a search to take place following a stop, PACE regulates the manner in which a search must be carried out. Except as regards an unattended vehicle, a plain clothes officer must produce his warrant card prior to the search (but not the initial stop) and every officer must state his name (or as regards terrorist offences, number), police station, the reasons for the search and the entitlement to a record of the search. A failure to provide the grounds for the search will render the search unlawful (*R. v. Fenneley* (1989)).

The search must be conducted in accordance with the Act and Code A. Every reasonable effort must be made to minimise potential embarrassment of the suspect (A: 3.1). The person or vehicle may be detained only for such time as is reasonable in all the circumstances and not beyond the time taken for the search (A: 3.3). In addition, the thoroughness and extent of the search depends upon what items the police are looking for. Since the Criminal Justice and Public Order Act 1994, the police may search the suspect's mouth.

The searched person cannot, however, be compelled to remove, in public, more than outer clothing (coat, jacket or gloves: s. 2 (9)) and, for these purposes, a deserted street is regarded as being 'in public' (A: 3A).

The removal of other clothing can only be required if there are reasonable grounds to consider it necessary and when the search is beyond public view (A: 3.5). There is nothing, however, to prevent an officer from requesting that a suspect voluntarily remove any clothing (A: 3A). A search involving the removal of more than outer clothing, headgear and footwear may only be made by (and in the presence of) an officer of the same sex (A: 3.5). No member of the opposite sex may be present unless the person searched specifically requests it. This could prove to be a useful safeguard where the suspect is accompanied by, for example, a spouse or parent. Intimate searches can be undertaken only on the authorisation of an inspector or officer of higher rank.

A further safeguard is the general obligation to make a contemporaneous, written record of any search undertaken, unless it is impractical to do so (s. 3 (1)). The Code advises that a record need not be made contemporaneously where the officer has immediate duties elsewhere or the weather is inclement (A: 4.2), but it must then be compiled as soon as it becomes practical (s. 3 (2)); and need not be compiled at all if it is a mass search or involves public disorder (A: 4.1). The record must name the person searched (or, if unknown, contain a description), disclose the suspect's ethnic origin and state the purpose of the search and details of its conduct and outcome (A: 4.5). The individual enjoys a right to a copy of this record, provided a request is made within 12 months of the date of the search (s. 3 (7), (8)). The documentation provisions apply only to compulsory searches (s. 3 (1)) and, accordingly, nothing in the Code affects the routine searching, with consent, of persons entering sports grounds or other premises or when search is a condition of entry (A: 1D). The annual reports of police authorities must contain statistical information about searches made within their areas, and these will provide a breakdown of the total monthly number of searches for stolen goods, offensive weapons and other prohibited articles, and details of the number of arrests arising from such searches (s. 5). This may serve to highlight any random use of the power within a particular force, but is limited in the sense that it does not cover the number of stops made without a subsequent search and may not accurately reflect the figures of voluntary stops and searches.

21.4.4   Road checks

Section 4 of PACE permits the setting up of 'road checks' (or 'road blocks') which, except as a matter of urgency, must be authorised in writing and by an officer of at least the rank of superintendent. The authorisation can last for up to seven days (28 days under the Terrorism Act 2000 provided it is confirmed by the Secretary of State) and may direct that the check be continuous or be conducted at specified times. Thereafter, and if the senior officer thinks that the road check 'ought' to continue, further seven-day extensions may be authorised. Section 4 leaves unaffected any other statutory power (e.g. or the Terrorism Act 2000, the Road Traffic Act 1988 the Criminal Justice and Public Order Act 1994) and the common law power in relation to a breach of the peace, and these powers are not regulated by s. 4.

The purpose of s. 4 is to enable the police to ascertain whether there is, in the vehicle stopped, someone who has committed, or is intending to commit, an offence, someone who has witnessed an offence or someone who is 'unlawfully at large' (e.g. an escaped convict or a person absconding while on bail). All searches are, therefore, for people and not for evidence. A road check cannot, however, be authorised in relation to any offence. The superintendent must reasonably 'believe' (a more onerous standard than 'suspicion') that it is 'a serious arrestable offence' (see below) and reasonably 'suspect' that the person who has committed it, or intends to commit it, is going to be in the locality where vehicles will be stopped. If the purpose is to seek witnesses, the requirement is merely that the superintendent believes, on reasonable grounds, that a serious arrestable offence has been committed. There is no locality condition. If the object is to apprehend someone unlawfully at large, it is necessary that there is reasonable suspicion that the person is, or is about to be, in the area.

Once a road check is authorised, the police may stop any vehicle, and, seemingly, at random. By implication, the motorist is under a duty to remain stationary for a reasonable period. The provision does not allow a subsequent search or other action, but where necessary such power will be available elsewhere (e.g. a search under s. 1). The stopped motorist is entitled, within 12 months, to obtain a written record of the reasons for the road check. Statistics concerning checks within each police area must be compiled and included in the police authority's annual report (s. 5(1)(b)). In this way the frequency and results of road checks can be monitored.

Under s. 24 an 'arrestable offence' is either an offence where the sentence is fixed by law (e.g. murder); or one for which a person may theoretically, on first conviction, be sentenced to a term of imprisonment of five years or more for the offence; or one which is specifically designated by statute as arrestable. Recent additions to the list include harassment (Protection from Harassment Act 1997), failure to comply with a police request to remove a mask, and certain offences of obscenity and indecency (Criminal Justice and Public Order Act 1994), a racially aggravated violent offence (Crime and Disorder Act 1998), carrying an offensive weapon (Offensive Weapons Act 1996), kerb crawling and failing to stop and report a road traffic accident (Criminal Justice and Police Act 2001). The definition of arrestable offence extends also to conspiracy or attempts to commit such an offence as well as the aiding and abetting of these offences (s. 24(3)). The number of arrestable offences will undoubtedly continue to increase.

A 'serious arrestable offence' is either one listed in Schedule 5 (e.g. murder, manslaughter, rape and kidnapping) or an arrestable offence which has led, or is intended or threatened to lead, to certain consequences (s. 116). The relevant consequences are serious harm to the state, serious interference with the administration of justice or criminal investigation, death or serious injury, substantial financial gain to any person or serious financial loss to any person. As regards the last, in *R.* v. *Samuel* (1988) an offence of burglary was elevated to a serious arrestable offence because of the loss caused to the householder. This subjective assessment might entail that the theft from a homeless person be regarded as a serious loss.

It should be appreciated that the concept of a serious arrestable offence has resonance beyond road checks and is relevant to search warrants, detention beyond 24 hours, the taking of intimate and non-intimate samples, delaying notification of detention to a third party, and delaying access to legal advice.

21.4.5 Special stop and search powers

In addition to the general power conferred by s. 1–3, there are number of independent statutory powers of stop and search. These are listed in Code A: Annex A, and include powers relating to drugs, firearms, poaching and terrorism. The Terrorism Act 2000, for example, gives wider powers of stop and search, particularly at ports and borders. The Act also allows the police to cordon off areas for purposes of a terrorist investigation and impose parking restrictions in order to prevent terrorist activity. The Criminal Justice and Public Order Act 1994 s. 60 gives the power to stop and search a person or vehicle for offensive weapons or dangerous instruments even without grounds for suspecting that the person is carrying them. This power applies only where a senior officer reasonably believes that violent incidents may take place and authorises the power to be exercised for a period of not more than 24 hours. The Act also allows a uniformed constable to require any person to remove any item worn for the purpose of concealing identity and to seize such item, a power extended by the Anti-Terrorism Crime and Security Act 2001 s. 90. These powers are regulated by the proprieties contained in PACE and Code A. In *DSS* v. *Avery* (2001), for example, a constable asked a demonstrator to remove a mask under the 1994 Act. It was held that the officer was not obliged to give his name, police station and reasons for the request. This was because the removal of a mask did not amount to a search.

21.5   Arrest

21.5.1   Meaning of arrest

The status of the suspect is crucial when determining the powers of the police and the corresponding rights of the individual. Lawful arrest is an exception to the right of liberty under Art. 5 of the ECHR. Of particular importance is the distinction between a volunteer (i.e. someone 'helping the police with their enquiries') and the person under arrest. Although he need not be told of this right unless cautioned, a volunteer can leave a police station at will (s. 29), whereas the arrested person cannot. Although there is no statutory definition of 'arrest', at common law it is the physical restraint by compulsion of the freedom of the individual. Accordingly, taking someone by the arm and saying 'You are under arrest' is a sufficient restraint (*DPP* v. *Hawkins* (1988)). As Lord Devlin explained in *Hussein* v. *Chong Fook Kam* (1970): 'An arrest occurs when a police officer states in terms that he is arresting or when he uses force to restrain the individual concerned. It occurs also when by words or conduct, he makes it clear that he will, if necessary, use force to prevent the individual from going where he may want to go.' Where words alone are used, the person must submit under the threat of compulsion (*Nichols* v. *Bulman* (1985)). The legal complications tend to arise, however, in the context of whether a power to arrest has arisen and, moreover, whether it is exercised lawfully.

21.5.2   Powers of arrest

An arrest for any offence may be authorised by the issue of a warrant by a single magistrate under s. 1 of the Magistrates' Courts Act 1980 this being a directive to the police, requiring the arrest of the named person in order to compel him to attend court. The normal procedure is that the police present and swear an information to a magistrate that a particular person has, or is suspected of having, committed an offence.

The warrant must specify the person to be arrested and the offence, and, moreover, may be 'backed for bail' (which entails that the arrested person must then be released on bail) or not (in which case the arrested person must be brought before the court as soon as is practicable). The warrant will normally be issued only in relation to an arrestable offence and need not be in the possession of the officer when the arrest is made. In such case, however, it must be shown subsequently on request and as soon as is reasonably practicable (s. 125 Magistrates Court Act 1980 as amended by s. 33 of PACE).

The police also enjoy wide powers to arrest without a warrant (i.e. summary arrest). In addition to a general power in s. 24 of PACE relating to an arrestable offence (see 21.4.4), there remain a large number of specific powers which allow arrest without a warrant. These relate to offences which are thought sufficiently important to require a power of arrest without the restrictions which apply to the more general powers. They are listed in Schedule 2 of PACE. They include powers under, for example, the Bail Act 1976 and the Prevention of Terrorism legislation. Non-listed statutory powers of summary arrest are repealed but only in the case of powers granted exclusively to the police. In *Gapper* v. *Avon and Somerset Constabulary* (1998) the Court of Appeal held that a power of summary arrest of a 'vagabond' under s. 6 of the Vagrancy Act 1824 still survived because it conferred a power of arrest on a private citizen. The Act also preserves the common law power to arrest for a breach of the peace (s. 25 (6); see *Albert* v. *Lavin* (1982)). Note that Art. 5 (1) (c) of the ECHR authorises arrest to prevent the commission of an offence, but not in order merely to preserve peace and general order: *Ireland* v. *UK* (1978).

PACE itself offers three avenues whereby a summary arrest can be made. These are as follows.

(i) *For an 'arrestable offence'*

An officer, and a private citizen, is empowered to arrest anyone who is committing an arrestable offence (s. 24 (4)). For this purpose it is not necessary to enter into an analysis of exactly when the offence is completed for, according to the Court of Appeal, to do so would deter public-spirited citizens from making arrests (*Stanley* v. *Benning* (1996)). In addition, an officer, but not a private citizen, may arrest a person who is about to commit an arrestable offence or is suspected, on reasonable grounds, to be about to commit such an offence (s. 24 (7)). This is an unusual power as it caters for acts preparatory to the commission of an offence which fall short of an attempt to commit it. The other arrest grounds are where there is reasonable suspicion that the person has committed an offence or reasonably considered necessary to prevent escape after committing an offence. The officer can arrest where he has reasonable grounds for suspecting both that an arrestable offence has been committed and that it was committed by the person arrested (s. 24 (6)). The private citizen enjoys a similar power, but this is more curtailed than that vested in the police: s. 24 (5). The major difference is that an arrest by a citizen, after an offence has allegedly been perpetrated, will be unlawful unless an arrestable offence has actually been committed, whether it be by the suspect or someone else (see *Walters* v. *W.H. Smith* (1914); *R.* v. *Self* (1992)).

In relation to the need for reasonable suspicion, there is no requirement for the police to have anything like a prima facie case and they need not explore every explanation before making the arrest (*Castorini* v. *Chief Constable of Surrey* (1988)). The emphasis is upon suspicion, for example that an arrestable offence has been committed, and not evidence. It is the purpose of detention which is important and not whether the individual is later charged. Under the ECHR, Art. 5 (1) (c) recognises 'reasonable suspicion' as a ground for arrest and this, as with the national law, involves an honest belief and objective evaluation on the part of the police: *Fox* v. *UK* (1990). It is to be appreciated, however, that even under the Convention, terrorist offences fall into a special category with reduced safeguards. It is for the court to subsequently determine whether the officer had sufficient information available, upon which to make his suspicion reasonable, at the time of the arrest. The suspicion may be thin and yet still be sufficient (*Ward* v. *Chief Constable of Avon* (1986)) and can be based solely on the words of an informant (*James* v. *Chief Constable of South Wales* (1991)). A remote possibility, however, will not suffice (*Chapman* v. *DPP* (1988)) and when an arrest is premature (i.e. without reasonable grounds) it is unlawful (*Plange* v. *Chief Constable of South Humberside* (1992)). The term 'reasonable' imposes an objective yardstick. In *Bull* v. *Chief Constable of Sussex* (1995) it was said that the test is what the reasonable person who knows both the law and the facts of the case would believe at the material time. The suspicion must, therefore, be based on information known to the officer at the material time (*O'Hara* v. *Chief Constable of the RUC* (1997)).

Once the suspicion arises, the officer must also exercise his executive discretion in accordance with the general principles of administrative law (i.e. *Wednesbury* reasonableness) so as not to constitute an *ultra vires* abuse of power. The exercise of this discretion could be challenged if the police do not make full enquiries before the arrest (see *Castorini* (1988)). Nevertheless, this appears not to unduly fetter the actions of the police. In *Mohamed-Holgate* v. *Duke* (1984), for example, an officer exercised his discretion to arrest someone he reasonably suspected, solely motivated by the psychology that the suspect was more likely to confess if detained in custody. This was held by the House of Lords to be a '*Wednesbury*' reasonable exercise of the power to arrest, and confirms that arrest is validly part of the investigative process.

(ii) *For any offence*

The Act offers the police (but not the citizen) a novel and general power of arrest for any non-arrestable offence (normally of a less serious nature than an arrestable offence) where one of the specified 'general arrest conditions' is satisfied and where the service of a summons (which on average takes 88 days) is impracticable or inappropriate (s. 25(1)). Accordingly, and unlike arrestable offences, non-arrestable offences are deemed insufficiently serious to justify the arrest of those who are simply suspected of having committed them, and other circumstances are necessary before an arrest can be made. The officer, moreover, must have reasonable grounds for suspecting both that a non-arrestable offence has been (or is being) committed or attempted and that the person arrested is the offender. This suspicion, seemingly, must arise before the general arrest conditions become relevant: *G* v. *DPP* (1989).

The general arrest conditions are listed in s. 25(3) as being where the name of the suspect is unknown, cannot be ascertained or is doubted; where a satisfactory address has not been furnished; where the suspect needs to be restrained so as to prevent either harm to himself or a third party, physical injury to himself, loss or damage to property, an offence against public decency or an obstruction of the highway; or where an arrest is appropriate in order to protect a child or other vulnerable person from the suspect. Many of the above conditions are dependent upon the officer having reasonable grounds to doubt the suspect or to believe that the specified consequence will occur. The purpose of s. 25 is to widen the power of summary arrest potentially to cover all offences (e.g. riding a bicycle along a public road in a dangerous manner: *Nicholas* v. *Parsonage* (1987)) and not wearing a seat belt: *Ghafar* v. *Chief Constable of West Midlands Police* (2000)). As well as the ground of arrest, the suspect must also be told of the general arrest condition relied on by the police.

(iii) *For fingerprinting*

Certain offenders may be required to attend a police station so that fingerprints may be taken (s. 27). If a person fails to comply, any constable may arrest him without a warrant. This power extends only towards a person who has been either convicted of, cautioned for or warned and reprimanded (under the Crime and Disorder Act 1998) in relation to a 'recordable offence' (i.e. all offences punishable by imprisonment and a few other statutory offences) and where fingerprints have not previously been taken. The later rule gives way, however, when the fingerprints previously taken are either an incomplete set or are of unsatisfactory quality. The request to attend the station must be made within one month of the conviction and the person must be given at least seven days in which to co-operate. The requirement can be made only on the authority of an officer of inspector rank (or above) and provided that there exist, reasonable grounds for suspecting the individual's involvement in a criminal offence and that fingerprints will tend to prove or disprove that involvement. If an arrest is then made, the fingerprints may be taken without consent (s. 61 (6)).

21.5.3   Method of arrest

For a lawful arrest to occur (whether by the police or a citizen) it is necessary both that the power of arrest has arisen and that its exercise is proper (*Murray* v. *Ministry of Defence* (1988)). It is also a requirement that the suspect be cautioned upon arrest (C: 10.3), but this strikes at the admissibility of evidence rather than the lawfulness of the arrest.

As regards the exercise of the power, s. 28 (1), (3), (5) of PACE requires certain information to be given to the arrested person. This need not, however, be given by the arresting officer himself. The person must be told of the fact of arrest and the ground for the arrest, either 'at the time' of the arrest or within a short but reasonable time afterwards (*Nicholas* v. *Parsonage* (1987)), or, if met with immediate resistance or the person escapes after the arrest, for example, as soon as is practicable afterwards (see *Lewis* v. *Chief Constable of South Wales* (1991)). If the information is not supplied when it becomes practicable to do so, the arrest from that stage becomes unlawful, but this does not invalidate previous acts (see *DPP* v. *Hawkins* (1988)). Similarly, an unlawful arrest may become lawful once the information is provided: *Wilson* v. *Chief Constable of Lancashire Police* (2001). These details must be furnished even if it is obvious that an arrest has been made and upon what basis (s. 28 (2), (4)). The underlying rationale of this provision is as explained by Viscount Simon in *Christie* v. *Leachinsky* (1947): '[It is] the elementary proposition that in this country a person is prima facie entitled to his freedom and is only required to submit to restraints on his freedom if he knows in substance why it is claimed that his restraint should be imposed.' In *Clarke* v. *DPP* (1997) it was unclear whether the arrest was for common assault (non-arrestable) or assault occasioning actual bodily harm (arrestable). The arrest was therefore unlawful. The minimum obligation, therefore, is to give the suspect sufficient information as to the nature of the arrest and to allow the suspect the opportunity to respond.

In the main, s. 28 reiterates the old common law approach (see *Christie* v. *Leachinsky* (1947)). But the information need not be expressed in technical terms: 'I am arresting you on suspicion of burglary' was insufficient in *R.* v. *Telfer* (1976) because the police should have informed the suspect of the particular burglary he was being arrested for. In *Murphy* v. *Oxford* (1985) the view was taken that the details should be such as to allow the detainee to explain his innocence. There, the words 'You are wanted on suspicion of burglary in Newquay' spoken to a person arrested in Liverpool were also held insufficient. As Donaldson MR explained: 'He [the detainee] is entitled to much fuller details in order that he may be able to deny the charge, if he is innocent, with conviction.' The information should have included the date and more exact geographic location of the offence. In *Ireland* v. *UK* (1978), it was not enough to tell the individual that he was being detained under emergency legislation. All turns on the facts of each case, and whether sufficient information has been given is for the jury to decide. For example in *R.* v. *Green* (1996) the arrest was unlawful because the accused was told only that 'you are wanted on a warrant and I am arresting you'. If, moreover, the wrong ground is provided, the arrest is unlawful (*Edwards* v. *DPP* (1993)) and continues to be so until the correct reason is stated (*Lewis* v. *Chief Constable of South Wales* (1991)).

Article 5(2) of the ECHR emphasises that an arrested person is to be promptly informed, in a language which he speaks, of the reason for the arrest in straightforward terms. This, seemingly, adds nothing to the common law.

21.5.4 Treatment of arrested persons

Unless released, the arrested person should normally be taken to a 'designated' police station, that is, one with suitable facilities for the detention of suspects (ss. 30, 35). This should be done as soon as is practicable, but delay may be justified in order to take the suspect elsewhere 'in order to carry out such investigations as it is reasonable to carry out immediately' (s. 30 (10)). Although a matter of degree, this would cover the situation where, for example, a constable takes an arrested person to an address in order to verify an alibi (*Dallison* v. *Caffrey* (1965)). It does not, however, give the officer carte blanche to carry out interrogation which ought properly to occur at the police station (*R.* v. *Khan* (1993)). This is also recognised in Code C (11.1) which expressly states that a suspect must not be 'interviewed' except at a police station unless a delay would lead to certain consequences, such as hindering the recovery of property. The aim of s. 30 is to ensure that the arrested person benefits from the various safeguards (e.g. access to a solicitor) which operate only on arrival at the police station (*R.* v. *Keane* (1992)). The Code does not apply to an interview carried out before the interviewee became a suspect (*R.* v. *Mellor* (1996)).

The problem that has emerged concerns how to distinguish an 'interview' from other forms of questioning (see *R.* v. *Cox* (1993)). The answer appears to be that an 'interview' is a question-and-answer session which relates to the involvement of the suspect with an offence (*R.* v. *Oransaye* (1993)).

As with the exercise of any power bestowed by the Act, the police officer (or citizen) can use 'reasonable force' in its lawful exercise (s. 117). What constitutes 'reasonable force' will clearly depend on the circumstances and is a question of fact (see *Sturley* v. *Metropolitan Police* (1984)). In *Pollard* v. *Chief Constable of West Yorkshire Police* (1998) a police dog bit a suspect on the ear. Although the crime concerned criminal damage amounting only to £18, the dog was assisting in the arrest and its actions did not constitute unreasonable force. In contrast, in *Murgatroyd* v. *Chief Constable of West Yorkshire Police* (2000) the use of a police dog to disable a potentially suicidal person was unreasonable force. The purpose of the police dog was to protect the police from harm rather than to counter a mere risk that a person will self-inflict harm. If there had been an immediate threat of harm, however, it is possible that the court would have felt the force to be reasonable. In any case the use of undue force does not render the arrest unlawful (*Simpson* v. *Chief Constable of South Yorkshire* (1991)).

21.6   Search Before and Following Arrest

The police are given a specific statutory power (PACE s. 17(1)), in addition to any other legislative provision and common law right, to enter and search premises without a warrant in order either to arrest someone for an arrestable offence; to recapture a person unlawfully at large who is in the process of being pursued (*D'Souza* v. *DPP* (1992)), to save life or limb, or to prevent serious damage to property (see generally *Chapman DPP* (1988)). Except for the life/limb condition, the requirement is that the constable must have reasonable grounds for believing that the person sought is actually on the premises. There is no power of search if the person is arrested on the driveway to, or front step of, the property: *R.* v. *Commissioner of Police for the Metropolis* (2001). As acknowledged in *O'Loughlin* v. *Chief Constable of Essex* (1998) an attempt is made to 'balance' the incommensurables of the public interest in effective policing and the individual's right to privacy and security. There the police did not comply with B: 5.4, which requires communication with the occupier and an explanation of the authority under which the police seek entry. Mrs O'Loughlin had barricaded herself into her house and after stating that they wished to speak with her the police broke the door down. The use of force was held to be unlawful. It would also, of course, violate Art. 8 of the ECHR.

Where arrest occurs outside the police station, a constable (but not a citizen) may also search the arrested person or premises on the satisfaction of certain conditions (s. 32). A personal search is lawful if the officer has reasonable grounds for believing that the detainee may present a danger to himself or others, or that the person has concealed anything which might be used to assist escape or is evidence. Any relevant item found may be seized and retained (unless it is subject to legal privilege). The powers of the police to seize and retain evidence have been considerably widened by the Criminal Justice and Police Act 2001 (see below). In addition, the constable is allowed to enter and to search any premises (whether or not occupied or controlled by the arrested person) in which the arrest was made or in which the person had been immediately before the arrest (s. 32 (2)). This search may, however, only be for evidence relating to the offence with which the arrest was concerned and must be based upon reasonable grounds for believing that such evidence is on the premises (*R.* v. *Beckford* (1991)). PACE does not, therefore, empower the police to search the premises of a suspect who is caught red-handed. Section 32 invests an immediate power and does not allow the police to return later in order to carry out the search (*R.* v. *Badham* (1987)). Items relating to any offence (even though it may not have founded the basis for the search) which are found may be seized under s. 32, or the general power of seizure contained in s. 19, provided that they are reasonably believed to be evidence and that seizure is necessary to prevent their concealment, loss or destruction. Under the Criminal Justice and Police Act 2001 items can also be seized when it is not reasonably practicable to determine whether it is evidence which is entitled to be taken away. Whether it is 'reasonably practicable' depends upon the time and manpower it will involve to decide whether it is a seizable item.

A complementary power to enter and search is contained in s. 18. This permits a constable to search any premises 'occupied or controlled' by a person arrested, whether in or out of the station, for an arrestable offence. The search can occur at any time subsequent to the arrest, provided that the police have reasonable grounds for suspecting that there is on the premises non-legally privileged evidence concerning that offence or similar or connected arrestable offence. Normally the authorisation of an officer not below the rank of inspector is required before the search can be carried out. This gives way when the arrest is outside the station and the search is 'necessary' for the effective investigation of the offence (s. 18 (5)). Searches without prior authorisation must be later notified to an officer of at least the rank of inspector and, in all cases, a separate record of the search must be made.

21.7   Police Searches during the Investigation of Crime

In the course of investigation the police may seek to conduct searches for evidence of the crime or the proceeds of crime, such as stolen property. This often arises before the police feel able to make an arrest. The police are not, however, allowed to go on fishing expeditions for evidence and, if they do so, evidence found is likely to be excluded at trial. PACE has significantly extended police powers to enter premises by giving a general power to search for evidence and to obtain warrants to authorise that type of search. This is backed up by a general power to seize items, in order to prevent their loss, damage or concealment, that are discovered and which are reasonably believed to be criminally obtained or evidence of any offence (s. 19). Inherent in the exercise of such powers, however, is the danger that the police may exceed their office and, thereby, forcibly enter premises without warning and without the occupier (who need not necessarily be connected with, or suspected of, a criminal offence) having the ability to oppose the action. Accordingly, the right of the police to search is closely monitored and, when it is exercised, Code B lays down a number of guidelines as to how the search should proceed.

Clearly, if what is to be searched is a public place where anyone may lawfully look around, or if the occupier of private premises consents to a search, then few legal problems arise. Nonetheless, Code B does set out certain proprieties which need to be observed in the making of voluntary searches. Unless the police have a search warrant or any other power of entry, the general rule is that the consent must be given in writing (on the notice of powers and rights which must be provided to the occupier: see below) before the search, and the officer must make enquiries as to whether that person was entitled to allow the entry to the premises (B: 4.1). In addition, certain preliminary information must be given to the consenting party concerning the purpose of the search, the absence of a duty to consent, the liability to have items seized and used in evidence, and, if appropriate, that the person is not a suspect (B: 4.2). Consent can be withdrawn at any time and is vitiated by duress (B: 4.3). If the occupier does not consent (or it is withdrawn), the police need to rely on their statutory rights to obtain a warrant or to enter without one. Consent is not required, however, in circumstances where seeking it would cause 'disproportionate inconvenience' to that party (B: 4.4). The *Notes for Guidance* provide the example where the police have arrested someone at night after a pursuit and it is necessary to make a brief check of gardens along the route of the pursuit (B: 4C).

21.7.1 Production orders

An alternative to a search warrant exists whereby the police can gain access to confidential material (see below) and this is through the mechanism of a production order. This order is governed by schedule 1 and may be granted by a circuit judge, but not a magistrate. The order requires the person in charge of material within a specified time (the minimum is seven days) either to produce the material for removal by a constable or to allow the constable access to it. The holder must be served with notice of the proceedings and given details of the documents, etc. sought. Once notice is served, the holder must not conceal, destroy, alter or dispose of the material in question. The order can be made only if certain 'access conditions' are satisfied, and these are discussed below in the context of the grounds for a search warrant granted by a circuit judge. A failure to comply with a production order is a contempt of court and a search warrant will then be sought.

21.7.2 Search warrants

The aim of PACE is to clarify the law and offer the police a general power for the grant of search warrants relating to serious offences, while preserving the property rights and privacy of the individual. Existing and piecemeal powers are preserved, but general rules are established which cover all search warrants and regulate the circumstances under which they may be granted and the type of material which may, or may not, be the object of the search. As mentioned earlier, Art. 8 of the ECHR protects rights of privacy, but this protection gives way on the public interest grounds specified therein. Accordingly, and provided that the police act within national law, searches and seizure will not be in breach of Convention rights.

A warrant is a document issued by a person with authority which legitimises the doing of an act (e.g. entry and search) which would otherwise be a trespass. Once issued, the search warrant authorises only one entry and must be executed within one month of its grant (ss. 15(5), 16(3)). If the premises comprise more than one dwelling the warrant must specify which part of the building it covers, otherwise the search is unlawful (*R.* v. *South West Magistrates Court* (1997)). PACE prescribes the machinery by which a search warrant for evidence (not persons) can be obtained from a magistrate (s. 8) or a circuit judge (s. 9; schedule 1).

This procedure is amplified within Code B. Two issues of importance emerge: first, whether the correct procedures have been followed; and secondly, whether the grant should be made on the merits of the case. The aim is to ensure that the police should not seek, and the magistrates and judges should not grant, search warrants unless there are good grounds for doing so. In practice, however, the procedure is routine and refusals rare, although most seizures take place following an arrest and/or a lawful entry to the premises.

The application
Before an application is made, several steps must be taken. The police must make a reasonable check that the information upon which the justification for the warrant is based is accurate, recent and has not been provided maliciously or irresponsibly (B: 2.1). The Code also states that if the information is supplied by someone unknown to the police, they must seek (but not necessarily obtain) corroborative evidence. The police must, moreover, ascertain as specifically as possible the nature of the articles sought and their believed location; and details should be obtained about the likely occupier, the nature of the premises and any previous searches (B: 2.2, 2.3; see *R.* v. *Central Criminal Court ex parte AJD Holdings* (1992)). In relation to a magistrates' warrant, and unless it is an urgent case whereby the senior officer on duty may give authority, the application must be authorised by an officer not below the rank of inspector (B: 2.4). No application to a circuit judge may be made without the authority of an officer of at least the rank of

superintendent (ibid.). Finally, where the proposed search 'might' have an adverse effect on community relations, the local police community liaison officer, except if it is an urgent search, must be consulted before the search takes place (B: 2.5).

The application may be made by any officer (armed with the necessary authority) and the proceedings are conventionally *ex parte*. The officer should be prepared to answer questions under oath and the application must be accompanied by an information in writing. Both the application and accompanying information must specify the ground upon which the application is based (see below), the statute under which the application is made (e.g. PACE, Knives Act 1997, Misuse of Drugs Act 1971, Firearms Act 1968), the items (or, where appropriate, people) sought, and the premises to be entered (s. 15 (2)).

Grounds for magistrates' warrant

A magistrate, whether in private or in open court, may issue a warrant under PACE s. 8 if satisfied that there are reasonable grounds for believing all of the following: that a serious arrestable offence has been committed by someone; there is material on the premises which is likely to be of substantial value to the investigation of this offence; this material is likely to comprise admissible evidence at a subsequent trial; the material does not *prima facie* include items subject to legal privilege, excluded material or special procedure material (see below); and one of the conditions listed in s. 8 (3) applies. These conditions are either that it is impracticable to communicate with any person able to grant entry to the premises or access to the evidence; that entry will not be granted unless a warrant is produced; or that the purpose of the search may be frustrated or seriously prejudiced unless immediate entry can be secured. If s. 8 is satisfied the warrant can also be issued in relation to an overseas investigation (Criminal Justice (International Co-operation) Act 1990).

Although there is no general rule that other means of obtaining documents should be attempted before the issue of a warrant (*R. v. Billericay Justices ex parte Harris* (1991)), previous co-operation by the occupier would normally destroy the basis of the application (*R. v. Reading Justices ex parte South West Meat Ltd* (1992)). When the magistrates should not have been satisfied that the material sought was not covered by legal privilege or that the above grounds for a warrant were established, the warrant is bad and can be quashed on appeal (*R. v. Guildhall Magistrates ex parte Primlaks* (1990)).

There are three types of confidential material, which because of their sensitivity are treated differently by PACE. The statutory provisions are detailed and complex and, within the confines of this chapter, only a brief examination is possible. A magistrate cannot issue a warrant for these types of material and the police must instead apply to a circuit judge. In some instances even the judge cannot grant a search warrant.

Legal privilege

Firstly, s. 10 aims to preserve the confidentiality of communications between client and lawyer. Included within legal privilege are communications (usually written, but could be taped or perhaps email) between professional legal adviser and client, provided they are made in connection with the provision of legal advice. A conveyance, for example, is not clothed with privilege, whereas correspondence offering advice appertaining to the transaction would be (*R. v. Crown Court at Inner London Sessions ex parte Baines and Baines* (1988)). Coverage extends also to communications with a third party (for example, medical and forensic reports), provided that the material relates to actual or pending legal proceedings. In addition, items lawfully in the possession of any person (for example, handwriting samples, blood specimens and accounts) which are enclosed with (or referred to in) exempt communications, are also immune.

Items subject to legal privilege are, except as regards items held 'with the intention of furthering a criminal purpose' (s. 10 (2)), wholly exempt from search and seizure (s. 9 (2)). Items seized which are discovered to be privileged must be returned as soon as is reasonably practicable. The wording of s. 10 (2) has been widely construed. The majority of the House of Lords in *Francis and Francis* v. *Central Criminal Court* (1988) decided that it is not necessary that the adviser have any criminal intention, and that the state of mind of a client can suffice. The provision also extends to offences which have been committed (e.g. a bank robber concealing the proceeds of crime). The onus of proof lies with the police, but even if the criminal intention is established the items are still likely to be special procedure material (see below) because they will be held in confidence.

Excluded and special procedure material

These two categories are not completely protected but seizure requires an application to a circuit judge. However, an officer can seize excluded and special procedure material during a search under post-arrest powers (see ss. 18, 32 above) or any other lawful search (s. 19). This goes some way to explaining the noticeable decline in the number of warrant applications made to a circuit judge for these types of material. It also circumvents the associated safeguards imposed by PACE.

Excluded material is regarded as the most sensitive, and is immune unless there is a pre-existing statutory right to gain access to it (e.g. under the Theft Act 1968). This restriction does not apply to special procedure material. Excluded material is defined in s. 11 as embracing personal records which are held in confidence and have been acquired in the course of any trade, business, profession or other occupation or for the purposes of any paid or unpaid office. The meaning of 'personal records' is given in s. 12 and refers to documentary and other records which identify an individual and relate to specified matters: that is, physical and mental health; and spiritual or personal welfare counselling or assistance. This would include, for example, medical and psychiatric reports; records held by personnel officers, social workers, educational institutions and advice agencies; and information held by religious bodies. Also expressly included within s. 11 are human tissue and tissue fluid taken for the purpose of diagnosis or medical treatment, and journalistic materials, which are, in all cases, held in confidence.

Special procedure material constitutes confidential material (e.g. bank accounts, correspondence, minutes of meetings and book-keepers' files) which does not fall within either the legally privileged or excluded categories (s. 14). In addition to having a confidential nature, it is necessary that the material be acquired or created in the course of any trade, business, profession or other occupation or paid or unpaid office.

An application to a circuit judge is relevant where the police wish to gain access to excluded or special procedure material for the purposes of a criminal investigation. In conjunction with schedule 1, s. 9 offers the means by which, in certain circumstances, the police may obtain an order so as to gain possession of such confidential documentary and other material. This may comprise a production order (see above) or a search warrant. In all cases, the safeguard is that the judge exercises his powers and discretion properly.

A search warrant (or a production order) may be issued by a circuit judge in strictly limited circumstances. Unlike a production order, the application for a warrant will normally be *ex parte* because the holder of the documents will often be under investigation (*R.* v. *Leeds Crown Court ex parte Switalski* (1991)). The Act provides two sets of 'access conditions' which are relevant to this matter (schedule 1, paras 2, 3). The first set applies to special procedure material, whereas the second relates also to excluded material. It will be appreciated that major differences exist between the two sets.

The first set, which deals with applications made under PACE, harks back to the criteria employed in s. 8 which govern the magistrates' ability to issue a warrant. This set requires that there are reasonable grounds for believing that a serious arrestable offence has been committed and that special procedure material exists which is likely to be both of substantial value to the investigation and material evidence. In addition, unless they appeared bound to fail, other methods to obtain the material must have been attempted and, moreover, the seriousness of the investigation requires that it is in the public interest that the police have access to the material. The police are, moreover, under an obligation to be open-handed in their application and set out all the information in their possession (*R.* v. *Acton Crown Court ex parte Layton* (1993)). It appears that where the material is evidence of a serious arrestable offence the court will readily grant the order (see *R.* v. *Crown Court at Bristol ex parte Bristol Press* (1986)).

The second, and least popular, set of access conditions applies where the confidential material is sought under legislative provisions other than PACE (e.g. the Drug Trafficking Act 1986 or the Forgery Act 1913). The conditions here are that there exist reasonable grounds for believing that there is excluded or special material on the premises and that, under the previous law, a search warrant could have been granted by a magistrate and would have been appropriate in the circumstances. There is no further guidance to be found within schedule 1, and the police do not have to show either that the offence is of a serious arrestable nature, that they have tried other means of gaining access, or that the evidence is material to the investigation. Appropriateness is the governing principle and, accordingly, a search warrant may be appropriate when a production order has previously been made under this second set of access conditions and has not been complied with. As mentioned earlier, the primary effect of schedule 1 is to transfer the authority to issue a warrant from the magistrate to the judge.

If it is a search warrant (and not a production order) which is sought, the police must establish certain additional criteria listed within schedule 1. Regardless of which set of access conditions is fulfilled, to gain a warrant the police must show that it is not practicable to communicate with the occupier of the premises and the person entitled to grant access to the material; or that the disclosure of the material will be in breach of statute (this would cover, for example, a proposed breach of the Official Secrets Act by a journalist); or that proceedings for a production order may seriously prejudice the investigation. If the case for a warrant is not made out, no further application will be entertained unless supported by additional grounds (B: 2.8).

21.7.3 Execution of the warrant

The warrant may be executed by any officer named on it or any other constable (s. 16(6)). As regards a warrant for confidential material, Code B requires that an officer not below the rank of inspector be in charge of the search (B: 5.13). The officer in charge is responsible for ensuring that the search is carried out so as to cause the least possible disruption to any business or activity carried out on the premises. There is, however, no guidance as to the number of officers to be involved in the search, and this remains a matter of operational policy.

The entry and search must take place within one calendar month from the date the warrant is issued and at a reasonable hour unless this would frustrate the purpose of the search (s. 16(3),(4)). In the determination of what is reasonable, the officer in charge should take on board such factors as the times that the premises are likely to be occupied and when the residents are likely to be asleep (B: *Notes for Guidance* 5A). When the premises are occupied at the time of the search, certain formalities must be adhered to. The constable must identify himself, make the original warrant available for inspection and furnish the occupier with a certified copy (s. 16(5)). If these requirements are not satisfied the search is unlawful and any items seized cannot be retained (*R. v. Chief Constable of Lancashire ex parte Parker and McGrath* (1993)). If the occupier is absent, but the officer sees someone who is in charge of the premises, this information and documentation must be supplied to that person (s. 16(6)).

It is required also that a notice identifying the powers of the police and the rights of the individual be given to the occupier (B: 5.7). The timing of when these actions should occur was considered in *R. v. Longman* (1988) where it was decided that the necessary preliminaries may take place after the entry of occupied premises, but must be undertaken before the search. The copy of the warrant must be provided at the first reasonable opportunity. The occupier can, however, be deprived of these safeguards by his own actions (as in *Longman* where the occupier rushed at the police with a knife). In the situation where no one is either in occupation or in charge when the warrant is executed, a copy of the warrant and notice must be left in a prominent place on the premises (s. 16(7); B: 5.7).

A number of general considerations are prescribed in Code B and these apply to all searches authorised under statute or warrant and most voluntary searches. The premises may only be searched to the extent necessary to achieve the object for which the warrant was granted (B: 5.9; i.e. this is dependent upon the size and nature of the items sought). Once the subject-matter of the warrant has been located, or it is concluded that the items are not on the premises, the search may not continue except in so far as it is permitted under any other statutory provision (e.g. ss. 17, 18, 32 of PACE). Any search must be carried out with no more disturbance than is necessary and with due consideration for the property and privacy of the occupier (B: 5.10). If the occupier wishes to ask a third party to witness the search, this must be permitted unless the officer in charge has reasonable grounds for believing that it would 'seriously hinder' the investigation (B: 5.11). Nevertheless, the police have no legal authority (short of arrest) to prevent an invitee from attending. If the request is acceded to, the police are obliged to wait a reasonable time for the third party to be present (B: 5.11).

Reasonable force can be used if necessary where the occupier fails to co-operate or that co-operation is insufficient. The Code makes it clear that such force can be used to secure entry to premises when access is refused, the premises are unoccupied or there are reasonable grounds for believing that communication would frustrate the object of the search or endanger any person (B: 5.6). As the authority to search carries with it an implied duty on the occupier to admit entry, refusal will normally amount to an obstruction of the police in the execution of their duty (*Lunt* v. *DPP* (1993)). Where the premises have been entered by force, it is the responsibility of the officer in charge to ensure that they are secure before leaving (B:5.12). This can be achieved by arranging for the occupier to be present and, thereby, discharging responsibility or by any other appropriate means (e.g. boarding up windows).

21.7.4 Post-search records

Where premises have been searched (except when consent is not required because it would cause disproportionate inconvenience to the person concerned: B: 4.4), the officer in charge shall, on return to the station, have compiled a record of the search (B: 7.1). This record must identify the premises searched; the date, time and duration of the search; the lawful basis for the search (i.e. the warrant, consent or statutory power); except as regards terrorist investigations, the officers who participated; whether (and if so why) force was used and the extent of any damage caused to the premises; and a list of any articles seized. If the search was under warrant, similar details must also be endorsed on that warrant (B: 7.2).

At each subdivisional police station, a search register must be maintained and all records required by Code B need to be entered or referred to in this register (B: 8.1). These records will assume a general research importance and may also be used in evidence in any proceedings.

21.8 'In the Station': an Outline

It is beyond the scope of this chapter to explore in depth the statutory provisions which regulate the reception, detention, accommodation and interrogation of the arrested person once inside the police station. It should, however, be appreciated that PACE and Codes C, D and E lay down detailed rules concerning the treatment and rights of detainees. In recognition of the general theme that the exercise of police powers should produce a minimum interference with the personal freedoms of the individual, these controls are designed to ensure that detention time is kept to a minimum; that the detainee is treated in a humane fashion; and that questioning is unoppressive and conducted fairly. These safeguards appear consistent with Art. 3 and Art. 5 of the ECHR. In order to achieve these ends, the powers of the police are clarified, the suspect is to be given notification of his rights, interviews will normally be tape recorded and there must be a documentary record of actions taken (and the reasons why), with the key decisions being reached (often on the basis of 'reasonable grounds') by senior officers unconnected with the investigation. This is, at least the theory. In practice, legal advice is often delayed, the suspect is encouraged to talk in the absence of a lawyer, and obtaining a guilty plea is plausibly the driving force of police practice.

PACE requires that a custody officer (not below the rank of sergeant and who also is unconnected with the investigation) takes responsibility for the progress of the person through detention and maintains a custody record which discloses much of what happens to that individual while in the station. The suspect is allowed to view the Codes of Practice and must have explained (orally and/or in written form) his fundamental rights. Detailed rules govern the conditions of detention and, for example, cells must be adequately heated, ventilated and clean; at least two light meals and one main meal must be provided in every 24-hour period; access to toilet and washing facilities must be afforded; and outdoor exercise should be permitted. The detainee should be visited every hour and the continuing need for detention must also be kept under regular review. The Criminal Justice and Police Act 2001 allows this review process to be undertaken by telephone or video conferencing facilities. In the normal course of events, the arrested person will not be detained more than 24 hours without being charged (s. 42). In certain circumstances a superintendent may authorise an additional 12 hours' detention in the case of a serious arrestable offence (s. 42). Detention beyond this time must, however, be authorised by a magistrate who may grant a warrant of further detention for up to 36 hours (s. 43). This warrant may be extended on subsequent application for further periods until a total ceiling of 96 hours' detention is reached (s. 44 (2), (3)). During the period of detention, the arrested person is given the fundamental rights to obtain legal advice (s. 58) and to notify a third party of the arrest and the whereabouts of detention (s. 56). The exercise of these rights may be delayed for up to 36 hours on strictly delimited grounds, but only if the offence is of a serious arrestable nature and the delay is authorised by an officer of at least the rank of superintendent, (legal advice) or inspector (third-party notification).

Under the Anti-Terrorism, Crime and Security Act 2001, there are increased powers to take fingerprints, to carry out a non-intimate body search, to photograph suspects and to remove head coverings, all for the purpose of identification.

Summary

21.1   Traditionally, in English law, the police were not regarded as having special powers, but changes in society and the nature of crime necessitated that the police became more organised and more effective. Today, the law (principally statute law) recognises the need of law-enforcers to have clear and specific powers to enable them to perform their functions and at the same time to enable the individual to know his rights.

21.2   Current legislation deals with police powers to stop and search individuals and vehicles, to make arrests and to carry out searches for the evidence of crime. In exercising these powers the police are often allowed to act only on the basis of reasonable suspicion or reasonable belief. The 1984 Act, and the associated Codes of Practice, provide guidelines as to what can and cannot constitute such suspicion or belief. In many respects the extent of police powers will turn upon the seriousness of the offence under investigation and the distinction between arrestable offences, non-arrestable ones and serious arrestable offences.

21.3   It is now possible to be more certain as to whether an arrest or search is lawful. Although redress following an unlawful exercise of these powers remains essentially the same as before (i.e. a criminal prosecution or civil action for trespass to the person or land), the admissibility of the Act and Codes as evidence, coupled with individual records of searches and arrests which are now to be compiled, greatly assists the individual in challenging police action. Whether wrongful action on the part of the police will lead to an exclusion, in a subsequent criminal trial of the suspect, of illegally or unfairly obtained evidence, remains, however, a matter for judicial discretion rather than clear legal rules.

21.4   Whether PACE strikes the right 'balance' between police powers and individual liberty is a meaningless question because these are incommensurables. The real question is whether there is an accommodation that is broadly acceptable to the community.

Further Reading

Feldman, *Civil Liberties and Human Rights in England and Wales*, chapter 5.
McCrudden and Chambers, *Individual Rights and the Law in Britain*, chapter 3.
Munday, R. (1996) 'Inferences from silence and human rights law', *Criminal Law Review*, 370.
Sharpe (1997) 'The European Convention, a suspect's charter', *Criminal Law Review*, 448.

Exercises

21.1   One night, PC Bell and PC Rogers, two patrolling police officers, are told by X, a householder, that a burglar had just tried to enter her house but had run off when X shouted at him. X's house is 200 yards away from the point where X spoke to the officers. X gets into the police car and is driven round the neighbouring streets in search of the suspect. After five minutes, PC Bell sees a man walking hurriedly along the pavement. 'Is that him?' Bell asks X. 'I can't be sure. The burglar was roughly that height', replies X. The police stop their car and PC Bell approaches the man, Thompson. Bell asks him who he is and where he is going, but Thompson replies 'None of your business', and moves to get past PC Bell. At this time, PC Bell puts out an arm to stop him, but Thompson pushes it away and walks on. PC Bell grabs him, saying 'You're coming with me.' Thompson asks 'Am I under arrest?' and PC Bell answers 'It certainly looks like it, doesn't it?' and pushes Thompson into the police car. Nothing more is said until Thompson arrives at the police station where he is interviewed. As a result of this interview, there emerge no grounds for suspecting Thompson of being a burglar, but he is charged with assaulting PC Bell in the execution of his duty. Discuss:
 (i)   the likelihood on these facts of Thompson being convicted,
 (ii) whether Thompson could maintain an action for unlawful arrest, and
 (iii) whether your answer to (ii) would be different if PC Bell had said to Thompson: 'I am arresting you on suspicion of burglary.'

21.2   Throughout January–April 2001, 'The Biker's Cafe' was frequented by members of motor-cycle groups, most of whom had long hair and leather jackets. On three occasions, in April 2001, police found that several patrons of the cafe were in possession of offensive weapons. In each case the person was a long-haired motor-cyclist and sporting a leather jacket. On 1 May, Detective Constable Bell visited the cafe and was not in uniform. He noticed Mick, a man aged about 21 years, who was wearing a leather jacket, carrying a crash helmet and had his hair tied back in a pony-tail. DC Bell observed that there was a bulge in one of the pockets of Mick's leather jacket and that the metallic tip of an object was protruding from that pocket. DC Bell immediately concluded that Mick had a knife in his pocket. He approached Mick saying 'Come outside laddie. I want to search you.' Mick, who was a law student at the local university, was not a member of a motor-cycle gang and had never been to 'The Biker's Cafe' before. Mick, somewhat startled by DC Bell's manner, asked 'Why?', and received the reply: 'I'm a police officer. You'd better do what I say.' Mick followed DC Bell out to the street and, without further conversation, allowed him to pull out the object in his (Mick's) pocket. It proved to be a torch.

(i) Discuss whether the search of Mick was lawful and consistent with the ECHR.

(ii) Suppose that, in searching Mick's pocket, DC Bell had discovered a packet of heroin. Would the discovery of the packet be admissible evidence against Mick in any subsequent trial?

21.3 Explain the procedures, under PACE, whereby the police may obtain access to evidence which it is thought will be of assistance in the investigation of any crime.

22 State Secrecy

The republican perspective which I introduced in Chapter 1 stresses open government as an important way of combating domination. There are two aspects to state secrecy. The first concerns a public right of access to information held by government. Our private law traditions mean that the basic position is that no such right exists. The state, like a private person, can control its information unless there is a positive law to the contrary. Apart from cases where the principles of natural justice apply (see Chapter 16), the common law gives no right to information. Indeed in *Burmah Oil Corporation* v. *Bank of England* [1980] AC 1090 at 1112, Lord Wilberforce did not believe that the courts should support open government. There are, however, certain statutory rights to information of which the Freedom of Information Act 2000 is the most general but is not yet in force. On the other hand public interest immunity in litigation and the absence of a general duty to give reasons for government action reinforce state secrecy.

The second aspect concerns claims by the state to suppress information held by others such as the media. Here the state is interfering with common law rights and also the right of freedom of expression under Art. 10 of the European Convention on Human Rights. The onus is therefore on the state to justify its intervention. In relation to government information, secrecy is re-enforced by many statutes, notably the Official Secrets Act 1989 forbidding disclosure of certain information, by the civil law of breach of confidence, and by employment contracts.

There is also a tradition of voluntary secrecy generated by the priority of efficiency over accountability and partly perhaps by the psychological condition of many persons who desire to hold public office. For example, such persons may favour secrecy to reinforce their self-importance and may also be disposed towards tribalism. In particular, ministers and senior civil servants agree to subject any memoirs they propose to publish to vetting by the Cabinet Office. 'All information obtained by virtue of office is regarded as held for the State and not for the benefit of the office holder or the interested reader' (Cmnd 6386 (1986), para. 62). Contemporary policies of privatisation and encouraging public bodies to follow commercial practices, including 'commercial confidentiality', also militate against openness in favour of a protective, defensive culture.

Access to government information as such is not protected by the ECHR. Nor does it fall within Art. 10 (freedom of expression). Article 10 has been said to protect people who wish to disclose information and does not force anyone to do so (see *Leander* v. *Sweden* (1987)). However this takes no account of the democratic interest in the free flow of information which the ECHR has recognised in the context of press freedom (see Chapter 19). There may, however, be a right to information, under Art. 6 (right to a fair trial) and Art. 8 (respect for family life; see *Gaskin* v. *UK* (1989) – adoption records – applied restrictively in *Gunn-Russo* v. *Nugent Care Housing Society* (2001)).

In addtion to general concerns about freedom, arguments in favour of 'open government' include the following:

- *Democracy*: officials should be accountable to a well-informed public opinion.
- *Autonomy*: people should be able to exercise informed choice in relation to their own affairs.
- *Justice*: in being able to correct false information.
- *Direct public participation*: in decision making as an end in itself.
- *Public confidence*: in government.

Arguments in favour of government secrecy are primarily efficiency based and include the following:

- Release of certain kinds of information might cause serious harm, e.g. national security, crime prevention, child care and some economic information.
- Expense and delay, bearing in mind that seekers of information may be cranks, enemies or maniacs.
- Freedom of information could weaken ministerial responsibility to Parliament.
- Frankness within government, e.g. the danger of policy making being inhibited by premature criticism or the quality of debate being diluted by the temptation to play to the gallery (see Birkinshaw, 2001, p. 283 et seq.).
- Public panic if disclosures are misunderstood.
- Vanity and self-protection by public officials so that it might be more difficult to make public appointments.
- The mystique of government emphasised by Bagehot as a source of stability (see Chapter 3).

22.1 Voluntary Disclosure of Information

There is nothing to prevent the government from giving information on its own terms. Indeed the Official Secrets Act provides for 'authorised' information to be disclosed and the Freedom of Information Act 2000 leaves government with a discretion to disclose the many matters that are exempt from a duty to disclose under the Act (below). From the republican perspective this is not satisfactory in that it is not conducive to human dignity that important rights should depend on the goodwill of those in power. For example, the government provides unattributed information to journalists who are willing to fall into line (the 'Lobby'). The press also accepts the 'D' notice system which relies on voluntary censorship by a committee of officials and press representatives and voluntary regulation by the Press Complaints Commission.

Pressures for 'open government' have also been met by the voluntary disclosure of information (but not documents) held by central government departments (see *Open Government* Cm 2290, 1993). This Code of Practice (1994) is subject to many exceptions notably, information the disclosure of which 'would harm the candour and frankness of internal discussion'. A charge can be made for supplying information and there is no enforcement mechanism other than general channels of complaints within departments. However, the Parliamentary Commissioner can make recommendations.

The Code is sometimes restrictive. For example, the government will 'normally' disclose, but only after the policy is announced, facts and analysis of the facts which the government considers relevant and important in framing major policy proposals or decisions. 'Information' also includes reasons for administrative decisions to those affected, information about how public services are run including costs, complaints procedures, range of services, targets and standards, in response to specific requests, information relating to policies, actions and decisions.

The exceptions are in some cases vague. They include harm to defence, security and international relations, information received in confidence from foreign governments, courts or international organisations, communications with the royal household, prejudice to the administration of justice, harm to public safety or public order; danger to the life or physical safety of any person, protection of confidential sources, environmental damage, immigration and nationality, effective management of the economy and tax collection, effective management and operations of the public service, public employment, including personnel records, public appointments and honours, 'unreasonable', voluminous or vexatious requests, information which will soon be published or where publication is premature, research statistics or analysis, individual privacy, third-party's commercial confidences, information given in confidence, disclosures prohibited by statute, international agreement or under parliamentary privilege.

22.2 Statutory Rights to Information

There are certain statutory rights to information held by the government. They are characterised by broad exceptions and weak or nonexistent enforcement mechanisms. None of them gives access to the inner workings of the central government.

The most important of them are as follows:

- Historical records (see Cm. 853 (1991)). These are, subject to exceptions, made available after 30 years (Public Records Acts 1958, 1967, 1975). The 1993 White Paper on open government (Cm. 2290) proposed that records be withheld beyond 30 years only where actual damage to national security, economic interests or law and order can be shown, or if disclosure would be a breach of confidence or cause substantial distress or danger. At present many records are subject to blanket exclusion. The Freedom of Information Act 2000 removes exemptions for communications within UK governments, court records, decision making and policy formation, legal professional privilege and trade secrets contained in historical records. Information relating to honours is to be protected for 75 years and law enforcement matters for 100 years.
- Personal information held on computer or in structured manual records (Data Protection Act 1998). However, the Act exempts much government data including national security matters, law and tax enforcement matters and data 'relating to the exercise of statutory functions'.
- Local government information. The Local Government (Access to Information) Act 1985 gives a public right to attend local authority meetings including those of committees and sub-committees and to see background papers, agendas, reports and minutes. There are large exemptions. These include decisions taken by officers, confidential information, information from central government, personal matters excluded by the relevant committee, and 'the financial or business affairs of any person'. The Act appears to be easy to evade

by using officers or informal groups to make decisions. It is not clear what counts as a background paper.

- The Public Bodies (Admission to Meetings) Act 1960 gives a right to attend meetings of parish councils and certain other public bodies. The public can be excluded on the grounds of public interest (see *R. v. Brent Health Authority ex parte Francis* (1985)).

- The Access to Personal Files Act 1987 authorises access to local authority housing and social work records by the subject of the records and in accordance with regulations made by the Secretary of State (see also Housing Act 1985 s. 106 (5)).

- The Environmental Information Regulations 1992 (SI 1992 no. 320) implementing EC Directive, (90/313) require public authorities to disclose certain information about environmental standards and measures. The information must be made available on request, but there are no specific requirements as to how this is to be done. A charge can be made. Requests can be refused on grounds including manifest unreasonableness or a too-general request (how does a citizen know what to ask for?), confidentiality, increasing the likelihood of environmental damage, information voluntarily supplied unless the supplier consents, international relations, national security. Under the Aarhus Convention on Access to Information, Public Participation and in Decision Making and Access to Justice in Environmental Matters (1998, Cm. 4736 (2000)) the government is required to make regulations giving a general right to environmental information subject to exceptions on public interest grounds. These will replace the present regulations and be integrated into the machinery of the Freedom of Information Act 2000 under s. 74 of that Act (see also HL 9 (1996–97), *Freedom of Access to Information on the Environment*).

22.3 The Freedom of Information Act 2000

The majority of democratic states possess freedom of information legislation giving the public a legal right of access to governmental information. The Freedom of Information Act 2000 is a weak version. It is not yet in force and is required to be in force by 2005 (s. 87). Some parts of it, in particular a requirement to prepare 'publication schemes' (s. 19), are already in force but these give no right to particular information.

Subject to many exemptions and, in some cases to a governmental veto the Act requires public authorities to disclose information on request and also to confirm or deny whether the information exists (s. 1). This is supervised and enforced by an Information Commissioner who also has advisory and promotional functions. The Information Commissioner will also supervise a Code of Practice on Access to Government Information and approve publication schemes. The Act does not *prevent* an authority from disclosing any information (s. 78).

The scope of the Act is potentially wide. Under Sched. 1, central government departments (but not the cabinet, the royal household or the security services), Parliament, the Welsh Assembly (but not the Scottish government), local authorities, the police, the armed forces, state educational bodies and NHS bodies are automatically public authorities as well as a long list of other specified bodies, as are companies which are wholly owned by these bodies (s. 6). The Secretary of State may also designate other bodies, office holder or persons as public authorities which appear to him to be exercising 'functions of a public nature' or who provide services under a contract with a public authority the functions of which include the provision of that service (s. 3 (1)). This might include, for example, a voluntary body acting on behalf of a government agency. The Secretary of State can, however, put limits on the kind of information that the bodies he lists can disclose (s. 7).

The Act gives certain rights to any person to request in writing (s. 8), information held by the authority on its own behalf or held by another on behalf of the authority (s. 3 (2)). Reasons do not normally have to be given for the request. However, disclosure can be refused if the applicant has not provided such further information as the authority reasonably requires to enable the requested information to be found (s. 1) although the authority must provide reasonable advice and assistance (s. 16). A request can also be refused if the cost of compliance exceeds a limit set by the Secretary of State or where the request is vexatious or repetitive (s. 14). A fee regulated by the Secretary of State can be charged (s. 9). The authority must respond promptly and within 20 working days. However, if the matter might involve an exemption there is no time limit other than a 'reasonable time to make a decision' (s. 10).

The Information Commissioner can require the authority to disclose information either on his own initiative (enforcement notice, s. 52), or on the application of a complainant whose request has been refused (decision notice, s. 50). Reasons must be given for a refusal and the Commissioner can, where appropriate, inspect the information in question and also require further information. An authority can refuse to disclose to the Commissioner any information which might expose it to criminal proceedings other than proceedings under the Act itself. Both sides may appeal to the 'Information Tribunal' on the merits with a further appeal to the High Court on a point of law (s. 57). The right to information can be enforced by the courts through the law of contempt but no civil action is possible (s. 56).

However, the government sometimes has a veto over the Commissioner's enforcement powers (s. 53). This applies to information held by the central government, the Welsh Assembly and other bodies designated by the Secretary of State. It applies to any request that falls within the exemptions. An 'accountable person' (a cabinet minister, or the Attorney General or their equivalents in Scotland and Northern Ireland), can serve a certificate on the Commissioner 'stating that he has on reasonable grounds formed the opinion' that there was no failure to comply with the duty to disclose the information. Reasons must be given and the certificate must be laid before Parliament. The certificate would also be subject to judicial review.

The right to information under the Act is subject to many exemptions contained in Part II. These apply both to the information itself and usually to the duty to confirm or deny. Most are blanket exemptions for whole classes of information. Some require a 'prejudice' test relating to the particular document. However, this is less onerous for the government than the 'substantial prejudice' that was originally envisaged (White Paper, (1997). Some exemptions are absolute. Those that are not absolute are subject to a public interest test (see below).

The absolute exemptions are as follows:

- information which is already reasonably accessible to the public even if payment is required (s. 21);
- information supplied by or relating to the intelligence and security services (s. 23). A minister's certificate is conclusive subject to an appeal to the Tribunal by the Commissioner or the applicant which in respect of the reasonableness of the decision is limited to the judicial review grounds (s. 60);
- information contained in court records widely defined (s. 32);
- information protected by Parliamentary privilege (s. 34);
- information that would prejudice the conduct of public affairs in the House of Commons or the House of Lords (s. 36);
- certain personal information, although some of this is available under the Data Protection Act 1998 (s. 40 (1) (2));
- information the disclosure of which would be an actionable breach of confidence (s. 41), a public interest test applies at common law (see below);

- information protected by legal obligations such as legal professional privilege or European Law (s. 44).

  In other cases the exemption applies only where it appears to the authority that 'the public interest in maintaining the secrecy of the information outweighs the public interest in disclosure' (s. 2 (1)b). The balance is therefore tipped in favour of disclosure. However, because this test is subjective, the Commissioner's powers may be limited to the grounds of judicial review.

  The main exemptions of this kind are as follows:

- information which is held at the time of request with a view to be published in the future (s. 22). No particular time for publication need be set although it must be reasonable that the information be withheld;
- information required for the purpose of safeguarding national security. There is provision for a minister's certificate as under s. 23 (see above);
- information held at any time for the purposes of criminal proceedings or investigations which may lead to criminal proceedings or relate to information provided by confidential sources (s. 30). This would include many inquiries into matters of public concern;
- information the disclosure of which would or would be likely to prejudice defence, foreign relations, relations between the United Kingdom devolved governments, the House of Commons or the House of Lords, law enforcement widely defined to include many official inquiries, the commercial interests of any person including the public authority holding the information, or the economic interests of the United Kingdom. Nor does the duty to conform or deny arise in these circumstances, (ss. 26, 27, 28, 29, 31);
- audit functions;
- communications with the royal family;
- health and safety matters;
- environmental information subject to regulations made under s. 74 (see above).
- information concerning the 'formulation or development' of government policy (s. 35). This also includes communications between ministers, cabinet proceedings, advice from the law officers and the operation of any ministerial private office. It also seems to include advice from civil servants. However, once a decision has been taken statistical background can be released.
- Information held by government departments, and the Welsh Assembly which 'in the reasonable opinion of a qualified person'

would or would be likely to prejudice collective ministerial responsibility or which would or would be likely to inhibit 'free and frank'
provision of advice or exchange of views or 'would otherwise prejudice or be likely to prejudice the effective conduct of public affairs'
(s. 36). This would again ensure that civil service advice remains
secret. A 'qualified person' is the minister or other official in charge
of the department. Because the test is subjective it appears that
the Commissioner would have no power to intervene except where
the qualified person's decision was 'unreasonable'. A question here
would be whether the minimal *Wednesbury* version of unreasonableness would apply.

22.4   Unlawful Disclosure of Government Information

22.4.1   The Official Secrets Acts: the criminal law

The Official Secrets Act 1989 protects certain kinds of government
information from unauthorised disclosure. It was enacted in response
to long-standing and widespread criticism of the Official Secrets Act
1911 s. 2 which covered all information, however innocuous, concerning the central government (see Franks Committee Report, Cmnd
6104 (1972)). A series of controversial prosecutions culminated in the
Ponting trial in 1995 where a civil servant who gave information to an
MP concerning alleged governmental malpractice during the Falk-
lands war, was acquitted by a jury against the judge's summing up.
Section 2 required the Crown to show that the disclosure was not
made under a duty to the 'state'. The judge emphasised that civil
servants owed absolute loyalty to ministers and held that the 'state'
meant the government of the day, thus making it clear the 'public
interest' could not justify disclosure. However, Ponting's acquittal
meant that the government could no longer resist reform.

The Official Secrets Act 1989 is narrower but more sharply focused.
It identifies four protected areas of government activity and provides
defences which vary with each area. The aim is to make enforcement
more effective in respect of the more sensitive areas of government.
The protected areas are as follows.

(1) *Security and intelligence* (s. 1). This applies (i) to a member of the
security and intelligence services; (ii) to anyone else who is 'notified' by
a minister that he is within this provision; (iii) to any existing or former
Crown Servant or government contractor. In the case of (i) and (ii) any
disclosure is an offence unless the accused did not know and had no

reasonable cause to believe that the information related to security or intelligence. The nature of the information is irrelevant. In the case of (iii) the disclosure must be 'damaging'. This includes cases where the actual disclosure is damaging and also where the information or document is of a kind where disclosure is likely to be damaging (s. 1 (4)).

'Damaging' does not concern the public interest generally but means only damaging to 'the work of the security and intelligence services'. This might include, for example, informing MPs that security agents are breaking the law. It is a defence that the accused did not know and had no reasonable cause to believe that the disclosure would be damaging.

It is arguable that these provisions which lack proportionality tests violate the Human Rights Act 1998. However in *R.* v. *Shaylor* (2001) the Court of Appeal held that there was no public interest defence to s. 1 or to s. 4 (information relating to criminal investigations). At best an accused might raise a defence of necessity on the basis of proportionate action taken in order to avoid an imminent peril of danger to life or serious injury to himself or to someone for whom he reasonably regarded himself as responsible. The accused, a former member of MI5, had handed over documents to journalists which according to him revealed criminal behaviour by members of the service including a plot to assassinate President Gadiffi of Libya. His motive was to have MI5 reformed in order to remove a public danger. It was held that the defence of necessity was not available because he could not identify particular individuals who would be protected by the disclosure. Lord Woolf also held that the blanket ban on disclosure was not disproportionate so as to violate the right to freedom of expression in the ECHR. This was because national security was a particularly important public interest which required a strong deterrent. Moreover the Act contained some protection for the individual in the form of a right to obtain authorisation for a disclosure (below) 'and to make his voice heard not only by his superiors but by those of undoubted integrity and independence'. Given that the press would pay well for security information this arrangement also helped to ensure objectivity. However, his Lordship did not specify who the objective authorisers were. The Act itself does not create any independent mechanism.

(2) *Defence* (s. 2). This applies to any present or former Crown Servant or government contractor. In all cases the disclosure must be damaging. Here damaging means hampering the armed forces, leading to death or injury of military personnel, or leading to serious damage to military equipment or installations. A similar defence of ignorance applies as in (1).

(3) *International relations* (s. 3). Again this applies to any present or former Crown Servant or government contractor. Two kinds of information are covered: (i) any information concerning international relations; (ii) any confidential information obtained from a foreign state or an international organisation. The disclosure must again be damaging. Damaging here refers to endangering the interest of the UK abroad or endangering the safety of British citizens abroad. The fact that information in this class is confidential or its 'nature or contents' may be sufficient in itself to establish that the disclosure is damaging (s. 3(3)). There is a defence of ignorance on the same basis as in (1) (s. 3(4)).

(4) *Crime and special investigation powers* (s. 4). This applies to any present or former Crown Servant or government contractor and covers information relating to the commission of offences, escapes from custody, crime prevention, detection or prosecution work. 'Special investigations' include telephone tapping under a warrant from the Home Secretary (Interception of Communications Act 1985), and entering on private property in accordance with a warrant under the Security Services Act 1989 (see below). Section 4 does not require that the information be damaging as such because damage is implicit in its nature. There is, however, a defence of 'ignorance of the nature' of the information (s. 4(4)(5)).

In all the above cases the disclosure must be 'without lawful authority'. In the case of a Crown Servant or 'notified person' (see above) this means 'in accordance with his official duty' (s. 7). In the case of a government contractor, lawful authority means either with official authorisation, or disclosure for the purpose of his functions as such, e.g. giving information to a subcontractor. In the case of other persons who may fall foul of the Act (see below), lawful authority means disclosure to a Crown Servant for the purpose of his functions as such or official authorisation. There is a defence of reasonable belief in lawful authority.

Section 5 makes it an offence to pass on protected information, for example to the press. Protected information is information which has come into a person's possession as a result of (i) having been 'disclosed' (whether to him or another) by a Crown Servant or government contractor without lawful authority; or (ii) entrusted to him in confidence; or (iii) disclosed to him by a person to whom it was entrusted in confidence. This does not seem to cover someone who receives information from a *former* Crown Servant or government contractor. If this is so, the publisher of the memoirs of a retired civil servant may be safe (cf. *Lord Advocate* v. *Scotsman Publications* (1989) where s. 5 was applied to a retired civil servant). Nor does the section seem to apply to a person who accidentally finds protected information (e.g. a civil servant leaves his briefcase in a restaurant). Could this be regarded as a 'disclosure'? (It is an offence for a Crown Servant or government contractor not to look after the protected information and for anyone to fail to hand it back if officially required to do so.)

The Crown must prove that the accused knew or had reasonable cause to believe that the information was protected under the Act and that it came into his possession contrary to the Act. In the case of information in categories 1, 2 and 3 (above) the Crown must also show that disclosure is 'damaging' and that he knew or had reasonable cause to believe that this was so.

Finally it is an offence for any person without lawful authority to make a 'damaging' disclosure of information relating to security or intelligence, defence or international relations, which has been communicated in confidence by or on behalf of the UK to another state or international organisation and which has come into his possession without the authority of that state or organisation (s. 6). Apart from the normal defence of ignorance, there is a defence (unique to this section) that the information has already been published with the authority of the state or organisation concerned (s. 6 (3)).

22.4.2   Civil liability: breach of confidence

Information given in confidence can be prevented from publication by means of an injunction. This may be attractive to governments since it avoids a jury trial, can be very speedy and requires a lower standard of proof than in a criminal case. Indeed a temporary injunction which against the press may destroy a topical story can be obtained from a judge at any time on the basis of an arguable case. An action for breach of confidence can be brought by anyone. However, a public authority must show positively that secrecy is in the public interest, which the court will balance against any countervailing public interest in disclosure. Section 12 of the Human Rights Act 1998 reinforces this (above p. 467). In the case of a private claimant the dependent must show that disclosure is in the public interest. A public authority can rely on a public interest in disclosure in order to override private confidentiality even where the information has been given only for a specific purpose (see *Hellewell* v. *Chief Constable of Derbyshire* (1998); *Woolgar* v. *Chief Constable of Sussex* (1999)).

In *A-G* v. *Guardian Newspapers Ltd (No. 2)* (1988) (*Spycatcher*), the House of Lords in principle supported the interests of government secrecy. Peter Wright, a retired member of the security service, had published his memoirs abroad revealing possible malpractice within the service. In *A-G* v. *Guardian Newspapers Ltd* (1987) the government had obtained a temporary injunction preventing publication of extracts from the memoirs. At the full trial, however, their Lordships refused to make the injunction permanent but only because the memoirs were no longer secret, having become freely available in Britain. It was held that, in principle, publication was unlawful because it was in the public interest that the security service should have blanket protection; and that the Crown could probably obtain compensation in respect of publication in the UK before the memoirs had been published abroad. This was confirmed by the ECHR as proportionate. In *Observer and Guardian* v. *UK* (1991) the ECHR held that in the area of national security an injunction is justifiable to protect confidential information even where the content of the particular information is not in itself harmful (see also *Sunday Times (No. 2)* v. *UK* (1991); *A-G* v. *Jonathan Cape* (1975)).

Spycatcher also confirmed that members of the security services have a 'lifelong duty of confidence'. In *A-G* v. *Blake* (1998), a former civil servant had been been convicted of spying but escaped to Moscow where he published his memoirs. The House of Lords held that, even though the content of the memoirs created no danger to national security and were no longer confidential, Blake was liable to account for his royalties to the government on the ground that he should not be permitted to profit from his wrong.

The exposure of 'iniquity' (serious wrongdoing or crime) by government officers can justify disclosure (see, e.g. *Lion Laboratories* v. *Evans* (1985)). In *Spycatcher*, serious iniquity was not established and it remains to be seen whether 'iniquity' overrides national security. The method of disclosure must be reasonable and the discloser must probably complain internally before going public (*Francombe* v. *Mirror Group Newspapers* (1984)). This suggests that a high standard of evidence is required given that *Spycatcher* involved allegations of criminal activity against security service members including a plot to destabilise the Labour government.

The Public Interest Disclosure Act 1998 protects employees against unfair dismissal who disclose information to a minister or to a person prescribed by a minister relating to criminal offences, breaches of legal duties, miscarriages of justice, danger to health and safety or danger to the environment. However, there is no protection where the disclosure is an offence, for example under the Official Secrets Act 1989 (see above), and employees working in national security areas can be excluded (s. 11). Exceptionally an employee can make a disclosure to another person or even to the press. However, this must be reasonable and applies only where either the matter is exceptionally serious or the discloser reasonably believes either that s/he will be victimised or that evidence will be concealed, or there is no prescribed person or the matter has already been disclosed to the employer.

22.4.3   The press and breach of confidence

It was held in *Spycatcher* (see above) that a third party such as a newspaper is bound by an obligation of confidence where it obtained the information knowing of its confidential source. However, Lord Keith distinguished between disclosure by the Crown Servant himself and disclosure by the press. His Lordship emphasised the importance of press freedom and took the view that, against the press, the Crown must show a positive public interest in secrecy based on the contents of the documents (see also *Lord Advocate* v. *Scotsman Publications* (1990)). Against a Crown Servant, on the other hand, 'the general public interest in confidentiality and in encouraging other crown servants to preserve it may be enough'. Moreover, in order to maintain its right of freedom of expression under Art. 10 of the ECHR, a newspaper is not required to obtain advance clearance from the government (*A-G* v. *Times Newspapers* (2001)).

Third parties are not directly bound by an injunction even if they are aware that the material falls within it. A third party will be liable only if it reveals information in such a way as knowingly to destroy the purpose of the injunction (see *A-G* v. *Punch Ltd* (2001); *A-G* v. *Times Newspapers Ltd* (1991)). However, a third party who has obtained the information from a person bound by an injunction might be guilty of aiding and abetting disobedience to an injunction (ibid.). In *A-G* v. *Punch Ltd* (para. 121), the Court of Appeal left it open whether in a national security case an injunction might be made binding on the whole world.

Under the common law the courts have been reluctant to protect press sources on the Dicean ground that the press have no special status in law. However, s. 10 of the Contempt of Court Act 1981 protects the anonymity of a publisher's sources of information except where the court thinks that disclosure is necessary on the grounds of the interests of justice, national security or the prevention of crime and disorder. Section 10 does not automatically require disclosure on these grounds but permits the court to exercise a discretion between the competing concerns.

On the whole the English courts have interpreted the exceptions broadly against the press. In *X Ltd* v. *Morgan Grampian Publishers Ltd*

(1991) the House of Lords held that a commercial interest in discovering the source of a leak outweighed press freedom. This was condemned by the European Court in *Goodwin* v. *UK* (1996) on the ground that limitations on the confidentiality of journalistic sources call for 'the most careful scrutiny'. Moreover the interference was not proportionate given that further dissemination of the leaked information had been stopped. It has also been held that 'necessary' does not mean essential but only 'important' (*Re an Inquiry under the Companies Securities (Insider Dealings) Act 1985* (1988)) and that, where national security or wrongdoing are involved the court will usually order disclosure (*X Ltd* v. *Morgan Grampian Publishers Ltd* (1991); *Ashworth Hospital* v. *MGN Ltd* (2001)). However, in *John* v. *Express Newpapers Ltd* (2000) which concerned the leaking of draft advice from a barrister, it was held that a confidential source should be publicly disclosed only as a last resort.

Section 10 cases provide a characteristic example of the subjective accommodation inherent in human rights problems. It is not clear what the overall criterion should be. Proportionality seems to be of little help since, as Palmer (1992) points out, freedom of expression is general and abstract whereas harm tends to be specific and immediate thus favouring disclosure. It is not therefore surprising that judicial attitudes differ.

22.5 Public Interest Immunity

An important aspect of government secrecy concerns the doctrine once called 'Crown privilege' and now known as 'public interest immunity'. A party to a legal action is normally required to disclose relevant documents and other evidence in his possession, but where public interest immunity applies, documents and the information in them must not be disclosed. In deciding whether to accept a claim of public interest immunity the court is required to 'balance' the public interest in the administration of justice against the public interest, in confidentiality. At one time the courts would always accept the government's word that disclosure should be prohibited. However, as a result of *Conway* v. *Rimmer* (1968) the court itself now does the balancing exercise.

Public interest immunity applies both to civil and criminal proceedings. However, in criminal cases the claim is likely to succeed only in exceptional circumstances (see *R.* v. *Brixton Prison Governor ex parte Osman* (1992); *R.* v. *Keane* (1994); cf *R.* v. *Horseferry Road Magistrates*

Court (1993), Scott, 1996b). Any person can raise a claim of public interest immunity. Claims are often made by ministers following a well-established procedure involving advice from the Attorney-General ostensibly acting independently of the government. PII is not a right that can be voluntarily exercised but a duty that must be exercised even against the interests of the person claiming it (see *Makenjuda* v. *Metropolitan Police Commissioner* (1992)). However a minister is not under a duty to make a claim whenever he believes that there is a public interest at stake but must personally do an initial balancing exercise. In *R.* v. *Brown* (1994) the court emphasised that it was objectionable for a minister merely to be guided by the Attorney. Other persons are probably required to put forward the claim to the court or to hand the matter to a minister (see *R.* v. *West Midlands Chief Constable ex parte Wiley* (1994)).

The person seeking disclosure must first satisfy the court that the document is likely to be necessary for fairly disposing of the case, or in a criminal case, of assisting the defence, a less difficult burden (see *Air Canada* v. *Secretary of State for Trade* (1983); *Goodridge* v. *Hampshire Chief Constable* (1999), Criminal Procedure and Investigations Act 1996 s. 3). The court can inspect the documents at this stage but is reluctant to do so in order to discourage 'fishing expeditions' (see *Burmah Oil Co. Ltd* v. *Bank of England* (1980)).

The court itself will then 'balance' the competing public interests involved, at this stage inspecting the documents. In a criminal case, if the government objects to the court looking at the documents, it must normally abandon the prosecution (*R.* v. *Ward* [1993] 1 WLR 619, 681). A successful public interest immunity claim means that there is unfairness to the individual which is outweighed by other more important concerns. Moreover, before the Human Rights Act, at least in civil cases, the court did not give special weight to the interests of justice but applied a balance of probabilities test.

In both respects, therefore, public interest immunity seems to violate the right to a fair trial in Art. 6 of the ECHR, particularly in criminal cases (see *Borgers* v. *Belgium* (1991)). Article 6 contains no overrides except to the extent that the press or public may in certain circumstances be excluded from a trial. Indeed in *R.* v. *DPP ex parte Kebelene* (1999), Lord Bingham, remarked that 'I can conceive of no circumstances in which, having concluded that that feature rendered the trial unfair, the court would not go on to find a violation of Art. 6'. In *Kostovski* v. *The Netherlands,* (1989), the European Court of Human Rights refused to allow the state to protect the anonymity of witnesses. It applied a test of whether the exclusion placed the accused at a substantial disadvantage. The court emphasised that the right to a fair trial 'cannot be sacrificed to expediency'.

On the other hand, as long as the trial as a whole is fair with 'equality of arms' between the parties, particular aspects of it need not be fair (*Brown* v. *Stott* (2001), *Soering* v. *UK* (1989)). The safeguards in UK law, particularly the fact that the balancing must be carried out by an independent court, create substantial protection for the individual (see *C* v. *S* (1999)). Moreover the proportionality test now applies which requires the government to show a pressing social need which cannot be met by less intrusive means. This might well exclude claims based for example on frankness and administrative efficiency (see below). Any difficulties to the defence must also be counterbalanced by other procedural measures (see *Rowe* v. *United Kingdom* (2000); refusal to disclose evidence from police informers held unlawful).

Grounds for refusing disclosure include national security, the protection of anonymous informers (*Rogers* v. *Home Secretary* (1973); *D* v. *NSPCC* (1978); cf. *Alfred Crompton* v. *Customs and Excise* (1974) information supplied under a legal duty had to be disclosed), economically or commercially sensitive material, the protection of children, and relationships with foreign governments. It has also been said that preventing 'ill-informed or premature criticism of the government' is in the public interest, thus justifying a refusal to disclose high-level policy documents such as cabinet minutes (*Conway* v. *Rimmer* [1968] AC 910 at 952). There is no automatic immunity for such documents but a specially strong case would have to be made for their disclosure (see *Burmah Oil Co. Ltd.* v. *Bank of England* (1980) and *Air Canada* v. *Secretary of State for Trade* (1981)). On the other hand the desire to protect candour and frankness within the public service is probably not a sufficient justification (*Conway* v. *Rimmer* (above) at 957, 976, 993–4, 995); *R.* v. *West Midlands Chief Constable* (above); *Williams* v. *Home Office (No. 2)* [1981] 1 All ER 1151 at 1155; *Science Research Council* v. *Nasse* [1980] AC 1028 at 1970, 108 – candour a 'private' interest; but see *Burmah Oil Co. Ltd.* v. *Bank of England* [1980] AC 1090 at 1132). The courts also consider the purpose for which the information was given. Information given in confidence for a particular purpose will not be disclosed for another purpose unless the donor consents in circumstances where disclosure would not be harmful to the public interest (*R.* v. *West Midlands Chief Constable* (1994); *Lonrho* v. *Fayed (No. 4)* (1994); cf. *Peach* v. *Metropolitan Police Commissioner* (1986) – nothing to lose).

A distinction is often made between 'class' claims and 'contents' claims. A class claim means that, even if the contents of a document are innocuous, it should still be protected, because it is a member of a class of document of which disclosure would prevent the efficient working of government. In *R. v. Horseferry Rd Magistrates Court ex parte Bennett* (1993), a class claim was upheld in principle but the court emphasised the need for flexibility. The claim was for the confidentiality of communications betwen UK and overseas law enforcement agencies. Class immunity was justifiable in order to encourage international co-operation and to protect criminal investigations. However, the court held that the Crown Prosecution Service should consider whether to make a voluntary disclosure particularly where this would help the defence. The consent in writing and recorded of the Treasury Solicitor would be necessary. This process would enable the court to monitor class claims. In *R. v. West Midlands Chief Constable* (above) it was claimed that evidence given to the police complaints authority was protected by class immunity. The House of Lords rejected this blanket claim, holding that immunity depended on whether the contents of the particular document raised a public interest, which on the facts they did not. Lord Templeman remarked (at 424) that the distinction between a class and a contents claim loses 'much of its significance'. The alleged public interest in preventing premature criticism of the government might, however, protect classes of document such as policy advice given by civil servants or diplomatic communications.

After the Scott Report (1996) into the 'Arms for Iran Affair' the then government undertook not to make class claims as such and to claim Public Interest Immunity only where disclosure would cause 'real damage or harm' to the public interest. It also conceded not to claim immunity for high-level policy documents as such but has never resiled from the position that frankness can be a matter appropriate for protection (see HC Deb. vol. 287 col. 949; HL Deb. vol. 576 col. 1507; Ganz, 1997). These concessions are not legally binding and do not cover other bodies such as the police who may claim public interest immunity.

22.6   Security and Covert Surveillance

State secrecy is at its strongest in national security cases. National security issues put traditional notions of constitutionalism to the test. They reflect the Hobbesian value that the safeguarding of order and the state itself is the highest duty of the state to which other values including democracy must give way. According to Simon Brown LJ (1994), 'the very words 'national security' have acquired over the years an almost mystical significance. The mere incantation of the phrase of itself instantly discourages the court from satisfactorily fulfilling its normal role of deciding where the balance of public interest lies'. The UK courts have traditionally been reluctant to review national security decisions. In *The Zamora* (1916) it was held that those responsible for national security must be the sole judge of what national security requires. The high watermark is represented by the majority of the House of Lords in the wartime case of *Liversidge and Anderson* (1942). They held that the Home Secretary need not objectively justify a decision to intern an alien even though the statute required him to have 'reasonable cause'. Lord Atkin famously dissented, deploring judges 'who when face to face with claims involving the liberty of the subject show themselves more executive minded than the executive'. He was subsequently ostracised by his colleagues.

Lord Atkin is now widely recognised as having been right (*see* Lord Diplock in *IRC* v. *Rossminster* [1980] AC 952, 1011). Nevertheless review in national security cases is still restrained. In *Council of Civil Service Unions (CCSU)* v. *Minister for the Civil Service* (1985) the House of Lords held that the court can require evidence that the matter is genuinely one of national security but, subject to that, the question whether the action taken, in that case denial of a right to be consulted, was necessary, was not for the court to decide and no further reasons have to be given (see also *R.* v. *Secretary of State for the Home Department ex parte Hosenball* (1977); *R.* v. *Secretary of State for the Home Department ex parte McQuillan* (1995); *R.* v. *Secretary of State for the Home Department ex parte Adams* (1995)). The court could perhaps interfere on the ground of irrationality or bad faith although these would be difficult to establish because reasons do not have to be given (see *R.* v. *Secretary of State for the Home Department ex parte Cheblak* (1991)).

Secrecy is justified under the European Convention on Human Rights particularly on the ground of national security and the prevention of crime but subject to the existence of independent safeguards and the test of proportionality (see *Klass* v. *Federal Republic of Germany* (1978); *Kruslin* v. *France* (1990)). The Convention gives states a wide margin of appreciation in relation to security matters and confidentiality has been held to be a legitimate state interest in that it advances the proper working of government (see *Ireland* v. *UK* (1978); *Leander* v. *Sweden* (1987); *Observer and Guardian Newspapers* v. *UK* (1991)). On the other hand in *McQuillan* (above), Sedley J pointed out that the English approach ignores the fact that not all national security considerations are necessarily of the same weight and importance, so that the present approach does not satisfy the proportionality test.

The European Court has emphasised the need for safeguards against abuse, as being necessary in a democratic society even for national security matters (*Lawless* v. *Ireland* (1961); *Klass* v. *Federal Republic of Germany* (1978), *Malone* v. *UK* (1984); *Brogan* v. *UK* (1988)). However, safeguards need not necessarily be judicial. For example, in *Leander* v. *Sweden* (1987) the applicant's claim to see secret reports on him made for the purpose of security vetting was denied. This was because there were safeguards against abuse, consisting of a right of appeal to an independent committee. In *R.* v. *Shaylor* (2001) which concerned an absolute prohibition on disclosing information under the Official Secrets Act 1989, the Court of Appeal held that an internal mechanism for obtaining authority from a superior helped to strike a fair balance between freedom of expression and national security (see also *Brannigan and McBride* v. *UK* (1993)).

22.6.1   The Security and Intelligence Services

The 'secret services' comprise the Security Services, the Intelligence Services and the government communications centre GCHQ. Traditionally they have operated under the general law without special powers other than the possibility of royal prerogative power. They were in principle accountable to ministers, ultimately to the Prime Minister, but there was no formal mechanism for parliamentary accountability. Their role has been primarily that of information gathering. Where powers of arrest or interference with property were required, the assistance of the police was requested. However, the 'Spycatcher' litigation brought to a head recurrent concerns that security agents were out of control and unaccountable and they have now been placed within a statutory framework. This relies heavily on the discretionary powers of ministers but contains certain independent safeguards, albeit judicial review is restricted.

   The Security Services (formerly MI6) deal with internal security (Security Services Act 1989). They report to the Prime Minister. Their responsibilities include 'the protection of national security and, in particular, its protection against threats from espionage, terrorism and sabotage, from the activities of agents of foreign powers, and from actions intended to overthrow or undermine parliamentary democracy by political or violent means' (s. 1). Section 1 (3) includes the safeguarding of 'the economic well-being of the UK against threats posed by the actions or intentions of persons outside the British Islands'. This is extremely wide and could extend to the lawful activities of pressure groups. Moreover the Security Services Act 1996 extends the functions of the security services to include assisting the police in the prevention and detection of serious crime. This is vaguely defined to include the use of violence, crimes resulting in substantial financial gain, or conduct by a large number of persons in pursuit of a common purpose or crimes carrying a sentence of three years or more. This is wide enough to include political public order offences and industrial disputes and may violate ECHR notions of clarity and proportionality.

The Director-General is responsible as both poacher and game-keeper for the efficiency of the service, and for making 'arrangements' for securing that information is neither obtained nor disclosed 'except in so far as is necessary for the proper discharge of its functions' or, in the case of disclosure, for the prevention or detection of serious crime. The service must not take action to further the interests of any political party (s. 2 (2)). Nor can its information be used 'in determining whether any person should be employed or continue to be employed' except with the consent of the Secretary of State (s. 2 (3)).

The Intelligence Services (formerly MI5 and GCHQ, Intelligence Services Act 1994) deal with threats from outside the United Kingdom. They are under the control of the Foreign Office but also report to the Prime Minister. Their functions are widely defined as being 'to obtain and provide information relating to the actions and intentions of persons outside the British Islands' and 'to perform other tasks relating to the actions and intentions of such persons'. Reflecting the language of the European Convention on Human Rights, the powers of the intelligence servives are limited to national security with particular reference to defence and foreign policies, the economic well-being of the United Kingdom in relation to the actions and intentions of persons outside the British islands and the prevention and detection of serious crime (ss. 1 (2), 3 (2)). GCHQ can monitor and interfere with electronic communications and 'other emissions' and can provide advice and information to the armed forces and other organisations specified by the Prime Minister.

22.6.2 Surveillance Powers

The exercise of surveillance powers involves the Art. 8 right of privacy against clear public interests in national security and the prevention and detection of serious crime. The absence of a distinctive privacy law meant that UK law lacked sufficient safeguards to comply with Art. 8 of the European Convention on Human Rights (see *Malone* v. *UK* (1985), *Klass* v. *Federal Republic of Germany* (1978), *Kruslin* v. *France*

(1990)). There is now a range of statutory provisions which authorise surveillance. The main powers are as follows.

The Interception of Communications Act 1985 empowers the Secretary of State to issue warrants to the police and to certain other public authorities authorising them to intercept public telecommunication systems on prescribed grounds such as serious crime or national security. It is an offence, knowingly to intercept without a warrant. Information must be used only for the authorised purpose and must be destroyed after use. Complaints relating to whether a warrant has been lawfully issued can be made to a tribunal and a commissioner who is a senior judge reviews the arrangements, reporting to the prime minister. The tribunal is limited to applying judicial review standards. The decisions of these persons cannot be challenged in the courts (s. 7(8)). Moreover, except in relation to a prosecution under the Act, and in certain employment cases, neither evidence obtained by tapping nor the fact of tapping, nor the question whether a warrant has been obtained can be used in legal proceedings (s. 9). The 1985 Act has been overtaken by technology. It does not apply to private telephone systems (*Halford* v. *UK* (1997)), nor apparently to cordless or mobile telephones. It does not protect the metering of calls, which is lawful for the purpose of investigating crime (see Telecommunications Act 1985 s. 45). Moreover the tribunal's powers are limited. It cannot investigate claims concerning interception without a warrant nor the use of information after interception. In *R.* v. *Preston* (1993) Lord Mustill remarked that the 1985 Act seemed to violate basic principles of fairness relying heavily on the good faith of the officials involved (see also Justice, 1998).

Part 2 of the Police Act 1997 gives the police additional power in connection with bugging devices. Section 92 makes it lawful to enter or interfere with property normally with the authorisation of the Chief Officer of Police (s. 93). The use of surveillance devices can be authorised only where the matter concerns a serious crime, and the action is necessary. A commissioner (below) must be immediately notified, who can quash the warrant. However, information already obtained does not have to be destroyed if it is to be used in court. Except in cases of urgency, prior consultation with a commissioner is required in the case of residences, hotel bedrooms, specified confidential information and personal or journalistic information.

The Regulation of Investigatory Powers Act (RIPA) 2000 is more comprehensive. It sets out to ensure that surveillance and the use of secretly obtained information by all public authorities including the security services complies with the European Convention on Human

Rights by controlling the interception, acquisition and use of information in relation both to public and private telecommunication systems. This includes telephone tapping, including mobile phones and intercepting electronic data. It also authorises the interception of 'communications data', this being information about the use made of communication systems, billing, websites etc. as opposed to content.

RIPA creates significant new powers of surveillance by making clear that certain forms of surveillance are lawful and also by imposing duties on communication providers such as Internet service providers to co-operate with the authorities by providing surveillance facilities. Government funding is available for this. It is an offence deliberately and without lawful authority to intercept a public telecommunication system and a private telecommunication system without the consent of the person in control of the system (s. 1). It is a tort, actionable in private law, to intercept communications in a private telephone system without the consent of the person in control of the system (s. 1(3)).

Lawful authority is provided by a warrant issued by the Secretary of State (s. 5). There are also cases where a warrant is not required (ss. 3, 4). In particular the Secretary of State can make regulations legitimating interception for the purpose of co-operating with overseas interception requests, monitoring or recording business activities and in prisons, and secure hospitals (s. 4). Under the *Telecommunications (Lawful Business Practices) (Interception of Communications) Regulations 2000*, (SI 2000, No. 2699), employers and service providers can intercept data on their own systems for the purposes of their business and in relation to certain crimes and public concerns (cf. Directive 97/666, EC).

A warrant can be issued by the Secretary of State on the application of the chief of the security, or intelligence services, a chief of police or the senior officers of the customs and excise or defence services (s. 3). 'Interception' includes modifying the system or its operation or monitoring its transmissions (s. 2(1)). Independent judicial supervision is not required, although this might arguably violate the ECHR. The Act also requires service providers to maintain an interception capability (s. 12). Government funding is available for this. Specific authorisation is required for intercepted information to be shared with other persons including public authorities.

The obtaining and use of 'communications data' (above) can be authorised by a wide range of senior police and other officials. Chapter II empowers the disclosure of communications or 'traffic' data, such as subscriber details, telephone bills and e-mail addresses. Authorisation can be given on wider grounds, including tax collection. Moreover authorisation does not require a warrant and can be internal from the head of the public authority concerned. This may also be questionable under the ECHR (see *Kopp* v. *Switzerland* (1998)). The Anti-Terrorism, Crime and Security Act Part 11 extends this power in order to require communications providers such as Internet service providers to make archived communications data available which can be trawled through at leisure.

Controversially, RIPA empowers anyone in lawful possession of intercepted information to require the disclosure of the key to protected (encryptified) data on the grounds of national security, serious crime and, more dubiously, that it is necessary for the performance of a public function (s. 49). The UK is the only leading democracy to allow this. A disclosure notice must be authorised by a circuit judge who must be satisfied that there is no other means of obtaining the required information and that the direction is proportionate to what is sought to be achieved. In the case of a company the notice must be served on a senior officer or employee (s. 49(5)) and the Secretary of State must contribute to the cost of compliance (s. 51). A disclosure notice requested by the police, the security services or the customs and excise commissioners can also contain 'tipping-off' provisions imposing life-long secrecy requirements as to the existence of the notice (s. 54).

Part II of RIPA provides for the authorisation of covert surveillance including bugging devices and 'covert human intelligence sources'. The latter are informers who form a personal relationship with a person for the purpose of obtaining information (s. 26). The Act provides that such activities are lawful for all purposes if authorised under the Act. This kind of surveillance is not otherwise unlawful and the Act does not make it so. However, without authorisation it is vulnerable to challenge under the Human Rights Act 1998 because of the absence of safeguards (see *Teixeira de Castro* v. *Portugal* (1999)). In *J.H. Ltd* v. *UK* (2001), the European Court held that bugging in a police station without safeguards was a violation of the right to privacy.

Intrusive surveillance is covert surveillance on or in relation to residential premises or in a private vehicle which involves either presence on the premises or in the vehicle, or use of a bugging device. However, if the device is not on the premises or vehicle, it is 'intrusive' only if the quality of information is as good as if it were (s. 26(5)).

These forms of surveillance can be authorised on a lower level than is the case with telephone interception (above), (see *Regulation of Investigatory Powers (Prescription of Offices, Ranks and Positions) Order 2000* (SI. 2000 no. 2417)). Intrusive surveillance requires a higher level of authorisation (s. 32(1)).

The circumstances in which these powers can be exercised reflects the European Convention on Human Rights, in particular the concept of proportionality and the overrides affecting the right to privacy (see e.g. ss. 5, 15, 32, 49, 74). These include national security, the prevention and detection of serious crime, the safeguarding of the economic well-being of the country and, in the case of conduct other than interception, the safeguarding of public health, public safety, tax collection, emergencies protecting life and health and 'other purposes specified by the Secretary of State' (s. 22).

22.6.3 Safeguards

Commissioners for intelligence services, interception of communications, and police surveillance operations review the exercise of the various powers of investigation and use of material under the legislation (Regulation of Investigatory Powers Act 2000, s. 59, Police Act 1997). The commissioners who are senior judges can report to the Prime Minister at any time. The Prime Minister must lay their annual reports before Parliament. There is also a Joint Intelligence and Security Committee of Parliament which examines the spending, administration and policy of the intelligence services (Intelligence Services Act 1994 s. 11).

RIPA creates a unified Tribunal to hear allegations of misuse of power by the security and intelligence services and also in relation to the interference with property, interception of communications, covert surveillance or misuse of information by the police and armed forces (s. 65). The Tribunal is also concerned with claims based on human rights for which it is made the only forum for actions against a public body under s. 7 of the Human Rights Act 1998. The tribunal is required to apply judicial review principles review (s. 67). In view of the wide powers involved this affords only a low level of review although this is likely to be enough to conform to the ECHR. The tribunal may award compensation, and make other orders including quashing warrants or authorisations and ordering records to be destroyed (ibid). In the case of a complaint about interference with property by the security services the tribunal must refer the matter to the Commissioner who must then investigate (Intelligence Services Act 1994 Schedule 1 (4) (1)). If a warrant has been issued, the Commissioner is banned from probing any deeper than would a court applying judicial review principles (ibid.). The Commissioner reports back to the tribunal (Schedule 1 (4) (2)).

In the case of the intelligence services the tribunal has power where they do not decide in favour of the complainant, to refer a matter to the Commissioner where they think it appropriate that there should be an investigation into 'whether the service has in any other respect acted unreasonably in relation to the complainant or his property'. The Commissioner may then report to the Secretary of State who can make an award of compensation (Schedule 1 (7)). It is doubtful however whether a single commissioner has the resources adequately to investigate complaints. The decisions of the Tribunal and the Commissioner cannot be questioned in the courts even on jurisdictional grounds (Intelligence Services Act 1994 s. 5 (4), RIPA s. 67 (8)), a provision that might violate the ECHR.

Summary

22.1   There is no general right to the disclosure of governmental information. There is a voluntary code subject to many exceptions, and the government proposes to introduce a freedom of information bill where information must be disclosed unless to do so would be harmful. Again there are exceptions.

22.2   There are certain statutory rights to the disclosure of specified information, but these are outnumbered by many statutes prohibiting the disclosure of particular information.

22.3   The Freedom of Information Act 2000 confers a right to 'request' the disclosure of documents held by public authorities. However, this can be overridden by the government and is subject to many exceptions particularly in relation to central government policy. The Act is not yet in force.

22.4   Under the Official Secrets Act 1989 certain categories of information are protected by criminal penalties. Except in the case of national security, the information must be damaging. There is also a defence of ignorance.

22.5   The law of confidence requires the court to balance the public interest in 'openness' against the public interest in effective government. The balance is struck differently according to context. The courts have endorsed the importance of freedom of expression and a public body is required to show a public interest in secrecy. The main remedy is an injunction. Third parties such as the press are not directly bound by an injunction but might be liable for contempt of court if they knowingly frustrate its purpose.

22.6   Public interest immunity allows the government to withhold evidence. The court makes the decision on the basis of balancing the public interest in the administration of justice against the public interest in effective government. The courts' approach to public interest immunity is affected by the Human Rights Act 1998 which requires that any claim satisfy the proportionality principle.

22.7   The Security and Intelligence Services are subject a certain degree of control largely through non-judicial mechanisms. There is detailed regulation of electronic surveillance. This gives the government wide powers of interception subject to the requirement for safeguards in respect of the obtaining and handling of information in particular proportionality and limitations on purposes. The courts give the executive a wide margin of discretion in relation to security matters.

Further Reading

Akdeniz *et al.* (2001) 'Regulations of Investigatory Powers Act 2000 (1): Big Brother. gov.UK: State Surveillance in the Age of Informatiion and Rights,' *Criminal Law Review* 73.
Leigh, I. and Lustgarten, L. (1991) 'The Security Commission: constitutional achievement or curiosity?', *Public Law*, 215–32.
Oliver, D. (1998) 'Freedom of information and ministerial accountability', *Public Law*, 171.
Palmer, S. (1990) 'Tightening secrecy law', *Public Law*, 243.
Scott, Sir R. (1996) 'The acceptable and unacceptable uses of public interest immunity', *Public Law*, 427.
Simon Brown, LJ (1994) 'Public Interest Immunity', *Public Law*, 579.
Uglow, S. (1999) 'Covert surveillance and the European Convention on Human Rights', *Criminal Law Review*, 287.
White Paper, *Your Right to Know: Freedom of Information* (1997) Cm 3818.
Whitty, Murphy, Livingstone, *Civil Liberties Law: The Human Rights Act Era*, Ch. 7.

Exercises

22.1 To what extent is the law relating to government secrecy affected by the Human Rights Act 1998?

22.2 'We have moved from a discretionary open government regime under a voluntary Code of Practice to a statutory open government regime in which the power to decide what is to be disclosed lies within the discretion of government and is denied to independent bodies', Nigel Johnson ((2001) 151 *New Law Journal* at 1031). Explain and discuss critically.

22.3 Sam is a member of the Intelligence Services. In connection with his work, he hears a rumour that terrorists are planning to infect certain television studios with a substance capable of infecting people with the disease anthrax. However, it is not clear which studios will be targeted. Sam's daughter Jill is a presenter at a local television studio in the north of England. Without consulting anybody, Sam informs Jill of the rumour. The rumour is subsequently revealed on the local television news broadcast from the studio in question. Sam and Jill are prosecuted under the Official Secrets Act 1989. Advise them.

22.4 Derek, a director of a company that supplies rail catering services, is prosecuted for insider dealing in the shares of an associated company that recently entered into a contract to provide travel facilities and 'entertainment' for the government. Derek claims that, when he dealt with the shares, the government's plans involved a different company altogether but were later vetoed by a special advisor to the Secretary of State and a cover-up put in place. Derek requests the production of letters between civil servants and the Secretary of State (the existence of which he learned of from an anonymous e-mail), which he claims would support his version of events. The government issues a PII certificate on the ground that the information is in a category the disclosure of which would inhibit free and frank discussion within the government. The minister who signed the certificate did not examine the information personally but relied on advice from the Attorney-General that the 'certificate is good for all cabinet level documents'. Advise Derek.

22.5   Dan, a property developer, enters into an agreement with Oldcastle Council under which he promises to provide the Council with a magnificent new headquarters in return for planning permission to build a shopping centre. Bill, the leader of the Council opposition, suspects that the project is financed by the proceeds of drugs dealing and wishes to intercept Dan's telephone conversations and e-mails and obtain access to his encrypted business records in order to establish this. Advise Bill.

Bibliography

Abel, R. (1994a) *Speech and Respect,* London: Stevens & Son.

Abel, R. (1994b) 'Public freedom, private constraint', *Journal of Law and Society,* 21(3), 374–382.

Akdenig, Taylor, Walker (2001) 'Regulation of Investigating Powers Act 2000(1): Big Brother.gov.uk: State Surveillance in the Age of Information and Rights', Crim. LR 73.

Alder, J. (2001) 'Incommensurable values and judicial review: the case of local government', *Public Law,* 717.

Allan, J. (1996) 'Bills of rights and judicial power: a liberal's quandary', *Oxford Journal of Legal Studies,* 16(2), 337–352.

Allan, T. (1985) 'The limits of parliamentary sovereignty', *Public Law,* 614–631.

Allan, T. (1993) *Law, Liberty and Justice: Legal Foundations of British Constitutionalism,* Oxford: Oxford University Press.

Allan, T. (1997) 'Parliamentary sovereignty: law, politics and revolution', *Law Quarterly Review,* 113, 443–452.

Allan, T. (1999) 'The rule of law as the rule of reason: consent and constitutionalism', *Law Quarterly Review,* 115, 221–244.

Allan, T. (2000) *Constitutional Justice: A Liberal Theory of the Rule of Law,* Oxford: Oxford University Press.

Allison, J. (1996) *A Continental Distinction in the Common Law: A Historical and Comparative Perspective on English Public Law,* Oxford: Clarendon Press).

Allott, P. (1990) 'Parliamentary sovereignty – from Austin to Hart', *Cambridge Law Journal,* 49(3), 377–380.

Armstrong Report (1986) *Civil Servants and Ministers: Duties and Responsibilities. Government Response to the Seventh Report from the Treasury and Civil Service Committee,* Cmnd. 9841, London: HMSO.

Atiyah, P. (1979) *The Rise and Fall of Freedom of Contract,* Oxford: Oxford University Press.

Bagehot, W. (1902) *The English Constitution,* 2nd edn, London: Kegan, Paul.

Bailey, S., Harris, D. and Jones, B. (1995) *Civil Liberties: Cases and Materials,* 4th edn, London: Butterworths.

Baldwin, R., McCrudden, C. and Craig, P. (eds) (1987) *Regulation and Public Law,* London: Weidenfeld & Nicolson.

Bamforth, N. (1999) 'The application of the Human Rights Act 1999 to public authorities and private bodies', *Cambridge Law Journal,* 58(1), 159–170.

Barber, N. (2000) 'Sovereignty re-examined: the courts, Parliament and statutes', *Oxford Journal of Legal Studies,* 131.

Barberis, P. (1998) 'The new public management and a new accountability', *Public Administration,* 76, 451–470.

Barendt, E (1985a) *Freedom of Speech,* Oxford: Clarendon Press.

Barendt, E. (1985b) 'Dicey and Civil Liberties', *Public Law,* 596–613.

Barendt, E. (1995) 'Separation of powers and constitutional government', *Public Law,* 599–619.

Barendt, E. (1998) *An Introduction to Constitutional Law,* Oxford: Oxford University Press.

Baxter, J.D. (1990) *State Security, Privacy and Information,* Hemel Hempstead: Harvester Wheatsheaf.

Beatson, J. and Tridimas, T. (1999) *New Directions in European Public Law,* Oxford: Hart Publishing.

Beetham, D. (1991) *The Legitimation of Power*, Basingstoke: Macmillan.

Bellamy, R., Bufacchi, V. and Castiglione, D. (eds) (1995) *Democracy and Constitutional Culture in the Union of Europe*, London: Lothian Foundation Press.

Bennion, F. (2000) 'What interpretation is "possible" under section 3(1) of the Human Rights Act 1998?, *Public Law*, 77–91.

Berlin, I. (1996) *The Sense of Reality: studies in ideas and their history* (ed. H. Hardy), London: Chatto & Windus.

Berlin, Sir I. (1969) *Four Essays on Liberty*, London: Oxford University Press.

Betten, L. and Grief, N. (1998) *EU Law and Human Rights*, New York: Longman.

Beyleveld, D. (1995) 'The concept of a human right and the incorporation of the European Convention on Human Rights', *Public Law*, 577–598.

Billings, P. and Ponting, B. (2001) 'Prerogative powers and the Human Rights Act: elevating the status of Orders in Council', *Public Law*, 21–27.

Bingham, Sir T. (1992) 'There is a world elsewhere: the changing perspectives of English law', *International Comparative Law Quarterly*, 41, 513–529.

Bingham, Sir T. (1993) 'The European Convention on Human Rights: time to incorporate', *Law Quarterly Review*, 109, 390–400.

Bingham, The Right Hon. Lord (1998) 'The way we live now: human rights in the new millennium', The Earl Grey Memorial Lecture: University of Newcastle-upon-Tyne, http://webjcli.ncl.ac.uk.

Bingham, The Right Hon. Lord (2002) 'Dicey revisited', *Public Law*, 39.

Birkinshaw, P. (1994) *Grievances, Remedies and the State*, 2nd edn, London: Sweet & Maxwell.

Birks, P. (ed.) (1997) *Privacy and Loyalty*, Oxford: Clarendon Press.

Blackburn, R. (1989) 'The summoning and meeting of new Parliaments in the United Kingdom', *Legal Studies*, 9, 165–176.

Blackburn, R. (1995) *The Electoral System in Britain*, New York: St Martin's Press.

Blackburn, R. and Busuttil, J. (eds) (1997) *Human Rights for the 21st Century*, London: Pinter.

Blackburn, R. and Plant, R. (eds) (1999) *Constitutional Reform: the Labour Government's Constitutional Reform Agenda*, London: Longman.

Blackstone, W. (1765–69) *Commentaries on the Laws of England*, 15th ed., 1809, Oxford: Oxford University Press.

Blasi, V. (1977) 'The checking value in First Amendment theory', *American Bar Foundation Research Journal*, 3, 521–649.

Bloustein, E. (1964) 'Privacy as an aspect of human dignity: an answer to Dean Prosser', *New York ULR*, 39, 962–971.

Bogdanor, V. (1981) *The People and the Party System: The Referendum and Electoral Reform in British Politics*. Cambridge: Cambridge University Press.

Bogdanor, V. (1995) *The Monarchy and the Constitution*, New York: Clarendon Press.

Bogdanor, V. (1999a) *Devolution in the United Kingdom*, Oxford: Oxford University Press.

Bogdanor, V. (1999b) 'Devolution: decentralisation or disintegration?' *Political Quarterly*, 70(2), 185–194.

Bogdanor, V. (1999c) 'Reform of the Lords: a sceptical view', *Political Quarterly*, 70(4), 375–381.

Bollinger, L. (1990) 'The tolerant society: a response to critics', *Columbia Law Review*, 90(1), 979–1003.

Boyle, A. (1984) 'Administrative justice, judicial review and the right to a fair hearing under the European Convention on Human Rights', *Public Law*, 89–111.

Boyron, S. (1992) 'Proportionality in English administrative law: a faulty translation', *Oxford Journal of Legal Studies*, 12, 237–264.

Bradbury, J. and Mitchell, J. (2001) 'Devolution: new politics for old', *Parliamentary Affairs*, 54(2), 257–275.

Bradley, A. (1994) 'Parliamentary sovereignty – in perpetuity?', in Jowell, J. and Oliver, D. (eds), *The Changing Constitution*, 3rd ed, Oxford: Clarendon Press.

Brady, R. (1999) 'Collective responsibility of the cabinet: an ethical, constituional or managerial tool?', *Parliamentary Affairs*, 52(2), 214–229.

Brazier, R. (1988) 'The financial powers of the House of Lords', *Anglo-American Journal*, 17(2), 131–161.

Brazier, R. (1989a) 'Government and the law: ministerial responsibility for legal affairs', *Public Law*, 64–94.

Brazier, R. (1989b) 'The constitutional role of the opposition', *Northern Ireland Legal Quarterly*, 40(2), 131–151.

Brazier, R. (1992) 'The non-legal rules of the constitution', *Northern Ireland Legal Quarterly*, 43(3), 262–287.

Brazier, R. (1994) *Constitutional Practice*, 2nd edn, Oxford: Clarendon Press.

Brazier, R. (1995) 'The constitutional position of the Prince of Wales', *Public Law*, 401–416.

Brazier, R. (1998) 'Defending the Hereditaries: the Salisbury convention', *Public Law*, 371–377.

Brazier, R. (1999) 'The constitution of the United Kingdom', *Cambridge Law Journal*, 58(1), 96–128.

Brennan, W. (1989) 'Why have a Bill of Rights?', *Oxford Journal of Legal Studies*, 9(4), 425–440.

Briggs, A. (1959) *The Age of Improvement 1783–1867*, London: Longman.

Browne-Wilkinson, Sir N. (1988) 'The independence of the judiciary in the 1980s', *Public Law*, 44–57.

Browne-Wilkinson, The Rt. Hon. Lord (1992) 'The infiltration of a Bill of Rights', *Public Law*, 397–410.

Butler, A. (1997) 'The Bill of Rights debate: why the New Zealand Bill of Rights 1990 is a bad model for Britain', *Oxford Journal of Legal Studies*, 17(2), 323–345.

Butler, D., Bogdanor, V. and Summers, R. (eds) (1999) *The Law, Politics and the Constitution: Essays in Honour of Geoffrey Marshall*, Oxford: Oxford University Press.

Buxton, R. (2000) 'The Human Rights Act and private law', *Law Quarterly Review*, 116, 48–65.

Cabinet Office (1987) *Notes of Guidance on the Duties and Responsibilities of Civil Servants in Relation to Ministers*, London: Cabinet Office.

Cabinet Office (1997) *A Code of Conduct and Guidance on Procedures for Ministers*, London: Cabinet Office.

Cabinet Office (1998) *Public Services for the Future: Modernisation, Reform, Accountability: Comprehensive Spending Review: Public Service Agreement 1999–2000*, Cm. 4181, London: HMSO.

Cabinet Office (2000a) *Executive Agencies*, 1999 Report Cm. 4658, London: HMSO.

Cabinet Office (2000b) *How to Review Agencies and Non-departmental Public Bodies to Improve the Quality and Effectiveness of Public Services*, http://www.gov.uk/eeg/2000.

Cabinet Office (2000c) *Executive NDPBs: 1999 Report*, Cm. 4657, London: HMSO.

Caenegem, R. van (1995) *An Historical Introduction to Western Constitutional Law*, Cambridge: Cambridge University Press.

Campbell, D. and Lewis, D. (1999) *Promoting Participation: Law or Politics*, London: Cavendish Publishing.

Campbell, T. (1999) 'Human rights: a culture of controversy', *Journal of Law and Society*, 26(1), 6–26.

Cane, P. (1995) 'Standing up for the public', *Public Law*, 276–287.

Card, R. (2000) *Public Order Law*, Bristol: Jordans.

Carmichael, P. and Dickinson, B. (eds) (1999) *The House of Lords: Its Parliamentary and Judicial Roles*, Oxford: Hart Publishing.

Carnwath, The Hon Sir R. (1996) 'The reasonable limits of local authority power', *Public Law*, 244–265.

Carter-Ruck, P. *et al.* (1992) *Carter-Ruck on Libel and Slander*, 4th edn, London: Butterworths.

Chandler, J. (1989) 'The liberal justification for local government: values and administrative expediency', *Political Studies*, 37(4), 604–611.

Citizen's Charter, *Raising the Standard*, Cm. 1599, London: HMSO.

Citizen's Charter, *Second Report: 1994*, Cm. 2540, London: HMSO.

Civil Service Department (1980) *Memorandum of Guidance for Officials Appearing before Select Committes*, London: Civil Service Department.

Clements, R. (1999) 'The Human Rights Act – a new equity or a new opiate: reinverting justice or repackaging state control?', *Journal of Law and Society*, 26(1), 72–85.

Clements, R. (2000) 'Bringing it all back home: "rights" in English law before the Human Rights Act 1998', *Human Rights Law Journal*, 21(4–7), 134–142.

Clothier, C. (1986) 'The value of an ombudsman', *Public Law*, 204–211.

Code of Practice (1994) *Access to Governmental Information*, London: HMSO.

Colvin, M. (1998) *Under Surveillance: Convert Policing and Human Rights Standards*, London: Justice.

Constantinesco, V. (1991) 'Who's afraid of subsidiarity?', *Yearbook of European Law*, 11, 33–55.

Convention for the Protection of Human Rights and Fundamental Freedoms, *Treaty Series*, 71, Cmd. 8969, London: HMSO.

Copp, D., Hampton, J. and Roemer, J. (eds) (1993) *The Idea of Democracy*, Cambridge: Cambridge University Press.

Coppel, J. (1999) *The Human Rights Act 1998: Enforcing the European Convention in the Domestic Courts*, Chichester: John Wiley.

Cosgrove, R. (1980) *The Rule of Law: Albert Venn Dicey, Victorian Jurist*, Chapel Hill: University of North Carolina Press.

Craig, P. (1990) *Public Law and Democracy in the United Kingdom and the United States of America*, Oxford: Clarendon Press.

Craig, P. (1992a) 'Once upon a time in the west: direct effect and the federalization of EEC law', *Oxford Journal of Legal Studies*, 12(4), 453–479.

Craig, P. (1992b) 'Legitimate expectations: a conceptual analysis', *Law Quarterly Review*, 108, 79–98.

Craig, P. (1994) 'The common law, reasons and administrative justice', *Cambridge Law Journal*, 53(2), 282–302.

Craig, P. (1997a) 'Directives: direct effect, indirect effect and the construction of national legislation', *European Law Review*, 22, 519–538.

Craig, P. (1997b) 'Formal and substantive conceptions of the rule of law: an analytical framework', *Public Law*, 467–487.

Craig, P. (1998) '*Ultra vires* and the foundations of judicial review', *Cambridge Law Journal*, 57(1), 63–90.

Craig, P. (1999) 'Competing models of judicial review', *Public Law*, 428–447.

Craig, P. (2001) 'The courts, the Human Rights Act and judicial review', *Law Quarterly Review*, 117, 589–603.

Craig, P. and Bamforth, N. (2001) 'Constitutional principle, constitutional analysis and judicial review', *Public Law*, 763–780.

Craig, P. and De Burca, G. (1998) *EU Law: Text, Cases and Materials*, 2nd edn, New York: Oxford University Press.

Craig, P. and Walters, M. (1999) 'The courts, devolution and judicial review', *Public Law*, 274–303.

Craig, P. and Harlow, C. (eds) (1998) *Lawmaking in the European Union*, London: Kluwer Law International.

Crick, B. (1986) 'Northern Ireland and the concept of consent', in C. Harlow (ed.), *Public Law and Politics*, London: Sweet & Maxwell.

Crick, B. (1990) 'The sovereignty of Parliament and the Scottish question', in N. Lewis *et al.* (eds), *Happy and Glorious: The Constitution in Transition*, Milton Keynes: Open University Press.

Curtin, D. (1993) 'The constitutional structure of the Union: a Europe of bits and pieces', *Common Market Law Review*, 30, 17–69.

Daintith, T. and Page, A. (1999) *The Executive in the Constitution: Structure, Autonomy and Internal Control*, New York: Oxford University Press.

Davies, A. and Williams, J. (1991) *What Next? Agencies, Departments and the Civil Service*, London: Institute for Public Policy Research.

de Burca, G. (1992) 'Giving effect to European Community directives', *Modern Law Review*, 55(2), 215–240.

de Burca, G. (1993) 'Fundamental human rights and the reach of EC law', *Oxford Journal of Legal Studies*, 13(3), 283–319.

de Tocqueville, A. (1945) *Democracy in America*. The Henry Reeve text as revised by Francis Bowen, now further corrected and edited by Phillips Bradley; foreword by Harold J. Laski, New York: A.A. Knopf.

Devlin, Lord (1976) 'Judges and lawmakers', *Modern Law Review*, 39(1), 1–16.

Dicey, A. (1915) *An Introduction to the Law of the Constitution*, 8th edn. Sl: sn 1915.

Dicey, A. (1959) *Introduction to the Study of the Law of the Constitution*, with introduction by E.C.S. Wade, 10th edn, London: St Martin's Press.

Dickson, B. (ed.) (1997) *Human Rights and the European Convention: The Effects of the Convention on the United Kingdom and Ireland*, London: Sweet & Maxwell.

Dowding, K. and Won-Taek, K. (1998) 'Ministerial resignations, 1945–97', *Public Administration*, 76, 411–429.

Downey (1997), *Committee on Standards and Privileges*, 1st Report HC 30-1 (1997–98).

Drewry, G. (1989) *The New Select Committees: A Study of the 1979 Reforms*, 2nd edn, ed. by Gavin Drewry for the Study of Parliament Group, Oxford: Clarendon Press.

Drewry, G. (1990) 'Next: the pace falters', *Public Law*, 322–329.

Drewry, G. (1993) 'Mr Major's charter, empowering the consumer', *Public Law*, 248–256.

Drewry, G. (1996) 'Judicial Inquiries and public reassurance', *Public Law*, 368–372.

Drewry, G. and Harlow, C. (1990) 'A "Cutting edge?", The Parliamentary Commissioner and MPs', *Modern Law Review*, 53(3), 745–769.

Dunleavy, P. (1991) *Democracy, Bureaucracy and Public Choice: Economic Explanations in Political Science*, London: Harvester.

Dworkin, R. (1986) *Law's Empire*, London: Fontana.

Dworkin, R. (1996) *Freedom's Law: The moral reading of the Constitution*, Oxford: Oxford University Press.

Dyson, K. (1980) *The State Tradition in Western Europe: A Study of an Idea and Institution*, Oxford: Martin Robertson.

Dyzenhaus, D. (ed.) (1999) *Recrafting the Rule of Law: The Limits of Legal Order*, Oxford: Hart Publishing.

Economides, K., Betten, L., Bridge, J., Shrubsall, V. and Tettenborn, A. (eds) (2000) *Fundamental Values*, Oxford: Hart Publishing.

Edwards, J. (1984) *The Attorney General, Politics and the Public Interest*, London: Sweet & Maxwell.

Elias, P. (1994) 'New direction in judicial review', in Jowell, J. and Oliver, D. *The Changing Constitution*, 3rd edn, Oxford: Clarendon Press.

Elliot, M. (1999a) 'The demise of parliamentary sovereignty? The implications for justifying judicial review', *Law Quarterly Review*, 115, 119–137.

Elliot, M. (1999b) 'The *ultra vires* doctrine in a constitutional setting: still the central principle of administrative law', *Cambridge Law Journal*, 58(1), 129–158.

Endicott, T. (1999) 'The impossibility of the rule of law', *Oxford Journal of Legal Studies*, 19, 1–18.

Ewing, K. (1999) 'The Human Rights Act and parliamentary democracy', *Modern Law Review*, 62(1), 79–99.

Ewing, K. and Gearty, C. (2000) *The Struggle for Civil Liberties: Political Freedom and the Rule of Law in Britain, 1914–1945*, Oxford: Oxford University Press.

Farran, S. (1996) *The UK before the European Court of Human Rights: Case Law and Commentary*, London: Blackstone Press.

Faulks, *Report of the Committee on Defamation*, Cmd. 5909, London: HMSO.

Feldman, D. (1993) *Civil Liberties and Human Rights in England and Wales*, Oxford: Oxford University Press.

Feldman, D. (1994) 'Discretion, choices and values', *Public Law*, 279–293.

Feldman, D. (1997) 'The developing scope of Article 8 of the European Convention on Human Rights', *European Human Rights Law Review*, 3, 265–274.

Feldman, D (1999a) 'Human dignity as a legal value, Part 1', *Public Law*, 61, 682–702.

Feldman, D. (1999b) 'The Human Rights Act 1998 and constitutional principles', *Legal Studies*, 19, 165–206.

Feldman, D. (2000) 'Human dignity as a legal value, Part II', *Public Law*, 62, 61–76.

Fenwick, H. and Phillipson, G. (1996) 'Confidence and privacy: a re-examination', *Cambridge Law Journal*, 55(3), 447–455.

Finer, F., Bogdanor, V. and Rudden, B. (1995) *Comparing Constitutions*, Oxford: Clarendon Press.

Fish, S. (1994) *There's No Such Thing As Free Speech And It's a Good Thing Too*, New York and Oxford: Oxford University Press.

Fleming, J.G. (1998) *The Law of Torts*, 9th edn, North Ryde, New South Wales: LBC Information Services.

Ford, R. (1999) 'Human rights in the UK: some lessons from Canada', *Statute Law Review*, 20(3), 251–261.

Forsythe, C. (1996) 'Of fig leaves and fairy tales: the *ultra vires* doctrine, the sovereignty of Parliament and judicial review', *Cambridge Law Journal*, 55(1), 122–140.

Forsythe, C., Hare, I. and Wade, Sir W. (eds) (1998) *The Golden Metwand and the Crooked Cord, Essays in Public Law in Honour of Sir William Wade*, Oxford: Clarendon Press.

Fredman, S. and Morris, G. (1994) 'The costs of exclusivity: public and private re-examined', *Public Law*, 69–85.

Freeden, M. (1991) *Rights*, Milton Keynes: Open University Press.

Freedland, M. (1994) 'Government by contract and public law', *Public Law*, 86–104.

Freedland, M. (1996) 'The rule against delegation and the *Carltona* doctrine in an agency context', *Public Law*, 19–30.

Freedland, M. (1998) 'Public and private finance – placing the private finance initiative in a public law Frame', *Public Law*, 288–307.

Freeman, S. (1990) 'Constitutional democracy and the legitimacy of judicial review', *Law and Philosophy*, 9, 327–370.

Fuller, L. (1969) *The Morality of Law*, revised edn, New Haven: Yale University Press.

Ganz, G. (1990) 'The depoliticisation of local authorities. The Local Government and Housing Act 1989, Part 1', *Public Law*, 224–242.

Gay, O. (2001) 'What's in a name? Political Parties, Lists and Candidates in the United Kingdom', *Public Law*, 245–255.

Gay, O. and Winitrobe, B. (1997) 'Putting out the Writs', *Public Law*, 385–393.

Gearty, C. and Tomkins, A. (eds) (1996) *Understanding Human Rights*, New York: Mansell.

Gibbons, T. (1996) 'Defamation reconsidered', *Oxford Journal of Legal Studies*, 16(4), 587–615.

Giddings, P. and Drewry, G. (1996) *Westminster and Europe: The Impact of the European Union on the Westminster Parliament*, A Study of Parliament Group, Basingstoke: Macmillan.

Graber, C. and Teubner, G. (1998) 'Art and money: constitutional rights in the private sphere?', *Oxford Journal of Legal Studies*, 18, 61–73.

Graham, C. (2000) *Regulating Public Utilities: A Legal and Constitutional Approach*, Oxford: Hart Publishers.

Gray, J. (1993) *Post-Liberalism: Studies in Political Thought*, London: Routledge.

Great Britain Treasury (1989) *Government Accounting: A Guide on Accounting and Financial Procedures for the Use of Government Departments*, 4th edn, London: HMSO.

Greenawalt, K. (1989) 'Free speech justifications', *Columbia Law Review*, 89(1), 119–155.

Griffiths, J. (1979) 'The political constitution', *Modern Law Review*, 42(1), 1–21.

Griffiths, J. (2001) 'The common law and the political constitution', *Law Quarterly Review*, 117, 42–67.

Griffiths, J. and Ryle, M. (1989) *Parliament: Functions, Practices and Procedures*, London: Sweet & Maxwell.

Gross, H. and Harrison, R. (1992) *Jurisprudence, Cambridge Essays*, Oxford: Clarendon Press.

Gurry, F. (1984) *Breach of Confidence*, Oxford: Clarendon Press.

Gutmann, A. and Thompson, D. 1996 *Democracy and Disagreement*, Cambridge, MA: Belknap Press of Harvard University Press.

Habermas, J. (1996a) 'The European nation state. Its achievements and limitations. On the past and future of sovereignty and citizenship', *Ratio Juris*, 9(2), 125–137.

Habermas, J. (1996b) *Between Facts and Norm: Contributions to a Discourse Theory of Law and Democracy*, Cambridge, MA: MIT Press.

Hadfield, B. (1998) 'The Belfast agreement, sovereignty and the state of the Union', *Public Law*, 599–616.

Hadfield, B. (1999) 'The nature of devolution in Scotland and Northern Ireland, key issues of responsibility and control', *Edinburgh Law Review*, 3, 3–31.

Hampshire-Monk, I. (1992) *A History of Modern Political Thought*, Oxford: Blackwell.

Harden, I. (1991) 'The constitution and its discontents', *British Journal of Political Science*, 21, 489–510.

Harden, I. (1993) 'Money and the constitution: financial control reporting and audit', *Legal Studies*, 13(1), 16–37.

Harden, I. (1994) 'The constitution and the European Union', *Public Law*, 609–624.

Harden, I. (1996) 'Democracy and the European Union' in Hirst, P. and Khilnani, S. (eds) *Re-inventing Democracy*, Oxford: Blackwell.

Harden, I., White, F. and Hollingsworth, K. (1996) 'Value for money and administrative law', *Public Law*, 661–681.

Harlow, C. (ed.) (1986) *Public Law and Politics*, London: Sweet & Maxwell.

Harlow, C. (1997) 'Back to basics: reinventing administrative law', *Public Law*, 245–261.

Harlow, C. (2000a) 'Export, import. The ebb and flow of English public law', *Public Law*, 240–253.

Harlow, C. (2000b) 'Disposing of Dicey: from legal autonomy to constitutional discourse', *Political Studies*, 48, 356–369.

Harlow, C. and Rawlings, R. (1997) *Law and Administration*, 2nd edn, London: Butterworths.

Harris, B. (1992) ' "The Third Source" of authority for government action', *Law Quarterly Review*, 108, 626–651.

Harris, D., O'Boyle, M. and Warbrick, C. (1995) *Law of the European Convention on Human Rights*, London: Butterworths.

Harvey, C.J. (1997) 'The procedural paradigm of law and democracy', *Public Law*, 692–703.

Hayek, F. (1973) *Law, Legislations and Liberty: A New Statement of the Liberal Principles and Political Economy*, London: Routledge & Kegan Paul.

Hazell, R. (ed.) (1999) *Constitutional Futures: A History of the Next Ten Years*, Oxford: Oxford University Press.

Hazell, R. (2001) 'Reforming the constitution', *Political Quarterly*, 39(1), 1–49.

Held, D. (ed.) (1991) *Political Theory Today*, Oxford: Polity Press.

Held, D. (1996) *Models of Democracy*, 2nd edn, Cambridge: Polity Press.

Held, D. (ed.) (1999) *Global Transformations: Politics, Economics and Culture*, Oxford: Polity Press.

Hennessey, P. (1986) *Cabinet*, Oxford: Basil Blackwell.

Hennessey, P. (1995) *The Hidden Wiring: Unearthing the British Constitution*, London: Gollancz.

Hennessey, P. (2001), *The Prime Minister: The Office and its Holders since 1945*, London: Allen Lane.

Hey, D. *et al.* (1975) *Albion's Fatal Tree: Crime and Society in Eighteenth-Century England*, London, Allen Lane.

Himsworth, C. (1996) 'In a state no longer: the end of constitutionalism?', *Public Law*, 639–660.

Himsworth, C. and Munro, C. (1999) *The Scotland Act 1998*, Edinburgh: W. Green/ Sweet & Maxwell.

Hobbes, T. (1974) *Leviathan*, introduction by K.R. Minogue, London: Dent.

Hoffmann, The Rt Hon Lord (1999) 'Human rights and the House of Lords', *Modern Law Review*, 62(2), 159–166.

Holliday, I. (2000) 'Is the British state hollowing out?', *Political Quarterly*, 72(2), 167–176.

Home Office (1999) *Interception of Communications in the UK*, London: Home Office.

Hooper, Sir A. (1998) 'The impact of the Human Rights Act on judicial decision making', *European Human Rights Law Review*, 6, 676–686.

Hope, Lord (2000) 'Human rights: where are we now?', *European Human Rights Law Review*, 5, 439–451.

Horwitz, M. (1977) 'The rule of law: an unqualified human good?', *Yale Law Review*, 86, 561–566.

Horwitz, M. (1997) 'Why is Anglo-American jurisprudence unhistorical', *Oxford Journal of Legal Studies*, 17, 551–586.

Hoskyns, J. (1983) 'Whitehall and Westminster, an outsider's view', *Parliamentary Affairs*, 36, 137–147.

House of Commons (1987) *Manual of Procedure in the Public Business*, 14th edn, London: HMSO.

House of Commons (1989) *The Financing and Accountability of Next Steps Agencies*, Cm. 914. London: HMSO.

House of Commons, *1st Report from the Liaison Committee, The Select Committee System*, HC 92 (1982–83), London: HMSO.

House of Commons, *2nd Report from the Select Committee on Procedure. The Working of the Select Committee System*, HC 19-1 (1989–90), London: HMSO.

House of Commons, *4th Report from the Defence Committee: Westland plc: The Government's Decision-Making: Report and Proceedings of the Committee*, HC 519 (1985–86), London: HMSO.

House of Commons, *8th Report from the Treasury and Civil Service Committee, Civil Service Management Reform: The Next Steps*, HC 494-1 (1987–88), London: HMSO).

House of Commons, *Government Reply to the 8th Report from the Treasury and Civil Service Committee*, Cm. 524, 1988, London: HMSO.

House of Commons, *5th Report: The Role of the Civil Service Treasury and Civil Service Committee*, Vol. 1, HC 27-1 (1993–94), London: HMSO.

House of Commons (1995) *Government Reply to the 5th Report: The Role of the Civil Service Treasury and Civil Service Committee*, Cm. 3931, London: HMSO.

House of Commons, *1st Report from the Liaison Committee: Accountability of Ministers and Civil Servants to Select Committees of the House of Commons*, HC 100 (1986–87), London: HMSO.

House of Commons, *Select Committee on Public Administration, 1st Report – Public Appointments*, HC 327 (1997–88), London: HMSO.

House of Commons, *Public Service Committee 2nd Report Ministerial Accountability and Responsibility*, HC 313 (1996), London: HMSO.

House of Commons, *Government Reply, Public Service Committee 1st Special Report – Government Response to the 2nd Report from the Committee on Ministerial Accountability and Responsibility*, HC 67 (1995–96), London: HMSO.

House of Commons, *5th Report: The Civil Service Pay and Conditions of Service Code*, HC 260 (1989–90), London: HMSO.

House of Commons, *7th Report from the Treasury and Civil Service Committee: Civil Servants and Ministers: Duties and Responsibilities*, HC 92-1 (1985–86), London: HMSO.

House of Commons (1995) *The government's response to the 1st Report from the Committee on Standards in Public Life*, Cm. 2931, London: HMSO.

Hunt, M. (1997) 'Human rights in English courts', in M. Taggart (ed.), *The Province of Administrative Law*, Oxford: Hart Publishing.

Hunt, M. (1998) 'The "horizontal effect" of the Human Rights Act', *Public Law*, 423–443.

Hunt, M. (1999) 'The Human Rights Act and legal culture: the judiciary and the legal profession', *Journal of Law and Society*, 26(1), 86–102.

Hunt, M. and Singh, R. (eds) (2001) *A Practitioner's Guide to the Impact of the Human Rights Act 1998*, Oxford: Hart Publishing.

Ibbs Committee, Jenkins, K., Caines, K. and Jackson, A. (1988) *Improving Management in Government: The Next Steps*, London: HMSO.

Irvine, D. (1996) 'Judges and decison-makers: the theory and practice of *Wednesbury* review', *Public Law*, 59–78.

Irvine, D. (1996) 'The development of human rights in Britain under an incorporated convention on human rights', *Public Law*, 221–236.

Jacob, J. (1996) *The Republican Crown: Lawyers and the Making of the State in Twentieth-Century Britain*, Aldershot: Brookfield.

Jaconelli, J. (1985) 'Comment', *Public Law*, 629.

Jaconelli, J. (1999) 'The nature of constitutional convention', *Legal Studies*, 19, 24–46.

Janis, M., Kay, R. and Bradley, A. (2000) *European Human Rights Law: Text and Materials*, 2nd edn, Oxford: Clarendon Press.

Jenkins, K., Caines, K. and Jackson, A. (1988) *Report to the Prime Minister: Improving Management in Government. The Next Steps*, London: HMSO.

Jenkins Report (1998) *The Report of the Independent Commission on the Voting System*, Cm. 4090–1, London: HMSO.

Jenkins, S. (1996) *Accountable to None: The Tory Nationalism of Britain*, Harmondsworth: Penguin.

Jennings, I. (1959) *The Law and the Constitution*, 5th edn, London: University of London Press.

Jones, D.L. (1988) *A Parliamentary History of the Glorious Revolution*, London: HMSO.

Jowell, J. (1999) 'Of *vires* and vacuums: the constitutional context of judicial review', *Public Law*, 448–460.

Jowell, J. and Lester, A. (1987) 'Beyond *Wednesbury*: substantive principles of administrative law', *Public Law*, 368–382.

Jowell, J. and Oliver, D. (eds) (2000) *The Changing Constitution*, 4th edn, Oxford: Oxford University Press.

Jowell, J. (2000) 'Beyond the rule of law: towards constitutional judicial review', *Public Law*, 671–683.

Justice (1998) *Under Surveillance: Covert Policing and Human Rights Standards*, London: Justice.

Kantorowicz, E. (1957) *The King's Two Bodies: A Study in Medieval Political Theology*, Princetown, NJ: Princetown University Press.

Kay, R. (1989) 'Substance and structure as constitutional protections: centennial comparisons', *Public Law*, 428–439.

Kay, R. (1990) 'Constitutional cultures: constitutional law', *University of Chicago Law Review*, 57, 317–325.

Keir, Sir D.L. (1969) *The Constitutional History of Modern Britain since 1485*, 9th edn, London: Black.

Kelman, M. (1988) 'On democracy-bashing: a skeptical look at the theoretical and "empirical", practice of the public choice movement', *Virginia Law Review*, 74(1), 199–273.

Kelsen, H. (1961) *General Theory of Law and State*, New York: Russell & Russell.

Kent, Sir H. (1979) *In on the Act: Memoirs of a Lawmaker*, London: Macmillan.

Kilbrandon (1973) *Royal Commission on the Constitution, 1969–1973*, Cmnd. 5460, London: HMSO.

King, T. (2000) *Does the United Kingdom still have a Constitution?* London: Sweet and Maxwell.

Kingdom, J. (1991) *Government and Politics in Britain*, Cambridge, MA: Polity Press.

Klug, F. (1999) 'The Human Rights Act 1998: Pepper *v.* Hart and all that', *Public Law*, 246–273.

Klug, F., Starmer, K. and Weir, S. (1996) *The Three Pillars of Liberty: Securing Political Rights and Freedom in the United Kingdom*, London: Routledge.

Klug, F. and Starmer, K. (2001) 'Incorporation through the "front door": the first year of the Human Rights Act', *Public Law*, 654–665.

Langbein J.H. (1983) 'Albion's fatal flaws', Oxford: Past and Present Society.

Lardy, H. (2000) 'Democracy by default: the representation of the People Act 2000', *Modern Law Review*, 64(1), 63–81.

Law Commission (1994) *Administrative Law: Judicial Review and Statutory Appeals*, HC 669 (1993–94), London: HMSO.

Laws, Sir J. (1998) 'The limitations of human rights', *Public Law*, 254–265.

Laws, Sir J. (1989) 'The ghost in the machine: principle of public law', *Public Law*, 27–31.

Laws, Sir J. (1992) 'Illegality: the problem of jurisdiction', in M. Supperstone and J. Gouldie, *Judicial Review*, London: Butterworths.

Laws, Sir, J. (1993) 'Is the High Court the guardian of fundamental constitutional rights?', *Public Law*, 59–79.

Laws, Sir, J. (1994) 'Judicial remedies and the constitution', *Modern Law Review*, 57(2), 213–227.

Laws, Sir, J. (1995) 'Law and democracy', *Public Law*, 72–93.

Laws, Sir. J. (1996) 'The constitution: morals and right', *Public Law*, 622–635.

Lawson R. and Schermers, H. (1997) *Leading Cases of the European Court of Human Rights*, Nijmegan: Ars Aequi Libri.

Le Sueur, A. (1992) 'Should we abolish the writ of *habeas corpus*?', *Public Law*, 13–20.

Le Sueur, A. and Sunkin, M. (1992) 'Applications for judicial review: the requirement of leave', *Public Law*, 102–129.

Leach, P.P. (2000) *Taking a Case to the ECHR*, London: Blackstone Press.

Leigh, I. (1986) 'A tapper's charter', *Public Law*, 8–18.

Leigh. I. (1999) 'Horizontal rights, the Human Rights Act and privacy: lessons from the Commonwealth?', *International and Comparative Law Quarterly*, 48, 57–87.

Leigh, I. and Lustgarten, L. (1991) 'The Security Commission: constitutional achievement or curiosity?', *Public Law*, 215–232.

Leigh, I. and Lustgarten, L. (1999) 'Making rights real: the courts, remedies and the Human Rights Act', *Cambridge Law Journal*, 58(3), 507–545.

Lenaerts, K. (1991) 'Some reflections on the separation of powers in the European communities', *Common Law Review*, 28(1), 11–35.

Lenz, C. (1989) 'The Court of Justice of the European communities', *European Law Review*, 14(3), 127–139.

Leopold, P. (1986) 'Leaks and squeaks in the Palace of Westminster', *Public Law*, 368–734.

Lester, A. (1993) 'English judges as law makers', *Public Law*, 269–290.

Lester, A. (2001) 'Developing constitutional principles of public law', *Public Law*, 684–694.

Lester, A., Pannick, D. and Carss-Frisk, M. (eds) (1999) *Human Rights Law and Practice*, London: Butterworths.

Lewis, N. (1993) 'The citizens charter and next steps: a new way of governing?', *Political Quarterly*, 64(3), 316–326.

Lewis, N. (1994) 'Reviewing change in government: new public management and next steps', *Public Law*, 105–113.

Lewis, N. (1998) 'A civil service act for the United Kingdom', *Public Law*, 463–488.

Lewis, N. and Longley, D. (1994) 'Ethics and the public service', *Public Law*, 526–608.

Leyland, P. and Woods, T. (eds) (1997) *Administrative Law Facing the Future: Old Constraints and New Horizons*, London: Blackstone Press.

Lively, J. and Lively, A. (1994) *Democracy in Britain, a Reader*, Oxford: Blackwell.

Lock, G. (1985) 'Parliamentary privilege and the courts: the avoidance of conflict', *Public Law*, 64–92.

Locke, J. (1632–1704) (1960) *Two Treaties of Government*, ed. P. Laslett, Cambridge: Cambridge University Press.

Longley, D. and Rhoda, J. (1999) *Administrative Justice: Central Issues in UK and European Administrative Law*, London: Cavendish.

Lord Chancellor's Department (1989) *Judicial Appointments, The Work and Organisation of the Legal Profession*, London: HMSO.

Loughlin, M. (1989) 'Law ideologies and the political–administrative system', *Journal of Law and Society*, 16(1), 21–41.

Loughlin, M. (1994) *The Constitutional Status of Local Government*, London: Commission for Local Democracy.

Loughlin, M. (1996) *Legality and Locality: The Role of Law in Central–Local Government Relations*, Oxford: Clarendon Press.

Loveland, I. (1996) 'A sign of things to come? The ECHR and a "public/private" divide in the civil law of defamation', *Communications Law*, 1(5), 193–197.

Loveland, I. (1998a) 'The constitutionalisation of political libels in English common law?', *Public Law*, 633–646.

Loveland, I. (ed.) (1998b) *Importing the First Amendment*, Oxford: Hart Publishing.

Loveland, I. (2001) 'Freedom of political expression: who needs the Human Rights Act?', *Public Law*, 233–244.

Lustgarten, L. (1986) *The Governance of the Police*, London: Sweet & Maxwell.

Lustgarten, L. and Leigh, I. (1994) *In from the Cold: National Security and Parliamentary Democracy*, Oxford: Clarendon Press.

MacCormick, N. (1978) 'Does the United Kingdom have a constitution? Reflections on MacCormick v. Lord Advocate', *Northern Ireland Law Quarterly*, 29, 1–20.

MacCormick, N. (1983) 'Jurisprudence and the Constitution', *Current Legal Problems*, 36, 13–30.

MacCormick, N. (1993) 'Beyond the sovereign state', *Modern Law Review*, 56(1), 1–18.

McCrudden, C. and Chambers, G. (eds) (1998) *Individual Rights and the Law in Britain*, Oxford: Clarendon Press.

MacDonald, R. St. J., Matscher, F. and Petzold, H. (eds) (1993) *The European System for the Protection of Human Rights*, Dordrecht: Nijhoff.

MacFarlane, L. (1985) *The Theory and Practice of Human Rights*, Hounslow: Temple Smith.

MacKay of Clashfern, James Peter Hymers, Baron (1994) *The Administration of Justice*, London: Steven & Sons.

Maclean, J. (ed.) (1999) *Property and the Constitution*, Oxford: Hart Publishing.

MacPherson, C. (1977) *The Life and Times of Liberal Democracy*, Oxford: Oxford University Press.

Mahoney, P. (1994) 'The doctrine of the margin of appreciation under the European Convention of Human Rights: Its legitimacy in theory and application in practice', *Human Rights Law Journal*, 1–6.

Mahony, P. (1999) 'Speculating on the future of the reformed European Court of Human Rights', *Human Rights Law Journal*, 1–4.

Maitland, F. (1901) 'The Crown as corporation', *Law Quarterly Review*, 17, 131–146.

Maitland, F. (1908) *The Constitutional History of England*, Cambridge: Cambridge University Press.

Maltby, N. (1993) '*Marleasing*: what is all the fuss about?', *Law Quarterly Review*, 109, 301–311.

Mancini, G. (1991) 'The making of a constitution for Europe', in R. Keohan and S. Hoffman, *The New European Community: Decision Making and Institutional Change*, Boulder: Westview.

Mancini, G. and Keeling, D. (1994) 'Democracy and the European Court of Justice', *Modern Law Review*, 57(2), 175–190.

Manin, B. (1987) 'On legitimacy and political deliberation', *Political Theory*, 15(3), 338–368.

Markesinis, B. (ed.) (1998) *The Impact of the Human Rights Bill on English Law*, Oxford: Oxford University Press.

Marks, S. (1995) 'Civil liberties at the margin: the UK derogation and the European Convention on Human Rights', *Oxford Journal of Legal Studies*, 15, 69–95.

Marr, A. (1995) *Ruling Britannia: The Failure and the Future of British Democracy*, London: Michael Joseph.

Marshall, G. (1971) *Constitutional Theory*, Oxford: Clarendon Press.

Marshall, G. (1984) *Constitutional Conventions: The Rules and Forms of Political Accountability*, Oxford: Clarendon Press.

Marshall, G. (ed.) (1989a) *Ministerial Responsibility*, Oxford: Clarendon Press.

Marshall, G. (1989b) 'Taking rights for an override: free speech and commercial expression', *Public Law*, 4–11.

Marshall, G. (1998) 'Interpreting Interpretation in the Human Rights Bill', *Public Law*, 167–170.

Marshall, G. (2001) 'Things we can say about rights', *Public Law*, 207–209.

May, T. Erskine (1997) *Erskine May's Treatise on the Law, Privileges, Proceedings and Usage of Parliament*, 22nd edn, D. Limon (ed.) *et al.*, London: Butterworths.

McAllister, L. (2001) 'Wales: Labour's devolution dilemma', *Parliamentary Affairs*, 54(1), 156–159.

McClean, I. (1999) 'Mr Asquith's unfinished business', *Political Quarterly*, 70, 382–389.

McHarg, E. (1999) 'Reconciling human rights and the public interest: conceptual problems and doctrinal uncertainty in the jurisprudence of the European Court of Human Rights', *Modern Law Review*, 62, 671–696.

Memorandum of Understanding and supplementary agreements between the UK Government, the Scottish Ministers, the Cabinet of the National Assembly for Wales and the Northern Ireland Executive Committee (1999), Cm. 4806, London: HMSO.

Mill, J. (1962) *Utilitarianism*, ed. M. Warnock, Glasgow: Collins/Fontana.

Mills, S. and Whitty, N. (1999) *Feminist Perspectives on Public Law*, London: Cavendish.

Mitchell, J. (1965) 'The causes and effects of the absence of a system of public law in the United Kingdom', *Public Law*, 95–118.

Mitchell, J. (1999) 'The creation of the Scottish Parliament: journey without end', *Parliamentary Affairs*, 52(4), 649–665.

Morison, J. (1998) 'The case against constitutional reform', *Journal of Law and Society*, 25(4), 510–535.

Morison, J. (2000) 'The government–voluntary sector compacts: governance, governmentality and civil society', *Journal of Law and Society*, 27(1), 98–132.

Morison, J. (2001) 'Democracy, governance and governmentality: civic public space and constitutional renewal in Northern Ireland', *Oxford Journal of Legal Studies*, 21(2), 287–310.

Morison, J. and Livingstone, S. (1995) *Reshaping Public Power: Northern Ireland and the British constitutional crisis*, London: Sweet & Maxwell.

Morris, D. (2000) 'The Human Rights Act 1998: too many loose ends?', *Statute Law Review*, 21(2), 104–125.

Mount, F. (1992) *The British Constitution Now*, London: Heinemann.

Mowbray, A. (1994) 'A New European Court of Human Rights', *Public Law*, 540–552.

Mowbray, A. (1997) 'The European Court of Human Right's approach to just satisfaction', *Public Law*, 647–659.

Mullender, R. (1996) 'Judicial review and the rule of law', *Law Quarterly Review*, 112, 182–186.

Mullender, R. (1998a) 'Privacy, paedophilia and the European Convention on Human Rights: a deontological approach', *Public Law*, 384–388.

Mullender, R. (1998b) 'Parliamentary sovereignty, the constitution and the judiciary', *Northern Ireland Legal Quarterly*, 49(2), 138–166.

Mullender, R. (1999) 'Defamation qualified privilege and the European Convention on Human Rights', *Cambridge Law Journal*, 58(1), 15–18.

Mullender, R. (2001) '*Prima facie* rights, rationality and the law of negligence' in M. Kramer (ed.), *Rights, Wrongs and Responsibilities*, London: Palgrave.

Munday, R. (1996) 'Inferences from silence and European Human Rights Law', *Criminal Law Review*, 370–385.

Munro, C. (1985) 'Dicey on Constitutional Conventions', *Public Law*, 637.

Munro, C. (1999) *Studies in Constitutional Law*, 2nd edn, London: Butterworths.

Nairn, T. (1988) *The Enchanted Glass: Britain and its Monarchy*, London: Radius.

Neill, Lord (1998) *5th Report of the Committee on Standards in Public Life*, Cm. 4057-1. *The Funding of Political Parties*, London: HMSO.

Neill Lord (2000a) *6th Report on Standards in Committee on Standards in Public Life*, Cm. 4557-1, *Reinforcing Standards*, London: HMSO.

Neill Lord (2000b) *7th Report of the Committee on Standards in Public Life*, Cm. 4903-1, London: HMSO.

Newton, Lord (2001) *Standards of Conduct in The House of Lords, The Challenge for Parliament; Making Government Work*, London: Hansard Society.

Nicholson, D. and Reid, K. (1996) 'Arrest for breach of the peace and the European Convention on Human Rights', *Criminal Law Review*, 764–775.

Nicholls (1999) *Joint Committee on Parliamentary Privilege (1998–19)*, HL 43, HC 34 (see Leopold [1999]) PL 604.

Nolan, Lord (1995), *First Report of the Committee on Standards in Public Life*, Cm. 2850-I, London: HMSO.

Nolan, Lord and Sedley, Sir S. (1997), *The Making and Remaking of the British Constitution*, London: Blackstone Press.

Norton, P. (1984) *The British Polity*, New York: Longman.

Norton, P (1993) *Does Parliament Matter?* Harvester, Wheatsheaf.

Nozick, R. (1975) *Anarchy, State and Utopia*, New York: Basil Books.

Oliver, D. (1987) 'Is the *ultra vires* rule the basis for judicial review?', *Public Law*, 543–569.

Oliver, D. (1989) 'Law convention and abuse of power', *Political Quarterly*, 60(1), 38–49.

Oliver, D. (1994) 'Law, politics and public accountability. The search for a new equilibrium', *Public Law*, 238–253.

Oliver, D. (1997) 'Common values in public and private law and the public/private divide', *Public Law*, 630–646.

Oliver, D. (1998a) 'Freedom of information and ministerial accountability', *Public Law*, 171–175.

Oliver, D. (1998) 'A negative aspect to legitimate expectations', *Public Law*, 558–562.

Oliver, D. (1999) *Common Values and the Public–Private Divide*, London, Butterworths.

Oliver, D. (2000) 'The frontiers of the state: public authorities and public functions under the Human Rights Act', *Public Law*, 76–493.

Oliver, D. (2002) 'Public law procedures and remedies', *Public Law*, 91.

Oliver, D. and Drewry, G. (1996) *Public Service Reforms*, London: Pinter.

Olowofoyeku, A. (1993) *Suing judges: A Study of Judicial Immunity*, Oxford: Clarendon Press.

Olowofoyeku, A. (1999) 'Decentralising the UK: the federal argument', *Edinburgh Law Review*, 3(1), 57–84.

Olowofoyeku, A. (2000) 'The Nemo Judex rule: the case against automatic disqualification', *Public Law*, 456–475.

O'Neill, A. (2001) 'Judicial politics and the judicial committee: the devolution jurisprudence of the privy council', *Modern Law Review*, 64(4), 603–618.

Paine, T. (1987) *The Thomas Paine Reader* (eds Foot, M. and Kramnick, I.) Harmondsworth: Penguin.

Palmer, S. (1990) 'Tightening secrecy law: The Official Secrets Act 1989', *Public Law*, 243–256.

Palmer, S. (1992) 'Protecting journalists. Sources: Section 10, Contempt of Court Act 1981', *Public Law*, 61–72.

Palmer, S. (1993) 'Freedom of expression, democracy and the European Convention on Human Rights', *Cambridge Law Review*, 52(3), 363–364.

Pannick, D. (1998) 'Principles of interpretation of Convention rights under the Human Rights Act and the discretionary area of judgement', *Public Law*, 545–551.

Paton, E. (1995) 'Respecting freedom of speech', *Oxford Journal of Legal Studies*, 15(4), 597–610.

Pettit, P. (1997) *Republicanism: A Theory of Freedom and Government*, Oxford: Oxford University Press.

Phillipson, G. (1999) 'The Human Rights Act, "horizontal effect" and the common law: a bang or a whimper', *Modern Law Review*, 62(6), 824–849.

Pliatzky, L. (1992) 'Quangos and agencies', *Public Administration*, 70, 555–563.

Poggi, G. (1990) *The State: Its Nature, Development and Prospects*, Cambridge: Polity Press.

Popper, Sir K.T. (1966) *The Open Society and its Enemies, II, The High Tide Of Prophecy: Hegel, Marx and the Aftermath*, 5th edn (revised), London: Routledge.

Posner, R. (1986) *Economic Analysis of Law*, 3rd edn, Boston: Little Brown.

Postema, G. (1986) *Bentham and the Common Law Tradition*, Oxford: Clarendon Press.

Prosser, T. (1982) 'Towards a critical theory of public law', *Journal of Law and Society*, 9(1), 1–19.

Prosser, T. (1995) 'Bringing constitutional principles back', in R. Bellamy *et al.* (eds), *Democracy and Constitutional Culture in the Union of Europe*, London: Lothian Foundation Press.

Prosser, W. (1960) 'Privacy', *California Law Review*, 48(3), 383–423.

Proudhon, P. (1969) *General Idea of the Revolution in the Nineteenth Century*, translated from the French by J.B. Robinson, New York: Haskell House Publishers.

Pugh, W. (1997) in T. Halliday and L. Karpik (eds), *Lawyers and the Rise of Western Political Liberalism: From the Eighteenth to Twentieth Centuries*, Oxford: Clarendon Press.

Raphael, D. (ed.) (1967) *Political Theory and the Rights of Man*, London: Macmillan.

Raphael, D. (1981) *Moral Philosophy*, Oxford: Oxford University Press.

Rasmussen, H. (1986) *On Law and Policy in the European Court of Justice: A Comparative Study in Judicial Policymaking*, Dordrecht: Nihoff.

Rawlings, R. (ed.) (1997) *Law, Society and Economy*, Oxford: Clarendon Press.

Rawlings, R. (1998) 'The new model Wales', *Journal of Law and Society*, 25(4), 461–509.

Rawlings, R. (2000) 'Concordats of the constitution', *Law Quarterly Review*, 116, 257–286.

Rawls, J. (1993) *Political Liberalism*, New York: Columbia University Press.

Raz, J. (1977) 'The rule of law and its virtue', *Law Quarterly Review*, 93, 195–211.

Raz, J. (1986) *The Morality of Freedom*, Oxford: Oxford University Press.

Raz, J. (1991) 'Free expression and personal identification', *Oxford Journal of Legal Studies*, 11(3), 303–324.

Rhodes, M. (ed.) (1995) *The Regions and the New Europe: Patterns in Core and Periphery Development*, Manchester: Manchester University Press.

Rhodes, R. (1991) 'The new public management', special issue of *Public Administration*, 69.

Rhodes, R. (1994) 'The hollowing out of the state: the changing nature of the public service in Britain', *Political Quarterly*, 65(2), 138–151.

Rhodes, R. (1996) 'The new governance: governing without government', *Political Studies*, 44, 652–667.

Richards, D. (1999) *Free Speech and the Politics of Identity*, Oxford: Oxford University Press.

Richardson, G. (1986) 'The duty to give reasons: potential and practice', *Public Law*, 437–469.

Richardson, G. and Genn, H. (eds) (1994) *Administrative Law and Government Action: The Courts and Alternative Mechanisms of Review*, Oxford: Oxford University Press.

Richardson, G. and Sunkin, M. (1996) 'Judicial review: questions of impact', *Public Law*, 79–103.

Riddall, P. (2000) 'The second chamber: in search of a complementary role', *Political Quarterly*, 70(4), 404–410.

Ridley, F. (1988) 'There is no British constitution – a dangerous case of the Emperor's Clothes', *Parliamentary Affairs*, 41(3), 340–361.

Robertson, G. (1993) *Freedom, the Individual and the Law*, 7th edn, Harmondsworth: Penguin.

Robson, W. (1928) *Justice and Administrative Law: A Study of the British Constitution*, London: Macmillan.

Rose, R. (1982) *Understanding the United Kingdom: The Territorial Dimension in Government*, London: Longman.

Rousseau, J. (1712–1778) (1968) *The Social Contract*, translated and introduced by M. Cranston, Harmondsworth: Penguin.

Russell, M. (2000) *Reforming the Lords: Lessons from Overseas*, Oxford: Oxford University Press.

Russell, M. and Cornes, R. (2001) 'The Royal Commission on the House of Lords: A House for the future?', *Modern Law Review*, 64(1), 82–99.

Sampford, C. (1987) ' "Recognize and declare": an Australian experience in codifying constitutional conventions', *Oxford Journal of Legal Studies*, 7(3), 369–417.

Schonberg, S. (2000) *Legitimate Expectations in Administrative Law*, Oxford: Oxford University Press.

Scott, C. (1999) 'Regulation inside Government: re-badging the Citizen's Charter', *Public Law*, 595–603.

Scott, Sir R. (1996a) 'Ministerial accountability', *Public Law*, 410–426.

Scott, Sir R. (1996b) 'The acceptable and unacceptable uses of public interest immunity', *Public Law*, 427–444.

Sedley, Sir S. (1994a) 'The sound of silence: constitutional law without a constitution', *Law Quarterly Review*, 110, 270–921.

Sedley, Sir S. (1995a) 'Human rights: a twenty-first century agenda', *Public Law*, 386–400.

Sedley, Sir S. (1995b) 'The moral economy of judicial review', in G. Wilson (ed.), *Frontiers of Legal Scholarship*, Chichester: Wiley.

Sedley, Sir S. (2001) 'The common law and the political constitution: a reply', *Law Quarterly Review*, 117, 68–70.

Sedley, Sir S. (2001a) 'Turning on turtles', *London Review of Books*, 15 Nov., 11.

Seidentop, L. (2000) *Democracy in Europe*, London: Allen Lane.

Sharpe, L. (ed.) (1979) *Decentralist Trends in Western Democracies*, London: Sage.

Sharpe, S. (1997) 'The European convention, a suspect's charter?', *Criminal Law Review*, 848–860.

Shaw, J. (1996) *Law of the European Union*, 2nd edn, Basingstoke: Macmillan.

Shaw, J. and More, G. (eds) (1995) *The New Legal Dynamics of European Union*, New York: Clarendon Press.

Sheehy, Sir P. (1993) *Inquiry into Police Responsibilities and Rewards*, Cm. 2280-1, London: HMSO.

Shell, D. (1988) *The House of Lords*, 2nd edn, Doddington: Philip Allen.

Shell, D. (1999) 'The future of the second chamber', *Political Quarterly*, 70(4), 390–395.

Short, E. and de Than, C. (1998) *Civil Liberties*, London: Sweet & Maxwell.

Shrimpton, M. (1993) 'In defence of *habeas corpus*', *Public Law*, 24–30.

Silk, P. and Wallers, R. (1987) *How Parliament Works*, London: Longman.

Simcock, A. (1992) 'One and many – the office of Secretary of State', *Public Administration*, 70, 535–553.

Steiner, J. (1993) 'From direct effects to *Frankovich*: shifting means of enforcement of community law', *European Law Review*, 18, 3–22.

Stevens, R. (1993) *The Independence of the Judiciary: The View from the Lord Chancellor's Office*, Oxford: Clarendon Press.

Stevens, R. (1999) 'A loss of ninocence? Judicial independence and the separation of powers, *Oxford Journal of Legal Studies*, 19, 365–402.

Stewart, J. (1999) *The Nature of British Local Government*, Basingstoke: Macmillan.

Stewart, J. and Walsh, K. (1992) 'Change in the management of public services', *Public Administration*, 70, 499–518.

Steyn, The Rt Hon Lord (1997) 'The weakest and least dangerous department of government', *Public Law*, 84–95.

Steyn, The Rt Hon Lord (2000) 'The new legal landcape', *European Human Rights Law Review*, 549–554.

Suerin, J.L. (1994) 'Towards a European constitution, problems of political integration', *Public Law*, 625–636.

Sugerman, D. (1983) 'The legal boundaries of liberty: Dicey, liberalism and legal science', *Modern Law Review*, 46(1), 102–111.

Sunkin, M. and Payne, S. (1999) (eds) *The Nature of the Crown: A Legal and Political Analysis*, Oxford: Clarendon Press.

Sunkin, M., Bridges, L. and Meszaros, G. (1996) *Judicial Review in Perspective*, 2nd edn, London: Cavendish.

Supperstone, M. (1994) 'The Intelligence Services Act 1994', *Public Law*, 329–331.

Syrett, K. (1998) 'Prerogative powers: New Labour's forgotten constitutional reform?', *Denning Law Journal*, 111–129.

Taggart, M. (ed.) (1997) *The Province of Administrative Law*, Oxford: Hart Publishing.

Taggart, M. (1999) 'Reinvented government traffic lights and the convergence of public and private law', *Public Law*, 124–138.

Taswell-Langmead, T.P. (1960) *English Constitutional History*, 7th edn, London: Stevens & Haynes.

Taylor, C. (1989) *Sources of the Self: The Making of the Modern Identity*, Cambridge: Cambridge University Press.

Taylor, H. (1992) *The Origins and Growth of the English Constitution*, Denver, CO: Rothman.

Temple-Lang, J. (1990) 'Community constitutional law: Article 5 of the EEC Treaty', *Common Market Review*, 27(4), 645–681.

Teubner, G. and Graber, C. (1998) 'Art and money: constitutional rights in the private sphere?', *Oxford Journal of Legal Studies*, 18, 61–73.

Thompson, E. (1963) *The Making of the English Working Classes*, 1980 edition, Harmondsworth: Penguin.

Thompson, E. (1975) *Whigs and Hunters: The Origin of the Black Act*, London: Allen Lane.

Tierney, S. (2000) 'Devolution issues and s. 2(1) of the Human Rights Act 1998', *European Human Rights Law Review*, 380–392.

Tivey, L. (1999) 'Constitutionalism and the political arena', *Political Quarterly*, 70(2), 175–184.

Tomkins, A. (1993) 'Public interest immunity after Matrix Churchill', *Public Law*, 650–668.

Tomkins, A. (1998a) (ed.) *Devolution and the British Constitution*, London: Key Haven.

Tomkins, A. (1998b) *The Constitution after Scott: Government Unwrapped*, Oxford: Clarendon Press.

Tomkins, A. (2001) 'Magna Carta, Crown and colonies', *Public Law*, 571–585.

Toulson, R. and Phipps, C. (1996) *Confidentiality*, London: Sweet & Maxwell.

Tribe, L. (1988) *American Constitutional Law*, 2nd edn, Mineola, New York: Foundation Press.

Tribe, L. (1988) *Constitutional Choices*, Cambridge, MA: Harvard.

Uglow, S. (1999) 'Covert surveillance and the European Convention on Human Rights', *Criminal Law Review*, 287–299.

Underhill, N. (1978) *The Lord Chancellor*, Lavenham: Dalton.

University of Cambridge Centre for Public Law (1998) *Constitutional Reform in the United Kingdom: Prctice and Principles*, Oxford: Hart Publishers.

Vincent-Jones, P. (2000) 'Central–Local relations under the Local Government Act 1999: a new consensus?', *Modern Law Review* 63(1), 84–103.

Vincenzi, C. (1998) *Crown Powers, Subjects, Citizens*, London: Pinter.

Wacks, R. (1995) *Privacy and Press Freedom*, London: Blackstone Press.

Wade, W. (1955) 'The basis of legal sovereignty', *Cambridge Law Review*, 172–197.

Wade, W. (1985) 'Procedure and prerogative in public law', *Law Quarterly Review*, 101, 180–199.

Wade, W. (1998) 'Human rights and the judiciary', *European Human Rights Law Review*, 5, 520–533.

Wade, W. (2000) 'Horizons of horizontality', *Law Quarterly Review*, 116, 217–224.

Wakeham, Lord (2000) *A House for the Future Royal Commission on the House of Lords*, Cm. 4534, London: HMSO.

Waldron, J. (ed.) (1984) *Theories of Rights*, Oxford: Oxford University Press.

Waldron, J. (1990) *The Law: Theory and Practice in British Politics*, London: Routledge.

Waldron, J. (1993) 'A right-based critique of constitutional rights', *Oxford Journal of Legal Studies*, 13(1), 18–51.

Waldron, J. (1998) *Law and Disagreement*, Oxford: Clarendon Press.

Walker, C. (1987) 'Review of the prerogative: the remaining issues', *Public Law*, 62–84.

Walker, D. (1953) 'The legal theory of the state', *Judicial Review*, 65, 255–261.

Walter, N. (1995) 'European constitutionalism and European integration', *Public Law*, 266–293.

Walker, N. (1999) 'Setting English judges to rights', *Oxford Journal of Legal Studies*, 19, 133–151.

Walker, P. (1995) 'What's wrong with irrationality?', *Public Law*, 556–576.

Ward, I. (1996) *A Critical Introduction to European Law*, London: Butterworths.

Ward, I. (1998a) *An Introduction to Critical Legal Theory*, London: Cavendish.

Ward, I. (1998b) 'Law, liberty and literature', *Anglo-American Law Review*, 27(2), 188–220.

Ward, I. (2000) *A State of Mind?: The English Constitution and the Popular Imagination*, Stroud: Sutton.

Wetherall, S. (1985) *Law and Integration in the European Communities*, Oxford: Oxford University Press.

Webb, P. (2001) 'Parties and party systems: modernisation, regulation and diversity', *Parliamentary Affairs*, 54(2), 308–321.

Weiler, J. (1987) 'The Court of Justice on trial', *Common Market Law Review*, 24, 555–589.

Weiler, J. (1993) 'Journey to an unknown destination: a retrospective and prospective of the European Court of Justice in the arena of political investigation', *Journal of Common Market Studies*, 31(4), 417–446.

White Paper (1985) *The Interception of Communications in the United Kingdom*, Cm. 9438, London: HMSO.

White Paper (1997a) *Rights Brought Home: The Human Rights Bill*, Cm. 3782, London: HMSO.

White Paper (1997b) *Your Right to Know: the Government's Proposal: Freedom of Information Act*, Cm. 3818, London: HMSO.

White Paper (1998) *A Mayor and Assembly for London. The Government's Proposal for Modernising the Governance of London*, Cm. 3897, London: HMSO.

White Paper (2001) *The House of Lords: Completing the Reform*, Cm. 5291.

White, F., Harden, I. and Donnelly, K. (1994) 'Audit, accounting officers and accountability: the Pergau Dam Affair', *Public Law*, 526–534.

White, G. (1996) 'The First Amendment comes of age: the emergence of free speech in twentieth-century America', *Michigan Law Review*, 95(1), 299–392.

Whitty, N., Murphy, T. and Livingstone, S. (2001) *Civil Liberties Law: The Human Rights Act Era*, London: Butterworths.

Widdicombe, D. (1986) *Report into the Conduct of Local Authority Business*, Cm. 9797, London: HMSO.

Wilke, M. and Wallace, H. (1990) *Subsidiarity: Approaches to Power-Sharing in the European Community*, London: Royal Institute of Economic Affairs.

Willett, C. (ed.) (1996) *Public Sector Reforms and the Citizen's Charter*, London: Blackstone Press.

Williams, D. (1984) 'Public order and common law', *Public Law*, 12–16.

Williams, D. (1987) 'Processions, assemblies and the freedom of the Individual', *Criminal Law Review*, 167–179.

Williams, E. (1960), *The Eighteenth-Century Constitution*, Cambridge: Cambridge University Press.

Wilson, D. (1999) 'Exploring the limits of public participation in local government', *Parliamentary Affairs*, 52, 246–259.

Wilson, D. (2001) 'Local government: balancing diversity and uniformity', *Parliamentary Affairs*, 54(2), 289.

Winterton, G. (1976) 'The British grundnorm: parliamentary supremacy re-examined', *Law Quarterly Review*, 92, 591–617.

Wolff, J. (1996) *An Introduction to Political Philosophy*, (Oxford: Oxford University Press).

Wong, G. (2000) 'Towards the nutcracker principle: reconsidering the objections to proportionality', *Public Law* 92–109.

Woodhouse, D. (1994) *Ministers and Parliament: Accountability in Theory and Practice*, Oxford: Clarendon Press.

Woodhouse, D. (1995) 'Politicians and the judiciary: a changing relationship', *Parliamentary Affairs*, 48(3), 401–417.

Woodhouse, D. (1997a) 'Ministerial responsibility: something old something new', *Public Law*, 262–282.

Woodhouse, D. (1997b) *In Pursuit of Good Administration: Ministers, Civil Servants and Judges*, Oxford: Clarendon Press.

Woodhouse, D. (1998) 'The Office of Lord Chancellor', *Public Law*, 617–632.

Woodhouse, D. (2001) *The Office of the Lord Chancellor*, Oxford: Hart Publishing.

Woodhouse, D. (2002) 'The reconstruction of constitutional accountability', *Public Law*, 73.

Woolf, Sir H. (1995) *Protection of the Public: A New Challenge*, London: Sweet & Maxwell.

Wright, J. (2001) *Tort Law and Human Rights*, Oxford: Hart Publishing.

Zuckerman, A. (1994) 'Public interest immunity – a matter of prime judicial responsibility', *Modern Law Review*, 57(5), 703–725.

Index